DISCARDED
P9-AAY-798

THE CAUSES OF HIGH AND LOW READING ACHIEVEMENT

THE CAUSES OF HIGH AND LOW READING ACHIEVEMENT

RONALD P. CARVER
University of Missouri–Kansas City

LAWRENCE ERLBAUM ASSOCIATES, PUBLISHERS
2000 Mahwah, New Jersey London

Lawrence Erlbaum Associates, Inc., Publishers
10 Industrial Avenue
Mahwah, NJ 07430

Cover design by Kathryn Houghtaling Lacey

Library of Congress Cataloging-in-Publication Data

Carver, Ronald P.
The causes of high and low reading achievement / by Ronald P. Carver
p. cm.
Includes bibliographical references and index.
ISBN 0-8058-3529-6 (cloth: alk. paper)
1. Reading. 2. Reading comprehension 3. Reading disability. I. Title.

LB1050.2 C27 2000
428'.4--dc21 99-053157

The final camera copy for this work was prepared by the author, and therefore the publisher takes no responsibility for consistency or correctness of typographical style. However, this arrangement helps to make publication of this kind of scholarship possible.

Books published by Lawrence Erlbaum Associates are printed on acid-free paper, and their bindings are chosen for strength and durability.

Printed in the United States of America

10 9 8 7 6 5 4 3 2 1

To Mary Lou, Melanie, Heather,

Bill, Jay, and last but not least, Joey.

CONTENTS

	Preface	ix
	Acknowledgments	xii
PART I.	THE FIRST PART	1
1.	The Causal Model	3
2.	Context for the Causal Model	24
PART II.	THEORETICAL CONSTRUCTS	45
3.	Efficiency Level, E_L	47
4.	Accuracy Level, A_L	61
5.	Rate Level, R_L	75
6.	Verbal Knowledge Level, V_L	90
7.	Pronunciation Knowledge Level, P_L	99
8.	Cognitive Speed Level, C_s	113
PART III.	THE PROXIMAL CAUSES	127
9.	Two Causes of Efficiency Level	129
10.	Two Causes of Accuracy Level	140
11.	Two Causes of Rate Level	153
12.	Two Causes of Verbal Level	163
13.	Two Causes of Pronunciation Level	175
14.	Two Causes of Cognitive Speed Level	192

PART IV.	GENERAL RESEARCH EVIDENCE	201
15.	Lower-Grade Readers	203
16.	Middle-Grade Readers	215
17.	Adult Readers	225
PART V.	DISABLED READERS	239
18.	The Rauding Diagnostic System	241
19.	Research on Dyslexia and Disabilities	258
PART VI.	THREE NON-CAUSAL FACTORS	277
20.	Intelligence and Reading	279
21.	Volume of Reading	298
22.	Whole-Language Approach	311
PART VII.	THE LAST PART	329
23.	The Rauding Approach	331
24.	Summary and Conclusions	355
Appendix A.	The Earlier Constructs of Rauding Theory	379
Appendix B.	The Three Laws of Rauding Theory	383
Appendix C.	The Equations of Rauding Theory	385
Appendix D.	Conversions Among Units of Rauding Rate	395
Appendix E.	List of Numbered Equations	397
	Glossary	399
	References	411
	Author Index	431
	Subject Index	439

Preface

In this book, an attempt will be made to describe all of the important factors which cause some students to have low reading achievement and other students to have high reading achievement. This book is most relevant to researchers. However, teachers and other stakeholders, such as parents, school district personnel, government agency personnel, and legislators should find it helpful.

Researchers who read this book should be able to organize their knowledge better, and thereby improve the way they design and conduct their research. Teachers who read this book should have a better idea of how to improve their instruction in reading. When this book is read by other stakeholders, such as parents, legislators, state department personnel, and government employees dealing with education, they should be better able to evaluate what is likely to work with respect to new programs designed to increase the reading achievement of students.

Great attention will be devoted to the main factors that influence how much a student gains in reading achievement during a year of school, or a calendar year. If we can increase the reading achievement of students, then they will automatically comprehend more of what they read whenever they read. An attempt will be made to answer the following question: what things can educators do to increase reading achievement, and what things are beyond the influence of educators?

This book will be directly concerned with achievement associated with normal or typical reading. Other types of reading such as skimming, scanning, learning from difficult text, or memorizing text will not receive much attention. This book will not be concerned with helping students learn to improve their study skills, or improve their study habits, or improve their motivation to read. Instead, much attention will be directed toward the things that teachers can do during an entire school year that are likely to improve the reading level and reading rate of students, which in turn, will increase their reading achievement.

The content of this book is unique in at least nine ways. First, it defies tradition by contending that a deficiency in a reading process is not a primary cause of low reading achievement. This book will not try to fix reading processes that are malfunctioning because it will be contended that poor reading achievement has little or nothing to do with how a student is looking at the words on the page. Second, tradition will also be defied by theorizing that beginning readers should not be asked to guess at the pronunciation of words; they should not be asked to guess from context via the whole-language approach or guess from letter-sound correspondences via the phonics approach. Third, this book treats spelling quite differently from traditional instructional methods. The teaching of correct spelling is usually done for the purpose of helping children write better. One major thrust of this book is that the teaching of spelling not only helps children increase their reading level but it also helps children learn to read faster. Fourth, this book defies a great deal of tradition by focusing upon reading rate. Most researchers ignore reading rate and most teachers ignore reading rate. A measure of reading rate is seldom used to evaluate reading progress or to diagnose reading problems, yet the normal rate at which individuals can read with accurate comprehension is a major factor affecting their reading achievement. Fifth, it is theorized that students who have not yet learned to pronounce all of the words they know when listening, should be given instruction that is different from those students who have already learned to pronounce all the words they know when listening. Sixth, this book is unique in that it attempts to organize the most important factors causing high and low reading achievement into a theoretical framework that should help researchers and teachers in their quest to increase the reading ability of all students. Seventh, two factors that have traditionally been thought to have a major influence upon reading achievement are IQ and the amount of time a student spends reading, yet those two factors do not seem to have a substantial effect upon reading achievement. Eighth, a system is presented for diagnosing disabled readers and dyslexics; from these diagnoses, the best instruction for remediating reading problems has been proposed. Ninth, a new approach to reading instruction has been recommended as a replacement for traditional approaches, such as whole-language, phonics, and skills. In the above nine ways, plus others, this book attempts to upgrade what we think we know about improving reading achievement.

This effort to specify the most important causes of high and low reading achievement represents an integration of the two disciplines of scientific psychology, namely, the discipline of the experimentalists and the discipline of the psychometricians (see Cronbach, 1957). The discipline of the experimentalist is involved in educational instruction, or treatments designed to improve reading achievement; experimentalists change conditions in order to study their consequences. The discipline of the psychometrician is involved in aptitudes for achievement; individual differences in aptitudes for learning are within the realm of psychometricians who study correlations between already existing variations between individuals. The root causes of high and low reading achievement involve influences within the individual (aptitudes) and influences outside the individual (instruction). These two general types of root causes, and their effects, will be studied in great detail via the following chapters. Throughout these chapters, there will be an attempt to bridge the gap that often exists between concepts used by educators (e.g., fluency) and concepts used by psychologists (e.g., automaticity); this gap is often bridged by using new theoretical constructs that try to extract the best from both worlds (e.g., rauding and raudamatized words).

The 24 chapters in this book are divided into seven major parts. Part I contains two chapters that provide an overview of the entire book and an introduction to the remaining chapters. The most important content in Part I is the presentation of a causal model of reading achievement, which involves several theoretical constructs and how they cause high and low reading achievement.

This model is an extension of rauding theory, which is based upon the similarities between comprehension during reading and comprehension during auding (or listening).

Part II of this book contains six chapters, each devoted to a detailed explanation of one of the theoretical constructs in the causal model, namely, efficiency level (achievement), accuracy level (reading level), rate level (reading rate), verbal level (listening), pronunciation level (decoding), and cognitive speed level (naming speed); each of these six chapters also contain a summary of relevant research (Chapters 3 to 8). Then, Part III also contains six chapters (Chapters 9 to 14), each one devoted to theory and research relevant to a particular causal connection in model. For example, verbal level (listening) and pronunciation level (decoding) are said to be the two proximal causes of accuracy level (reading level) in the model, so Chapter 10 contains theory and research relevant to listening and decoding being the two main causes of high and low reading levels.

Part IV contains general research evidence supporting the relevance of the causal model to lower-grade readers (Chapter 15), middle-grade readers (Chapter 16), and adult readers (Chapter 17); the research evidence presented in Part IV will be relevant to disparate parts of the causal model, such as distal causes and non-causal connections.

Part V is devoted to disabled readers. It explains how the causal model can be used to diagnose reading disabilities that are relevant to dyslexics and other handicapped readers (Chapter 18). Then, this new diagnostic system is compared to the traditional conceptions of disabled readers and dyslexic readers that are held by researchers (Chapter 19).

Part VI relates the causal model to three factors that are not considered to be important causes of high reading achievement, namely, intelligence (Chapter 20), volume of reading (Chapter 21), and the whole-language approach to reading instruction (Chapter 22).

Part VII, the last part, includes a chapter on a newly developed "rauding approach" to reading instruction (Chapter 23). This last part also attempts to summarize and draw conclusions based upon the theory and empirical evidence presented in the earlier parts of the book (Chapter 24).

Finally, at the back of this book, there is a glossary containing definitions of concepts and constructs. There are also appendices that (a) explain rauding theory, (b) explain the three laws of rauding theory, (c) explain the equations that can be used to predict the accuracy of reading comprehension, (d) provide conversions among units of rauding rate, and (e) list the numbered equations presented in this book.

Ronald P. Carver

Acknowledgments

This book was six years in the making and my wife, Mary Lou, contributed to my long periods of productive concentration by being patiently supportive.

I am grateful that the University of Missouri at Kansas City gave me a research leave of one semester in 1994, to get the book started.

Thanks also to the hundreds of researchers who have published data relevant to the theory underlying this book; the hard work of those researchers provided ideas and empirical evidence that made my efforts possible. In this regard, I need to point out that the theory in this book was highly influenced by (a) the simple view of reading espoused by Philip Gough and colleagues, (b) verbal efficiency theory espoused by Charles Perfetti and colleagues, and (c) the spelling/reading theory espoused by Linnea Ehri and colleagues.

During the past 6 years, all the words that I have hand written and rewritten have been typed by Darlene Beeman, with a high level of speed and accuracy that continues to amaze me; without her excellent help I am sure that this book would have taken many more years to finish.

I am indebted to the following researchers who gave me helpful criticisms of draft chapters: Patricia G. Bowers, Susan W. Clark, G. Reid Lyon, Frank R. Manis, Michael C. McKenna, Louisa C. Moats, Ann J. Pace, Charles A. Perfetti, John P. Sabatini, Steven A. Stahl, William E. Tunmer, W. James Wagner, Victor L. Willson, and Maryanne Wolf.

I would especially like to thank the two anonymous reviewers of the first version of this book, which was over 900 pages long in manuscript form; they convinced me that the manuscript needed to be drastically cut. I did cut over 250 pages, so they get credit for helping to make the book much more readable.

Finally, I would like to acknowledge the life long caring of my parents, Ramon Edison Carver (deceased, 1995) and Byrl Berniece Carver.

PART I

THE FIRST PART

Part I, which follows, contains two introductory chapters. Chapter 1 contains an overview of a causal model which purports to explain and describe the causes of high and low reading achievement. This first chapter contains theoretical constructs, their causal connections, and how they relate to more traditional concepts in reading and reading research. Chapter 2 puts this causal model into the context of prior research and theory about reading; it elaborates upon what the model attempts to describe, explain, predict, and control, and what lies outside its purported relevance.

CHAPTER

1

THE CAUSAL MODEL

The main purpose of this book is to present an explanation of why some students achieve at high levels in reading while others achieve at low levels, or fail to read well. This explanation will include implications for what we should be doing to help all readers achieve at higher levels, whether they read poorly or not. The explanation will take the form of a causal model. This model involves theoretical constructs and their causal connections. Later in this chapter, an overview of the causal model will be presented.

The causal model is based on rauding theory, so it will be necessary to explain what "rauding" means and what "rauding theory" entails, before presenting the causal model. The theoretical constructs in this model will be new for many readers, such as accuracy level and rate level, so they will be described briefly. After the model is presented, several measures of the constructs in the model will be described to help the reader understand the constructs better. Then, in subsequent chapters, each construct will be described in greater detail.

Rauding and Rauding Theory

The term "rauding" was derived from a combination of two words, reading and auding; reading usually means to attempt to comprehend language in the form of printed words, and auding usually means to attempt to comprehend language in the form of spoken words. The term rauding was developed (Carver, 1977) to focus on the similarity between reading comprehension and listening comprehension when individuals are comprehending sentences in textual materials, without regard for whether the words in the sentences are (a) being read as they are looked at in printed text, or (b) being auded as they are read aloud by someone else.

Rauding is the process of comprehending sentences, or complete thoughts, during reading or auding. So, rauding focuses upon the similarities between the comprehension of sentences during both reading and auding. This common comprehension process has long been recognized by researchers. As early as 1972, Sticht acknowledged that reading and listening comprehension represented the same internal processes when he stated that "there is only one, holistic ability to comprehend by language, and one should be able to comprehend equally well by listening or by reading, if one has been taught to decode well and other task variables are equalized" (pp. 293-294).

Figure 1-1 depicts the theoretical connections among reading, auding, and rauding. The term "reading" usually involves looking at printed words in the form of sentences in order to comprehend the thoughts the author intended to communicate; however, reading may occur without comprehension. The term "auding" usually involves listening to spoken words in the form of sentences in order to comprehend the thoughts the speaker intended to communicate; however, auding may occur without comprehension. Rauding means that an individual is comprehending most, if not all, of the thoughts during reading or auding.

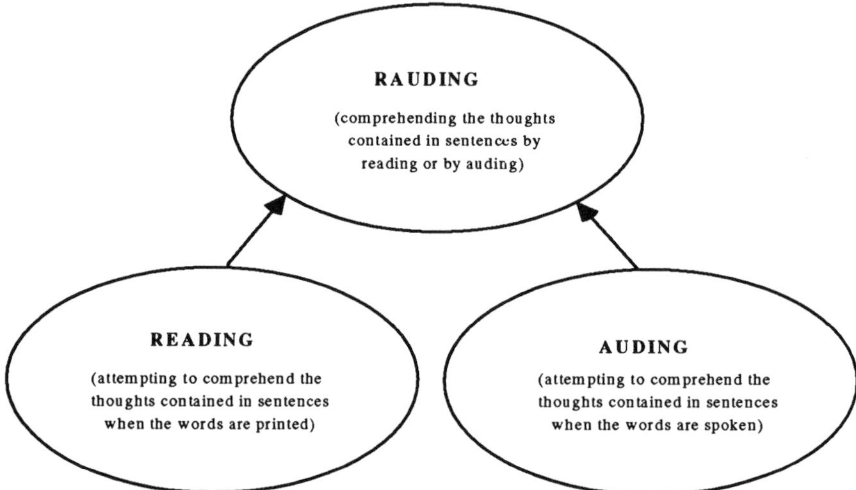

Figure 1-1. The theoretical connections among reading, auding, and rauding.

Before continuing, it should be acknowledged that there are many differences between listening and reading as they occur naturally in language situations (e.g., see Danks, 1980). When people are engaged in conversation there are many factors which would make a written transcript of the conversation more difficult to comprehend. For example, comprehension of conversation can involve cues from tone of voice and body language but this information is not available during reading. However, there are few differences between the process involved in comprehending relatively easy text when reading, and the process involved in comprehending the same text when it is read aloud for the individual at the typical reading rate of the individual.

During reading, rauding is similar to what has traditionally been referred to as ordinary reading, normal reading, typical reading, or simple reading. In this book, which is directed toward reading achievement, rauding will mean that an individual is recognizing each consecutive word in the sentences of printed text, and simultaneously understanding all, or almost all, of the complete thoughts in these sentences as they are being read. As will be explained in more detail in later sections, rauding refers to a particular reading process that is different from other reading processes that can be operated on text, such as scanning the words, skimming the sentences, learning from the text, and memorizing the text.

Rauding has a great deal in common with what is often called "fluency in reading." Individuals are said to be "fluent" readers when they read text orally (aloud) with accuracy of pronunciation and with appropriate expression which suggests that they are understanding the thoughts represented by the words they are saying aloud. A person who is reading relatively hard material aloud is not likely to be described as a fluent reader because the text is likely to contain (a) words incorrectly pronounced because they are unknown, and (b) incorrect expression because the thoughts are not being understood. Expressiveness is an important ingredient of oral reading because that is the only clue another person has about whether the reader is understanding what is being read. Yet, expressiveness can be faked, and it is only important for oral performance when the purpose is to help others comprehend or to entertain them; expressiveness is not a necessary ingredient for the accuracy of text comprehension by the readers themselves. Rauding and fluent reading are very similar except that rauding ordinarily refers to silent reading and fluency ordinarily refers to oral reading.

Although fluency in reading is a term usually applied to a speaker whose textual rendition is fluid or facile, the term may also be applied to silent reading or to the rapid identification of lists of isolated words so that fluency is sometimes used synonomously with skilled reading (e.g., see Beck & Carpenter, 1986). If the term "fluency" is used to refer to the silent reading of relatively easy text wherein the words are recognized effortlessly at the typical reading rate of the individual while the complete thoughts in these sentences are being comprehended as they are read, then "fluency" and "rauding" are synonymous terms.

With respect to reading, rauding means to read normally with high accuracy of comprehension. A theory of rauding, or rauding theory, refers to all the theoretical constructs, laws, equations, and models that have been developed to describe, explain, predict, and control rauding (e.g., Carver, 1977; 1981; 1990a; 1997). An overview of the earlier constructs of rauding theory plus an overview of its laws and equations is presented at the back of this book in Appendices A, B, and C. Those earlier ideas and terminology will be used and built upon in this book. Definitions of many important terms are contained in a glossary at the back of this book. Rauding theory has been used as the foundation for developing a causal model of reading achievement, which is the focus of this first chapter and the focus of this book.

Overview of the Causal Model

This section will present a brief overview of the main factors which cause high and low reading achievement. These causes are organized into a theoretical framework, or a causal model. In order to understand this model, it will be necessary to learn new terminology. These new terms have meanings that are similar to older and more familiar concepts, but the new terms have meanings that are more precise and often different in important ways from earlier concepts. Because new terms are involved in the causal model, this overview will be difficult for most readers of this book to comprehend. However, immediately following this section, a more lengthy description of the causal model will be given, along with a graphic summary. The second and more lengthy description will provide redundancy and reinforcement of the new terms and causal connections which are presented later in this section. It may also help to remember that Chapters 3 through 14 of this book provide a detailed elaboration of the causal model. In the paragraphs which follow, the causal model will be outlined using theoretical constructs, but their similarities to older more traditional terms, called concepts, will also be pointed out along the way.

The focal point of the causal model is reading achievement. In order to explain what factors cause the most improvement in reading achievement during a school year, it is necessary first to define what is meant by the term "reading achievement." Traditionally, reading achievement has been measured by standardized reading comprehension tests. These tests usually involve (a) reading passages that vary in difficulty, (b) answering questions on each passage, and (c) working under a time limit. These tests provide a crude operational definition of general reading ability; high scores on one of these tests means high reading achievement and low scores mean low reading achievement. This traditional concept of reading achievement will be refined and clarified by using a newer construct called rauding efficiency level (E_L). This means that the older concept of reading achievement is being upgraded by a newer theoretical construct, which is symbolized as E_L and is usually referred to as "efficiency level." So, using more precise terminology, this book will be devoted to the primary causes of efficiency level, E_L. Later in Chapter 3, a more extensive description of the E_L construct will be given.

One primary cause of gain in efficiency level, E_L, is the gain in rauding accuracy level (A_L), according to the causal model. Accuracy level, A_L, is a construct that is similar to the traditional concept of reading level. For example, if a student is found to be reading at the ninth-grade level by an informal reading inventory, then this student is also likely to have an accuracy level around the ninth-grade level ($A_L = 9$). A_L actually refers to the most difficult text a student can accurately read when it is read at the student's normal reading rate. This book will elaborate upon and clarify the connection between reading level and general reading ability by explaining how accuracy level, A_L, is a primary cause of efficiency level, E_L. An extensive description of A_L is provided in Chapter 4, and then Chapter 9 elaborates upon how A_L is a proximal cause of E_L.

The other primary cause of high and low efficiency level, E_L, is rauding rate level (R_L). This construct is similar to normal reading rate. For example, if a student is found to be reading at a rate equal to an average student in grade 4, then this student is likely to have a rate level around the fourth-grade level ($R_L = 4$). Most researchers are aware that the fastest rate at which an individual can accurately comprehend text does affect reading achievement. This book will make it clearer how normal reading rate affects reading achievement by explaining how gains in rate level, R_L, impact upon gains in efficiency level, E_L. An extensive description of rate level is given in Chapter 5, and Chapter 9 elaborates upon how R_L is a proximal cause of E_L.

Figure 1-2 depicts how reading level and normal reading rate are the two causes of high and low reading achievement, or how A_L and R_L are the two causes of high and low general reading ability. For example, a student in grade 6 might have a high reading level ($A_L = 9$) but a low reading rate ($R_L = 4$), which combine to cause an average level of reading achievement ($E_L = 6$). If accuracy level, A_L, and rate level, R_L, are the two proximal causes of high and low reading achievement, that is, high and low efficiency level, E_L, then it is important to determine what causes gains in A_L and R_L.

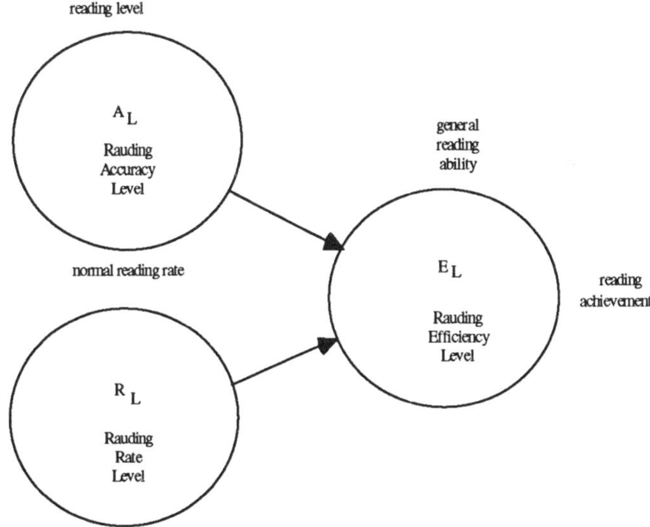

Figure 1-2. A graphic depiction of how A_L (reading level) and R_L (normal reading rate) are the two proximal causes of E_L (reading achievement or general reading ability).

With respect to accuracy level, A_L, it has always been recognized that how much a person knows affects their reading level, and that idea has been clarified by advancing the theoretical construct of verbal knowledge level (V_L). This construct has much in common with the more traditional concepts of general knowledge, world knowledge, verbal knowledge, or the most difficult text a student can accurately comprehend when listening, called listening capacity. If we want to improve an individual's accuracy level, A_L, then we can do that by improving their verbal level, V_L. An extensive description of verbal level is contained in Chapter 6, and Chapter 10 explains in detail about how V_L is causal for A_L.

Another way we can improve the accuracy level, A_L, of most students in elementary school is by helping them increase the number of words they can accurately pronounce, called pronunciation knowledge level (P_L). It has long been recognized by researchers that the ability to accurately decode or pronounce isolated words has a major impact upon reading level. This ability to identify isolated words has also been called word recognition, or word identification. The causal connection between decoding ability and reading level can be translated into the terminology of the causal model by saying that increases in pronunciation knowledge level, P_L, cause increases in accuracy level, A_L. A more detailed description of pronunciation level is provided in Chapter 7, and then Chapter 10 explains how P_L is a proximal cause of A_L.

Figure 1-3 contains a graphic depiction of how verbal level (listening) and pronunciation level (decoding) are the two proximal causes of high and low accuracy level (reading level). For example, a student in grade 4 may have a high listening level ($V_L = 8$) but a low decoding level ($P_L = 2$), which combine to cause an average reading level ($A_L = 4$).

With respect to improving rate level, R_L, it turns out that increases in pronunciation level, P_L, are also purported to cause increases in rate level, R_L. So, improving pronunciation level has a double dividend. That is, gain in P_L is likely to improve both A_L and R_L, and therefore have a doubly high impact upon gain in E_L, or reading achievement. A lengthy description of how P_L is an important cause of improvement in R_L is given in Chapter 11.

The other primary factor which purportedly influences rate level, R_L, besides pronunciation level, P_L, is cognitive speed level (C_s). This construct is similar in concept to an older concept in reading called "thinking rate." It is also similar to a newer concept in reading called "naming speed." The causal connection between thinking rate, or naming speed, and reading rate has been translated into the terminology of the causal model by saying that increases in cognitive speed level, C_s, cause increases in rate level, R_L. The cognitive speed level construct is described in great detail in Chapter 8, and then Chapter 11 explains how C_s influences R_L.

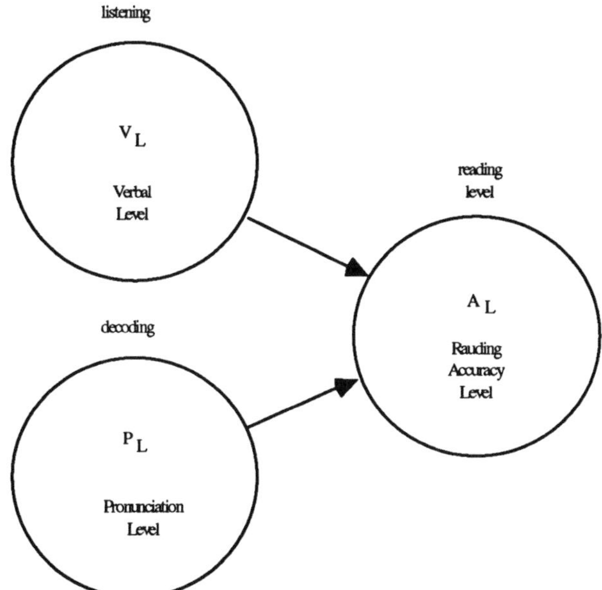

Figure 1-3. A graphic depiction of how V_L (listening level) and P_L (decoding level) are the two proximal causes of A_L (reading level).

Figure 1-4 depicts how pronunciation level (decoding) and cognitive speed level (naming speed) are the two proximal causes of rate level (normal reading rate). For example, a student in grade 4 may have a low decoding level ($P_L = 2$) but a high naming speed level ($C_s = 8$), which combine to cause an average level of normal reading rate ($R_L = 4$).

The connections between traditional concepts in reading research and the six theoretical constructs of E_L, A_L, R_L, V_L, P_L, and C_s, have been summarized in Table 1-1 for reference purposes. For example, it can be seen in Table 1-1 that the traditional concepts of reading achievement, general reading ability, and the ability to read efficiently have been replaced by the theoretical construct of rauding efficiency level, which is symbolized as E_L and is commonly called "efficiency level."

In summary, a gain in E_L requires a gain in A_L or a gain in R_L. Gains in A_L and R_L require gains in V_L, P_L, or C_s. Therefore, increases in efficiency level, E_L, come from increases in accuracy level and rate level, A_L and R_L, which in turn are caused by increases in verbal level, pronunciation level, or cognitive speed level—V_L, P_L, or C_s.

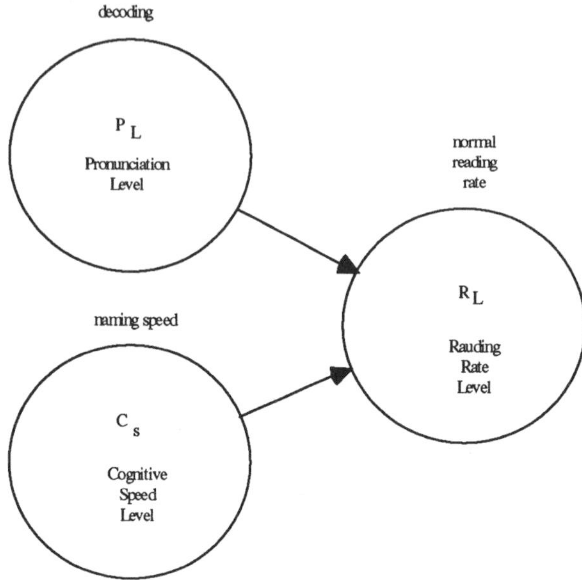

Figure 1-4. A graphic depiction of how P_L (decoding) and C_s (naming speed) are the two proximal causes of R_L (normal reading rate).

Verbal level, V_L, and pronunciation level, P_L, are themselves influenced by extremely important root factors in the causal model that are not included in Table 1-1, such as teaching and learning experiences plus aptitudes. Any attempt to inprove verbal level, V_L, by instruction will also be influenced by the verbal knowledge aptitude of the individual, symbolized as "g_v." Also, any attempt to improve pronunciation level, P_L, by instruction will be influenced by the pronunciation knowledge aptitude of the individual, symbolized as "g_p." Finally, it is theorized that cognitive speed level, C_s, cannot be improved by instruction or learning; C_s can only be improved via maturation, or increases due to the passage of time during the school year. Differences between individuals in C_s at the same age are referred to as "cognitive speed aptitude," and are symbolized as "g_s."

From this brief overview of the causal model, it can be seen that the most effective way to increase reading achievement during a school year, is to concentrate on providing the best instruction for increasing verbal level, V_L, and the best instruction for increasing pronunciation level, P_L. However, the amount of gain in reading achievement will also be importantly influenced by the individual's aptitude for verbal learning, g_v, aptitude for pronunciation learning, g_p, and aptitude for cognitive speed, g_s. That is, the root causes of high and low reading achievement are (a) excellent or poor teaching with respect to increasing an individual's verbal knowledge level and increasing an individual's pronunciation knowledge level, and (b) high or low aptitude in verbal knowledge, pronunciation knowledge, and cognitive speed.

Table 1-1
Six Theoretical Constructs, Their Symbols, Their Corresponding Traditional Concepts, and Their Commonly Used Names

Symbol	*Theoretical Construct*	*Similar Traditional Concepts*	*Commonly Used Name*
E_L	Rauding efficiency level	Reading achievement, general reading ability, or ability to read efficiently.	Efficiency level
A_L	Rauding accuracy level	Reading level, or most difficult text that can be accurately comprehended during reading.	Accuracy level
R_L	Rauding rate level	Normal reading rate.	Rate level
V_L	Verbal knowledge level	General knowledge, or the most difficult text that can be accurately comprehended during listening.	Verbal level
P_L	Pronunciation knowledge level	Decoding ability, or the number of words that can be accurately identified.	Pronunciation level
C_s	Cognitive speed level	Rate of naming letters or numbers—or thinking speed.	Cognitive speed level

In this brief overview of the causal model of reading achievement, older concepts have been used to help explain the new and upgraded constructs of the causal model. The same causal model will be presented again in the next section, but this time it will be described in more detail.

The Causal Model in More Detail

Introduction. The causal model for reading achievement, outlined briefly in the previous section, is graphically depicted in Figure 1-5—a slightly modified version of Figure 5 in Carver (1997). This figure contains all the factors described earlier that purportedly cause high and low reading achievement; the theoretical constructs described earlier are inside the circles in Figure 1-5. For example, efficiency level, E_L, is inside the circle at the far right side of the figure; traditional concepts that are similar to each theoretical construct are noted above the circles. Notice that "general reading ability" is located above the circle containing E_L. Also notice that when one construct is the cause of another construct, this is indicated by an arrow on a line connecting the two constructs. For example, a line connects the A_L construct with the E_L construct, and the direction of the arrow indicates that A_L is the cause of E_L.

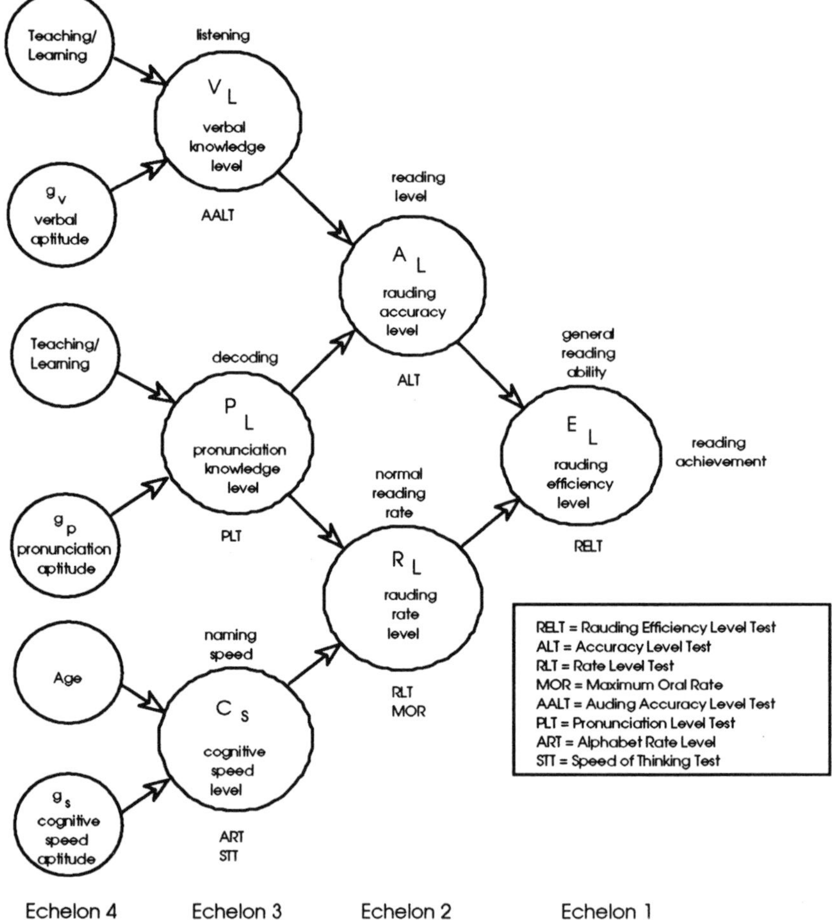

Figure 1-5. The Causal Model of Reading Achievement.

Below each circle is the abbreviated name of a test (or tests) that has been used to measure the construct, such as RELT located below the E_L circle.

These abbreviated test names have been spelled out in a box in Figure 1-5, such as Rauding Efficiency Level Test for RELT. These tests will be described in more detail in the six chapters contained in Part II of this book.

Notice that there are four vertical columns of circles in the figure and they are labeled at the bottom of the figure as Echelons 1, 2, 3, and 4; E_L is in the only circle in Echelon 1. The remainder of this section will be organized in terms of these four echelons.

Echelon 1. As was noted earlier, the focal point of the causal model is "reading achievement," which is written beside the E_L circle in Figure 1-5. Also, as noted earlier, general reading ability is above the E_L circle because the E_L construct replaces this more traditional concept. E_L is a theoretical construct that represents the highest grade level of text difficulty (D_L) that an individual can comprehend accurately (64% or more) when the material is presented at a rate that is equal to the level of text difficulty. For example, if an individual has $E_L = 4$, this means that this person could accurately comprehend text at grade level four in difficulty when the text was presented for a length of time equal to a fourth-grade reading rate, but this individual could not accurately comprehend material at the fifth-grade level when it was presented for a length of time equal to a fifth-grade rate. This E_L construct is similar to what Perfetti (1985) called "general reading ability," because it involves both accuracy and rate.

Measures of E_L should correlate highly with scores on reading comprehension tests because these traditional reading tests usually contain texts to read that increase in difficulty, and these reading tests usually have time limits that make reading rate a factor that influences the test scores. Indeed, a number of research studies have provided support for the hypothesis that individual differences in E_L and individual differences on standardized reading comprehension tests are usually measuring the same factor (e.g., see Carver, 1992a, 1992b).

In summary, reading achievement is the focal point of the causal model and it is represented by the theoretical construct called efficiency level. This E_L construct also is (a) similar to the more traditional concept of general reading ability, and (b) similar to what is being measured by traditional standardized reading comprehension tests with time limits that put a premium on both accuracy and rate of comprehending textual material that varies in difficulty.

Echelon 2. In Figure 1-5, A_L and R_L are inside the two circles in Echelon 2; they are purported to be the two proximal causes of E_L, or reading achievement.

As noted earlier, A_L symbolizes the construct called rauding accuracy level which is very similar to the more traditional concept of reading level. For example, students who purportedly are reading at the third-grade level are likely to be found to have $A_L = 3$.

As noted earlier, R_L symbolizes the construct called rauding rate level, which is very similar to the traditional concept of normal reading rate expressed in grade equivalent (GE) units. For example, students who purportedly read at the normal rate of fifth-graders are likely to be found to have $R_L = 5$.

Defined in more technical terms, accuracy level, A_L, is the highest level of text difficulty, D_L, that individuals can accurately comprehend (64% or higher) when they read this material at their own rauding rate (R_r). Rauding rate, R_r, is the relatively constant rate at which individuals read normally; it is also the rate at which they operate their rauding process on relatively easy material ($A_L > D_L$) and are accurately comprehending (64% or higher). Individuals normally read relatively easy material at a relatively constant rate, called their rauding rate (Carver, 1990a), because it is also their most efficient rate (Carver, 1982). When rauding rate, R_r, is expressed in GE units, it is called rauding rate level, R_L (see Appendix D).

A_L and R_L are the two proximal causes of gain, growth, or improvement in efficiency level, E_L. This causal relationship between A_L and R_L at Echelon 2 and E_L at Echelon 1, has been expressed mathematically (Carver, 1997) as follows:

$$E_L = \sqrt{A_L R_L} \tag{1-1}$$

This equation means that efficiency level is purported to be equal to the square root of the product of accuracy level and rate level, or stated differently, E_L is the average of A_L and R_L when the geometric mean is used to get the average. For example, if an individual is at the ninth-grade level of reading accuracy ($A_L = 9$) and is at the fourth-grade level of reading rate ($R_L = 4$), then the efficiency level of this student would be at grade 6 ($E_L = 6$) because the product of 9 and 4 is 36 and the square root of 36 is 6.

Equation 1-1 succinctly summarizes how the reading achievement of individuals is a function of their reading level and their normal reading rate. If we want to improve the reading achievement of students, then we must help them increase their accuracy level, A_L, or help them increase their rate level, R_L; according to this causal model there are no other choices.

Echelon 3. Next to be discussed are the three factors in Echelon 3 which are purported to be the proximal causes of A_L and R_L in Echelon 2.

The two proximal causes of high and low accuracy level, A_L, are verbal knowledge level, V_L, and pronunciation knowledge level, P_L. Verbal level, V_L, is a construct that represents the level of verbal knowledge acquired by individuals, in GE units. V_L represents level of knowledge in the form of oral language, or spoken words, so it is similar to the traditional concept of listening comprehension, or listening capacity. Therefore, measures of V_L would include listening vocabulary tests, listening comprehension tests, and general knowledge tests that were administered auditorily.

P_L is the number of real words an individual can accurately pronounce, expressed in GE units; it is similar to the more traditional concept of decoding ability, or decoding knowledge. Measures of P_L would include word identification tests, and word recognition tests.

Theory and data already exist relevant to the above hypothesis which holds that the two primary factors causing improvement in reading level, A_L, are verbal level, V_L, and pronunciation level, P_L. That is, Gough and Tunmer (1986), as well as Hoover and Gough (1990), have advanced the simple view of reading which posits that reading is comprised of decoding and listening. The connections between this "simple view of reading" and the theory that V_L and P_L are the two proximal causes of A_L will be examined in more detail later in Chapter 10.

The causal relationship between V_L and P_L at Echelon 2, and A_L at Echelon 3, has been expressed mathematically (Carver, 1997) as follows:

$$A_L = \sqrt{V_L P_L} \qquad (1\text{-}2)$$

This equation means that accuracy level, A_L, is purported to be equal to the square root of the product of V_L and P_L, or reading level is the average of listening level and decoding level when the geometric mean is used to get the average. For example, if an individual is able to comprehend text at the sixth-grade level when listening ($V_L = 6$) and is also able to correctly pronounce words at a grade equivalent level of 4.2 ($P_L = 4.2$), then this student would be reading at the fifth-grade level ($A_L = 5$) because $5 = \sqrt{6 \text{ x } 4.2}$.

Equation 1-2 succinctly summarizes how reading level is a function of listening and decoding. If we want to increase the reading level of students, then we must help them increase their verbal level, V_L, or help them increase their pronunciation level, P_L; according to this causal model there are no other choices. It should be noted that when students become advanced readers, then Equation 1-2 is no longer valid. That is, when individuals have reached the eighth-grade level in both V_L and P_L, then Equation 1-2 no longer holds; this is explained in more detail in Chapter 17.

The two proximal causes of high and low rate level in Echelon 2 are pronunciation level, P_L, and cognitive speed level, C_s, which are in Echelon 3 of Figure 1-5. Note again that P_L is considered to be a proximal cause of both A_L and R_L, whereas V_L is only a proximal cause of A_L, and C_s is only a proximal cause of R_L.

C_s is similar in concept to the more recent concept of naming speed (Wolf, 1991), and it is also similar to the more traditional concept of thinking speed (Buswell, 1951). Measures of C_s would include the ability to read aloud quickly the letters of the alphabet in random order, e.g., using the Alphabet Rate Test, ART, as is explained in more detail in Chapter 8.

The causal relationship between P_L and C_s at Echelon 3 and R_L at Echelon 2 has been expressed mathematically as follows:

$$R_L = \sqrt{P_L C_s} \qquad (1\text{-}3)$$

This equation means that rate level is purported to be equal to the square root of the product of pronunciation level and cognitive speed level, or that reading rate level is the average of decoding level and naming speed level when the geometric mean is used to get the average. For example, if an individual is able to pronounce words at the second-grade level ($P_L = 2$) and has a cognitive speed at the eighth-grade level ($C_s = 8$), then the rate level of this student would be at grade 4 ($R_L = 4$), because $4 = \sqrt{2 \times 8}$.

Equation 1-3 succinctly summarizes how the reading rate of individuals is a function of their decoding level and naming speed. If we want to improve the rate level, R_L, of students, then we must help them increase their pronunciation level, P_L; we cannot help individuals improve their cognitive speed level, C_s, as will be explained in more detail in Chapter 8 and Chapter 14.

Echelon 4. Next, the proximal causes of V_L, P_L, and C_s in Echelon 3 will be described by reference to their causal factors located in Echelon 4.

The proximal causes of verbal level, V_L, are theorized to be (a) teaching and learning experiences (T/L), and (b) verbal knowledge aptitude, g_v. In the causal model it is assumed that the V_L of individuals can be improved if they (a) listen to new ideas such as those advanced by their teachers, (b) view and listen to the voice track on documentary films and videos, and (c) read new ideas in textbooks or other expository texts. Measurement of this T/L factor might include the amount of time a student was engaged in quality learning or a measure of the quality of instruction with respect to learning new information of a verbal nature. However, equal exposure of individuals to new ideas, concepts, and words will not result in an equal increase in V_L. Individuals are not equal with respect to how much they can learn from what they have been told orally or in print, that is, some individuals have more verbal aptitude than others. Verbal knowledge aptitude has been symbolized in the causal model as g_v. This causal factor, g_v, influences how much an individual learns from being told. Measures of g_v would include memory for words on an auditorily presented reading span test (see Daneman and Carpenter, 1980, and Chapter 12).

Similar to V_L discussed above, there are also two proximal causes of P_L; they are (a) teaching and learning experiences (T/L), and (b) pronunciation knowledge aptitude, g_p. If we want to improve P_L, then we can try to get individuals involved in teaching and learning activities designed to improve P_L, such as learning to decode and spell. However, individuals are not equal with respect to how much instruction or repetition they need to learn sound-symbol connections, that is, some individuals learn faster than others. This aptitude for learning to pronounce words correctly has been symbolized in the model as g_p. Measurement of g_p would include tests of the basic ability to learn the somewhat consistent associations between the sounds within spoken words and the letters within printed words (see Chapter 13).

Finally, in Echelon 4 there are two primary proximal causes of C_s; they are age and cognitive speed aptitude (g_s). C_s advances one GE each year due to maturation, and there are no known instructional techniques which can increase C_s. However, at each age some individuals have more of this ability than others, due to an aptitude, or trait. Notice that C_s and g_s represent the same ability or aptitude with respect to cognitive speed, except that C_s is measured in GE units, which reflect absolute amounts, and g_v is measured in standard score units, which reflect individual differences at a particular age.

The root causes of high and low reading achievement, located at Echelon 4 in the causal model, reflect an interaction between nature and nurture factors. Vellutino et al. (1996) have articulated the importance of such an interaction as follows: "... any given level of reading achievement is a by-product of a complex interaction between one's endowment and the quality of one's literacy experience and instruction, such that the child who is endowed with an adequate mix of the cognitive abilities underlying reading ability is better equipped to profit from experience and instruction in learning to read than is the child who is endowed with a less than adequate mix of these abilities" (p. 602). Also, Olson et al. (1999) studied the genetics of learning disabilities and they concluded that the evidence for genetic influence helps explain why extra teaching and learning may be needed for some children.

Summary. The causal model of reading achievement has been summarized graphically in Figure 1-5, as was presented earlier. In this model, reading achievement is represented by a more precise theoretical construct called efficiency level, symbolized as E_L. The two proximal causes of E_L are accuracy level, A_L, and rate level, R_L. A_L is similar to the concept of reading level in GE units. R_L is similar to normal reading rate in GE units. The two proximal causes of A_L are verbal level, V_L, and pronunciation level, P_L. V_L is similar to listening level measured in GE units. P_L is similar to decoding level measured in GE units. The two proximal causes of R_L are pronunciation level, P_L, and cognitive speed level, C_s. P_L was described above, and C_s is similar to naming speed measured in GE units. The two proximal causes of V_L are teaching and learning experiences, T/L, and verbal knowledge aptitude, g_v, which is the ability to learn and remember verbal information. The two proximal causes of P_L are teaching and learning experiences, T/L, and pronunciation knowledge aptitude, g_p, which is the ability to learn and remember sound-symbol correspondences. The two proximal causes of C_s are age and cognitive speed aptitude, g_s, which is the ability to name a series of simple stimuli quickly. The root causes of high and low reading achievement are at Echelon 4 in the causal model; they are teaching and learning with respect to verbal knowledge and pronunciation knowledge, as well as verbal aptitude, pronunciation aptitude, cognitive speed aptitude, and age.

Measures

Introduction. The causal model can be grounded in the context of prior reading theory and prior reading research by describing how its constructs are measured and how these constructs relate to earlier measures used in reading.

One fundamental notion underlying the causal model is that each factor in the model can be measured in different ways. This idea was articulated by Cronbach (1957) as follows: "When there are many response variables, however, it is mandatory to subsume them under constructs, since otherwise we must have a separate set of laws for every measure of outcome" (p. 676). Thus, each construct in the causal model can be measured in different ways, although some ways are likely to be more valid than others.

Types of Measures. Three different types of measures can be used to test the hypotheses involved in the causal model—direct measures, indicants, and indirect measures. A direct measure of a theoretical construct is a measure designed directly from a definition of the construct; therefore it is measured in the units of the construct. For example, the walking distance from the front door of my home to the closest grocery store can be determined by two persons using a 100 foot tape measure—yielding 934.6 feet, for example, as a direct measure.

An indicant is a measure that theoretically should be measuring something that is either very similar to the theoretical construct or is likely to be correlated very highly with the construct. For example, I might count the number of walking strides between the front door of my home and the nearest grocery store—yielding 370 strides, an *indicant* of the distance.

An indirect measure is an indicant that has been rescaled into the same units as a direct measure. For example, I might multiply the number of strides to the grocery store by my estimated stride length (e.g., 2.5 feet)—yielding a total of 925 feet, for example, as an indirect measure.

A direct measure should ordinarily be the most valid. However, it is possible for an indirect measure to be more valid than a direct measure. For example, if a tape measure was used to provide a direct measure of the distance to the grocery store, and the two persons using the tape measure were not reliable in writing down their successive measurements and adding them up, then it is possible that a person who walked to the grocery store counting strides that were a consistent length would produce a more valid measure.

One disadvantage inherent in indicants and indirect measures is that experimental research may be required to prove beyond a reasonable doubt that these measures are valid for reflecting changes within individuals. For example, if an indirect measure shows the effect of a treatment, would a direct measure show the same effect?

The above fundamental ideas about measurement will be applied in the following subsection to the constructs in the causal model.

Measuring the Constructs. Past research on rauding theory has usually involved indicants and indirect measures. For example, accuracy level, A_L, is the most difficult level of text difficulty, D_L, that an individual can read accurately ($A > .64$) when the text is read at the individual's own rauding rate. With this definition of A_L, a direct measure of A_L would involve the presentation of increasingly difficult texts at the individual's own rauding rate, until the most difficult one that can be comprehended accurately is determined. However, most research on A_L has involved a vocabulary test as an indicant that has been rescaled into GE units to provide an indirect measure of A_L. It has been determined empirically that a more direct measure of A_L correlates highly with a vocabulary test that contains increasingly difficult words (Carver, 1994a). So, this vocabulary test has been scaled into GE units and used as an indirect measure of A_L. Indirect measures are indicants of a construct that can be used as an index or a surrogate to investigate the construct. In the example above, the scores on the vocabulary test (an indicant of A_L) were rescaled into the same GE units as a direct measure of A_L, so those scores can be said to provide an indirect measure of A_L.

Table 1-2 contains the three theoretical constructs at Echelons 1 and 2 of the causal model, along with related traditional concepts plus direct measures, indirect measures, and indicants. For example, rauding efficiency level (a) is a theoretical construct at Echelon 1 which is symbolized as E_L, (b) is similar to such traditional concepts as reading achievement, general reading ability, and reading efficiency, (c) can be measured directly by the Rauding Efficiency Level Test (see Chapter 3), (d) can be measured indirectly by the average of A_L and R_L (see Chapter 9), and (e) can be measured by an indicant such as the score on a standardized reading achievement test (see Chapter 3). Also, notice that indicants of A_L are untimed or unspeeded standardized reading comprehension tests, and indicants of R_L are standardized reading rate tests.

Table 1-3 contains information similar to Table 1-2 except it is for the three theoretical constructs at Echelon 3 in the causal model, namely, V_L, P_L, and C_s. Notice that decoding knowledge and word identification knowledge are traditional concepts related to pronunciation level, and that P_L can be measured by an indicant such as the score on a word identification test. Also, notice that verbal speed is another traditional concept similar to cognitive speed level, C_s.

Table 1-2
Theoretical Constructs, Symbols, Related Concepts, and Measures for E_L, A_L, and R_L at Echelons 1 and 2

Symbol	*Construct*	*Related Traditional Concepts*	*Measures*
E_L	Rauding efficiency level	(1) reading achievement (2) general reading ability (3) reading efficiency	Direct Measure: RELT, Rauding Efficiency Level Test (see Chapter 3) Indirect Measure: $E_L' = \sqrt{A_L R_L}$ (see Chapter 9) Indicant: standardized reading achievement test (see Chapter 3)
A_L	Rauding accuracy level	(1) reading level (2) reading comprehension level	Indirect Measure: ALT, Accuracy Level Test (see Chapter 4) Indicant: untimed (or not speeded) reading comprehension tests such as the Degrees of Power test, DRP (see Chapter 4)
R_L	Rauding rate level	(1) normal reading rate (2) rate level	Indirect Measures: RLT, Rate Level Test, or MOR, Maximum Oral Rate (see Chapter 5) Indicants: typical reading rate, or reading rate as measured by standardized tests such as the Nelson-Denny Reading Test (see Chapter 5)

Table 1-4 also contains information similar to Tables 1-2 and 1-3 except it is for three theoretical constructs at Echelon 4, namely, g_v, g_p, and g_s. Notice that (a) a listening span test measuring recall of verbal content could be developed into an indirect measure of g_v, and (b) verbal intelligence and crystallized intelligence are traditional concepts that are similar to g_v. Also, notice that an indicant of g_p would include a test of phonological awareness. Finally, notice that indicants of g_s would include: (a) a test of naming speed for colors, and (b) a test of naming speed for digits.

Not included in any of Tables 1-2, 1-3, and 1-4 is a measure of the two teaching and learning, T/L, factors at Echelon 4. If growth in V_L, P_L, and C_s for a school year was being measured, then it would be necessary to have measures of these T/L factors at Echelon 4 as well as measures of g_v, g_p, and g_s in order to predict this growth. The best indicants of T/L would probably measure the amount of time each student was involved in teaching and learning experiences directly related to improving V_L or P_L. Another indicant of T/L would be the number of basal readers covered in a year, or the number of instructional units mastered. Measuring T/L for V_L, T/L for P_L, g_v, g_p, and g_s is a challenge that must be met, eventually, for the causal model to be fully tested.

Table 1-3
Theoretical Constructs, Symbols, Related Traditional Concepts, and Measures for V_L, P_L, and C_s at Echelon 3

Symbol	*Construct*	*Related Traditional Concepts*	*Measures*
V_L	Verbal knowledge level	(1) listening comprehension level (2) listening vocabulary (3) general knowledge	Indirect Measure: AALT, Auding Accuracy Level Test (see Chapter 6) Indicants: listening comprehension tests, listening vocabulary tests, and auditory tests of general knowledge (see Chapter 6)
P_L	Pronunciation knowledge level	(1) decoding knowledge (2) word identification knowledge	Indirect Measure: PLT, Pronunciation Level Test (see Chapter 7) Indicants: word identification tests, word recognition tests, and decoding tests (see Chapter 7)
C_s	Cognitive speed level	(1) naming speed (2) thinking speed (3) verbal speed	Indirect Measures: ART, Alphabet Rate Test, STT, Speed of Thinking Test (see Chapter 8) Indicants: naming speed for overlearned language symbols (see Chapter 8)

Summary, Conclusions, and Implications

The root causes of high and low reading achievement, or E_L, are contained in Echelon 4 of the causal model. This echelon contains the three aptitudes that influence reading achievement, namely, verbal knowledge aptitude, g_v, pronunciation aptitude, g_p, and cognitive speed aptitude, g_s. This echelon also contains the teaching and learning experiences that elicit improvement in V_L and P_L.

Metaphorically, there are only two buttons which educators can push in the causal model (or circles in Figure 1-5) to get improvement in reading achievement, or E_L. The harder educators depress the teaching/learning button in Echelon 4 that is connected to verbal level, the bigger the effect they will have upon V_L at Echelon 3, and in turn the bigger the effect they will have on A_L at Echelon 2, and in turn the bigger the effect they will have on E_L at Echelon 1. The harder they depress the other teaching/learning button in Echelon 4 that is connected to pronunciation level, the bigger the effect they will have upon P_L at Echelon 3, and in turn the bigger the effect they will have on A_L and R_L at Echelon 2, and in turn the bigger the effect they will have on E_L at Echelon 1. Since E_L is completely determined by A_L and R_L, and since A_L and R_L are completely determined by V_L, P_L, and C_s, this means that the only way that educators can influence reading achievement, or E_L, is by their influence upon verbal level, V_L, and pronunciation level, P_L, at Echelon 3—educators cannot influence the other factor at Echelon 3, namely, C_s. Again, the root causes of reading achievement, or E_L, are teaching and learning with respect to verbal knowledge and pronunciation knowledge, as well as age and the three aptitude factors called verbal knowledge aptitude, pronunciation knowledge aptitude, and cognitive speed aptitude.

Table 1-4
Theoretical Constructs, Symbols, Related Concepts and Measures for g_v, g_p, and g_s at Echelon 4

Symbol	*Construct*	*Related Traditional Concepts*	*Measures*
g_v	Verbal knowledge aptitude	(1) verbal aptitude (2) verbal intelligence (3) crystallized intelligence	Direct Measure: listening span tests measuring recall of verbal content (see Chapter 12) Indicants: verbal intelligence tests such as the Peabody Picture Vocabulary Test, and verbal ability tests such as the SAT and GRE (see Chapter 12)
g_p	Pronunciation knowledge aptitude	(1) decoding aptitude (2) phonological awareness	Indicants: phonological awareness tests and letter-name accuracy tests (see Chapter 13)
g_s	Cognitive speed aptitude	(1) naming speed ability (2) speed of thinking (3) verbal speed	Indirect Measures: age normed scores on ART and STT (see Chapter 14) Indicants: naming speed for colors, and naming speed for digits (see Chapter 14)

This causal model contains ideas that are somewhat different from much conventional wisdom. That is, it holds that three primary factors completely determine reading achievement, or general reading ability. If you know the grade level scores for listening (verbal knowledge), word identification (pronunciation knowledge), and naming speed (cognitive speed), then reading achievement in grade level units is mathematically determined, or predicted with little error. Because cognitive speed is not amenable to improvement by education, this means that if we want to improve reading achievement of students, then (a) we have to improve their verbal knowledge or how much they know auditorily, or (b) we have to increase how many words they can accurately pronounce in isolation.

From this theory, it can be inferred that instruction in reading should be directed first toward activities that will produce the most gain in the number of words that individuals can accurately pronounce in a list, not pronounce in the context of a sentence. This instruction should continue until students can accurately pronounce all the words in print that they know when listening. When students are able to do this, instruction should then be directed toward increasing verbal knowledge and pronunciation knowledge simultaneously. For example, any new words learned by listening should simultaneously be learned by reading; newly learned spoken words should be practiced in written form until they can be spelled accurately and recognized quickly.

The causal model is being presented as a theory which purports to explain all of the variance in reading achievement for students in elementary school, high school, and college—as well as adults. That is, all of the variance in reading achievement, or E_L, is purportedly explained by variation in A_L, the rauding accuracy level of students, and R_L, the rauding rate level of students. All of the variation in A_L and R_L in students is purportedly explained by variation in their verbal knowledge level, V_L, their pronunciation knowledge level, P_L, and their cognitive speed level, C_s. Finally, it is likely that almost all of the variation in V_L, P_L, and C_s in students can be explained by the following: their age, their teaching/learning experiences, their verbal knowledge aptitude, their pronunciation knowledge aptitude, and their cognitive speed aptitude. V_L, P_L, and C_s completely determine reading achievement and the way to cause gain in these three primary factors is via appropriate instruction, but the effects of instruction are greatly influenced by individual aptitudes in the three specific areas noted above—g_v, g_p, and g_s.

The remainder of this book will be devoted to explaining this causal model in greater detail, as well as reviewing theory and research data relevant to the model. By the end of this book, the model should be understood very well, well enough to know its strong points and its weak points. Furthermore, it should be possible to use the model to cause improvement in reading achievement. Knowing the main factors which cause high and low reading achievement should help everyone who is devoted to increasing reading achievement in students.

CHAPTER

2

CONTEXT FOR THE CAUSAL MODEL

In this chapter, the causal model presented in the preceding chapter will be placed into the context of prior theory and research.

The next section will be devoted to explaining how the rauding process fits into the context of several other processes involved when individuals read text, namely, scanning, skimming, learning, and memorizing. Then, a section will be devoted to explaining how the slice of time that is most relevant to the causal model is 1 year, but that reading for 1 second and reading for 1 minute are also indirectly relevant to the causal model. A subsequent section will put the model into context with respect to age (lower graders, middle graders, and adults) and skill categories (beginning readers, intermediate readers, and advanced readers). Then, the model will be compared to other theoretical approaches to reading.

Basic Reading Processes

Introduction. An overview of the five basic reading processes will be given later in this section. Then, the rauding process will be described in more detail because it is the basic reading process that is relevant to the causal model. A subsection will also be devoted to a detailed explanation of how the rauding process can be induced in research.

Overview. In rauding theory (Carver, 1990a), five basic reading processes (or reading gears) are purportedly involved when individuals are reading textual materials, namely, memorizing (Gear 1), learning (Gear 2), rauding (Gear 3), skimming (Gear 4), and scanning (Gear 5). Table 2-1 contains the culminating component and the rates associated with each of these five basic processes, or gears. Notice that college students can operate a scanning process, Gear 5, at around 600 standard length words per minute (Wpm) because only one component is involved in the process, lexical accessing. An example of such a process would be a college student scanning a book to see if it mentioned a particular topic or word. A skimming process (Gear 4) involves two components—lexical accessing and semantic encoding—so it generally operates slower at around 450 Wpm for college students. An example of such a process would be a student skimming a chapter to get an overview of the content; it should also be noted that Carver (1972; 1992e) has contended that speed reading is really a skimming process.

Table 2-1
Five Basic Reading Processes or Reading Gears

Gear	*Process*	*Culminating Component*	*Typical Rate for College Students*
5	Scanning	Lexical accessing	600 Wpm
4	Skimming	Semantic encoding	450 Wpm
3	Rauding	Sentence integrating	300 Wpm
2	Learning	Idea-remembering	200 Wpm
1	Memorizing	Fact-rehearsing	138 Wpm

Note: Wpm symbolizes standard length words per minute; a standard length word is six character spaces, or six letters and spaces.

The rauding process (Gear 3) involves three components—lexical accessing, semantic encoding, and sentence integrating—so it operates slower at around 300 Wpm for college students; the rauding process also involves the internal articulation of the words in sentences, as they are lexically accessed, semantically encoded, and sententially integrated. A learning process (Gear 2) involves the three components just noted for rauding, plus an idea-remembering component which slows the process further to around 200 Wpm. An example of such a process would be a college student reading a difficult chapter in a textbook in preparation for a multiple-choice examination. Finally, a memorizing process involves the four components just noted plus a fact-rehearsing component which slows this process further to around 138 Wpm for college students. An example of such a process would be a student studying a textbook in preparation for an essay examination which the student expects will require a recitation of almost all the material, almost verbatim.

The idea that reading text may involve different processes is not new. For example, as early as 1975, Jackson and McClelland stated that "the term 'reading' has been used to refer to a number of different processes" (p. 565). Furthermore, Gibson and Levin (1975) contended that a skilled reader sometimes skims, sometimes skips, and sometimes concentrates, and that "there is no single reading process" (p. 438). Rauding theory has simply identified five basic processes and featured the one that is normally or typically used—the one called rauding. However, it should be acknowledged that other reading theorists (e.g., Goodman & Goodman, 1979) have contended that "there is only one reading process" (p. 148).

The Rauding Process. The rauding process is relatively simple in that it involves only three components—lexical access, semantic encoding, and sentence integrating—as the process is carried out on each word in text. All readers, good and poor, use this same process when they are reading normally, that is, when they are reading relatively easy text at their own normal rate and they are trying to comprehend the complete thought in each sentence as they read each word.

The rauding process is also unique in that it is the only basic reading process which has as its goal the comprehension of sentences. By internally articulating each word in a sentence as it is recognized, the individual is better able to remember the ideas associated with these words from the beginning to the end of the sentence. Evidence that each successive word in a sentence is automatically integrated with what has been understood up to that point in the sentence, comes from the research of Masson (1986). The rauding process involves the "immediacy assumption," which has been articulated by Beck and Carpenter (1986) as follows: "... a reader (or listener) usually tries to encode and access each word and integrate it with the context immediately upon encountering it, rather than waiting to make an interpretation until he or she has encountered a number of words ..." (p. 1099). In order for the rauding process to operate successfully, the sentence integration component must be involved as each word in text is encountered.

The rates associated with each basic process, given earlier in Table 2-1 can also be expressed as msec per word. The lengthy quotation given below from Carver (1990a) illustrates the time required for the operation of each component involved in the rauding process, Gear 3:

> Context can facilitate the rate that words can be identified, but there appears to be a limit to this facilitation. This limit is reached when known words are presented under standard viewing conditions, i.e., about 100 msec per standard length word for typical college students. Having to determine the meaning of those words within a sentence, i.e., semantically encode them, slows a reading process about 33 msec so that a typical college student requires about 133 msec per standard length word. Having to integrate the meaning of the word into the meaning of the sentence within the context of the passage slows this process another 67 msec so that a typical college student can do this at the rate of about 200 msec per standard length word. (p. 268)

In this quote, the three components of the rauding process are described in terms of the msec required for each added component. The 200 msec per standard word needed for a typical college student to operate this rauding process is exactly the same rate as the 300 Wpm noted in Table 2-1 for the rauding process.

A great deal of the earlier research in reading has not involved the rauding process, but has involved learning and memorizing processes, Gears 1 and 2. For example, the research of Kintsch (1994) on text comprehension, memory, and learning is more closely related to Gears 1 and 2, because individuals in that type of research are usually given more than enough time to read the text once, and the material being read is usually relatively hard for the readers. Kintsch (1994) makes a distinction between (a) remembering a text, which for him means that "one can reproduce it in some form, more or less verbatim and more or less completely, at least its gist" (p. 294), and (b) learning from a text which for him "implies that one is able to use the information provided by the text in other ways, not just for reproduction" (p. 294). However, Kintsch also contends that remembering and learning "... are correlated, so that text memory becomes a prerequisite for learning, although that is not necessarily so" (p. 294). Notice that Kintsch is interested in reading processes that allow readers to reproduce text verbatim (Gear 1) and using the text in a manner that indicates learning (Gear 2), and that Kintsch does not seem to be interested in simply comprehending the sentences (Gear 3). The point to be emphasized here, is that the theory developed by Kintsch is not directly relevant to the rauding process, Gear 3, or the causal model because it is directly relevant to a learning process, Gear 2, and a memorizing process, Gear 1.

Inducing the Rauding Process. If a researcher wants to study the rauding process, how can it be induced in a research study? There are three primary factors that influence whether readers are likely to be engaged in the rauding process (see Carver, 1990a). The first factor is the relative difficulty of the textual material, or passages, involved. If relatively easy passages are presented ($D_L < A_L$), then the rauding process is more likely to be executed by the reader. On the other hand, if the material presented is relatively hard ($D_L > A_L$), the rauding process is not likely to be engaged. That is, if the level of difficulty of the text is higher than the than the level of ability of the individual, $D_L > A_L$, then the rauding process is not likely to be used.

The second primary factor influencing whether or not the rauding process will be used is the way in which the instructions are presented by the researcher. If individuals are asked to read the material once as they would normally or ordinarily read, then they will probably use their rauding process. On the other hand, if individuals are asked to learn the essential elements of the text, they are likely to shift out of Gear 3, the rauding process, into Gear 2, a learning process. Or, if individuals are asked to read very carefully so they can recall the details later, they are more likely to shift out of the rauding process into a memorizing process, which is Gear 1.

The third primary factor influencing a reader's choice of gears is the objective consequences. If individuals are asked to identify incomplete thoughts or anomalous sentences, they are likely to use Gear 3, their rauding process. On the other hand, if individuals know they are going to be required to answer difficult multiple-choice questions, they are likely to shift down to Gear 2, a learning process. Or, if they know they are going to have to write down everything they can remember, they are likely to shift further down into Gear 1, a memorizing process.

Finally, if the researcher wants some *post hoc* evidence relevant to whether the rauding process was actually engaged or not, then the reading rate of the individual can be measured during the data collection. If college students were in fact reading the passages at rates around 260 to 300 words per minute, on the average, then the rauding process was probably engaged. On the other hand, if the reading rates averaged 450 to 600 words per minute or 100 to 200 words per minute, then the rauding process probably was not being executed for most of the college students involved (see Carver, 1990a).

Concluding Comments. This book will only deal with the rauding process, or typical reading, and how it is involved in reading achievement. This book will not deal with other of the basic reading processes, such as those processes involved in scanning text, skimming text, learning from text, or memorizing text.

Slices of Time

Introduction. The three major categories of time, or slices of time, that are relevant to theory and research in reading are 1 second, 1 minute, and 1 year (Carver, 1997). One second of time is highly important to researchers who study the cognitive components involved in reading processes. One minute of time is highly important to researchers who study how much of a passage, or piece of text, has been comprehended after it has been read. One year of time is highly important to researchers who study what kind of instruction causes the most gain in reading achievement during a school year. Each of these major slices of time will be discussed in detail, and related to the causal model. The causal model is relevant to all three of these slices of time but the focus of this book is only upon 1 year of time.

One Second of Reading. In this section, the relationship between the causal model and 1 second of reading will be explained. One second of reading, or one fixation of the eye on a word, has much in common with research on complex cognitive processes (see a historical perspective by Venezky, 1977) and much in common with research on "the" reading process. Therefore, this subsection on 1 second of reading will contain an elaboration upon the connections among rauding theory, the causal model, and research on reading processes.

Researchers who study the processes involved in reading often create tasks which involve reading for time periods around 1 second, or 1000 msec. For example, Perfetti and Roth (1981) presented a word and measured the latency or time required to orally respond to the word in msec. Perhaps the most famous ideas relevant to 1 second of reading were presented by Gough (1972), via a model of the cognitive processes involved in reading, such as memory retrieval and storage components. Later, Perfetti (1985) presented a theory, called verbal efficiency theory, which holds that the comprehension that occurs during these brief moments of reading depend upon the rate and accuracy of basic processes, primarily lexical access. More recently, Seidenberg and McClelland (1989) have presented an upgraded model of the components involved during one eye fixation or 1 second of reading isolated words, and their connectionist model has been elaborated upon by Adams (1990).

This research involving 1 second of reading has an indirect connection with the causal model presented in Chapter 1—that connection involves accuracy level, A_L, and rate level, R_L. If the accuracy level of the reader, A_L, is higher than the difficulty level, D_L, of the text being read, then individuals are likely to operate their rauding process because the text is relatively easy, as noted earlier in this chapter. Furthermore, the msec of time needed to operate this process on a standard length word, or the time in msec needed to raud a standard length word (t_r) can be calculated by the following formula:

$$t_r = \frac{60{,}000}{R_r} \qquad (2\text{-}1)$$

This formula is only appropriate when R_r is expressed in standard words per minute (Wpm), instead of standard sentences per minute (Spm) or instead of rate level, R_L, which is in GE units (see Carver, 1990a). For example, suppose a college student has a rauding rate, R_r, at 300 Wpm. By substituting 300 into Equation 2-1, we find that this individual would need 200 msec to raud a standard length word, or that 1 second would be needed to raud five standard words. Notice that A_L can be used to predict when the rauding process is likely to occur on text of known difficulty level, and R_L (converted into Wpm via Appendix D) can be used to predict how much time is needed to raud one word or how many words can be rauded in 1 second of reading.

Much of the research on reading processes has involved individuals at a particular age or grade, reading material at approximately that grade level of difficulty; for example, students in grade 4 are often given text at the fourth-grade level of difficulty to read (D_L = 4). Under these typical research conditions, the good readers (e.g., A_L = 6) can use their rauding process because the text will be relatively easy for them, $A_L > D_L$. The poor readers (e.g., A_L = 2) cannot operate their rauding process successfully because the text is relatively hard for them, $D_L > A_L$. Under these typical research conditions, there are likely to be major individual differences in the processes involved in reading. The poor readers (e.g., A_L = 2) are likely to encounter many unknown words and read in a manner that requires an interactive compensatory mechanism to explain their accuracy and rate of word recognition (see Stanovich, 1980). On the other hand, suppose the good readers (A_L = 6) are given relatively hard texts to read D_L = 8), and the poor readers are given relatively easy texts to read (D_L = 1), then the good readers will appear to have something wrong with their reading process because they will have trouble comprehending whereas the poor readers will seem to have nothing wrong with their reading process because they will be rauding. This idea was articulated by Dole, Duffy, Roehler, and Pearson (1991) as follows:

> ... even novice readers can behave like experts when presented with texts and tasks for which they possess appropriate knowledge. Conversely, even expert readers can be reduced to novices when presented with obscure or ambiguous texts. (p. 241)

Next, a situation will be examined where the good readers (A_L = 6) are given a passage to read once at the fifth-grade level (D_L = 5), and the poor readers (A_L = 2) are given a passage to read once at first-grade level (D_L = 1). Then, the relative difficulty of the text for the good readers will equal the relative difficulty of the text for the poor readers (A_L - D_L = 1), and both will likely operate their rauding process successfully. This means that when students at various levels of ability, A_L, are all given text to read that is relatively easy for them, $A_L > D_L$, and they are given instructions and tasks that are likely to induce their rauding process, then there will be no individual differences in the process they use because they will all execute the same process. Furthermore, according to the formula given in Appendix C (Equation C-7), both the good readers and the poor readers in this example would comprehend 68% of the text. That is, the accuracy of comprehension of the text is likely to be 68% for both the good readers and the poor readers in this example. Both good and poor readers are likely to operate their rauding process equally well with the same effect from an accuracy of comprehension standpoint.

Poor readers exist in a certain grade level in school because they cannot read more difficult text at the same accuracy and rate as good readers in that same grade. However, poor readers can accurately comprehend easier text at their own slower rate of reading. This means that poor readers can raud, that is, they can successfully operate their rauding process on text that is relatively easy for them. Their slow rate does not cause a breakdown or malfunction of their rauding process. There are no qualitative differences between the rauding process of good readers and the rauding process of poor readers when relatively easy text is being read. Good and poor readers both lexically access each word, semantically encode it, and sententially integrate it into the sentence of the text during an amount of time in milliseconds that can be predicted from the individual's rauding rate, R_r (or rate level, R_L). There has been no evidence collected which directly supports the contention that a slow rate of reading words prohibits the successful operation of the rauding process. For example, no one has shown that poor reading twelfth graders who read at the sixth-grade level of accuracy (e.g., $A_L = 6$) and read at the sixth-grade level of rate (e.g., $R_L = 6$), cannot accurately comprehend text at the fourth-grade level of difficulty ($D_L = 4$) while reading it at their own normal reading rate.

A major thesis of this book is that all individuals process words during normal reading almost exactly the same way. There will be no attempt to find and magnify differences between individuals in how they process words during reading because they operate a common reading process, called the *rauding* process. This rauding process is ordinarily the same across different individuals as long as they are reading relatively easy material at their normal reading rate. Therefore, A_L and R_L can be considered as factors which are causal for the rauding process to occur. So, A_L and R_L are not only causal for E_L in the model described in Chapter 1; A_L and R_L are also factors that are causal for whether the rauding process will be operated successfully during 1 second of reading. However, the focus of this book is upon the factors that are causal for A_L and R_L, not how A_L and R_L affect what happens during 1 second of reading. It is simply assumed that A_L and R_L affect (a) when the rauding process will occur, and (b) how much time will be required to process each word when it does occur.

Recently, Share and Stanovich (1995) have claimed that reading-disabled individuals have a *processing* deficit associated with turning spellings into sounds. Yet, these poor readers are not likely to have anything wrong with their rauding process; their 1 second of rauding is not likely to have malfunctions or deficiencies associated with the cognitive components. As long as the text being read is relatively easy, $A_L > D_L$, then even disabled readers are likely to operate their rauding process without any noticeable problem or malfunction with respect to their accuracy of comprehension. That is, poor readers should be able to turn spellings into sounds (internally articulate words) and comprehend just as accurately as good readers when poor readers are operating their rauding process on relatively easy text.

At one time, it was thought that slow decoding was a likely candidate for causing a breakdown of comprehension during reading, that is, a reading process dysfunction that explained why some individuals read poorly. In fact, much of the importance of the automaticity idea as advanced by LaBerge and Samuels (1974) is predicated on the contention that slow decoding of individual words soaks up attention and memory capacity so that comprehension suffers. However, Fleisher, Jenkins, and Pany (1979) conducted a research study that clarifies the problem with this theory. They found that training children to read words in isolation faster was effective in getting them to read text containing these words faster, yet the text was not comprehended any better. Their data showed that the lack of comprehension during 1 second of reading is not necessarily due to a slow rate of reading. That is, the accuracy of comprehension accompanying the rauding process (A_r) is solely affected by the relative difficulty of the material, A_L - D_L (Carver, 1990b), and this is explained in more detail in Appendix C.

Educators should not be trying to figure out how to fix a broken rauding process, because this process generally works successfully for all readers. The real problem is that many readers cannot operate the process successfully on anything but very easy material; they need to be able to gain each year with respect to being able to operate their rauding process successfully (accurately) on increasingly difficult material. This means that educators need to be focusing upon gain in A_L so that more difficult material can be rauded. Another real problem is that many readers operate their rauding process very slowly—they need to be able to gain each year with respect to being able to operate this process successfully (accurately) at a faster rate. Translated, this means that students need to make substantial gains each year in their accuracy level, A_L, and their rate level, R_L, which in turn will improve their reading achievement, or efficiency level, E_L. These gains in A_L and R_L will also improve what happens during 1 second of reading because more textual materials will be raudable and the time required to operate the rauding process on each word in the text will be shorter.

The reading process is often regarded as a complex perceptual and cognitive skill consisting of many components (e.g., see Schustack, Ehrlich, & Rayner, 1987). This kind of conventional wisdom is also evident in the earlier research of Just and Carpenter (1980), wherein 22 different variables were needed to explain 98.5% of the variance in the time required to read lines of text. Yet, this research has been critiqued by Coleman (1990) who pointed out that the *length* of the lines read by the subjects in this research could explain almost as much variance as the 22 cognitive variables, 97.7%. Thus, reading may not be as complicated as has been thought. If we can eliminate 22 complex cognitive variables related to the time required to read a line of print and replace them with one simple variable—the length of the line in terms of the number of letters in the words—then it seems possible that we can reduce the complexity in other areas as well. Indeed, one of the goals of this treatise is to reduce the complexity of reading research, at least that part of reading research related to reading achievement as it applies to normal reading or what has been called the rauding process.

In conclusion, what happens during 1 second of reading, or one eye fixation, is highly important to research on the cognitive components involved in a reading process. However, most of that research is not relevant to the rauding process because research conditions conducive to the rauding process are generally not used. The major connection between research involving 1 second of reading and the causal model is that if this research wants to study the rauding process, then it needs to pay attention to Echelon 2 of the causal model, that is, A_L and R_L of the readers involved. If A_L is not higher than D_L, then the rauding process is not likely to occur. Also, if the time allowed to read a standard length word is not at least equal to 60,000/R_r in msec, then the rauding process is not likely to occur because not enough time has been allowed for the three cognitive components of rauding to operate successfully—lexical access, semantic encoding, and sentence integrating. Much of the earlier research on reading processes and their cognitive components has assumed that poor readers have malfunctioning cognitive components or lack a particular cognitive component. That theory and research is inconsistent with rauding theory which holds that all readers (good and poor, or low and high achievers) use the same three cognitive components during rauding, and that these three components all operate without error or malfunction as long as the text being read is relatively easy.

One Minute of Reading. Research involving 1 minute of reading has ordinarily involved asking individuals to read about 100 to 300 words of text. This research normally has been concerned with the accuracy of text comprehension (A), the rate of text comprehension (R), or the efficiency of text comprehension (E). There are many examples of this type of research; see Frase (1967), Rothkopf (1966), J. R. Miller & Kintsch (1980), and Graesser, Hoffman, & Clark (1980). Most of these researchers who have individuals read passages for around 1 minute would probably contend that their results would generalize to longer passages and longer times, such as 1 hour, or even 10 hours. For an overview of how the accuracy of text comprehension, A, can be predicted after 1 minute of reading, see Carver (1997) or Appendix C.

Most of the earlier research involving rauding theory has been devoted to measuring how much of a short passage has been comprehended when it is at a particular difficulty level, D_L, and when it was read by individuals at particular levels of A_L and R_L for about 1 minute of time. So, this past research has not focused on growth or improvement in E_L, A_L, or R_L over a year, as is the context for the causal model.

Rauding theory includes equations which explain and predict individual differences in the accuracy of text comprehension for all readers who operate their rauding process. As is explained in some detail in Appendix C of this book, the accuracy of text comprehension is symbolized as A, and is determined by (a) the time that the text is presented, t, (b) the difficulty level of the text, D_L, (c) the accuracy level of the reader, A_L, (d) the length of the passage (T_p), and (e) the rauding rate, R_r, or rate level of the individual, R_L. Formulas are also presented in Appendix C, and elsewhere (Carver, 1981, 1990a), for predicting the accuracy of comprehension of text from t, D_L, A_L, T_p, and R_r (see Equation C-10); the research evidence supporting those formulas has been reviewed elsewhere (Carver, 1997).

Out of the five factors just listed which affect the accuracy of text comprehension, A, the two main individual difference variables are the accuracy level and rate level of the reader, that is, A_L and R_L. From Chapter 1, it may be remembered that these two variables also determine reading achievement, general reading ability, or E_L in the causal model. So prior research in rauding theory has focused on A_L and R_L as being the primary individual difference factors which affect accuracy of text comprehension, A, and this book focuses on how to increase or improve A_L and R_L—which determine reading achievement, or E_L. It should not go unnoticed that if the causal model helps us learn how to improve E_L during a year, then we will also be automatically increasing A_L and R_L, and thereby increasing the accuracy of text comprehension, A, for all the texts read by these individuals.

When the amount of time allowed to read a particular text is equal to the rauding rate of the individual, so that $R = R_r$, then the accuracy that accompanies the rauding rate, A_r, is determined solely by the relative easiness of the text, $A_L - D_L$. The equation which shows how increases in A_L cause an increase in the amount of text comprehension during 1 minute of reading (taken from Carver, 1990b) has been reproduced below (see also Equation C-7 in Appendix C):

$$A_r = .04\,(A_L - D_L) + .64 \qquad (2\text{-}2)$$

This equation shows that rauding accuracy, or the accuracy of text comprehension while operating the rauding process, is a function of the accuracy level of the individual, A_L, and the difficulty level of the text, D_L.

In conclusion, the causal model has been designed to increase reading achievement, or E_L, and it has not been directly designed to increase the accuracy or rate at which individuals can comprehend text during 1 minute of reading. However, one of the major effects of increasing reading achievement is to automatically increase the accuracy and rate at which individuals comprehend text. In order to increase reading achievement, or E_L, it is necessary that A_L or R_L at Echelon 2 be increased, and any increase in A_L or R_L for individuals will automatically increase the accuracy and rate accompanying the reading of almost all texts. Even though this book does not focus upon increasing the accuracy and rate of text read for 1 minute, or 10 hours for example, it is a necessary outcome that this increase will occur whenever reading achievement is increased. The formulas for predicting increases in the accuracy of text comprehension—A or A_r—due to increases in A_L and R_L are presented in Appendix C, as noted earlier.

One Year of Reading. The causal model presented in Chapter 1 is directly relevant to the factors that cause high and low reading achievement during 1 year of reading. Reading for 1 year refers to the teaching and learning experiences relevant to reading achievement that ordinarily occur inside or outside of the classroom during a school year. For example, the research of Juel, Griffith, and Gough (1986), followed student gains over a 4-year period. Also, the classic first-grade studies (Stauffer, 1967) would be an example of research relevant to 1 year of reading.

Remember that A_L and R_L were the two factors that were mentioned in connection with 1 second of reading which determined whether the rauding process was likely to be operating and how long it would take to operate it on a standard length word. Remember also that A_L and R_L were the two factors relevant to 1 minute of reading which determined the accuracy of text comprehension, A. Finally, remember that A_L and R_L are the two factors relevant to 1 year of reading which cause increases in reading achievement, or E_L, in the causal model. Notice that A_L and R_L are the two constructs which unify all of the theory relevant to 1 second, 1 minute, and 1 year of reading. From the causal model it can be inferred that reading achievement can be improved the most during 1 year by focusing on teaching and learning experiences which increase V_L and P_L the most during a year, which in turn will increase A_L and R_L, which in turn (a) increases reading achievement, E_L, and (b) increases the accuracy of comprehension of almost all the text that individuals read, A. So, this book is devoted to the gain in reading achievement, or E_L, during 1 year of reading, but it is also indirectly relevant to 1 second of reading or 1 minute of reading via gain in A_L and R_L.

Skill and Age Categories

With respect to rauding skill, there are three major categories: beginning readers, intermediate readers, and advanced readers. These skill categories have their counterparts in terms of age or grade categories; that is, beginning readers are mostly in the lower grades (kindergarten, grade 1, and grade 2), intermediate readers are mostly in the middle grades (grades 3 through 7), and advanced readers are mostly adults (grade 8 or higher).

Figure 2-1 contains an estimate of the percentage of students in each age category who are in each rauding skill category. For example, out of all middle grade readers, it is estimated that about 20% are beginning readers, about 75% are intermediate readers, and about 5% are advanced readers. The criteria for each category are also given in Figure 2-1. Notice that a beginning reader is defined as having a verbal level or a pronunciation level that is below grade 3.0. An intermediate reader has been defined as having a verbal level at 3.0 or higher and a pronunciation level at 3.0 or higher, but having a verbal level below 8.0 or having a pronunciation level that is below 8.0 An advanced reader is defined as having a verbal level at 8.0 or higher and a pronunciation level at 8.0 or higher.

	Skill Categories		
	Beginning Readers	Intermediate Readers	Advanced Readers
	($V_L < 3.0$ or $P_L < 3.0$)	($V_L \geq 3.0$ and $P_L \geq 3.0$; $V_L < 8.0$ or $P_L < 8.0$)	($V_L \geq 8.0$ and $P_L \geq 8.0$)
Age Categories			
Lower Graders (Below AgeGE 3.0) (Age < 8.4 years) (100%)	(90%)	(10%)	(0%)
Middle Graders (AgeGE 3.0 to 7.9) (8.4 yrs. < Age < 13.4 yrs.) (100%)	(20%)	(75%)	(5%)
Adults (AgeGE 8.0 and above) (Age ≥ 13.4 yrs.) (100%)	(5%)	(45%)	(50%)

Figure 2-1. Criteria for age categories and rauding skill categories, along with the estimated percentage of individuals in each rauding ability category for each age category.

The causal model presented in Chapter 1 is relevant to most beginning readers and most intermediate readers in all three age categories—lower graders, middle graders, and adults. However, for advanced readers certain parts of the model have been modified as follows: (a) A_L at Echelon 2 is equal to V_L at Echelon 3, (b) P_L at Echelon 3 is no longer causal for A_L or R_L at Echelon 2, (c) g_s at Echelon 4 is synonymous with C_s at Echelon 3, and (d) R_L is equal to C_s. This modified causal model for advanced readers is explained in more detail in Chapter 17.

When talking about the causal model in this book, these three categories of rauding skill will be used—beginning, intermediate, and advanced, and these three age categories will be used—lower graders, middle graders, and adults. Furthermore, from now on, the term "poor readers" will be used to refer to individuals who have low reading achievement for their age (low E_L for age), and the term "good readers" will be used to refer to individuals who have high reading achievement for their age (high E_L for age).

Many of the terms used in connection with the causal model will have a more specific meaning than they have had in the past. For example, it has not always been clear what constituted a "skilled" reader when this term has used in the earlier research literature. Often a skilled reader is operationally defined in a manner which means that the readers are above average in ability for age or grades, that is, a good reader as defined earlier. Other times, a skilled reader would seem to be synonymous with an intermediate reader or an advanced reader, as compared to a beginning reader.

The age categories and rauding skill categories depicted in Figure 2-1, along with poor readers and good readers, will be used to describe readers, and such terms as "skilled reader," "fluent reader," or "mature reader" will not be used in connection with the causal model.

Other Theoretical Perspectives

Introduction. From the information given earlier in this chapter it is evident that rauding theory is relevant to the rauding process as it is being operated for 1 second, 1 minute, or 1 year, by lower graders, middle graders, and adults. Furthermore, the causal model derived from rauding theory is directly relevant to the rauding process but it is not directly relevant to the other reading processes such as scanning, skimming, learning, or memorizing. The causal model is directly relevant to the gains in reading achievement, or E_L, that occur during 1 year of schooling, for beginning readers, intermediate readers, and advanced readers, and it is also indirectly relevant to 1 second of reading or 1 minute of reading.

Now that the causal model has been placed into the context of the five basic processes involved in reading, the three slices of time involved in reading research, and the three age and skill categories, it will be placed into the context of other theoretical approaches in reading. More specifically, rauding theory and the causal model will be compared to verbal efficiency theory, schema theory, and the whole-language approach to reading instruction.

Verbal Efficiency Theory. The causal model, and rauding theory, will be compared to verbal efficiency theory as developed by Perfetti (1985, 1988). He hypothesized that the efficiency of lexical access is an important variable that is implicated in high- and low-ability readers; the reason that slow efficiency of lexical access adversely affects reading is because it is more difficult for working memory to carry out prepositional text work. This means that poorer readers execute their reading process, during 1 second of reading, in a manner that is defective or less competent than better readers. Again, the problem to be solved by Perfetti's theory is an assumed defective or poorly functioning reading process. As discussed earlier, a defective or malfunctioning reading process is not assumed to be a problem from the perspective of the causal model. Instead, the rauding process for every student is assumed to work well and to work similarly, as long as the material being read is relatively easy and the students can read at their own pace.

In the causal model, the concepts of verbal efficiency and efficiency of lexical access have no direct counterparts because these concepts have been designed to help explain why the reading process of poor readers is not as proficient as the reading process of good readers. In rauding theory and the causal model, it is theorized that there are several basic reading processes but the one that is most important and most often used is the rauding process. Furthermore, both good and poor readers use exactly the same process so that the main difference between good and poor readers cannot be found in the components of this process. Instead, it is the level of material difficulty that the rauding process can operate, as reflected by A_L, and the fastest rate at which the rauding process can operate accurately, R_L, which limit the amount of text an individual can accurately read during a fixed time period, or how long it will take to raud the entire text. When students at a particular age or grade in school, such as grade 5, are given material to read at that grade level ($D_L = 5$), then the better readers (such as $A_L = 7$) will be able to use their rauding process and the differences in the accuracy of comprehension for these good readers ($A_L = 7$) are likely to be minimal unless time limits are imposed. When time limits for reading a particular piece of text are imposed, then those students with higher R_L will comprehend more than those with lower R_L, and the proportion of the text, A, that was comprehended by each of these good readers can be predicted from rauding theory (see Appendix C). On the other hand, in this example the poorer readers (e.g., $A_L = 3$) will not be able to operate their rauding process on this material because it is likely to contain words that will be recognized slowly from context plus words that are not known at all. Therefore, the reader may shift gears to another basic reading process, such as a learning process. In any event, it is misleading to suggest that there is something defective about the process being used by the poor readers because they are likely to be able to operate exactly the same rauding process as the good readers if they were also given relatively easy materials to read. Both the good and poor readers have efficient enough lexical access to operate their rauding process on relatively easy materials and still comprehend the complete thoughts in sentences without any overloads on working memory.

The main difference between verbal efficiency theory and the causal model is that the former concentrates more on reading processes and what occurs during 1 second of reading. Or, stated differently, verbal efficiency theory seems to want to explain high and low reading achievement by reference to individual differences in the efficiency of a reading process or what happens during 1 second of reading, whereas the causal model attempts to explain what happens during the rauding process by reference to high and low reading achievement. The causal model can explain (a) why low A_L individuals cannot successfully operate their rauding process on a relatively hard passage (low V_L and/or low P_L), and (b) why low R_L individuals operate their rauding process relatively slowly (low P_L and/or low C_s).

Verbal efficiency theory seems to deal primarily with typical reading, learning, and memorizing as they occur during 1 second of reading for lower graders, middle graders, and adults. Verbal efficiency theory does not make strong claims about the accuracy of text comprehension that occurs during 1 minute of normal reading. Furthermore, verbal efficiency theory does not make strong claims about scanning and skimming.

Schema Theory. The fundamental idea underlying schema theory is that reading comprehension involves integrating new knowledge in text with old prior knowledge. It has been contended that schema theory is not likely to have much relevance when an individual is "simply reading" (Anderson & Pearson, 1984). Because "simply reading" is one way to describe the rauding process, this means that schema theory is not directly relevant to the causal model. It has also been contended by Anderson and Pearson (1984) that schema theory is most appropriate "when a person is studying a text—that is reading with the deliberate intention of learning ideas and information" (p. 277). Furthermore, most of the research on schema theory has involved college students, or advanced readers. Notice that schema theory does not even purport to be directly relevant to the rauding process or the gain in reading achievement that occurs during 1 year of reading. Therefore, it seems to have no direct overlap with the causal model. However, it should be noted that the main way that advanced readers, such as college students, improve their verbal level, V_L, is by reading or studying relatively hard texts. Therefore, schema theory would seem to be relevant to the teaching/learning factor (at Echelon 4) which improves V_L, especially for advanced readers. This improvement in V_L would also involve a simultaneous improvement in A_L, which would automatically improve E_L, or reading achievement. So, schema theory is distally relevant to increases in reading achievement via the teaching/learning factor at Echelon 4 which affects V_L and A_L for advanced readers.

Perfetti (1988) has pointed out that schema theory makes it explicit that "comprehension depends on knowledge" (p. 116) but that this is "... not very powerful when applied to individual differences in reading ability" (p. 116). He says that if some individuals are better comprehenders when reading about fly-fishing and others are better comprehenders when reading about baseball, then there would be no general ability. And, he contends that a general reading ability does exist so that "individual differences in specific knowledge cannot be the central explanatory factor in reading ability" (p. 117). Translated into the terminology of the causal model, verbal level is an indicator of a level of schema knowledge for text presented auditorily, and accuracy level is an indicator of a level of schema knowledge for printed text. Therefore, when relatively easy material is being read, $A_L > D_L$, then the individual has all of the prerequisite schema or background knowledge needed to comprehend the text.

One of the implications of schema theory has been the proposed efficacy of prior knowledge and prediction activities. That is, it has been inferred from schema theory that having students engage in predicting what is in a text before it is read and giving them prior knowledge about what they will read, will improve the reading process so that higher comprehension will result. This means that prediction activities and prior knowledge have been hypothesized as proximal causes of high and low reading achievement, or E_L. This hypothesis is counter to rauding theory and the causal model; prediction activities and prior knowledge should not increase scores on reading achievement tests that require the answering of questions on passages under a time limit that is conducive to the rauding process.

Evidence relevant to the hypothesis advocating high potency for prediction activities and prior knowledge has been collected by Valencia and Stallman (1989), and there was no support for this hypothesis. They had three experimental treatment groups involving about 2,400 students in grades 3, 6, 8, and 10. One group was given two or three sentences about what they would read later (prior knowledge) and then they were asked to make predictions about what they would read in the form of multiple-choice questions. Another group was given the same two or three sentence prompt (prior knowledge) but was then asked to write down the ideas they thought would be in a passage (prediction activities). A control group was not given prior knowledge and did not engage in prediction activities.

With respect to the results, the only statistically significant differences found were in favor of the controls who were given no prior knowledge and engaged in no prediction activities. Because the tests were given under conditions likely to induce the rauding process for most students, it seems reasonable to conclude that these data provide support for the causal model given in Chapter 1. That is, there is no evidence that the amount of knowledge a student has about a passage that is specific to the passage (e.g., specific knowledge about fly-fishing or specific knowledge about baseball) is a major factor affecting how much is comprehended during the execution of the rauding process. These data also support the contentions of Perfetti (1988) noted earlier, and they support the causal model in that knowledge specific to each passage being read is not a major factor that should be accounted for in the causal model.

It should be noted before continuing that the students in this research were likely to have been using their rauding process because the material they were given to read was not relatively hard and there was no indication that the students were allowed or instructed to read the material more than once. Therefore, their accuracy of text comprehension, A_r, is predictable from Equation 2-2 given earlier in this chapter. In that equation, there is no provision for an adjustment due to prior knowledge specific to the type of text being read and no adjustment for whether or not the individual engaged in prediction activities immediately prior to reading the text. Instead, the only thing that is needed to predict the amount of text comprehension, A_r, is the difficulty level of the text in GE units, D_L, and the accuracy level of the reader in GE units, A_L. The Valencia and Stallman (1989) research could have gotten results that would have invalidated Equation 2-2, and thereby could have invalidated a major part of rauding theory including the causal model, but they did not. Instead, their data can be interpreted as providing support for rauding theory and the causal model.

This research conducted by Valencia and Stallman (1989) was critiqued by Carver (1992c), and he also found evidence in their data that the type of text—expository versus narrative—is not an important variable to consider when generalizing about the rauding process. This finding is counter to schema theory because an individual is supposed to comprehend better when the schema underlying the text is known. Because story schema is easy to learn and ubiquitous in children's fiction, it would be inferred that narrative text would be comprehended more accurately than expository material for students in grades 3, 6, 8, and 10. However, in Carver's reanalysis of their evidence, he contended that there was no support for narrative text being different from expository text. That is, Equation 2-2 does not need to be adjusted to account for whether the text being read is expository or narrative; instead, knowing the difficulty level, D_L, of the text is all that is needed to predict accuracy of comprehension when the rauding process is executed once on the text.

The reason why Valencia and Stallman found no support for schema theory was probably because they were in fact investigating the rauding process in their research instead of investigating a learning process or a memorizing process. Remember that Anderson and Pearson (1984) contended that schema theory is most appropriate when individuals are "studying" a text, and Valencia and Stallman did not design their research in a way that would induce studying. For example, they did not make a case for the text being relatively hard for most of the students and they did not ask their students to read the text more than once or to study it with the deliberate intention of learning ideas and information.

With the advantage of hindsight, it is easy to see why the Valencia and Stallman research supported rauding theory and the causal model, and did not support schema theory. Their research involved the rauding process and therefore supported rauding theory. Their research did not involve "studying" and therefore did not support schema theory. Schema theory is relevant and useful for understanding why some individuals are able to learn more from certain texts compared to other texts. For example, (a) an educational psychologist is likely to learn more in 1 minute of studying an article in the *Journal of Educational Psychology* than a physician specializing in internal medicine, and (b) a physician specializing in internal medicine is likely to learn more in 1 minute of studying an article in a journal for internists than is an educational psychologist. This difference in accuracy of comprehension cannot be predicted from rauding theory or the causal model, because (a) learning processes will be involved, and (b) content specific matches between the text and the reader are not taken into account by measures of A_L and D_L.

Notice that schema theory is quite different from the causal model and rauding theory in that schema theory is most relevant to the basic reading process called learning whereas the causal model is most relevant to the basic reading process called rauding. Schema theory also focuses directly upon the accuracy of text comprehension that occurs during 1 minute of reading whereas the causal model focuses directly upon the gain in reading achievement that occurs during 1 year of reading. Finally, schema theory is most relevant to advanced readers who are studying to learn ideas whereas the causal model is relevant to lower graders, middle graders, and adults who are using their rauding process, or reading normally. The only point of overlap between schema theory and the causal model is that schema theory is relevant to the teaching/learning factor for increasing V_L at Echelon 4, especially for advanced readers. This means that educators should be able to cause growth in V_L by getting some students to operate their learning process on relatively hard text, $D_L > A_L$, and schema theory is relevant in those situations.

Whole Language. The causal model will be compared next to the whole-language approach to reading instruction, using an article by K. S. Goodman (1989) as the exemplar of this approach. This approach involves the guessing of unknown words from context and the use of whole words (not letters) and whole sentences (not isolated words) in reading instruction. On the basis of Goodman's description of the whole-language approach, it does seem to be relevant to normal reading, or the rauding process, in spite of the fact that beginning readers are often encouraged to read text that contains words that are unfamiliar. Also, the whole language approach does seem to be relevant to the gains in reading achievement that occur during 1 year of schooling, or instruction, in spite of the fact that standardized reading achievement tests would probably not be recommended for measuring such growth (see K. S. Goodman, 1992). The whole language approach seems to be mainly concerned with the teaching/learning factor at Echelon 4 for beginning readers. It has little relevance to intermediate readers or advanced readers.

The whole-language approach will not be examined in detail, here, because an entire chapter has been devoted to this approach; see Chapter 22. It should be sufficient, at this point, to say that whole language and the causal model seem to share a concern for what can be done during a year to improve normal reading or reading achievement, but whole language seems to be mostly concerned with lower graders whereas the causal model is concerned with lower graders, middle graders, and adults.

Summary and Conclusions

The causal model can be put into a larger context several ways. It claims to be relevant to beginning readers, intermediate readers, and advanced readers, as well as lower graders, middle graders and adults. It is mostly relevant to normal reading, or the rauding process, which is one of five basic reading processes called scanning, skimming, rauding, learning, and memorizing; the causal model is not directly relevant to scanning, skimming, learning, or memorizing. The causal model is primarily relevant to 1 year of reading, that is, the yearly gains that occur in reading achievement, or the yearly gains in the level of efficiency at which the rauding process operates. The causal model is also relevant to 1 second of reading, because two of the constructs in the model are directly relevant to whether the rauding process is likely to occur during 1 second of reading, namely, A_L and R_L. The causal model is also relevant to the text comprehension that occurs during 1 minute of reading because A_L and R_L from the causal model are two very important factors which influence how much of a text will be comprehended, A, when it is read.

The causal model may also be put into context by comparing it to other theoretical perspectives. Verbal efficiency theory is not directly relevant to 1 year of reading. Schema theory is not directly relevant to normal reading or 1 year of reading. Whole language is a theoretical approach to reading instruction which seems to be relevant to normal reading and 1 year of reading or schooling, but does not seem to be relevant to middle graders or adults. The causal model seems to be the only theoretical perspective that is relevant to lower graders, middle graders, and adults when they read normally for 1 year, that is, it is relevant to their gain in reading achievement, or efficiency level.

This book is uniquely concerned with the most important factors that cause lower graders, middle graders, and adults to improve their normal reading, or typical reading, during a school year or a year's time. Stated differently, the main goal of this book is to determine the root causes of high and low reading achievement for all readers, and to determine how the root causes exert their effects on reading achievement. Any increases in reading achievement, or E_L, will automatically result in a higher accuracy of text comprehension during 1 minute of reading, and will also automatically result in either (a) more difficult text being read more accurately or (b) words being read faster during 1 second of reading. Outside the context of this book are all the reading situations that involve skimming, scanning, learning, and memorizing, as well as all studying situations that involve notetaking, rereading, underlining, etc. The causal model is primarily relevant to the gain in reading achievement, or E_L, that occurs during 1 year of reading and everything else that does not directly affect E_L is likely to be outside the scope of this book.

Restricting the focus of this book to reading achievement, or E_L, may be perceived as too narrow. However, this focus is still broad enough to include implications and recommendations for (a) how to help dyslexics and other disabled readers learn to read better (Chapters 18 & 19), (b) how to help beginning readers learn to read better (Chapter 24), and (c) how to help all English speaking individuals learn to become advanced readers (Chapter 24). Furthermore, anytime that the reading achievement of students can be increased, then these students will be able to comprehend all of the text they read more efficiently.

The remaining chapters of this book will explain in great detail how the causal model can be validly used to describe, explain, predict, and control the main factors which cause high and low reading achievement for lower graders, middle graders, and adults—plus disabled readers.

PART II

THEORETICAL CONSTRUCTS

In Part I, the causal model was presented in the form of an overview, and put into context with respect to other theory and research. Part II will elaborate upon the six theoretical constructs located in Echelons 1, 2, and 3 of the model. A separate chapter will be devoted to each of these constructs—E_L (Chapter 3), A_L (Chapter 4), R_L (Chapter 5), V_L (Chapter 6), P_L (Chapter 7), and C_s (Chapter 8). Each chapter will contain (a) a detailed definition of the theoretical construct, (b) a detailed description of how the construct relates to traditional concepts, (c) a description of tests that can be used to measure the construct, and (d) a short summary of the evidence supporting the existence of the construct.

CHAPTER

3

EFFICIENCY LEVEL, E_L

Efficiency level, E_L, was advanced in Chapter 1 as a theoretical construct that is an upgrade of the more common concept of reading achievement. Because the focal point of the causal model is efficiency level, E_L, it is crucial that a strong case be made that this construct is an appropriate theoretical substitute for reading achievement. It should be acknowledged here at the outset of this chapter that the validity of the causal model presented in Chapter 1 can be tested by using traditional reading comprehension tests as measures of the E_L construct.

This chapter will present the case for the theoretical existence of the E_L construct as an upgrade of the concept of reading achievement, and it will also describe in some detail how the E_L construct can be measured. Major limitations of traditional standardized reading comprehension tests will also be given. Then, a summary of empirical evidence will be presented which supports the theory underlying E_L, and its measurement.

Theoretical Construct

Although efficiency level is similar in concept to reading achievement, it has a much more precise definition as a theoretical construct in the causal model. Rauding efficiency level, E_L, is the highest level of text difficulty, D_L, at which an individual can accurately comprehend ($A > .64$; see Appendix C), when the individual is allowed to read the text at an average rate that is equal to the difficulty level of the text when both are in GE units, that is, $R_L = D_L$. For example, suppose a student is given a passage to read at the fifth-grade level of difficulty, $D_L = 5$, and this student is given an amount of time to read the passage so that students with $R_L = 5$ would just finish reading it at the completion of the time limit. Suppose this student accurately comprehended 80% of the sentences in the passage. Furthermore, suppose this same student was given another passage at the next higher level of difficulty, $D_L = 6$, with the time limit based on $R_L = 6$, and the student only accurately comprehended 60% of the sentences in the text, partly because the time limit was too short for this student with $R_L = 5$ to finish. In this example, this hypothetical student would be at the fifth-grade level of rauding efficiency, $E_L = 5$, because the passage at the fifth-grade level of difficulty is the most difficult passage at which the student could accurately comprehend ($A > .64$) when the passage was presented for an amount of time such that $R_L = D_L$.

Even though the E_L construct is usually referred to as "efficiency level," it should not be forgotten that its full name is rauding efficiency level. The rauding process is based upon comprehending the complete thoughts in sentences (or independent clauses) so E_L represents the highest level of material difficulty, in GE units, at which individuals can efficiently operate their rauding process; E_L is their level of efficiency of comprehending sentences in text. It is very important that the ability reflected by E_L be dependent upon the type of reading that involves the accuracy and rate at which sentences can be comprehended in texts that vary in difficulty.

The choice of the sentence as a basic unit of comprehension can be traced as far back as Huey (1908) who said that "language begins with the sentence" and that "a sentence is the unitary expression of thought" (p. 123). This theoretical choice was also affirmed by Dolch (1948) who said that "It is obvious that words make up sentences, and that the sentence is the real unit of thought and thus the essential unit of reading" (p. 242). The importance of sentences to the rauding process has been shown by Carver (1970) who investigated the effect of eliminating sentence punctuation clues in text. In this research, the beginning words of sentences were not capitalized and the ending period was omitted. The effect of eliminating these sentence markers in text was that (a) reading rate dropped 14%, and (b) accuracy of comprehension dropped 20%. This means that the combined detrimental effect upon efficiency would have been substantial.

Efficiency level, E_L, provides an appropriate index of reading achievement because it indicates the most difficult level of material in GE units that an individual can accurately read given a length of time that is typical or average for individuals at that same grade level. A group of ordinary students (not disabled) who have had average reading instruction in school should have an average E_L that is about equal to their grade in school. For example, a large group of typical students in grade 4 should have an average efficiency level around GE = 4. Furthermore, these students should also average around grade 4 on most standardized reading achievement tests that report scores in GE units, such as the Iowa Test of Basic Skills (ITBS).

Remember that E_L is the focal point of the causal model (see Figure 1-5 in Chapter 1). If a traditional reading achievement measure is placed at the focal point, this causal model should still be valid. However, the more that a standardized reading achievement test relies on inferential questions or reading relatively hard materials, the less the causal model will be valid. That is, the more that the reading achievement test requires novel problem solving such as is usually required by reading difficult texts and answering inferential questions, the more that fluid intelligence (Gf) becomes a causal factor. Furthermore, those reading achievement tests that do rely heavily on the ability to make inferences should show less yearly gain due to the quality of schooling, or education. This means that when E_L is measured by a standardized reading achievement test that requires a great deal of inferencing, then the causal model may be less than perfectly adequate because fluid intelligence would then be a primary causal factor (see Chapter 20).

The E_L construct was created to achieve a goal articulated many years ago by Cronbach (1957). He said "we depend wholly on the creative flair of the theorist to collate the experiments and to invent constructs which might describe particular situations, reinforcements, or injunctions in terms of fundamental variables" (p. 677). Efficiency level, E_L, has been created to capture the essence of reading achievement, as measured by most standardized reading comprehension tests which require individuals to read increasingly difficult material with both accuracy and speed.

Related Traditional Concepts

Introduction. In this section, E_L will be compared to related concepts that are more traditional in reading and reading research. First, E_L will be compared to what is usually being measured by standardized reading comprehension tests. Then, E_L will be compared to the concept of general reading ability. Finally, E_L will be related to earlier reading research involving factor analyses of reading measures which sometimes found one factor and other times found two or more factors.

Standardized Reading Comprehension Tests. Reading achievement has traditionally been measured by tests of reading comprehension which contain multiple-choice questions on passages that vary in difficulty and are administered under a time limit so that many individuals do not have time to finish. On these traditional standardized reading comprehension tests, the easiest passage is likely to be relatively hard for the lowest achieving students and is likely to be relatively easy for the highest achieving students, whereas the hardest passage may be relatively hard for almost all the students being tested. These tests may be considered as providing indicants of individual differences in E_L.

With respect to constructing a good test of reading comprehension, or a good measure of reading achievement, Anderson (1972) advanced helpful criteria. He advocated the use of paraphrase questions to measure the comprehension of concepts and principles in text. It should be pointed out that Anderson's ideas about developing paraphrase questions to measure comprehension has been upgraded and applied to sentences by Royer and associates (e.g., see Royer, Greene, & Sinatra, 1987; Royer, Hastings, & Hook, 1979), under the rubric of the sentence verification technique (SVT). However, most standardized tests of reading comprehension do not include paraphrase questions; they usually include a combination of literal and inferential questions. Anderson also pointed out that traditional reading comprehension tests are usually developed by selecting test items with difficulty values near .50; this practice maximizes discriminating power while emphasizing aptitude and de-emphasizing achievement (see Carver, 1974).

When Anderson (1972) advanced his criteria for measuring comprehension accuracy, he disregarded any mention of time or rate. Yet, standardized reading tests ordinarily have a time limit so that the scores are also influenced by the reading rate of the individual. Therefore, scores on standardized tests of reading comprehension are very likely to be strongly influenced by accuracy level, A_L, and by rate level, R_L. From Chapter 1, it may be remembered that A_L and R_L are also the two causes of E_L. A_L and R_L are also likely to be the primary causes of high and low scores on reading comprehension tests. Therefore, it follows that E_L and traditional reading comprehension test scores are likely to be highly related. The case for a close connection between E_L and scores on these tests can be made in a more technically precise manner using rauding theory and the causal model, as will be explained next.

Traditional standardized tests of reading comprehension ordinarily require that individuals read passages and answer multiple-choice questions on them under a time limit, which makes the test speeded, as has been noted several times earlier. On these tests, the proportion of questions answered correctly on each piece of text is a measure of the accuracy of text comprehension, A. This value of A can be predicted using Equation C-10 from Appendix C, which is reproduced below:

$$A = [.04(A_L - D_L) + .64]\ R_r(t/T_p) \qquad (3\text{-}1)$$

Notice that the accuracy of text comprehension, A, depends upon A_L. Also, notice that A depends upon rauding rate, R_r, and when R_r is expressed in GE units, it is R_L (see Appendix D). So, the accuracy of text comprehension, A, on a reading comprehension test depends upon A_L and R_L, which are also the two proximal causes of E_L according to the causal model presented in Chapter 1. This means that the accuracy of passage comprehension on these reading comprehension tests depends upon the same two factors which purportedly cause E_L, namely A_L and R_L.

It can also be seen from Equation 3-1 that A depends upon other factors, or variables, besides A_L and R_L (or R_r). Yet, these other factors—D_L, t, and T_p—happen to be constant for everyone taking the test. D_L, the average difficulty level of all the passages on the test, is the same for everyone taking the test so it is constant across individuals. The value of "t" is also constant across all individuals because all the individuals taking the test have the same fixed time limit. Furthermore, the value of T_p is constant across individuals because the passages on the test are the same length for everyone. The only two factors that vary across individuals are A_L and R_r (which is R_L in GE units), and these are the two factors at Echelon 2 in the causal model that cause E_L. This means that the raw score on a reading comprehension test, which is usually the number of correctly answered multiple-choice questions, is an indicant of the accuracy of text comprehension, A, and should correlate very highly with a direct measure of E_L because both A and E_L are determined by the same two factors, A_L and R_L. Therefore, most standardized reading comprehension tests yield individual difference scores which are indicants of E_L because the accuracy of comprehension on these tests is directly determined by A_L and R_L, as demonstrated mathematically via Equation 3-1.

In summary, the equations of rauding theory (see Appendix C) can be used to explain why scores on most standardized reading comprehension tests should provide indicants of rauding efficiency level, E_L. These test scores are indicants of the accuracy of text comprehension, A, because D_L, t, and T_p are constant under these conditions, so that individual differences in A are only affected by individual differences in A_L and R_L. Because E_L is completely determined by A_L and R_L from Equation 1-1, and since A is completely determined by A_L and R_L via Equation 3-1, then it necessarily follows that the scores on a speeded reading comprehension test are likely to be highly correlated with a measure of E_L. Thus, efficiency level, E_L, and reading achievement measured by traditional standardized tests of reading comprehension are conceptually almost the same.

It should be remembered, however, that E_L is measured in GE units and it is also measured in a way that minimizes the influences of fluid intelligence, or the ability to draw inferences in novel situations. In contrast, speeded reading comprehension tests (a) often are highly loaded on inferential questions that emphasize fluid intelligence, and (b) vary with respect to the relative influence of A_L and R_L, depending upon the length of the time limits. Therefore, scores on standardized reading comprehension tests should not be expected to correlate perfectly with E_L. Another reason why these test scores should not be expected to correlate perfectly with E_L is that each of these tests have different time limits that vary the relative influence of A_L and R_L in a manner that is very unlikely to be equal to the average of A_L and R_L, which is E_L.

General Reading Ability. Another traditional concept that is highly related to reading achievement and efficiency level, E_L, is general reading ability (see Perfetti, 1985). As early as 1954, we find Holmes discussing this concept as follows: "... general reading ability is a composite of 'speed' and 'power' of reading, and that underlying each component is a multiplicity of related and measurable factors" (p. 7). Holmes' concept of general reading ability translates directly into efficiency level because E_L is composed of A_L (accuracy or power) and R_L (rate or speed).

More recently, Perfetti (1989) devoted an entire article to an argument for the existence of general reading ability, from a theoretical standpoint; the title of his article was as follows: "there are generalized abilities and one of them is reading." He noted that the arguments against the existence of general reading ability usually involved the role of knowledge—general knowledge and specific knowledge. Perfetti contended that general reading ability cannot be identified with general knowledge even though specific knowledge can be critical to reading comprehension. These ideas of Perfetti's are consistent with the causal model. General reading ability, E_L, cannot be identified directly with general knowledge or verbal knowledge, V_L, because E_L is also influenced by pronunciation level, P_L, and cognitive speed level, C_s, according to the causal model (see Chapter 1). Perfetti also pointed out that general reading ability is not substantially influenced by the ability to draw inferences or make elaborations. This idea also translates well into the causal model because E_L is not substantially influenced by fluid intelligence (see also Chapter 20).

In conclusion, the earlier theory and evidence relevant to the existence of general reading ability can be used to support the case for the existence of efficiency level, E_L. The advantage of E_L over the concept of general reading ability is that E_L is more precisely defined and its relationship to the accuracy of text comprehension is very precise.

Factors in Reading Ability. Both the concept of reading achievement and the concept of general reading ability suggest the existence of one culminating factor, or one summarizing factor, in reading ability. Similarly, in the causal model there is one criterion variable which is called efficiency level. However, E_L is composed of two subfactors, A_L and R_L, thereby elevating rate or speed to a level of importance equal to accuracy. This means that research on the number of factors involved in reading ability should (a) find one factor, which is reading achievement, E_L, or (b) find two factors, which are accuracy and rate, A_L and R_L.

There has been a great deal of factor analytic research in reading, with mixed results. However, it is not surprising that the results have been mixed with respect to the number of primary factors involved because there is one criterion variable, E_L, which is caused by, or composed of, two other variables, A_L and R_L, which in turn are caused by three more variables, V_L, P_L, and C_s. An example of mixed results comes from an early article by Lennon (1962) who reviewed the factor analytic literature relevant to reading tests and reported that about half of the studies found a single general factor and the remainder found two or more factors. The causal model and the theory behind it provides three explanations for these conflicting results. First, there are six factors represented in Echelons 1, 2, and 3 in the causal model, so it should not be surprising that one, two, or more of these factors are often evident in factor analytic studies that contain indicants of these factors. If a factor analytic study involved several accuracy of reading measures and several rate of reading measures, then it should not be surprising if two factors were found, A_L and R_L, as long as the two factors are lowly correlated and orthogonal factors are fit to the data. Second, because the two primary subcomponents of efficiency level, E_L, are accuracy level, A_L, and rate level, R_L, studies that use measures *not* involving time limits, or rate, are very likely to find only one factor, A_L. Also, those studies that fit correlated factors when accuracy and rate are substantially correlated are likely to find only one factor. In the past, most of the factor analytic studies have forced the factors to be orthogonal, or uncorrelated, even though A_L and R_L are more likely to be correlated factors. Third, the empirical technique of factor analysis is ill equipped to sort out the primary factors involved in reading ability into the echelons of causality as depicted earlier in Figure 1-5, unless the factor analysis is guided by theory.

Later in Chapter 9, a great deal of empirical evidence will be presented relevant to the existence of only one general factor, E_L—unless E_L is broken down into its causal components, A_L and R_L, in which case two factors are more likely to be found. Because A_L and R_L are substantially correlated in beginning readers and intermediate readers (Carver, 1992a), research at those levels is more likely to find only one factor, E_L. Because A_L and R_L are lowly correlated in advanced readers, research at this level is likely to find two factors. The reason why A_L and R_L are much more highly correlated in beginning readers and intermediate readers, as compared to advanced readers, is probably because pronunciation level causes both A_L and R_L for beginning and intermediate readers (see Chapter 1) but P_L is not causal for either A_L or R_L for advanced readers (see Chapter 17).

Given the wisdom of hindsight, it is now easy to see (a) why Farr (1968) found one factor in one study and two uncorrelated factors in another study, (b) why Sassenrath (1972) reported that "Speed and comprehension in reading were separate factors at the college level but were combined into one factor of general reading ability at the two younger age levels" (p. 304), (c) why R. L. Thorndike (1974) was able to reanalyze the test data collected by F. B. Davis (1972) involving no speeded measures and find one factor, (d) why Rost (1989) found one factor at the elementary level for 220 German second graders, and (e) why Zwick (1987) found one factor involving scores on unspeeded test items from 83,353 students in grades 4, 8, and 11.

Relevant Tests

Introduction. This section contains a description of a direct measure of E_L, the Rauding Efficiency Level Test (RELT), and two standardized tests which provide indicants of E_L, namely the Nelson-Denny Reading Test (NDRT) and the Iowa Test of Basic Skills (ITBS). Also, comparisons will be made among various measurement techniques.

The RELT. The Rauding Efficiency Level Test, RELT, has been developed to provide a direct measure E_L (Carver, 1987b, 1998a). On this test, students are presented with passages that are about 100 words in length and vary in difficulty level from grade 1 to grade 18. Each passage is presented for reading under a time limit that decreases as the difficulty level, D_L, of the passage increases; the amount of time is reduced so that the average rate for reading the passage is equal to the average rate of individuals at that grade level, that is, $R_L = D_L$. This means that the rate of passage presentation, R, is equal to the rauding rate of an individual who is at that same level in GE units, that is, $R_L = D_L$. Again, this also means that the time limits allowed for reading the passages get shorter as the passages increase in difficulty from 1 to 18 because if the average reading rate increases as the difficulty increases, then the time allowed to read must decrease as the difficulty increases.

After a passage has been presented for a fixed amount of time on the RELT, then a test is administered that contains 5 paraphrase type items. Each of the five items consists of two sentences, one is a paraphrase of 1/5 of the passage and the other is not a paraphrase of the same 1/5 of the passage. The task for the examinee is to decide which one of the two sentences is the paraphrase. The final score on the RELT, in GE units, is the highest level of passage difficulty that a student can pass the paraphrase test. A student must score higher than 60% on one of these paraphrase tests in order to pass that level of difficulty. For example, if a student has $E_L = 5$ from the RELT, this means that the fifth-grade passage is the most difficult passage that the student could read accurately when it was presented for an amount of time equal to that required by students with $R_L = 5$ to finish reading the passage once.

The RELT seems to be an improvement upon traditional standardized reading comprehension tests, from a theoretical standpoint. The RELT incorporates the best of all the ideas that have been advanced by Anderson (1972) and Royer, Greene, and Sinatra (1987), noted earlier, because it uses paraphrase questions on sentences to measure the accuracy of comprehension of passages, A. The RELT also maintains strict time limits on the reading of passages, but not on answering test items, so that rate, R, is precisely controlled. This represents an improvement over traditional tests because their time limits apply both to passages and test questions in an arbitrary manner which allows the relative influence of A_L vs. R_L to vary from one test to another. On the

RELT, the difficulty level, D_L, of the passages vary in a controlled manner from $D_L = 1$ to $D_L = 18$, whereas the passages on traditional tests are seldom selected to precisely represent any particular measured grade level of difficulty. The RELT also avoids scores that load highly in fluid intelligence, Gf (see Chapter 20), by using paraphrase questions and by not using item selection criteria that tend to make the test as much of an aptitude measure, Gf, as an achievement measure, E_L. However, it is possible that the RELT is less valid than a traditional reading comprehension test as a measure of the E_L construct because the RELT may be less reliable. In the manual for the RELT (Carver, 1987b), there was no alternate form or internal consistency estimate of reliability given. As noted in Chapter 1, it is possible for an indicant to be more valid than a direct measure, such as this version of the RELT.

The NDRT. The Nelson-Denny Reading Test, NDRT, is a standardized reading comprehension test that includes a Comprehension section which should provide an indicant of efficiency level, E_L. The NDRT contains passages that vary somewhat in difficulty level for college students, and the 36 multiple-choice questions on the eight passages must be answered under a time limit of 20 minutes. Thus, it seems to be a somewhat speeded test, and the raw score should provide an indicant of E_L, even though some of its questions require a great deal of inference and some of its passages are likely to be difficult for poorer-reading college students.

The ITBS. The Iowa Test of Basic Skills, ITBS, is a battery of achievement tests for elementary school students, and it contains a Reading Comprehension part which should provide an indicant of efficiency level, E_L. The passages vary in difficulty, and there is a time limit for reading the passages and answering the questions which should put a premium on rate. Thus, it seems to be a speeded test, and the raw score should provide an indicant of E_L even though some of its questions are inferential in nature. The GE scores on the ITBS-Comprehension would provide an indirect measure of E_L.

Comparisons. Table 3-1 contains a summary of how reading achievement measured by the RELT (a) compares to tests of reading comprehension developed by the criteria of Anderson, and (b) compares to most standardized reading comprehension tests. For example, in Table 3-1 it can be noted that the RELT uses paraphrase questions, as is advocated by Anderson, whereas most standardized tests use a variety of inferential and literal questions, not necessarily paraphrase.

The RELT has been designed and constructed to measure reading achievement in a manner that directly reflects E_L by measuring the accuracy of text comprehension, A, for passages that systematically vary in R_L and D_L. This is in contrast to the design and construction of traditional standardized reading comprehension tests which also measure A, while varying rate and text difficulty but do it in a less systematic manner that also allows fluid intelligence to become a major influence. Therefore, the scores on various standardized reading comprehension tests will be likely to fluctuate with respect to their correlations with A_L, R_L, E_L, and Gf.

Table 3-1
Measuring Reading Achievement

Aspect	*RELT*	*Anderson Criteria*	*Most Standardized Tests*
Questions	Uses paraphrase questions	Advocates paraphrase questions to measure comprehension of principles.	Use a variety of inferential and literal questions, not necessarily paraphrase.
Rate, or time limits	Involves time limits, or rate.	No mention of time, or rate.	Have scores that are influenced by rate via a time limit on the test.
Efficiency Level, E_L	Involves A_L, R_L, and D_L to measure E_L	No mention is made of efficiency, rate, or difficulty level; mostly relevant to measuring A_r, *not* E_L.	Correlate highly with E_L because accuracy of comprehension of increasingly difficult passages is measured under a time limit so the scores depend on A_L, R_L, & D_L.
Fluid Intelligence, Gf	Avoids high loading on Gf by using paraphrase questions and no use of $p = .50$ to select items.	Avoids high loading on Gf via paraphrase questions and no use of $p = 50$ to select items.	Likely to load substantially on Gf due to inferential questions and item selection techniques based on $p = .50$.

Nevertheless, the most important aspect of learning to read well can be assessed by traditional standardized reading comprehension tests, which are also generally regarded as reading achievement measures. These tests tap the skills that we want students to learn from schooling. If students are not learning to comprehend increasingly difficult text in a timely manner (at a reasonable rate), and showing this ability by answering questions about what they have read, then it would seem that everyone with a vested interest should have a right to know about this failure, especially students, teachers, principals, superintendents, school boards, parents, and taxpayers. The best measures of reading comprehension, or reading achievement, will put a premium on speed by use of a time limit that prevents a substantial number of the examinees from finishing the test when they read at their normal rate. That is, the best tests will load substantially on both A_L and R_L. On the other hand, there is nothing wrong with a reading comprehension test that is designed to measure A_L by allowing excessively long time limits, or by letting the examinees read at their own rate as is usually done on individually administered reading comprehension tests. However, it should be recognized that these unspeeded reading comprehension tests will not be influenced by R_L in a major way; they will not be good indicants of E_L because they are good indicants of A_L.

It is very important that reading achievement be measured in a way that rate level influences the scores as much as accuracy level. This means that the validity of a standardized test of reading comprehension as an indicant of E_L depends upon the time limit used on the test. These time limits usually are somewhat arbitrary, and vary considerably from one test to the next. Therefore, the extent to which the score on a standardized reading comprehension test is valid as an index of E_L varies to the extent that R_L is made a factor by lowering the time limit to weigh R_L more at the expense of A_L. Two standardized reading comprehension tests would never be expected to correlate perfectly (as might be idealized) even if they were perfectly reliable, because they could never be expected to give exactly the same weighting to A_L and R_L. Given that increasing or decreasing the time limits on a standardized reading comprehension test will decrease or increase the extent to which the test reflects R_L, it is almost impossible for any such test to be perfectly valid as a measure of E_L. Again, scores on a standardized reading comprehension test would not be expected to correlate perfectly with a direct measure of E_L, even if both were perfectly reliable. Also, reading comprehension tests do not always report GE scores and often do not purport to be achievement measures. The tests that do purport to provide GE scores ordinarily have derived them using norm-referenced techniques that may make them somewhat different from an E_L score which is also criterion-referenced.

The use of standardized reading achievement tests is often deprecated by those who advocate the whole-language approach to reading instruction (Clarke, 1987; K. S. Goodman, 1992). Whole-language advocates may contend that (a) their approach involves much more than what is measured by these tests, (b) this criterion is not authentic, and (c) this criterion favors a skills approach. It is true that the whole-language approach often has much wider goals, such as creating a love for reading. However, it is not true that a traditional reading comprehension test is not authentic. Such tests involve reading passages (ordinarily taken from previously published literature) and answering multiple-choice questions about these passages under a time limit. Answering multiple-choice questions on what one has read previously is involved in many real-world situations that are extremely important, e.g., getting a license to be a motor vehicle operator, a beauty operator, a barber, an engineer, a lawyer, and a medical doctor, to name a few of such situations—not to mention doing well on academic tests that are also a big part of the schooling world. So, doing well on a multiple-choice reading test under a time limit seems to be much more authentic and important for the real world than learning to love and appreciate the reading of novels which are fiction and not true, and therefore are in some sense *not* authentic.

Standardized tests of reading comprehension will vary with respect to how much they measure fluid intelligence, Gf, depending upon the number of good inferential questions left on the test after many are eliminated because their item difficulties deviate from $p = .50$. In this regard, consider the surmissal of Perfetti (1989) who stated that reading ability "... depends much less on abilities to draw inferences, to make elaborations, and more generally to apply interpretive schemata to the outcome of meaning comprehension" (p. 324). Perfetti is attempting to delineate reading ability as conceptually distinct from reasoning ability, or fluid intelligence. Translated, Perfetti would seem to agree that efficiency level, E_L, should not be measured in a manner that makes the test scores highly influenced by the ability of the reader to draw inferences, make elaborations, or apply interpretive schemata, as is the case for many standardized reading comprehension tests.

Even though the above problems are usually inherent in standardized reading comprehension tests, those tests would still be expected to correlate highly with a direct measure of E_L. That is, any standardized reading comprehension test that involved a time limit short enough to be a speeded test for a substantial number of examinees would be expected to correlate highly with an empirical measure of E_L even if the reading comprehension test contained many inferential questions.

Later in Chapter 9, a great deal of evidence will be presented relevant to the theory that measures of reading efficiency are measuring almost the same thing as what is measured by traditional standardized tests of reading comprehension.

Summary of Theory

Rauding efficiency level, E_L, is the highest level of text difficulty, D_L, that an individual can accurately comprehend ($A > .64$) when the time allowed to read is equal to that required for an individual at that rate level to finish reading the text once, that is, $R_L = D_L$. Efficiency level, E_L has much in common with the traditional concept of general reading ability.

E_L also has much in common with what is measured by tests of reading achievement, or traditional standardized reading comprehension tests; these tests require individuals at varying reading levels, A_L, to read and answer questions on texts that increase in difficulty level, D_L, under a time limit which makes the test speeded. Scores on traditional standardized reading comprehension tests provide indicants of the accuracy of text comprehension, A. Individual differences in the accuracy of text comprehension, A, on standardized reading comprehension tests are directly caused by A_L and R_L via Equation 3-1, because all the other factors influencing A are constant on one of these tests. E_L is also directly caused by A_L and R_L via Equation 1-1, given in Chapter 1. Because both E_L and the scores on these reading comprehension tests (indicants of A) are caused by the same two factors (A_L and R_L), this means that scores on standardized reading comprehension tests are also indicants of E_L.

Some standardized reading comprehension tests require that students answer inferential questions on very hard texts under long time limits that make the test relatively unspeeded. Therefore, these latter tests will be less valid as indicants of E_L. In general, the more that reading comprehension tests rely on inferential questions, the more they rely on relatively hard texts, and the more time they allow for reading, the less these tests will be indicants of E_L.

Summary of Evidence

Traditional concepts of general reading ability have involved both the ability to comprehend accurately and the ability to comprehend quickly (Perfetti, 1985). Traditional tests of reading achievement have usually been standardized reading comprehension measures that involved reading passages at varying difficulty levels and answering questions under a time limit that puts a premium on both accuracy and rate of comprehension. Accuracy and rate, or power and speed, are the two components of efficiency, and accuracy and rate have long been considered to be the essence of general reading ability (Holmes, 1954).

Indicants of efficiency level, E_L, correlate substantially (.55 to .72) with scores on traditional tests of reading comprehension (Carver, 1992a; Carver & Darby, 1971, 1972), and when these correlations are corrected for the unreliability of each measure involved then they are considerably higher. Factor analytic studies have generally found one or two factors (e.g., Farr, 1968; Rost, 1989; Sassenrath, 1972; R. L. Thorndike, 1974; Zwick, 1987), and this is consistent with the theory that (a) one factor will be found when A_L and R_L are substantially correlated so that only E_L is prominent, (b) one factor will be found when the comprehension measures are not speeded so only A_L is being measured, and (c) two factors will be found when both A_L and R_L are represented but not substantially correlated.

The RELT is the only existing test designed to provide a direct measure of E_L, and it seems to have been developed in a manner that builds upon the best of what we have learned from theory and research (Carver, 1987b). It explicitly focuses upon the ability to raud, that is, the ability to accurately and rapidly execute the rauding process on increasingly difficult material. The RELT does not require the ability to draw inferences or reason abstractly in novel or complex situations. From a theoretical standpoint, traditional reading comprehension tests are less desirable measures of reading achievement, or E_L, because these tests (a) have not been designed to systematically handle the varying influence of rauding rate level, R_L, (b) have not been designed to systematically account for the varying influence of the types of questions asked, e.g., literal, influential, paraphrase, etc., and (c) have not been designed to systematically control the varying difficulty level of the texts used. However, the existing version of the RELT only has five two-choice questions at each level of difficulty, so it may be low in reliability and not as valid for measuring E_L as traditional standardized reading comprehension tests.

Forget Me Nots

Rauding efficiency level, E_L, is a theoretical construct that tries to incorporate all of the good ideas that have traditionally been associated with the following: (a) reading achievement, (b) general reading ability, and (c) scores on standardized reading comprehension tests. These earlier concepts have been upgraded by the E_L construct which is more precisely defined, both from a theoretical and an operational standpoint; it is measured in GE units, for example, an individual may have a fourth-grade level of rauding efficiency, $E_L = 4$.

CHAPTER

4

ACCURACY LEVEL, A_L

If it is agreed that reading achievement can be replaced by the more precise construct of efficiency level, E_L, as was advocated in the preceding chapter, then it becomes important to analyze the primary factors that influence E_L. In the causal model, accuracy level is one of the two factors at Echelon 2 that are causal for E_L—along with rate level which will be described in detail in the next chapter.

As was noted earlier in Chapter 1, the theoretical construct called A_L is very similar to the traditional concept of reading level. Rauding accuracy level, or A_L, is simply an upgraded version of the reading level concept. Therefore, A_L is a very traditional concept with a new name, a more precise theoretical definition, and a new technique for measuring it, as will be explained later.

High accuracy level, A_L is purported to be a necessary, but not sufficient condition for high reading achievement. Individuals cannot become very good readers unless they have a high accuracy level, A_L. However, it is possible to have high A_L but still not have high reading achievement (high E_L) because rate level, R_L, is low.

This chapter contains a detailed definition of the A_L construct, explains how it relates to similar traditional concepts, explains how it can be measured, and gives a brief summary of empirical evidence supporting its existence.

Theoretical Construct

Accuracy level, A_L, is the highest level of text difficulty in GE units, that individuals can accurately read, when they are reading at their rauding rate, R_r. The operational definition of what it means to read text accurately has conventionally been taken to be 75% (e.g., see Betts, 1946), but this cutoff criterion has been operationally refined on the basis of empirical data to be 64% (Carver, 1990b). For example, suppose individuals with a rauding rate of 150 Wpm (R_L = 4.5; R_r = 9 standard sentences per minute; see Appendix D) are given passages to read at varying levels of difficulty. If their accuracy of text comprehension in this situation, A_r, is .80 for a fifth-grade level passage but is only .60 for a sixth-grade passage, then their accuracy level is at the fifth-grade level (e.g., A_L = 5.5), because the fifth-grade level of passage difficulty is the most difficult level that these individuals can accurately read (A > .64) at their own rauding rate.

Remember that the words in texts that are relatively easy, $A_L > D_L$, have been practiced so often that they are recognized at the rauding rate of the individual. For example, if an individual has an accuracy level at grade four (A_L = 4), then it is assumed that at least 99% of the words in text at D_L = 3 and below are accurately recognized and successfully processed at the rauding rate (see Carver, 1994b). All of these words that an individual can accurately process at the rauding rate will be called "raudamatized words." Therefore, all of the words in texts at $D_L < A_L$ should be raudamatized words; those words will be symbolized as A_LWords. This means that a measure of A_L and a measure of A_LWords should correlate almost perfectly because the A_L construct and the A_LWords construct are inherently very closely related, such that the number of raudamatized words, A_LWords, is an indicant of A_L.

Related Traditional Concepts

Introduction. In this section, the concepts of reading level, automaticity, autonomous lexicon, and unitized words, will be related to the A_L construct.

Reading Level. The concept of reading level was explicated by Betts (1946) when he described the independent, instructional, frustration, and capacity levels. The lowest level of Betts' was the independent level—also referred to as the basal level. For example, if an individual had an independent level at second grade, then this student should be able to read material at the second-grade level of difficulty, such as a book, without help from a teacher, parent, or anyone else and achieve at least 90% comprehension with 99% accurate pronunciation of the words in the text. The next higher level was the instructional level, which should be higher than the independent level; it is the teaching level, and is the level that is most similar to accuracy level, A_L. For example, if an individual has a third-grade instructional level, or A_L = 3, then this individual should be taught using materials at the third-grade level because they are challenging but not too difficult. The individual is supposed to achieve around 75% comprehension when reading at the instructional level, with 95% accuracy of pronunciation. The frustration level should be higher than the instructional level; it is to be avoided. For example, if an individual has a fourth-grade frustration level, then this is the lowest level of difficulty at which this individual is unable to understand. For this individual, material at the fourth-grade level is too difficult and frustrating because less than 50% will be comprehended. The highest level of all should be the capacity level, or hearing level. It is the highest level of material difficulty that a student can understand when listening to someone else read the material aloud. For example, individuals who have a fifth-grade capacity level, can comprehend 75% of the material from a book at fifth-grade level when someone reads it aloud to them.

Informal reading inventories are often based upon the above criteria of Betts. These inventories often ignore rate measurement, and none of the criteria presented by Betts involved rate. For example, Fuchs, Fuchs, and Deno (1982) conducted a study of the reliability and validity of curriculum-based informal reading inventories (IRIs), and none of the seven criteria they investigated for determining reading level involved a rate requirement. Another example comes from Cadenhead (1987), who traced the history of the concept of reading level in his effort to eliminate the concept, and rate was not involved. Although IRIs theoretically do not involve rate, the measurement of a student's reading level by a classroom teacher may involve rate in a manner that makes the result more similar to efficiency level, E_L. Furthermore, IRIs traditionally involve oral reading with all the measurement problems that accompany this practice (see Carver, 1990a). Therefore, when reading level is measured by use of an IRI, it may reflect efficiency level, E_L, more than accuracy level, A_L, because it may involve both accuracy and rate via oral reading rate and accuracy of word pronunciation. Nevertheless, the traditional concept of reading level ordinarily does not denote or connote a rate dimension. So, the concept of instructional reading level can be used to help communicate the meaning of A_L, in spite of the fact that some measures of reading level using IRIs may correlate higher with E_L than A_L, and some may correlate relatively low with both because these informal reading measures are often unreliable.

In summary, Betts' instructional reading level is conceptually similar to rauding accuracy level, A_L; however, Betts' uses a 75% comprehension criterion, and rauding theory uses a 64% comprehension criterion because empirical data suggests that 64% of passages will be comprehended when the accuracy level matches or equals the difficulty level ($A_L = D_L$), or the relative difficulty is zero ($D_L - A_L = 0$). From one standpoint, rauding theory has provided a rather precise definition of reading level which can be operationally applied, that is, the traditional concept of instructional reading level means rauding accuracy level. The construct A_L is an upgraded version of the reading level construct because it specifies that individuals must be reading at their own rauding rate—normal or typical silent rate—when determining the most difficult level of text that can be read accurately.

Automaticity. Raudamatized words, as defined earlier, would probably be considered "automatized" words by many researchers. However, the concept of automaticity that has been advanced by LaBerge and Samuels (1974) is associated with a general ability that has been learned by the individual rather than a property of a particular word with respect to a particular individual. Furthermore, their concept of automaticity is defined directly in terms of a "lack of attention," whereas raudamatized words are defined in terms of rate, not attention.

The criterion that LaBerge and Samuels used for deciding if a skill had reached automaticity was whether "it can complete its processing while attention is directed elsewhere" (p. 295). They thought that automaticity was a general skill that an individual learned which could be applied to all the words an individual read. That is, they contended that "... during the development of automaticity the person may either attempt to reorganize smaller units (e.g., words) into larger units (e.g., word phrases) or he may simply stay at the word unit level" (p. 316). Thus, for LaBerge and Samuels each word did not become automatized for the individual so that each individual had some words that were automatized and some that were not. Instead, each individual had varying degrees of automaticity for all words and those who do not develop automaticity do not succeed in becoming "fluent" readers. They carried this idea of automaticity for larger and larger units (letters to words to phrases) even further by using it to explain fast reading, even speed reading, as the following quotations attest:

> For example, when the child reads text in which the same vocabulary is used over and over again, the repetitions will certainly make more automatic the perceptions of each word unit, but if he stays at the word level he will not realize his potential reading speed. If, however, he begins to organize some of the words into short groups or phrases as he reads, then further repetitions can strengthen those units as well as word units. In this way he can break through the upper limit of word-by-word reading and apply the benefits of further repetitions to automatization of larger chunks. (p. 315)
>
> We do not know specifically how to train a child to organize codes into higher units although some speed-reading methods make claims that sheer pressure for speed forces the person out of the word-by-word reading into larger units. (p. 315)

It seems clear from the above quotes that LaBerge and Samuels were offering a theory as to why some individuals are able to comprehend accurately while reading fast (are "fluent" readers) while others are slow (and not "fluent"). Supposedly, the fast readers have learned to chunk the information contained in text into larger units (from letters to words to phrases) by practicing this process whereas the slower readers have not learned to do this, probably because they never practiced this process by forcing themselves to process larger and larger chunks. This idea that the reader needs to achieve a phase or stage of automatic reading has recently been articulated by Stahl (1997). He said that "the transition from accurate to automatic word recognition occurs over a number of years, conventionally from the end of first grade to the end of third grade" (p. 17). Notice that this idea seems to suggest that typical readers by the fourth grade can rapidly read all words, seemingly without practice on them, because they have become automatic readers. Furthermore, this idea seems to suggest that typical readers in second and third grade are not able to recognize any words automatically even with hundreds or thousands of practice trials on such words as "the," "and," "you," etc.

In summary, the general idea of automaticity has been upgraded in the causal model by the A_L construct and raudamatized words, because the original concept of automaticity does not seem to be valid.

Autonomous Lexicon. Fries (1963) seems to be the first to talk about the "automatic recognition" of words. He says that "as great skill develops they become automatic habits and the recognition response itself sinks below the threshold of attention" (p. 177). He has elaborated upon this automatic word recognition as follows:

> The major spelling patterns of present-day English are fortunately few in number, but for those the reader must develop, through long practice, high-speed recognition responses. These responses must become so habitual that practically all the clues that stimulate them eventually sink below the threshold of attention leaving only the cumulative comprehension of meaning. (p. xvi)

Perfetti (1991a) has defined the autonomous lexicon as consisting of all the printed words an individual can recognize automatically, or quickly. Therefore, conceptually there is no difference between the autonomous lexicon and A_LWords as defined earlier. That is, the lexicon of raudamatized words and the autonomous lexicon are synonymous in concept. The only justification for creating a new term, "raudamatized" to replace "autonomous" or "automatized" words, is that these latter words carry the unwanted connotations of limited attention capacity and a general skills affecting all words. Translated into rauding theory and the causal model, all the words in relatively easy material, $A_L > D_L$, should be in an individual's autonomous lexicon because they should be accurately and quickly recognized, and comprehended, at the individual's rauding rate, R_r. Any treatment that successfully increases A_L should also produce a corresponding, or proportional, increase in the size of the autonomous lexicon, or A_LWords, and any treatment that successfully increases the size of the autonomous lexicon, or A_LWords, should produce a corresponding, or proportional, increase in A_L.

Given the above connections among A_LWords, A_L, and the autonomous lexicon, it will be helpful to note what Stanovich (1980) said about automaticity and reading that is also relevant to raudamatized words, or A_LWords. He has articulated the relationship between automaticity and reading as follows:

> ... during the time that automaticity is developing, and even after a word is fully automatized, recognition time continues to decrease. The latter point is often lost in discussions that center on the automaticity concept itself, even though there is ample evidence in the

> literature documenting the fact that recognition time continues to decrease after words have become fully automatized. (p. 60)

In the above research referred to by Stanovich, the criterion for reaching automaticity was the point where attention was no longer directed toward recognition of the word but could be directed elsewhere, such as to comprehending the complete thought in the sentence. Notice that these ideas of Stanovich about automaticity make it clear that for him, automaticity refers to a particular word for a particular individual. These ideas articulated by Stanovich may be readily translated into the following: An automatized word is not necessarily a raudamatized word because further practice on an automatized word may be needed to get it up to the rauding rate; however, a raudamatized word is necessarily an automatized word because a raudamatized word has been practiced to a rate well beyond the point where it can be recognized without attention. Raudamatized words are likely to be recognized at a faster rate than the slower rate associated with automatized words.

In summary, the size of the autonomous lexicon as conceived by Perfetti (1991a) should be equivalent in concept to A_LWords; therefore, measures of the size of the autonomous lexicon should also correlate highly with measures of the A_L construct.

Unitized Words. In 1983, Ehri and Wilce further clarified the connection between automaticity and reading by testing their theory (Ehri & Wilce, 1979b) that skilled word recognition develops in the following three phases:

> In Phase I, unfamiliar words become familiar and are recognized *accurately* by readers directing their attention to component letters as they map sounds. During Phase 2, as a result of more practice, familiar words come to be recognized *automatically* as wholes without attention and without deliberate processing of component letter-sound relations. In Phase 3, the *speed* of processing familiar words increases to a maximum as the components involved in stimulus recognition and response production become consolidated or "unitized" in memory. (p. 3)

Notice that Ehri and Wilce make the same kind of distinction that Stanovich (1980) made; an automatized word is processed at a slower rate than a "unitized" word. The concept of a unitized word used by Ehri and Wilce is very similar to the concept of a raudamatized word, so these two concepts need further elaboration.

There is a major problem with using the word "unitized" to describe the point at which the speed of word recognition no longer increases due to practice or experience. Ehri and Wilce had the idea that each unitized word could be recognized at exactly the same rate or speed. Yet, this is not possible during rauding. Carver (1976) has shown that when reading rate is measured using actual words per minute, then shorter words are read faster; however, when rate is measured in standard length words per minute, then rate is constant at the rauding rate, R_r. This means that shorter words are processed faster than longer words during rauding. Therefore, the concept of a unitized word is misleading because there is not likely to be a constant amount of time needed per actual word. Instead, as discussed in Chapter 2, there is likely to be a certain amount of time needed per standard length word. So, words that have reached asymptote on a learning curve will not be described as "unitized," mainly because that would erroneously suggest a unitary rate of word recognition for a particular individual, no matter how long the word was in letters, phonemes, or syllables. Yet, it should not go unnoticed that the earlier concept of a unitized word advanced by Ehri and Wilce is very similar to the raudamatized concept introduced earlier in this chapter.

In summary, all of the A_LWords and all of the words in the autonomous lexicon should be raudamatized words that Ehri and Wilce (1983) would call unitized words, except all raudamatized words are only recognized at the same rate, or a unitary rate, if rate is measured in standard length words.

Relevant Tests

Introduction. There are two tests that would seem to provide highly valid measures of A_L, and they will be described in some detail. Then, a few other measures of A_L will be briefly acknowledged.

Degrees of Reading Power (DRP). The DRP test includes passages that increase in difficulty level along with questions which must be read and answered without a time limit. Therefore, this test provides an indicant of accuracy level because the nature of the test follows closely the definition of accuracy level. This test does not provide GE scores that have been scaled to reflect A_L; so, it provides an indicant of A_L instead of an indirect measure. However, it should be noted that Carver (1990c) has rescaled the scores on this test into GE units so these scores may provide a valid direct measure of A_L, though their validity for providing absolute levels of A_L has not been investigated.

The DRP, described above, measures reading ability in a manner very similar to what would be expected if it had been explicitly designed to measure the A_L construct. That is, it requires items to be answered covering passages of increasing difficulty, and the examinees are given the following instructions:

> You are not expected to read at the same rate as other people or to answer the same number of questions. As you work on this test you will find that the passages become harder to read... . You will be given as much time as you need.

Accuracy Level Test (ALT). The ALT is a reading vocabulary measure of A_LWords; therefore, it is an indicant of A_L. It has been used previously to investigate rauding theory; it is the measure noted in the causal model, from Chapter 1. This test was originally developed in 1987, with 100 vocabulary items spanning the range of 0.0 to 15.8 GE units. It is also purported to be an indirect measure of accuracy level, A_L, because it involves a measure of A_L-Words scaled in GE units. It was later revised (Carver, 1994a) by including 20 more items at the top of the test; now, it measures across 120 items which cover the range between 0.0 and 19.0 GE units.

The idea that vocabulary tests are indicants of reading level, or A_L, has been articulated (a) by Sternberg (1987) who said that "... one's level of vocabulary is highly predictive of one's level of reading comprehension" (p. 90), and (b) by Anderson and Freebody (1981) who said that "an assessment of the number of meanings a reader knows enables a remarkably accurate prediction of this individual's ability to comprehend discourse" (p. 77). The more printed words known by an individual, the more likely the individual will be able to comprehend more difficult texts that contain less frequently used words. Furthermore, individuals who can comprehend text at higher levels of difficulty are more likely to know the meaning of more words that occur less frequently. Therefore, a measure of reading vocabulary should constitute an indicant of A_L.

The ALT is somewhat different from traditional reading vocabulary tests which ordinarily include alternative wrong answers (foils) that are somewhat plausible, so that many of the examinees have to use their reasoning ability to determine which answer is best. Instead, the correct answer to a vocabulary item on the ALT is always a synonym that is an even easier word than the stem, that is, at a higher frequency of usage, and is the only one of the three alternatives that is close in meaning to the stem. This procedure for developing the ALT helped assure that a higher score on the test would reflect a proportionally greater number of words known; i.e., a greater number of A_LWords. In fact, in the manual for the test, a table is provided for transforming a raw score on the ALT into an estimate of words known, A_LWords, based upon the sampling from the Carroll, Davies, and Richman (1971) ranked list.

The manual for the ALT also contains reliability estimates (Carver, 1994a). The standard error of measurement is around 0.7 GE units in each of grades 3 through 12, plus college and graduate school, and the average alternate form reliability coefficient is .85 in grades 3 through 12; the corresponding reliability coefficients in college and graduate school are comparable or higher.

One way to evaluate the validity of the ALT, as an indicant of A_L, is to relate it to the RELT as a measure of E_L. Carver (1987b) reported that the ALT correlated .73 with the RELT—with grade level in school partialled out, for 107 students in grade 3 to graduate school. This is a very high correlation considering that E_L is made up of both A_L and R_L, in roughly equal proportions; the corresponding partial correlation for an indicant of R_L in this same research was .77.

The validity of these GE scores for A_L has also been established by asking 568 students in grades 3 through 12 and graduate school, to read passages once at varying difficulty levels, D_L, and then to make a judgment or estimate of their percentage of comprehension of the passage (Carver, 1990b). These percentages constitute a measure of rauding accuracy, or A_r. Notice that A_r represents the accuracy of comprehension, A, that accompanies the rauding rate when the individuals are instructed to read the passage once at their normal reading rate. These students were also given the ALT, so that the relative easiness of the passage, A_L - D_L, could be related to the estimates of accuracy of comprehension, or A_r. For the means of rauding accuracy at 17 levels of relative difficulty, the relationship between A_r and A_L - D_L was almost perfect (r = .992). The equation of the straight line that fit these data was as follows: $A_r = .04\ (A_L - D_L) + .64$, which is Equation 2-2, referenced earlier. So there is a high relationship between the percentage of a passage that was accurately comprehended, A_r, and the relative easiness of the passage, A_L - D_L, when the indicant of A_L was a reading vocabulary test. Any measure of A_r for texts at a constant level of difficulty, D_L, would automatically provide an indicant of A_L because variations in A_r would be linearly related to A_L according to Equation 2-2.

Other Standardized Tests. There are several standardized tests of reading comprehension that are administered individually and are untimed or unspeeded; these tests should provide indicants of accuracy level, A_L. One example is the Woodcock Reading Mastery Tests (WRMT) - Passage Comprehension. On this measure, an individual must read short paragraphs which increase in difficulty. Each of these paragraphs have had one word deleted and replaced with a blank. The individual must figure out what word goes into the blank, with more than one word being scored as correct because synonyms or equivalents of the correct word are equally correct. It is likely that this particular indicant of A_L would load higher on fluid intelligence, Gf, than would the ALT, because more abstract reasoning is likely to be involved in figuring out what word best fits into the puzzle of the missing word. That is, information needs to be gathered from all the context surrounding the missing words, possible words need to be generated, and a decision needs to be made regarding the best word.

There are two other tests that can be mentioned that are similar to the WRMT- Passage Comprehension, and would provide indicants of A_L. They are the Peabody Individual Achievement Tests (PIAT) - Passage Comprehension and the Woodcock-Johnson Tests of Achievement-Passage Comprehension.

Other Tests. A time-limited word identification test would also provide a measure of raudamatized words, or A_LWords, and would constitute an indicant of A_L. On this type of test, words that vary in frequency of usage are each presented for a brief period of time, such as 1 or 2 seconds. For example, Olson, Wise, Ring, and Johnson (1997) recently administered such a test to poor readers in grades 2 through 5; they described the experimental test as "... a difficulty-ordered list of words presented individually for 2 sec. on the computer screen" (p. 245). On this type of test, if the word presented was a known word that had been practiced until it was overlearned, then it should be quickly recognized and pronounced correctly during the brief time limit. Words presented that are not known or had not been overlearned from practice, probably would not be pronounced correctly because there would not be enough time to develop a reasonable guess. Therefore, the number of correctly pronounced words on this type of test should be an indicant of the size of the lexicon of known words, A_LWords, and an indicant of A_L.

The instructional level from an informal reading inventory, IRI, would ordinarily provide an indirect measure of A_L. These IRIs are often constructed by teachers from a basal reading series which require the student to read aloud from successively higher GE levels with comprehension sometimes assessed at each level. Ordinarily, the students read increasingly difficult material at an oral rate of their own choosing, until they no longer can accurately comprehend or accurately pronounce the words. These tests are not standardized and are not likely to be reliable, but it can be seen that they would be measuring a level of reading comprehension in GE units that is somewhat similar to accuracy level, A_L, in that both require increasingly difficult text to be accurately read and both yield GE units.

Another kind of test providing an indicant of A_L is the score on an untimed or unspeeded measure of reading comprehension. It may be remembered that when an individual is allowed to read a passage once, the accuracy of text comprehension is called rauding accuracy, or A_r, and it is equal to .04 (A_L - D_L) + .64 (from Equation 2-2, or Equation C-7). If everyone is given the same text to read in this situation, then the measure of text comprehension, A_r, would reflect only individual differences in A_L because D_L would be constant in Equation 2-2. That is, a measure of A_r in this situation should correlate almost perfectly with A_L, as noted earlier. In actual research situations, the tested individuals are often given as much time as they want to read so some may read the text more than once. However, when individuals are allowed to read text longer than the time they need to read it once (see Equations C-3 and C-4 in Appendix C), the increase in the accuracy of text comprehension is not so large, relatively, that such reading comprehension measures, A, are rendered invalid as indicants of A_L. This means that reading comprehension tests that happen to have ample time limits so that almost everyone can finish the test without hurrying or feeling time pressure will correlate higher with A_L than they will with R_L or E_L. As the time limits on the comprehension test are shortened, then rate level, R_L, becomes more of a factor so the test starts to become a better indicant of efficiency level, E_L. If the test has a very short time limit then it could become much more of an indicant of R_L than A_L or E_L.

Concluding Comments. The close connection between the number of printed words known (reading vocabulary, or A_LWords) and the ability to accurately comprehend text of increasing difficulty, A_L, is assumed to involve a causative connection. That is, it is assumed that it would be impossible to gain one GE on the ALT test without also gaining 1 GE on a more direct measure of A_L such as the DRP. For example, a program designed to increase vocabulary knowledge might be thought to provide an artifactual increase in ALT with no increase in the DRP. Yet, it seems unlikely that individuals could learn and remember the meanings of the hundreds of words necessary to increase ALT one GE without gaining the associated verbal knowledge that would also allow text at the next GE to be accurately comprehended on the DRP. Conversely, it is assumed that it would be impossible to gain one GE on a more direct measure of A_L, such as the DRP, without also gaining one GE on the ALT. It seems unlikely that a person would be able to accurately comprehend text at the higher level of difficulty on the DRP without learning the thousands of concepts in the form of words that would also result in a one GE gain on the ALT.

The above assumptions seem to be endorsed by several other researchers. For example, Curtis (1987) contended that vocabulary growth increases comprehension ability and that better reading comprehension enhances vocabulary. Also, Stanovich (1986) has argued for a reciprocality between vocabulary and reading deficits, such that a problem in reading will lower vocabulary development.

Summary of Theory

Accuracy level, A_L, is a very important theoretical construct because it is one of only two factors that are directly causal with respect to high and low reading achievement, or E_L. A_L is actually rauding accuracy level, which is defined as the most difficult text, in GE units, that an individual can read accurately when the text is read at the individual's rauding rate. A_L is similar to the traditional concept of reading level, or Betts' (1946) instructional level. The Degrees of Reading Power test measures the most difficult text that an individual can accurately comprehend under unspeeded conditions so it provides an indicant of A_L.

The number of words that can be accurately and quickly pronounced is a measure of A_LWords, or raudamatized words. Reading vocabulary is a measure of A_LWords that is so closely connected to the accuracy of text comprehension that it is also an indicant of A_L. Also, text that is relatively easy, $A_L > D_L$, contains words that can be accurately processed at the rauding rate, so these words in relatively easy texts are raudamatized words. Therefore, the size of the lexicon of raudamatized words, called A_LWords, is likely to be almost exactly the same as the size of the *autonomous* lexicon as conceptualized by Perfetti (1991a), or the number of unitized words as conceptualized by Ehri and Wilce (1983). The lexicon of raudamatized words may not be exactly the same as the lexicon of automatized words, because words can become automatized (not requiring much attention) at a lower rate than raudamatized words. Automaticity and automatized words have been tied so closely to attention capacity and to an attribute of the reader (LaBerge & Samuels, 1974), that it is likely to be more confusing than illuminating to talk about automatized words, or automaticity, in connection with the causal model and rauding theory.

The A_L construct integrates measures of reading level, reading vocabulary, and the number of words on a time-limited word identification test. For example, a factor analysis of scores on the Passage Comprehension test from the Woodcock Reading Mastery Tests, the Vocabulary test from the Iowa Test of Basic Skills, and the time-limited word identification test used by Olson et al. (1997) should result in one factor—the A_L factor. There are many unspeeded standardized tests of reading comprehension that should provide indicants of accuracy level, A_L, such as the aforementioned Degrees of Reading Power test and the Woodcock Reading Mastery Tests—Passage Comprehension. At present, the best indirect measure of A_L is probably the Accuracy Level Test, ALT, which is a reading vocabulary test that seems to be reliable, valid, and quickly administered. There are no standardized direct measures of A_L available, at present, although the DRP test is close to meeting this criterion.

Summary of Evidence

Measures of reading vocabulary, A_LWords, and unspeeded measures of the accuracy of comprehension, A_L, are highly related (Anderson & Freebody, 1981; Beck, McKeown, & Omanson, 1987; Carroll, 1993; Holmes, 1954; R. L. Thorndike, 1973; Thurstone, 1946). The correlation between perfectly reliable measures of reading vocabulary tests, A_LWords, and measures of the accuracy of comprehension, A_L, can be estimated to approach 1.00 under optimum conditions (Sticht, Hook, & Caylor, 1982). These data suggest that the level of reading comprehension is very similar to the level of reading vocabulary, A_L-Words, which in turn supports the existence of the theoretical construct called rauding accuracy level, A_L, and supports the use of a reading vocabulary test scaled into GE units as an indirect measure of A_L.

The validity of the ALT as an indicant of A_LWords and the DRP as an indicant of A_L has been researched by correlating scores on these two tests with each other. In grades 7 and 8, the ALT correlated .80 with scores on the Degrees of Reading Power, DRP, test (Carver, 1992a). The ALT and the DRP also have been factor analyzed along with other tests; the ALT loaded on an accuracy factor about equally with the DRP (.92 for DRP vs. .90 for ALT).

Finally, evidence which seems to support the existence of raudamatized words comes from the eye movement research of Rayner and Duffy (1986). They found that fixation times for low-frequency words were higher than fixation times for high-frequency words even when word length was controlled. This result can be explained as follows: The low-frequency words probably were raudamatized whereas the high frequency words probably were not raudamatized.

Implications

Researchers need to know what they are measuring when they administer a standardized test of reading comprehension, or a reading achievement test. For example, Stone and Brady (1995) administered the Passage Comprehension subtest of the Woodcock Reading Mastery Test, and then generalized about "reading achievement." In a general sense, it is true they were measuring achievement in reading. However, they were not measuring E_L, because this Woodcock test is untimed and unspeeded so that it does not involve rate, or R_L. Therefore, Stone and Brady were likely to be measuring accuracy level, A_L. We need to know relatively precisely what we are measuring from a theoretical standpoint, so our theories are more likely to be testable, and therefore more readily refutable. Researchers need to be more aware of the difference between A_L and E_L, so that they can be more precise about whether they are measuring A_L or E_L; this distinction is important because C_s is a distal cause of E_L but C_s is neither a distal or proximal cause of A_L.

It would seem to be almost impossible to investigate lawful behavior in reading, without the A_L construct. Reading level and instructional level, are similar in concept to A_L but A_L is defined much more precisely; for example, reading level contains no qualifications with respect to rate and it is often determined under oral reading conditions. If the A_L construct is accepted, then it seems best to fuse it with (a) the concept of reading vocabulary size, (b) the concept of the accuracy of text comprehension under unspeeded conditions, and (c) the concept of time-limited word identification. Furthermore, if the A_L construct is accepted, then it is almost impossible to avoid accepting the lexicon of raudamatized words, or A_LWords.

Forget Me Nots

Rauding accuracy level, A_L, is a theoretical construct that tries to incorporate all of the good ideas that have traditionally been associated with the following concepts: (a) reading level, (b) level of reading comprehension, and (c) level of reading vocabulary. These earlier concepts have been upgraded by the A_L construct, which is more precisely defined both from a theoretical and an operational standpoint. Accuracy level, A_L, is the most difficult level of text that individuals can read accurately when they read at their own typical rate. For example, an individual may have a fourth-grade accuracy level, $A_L = 4$, as measured by a reading vocabulary test.

CHAPTER

5

RATE LEVEL, R_L

A high rate level, R_L, is necessary for high reading achievement. However, a high R_L is not sufficient for high reading achievement. In the causal model presented in Chapter 1, R_L is one of two factors at Echelon 2 that are the proximal causes of reading achievement, or E_L. The other proximal cause of E_L is accuracy level, A_L, as explained in the previous chapter.

The R_L construct is very helpful for explaining why some people are better readers than others, even though their accuracy of comprehension is not different. As noted earlier, rauding rate, or rate level, has been ignored by many researchers and many educators, and this chapter presents the case that rate level should be ignored no longer. The case for R_L belonging with A_L at Echelon 2 was supported by Carroll (1993) who stated that:

> There is good factorial evidence for distinguishing reading speed from reading comprehension. That is, it seems to be confirmed that individuals can attain equal degrees of comprehension at different speeds. (p. 165)

Carroll goes on to summarize the evidence that he reviewed as follows: "the weight of evidence from these studies indicates that reading speed is a cardinal variable in reading performance, and that it is associated with speed of accessing the memory codes involved in word recognition" (p. 166).

The idea of rate level, R_L, or a constant reading rate, is somewhat foreign to many reading researchers, as well as many educators. The reading rate of a student has traditionally been regarded as being fluid or flexible, that is, changing with one's purpose (Hoffman, 1978). So, it is somewhat unconventional to think that each student has a normal, typical, or optimal rate that is relatively constant, which allows one student to be compared to another student. Likewise, it is a somewhat foreign idea that this normal rate, R_r, could be measured in GE units (see Appendix D), and thereby be scaled in a manner comparable to accuracy level, A_L.

In this chapter, the R_L construct will be defined and related to traditional concepts. Then, tests measuring the construct will be described. Also, empirical evidence relevant to the existence of R_L will be summarized.

Theoretical Construct

Rauding rate level, R_L, is based on rauding rate, R_r. Rauding rate is defined as the relatively constant rate at which individuals successfully operate their rauding process. This theoretical construct, R_r, is somewhat similar to the more traditional concept of normal reading rate. When R_r is measured in GE units, it is symbolized as R_L and called rauding rate level, or rate level. For example, if an individual has a rauding rate of 162 Wpm, then this can be transformed into a grade equivalent of 5.5, so that $R_L = 5.5$ (see Carver, 1994c, or Appendix D).

The rauding rate of an individual, R_r, is also likely to be the fastest rate at which the individual can read relatively easy material and still comprehend accurately. Relatively easy material has already been defined as text which has a difficulty level lower than the accuracy level of the individual, $D_L < A_L$. To comprehend accurately has already been operationally defined as 64% comprehension or higher ($A > .64$), and the successful operation of the rauding process would require accurate comprehension. Rauding rate is very similar to the following concept advanced by Holmes (1954): "Speed of reading is used in this study to denote the rate of comprehension of relatively easy material ..." (p. 8).

Rauding rate can be measured in several different units, besides the GE units of R_L (Carver, 1990a). It can also be measured in standard length words per minute. A standard length word is six character spaces in length—such as five letters and one blank space between words. Actual words per minute will be designated using lower case letters, that is "wpm," while standard words per minute will be capitalized, that is "Wpm." For example, students at the college level of reading have rates around 260 Wpm ($R_L = 13.3$) to 300 Wpm ($R_L = 16.3$). Traditionally, reading rate has been measured by counting actual words read per minute, but easier material contains shorter words than harder material. Therefore, rauding rate is *not* constant across different levels of text difficulty when rate is measured in wpm (Carver, 1990a); rauding rate is constant across different levels of text difficulty (varying D_L) when rauding rate is measured in Wpm and the differing levels of text difficulty are all relatively easy for the individual, $A_L > D_L$ (Carver, 1976).

Rauding rate, R_r, can also be measured in standard length sentences per minute (Spm); a standard length sentence is defined as 16.67 standard length words (Carver, 1990a). In the equations of rauding theory that are used to predict the accuracy of text comprehension (see Appendix C), the value of R_r must be in Spm.

When word length is measured in a standard manner, such as standard words per minute, Wpm, then individuals normally read relatively easy material, $D_L < A_L$, at a relatively constant rate, as noted above. The first law of rauding, Law I (Carver, 1981), is that individuals attempt to comprehend thoughts in passages at a constant rate, called their rauding rate, R_r, unless they are influenced by situation-specific factors to change that rate (see Appendix B). Ordinarily, the average rate of comprehending a passage, R, is the rauding rate of the individual, R_r, that is, ordinarily $R = R_r$. This means that when individuals are reading text as they normally read, their text rate or average rate, R, is ordinarily the same as their rauding rate, R_r, because there is no time limit that makes the average rate that the text was read different from R_r.

Individuals are not likely to shift out of their rauding rate under normal reading conditions because this rate is also their optimal rate. That is, at rates other than their rauding rate, their efficiency of text comprehension (E) is likely to be lower. This means that they are likely to comprehend less sentences each minute they read when they read at a rate different from their rauding rate; their maximum efficiency of sentence comprehension occurs at their rauding rate. So, R_r is the rate at which efficiency, E, is at a maximum. Most individuals have a constant rate of reading relatively easy text because this rate, called their rauding rate, is the rate that maximizes their efficiency of reading. If they varied their reading rate so it was higher or lower, then the number of sentences they comprehended in a minute of reading would be less (Carver, 1982). The preceding theory has been labeled as the Third Law of Rauding (see Appendix B).

In research situations, individuals may shift out of their rauding process, which they ordinarily operate at a relatively constant rate of R_r. They are likely to shift to a higher gear (skimming or scanning) or to a lower gear (learning or memorizing) whenever (a) the instructions request faster or slower reading, (b) the objective consequences of the experimental task, such as a test, requires more or less than simply comprehending the thoughts in the sentences, (c) the material is relatively hard, $D_L > A_L$, (d) the time limits are so short that the individual does not have time to finish at the rauding rate, or (e) the time limits are so long that the individual has time to finish at the rauding rate (see Chapter 2).

In summary, the rauding rate of individuals is the rate at which they operate their rauding process. This rate is often expressed in standard words per minute, Wpm. When this rate is expressed in GE units, it is called rauding rate level and symbolized as R_L. Individuals tend to read normally at a constant rate because this rate optimizes their efficiency, that is, the number of sentences comprehended each minute of reading is likely to be less at rates other than their rauding rate. So, rauding rate level, R_L, is an indicator of rauding ability and a proximal cause of reading achievement, or E_L.

Related Concepts

Introduction. In this section, rauding rate level will be related to the concepts of reading rate, raudamatized words, rapid single-word decoding speed, word recognition speed, and apping.

Reading rate. The main thing to remember about reading rate, as a traditional concept, is that it is completely empirical; it can be used to measure how fast a person covers words during reading but it does not necessarily reflect a stable attribute of the individual. Individuals can shift gears when reading (Carver, 1992e), so they read at different rates (see Chapter 2). Most college students, for example, will vary their reading rate from around 138 words per minute when they know they will have to recall words in a passage later (Gear 1, a memorizing process) to around 600 words per minute when they only have to locate target words in passages (Gear 5, a scanning process). Individuals operate their rauding process (Gear 3) at their rauding rate, but they can shift out of this gear into other reading processes that operate at different reading rates. An individual may want to be able to remember the ideas better, and therefore shift gears down to a learning process (Gear 2); it proceeds at a slower reading rate because it involves more than simply comprehending the thoughts in the sentences. Or, an individual may want to get an overview of the material, and therefore shift gears up to a skimming process (Gear 4); it proceeds at a faster reading rate because it does not involve the time consuming sentence integration component of the rauding process. Extensive empirical evidence supporting the existence of these five reading gears, or five basic reading processes, has been reviewed by Carver (1990a).

Reading rate is highly contextual and task dependent, varying from gear to gear for an individual. In contrast, rauding rate is relatively constant; it is relatively constant for an individual across different purposes, such as preparing for a test, identifying main ideas, or analyzing author motives (see review of Hill, 1964, by Carver, 1990a). Rauding rate is also relatively constant across different levels of text difficulty, as long as the text is relatively easy; for example, individuals at $A_L = 12$ and higher will read textual materials varying in difficulty level from $D_L = 2$ to $D_L = 11$ all at the same rate in Wpm (Carver, 1983). Rauding rate is a constant reading rate for an individual, but it does vary between individuals. Some individuals can comprehend relatively easy material faster than others; some individuals operate their rauding process faster than others. This relatively constant rate of reading is their rauding rate, and when it is expressed in GE units it is called their rauding rate level, R_L. So, reading rate varies within an individual who shifts from one to another of the five basic reading processes or reading gears, but the reading rate at which individuals operate their rauding process is relatively constant.

Raudamatized Words. The concept of raudamatized words that was introduced in the last chapter on A_L, as an upgrade of the concept of automaticity, also has a direct connection to R_L. Remember that a raudamatized word is one which can be processed during rauding at the rauding rate of the individual. It was also theorized that raudamatized words are overlearned words such that further practice or experience with these words will not decrease the time needed to process them, t_r, because they have reached an asymptote that is common to all raudamatized words of standard length.

Notice that the rauding rate of an individual is also the rate at which standard-length words are read in context when these words are raudamatized words. Also, notice that there is a direct connection between raudamatized words and rate level, because R_L should be measured only when raudamatized words are purported to be involved, for example, using texts that are relatively easy, $D_L < A_L$, because they purportedly contain 100% (or 99% to 100%) raudamatized words (Carver, 1994b).

If raudamatized words are taken from relatively easy texts and presented in a randomized list, and then randomized again each time the list is presented, then individuals should not be able to improve the rate at which these words are read aloud; these words should be at asymptote with respect to the effect of practice upon rate of processing. Indeed, it is the naming of raudamatized words at a maximum rate that forces the constancy of R_r across difficulty levels as long as the text is relatively easy, $A_L > D_L$. An overlearned task cannot be improved with additional practice trials because it has reached maximum performance. Notice that it is not a lack of attention resources, *a' la* automaticity, that is being invoked as the mechanism that limits R_r, or R_L.

The effect of practice on the raudamatization of words was studied by Manis (1985). He gave students in grades 5 and 6, instruction and practice on 24 words they did not know. First, they learned the meaning of these words to an accuracy of 23 out of 24 correct in a trial. Then, they were asked to pronounce each word as fast as they could after it appeared on a computer screen, and latencies were measured. Results were reported in Sessions 1, 2, and 3. The results for Session 1 indicated that these "normal readers" pronounced these newly learned words slower than high-frequency control words. However, the results for Session 3 indicated that these students had overlearned (raudamatized) these 24 previously unknown words because they were pronounced just as fast as the control words. The results were somewhat different for a group of "disabled readers" who also were in grades 5 and 6. They were slower than the normals on all words in Session 1 and these disabled readers were not able to pronounce the 24 words as fast as the control words in Session 3. This means that the disabled readers had not raudamatized these 24 words by Session 3. However, they were clearly improving with practice and would very likely have been able to raudamatize these new words with additional practice sessions. That is, they would be able to recognize them as fast as the control words which they had already raudamatized. Keep in mind that the reading-disabled students had a slower rate of recognizing the control words, which means that they had a lower R_L. Also, remember that the normal-reading students were able to raudamatize the new words with the practice afforded by three sessions, whereas the reading-disabled students improved with the practice afforded but they were not able to raudamatize these words in only these few sessions.

Before continuing, it should be pointed out that in Chapter 2, a formula was given (Equation 2-1) for determining the number of milliseconds required for individuals to operate their rauding process on a standard length word in relatively easy text. The formula required that the rauding rate in Wpm be divided into 60,000; for example, if a college student had R_r = 300 Wpm, then this college student would require 60,000/300, or 200 msec per standard word. This 200 msec can now be interpreted as 200 msec per a standard length word that has been raudamatized, or 200 msec for each raudamatized word of standard length in the context of relatively easy text. Therefore, there is an inherent connection between raudamatized words and R_L. When the R_L construct is expressed in Wpm, then the amount of time needed to process a raudamatized word of standard length in context is the inverse of R_r. So, rauding rate expressed in GE units is rate level, R_L, and when rauding rate is expressed in msec per word, it is the time required to read a raudamatized word of standard length in context.

Rapid single-word decoding. The ability to read a list of isolated words quickly has long been considered an important ability in reading (Stanovich & West, 1979), and has been a cornerstone concept in verbal efficiency theory (Perfetti, 1985). This ability has been shown to correlate so highly with rauding rate that it is considered to be an indicant of rate level, R_L (Carver, 1991). Therefore, it would appear that much of the research involving speed of decoding isolated words can be alternately considered as research on rauding rate, or research on rate level, R_L. Lists of words that can be accurately pronounced without hesitation are likely to be raudamatized words so individual differences in their rate of decoding, or rate of pronunciation, are likely to correlate very highly with their rate of recognition during the rauding process. If the word lists used in the research contain all raudamatized words (well known to the readers with very high pronunciation accuracy and high speed of recognition), then this measure can be considered as an indicant of rauding rate, R_r, or as an indicant of rate level, R_L.

Given the above interpretations, it is easy to agree that rapid single-word decoding is a very important factor that distinguishes good from poor readers because individual differences in this ability are almost indistinguishable from rate level, R_L, which is a proximal cause of reading achievement, or E_L. More specifically, individual differences in the rate at which a list of raudamatized words can be read aloud is likely to be an indicant of R_L and correlate very highly with another measure of R_L. Stated differently, the ability to rapidly decode isolated known words is empirically almost exactly the same ability represented by the theoretical construct, R_L.

Notice that the R_L construct incorporates rapid single-word decoding so that prior research on this variable can be interpreted as a proximal cause of reading achievement, or E_L. That is, if rapid single-word decoding is scaled into GE units, then it purportedly has lawful relationships to E_L, P_L, and C_s via Equations 1-1 and 1-3.

Speed of word recognition. According to Perfetti (1985), speed of word recognition is a very important factor in reading skill. The speed of recognizing the meaning of known words in context and the speed of rapidly pronouncing isolated known words could both be referred to as "speed of word recognition." Yet, individuals can recognize and pronounce known words in context about twice as fast as they can recognize and pronounce isolated known words. For example, Carver (1991) had students in grades 2 to 10 read a passage aloud as fast as possible and also read the words aloud in randomized order, and he found that the mean rate was 140.5 Wpm for words in the meaningful text and 81.6 Wpm for the same words when they were randomized. In this research, individual differences in both of these measures loaded highly on a rate level factor (.89 & .85), which was defined (a) by a measure of typical silent reading rate, and (b) by an objective test of reading rate. Therefore, speed of word recognition is likely to be highly related to the R_L construct as long as the words are overlearned, or raudamatized words. Stated differently, speed of word recognition is likely to be highly correlated with R_L as long as the words are likely to be raudamatized words for all the individuals involved. Speed of word recognition is an indicant of rate level, R_L. Thus, most previous research on speed of word recognition involving overlearned words can also be interpreted as research involving individual differences in rauding rate, or rate level, R_L, with lawful relationships to reading achievement, or E_L (Equation 1-1), and lawful relationships to pronunciation knowledge and cognitive speed level (Equation 1-3).

Apping. In rauding theory, it is contended that readers have learned to move their eyes down a line of printed words in a habitual manner that requires no conscious attention; this is an overlearned psychomotor habit that can be done while comprehending the meaning of the words and forming the complete thought in the sentence. These habitual eye movements have been called "apping," a word derived from the initial letters of **A**utomatic **P**ilot for **P**rose (Carver, 1990a). During normal reading, or rauding, apping means that readers can think about the meaning of the words as they construct the thought in each sentence without thinking about where their eyes should move next. The eyes have been programmed by practice to automatically move down the line so that almost every word over 4 letters in length is fixated and each word can be perceived, lexically accessed, semantically encoded, and sententially integrated into the thought represented by the sentence. In this regard, Rayner (1997) has reviewed eye movement research and contends that "the optional strategy would be to fixate near the middle of each successive word" but "because short words can often be identified when they are to the right of the currently fixated word, they are often skipped" (p. 325).

Apping allows reading to be as efficient as auding, or as efficient as listening to an oral rendition of the same text when presented at the rauding rate of the individual. Apping also allows the reading of printed text to be as efficient as it would be if no eye movements were required, that is, as efficient as when each word is presented in the middle of a computer screen for a length of time in msec determined from the rauding rate of the individual and converted into msec per letter or msec per syllable. Indeed, research data exists which shows that eye movements are not needed to efficiently comprehend printed text (Masson, 1986). For example, Potter, Kroll, and Harris (1980) used the rapid serial visual presentation (RSVP) technique, developed by Forster (1970), to show that the number of idea units recalled were the same under the following three presentation conditions: (a) RSVP at 240 wpm, (b) reading printed text for a length of time equal to 240 wpm, and (c) listening to tape-recorded versions of the text at 240 wpm.

It should not go unnoted that the typical eye movement length of 6 character spaces, found by McConkie and Zola in 1984, is exactly equal to the length of a standard word in rauding theory, as defined earlier by Carver in 1976. This equivalency is not likely to be an accident. Carver (1976) reported that the average number of character spaces in college level words ($D_L = 13$) is 6. Because words read by college students tend to average around 6 character spaces in length (some longer and some shorter), and because college students normally fixate upon almost every word in the text during normal reading (see review of evidence by Carver, 1990a), it would be consistent for McConkie and Zola (1984) to find that college students most often have eye movements 6 character spaces in length.

In summary, apping is a psychomotor skill involving eye movements, which allows the rauding process to operate at the rauding rate of the individual, whether the text is being read or auded.

Relevant Tests

Introduction. Different tests that can be used to measure R_L will be described in some detail—the Rate Level Test, the Typical Silent Rate test, the Maximum Oral Rate test, the Nelson-Denny Reading Test-Rate, and other tests.

Rate Level Test (RLT). The RLT is a standardized test which uses a modified cloze task as an indicant of R_r and R_L. It is a 2-minute timed test that requires individuals to read short passages at the second grade level of difficulty

($D_L = 2$). These passages have been modified so that every fourth word offers a choice between two words—the word that belongs in the passage (right choice) or an alternative word that obviously does not belong in the passage (wrong choice); the wrong choice is obvious to those individuals who are at the second-grade reading level ($A_L = 2$) and higher. That is, the words on the test should be raudamatized words for students who are reading at a level above the first-grade. Accuracy on this test is typically 100% or very close to 100% so that the primary variable in the situation is how fast the correct answers (right choices) can be marked. The number of right choices marked in 2 minutes (corrected for guessing) is the Raw Score. The test manual (Carver, 1994c) explains how this raw score can be converted into Wpm for R_r or GE units for R_L (see also Appendix D).

The test manual, noted above, also contains extensive information regarding reliability and validity. Scores on Form A and Form B were compared for students in grades 3 through 12, college, and graduate school; the standard error of measurement was consistently around 1.2 GE units, and the average alternate form reliability coefficient across grades was .84. With respect to validity, the RLT was administered to students in grades 2 to 10, along with three other indicants of R_L (Carver, 1991). From a factor analysis of the correlations involved, controlled for grade level using partial correlations, (a) the RLT loaded .84 on an R_L factor, (b) typical silent rate loaded .80, on the R_L factor, (c) maximum oral reading rate loaded .89 on the R_L factor, and (d) speed of reading isolated words loaded .85 on the R_L factor. Notice that the RLT loaded higher than silent reading rate, about the same as the rate of reading isolated words, and a little lower than maximum oral reading rate.

Typical Silent Rate (TSR). On this test, which is part of the CARD battery (Carver, 1996), individuals are given a passage at the second-grade level of difficulty ($D_L = 2$) to read silently. Remember that rauding rate, R_r, can be directly measured whenever the rauding process is operating. This process is likely to be operating when individuals (a) are given relatively easy passages to read, $A_L > D_L$, (b) are asked to read these passages as they would read normally, and (c) are timed for how long it takes them to read the passages. Then, a measure of rauding rate can be obtained by counting the number of standard-length words in the passages, and then dividing by the elapsed time, in minutes, to get Wpm, as is the case for TSR.

Formulas have been given elsewhere (Carver, 1990a) for converting from various units into Wpm, such as from syllables per minute or from the printer's "em" unit. The obtained value in Wpm can also be divided by 16.67 to get rauding rate, R_r, in Sentences per minute, Spm, as was noted earlier in this chapter. However, R_r is more often expressed in GE units, as R_L, and Carver (1989, 1990a) has provided tables for translating Wpm into R_L. The Carver (1990a) transformation has subsequently been improved by Carver (1994c), that is, upgraded slightly by more recent research (see Appendix D).

The procedure just described for obtaining a direct measure of rauding rate, R_r (or R_L), works very well when averaging individual scores for groups (see Carver, 1983). However, it can produce unreliable data for a single individual because it is not entirely objective. For example, an individual may shift out of the rauding process into a higher gear (faster rate) or lower gear (slower rate) under the guise of being in Gear 3. The best direct measures of rauding rate would involve some evidence that the relatively easy text being read was also being comprehended accurately ($A_r > .64$).

Maximum Oral Rate (MOR). The MOR test is used in the CARD, Computer Assisted Reading Diagnosis (Carver, 1996). Students are given a short passage (about 100 words) that is very easy ($D_L = 2$), and asked to read it once silently to themselves (see TSR above). When finished, they are then asked to read aloud exactly the same passage again, as fast as they can; this procedure provides a measure of maximum oral rate, MORR, which is the number of standard words in the passage divided by the time required to read it aloud, in minutes. Carver (1990a) has hypothesized that R_r = MORR + 25 Wpm. However, a linear equating technique has subsequently been used to convert MORR into GE units, or R_L, for the CARD (Carver, 1996). This test also has an equivalent form, i.e., Form A and Form B.

The case for the MORR task being a good indicant of R_L is supported by Carroll (1993) who stated that "reading speed would seem to involve comprehension only minimally; the measure is simply the time to read a passage aloud as fast as possible, i.e., to recognize the words (in sentences) and utter them" (p. 165).

Carver (1991) has presented data, noted earlier in connection with the RLT, which indicates that the MOR test measures the rate level factor better than the RLT, better than typical silent rate, and better than the speed of reading isolated words; the MOR loaded the highest, .89, on the R_L factor. However, the RLT is a group test and MOR must be administered individually.

It should be noted that the rate of reading text orally is generally not a good indicant of R_L. Carver (1990a) has discussed how individuals who are asked to read text aloud (a) may choose to accent a good oral rendition for others, and not try to comprehend what is being read, or (b) may focus on comprehending, while disregarding how the rendition may sound to others. The rates that accompany these traditional oral reading situations cannot be relied upon to provide a good indicant of R_L. For example, on some reading tests a child is asked to read aloud and at the same time comprehend what is being read so that questions can be answered accurately later. The score on the comprehension test *may* provide an indicant of A_L and the rate of oral reading *may* provide an indicant of R_L. In these situations, the score on the test questions on the text *may* provide a better indicant of E_L than A_L. It should also be recognized that there will always be a certain amount of tradeoff between accuracy and rate during typical oral reading situations, because slowing down will lower rate and increase accuracy while speeding up will increase rate and decrease accuracy. Thus, variation in strategy during typical oral reading will likely change the correlation of oral reading rate with A_L and R_L.

In summary, maximum oral reading rate is an exceptional type of oral reading because (a) it requires that the text to be read be relatively easy and already have been read once silently for comprehension, (b) it requires that the text be read as fast as possible, and (c) it is relatively objective, reliable, and valid as a measure of R_L.

The Nelson-Denny Reading Test (NDRT). The NDRT provides a measure of reading rate, so it will be instructive to analyze this measure. Students are asked to read a passage that is about 600 words in length for 1 minute. At the end of this time period the examiner asks the individual to circle the word, or the line, they are reading. Then, reading rate is the number of words covered during this 1 minute of reading. For example, if the individual circled word number 279 (counting from the first word in the passage), then reading rate would be 279 wpm.

As early as 1968, Farr concluded that the rate measure on the NDRT "should probably not be used at all" (p. 190). Later, Carver (1992a) showed that this rate measure provides a poor indicant of the rate level factor. Theoretically, this NDRT rate measure would not provide a good measure of rauding rate, R_r, because it is likely to involve a passage that is relatively hard, $D_L > A_L$, for some college students. Also, because these individuals are expecting to be tested on what they have read, many are likely to shift into a learning process, or Gear 2, instead of using their rauding process (see Chapter 2). Finally, the words covered on the test would need to be converted into standard length words in order to provide a measure of rauding rate, or rate level, R_L.

Other Tests. A great deal of research has been conducted on the latency of word recognition and the speed of word recognition (see Perfetti, 1985). This research has unintentionally involved an indicant of rate level, R_L, because it involves the rate at which isolated raudamatized words are named (recognized or identified). As noted earlier, researchers have often acknowledged the importance of word recognition speed, even though it has not been generally acknowledged to be an indicant of R_L. For example, consider the following quotation from Stanovich (1980):

> Since the speed of recognition is now widely acknowledged as being crucial to reading (even among investigators of vastly different theoretical persuasions—see Biemiller, 1977; Doehring, 1976; LaBerge & Samuels, 1974; Smith, 1971; Smith & Holmes, 1971), it would seem necessary to focus on how readers of different abilities use orthographic structure to speed word recognition. (p. 38)

So, any measure of the speed at which overlearned words—raudamatized words—can be recognized is likely to provide an indicant of R_L. Again, prior research on individual differences in the speed of word recognition may be reinterpreted as investigations of reading rate, or rauding rate level, as long as the text was relatively easy, or raudamatized words were used.

In general, any measure of the time, rate, or latency at which readily identifiable words are correctly named (or pronounced) should be a good indicant of R_L. It is not necessary that the words be in meaningful order, or in context. It is only necessary that the words involved be raudamatized so they can be named accurately and relatively quickly. On the other hand, reading rates measured under conditions likely to induce memorizing, learning, skimming, or scanning processes are not likely to provide good indicants of R_L. Also, it should also be mentioned that the speed of pronouncing pseudowords has a special relationship to R_L, as will be explained in detail later in Chapter 11.

Summary of Theory

The rate at which individuals operate their rauding process is their rauding rate. Individuals normally read relatively easy materials at a relatively constant rate, which is their rauding rate; when this rate is measured in standard-length words and expressed in GE units, it is called rauding rate level, R_L. Whereas the reading rate of an individual may vary when other reading processes are operating, such as scanning, skimming, learning, and memorizing, rauding rate is relatively constant at a certain level, called R_L. Rauding rate is also the optimal rate, that is, the most efficient rate of comprehending sentences in text, whether the text is read or auded.

The words in relatively easy material that can be accurately and rapidly processed at the rauding rate during the operation of the rauding process are called raudamatized words. Raudamatized words are overlearned words that require a fixed or constant amount of time to process when they are standard in length, and this amount of time is the inverse of the rauding rate, or $1/R_r$. When reading these raudamatized words in relatively easy text, the eye movements involved are habitual and require little or no attention. These rhythmic eye movements are called apping—a term derived from automatic pilot for prose. Apping involves a fixation on almost every word; these fixations during apping involve lexically assessing, semantically encoding, and sententially integrating every word in a sentence of text. Apping allows printed raudamatized words to be successfully processed during the rauding process at the same rate as these words would be successfully processed (a) when no eye movements are involved during auding, or (b) when no eye movements are involved during the presentation of one word at a time in the middle of a computer screen. Rauding rate is relatively constant across varying levels of text difficulty, as long as $D_L < A_L$, because all of these words are raudamatized and therefore processed at the same rate even across varying purposes.

Indicants of R_L include (a) typical silent reading rate for relatively easy text, (b) the fastest rate at which raudamatized words in context can be pronounced aloud, called maximum oral reading rate, and (c) the fastest speed at which lists of raudamatized words can be pronounced aloud. The Rate Level Test, RLT, can be used as an indirect measure of R_L for students above the first-grade level because it is likely to contain raudamatized words for those individuals. The Rate score on the Nelson-Denny Reading Test would not provide a very good indicant of R_L because (a) some individuals are likely to shift into a learning process (Gear 2) in order to answer the test questions more accurately, (b) some of the words may not be raudamatized for some of the readers, and (c) the rate is not measured in standard length words per minute, Wpm.

Summary of Evidence

There is a great deal of data from many different research studies which provide strong support for the constancy of reading rate in standard words per minute when individuals are reading relatively easy material in a normal or typical manner (see Carver, 1990a, for a review of Ballantine, 1951; Carver, 1971a, 1971b, 1976, 1981, 1983; Coke, 1974; G. R. Miller & Coleman, 1971; Morse, 1951; Rothkopf & Coatney, 1974; Zuber & Wetzel, 1981); this evidence supports the existence of the R_r construct, and the R_L construct. The concept of apping, which accompanies normal reading of text and occurs at the rauding rate, has been supported by research which has found that random spaces inserted between the words of text has the effect of slowing reading rate (Lloyd & McKelvie, 1992).

The earlier idea that readers continually change their rate to match continually changing purposes and continually changing material difficulty (e.g., Hoffman, 1978), has no empirical support when normal or typical reading of relatively easy text is involved (see Carver, 1990a for a review of Hill, 1964).

The earlier idea that readers vary their rate with the number of propositions in a text (Kintsch & Keenan, 1973; Keenan & Brown, 1984), is relevant to a learning process or a memorizing process but is not relevant to the rauding process or normal reading. Therefore, this research should not be interpreted as evidence against rate level, R_L.

The earlier idea that the amount of context influences reading rate is not relevant to the rauding process, or normal reading (Gough, 1984). That is, Stanovich (1980) reviewed data which seems to have effectively demolished the idea that individuals use hypothesis testing and predictions to speed up word recognition (an idea espoused by Smith, 1971; Goodman, 1967; Levin & Kaplan, 1970; Williams, 1977). For example, Mitchell and Green (1978) found that the more predictable parts of text were *not* read faster.

Finally, speed of word recognition, which is an indicant of R_L, has long been considered to be an important determiner of reading ability (Carroll, 1993; Perfetti, 1985; Stanovich, 1980).

Given the amount of data supporting the existence of the R_L construct, and the lack of any conflicting data collected during the past 25 years, it is very surprising to find as late as 1995 that Rayner, Raney, and Pollatsek disregarded this prior theory and supporting research when they interpreted the data they collected involving reading rate and text difficulty data. They had 10 college students read six different passages that varied in difficulty from "light fiction" to "biology." The six mean rates they reported decreased from a high of 365 wpm for the light fiction passage to 233 wpm for the biology passage. They suggested that there was a dramatic influence of text difficulty, and that "familiarity with the material allows people to read text faster" (p. 14). In this interpretation of theirs, notice that (a) they did not mention the measured difficulty level of the text, (b) they made no distinction between the rates for relatively easy text and relatively hard text, and (c) they did not control for word length, by using standard-length words per minute, Wpm. Their data have been reanalyzed on the basis of some reasonable assumptions about the relative difficulty level, D_L - A_L, of their passages, and their lengths in standard words; it also seemed reasonable to assume that their college students were at the middle of college, $A_L = 14.5$. Therefore, the light fiction, history, and psychology passages were assumed to be relatively easy, $A_L > D_L$; these rates varied only from 313 Wpm to 334 Wpm. This is hardly a dramatic difference (31 Wpm) considering that the light fiction passage was read only 4% faster than the history passage and only 6% faster than the psychology passage. Furthermore, with regard to the economics passage, the physics passage, and the biology passage, they were assumed to be relatively hard, $D_L > A_L$, so it is not surprising that these students would shift down to a learning process; these passages were read considerably slower than the light fiction—18% slower for economics, 26% slower for physics, and 28% slower for biology. These data therefore may be alternately interpreted as supporting the theory that reading rate is relatively constant at R_L for relatively easy material.

Implications

We need to consider the strong probability that one theoretical construct, R_L, explains individual differences in many different rate measures, such as the following: (a) typical rate of reading relatively easy material silently, (b) fastest rate of reading aloud raudamatized words in context, and (c) fastest rate of pronouncing isolated lists of raudamatized words. When one of these measures is used in research it should be considered as an indicant of R_L, and therefore a measure of one of two proximal causes of reading achievement, or E_L.

Although rauding rate level, R_L, is an extremely important attribute of all readers including lower graders and middle graders, it is often ignored by educators. For example, school districts often administer standardized reading comprehension tests (indicant of E_L) and standardized reading vocabulary tests (indicant of A_L) but they do not ordinarily administer standardized tests that attempt to measure normal reading rate (indicant of R_L). Because R_L is a proximal cause of reading achievement, or E_L, it does not make sense to ignore it while measuring A_L, which is the other secondary cause of E_L. Furthermore, by administering a measure of rate level, it seems likely that many school districts would find that the whole-language approach and the phonics approach to instruction were causing their students to be slower readers, that is, lowering their R_L (see Chapters 22 and 23).

Rauding rate, rate level, raudamatized words, and apping, are theoretical constructs that have considerable empirical support. Furthermore, the R_L construct integrates and clarifies several previous concepts in reading, such as typical silent reading rate, fastest rate of reading text aloud, rapid single-word decoding, and automaticity. Acceptance of the R_L construct, which includes acceptance of a constant rauding rate for relatively easy materials, necessarily means that the traditional concepts of automaticity and rapid single-word recognition have been superseded, or upgraded.

Forget Me Nots

Rauding rate level, R_L, is a theoretical construct that tries to incorporate all of the good ideas that have traditionally been associated with normal reading rate and the rate at which lists of known words can be decoded. These earlier concepts have been upgraded by the R_L construct, which is more precisely defined both from a theoretical and operational standpoint. Rate level, R_L, is the rate at which an individual typically reads relatively easy text when that rate is measured in grade equivalent units; for example, an individual may have a fourth-grade rate level $R_L = 4$.

CHAPTER

6

VERBAL KNOWLEDGE LEVEL, V_L

Verbal knowledge level, V_L, is one of three primary causal factors at Echelon 3 in the causal model, along with pronunciation knowledge level, P_L, and cognitive speed level, C_s. Remember also from Chapter 1 that verbal level is one of the two proximal causes of accuracy level, along with pronunciation level. An individual cannot achieve highly in reading without a high level of verbal knowledge, V_L, but having a high verbal knowledge level is not enough to guarantee high reading achievement as the documented cases of some dyslexics attest (Levine & Osbourne, 1989).

Verbal knowledge is a prerequisite for growth in accuracy level, A_L, when children are beginning to learn to read. Without basic knowledge of the language, children in the early grades will not gain much in A_L during a school year. However, beginning readers who have high levels of V_L do not have a great advantage over those with moderate or average levels of V_L; individual differences in pronunciation level, P_L, are of much more consequence than individual differences in verbal level, V_L in their effect upon A_L for beginning readers. For most intermediate readers, V_L and P_L are two equally important factors influencing accuracy level, A_L. For advanced readers, verbal level becomes inextricably tied to accuracy level, A_L, so that a gain in one automatically results in a corresponding gain in the other. This means that for many adults, the amount of verbal knowledge and the level of difficulty of material that a student can accurately comprehend while reading or listening are all so closely tied together that they cannot be empirically or theoretically differentiated (see Chapter 17).

In this chapter, the V_L construct will be defined, and then traditional concepts that are related to V_L will be described. Then, relevant tests measuring V_L will be described. Empirical evidence relevant to the existence of V_L will also be reviewed.

Theoretical Construct

Verbal knowledge level, V_L, is the amount of verbal knowledge a person has, measured in GE units; this construct will generally be referred to by its shortened name of "verbal level" or by its symbol, V_L. This theoretical construct refers to all the world knowledge, background knowledge, or general knowledge a person has accumulated and remembers that is in the form of spoken words or language.

The V_L construct was created to achieve the goal advanced by Cronbach (1957) when he encouraged the creation of variables with minimum redundancy, that "... permit us to obtain maximum information from a minimum of experimental investment" (p. 677). With respect to the present goal of delineating the primary causes of high and low reading achievement, there does not seem to be any justification for trying to keep levels of verbal knowledge separate from (a) levels of ability to comprehend while listening to text being read aloud at varying levels of difficulty, (b) listening vocabulary, or levels of knowledge of the meaning of spoken words that vary in difficulty, or frequency of usage, or (c) levels of general knowledge that involves speaking and listening. For example, it would seem to be very unlikely for an individual to have a fifth-grade level of verbal knowledge, or V_L, and have a substantially different level of listening comprehension, have a substantially different level of listening vocabulary, or have a substantially different level of general knowledge, no matter how these concepts were measured—unless, of course, the measures were not highly reliable. The close connection between V_L and A_L in the causal model is mirrored by the traditionally close connections among general knowledge, vocabulary, listening, language, and reading.

The above definition of verbal knowledge level has much in common with the definition of "conceptual knowledge," given by Alexander, Shallert, and Hare (1991). They state that conceptual knowledge is made up of content knowledge and discourse knowledge with word knowledge (or vocabulary knowledge) overlapping with both content and discourse knowledge. For example, conceptual knowledge about human biology would involve knowledge of the systems of the body (content) and knowledge of how the concepts are related via language (discourse) as well as a knowledge of the words involved (what a "brain" is and that this word is used as a noun not a verb). Verbal knowledge is inextricably tied to vocabulary knowledge, yet it refers to more than the knowledge of the meaning of individual words. Verbal knowledge also involves what Alexander, Shallert and Hare (1991) call declarative (factual), procedural (how), and conditional (when and where) knowledge as long as these types of knowledge involve words or language.

Verbal knowledge does not refer to certain skills, such as knowing how to ride a bicycle—a psychomotor skill that is not represented in the form of words. It also does not refer to metacognitive knowledge, that is, knowledge of regulating one's cognition.

In short, verbal knowledge refers to all the conceptual knowledge that is useful for understanding sentences when listening to them being spoken, i.e., auding. Verbal knowledge level measured in GE units refers to increasing amounts of verbal knowledge that allow the sentences in increasingly difficult texts to be comprehended when they are auded.

The V_L construct also has a close connection to another theoretical construct, called audamatized words—not to be confused with automatized words. Words that can be comprehended when presented auditorily at the rauding rate of the individual, are called audamatized words. The size of the lexicon of audamatized words (V_LWords) is an indicant of V_L.

When individuals are listening to spoken sentences, or when written text is being read to them, the words are likely to be audamatized. That is, when textual material is being read aloud to the individual, and the individual is comprehending the sentences, then the words in the sentences are audamatized because they are readily recognized and comprehended. The learning curve for transforming an unknown spoken word into an audamatized word, is ordinarily not of direct interest to reading researchers. However, the concept of a lexicon of audamatized words, V_LWords, seems to be just as important for spoken words as the concept of raudamatized words, A_LWords, is important for printed words. Raudamatized words are audamatized words that can be comprehended just as accurately and quickly in print as they are when they are auded.

Related Traditional Concepts

Introduction. Chall (1983) has related knowledge, vocabulary, and reading as follows:

> "World knowledge" and vocabulary, both developed through wide reading, are also essential for reading development. Thus, education and reading are circular—the more a person has of one, the better the development of the other. The more the knowledge, the better the reading; the better the skill and uses of reading, the better the knowledge. (p. 8)

Similarly, Carroll (1993) states that "language acquisition is, in fact, largely a matter of the development of long-term semantic memory-information, that is, about the meanings and uses of words and other aspects of language structure" (p. 194); he goes on to say that "tests of vocabulary are in the main tests of knowledge" (p. 198).

The next subsection will describe in more detail how V_L is related to listening comprehension. Then, V_L will be related to three other concepts often used in psychology, namely, verbal ability, verbal intelligence, and verbal comprehension.

Listening comprehension. The concept of listening comprehension connotes an on-line process that is likely to be more relevant to 1 second of reading or 1 minute of reading, instead of 1 year of reading. Because V_L is a construct that is directly relevant to 1 year of reading, then it is more similar to the concept of listening comprehension ability or listening level. The more traditional concepts of listening comprehension, language knowledge, or linguistic comprehension are similar to V_L as long as these concepts are considered to be individual difference factors rather than within individual processing factors. Any listening comprehension measure that involves words of varying frequencies of usage, or passages of varying difficulty, should correlate highly with any purported measure of V_L.

The close connections among listening vocabulary, listening comprehension, and V_L are evident from a definition of listening comprehension given by Hammill and McNutt (1980), prior to their review of research in this area. They stated that "the construct of listening comprehension includes all tests or subtests designed to measure oral receptive language" (p. 271), and that "the tests or subtests designed to measure listening comprehension usually relate to one or two specific constructs: receptive vocabulary and contextual listening" (p. 271). Translated, this means that the number of V_LWords should be highly correlated with a listening comprehension measure of V_L.

The close connection between V_L and listening level was even more obvious in earlier published research on rauding theory. In those publications prior to 1994, the V_L construct was symbolized by $AudA_L$ and it was called auditory accuracy level, or auding accuracy level. Because auding and listening are the same concepts in the context of language comprehension, it can be seen that V_L evolved from a concept of listening comprehension level.

There is a very close connection between the traditional concepts of listening comprehension, or language knowledge, and V_L.

Verbal ability. The meaning of "verbal ability" has been discussed at some length by Campito (1994). He said that verbal ability was "a technical term used by cognitive and educational psychologists to refer to (1) the amount and structure of one's verbal knowledge, often called vocabulary knowledge, and (2) the ability to reason by using this verbal knowledge" (p. 1107). Campito goes on to say that verbal ability has "two broad facets: a knowledge facet and a cognitive processing facet" (p. 1107). The part of Campito's definition of verbal ability which refers to the amount and structure of one's verbal knowledge, often called vocabulary knowledge, has much in common with the V_L construct. However, the part of Campito's definition of verbal ability which deals with the ability to reason does not have much in common with the V_L construct.

Campito also stated that "verbal ability, represented by such behaviors as 'displays a good vocabulary,' 'reads with high comprehension,' 'is verbally fluent,' and 'converses easily on a variety of subjects,' was found by Sternberg, Conway, Ketron, and Berstein (1981) to be the first of three major factors defining intelligence for both experts in the field of intelligence and lay people" (p. 1107). So, V_L not only has much in common with verbal ability but it is also indirectly associated with verbal intelligence.

E. Hunt (1978) noted that "one of the reasons verbal ability tests do predict performance is that they test knowledge, and the amount of knowledge one possesses is a good guide to general cognitive competence" (p. 111). Thus, Hunt has strengthened the case for V_L having much in common with the traditional concept of verbal ability because verbal ability is closely associated with knowledge.

In summary, there is a very close connection between V_L and the knowledge aspect of verbal ability, but the reasoning aspect of verbal ability is not closely related to V_L (see Chapter 20 which relates reasoning to reading).

Verbal intelligence. There is a very high relationship between verbal intelligence and the V_L construct. Anderson and Freebody (1981) have stated that "the strong relationship between vocabulary and general intelligence is one of the most robust findings in the history of intelligence testing" (p. 77). Furthermore, the concept of verbal intelligence is very closely related to crystallized intelligence because both involve verbal knowledge or word knowledge. Later, Chapter 20 expounds upon how crystallized intelligence, Gc, which is the breadth and depth of knowledge of the individual's culture, relates to reading achievement.

In the causal model presented in Chapter 1, a distinction was made between g_v and V_L, where g_v is an aptitude or intelligence type of construct that represents a kind of ability not strongly influenced by education or instruction, whereas V_L was influenced by teaching and learning as well as g_v. The traditional concepts of verbal intelligence and crystallized intelligence connote more of a focus upon g_v than V_L, yet, this distinction is often blurred when the operational definitions in research involve measures that may involve V_L as much as g_v. That is, some tests of verbal intelligence, verbal aptitude, and crystallized intelligence are likely to contain items that are highly influenced by teaching and learning, and therefore may have as much in common with V_L as g_v.

In summary, verbal intelligence is a concept that is similar to both V_L and g_v, but most measures of verbal intelligence are more highly related to g_v than to V_L.

Verbal comprehension. It will be helpful to compare the construct of verbal level, V_L, to the concept of "verbal comprehension" as used by Sternberg and Powell (1983). They define this latter concept as "a person's ability to understand linguistic materials, such as newspapers, magazines, textbooks, lectures, and the like" (p. 878). A person's ability to understand newspapers, magazines, and textbooks would often be referred to as reading comprehension, or A_L, and a person's ability to understand lectures might be referred to as listening comprehension, or V_L. So, verbal comprehension seems to mean the same as reading and listening comprehension. Sternberg and Powell go on to state that verbal comprehension "... can be operationalized in a number of different ways" (p. 878) and that "most often, it is directly measured by tests of vocabulary, reading comprehension, and general information" (p. 878). They go on to note that learning vocabulary from the context of what is heard or read "can facilitate vocabulary level at the same time that a higher vocabulary level can facilitate learning from context" (pp. 880, 881).

From this operational definition of verbal comprehension given by Sternberg and Powell, it can be seen that it has much in common with V_L, in that both can be measured by vocabulary tests and tests of general information, or world knowledge. However, V_L for early and middle graders would ordinarily be measured by a listening comprehension test rather than a reading comprehension test, as noted at the outset of this chapter. This apparent difference between listening and reading evaporates, however, when dealing with many adult readers, such as most college students (see Chapter 17). When dealing with advanced readers, the concept of verbal comprehension as discussed by Sternberg and Powell seems to be very similar to the construct of V_L in the causal model. Sternberg and Powell go on to state that "vocabulary has been recognized not only as an excellent measure of verbal comprehension but also as one of the best single indicants of a person's overall level of intelligence" (p. 878).

The main thrust of Sternberg and Powell (1983) was to present their own theory of verbal comprehension, or general verbal ability, which is actually a theory of learning new vocabulary from context. In short, they presented a model of the factors that influence the learning of the meanings of words from context, and therefore it is a theory of what causes an increase in V_L, a subject that will be focused upon later in Chapter 12.

In summary, there is an extremely close connection between the concept of verbal comprehension and the V_L construct.

Relevant Tests

Introduction. Two tests that are relevant to measuring V_L are the Auding Accuracy Level Test, AALT, and the General Information subtest from the Peabody Individual Achievement Test, PIAT. These two tests will be described, and then some theory about testing V_L will be presented.

Auding Accuracy Level Test. In previous research on rauding theory, the construct of V_L (or $AudA_L$ prior to 1994) has been measured using a listening vocabulary test, called the Auding Accuracy Level Test (AALT). On this test, the individual is presented a target word auditorily, and then is presented three alternative answers (see Carver & Clark, 1998). One of the three alternative words means about the same thing as the target word (a synonym), and the other two alternatives have a meaning that is not close to the target word or its synonym. The scores on this test are scaled into GE units thereby providing an indirect measure of V_L.

The AALT is actually the same test as the ALT, described earlier in Chapter 4, except the words on the ALT are read aloud to the examinees on the AALT. Some researchers may question the use of the AALT as a measure of V_L from three standpoints. First, listening vocabulary tests used to measure verbal knowledge level is an indicant, and therefore not as authentic as a direct measure. However, as contended earlier, listening vocabulary knowledge is an important part of verbal knowledge or conceptual knowledge, so it would seem reasonable to use a person's knowledge of increasingly difficult (lower frequency) words presented auditorily as an indicant of V_L.

The second objection to the AALT is likely to be a procedural one. The words are presented on the AALT auditorily at the same time as they are presented in print, or on the computer screen. This procedural condition might contaminate the listening measure with unwanted effects due to variation in reading ability. However, Carver (1998c) has presented evidence that mitigates against this procedural detail being an important problem.

The third objection to the AALT as an indicant of V_L is also likely to be procedural—the administration of the same vocabulary words first by reading on the ALT and then by listening on the AALT. That is, if Form A of the ALT is administered and Form A of the AALT is administered, then the individual will be given exactly the same words on both tests. This procedural condition could produce a major practice effect. However, in the same research just noted (Carver, 1998c), the results indicated that no advantage accrued to those who had seen the same words earlier.

General Information. The Peabody Individual Achievement Test, PIAT, contains a General Information subtest that should provide a measure of V_L. It contains questions that are read aloud to the individual by an examiner. Because the raw score can be converted into a GE score, this test should provide a direct measure of V_L.

Test Theory. A direct measure of verbal level, V_L, would involve a sampling of all the verbal knowledge that a person has. That is, a direct measure would try to sample everything a person knows in the form of words, and then scale this knowledge into GE units.

Measures of listening comprehension that involve passages at varying levels of difficulty should provide excellent indicants of V_L. Furthermore, any auditorily administered measure of general knowledge, world knowledge, background knowledge, or cultural literacy should sample much the same universe of knowledge as that defined as verbal knowledge, and therefore should provide an indicant of V_L. That is, accuracy measures that involve auditorily presented words varying in difficulty—where a premium is not put on the ability to read and a premium is not put on rate—should provide a good indicant of V_L. This means that most auditorily administered vocabulary tests should also provide excellent indicators of V_L. However, it would seem possible to develop vocabulary tests so that they maximally discriminated between individuals at a particular age and therefore evolved into measures that were more highly related to verbal aptitude, g_v, than with verbal knowledge level, V_L.

A vocabulary test that has been designed to measure IQ, such as the vocabulary section of the Stanford Binet Intelligence Test, has also been designed to maximally discriminate between individuals at the same age level. This means that the items have not been selected to measure learning, gain, or progress. Because of this difference between psychometrically developed tests and edumetrically developed tests (Carver, 1974), listening vocabulary measures developed for an IQ test are likely to be better indicants of g_v than V_L.

Summary of Theory

Verbal knowledge is all the knowledge that an individual possesses in the form of words, and verbal knowledge level is that knowledge scaled into GE units. Therefore, verbal level, V_L, is a theoretical construct that attempts to incorporate several traditional concepts, such as general knowledge, world knowledge, background knowledge, conceptual knowledge, language knowledge, and listening vocabulary. V_L also attempts to incorporate the concept of listening comprehension or verbal comprehension, that is, the ability to comprehend auditory presentations of increasingly difficult text. V_L is also related to the concepts of verbal ability and verbal intelligence except that these concepts are likely to involve more reasoning, or fluid intelligence, Gf, and therefore are likely to be more related to verbal knowledge aptitude, g_v.

A direct measure of V_L would involve a sampling of all the verbal knowledge possessed by an individual, whereas indicants of V_L would include measures of listening comprehension, and auditory measures of general knowledge. A measure of all the words that an individual could recognize and comprehend when listening, called audamatized words or V_LWords, should be a good indicant of V_L, and would provide an indirect measure of V_L when scaled into GE units. One existing indirect measure of V_L is an auditorily administered vocabulary test, called the Auditory Accuracy Level Test, AALT. An existing direct measure of V_L would be the General Information test from the PIAT.

Summary of Evidence

Scores on listening vocabulary tests are almost perfectly correlated with scores on listening comprehension tests when both measures are corrected for attenuation (*r* = .91, from Sticht, Hooke, & Caylor, 1982). These data strengthen the case for V_L being a construct that encompasses both listening vocabulary knowledge and listening comprehension.

Measures of cultural literacy (or general knowledge) and vocabulary for adults are highly correlated, especially when corrected for attenuation (*r* = .78, from West, Stanovich, & Mitchell, 1993). These results strengthen the case that V_L incorporates both general knowledge and vocabulary.

Implications

Verbal knowledge level, V_L, is an extremely important construct when investigating the causes of high and low reading achievement. It incorporates other very important concepts in education and psychology, namely, level of listening comprehension, level of listening vocabulary, and level of general knowledge or world knowledge. V_L needs to be measured separately from verbal ability and verbal intelligence which are likely to be more highly related to fluid intelligence, Gf, and verbal knowledge aptitude, g_v.

Forget Me Nots

Verbal knowledge level, V_L, is a theoretical construct that tries to incorporate all of the good ideas that have traditionally been associated with the following concepts: (a) level of listening vocabulary, (b) level of listening comprehension, and (c) level of general knowledge, world knowledge, or conceptual knowledge. These earlier concepts have been upgraded by the V_L construct, which is more precisely defined both from a theoretical and an operational standpoint. Verbal level, V_L, is the amount of verbal knowledge an individual has when that knowledge is scaled into grade equivalent units; for example, an individual may have a fourth-grade verbal level, $V_L = 4$.

CHAPTER

7

PRONUNCIATION KNOWLEDGE LEVEL, P_L

A high level of pronunciation knowledge is necessary for high reading achievement. Individuals who have a low pronunciation knowledge for their age are very likely to be low in reading achievement. Pronunciation knowledge, P_L, is therefore a major factor affecting reading achievement. However, a high P_L is not sufficient to guarantee high reading achievement because reading achievement is also affected by two other factors at Echelon 3 in the causal model, namely, verbal knowledge level, V_L, and cognitive speed level, C_s.

The P_L construct is perhaps the most important one in the causal model because (a) it has a very important effect upon reading achievement, and (b) it is the factor that is unique to reading instruction. Without P_L there would be no need for reading instruction, and with P_L there is a major need for instruction in reading. You must understand the P_L construct in order to understand the causes of high and low reading achievement because P_L is at the core of the causal model. Reading educators who ignore P_L or minimize its importance put their students at risk.

In this chapter, the P_L construct will be defined, and then related to other traditional concepts that are similar. Then, tests that can be used to measure P_L will be described. Also, empirical evidence relevant to the existence of P_L will be summarized.

Theoretical Construct

Pronunciation knowledge level, P_L, is the number of words an individual can accurately pronounce out of context, or in a list, when scaled into GE units. One way to conceive of this construct is to (a) consider all of the main entries in a dictionary, (b) determine how many of these words an individual can correctly pronounce, and (c) transform this amount into a GE unit. A word that can be correctly pronounced by an individual is called a pronounceamatized word, so the number of pronounceamatized words scaled into GE units is pronunciation knowledge level, P_L. The lexicon of pronounceamatized words for an individual will be symbolized as "P_LWords," so P_L is also the number of P_LWords scaled into GE units.

The concept of pronounceamatized words, or P_LWords, has many theoretical implications relevant to the P_L construct. The lexicon of pronounceamatized words, or P_LWords, is simply all the printed words that an individual can pronounce correctly. Some of these P_LWords can be pronounced because they are raudamatized words, or A_LWords, and the remainder of the P_LWords can be pronounced correctly because of pure cipher knowledge. All the words that are unknown when listening but can be correctly pronounced using pure cipher knowledge, are in the lexicon of ciphermatized words (c_kWords). This means that P_LWords are composed of A_LWords and c_kWords such that

$$P_L\text{Words} = A_L\text{Words} + c_k\text{Words} \qquad (7\text{-}1)$$

For example, if an individual correctly pronounced 50 words on a word identification test (P_LWords = 50), and 40 of these words were known words, i.e., raudamatized words (A_LWords = 40), then 10 must have been ciphermatized words (c_kWords = 10), because 50 = 40 + 10. When c_kWords are scaled into GE units, they are symbolized as c_k.

It seems likely that when all of P_LWords, A_LWords, and c_kWords are scaled into GE units, then P_L would equal the average of A_L and c_k,

$$P_L = (A_L + c_k)/2 \qquad (7\text{-}2)$$

Those unknown real words that can be correctly pronounced are called ciphermatized words. Pseudowords that can be correctly pronounced are called pseudomatized words. They provide a measure of pure decoding knowledge. This lexicon of pseudomatized words representing pure decoding knowledge can be symbolized as d_kWords. When d_kWords are scaled into GE units, they are symbolized as d_k. Individual differences in d_kWords are likely to be almost perfectly correlated with individual differences in c_kWords, because unknown real words are not substantially different from pronounceable nonwords from the standpoint of the individual. Therefore, when c_kWords and d_kWords are scaled into GE units, they would be equal, that is,

$$c_k = d_k \qquad (7\text{-}3)$$

This also means that if d_k is substituted into equation 7-2 for c_k, then

$$P_L = (A_L + d_k)/2 \qquad (7\text{-}4)$$

That is, the GE score on a word identification test should equal the average of the GE scores from a measure of reading level (or reading vocabulary) and a measure of word attack (or pure decoding knowledge).

Equations 7-2, 7-3, and 7-4 are likely to be valid for beginning and intermediate readers, but may not be valid for advanced readers who have P_L scores greater than 7.9 and who may also have d_k scores greater than 7.9. The measurement of P_L and d_k at 8 and higher becomes questionable, and it has been theorized that P_L is no longer a causal factor for A_L or R_L when P_L is 8 or higher (see Chapter 17).

Given the proliferation of new constructs and symbols, Table 7-1 contains a summary of the new ones introduced in this chapter, plus similar ones introduced in earlier chapters. For example, the V_L construct was introduced in the preceding chapter as being similar to the concept of listening vocabulary, and its corresponding lexicon is audamatized words—-symbolized as V_LWords.

Related Concepts

Introduction. The P_L construct has much in common with word identification, cipher knowledge, spelling knowledge, lexical knowledge, decoding, and orthographic knowledge; these conceptual connections will be explained in this section. The P_L construct is not the same as the autonomous or functional lexicons introduced by Perfetti (1991a), but there are some important connections which also will be explained at the end of this section.

Word Identification. The theoretical construct of P_L has been studied by many researchers under the rubric of word identification. For example, word identification tests usually contain many words that vary in difficulty, or frequency of usage, and the individual is asked to pronounce each word on this difficulty-ordered list. Referring to such measures as "word identification tests" may suggest to some that if the individual pronounces the word correctly, then it is a known word that has been identified. Yet, many of the words pronounced correctly on a test designed to measure pronunciation level, P_L, will be words that are not known when reading (not raudamatized) because they are also not known when listening (see Carver, 1993a). For example, few children in the middle grades will know the meaning of the word "rebut" when it is presented in a list of words (out of context), yet most can pronounce it accurately. So, the term "pronunciation level" is much more neutral than "word identification" because it does not suggest that the individual knows the meaning of the words that are accurately pronounced.

The term "word recognition" is another term that is very similar to "word identification"; both suggest that a word known when listening can be correctly pronounced. However, P_L refers to the correct pronunciation of words whether or not their meaning is known when perceived auditorily or visually, that is, P_L refers to the number of words that can be correctly pronounced, whether or not the words are audamatized or raudamatized. The P_L construct refers to a knowledge of word pronunciation that includes both raudamatized words, A_L-Words, and ciphermatized words, c_kWords.

Table 7-1
Rauding Constructs, Their Corresponding Lexicons, and Their Corresponding Traditional Concepts

Constructs	*Corresponding Lexicons*	*Traditional Concepts*
V_L	V_LWords, audamatized words	listening vocabulary
A_L	A_LWords, raudamatized words	pure lexical knowledge, reading vocabulary, automatized lexicon
P_L	P_LWords, pronounceamatized words	word identification knowledge
c_k	c_kWords, ciphermatized words	cipher knowledge
d_k	d_kWords, pseudomatized words	decoding knowledge, pseudoword knowledge

The concept of word identification knowledge is conceptually almost the same as the P_L construct. Word identification knowledge is (a) ordinarily defined empirically as a GE score on a standardized word identification test, and (b) not defined as a theoretical construct. Notice that a fundamental difference between word identification knowledge and pronunciation knowledge is that P_L is defined more precisely as a theoretical construct, that is, the number of real words that an individual can correctly pronounce when scaled into GE units.

Cipher Knowledge. Reading and spelling are both based upon what Gough, Juel, and Griffith (1992) call the "cipher," that is, the somewhat systematic connections between letters and sounds in words. They make a distinction between code learning and cipher learning. For example, learning to associate 007 with James Bond is what they call learning a code whereas learning to associate Kbnft Cpoe with James Bond is what they call learning a cipher because there is a systematic relationship between each letter in Kbnft and each letter in James. Although the connections between letters in words and their sounds are not perfectly systematic, these connections are close enough so that learning them (learning the cipher) is what Gough, Juel, and Griffith call the foundation of reading and spelling. They presented evidence that "beginning readers read and spell in the same way on different occasions; they simply do so inconsistently" (p. 46).

Cipher knowledge is a concept that refers to the somewhat systematic spelling-sound correspondences which helps individuals correctly pronounce difficulty-ordered lists of printed real words, whether the words are known auditorily (audamatized) or unknown (ciphermatized). Cipher knowledge is also helpful for pronouncing pseudowords accurately and for spelling words accurately.

In summary, cipher knowledge is conceptually related to the knowledge represented by P_L, A_L, and d_k. However, pure cipher knowledge, c_k, was defined earlier as the number of ciphermatized words, c_kWords, scaled into GE units.

Spelling Knowledge. The ability to pronounce increasingly difficult words correctly is dependent upon the ability to learn and remember sounds that are associated with letters, whereas the ability to spell increasingly difficult words correctly is dependent upon the ability to learn and remember letters that are associated with sounds. Stated differently, P_L represents the number of words which can be pronounced accurately, and spelling knowledge can be defined as the number of words which can be spelled accurately. The level of spelling knowledge in GE units will be referred to as spelling level, and symbolized as S_L.

As noted earlier, cipher knowledge underlies both S_L and P_L. Vellutino, Scanlon, and Tanzman (1994) have stated that "... word identification, alphabetic mapping, and spelling are closely related skills" (p. 323). Ehri (1997) has recently built a strong case, both theoretically and empirically, that the learning involved in decoding and spelling are almost exactly the same. As noted earlier, Gough, Juel, and Griffith (1992) have presented evidence that words which can be spelled correctly are likely to be pronounced correctly. According to Juel, Griffith, and Gough (1986), "the relationship between word recognition and spelling was shown to be especially strong, because the development of both skills seem to rely on the same knowledge" (p. 243).

P_L not only can be considered as representing a level of pronunciation knowledge, but it may also be considered as representing a level of spelling knowledge, S_L. Given the above definitions of P_L and S_L, the precise relationship can be represented mathematically as follows:

$$S_L = P_L \quad (7\text{-}5)$$

In summary, spelling knowledge and pronunciation knowledge have a great deal in common because both depend upon a common knowledge of the cipher. The connection between S_L and P_L is so close that S_L should equal P_L, that is, when spelling knowledge and pronunciation knowledge are both measured in GE units, then S_L equals P_L.

Lexical Knowledge. A knowledge of the meaning of printed words can be defined as lexical knowledge. The connection between lexical knowledge and pronunciation knowledge is that pronunciation knowledge includes lexical knowledge. This means that P_LWords includes words that can be recognized in print because their meaning is known.

Earlier in this chapter, the number of printed words that are raudamatized was symbolized as A_LWords. Therefore, the amount of lexical knowledge an individual has can be measured by A_LWords. This means that pronunciation knowledge includes lexical knowledge, and the lexicon of P_LWords includes the lexicon of A_LWords, as expressed mathematically by Equation 7-1.

Support for Equation 7-1, which holds that P_LWords can be divided into A_LWords and c_kWords, comes from Ehri and Wilce (1987a). They contended that spelling and word recognition are caused by lexical knowledge and cipher knowledge, which is about the same as saying that P_L (word recognition or spelling knowledge) is composed of two parts, A_L (lexical knowledge) and c_k (pure cipher knowledge).

Juel, Griffith, and Gough (1986) also provide support for these connections among lexical, cipher, and pronunciation knowledge. They use the word "decoding" to mean word recognition, and they contend that decoding requires cipher knowledge and specific lexical knowledge. Notice that if decoding knowledge is measured by P_LWords, if specific lexical knowledge is measured by A_LWords, and if cipher knowledge is measured by c_kWords, then these contentions of Juel, Griffith, and Gough are consistent with Equation 7-1. Furthermore, this equation is a quantified translation of their statement that "we posit that both decoding and spelling are composed of (a) the cipher, and (b) knowledge of specific lexical items, or what we call lexical knowledge" (p. 245).

In summary, the connections among pronunciation knowledge, pure lexical knowledge, and pure cipher knowledge are such that the P_LWords equals the A_LWords plus the c_kWords (Equation 7-1), and P_L equals the average of A_L and c_k (Equation 7-2).

Decoding. Decoding is a conventional concept which sometimes refers to the pronunciation of real words, and sometimes refers to the pronunciation of pseudowords. When decoding refers to the ability to pronounce varying numbers of real words, measured in GE units, then that concept is little different from P_LWords, or the P_L construct. When decoding refers to the ability to pronounce pseudowords, then it is little different from d_kWords, or the d_k construct.

The ability to learn and remember how strings of letters are pronounced in real words will help with the ability to pronounce unknown words and pseudowords. This connection between the pronunciation of known words, P_L, and the correct pronunciation of letter strings in unknown words, c_k, and pseudowords, d_k, has been explained by Reitsma (1983) as follows:

> If word recognition memory entails recognition of patterns of letters co-occurring within words, this might also be used for pronouncing a new string of letters by analogy to similarly spelled words; spelling patterns may be generalized to novel examples. (p. 337)

The ability to correctly pronounce increasingly difficult pseudowords accurately has been called "pure decoding ability" by Roth & Beck (1987), and their wording stimulated the naming of the d_k construct as "pure decoding knowledge." The connection between d_k and pronunciation knowledge comes from the close connection between pure cipher knowledge and pure decoding knowledge. As noted earlier, pure cipher knowledge, c_k, should equal pure decoding knowledge, d_k, because unknown real words are likely to be mostly indistinguishable from pseudowords. In this regard, Gough and Juel (1991) have stated that "the child's mastery of the cipher is directly reflected in his ability to pronounce pseudowords" (p. 51). However, pseudowords are usually constructed by researchers and test makers so that there is only one correct pronunciation based upon highly probable sound-symbol correspondences, even though the pseudowords have never been seen before. On the other hand, cipher knowledge is likely to include more knowledge of the spellings of real words which are likely to be pronounced in more than one way when they have never been seen before. Stated differently, a student who has spent more time learning phonics rules may have slightly higher d_k than a person who has spend more time learning to pronounce audamatized words, and a student who has spent more time learning to pronounce audamatized words may have slightly higher c_k than a person who has spent more time learning phonic rules.

In summary, when decoding knowledge is interpreted as meaning the ability to pronounce real words, then it is conceptually similar to pronunciation knowledge, or P_L. However, when decoding knowledge is interpreted as meaning the ability to pronounce pseudowords, then it is called pure decoding knowledge, d_k, and it is conceptually more similar to pure cipher knowledge, c_k, such that d_k equals c_k (in GE units). Finally, the connection between pure decoding knowledge and the P_L construct has been precisely represented by Equation 7-4.

Orthographic Knowledge. The spelling of words in accordance with conventional practices is called orthography, and knowledge of these conventional practices is called orthographic knowledge, or orthographic skill. This knowledge is relevant to pronunciation level, because P_L is so highly related to spelling knowledge (Equation 7-5). In research related to reading, if the researcher pronounces the word and then asks the individual to produce the correct order of letters in the word, then this is usually called "spelling." However, if the researcher provides two or more printed spellings of a word, and then asks the individual to choose the correct spelling (e.g., bote vs. boat), this is more likely to be referred to as research on orthographic knowledge or skill (see Barker, Torgesen, & Wagner, 1992).

Orthographic knowledge or skill can be contrasted with phonological knowledge or skill. Knowing that "bote" and "boat" are both pronounced the same, is phonological knowledge; knowing that "boat" is a meaningful word but "bote" is not, is orthographic knowledge. However, knowing that "boat" is a meaningful word is more likely to come from knowing the word, called lexical knowledge, rather than being an inference made from knowledge about spelling rules. Orthographic knowledge would also refer to (a) knowing that spelling /boat/ with the letter string "bote" would involve putting letters together in a way that does not represent a conventional word, and (b) knowing that the letter string "bote" would not be a correct spelling of a word but it would still follow conventional spelling practices because it is readily pronounceable (see Assink & Kattenberg, 1993).

Orthographic knowledge includes knowing about orthographic redundancies. These are the statistical probabilities associated with the order of letters within words. For example, the letter "u" always follows the letter "q" in a word. Orthographic knowledge is usually associated with what is known about permissible letter patterns in words that is not necessarily taught in school whereas spelling is usually associated with the correct letter patterns for words that is often taught in school. Spelling usually involves explicit learning whereas orthographic knowledge usually involves implicit learning.

There is a major problem with recent research involving orthographic knowledge. Many of the measures used in this research have combined accuracy with rate, so as to measure orthographic skill or orthographic ability. The *accuracy* associated with orthographic skill would likely correlate highly with P_L, or A_L, whereas the *rate* associated with orthographic skill would likely correlate highly with R_L. A combination measure of accuracy and rate for orthographic skill is likely to create an *efficiency* type variable that would correlate highly with E_L. An example of the problem of combining accuracy and rate into one variable comes from the research of Barker, Torgesen, and Wagner (1992) who studied "the role of orthographic processing skills on five different reading tasks." Two of their five tasks were orthographic. For one of these, called orthographic choice, a student was asked to choose the correct spelling from two choices that sounded alike, such as the "bote" vs. "boat" example given earlier. In the other task, called homophone choice, the student read a sentence such as "What can you do with a needle and thread?" Then, "so" and "sew" immediately came up on the computer screen. In each task, latency and the accuracy were both measured. In their results section, it was not made perfectly clear how the variable representing each task was measured, but it is a reasonable assumption that it was an average of accuracy and rate, and was therefore a measure of efficiency. Therefore, it is not helpful to try to relate the results of this research to the P_L construct in the causal model.

Much of the research that has been conducted on orthographic processing has been summarized by Vellutino, Scanlon, and Tanzman (1994) as follows:

> ... we remain skeptical that the measures purported to assess orthographic coding ability and most often used to evaluate this ability, actually are measuring anything more than word identification and spelling ability, along with the assortment of visual and linguistic abilities that underlie word identification and spelling ability. (p. 324)

Translated into the constructs of the causal model, Vellutino, Scanlon, and Tanzman seem to be saying that orthographic coding ability is trivially different from P_L because orthographic coding ability involves word identification knowledge and spelling knowledge.

In conclusion, orthographic knowledge, orthographic coding ability, and orthographic processing skills that can be measured by accuracy of performance seem to be so closely related to spelling knowledge level, S_L, and pronunciation knowledge level, P_L that there is no need to include a separate construct in the causal model devoted to these orthographic skills, knowledges, or abilities.

Autonomous and Functional Lexicons. Perfetti (1991a) has theorized about the acquisition of the word representations that are used during the reading of text, using the concepts of autonomous and functional lexicons. Those concepts will be explained in this subsection after his ideas about word recognition have been presented.

Perfetti contends that it is the quality and quantity of graphemically accessible words that primarily differentiates between skilled and unskilled readers. He states that "learning to read does not involve learning rules but is rather a matter of incrementing a store of graphemically accessible words" (p. 33). By the quality of the representation of words, he means how well the word can be spelled. For example, a student might spell the word "iron" poorly as "irn," so this would not represent high quality representation of the word even though the word may be correctly recognized in the context of a sentence. Thus, a student who can spell "iron" correctly is more likely to be able to recognize the word out of context, and for Perfetti "skilled word recognition is context-free" (p. 34).

Perfetti goes on to distinguish between the autonomous lexicon of individuals and their functional lexicon. The autonomous lexicon was discussed earlier in Chapter 4; it is all the printed words that the individual can rapidly identify out of context, or in a list. The autonomous lexicon is therefore conceptually similar to the lexicon of raudamatized words, A_LWords, as defined earlier in Chapter 4. Notice that for Perfetti, it is the individual words that become "autonomous," whereas it was the children who became "automatic" under automaticity theory (LaBerge & Samuels, 1974). So, this concept of the autonomous lexicon seems to be almost exactly the same as the raudamatized lexicon, which is the number of words that can be processed at the rauding rate during the execution of the rauding process, A_LWords.

Whereas the autonomous lexicon described by Perfetti contains the population of words that can be rapidly recognized, his "functional lexicon" contains all the words that can be recognized in context but are *not* in the autonomous lexicon. The functional lexicon consists of the words that an individual can eventually recognize with difficulty in the context of sentences, but are not raudamatized. In the causal model, P_L is an indicant of the population of words that can be accurately pronounced out of context, P_LWords, and therefore does not directly represent either the autonomous or the functional lexicons as defined by Perfetti.

In summary, the lexicon of words represented by P_LWords (a) would include Perfetti's autonomous lexicon, or A_LWords, and (b) would not include words in Perfetti's functional lexicon.

Relevant Tests

Introduction. In this section, four tests that could be used as measures of P_L will be described—Pronunciation Level Test, Wide Range Achievement Test-Reading, Wide Range Achievement Test-Spelling, and the Woodcock-Johnson Tests of Achievement—Letter-Word Identification Test. A few other tests will be mentioned as additional examples.

Pronunciation Level Test (PLT). The PLT was developed using a strategy that is slightly different from the dictionary approach outlined at the outset of this chapter (see Carver & Clark, 1998). Instead, each word was sampled from every 500 words on the Carroll et al. (1971) list of words ranked according to frequency of usage in printed school materials. The number correct on this measure is an indicant of P_LWords. The PLT also provides a direct measure of P_L in that it attempts to estimate the total number of words an individual can correctly pronounce, in GE units.

Wide Range Achievement Test—Reading (WRAT-R). This standardized measure requires individuals to correctly pronounce increasingly difficult words, and it provides a score in GE units. Therefore, this measure qualifies as an indirect measure of P_L. This measure does not claim to have sampled the words on the test in a manner that would allow an estimate of the number of real words that could be correctly pronounced, so it has been categorized as an indirect measure rather than a direct measure.

Wide Range Achievement Test—Spelling (WRAT-S). This standardized measure requires individuals to spell words that increase in difficulty and it provides a GE score, so it qualifies as an indirect measure of S_L. In the manual for the WRAT, correlations are reported between WRAT-S and WRAT-R (described above) for students at each of ages 9 to 14. These correlations are extremely high, ranging from .88 to .92. When these correlations were corrected for unreliability of the two measures involved, the resulting correlations ranged from a low of .97 at age 13 (AgeGE = 8) to a high of 1.16 at age 14 (AgeGE = 9). The mean of the six correlations was 1.03, which suggests that the correlation between a perfectly reliable measure of pronunciation knowledge and a perfectly reliable measure of spelling knowledge would be perfect, or 1.00. These data also empirically validate spelling knowledge level, S_L, as an indicant of P_L, and provide strong evidence for $S_L = P_L$ (Equation 7-5).

Because this spelling test is also scaled into GE units, it is appropriate to consider the WRAT-S to be an indirect measure of P_L.

The Woodcock-Johnson Tests of Achievement—Letter-Word Identification Test. The items on this test start out with identifying letters but most of the items require that 47 real words be pronounced correctly. This test will be described by comparing it to the Pronunciation Level Test, PLT, described above.

The PLT was developed by sampling 1 word every 500 words, from word frequency rank 1 to word frequency rank 40,000, and the two tests can be compared using these rankings. For the Woodcock-Johnson, (a) 25 of the 47 words on the test were between the ranks of 1 and 2499, (b) 12 were between the ranks of 2,500 and 40,000, and (c) 10 were lower in frequency of usage, that is, ranked above 40,000. Whereas the Woodcock-Johnson has only 12 words covering ranks 2,500 to 40,000, the PLT has 75 words covering this range.

Given the description of items described above, it seems likely that the Woodcock-Johnson would be more discriminating and therefore more reliable for beginning readers, but the PLT would be more discriminating and therefore more reliable for intermediate readers. This means that it is likely that correlations involving the Woodcock-Johnson as an indicator of P_L would provide much lower correlations with other variables in grades 3 through 7, because such correlations would likely be severely attenuated due to lower reliability and therefore lower validity at these grade levels.

Other Tests. There are many standardized tests of word identification that would either be indicants or indirect measures of P_L. The following two will be named to provide more examples: (a) Woodcock Reading Mastery Tests—Word Identification, and (b) Peabody Individual Achievement Test—Reading Recognition.

Summary of Theory

The P_L construct is the number of words that an individual can correctly pronounce—called pronounceamatized words, or P_LWords—scaled into GE units. This construct is trivially different from whatever it is that has traditionally been measured by word identification tests, because these tests require that increasingly difficult (or less frequent) words be correctly pronounced. However, traditional word identification tests ordinarily have not been designed to sample systematically the population of words that can be accurately pronounced. P_L is also highly related to spelling knowledge level, S_L, which is the number of words an individual can spell correctly in GE units, such that $S_L = P_L$ (Equation 7-5). Because the P_L construct is so closely related to S_L, it follows that the P_L construct is also closely related to orthographic knowledge because this kind of knowledge is little different from spelling knowledge.

The lexicon of pronounceamatized words, P_LWords, includes the lexicon of raudamatized words, or A_LWords, plus those unknown words that can be correctly pronounced using pure cipher knowledge, called ciphermatized words, or c_kWords (Equation 7-1). When expressed in GE units, P_L is the average of A_L and c_k (Equation 7-2). Because the number of c_kWords should be almost perfectly related to the number of pseudowords that can be accurately pronounced, called d_kWords, it follows that when both are measured in GE units then d_k equals c_k (Equation 7-3). Therefore, P_L is also the average of A_L and d_k (Equation 7-4). This means that an indicant of A_L (passage comprehension) and an indicant of d_k (word attack) can be used to predict P_L (word identification), using Equation 7-4.

Summary of Evidence

There is evidence that indicants of A_L (passage comprehension) and d_k (word attack) can account for almost all of the reliable variance in P_L (word identification), that is, the relevant multiple correlations involving measures corrected for attenuation are around .95 (from Torgesen, Wagner, Rashotee, Burgess, & Hecht, 1997; from Woodcock, 1973). These data are highly consistent with the theory underlying Equations 7-1, 7-2, 7-3, and 7-4.

There is also evidence for Equation 7-5 that $S_L = P_L$. Measures of word identification and spelling knowledge are generally correlated around .90 or higher when they are corrected for attenuation (Calfee, Lindamood, & Lindamood, 1973). Furthermore, there is strong evidence from factor analytic research that pronunciation knowledge and spelling knowledge are identical factors (Carroll, 1993).

On the other hand, data exist which have been interpreted by Frith (1980) as suggesting that there are individuals who are high in P_L (good readers) and low in S_L (poor spellers), but a close examination of those results may be interpreted as providing no support for these claims. Frith worked with a group of 120 twelve-year-olds, that is, sixth and seventh graders. She selected 10 who were good readers and good spellers (Group A), 10 who were good readers and poor spellers (Group B), and 10 who were poor readers and poor spellers (Group C). She described the tests used to measure reading and spelling, but she did not report the details of the procedures used to select the individuals in each group. She did report the means and SDs of each group on both reading and spelling, and these data seem to undermine her interpretations. Group A and Group B both purportedly contained good readers except the mean for Group A on the indicant of P_L was .8 of an SD higher than the corresponding mean for Group B; this is a large effect size according to Cohen (1977). Therefore, it is misleading to compare these two groups as if they were equally good readers. Similarly, Group B and Group C were both supposedly composed of poor spellers. However, the spelling mean for Group C was .8 of an SD lower than the corresponding mean for Group B; again a large effect size. Therefore, it would be misleading to compare these two groups as if they were equally poor spellers. For example, Frith (1980) states that "Group C who had more nonphonetic misspellings, and hence must be worse at using letter-sound correspondence rules, managed nevertheless to do as well as Group B on the spelling test" (p. 500). In fact, however, Group C did not spell as well as Group B according to her own data. Notice that when Frith selected her group of poor spellers and good readers (Group B), she could not find a control group that was equally good in pronunciation knowledge (Group A), and she could not find a control group that was equally poor in spelling knowledge (Group C). The results that she reported are exactly the results that would be predicted from the contention in this chapter that level of ability to spell words is the same as level of ability to pronounce words, or that S_L is an indirect measure of P_L such that $S_L = P_L$. Therefore, these data may be alternately interpreted as providing strong evidence that word identification tests and spelling tests are both measures of P_L.

Implications

It is not necessary to administer a word-identification test plus a spelling test because the GE scores on both tests will be approximately the same; both types of tests are measuring the P_L construct. Furthermore, it is probably not necessary to administer a word attack type of test, involving pseudowords (indicant of d_k) along with a word identification test (indicant of P_L) and an unspeeded comprehension test (indicant of A_L), because d_k is not independent of

P_L and A_L. That is, P_L is purported to be equal to the average of A_L and d_k, so only two of these three tests need to be administered; the score on the third test can be determined from the scores on the other two tests.

For most students in the lower and middle grades, pronouncing many isolated words accurately and spelling many words accurately represent a level of knowledge that strongly affects reading achievement, or E_L. This knowledge is represented theoretically by the P_L construct. This P_L construct should be taken into account when trying to understand the causes of high and low reading achievement, and when trying to help many poor readers become better readers. Educators who disregard pronunciation knowledge level, P_L, and spelling knowledge level, S_L, are doing their students a disservice, especially those poor readers who are relatively low in P_L and S_L.

Forget Me Nots

Pronunciation knowledge level, P_L, tries to incorporate all of the good ideas that have traditionally been associated with the following concepts: (a) word-identification knowledge, (b) decoding knowledge, (c) spelling knowledge, and (d) orthographic knowledge. These earlier concepts have been upgraded by the P_L construct, which is more precisely defined both from a theoretical and an operational standpoint. Pronunciation level, P_L, is the number of words an individual can correctly pronounce when the words are presented out of context in a list, and then scaled into grade equivalent units; for example, an individual may have a fourth-grade pronunciation level, $P_L = 4$.

CHAPTER

8

COGNITIVE SPEED LEVEL, C_s

A high cognitive speed level, C_s, is necessary for high reading achievement (high E_L), that is, individuals are not likely to become high achievers in reading (high E_L), with a low cognitive speed level, C_s. However, having a high C_s does not guarantee high reading achievement. Remember that C_s is one of three primary causes of reading achievement at Echelon 3, along with V_L and P_L discussed in the two preceding chapters.

Cognitive speed, as defined more precisely later, is directly involved in the rate of naming things, such as colors, letters, and digits. Research in this general area dates back over 100 years to J. M. Cattell (1886); he published an article in *Mind*, entitled "The time it takes to see and name objects." Cattell found that "it takes about twice as long to read (aloud, as fast as possible) words which have no connection as words which make up sentences ..." (p. 64). Cattell did not study *individual differences* in naming speed, which is a much more recent development in research (see Denckla & Rudel, 1974; Spring & Capps, 1974; Wolf, 1991).

Later in this chapter, the C_s construct will be defined, and then it will be related to several other concepts that are similar. Then, existing tests that can be used to measure C_s will be described. Empirical evidence will also be summarized which supports the existence of the C_s construct.

Theoretical Construct

Cognitive speed is the fastest rate, in items per minute, at which a lengthy series of simple stimuli can be accurately named when there are no meaningful connections between adjacent stimuli and each stimulus is overlearned. Cognitive speed level is cognitive speed measured in GE units, and symbolized as C_s.

College students probably can name a list of randomized digits, or letters, faster than any other series of stimuli; an example of their cognitive speed for these items might be around 150 items per minute. On the other hand, many kindergarten students may be able to name randomized colors or pictures faster than any other stimulus; an example of their cognitive speed might be around 20 items per minute, as measured by their fastest rate of naming an overlearned series of color patches.

It also seems likely that kindergartners might be able to name speech sounds faster than they can say aloud the names of color patches. That is, if a tape recording was made of randomized color names presented at 25 items per minute, these students may be able to repeat aloud the names they heard at this rate. This example would suggest that the cognitive speed of these students was not the 20 items per minute for naming visually presented colors because they were not yet overlearned. Instead, their cognitive speed was actually higher at 25 items per minute because they could name overlearned auditorily presented colors faster.

This fastest naming speed will also likely occur when responding to those overlearned language symbols which are the simplest to say aloud, that is, no two-syllable names or multi-syllable names. In order to be sure that the individual is actually perceiving the stimulus, instead of reading it out of memory, the adjacent stimuli should not have meaningful connections among them. For example, cognitive speed could not be measured by asking individuals to name the letters of the alphabet in order, from A to Z, as fast as possible, but could be measured for most individuals by presenting these same printed letters in random order.

For most students in grade 2 or higher, the rate at which the randomized letters of the alphabet can be named aloud should reflect cognitive speed. This task should reflect cognitive speed because after hundreds of practice trials with recognizing the letter B (or any other letter of the alphabet) an asymptote should be approached on a learning curve such that further practice or experience with the letter will not substantially lower the amount of time required to lexically access it (see Ehri & Wilce, 1983). This asymptote will gradually increase with maturity, that is, students in grades 3 and 4 will have a higher cognitive speed than they did in grade 2 (see Chapter 14).

The C_s construct in the causal model of reading achievement receives support from (a) Biemiller (1977), who was one of the first to suggest that letter-naming speed represents a general ability that affects reading rate, and (b) E. Hunt, Davidson, and Lansman (1981), who were among the first to suggest that "the process of accessing overlearned materials is one of the important individual difference variables that underlies skilled verbal performance" (p. 608).

Related Concepts

Introduction. In this section, the cognitive speed construct will be related to several concepts used in research. The definition of C_s given in the preceding section is similar to, but somewhat different from (a) the older concepts of thinking speed and speed of cognitive performance, and (b) the newer concepts of naming speed, decoding speed, and verbal ability. Each of these five concepts will be discussed in turn. Then, the concepts of automaticity and basic information processing will be related to C_s.

Thinking Speed. The idea of a basic speed factor in mental tests dates back at least as far as the research of DuBois in 1932. He constructed four speed tests, each having two forms, involving arithmetic computation, analogies, directions, and arithmetic problems; each test had low item difficulty so that accuracy was close to perfect, and the reliability estimate was greater than .90 for each test. He concluded from his factor analyses of the data that there was "evidence for the existence of a factor common to the speed tests ..." (p. 36). It seems likely that this common factor he found is a close relative of cognitive speed level, C_s, because these tasks all required naming.

Later, in 1934, Traxler investigated a processing determinant of slow reading which he called "speed of association of ideas." He speculated that this was a causal factor because "slow thinkers tend to be slower readers" (p. 357). His research, and that of Bear and Odbert (1940), Stroud (1945), and Buswell (1951), has been reviewed in some detail by Carver (1990a); it was concluded by Carver that this early research marked "an era where theory and research were generally supportive of the idea that reading rate was limited or influenced by a more basic thinking rate" (p. 254). This early research on thinking speed, or mental speed, in the 1930s and 1940s was not continued into the decades of the 50s, or 60s. However, as late as 1977, Rozin and Gleitman contended that "... the speed of thinking is a major determinant of the speed of reading" (p. 65). Also in 1977, Carver contended that "rauding rate, R_r, is limited by an individual's basic thinking rate" (p. 20).

In summary, thinking speed has long been a vaguely defined concept in mental testing and reading. It has been used to explain why some individuals read faster than others. Cognitive speed level can be used as a replacement for the older concept of thinking speed because C_s is more precisely defined and can be measured more directly.

Cognitive Performance Speed. In 1971, R. B. Cattell advanced a speed of cognitive performance factor; he symbolized this factor as g_s, which is the same symbol as was used in Chapter 1 for cognitive speed aptitude in the causal model—to be discussed in more detail later in Chapter 14. However, Cattell's concept of cognitive performance speed was not restricted to naming. It included speed of performing any mental task such as "crossing out" tasks where a certain letter, such as "t," might be crossed out as it occurs along with other randomized letters of the alphabet. This performance speed factor of Cattell's has also been measured by (a) a visual matching task that involves the ability to rapidly find and circle numbers in a row of numbers, and (b) a cross-out type of task that involves the ability to rapidly scan a row of 20 drawings and mark those that match the target drawing (Woodcock, 1990). Notice that these processing-speed tasks could be conceptualized as perceptual-speed tasks because they involve the speed of perceiving matches between shapes, and they do *not* directly involve the speed of naming. This performance-speed factor of Cattell's is also similar to the speed factor advanced by Carroll (1993), which is one of his eight sub-abilities under general intelligence, *g*.

In summary, this general speed factor in cognitive performance includes broader cognitive abilities than does the C_s construct which is specific to naming speed. Therefore, it is necessary that C_s not be confused with cognitive performance speed, perceptual speed, processing speed, or a general speed factor. In contrast, C_s is restricted to the fastest speed at which a series of overlearned stimuli can be named; it is therefore somewhat different from perceptual speed or cognitive performance speed.

Naming Speed. In 1963 Mackworth laid the theoretical and empirical groundwork for naming speed and the C_s construct by his latency research on the naming of digits. He reasoned that because individuals can count aloud faster than they can read a list of randomized digits aloud, then the rate of reading randomized digits aloud cannot be limited by articulation speed. Instead, reading a list of randomized digits must be limited by how fast the stimuli can be recognized and named.

In 1972, Denckla appears to be the first to study the rapid oral naming of a continuous series of stimuli which probably were overlearned. Denckla's task involved "rapid color-naming of a chart of 50 squares of color, consisting of 10 randomly ordered repetitions of red, green, yellow, blue, and black, timed in seconds, and errors recorded as spoken" (p. 165). Notice, however, that these five responses are not likely to be equal in production time because "yellow" is two syllables in length.

Later in 1974, Spring and Capps reported that dyslexic boys named continuous digits, colors, and pictures slower than normal readers. Also in 1974, Denckla and Rudel, studied the naming speed of 180 normal boys and girls from age 5 to age 11. They used tests similar to the ones described above in the 1972 research of Denckla, that is, time to name 50 items in 10 rows of five each. They called this rapid "automatized" naming (R.A.N.).

During the 1970s and 1980s, there was a great deal of research conducted on naming speed; over 25 research articles were reviewed by Wolf (1991). She used the term "naming speed" to refer to the speed that a verbal label for a visual stimulus can be retrieved. The early research on naming speed, described above, involving lists of overlearned stimuli, may be alternately interpreted as providing support for the existence of the C_s construct.

In summary, naming speed does not have to involve a series of overlearned stimuli (asymptoted learning curve) whereas cognitive speed does. Naming speed may be measured in tasks that involve latencies to discretely presented stimuli, but cognitive speed may not be measured this way. Finally, and most importantly, cognitive speed level is a relatively stable attribute of an individual at a particular point in time whereas the naming speed of an individual may vary considerably from task to task depending upon whether the stimuli are overlearned or not, and depending upon the length of the oral response in syllables or phonemes.

Decoding Speed. Another concept that is related to cognitive speed is *decoding* speed. Stanovich (1981) used this term to refer to naming speed for visual language symbols, such as numbers, letters, and words.

Some of the results involving decoding speed seem to implicate cognitive speed as an explanatory factor. For example, Hogaboam and Perfetti (1978) have suggested that "faster decoding speeds of skilled readers are due to superior word-decoding processes rather than to simple frequency of exposure to particular words" (p. 717). Indeed, superior readers are likely to have higher cognitive speed levels, C_s, and this could explain why they had higher word decoding speeds, R_L, in their research (see Chapter 7).

Because decoding speed has a great deal in common with both cognitive speed level and naming speed, it will be helpful to consider more carefully the similarities and differences involved. Table 8-1 contains a systematic analysis of the relationships among cognitive speed level, decoding speed, and naming speed with respect to their relevance to tasks that have been used in research. In the table, notice first that the speed at which a series of overlearned language symbols are read, such as numbers and letters, can be properly referred to as cognitive speed, naming speed, or decoding speed. Notice second that cognitive speed level is relevant to the speed at which overlearned sound representations of language can be perceived but neither decoding speed nor naming speed is relevant to this type of auding rate. Notice third that cognitive speed level is not directly relevant to tasks that involve measuring the latency of response to visual language stimuli, whereas decoding speed and naming speed are directly relevant to this type of task. Notice fourth that cognitive speed level is not directly relevant to the speed at which newly learned words can be named, but naming speed and decoding speed are directly relevant to this type of research task. Notice fifth that cognitive speed level and naming speed are both relevant to the speed of naming patches of color, but decoding speed is not relevant to this task.

Verbal Ability. The traditional concept of verbal ability has received a great deal of attention by researchers, and one small part of this research is related to cognitive speed. Relevant research has been conducted primarily by E. Hunt and his colleagues. In 1978, E. Hunt reviewed what he called the "mechanics of verbal ability." He claimed that "individual cognitive competence depends on the knowledge an individual possesses and the individual capacity for manipulating information regardless of its meaning" (p. 109), and that "we can think of such capacities as mechanistic processes for thinking" (p. 109). Notice that Hunt has defined verbal ability so that it has two parts, or two components, verbal knowledge and verbal speed. In his own research, he used what has been called the Posner task (Posner & Mitchell, 1967) to measure the verbal speed part, or what he called "mechanistic processes for thinking." The Posner task involves asking individuals to decide as fast as possible whether pairs of letters have the same name or not, for example, "Aa" have the same name whereas "aB" do not. Notice that Hunt is measuring the verbal speed part of verbal ability in a manner that seems to require the rapid naming of letters. Because he considers this to be a measure of the individual's capacity for rapid mechanistic thinking, it appears that Hunt's research on verbal ability, or verbal speed, can be alternately interpreted as research on thinking speed, or research on naming speed for letters which may also be called research on cognitive speed level, C_s.

Table 8-1
Relevance of Cognitive Speed Level, Naming Speed, and Decoding Speed to Five Naming Tasks

Naming Task	*Cognitive Speed Level*	*Naming Speed*	*Decoding Speed*
1. Simple language symbols presented continuously, that are overlearned, such as rate of naming a series of randomized letters or numbers.	Yes	Yes	Yes
2. Nonvisual stimuli, such as sounds (e.g., rate of naming randomized digits presented by a tape recorder).	Yes	No	No
3. Discrete visual language stimuli, such as time taken (latency) to start to pronounce the names of letters or symbols.	No	Yes	Yes
4. Visual language symbols that are not necessarily overlearned, such as the rate of naming newly learned words.	No	Yes	Yes
5. Known stimuli, such as rate of naming patches of colors.	Yes	Yes	No

In summary, verbal ability includes two components as defined by Hunt (1978), verbal knowledge and verbal speed. The C_s construct seems to be very similar to the concept of verbal speed.

Automaticity. The concept of automaticity was described in Chapter 4 and discussed again in Chapter 5; its relationship to cognitive speed level is problematic, as will be explained in some detail in this subsection.

The connection between automaticity and naming speed was discussed by Wolf (1991), in her review of naming speed research. She said that "naming speed can be considered one index of what is commonly referred to as *auto-*

maticity in lower level processes" (p. 126). She said that "the term automaticity could be reserved only for those categories whose stimuli can, in fact, be named at uniquely rapid levels of speed" (p. 129), and that "such stimuli are commonly referred to as *automatized*" (p. 129). For Wolf, symbols that can be named so rapidly that the naming can be accomplished with limited attention resources, are referred to as *automatized.* Notice that when Wolf associates automaticity more with a particular stimulus and with particular words, then automaticity becomes more related to raudamatized words and less related to cognitive speed level, because C_s is a relatively stable attribute of the individual.

The connection between automaticity and naming speed has also been addressed by Bowers, Steffy, and Tate (1988). They used the term *naming automaticity*, and they operationally defined it by using "... Digit Naming Speed as an index of the ease of automatizing the retrieval of name codes from any visual symbol" (p. 317). Thus, these researchers seem to have defined naming automaticity in a manner that is almost the same as cognitive speed. For those researchers who define automaticity as an attribute of the individual, C_s might be considered as a measure of automaticity.

The term *automaticity* was defined more recently by J. M. Davis and Spring (1990) as "... the ability of individuals, after sufficient practice, to perform tasks rapidly and without the need for conscious attention" (p. 16). However, the measure of digit naming speed that they administered included no measure of attention, only speed or rapidity.

A major problem with the term *automaticity* is that it has varying connections with naming speed, attention, memory capacity, individual differences, and stimulus differences, depending upon who is using the term. It suffers tremendously from the lack of a commonly accepted operational definition. Yet, it enjoys wide usage. It can be bent or molded to fit several of the ideas underlying various constructs and concepts in rauding theory and the causal model. That is, automaticity has connections with (a) cognitive speed level, which is a relatively constant attribute of an individual that is not amenable to improvement due to education or experience but does gradually increase with maturity, (b) rate level, or rauding rate, which is a relative stable characteristic of the individual but can be improved by education and experience, and (c) raudamatized words, which is a characteristic of particular words for a particular individual.

The advantage of replacing the older concept of automaticity with the newer constructs involved in the causal model—C_s, R_L, and raudamatized words—is that these newer constructs reduce ambiguity and eliminate confusions because they involve more precise definitions and the relationships among constructs are more precisely defined.

Basic Information Processing. Another construct that is importantly related to cognitive speed is the BIP (Basic Information Processing), as advanced by Lehrl and Fischer (1990). The BIP is the shortest possible time during which a subject can process one bit of information, and it is measured by the speed at which a continuous list of 20 randomized letters can be named. Thus, BIP appears to be naming speed for overlearned letters, and therefore could also be used to measure cognitive speed level. However, there are two points that must be made about BIP. First, Lehrl and Fischer consider it to be the "basic determinant of intelligence" (p. 265). Second, by measuring BIP using short lists of only 20 letters, they are measuring their intelligence factor in a manner that might not give the same results as for longer periods. That is, they state the following:

> BIP, which is a capacity, can be measured during the time of about 10s of maximum effort. Then, the capacity drops. (p. 265)

This means that this empirical restriction on measurement may make the BIP somewhat different from cognitive speed, which does not depend upon short bursts of capacity effort involving less that 10 seconds.

Relevant Tests

Introduction. Previous research on rauding theory and the causal model has used two tests to measure cognitive speed level, C_s, namely, the Alphabet Rate Test (ART) and the Speed of Thinking Test (STT). After these two tests have been described, relevant test theory will be presented.

Alphabet Rate Test (ART). The ART has been designed to provide a direct measure of C_s (Carver, 1991). This test requires individuals to read aloud the letters of the alphabet, in random order, as fast as possible. The letter "W" has been omitted from the test because it is the only letter in the English alphabet which requires more than one syllable to pronounce. The ART has been administered by presenting the 25 letters of the alphabet (not W) in random order on the computer screen and then the same 25 letters have been randomized again and presented on the screen immediately following the first set with no obvious distinction between the two sets. The examinee must read each of the 50 letters aloud as fast as possible. The time taken is converted into a rate, and then this rate has been rescaled into GE units.

The ART is a measure that is similar to many such measures that have been used in research involving naming speed for letters (e.g., see Denckla & Rudel, 1976).

Speed of Thinking Test (STT). The STT is purported to provide an indirect measure of C_s. It is based upon the Posner task (Posner & Mitchell, 1967) that was described earlier, and it has been involved in many research studies involving rauding theory (e.g., Carver, 1991). It contains pairs of upper- and lower-case letters for which the individual must decide as fast as possible whether they have the same name or different names. For example, Aa and bB have the same name but bA and Ba have different names. For the printed version of this test (Carver, 1992d), the individual puts an X mark on the left side of the pair of letters if they are the same, and puts an X mark on the right side of the pair of letters if they are different. The raw score is how many items can be completed in 2 minutes.

The raw score on the STT has been rescaled into GE units using linear equating, that is, an equation for a straight line is used to convert the raw scores into GE units that are comparable to the GE units of other constructs presented earlier. The STT can also be administered by a computer (Carver, 1991), which requires the individual to press one key if the two letters have the same name, and another key is pressed if the two letters have a different name. Most of the earlier research employing the Posner task has involved the measurement of latencies to stimuli presented discretely, instead of continuously. The STT appears to be the only group test involving the Posner task that is currently being used in research.

Test Theory. A direct measure of cognitive speed level requires a task which involves a lengthy series of overlearned simple stimuli, such as randomized digits or letters. If the individuals being measured are typical students in grade 2 or higher, then it is often reasonable to assume that almost all of them have overlearned the names of digits (1 to 9) and the names of the letters of the alphabet (A to Z). That is, if those individuals are given additional practice trials on naming randomized digits or letters (randomized again on each new trial), they should not improve their scores substantially. So, naming a lengthy series of randomized numbers or digits (such as 50 in a row) as fast as possible provides a direct measure of cognitive speed level, when expressed in GE units, as least as long as it can reasonably be assumed that these stimuli are overlearned for the individuals involved.

For other tasks, and for many lower-grade students, a direct measure of C_s is more problematic. Many students in kindergarten, and some students in grade 1, probably have not overlearned their numbers or their letters, so this task cannot be used as a direct measure of C_s. Also, naming colors could present a problem because some colors are not simple in terms of a speech response (e.g., yellow has two syllables). It is also questionable whether a color-naming task involves overlearned names on the first trial, especially in kindergarten and grade 1; most of these students have learned their colors but it needs to be determined whether these names have been overlearned for all the particular color patches involved in the testing. Ideally, the color-naming task would be administered repeatedly to every individual until there was no further gain in speed due to practice—an asymptote was reached. That is, it seems likely that some students would gain speed much more than others on a second, third, or fourth trial. Color naming probably represents the best measure of C_s possible for students in kindergarten, as long as they have been given several trials to allow them to exhibit their fastest possible naming speed. Furthermore, the color-naming task that would likely produce the fastest rate would be one where only single syllable names were used, e.g., red, blue, green, white, etc.

Object naming from line drawings for example, could also present problems similar to those described above for letters and colors. Ideally, measures involving object naming would be repeated until there was no further gain due to practice. When the naming of colors, objects, letters and numbers has been practiced until there is no further gain due to practice on a R.A.N. task (described earlier), then the one that was the fastest in items per minute would be a direct measure of cognitive speed level, when converted into GE units. One advantage of the R.A.N. task for younger children is that only five different stimuli are used (randomized on each of 10 lines), so that five letters can be selected that are most likely to have been learned (e.g., not Q or X, but A, B, C, D, or E).

Measuring the latencies involved in naming discrete (not continuous) letters or digits would likely correlate substantially with C_s. and would provide imperfect indicants of C_s. There is no short-term memory involved in a latency measure, and that is probably why it is not a highly valid measure of C_s. Although latencies of naming overlearned discrete stimuli would likely be somewhat poor indicants of C_s, from an individual difference standpoint, when the means of groups are compared this measure should show differences similar to direct measures of C_s.

Summary of Theory

The theory is that individuals differ with respect to how fast they can name serially presented simple stimuli that have been overlearned, whether the stimuli are presented visually or auditorily. When the fastest speed of naming a series of overlearned stimuli is rescaled into GE units, it is called cognitive speed level. The C_s construct can be directly measured for almost everyone in the middle grades, as well as adults, by the naming speed for lists of randomized letters, or digits. Direct measures of C_s for many lower graders need to involve other overlearned stimuli, such as colors or objects, because many of those students have not learned to accurately and rapidly name letters and digits. Latency measures represent the least desirable measure of C_s because no short-term memory is involved as it is involved in reading. The Alphabet Rate Test, ART, purports to provide a direct measure of C_s by requiring that individuals read aloud randomized letters of the alphabet.

Several traditional concepts are related to cognitive speed. Thinking speed is a concept used by early researchers in reading that was not precisely defined but it is similar to cognitive speed in that both are used to explain how the reading rate of an individual is limited by a more basic ability or aptitude factor. Naming speed is a more recently researched concept that is part of the cognitive speed; that is, cognitive speed is the fastest rate at which a series of overlearned stimuli can be named. Naming speed also refers to the speed (latency) of naming discrete stimuli, which is not part of the C_s construct. Naming speed has not been used to refer to the speed of naming auditorily presented stimuli, which is part of the C_s construct. Decoding speed usually refers to the speed of naming printed language stimuli, such as letters and words, so the fastest rate that randomized letters could be named when they were overlearned could be said to involve both decoding speed and cognitive speed. However, decoding speed would not be relevant to the naming of color patches or the naming of auditory stimuli, whereas C_s would be relevant to this type of naming when it was overlearned. Decoding speed would also be relevant to the speed of naming newly learned words and the latencies to visually presented words, whereas C_s could not be measured by these tasks even though C_s would likely be a major influence upon how fast individuals could complete these tasks.

Cognitive speed seems to be similar to the part of verbal ability which has been called mechanistic, that is, the verbal speed part of verbal ability. Cognitive speed is different from cognitive performance speed which includes perceptual speed, or speed of processing stimuli that does not involve rapid naming.

Cognitive speed does have indirect connections to the concept of automaticity as it has been operationally defined and researched. For those researchers who consider automaticity to be an attribute of an individual, then C_s could be a measure of automaticity. However, the concept of automaticity has been used in many different ways, and it often has closer connections to raudamatized words than it does to C_s.

Finally, cognitive speed has a close theoretical connection to BIP, or Basic Information Processing, because BIP and C_s both refer to the fastest speed at which overlearned letters can be named. However, BIP puts a tight restriction on maximum measurement time, 10 seconds, so as to focus on bursts of capacity and intelligence. Therefore, the empirical connection between BIP and C_s may not be close.

Summary of Evidence

Much of the early research relevant to cognitive speed level has been conducted using other labels, such as naming speed (Spring & Capps, 1974), encoding speed (Spring & Capps, 1974), phonological coding speed (Spring & Farmer, 1975), naming rate (Torgesen, 1985), and rapid automatized naming, R.A.N. (Denckla & Rudel, 1976). However, most of the more recent research has been conducted under the rubric of naming speed, that is, letter, digit, color, and object naming.

Naming speed for letters and digits are highly related for second graders (Bowers & Swanson, 1991; Wagner, Torgesen & Rashotte, 1994). Letters and digits seem to provide equally good indicants of cognitive speed level, C_s, at least for most students in grade 2 and above. This means, for example, that the digit-naming tasks used by Spring and associates (J. M. Davis & Spring, 1990; Spring & Capps, 1974; Spring & Farmer, 1975; Spring & Perry, 1983; Spring & Davis, 1988) should provide results interchangeable with the letter-naming task involved on the Alphabet Rate Test, or R.A.N. letters, described earlier. It is possible that rapid digit naming may have a small advantage over rapid letter naming in that numerals seemed to be named more accurately than letters in the early grades (see Denckla & Rudel, 1974). Also in grade 2, letters, numbers, colors, and objects have all been found to correlate about equally with a standardized test of reading ability (Wolf, Bally & Morris, 1986), thereby indicating that the potency of rapid naming is not limited to the naming of language stimuli such as letters, numbers, and words (see also, Bowers, Steffy & Tate, 1988).

Naming speed research involving latencies to discretely presented stimuli, instead of the continuous lists of stimuli, has sometimes found distinctly positive relationships with reading ability (e.g., Bowers & Swanson, 1991; Bowers, 1995; Ellis & Miles, 1978; M. D. Jackson & McClelland, 1979), and other times has found very low relationships (e.g., Curtis, 1980; Perfetti, Finger, & Hogaboam, 1978; Stanovich, Nathan, & Vala-Rossi, 1986; Stanovich, 1981; Stanovich, Feeman, & Cunningham, 1983; Walsh, Price, & Gillingham, 1988). Because latency measures do not involve memory capacity whereas more direct measures of C_s do involve moderate amounts of memory capacity (e.g., Carver, 1998b), it seems likely that latency measures show lower relationships with reading because they do not involve memory capacity as does reading. In this regard, Bowers, Steffy, and Tate (1988) state that "several studies have shown that naming speed and verbal short-term memory are correlated (Lorsbach & Gray, 1986; Spring & Capps, 1974; Spring & Perry, 1983; Torgesen & Houck, 1980)" (p. 308); these researchers themselves reported a correlation of .30 between short term memory for digits and R.A.N. letters. Also, in another study, Bowers, Steffy, and Swanson (1986) found that digit span correlated .51 with letter naming.

Letter and digit naming speed is generally lower for disabled and dyslexic readers (e.g., Spring & Capps, 1974), and this may be interpreted as support for the C_s construct as it is positioned in the causal model as a distal cause of reading achievement, or E_L.

It has been found that the rate at which the efficiency of comprehending text is the highest during reading, is the same as the rate at which the efficiency of comprehending text is the highest during listening (Carver, 1982). These data may be interpreted as supporting the existence of cognitive speed level because C_s seems to be the factor which limits rauding rate during both reading and auding. Other supporting data for the auditory aspect of the C_s construct comes from Cermak (1983) who used auditory and visual tasks including the Posner task with learning-disabled (LD) children, and found that "these young LD children process information more slowly than normal readers (even when the material is presented aurally)" (p. 605). Other auding research supporting the existence of the C_s construct comes from Kagan (1982); their reading-disabled group was much slower than the controls in responding to auditory verbal tasks, and this suggests that poor reading is at least partially due to a lower cognitive speed level that affects both auding and reading.

Evidence relevant to the STT and the ART being measures of C_s comes from Carver (1991). The STT (as an indirect measure of C_s) correlated .60 with the ART (a direct measure of C_s); this correlation was almost as high as the estimated reliability of the STT at .63. In this research reported by Carver (1991), a factor analysis of the rate-related data was also conducted. The results of this analysis were as follows: (a) an R_L factor and a C_s factor resulted, and (b) the STT and the ART both loaded high and equally on the C_s factor, .88 and .88.

Implications

Earlier research on naming speed with lower graders has involved naming tasks in which all the stimuli probably were not overlearned (such as letters), and some tasks in which the stimuli may not be overlearned on the first few trials (such as colors). For these lower graders, research is needed which determines whether or not overlearned colors, objects, letters, and numbers all provide equally valid indicants of C_s. For example, it needs to be determined whether practice on naming colors until an overlearning criterion has been reached would provide a highly valid measure of C_s for lower graders.

Research is also needed to determine how much variance specific to the task used to measure C_s influences the validity of the measure. For example, younger children may have large individual differences in psychomotor skill so that any speeded task involving the movement of a pencil or the pressing of different keys on a computer keyboard may substantially lower the validity of the measure. More specifically, it has been theorized that the Posner naming task (e.g., Aa = same name; aB = different name) can provide an indicant of C_s but the validity of this indicant for lower graders needs to be determined because it depends heavily on psychomotor skill. Also, it is possible that on tasks requiring rapid oral responses, there is considerable variance specific to speech articulation speed for some readers, so that naming tasks that involve an articulation response may not correlate highly with naming tasks that require a psychomotor response, even though both involve C_s.

In the future, measures of cognitive speed level need to involve tasks where 99 - to 100% accuracy of naming is involved and the stimuli have been overlearned so that new learning is not a factor on the task itself. Also, because cognitive speed level seems to involve moderate amounts of short-term memory, it is important that latency measures not be used. Also, it is important that simple stimuli be used, such as one-syllable spoken words and one-character visual stimuli, and it is important that relatively long tasks be used, such as 50 randomized letters, so that short bursts of motivation or articulation do not contaminate the scores. Furthermore, rate should be used as the measure, not time, because the distribution of time scores are more likely to be highly skewed and less reliable (see Carver, 1990a). Finally, the importance of C_s should not be investigated using untimed or unspeeded measures of reading ability because these kinds of measures provide an indicant of A_L; C_s and A_L are neither proximally nor distally related in the causal model so a low relationship between measures of C_s and A_L would be expected.

Forget Me Nots

Cognitive speed level, C_s, is a theoretical construct that tries to incorporate all of the good ideas that have traditionally been associated with the following concepts: (a) naming speed, (b) thinking speed, (c) decoding speed, (d) verbal speed, and (e) automaticity. These earlier concepts have been upgraded by the C_s construct, which is more precisely defined both from a theoretical standpoint and an operational standpoint. Cognitive speed is the fastest rate, in items per minute, that individuals can accurately name a randomized series of overlearned stimuli, such as letters or digits. Cognitive speed level is cognitive speed scaled into GE units; for example, an individual may have a fourth-grade cognitive speed level, $C_s = 4$.

PART III

THE PROXIMAL CAUSES

Earlier in Part II, the six theoretical constructs in Echelons 1, 2, and 3 of the causal model were described in detail, that is, E_L, A_L, R_L, V_L, P_L, and C_s. Each of these six constructs has two proximal causes, according to the causal model given in Chapter 1. In Part III which follows, the two proximal causes of each of the above six constructs will be described in detail, and empirical evidence supporting these causal relationships will be summarized. This means that there will be six chapters in Part III, one chapter devoted to the two purported proximal causes of E_L, A_L, R_L, V_L, P_L, and C_s.

When gathering evidence relevant to causation, researchers often take a two-hurdle approach. The first hurdle is to collect correlational data showing that A correlates with B in a manner consistent with the hypothesis that A causes B. If the data indicate that the first hurdle has been successfully negotiated, then the second hurdle is approached. The second hurdle involves the collection of experimental data indicating that if A is changed, then B is also changed in accordance with the causal hypothesis. If the researcher decides to leap the second hurdle first, and is successful, then the first hurdle is not relevant.

If the second hurdle is most critical, then why do researchers collect so much correlational data relevant to the first hurdle? The answer is that it is much easier to collect correlational data with humans. Describing the way things are, involves procedures that are much more likely to be approved by teachers and parents in schools. Giving one treatment to one group and no treatment to another group (or a different treatment) poses many practical problems, and sometimes ethical problems. So, we set up the first hurdle and if we cannot jump over it successfully then we know that our hypothesis is no good, and we have no need to expend the extra effort on trying to negotiate the second hurdle. On the other hand, if we make it over the first hurdle, we are encouraged and have stronger grounds for expending the resources necessary to try to jump the second hurdle. As will be seen more clearly, later, most of the research relevant to the causal model reported in Part III will be correlational research, and is therefore only relevant to the first hurdle. However, it should never be forgotten that eventually evidence must be collected relevant to crossing the second hurdle, otherwise our knowledge will always be somewhat suspect.

CHAPTER

9

TWO CAUSES OF EFFICIENCY LEVEL

The two proximal causes of efficiency level, E_L, are accuracy level, A_L, and rate level, R_L, as was purported in Chapter 1. Because reading achievement is being represented in the causal model by E_L, this also means that the way to increase reading achievement is to increase A_L or to increase R_L.

In reading research, reading achievement is usually measured by a standardized test of reading comprehension, as was discussed earlier in Chapter 3. These tests ordinarily contain passages that vary in difficulty and must be read under a time limit. Therefore, the number of test questions answered correctly reflects the accuracy of text comprehension, A. It was shown in Chapter 3 that the accuracy of text comprehension, A, on one of these tests is determined by accuracy level and rate level, that is, A_L and R_L are causal for A. Therefore, A_L and R_L (a) are causal for the scores on reading achievement tests, A, and (b) are also causal for reading efficiency, E_L.

This rather simplistic idea that A_L and R_L are the two proximal causes of E_L has not always been accepted. For example, school district personnel who use reading achievement tests to evaluate their students and their instructional system, may not realize that these tests often measure both accuracy and rate, or efficiency. These tests may measure the rate level of students almost as well as they measure accuracy level (see Carver, 1992a). And, researchers who use these tests may also ignore the importance of rate. Our efforts to increase the reading achievement of students will be hampered severely as long as researchers and practitioners fail to recognize that reading achievement tests often measure reading efficiency, and that efficiency is made up of accuracy and rate.

The remainder of this chapter will be devoted to (a) a more detailed description of the theory underlying the purported causal connections among A_L, R_L, and E_L, (b) a review of related ideas in the research literature, and (c) a review of the empirical evidence supporting the causal theory. The intention is to convince the readers of this book that there is adequate theory and data to support the case that rauding accuracy level, A_L, and rauding rate level, R_L, are the two proximal causes of rauding efficiency level, E_L, such that improvement in E_L cannot occur without improvement in A_L or R_L.

Theoretical Relationships

The essence of "efficiency" according to Cronbach (1977) is that it "... is an index of how well the system functions as a whole" (p. 275). Rauding efficiency level, E_L, is an index of how well an individual's rauding system functions as a whole, that is, an index of how well an individual can raud. Remember from Chapter 3 that efficiency level was defined as the most difficult level of textual material that an individual can accurately read when the individual is allowed to read this material at a rate that is equivalent to the difficulty of the text, that is, the rate level of the individual is equal to the difficulty level of the material, $R_L = D_L$.

The proximal causes of efficiency level, E_L, are purported to be accuracy level, A_L, and rate level, R_L, according to Equation 1-1 presented in Chapter 1. In order to investigate the above hypothesis, it is necessary to discriminate between a direct measure of E_L, such as that provided by the RELT (described in Chapter 3), and E_L derived from measures of A_L (see Chapter 4) and R_L (see Chapter 5). So, E_L derived from measures of A_L and R_L will be symbolized with an attached prime, that is,

$$E_L' = \sqrt{A_L R_I} \qquad (9\text{-}1)$$

This means that the average of A_L and R_L (their geometric mean) yields an indirect measure of E_L, or an estimate of E_L, which is symbolized as E_L'. A measure of E_L should give the same result as E_L' determined from measures of A_L and R_L via Equation 9-1, that is, theoretically we should find empirical evidence that $E_L = E_L'$.

During 1 year of schooling, improving efficiency level one GE would seem to be an extremely important goal. As noted earlier, E_L can be improved in two primary ways, (a) by increasing the most difficult material that an individual can read accurately, called A_L, and (b) by increasing the rate of which an individual normally reads with accurate comprehension, R_L. So, the theory is that A_L and R_L are the proximal causes of E_L, and that A_L and R_L can be averaged to form an estimate of E_L, called E_L', using Equation 9-1.

Related Ideas

In the research on rauding theory published prior to 1995, E_L was estimated by using the arithmetic average of empirical indicants of A_L and R_L, that is

$$E_L' = (A_L + R_L)/2 \qquad (9\text{-}2)$$

This arithmetic mean was replaced later by the geometric mean given by Equation 9-1. The arithmetic mean and the geometric mean are both averages that predict E_L using measures of A_L and R_L, and the results from both formulas are almost perfectly correlated. For example, Carver (1998c) reported that for 135 students in grades 1 to 6, the correlation was .99 between E_L' from Equation 9-1 and E_L' from Equation 9-2, when controlled for grade level in school. So, there is very little empirical difference between E_L' determined from the average using the geometric mean in Equation 9-1 and the earlier estimates based on the average using the arithmetic mean in Equation 9-2.

The general idea that reading ability can be broken down into two primary subcomponents of accuracy and rate was suggested as early as 1921 by Gates. He collected data on many reading tests and concluded that "... rate and comprehension can be differentiated, although most of our tests do not do so" (p. 464), and (b) "usually the so-called 'rate' tests measure *comprehension* as well as rate, and the so-called 'comprehension' tests measure *rate* as well as comprehension" (p. 462). It is mildly embarrassing to be devoting an entire chapter to this idea that general reading ability, as measured by most reading achievement tests, is actually composed of accuracy of comprehension and rate of comprehension, considering that Gates seemed to grasp the basics of this truism over 70 years ago.

Many reading researchers through the years since 1921 have accepted the idea that general reading ability is composed of two components, one being a power, or accuracy of comprehension factor, and the other being a speed, or rate of comprehension factor. In 1954, Holmes contended that general reading ability is a composite of "speed" and "power," which are synonyms of "rate" and "accuracy." Then, in 1985, Perfetti based much of his verbal efficiency theory on the idea that "the definition of reading ability comes from considering both speed and comprehension" (p. 12). Again, Perfetti's speed and comprehension can be readily translated into rate and accuracy, respectively. More recently, Mills and Jackson (1990) contended that "... both speed and accuracy need to be considered in any full description of a child's performance" (p. 418). It can be seen that through the years many researchers seem to be endorsing the general idea that rauding efficiency level, E_L, is influenced by rauding accuracy level, A_L, and rauding rate level, R_L.

In summary, the old but true ideas outlined here have been upgraded. More precisely defined constructs and a mathematical formula have been used to express the nature of the relationships among reading achievement, or E_L, and its two proximal causes, A_L and R_L.

Empirical Evidence

Introduction. This section contains empirical evidence relevant to A_L and R_L being the proximal causes of E_L. This evidence has been divided into two parts. The first subsection contains evidence from factor analytic research. The second subsection contains empirical evidence relevant to the relationships among A_L, R_L, and E_L.

Factor Analytic Research. If the two proximal causes of efficiency level are accuracy level and rate level, then measures of efficiency level should be explained by two subfactors. In several studies, to be described later, many measures of reading ability have been factor analyzed with the resulting data supporting the theory that efficiency level is composed of two subfactors, namely, accuracy level and rate level.

In these earlier empirical studies, the same type of result occurs almost invariably. An efficiency factor results whenever a factor analysis of the data involves a single factor (either naturally occurring or a forced fit). Furthermore, whenever there are two factors (either naturally occurring or a forced fit), one of the two factors will be an accuracy factor and the other will be a rate factor. In this research, a data analysis strategy has been employed which involves either finding (a) one factor in the first analysis, and then forcing two factors for the second analysis, or (b) finding two factors in the first analysis and then forcing one factor in the second analysis. Either way, this strategy always results in a total of 3 factors. This factor analytic strategy will be called the 1-2-3 approach; it is called the 1-2-3 approach because it always produces the same factors—one general factor (efficiency) and two subfactors (accuracy and rate), for a total of three factors. Therefore, each variable involved in this data analysis strategy has three factor loadings—one for accuracy, one for rate, and one for efficiency.

Whenever the loadings on all three of the above factors are considered (accuracy factor, rate factor, and efficiency factor), many different standardized tests of reading comprehension should all load higher on the efficiency factor than they do on the accuracy or rate factors. That is, because scores on standardized reading comprehension tests are purported to measure efficiency level, then these tests should load higher on an efficiency factor than they load on either an accuracy or rate factor. Also, accuracy type measures of reading ability (unspeeded) should load higher on an accuracy factor than they load on a rate or efficiency factor. Furthermore, rate type measures of reading ability (speeded) should load higher on a rate factor than they do on an accuracy or efficiency factor. These predictions were tested by reviewing a great deal of data collected using the 1-2-3 approach.

Table 9-1 contains a summary of the factor analytic results from 20 standardized tests of reading ability that have no direct connections with rauding theory or the causal model. The table includes loadings for each test on the accuracy, rate, and efficiency factors obtained from the 1-2-3 approach, described earlier, plus the reference for the study wherein the data were obtained. The factor loading, out of three for each test, which was predicted to be the highest has an asterisk beside it, and the factor loading which was actually the highest of the three is in parentheses; therefore, when the asterisk is inside the parentheses, (*), then the prediction was confirmed. These 20 measures have also been subdivided into 7 accuracy tests, 5 rate tests, and 8 efficiency tests based upon the theory about the measures involved as presented in Chapters 3, 4, and 5.

Table 9-1
Summary of the Factor Analytic Results From 20 Tests

Measure	*Research*	*Factors*		
		Accuracy	*Rate*	*Efficiency*
ACCURACY MEASURES				
1. Davis Reading Test-Level	(Carver & Darby, 1972)	(.93*)	-.09	.76
2. Degrees of Reading Power	(Carver, 1992b)	(.92*)	.72	.92
3. NDRT Vocabulary	(Carver, 1992a)	(.92*)	.42	.83
4. ITBS Vocabulary	(Carver, 1992a)	(.90*)	.49	.84
5. NDRT Vocabulary	(Carver, 1992b)	(.87*)	.51	.82
6. Peabody Vocabulary	(Carver, 1992b)	(.80*)	.50	.77
7. Washington Vocabulary	(Carver, 1990a)	(.87*)	.32	.81
RATE MEASURES				
8. NDRT Rate	(Carver & Darby, 1972)	-.35	(.86*)	.43
9. Tinker Speed	(Carver & Darby, 1972)	.29	.61*	(.79)
10. NDRT Rate	(Carver, 1990a)	.40	(.92*)	.64
11. Minnesota Rate	(Carver, 1990a)	.32	(.86*)	.55
12. NDRT Rate	(Carver, 1992a)	.35	(.65*)	.58
EFFICIENCY MEASURES				
13. NDRT Comprehension	(Carver & Darby, 1972)	.67	.27	(.83*)
14. NDRT Comprehension	(Carver, 1992b)	.72	.65	(.83*)
15. ITBS Comprehension	(Carver, 1992a)	.85	.67	(.87*)
16. NDRT Comprehension	(Carver, 1992a)	.76	.54	(.79*)
17. NDRT Comprehension	(Carver, 1990a)	.86	.55	(.88*)
18. Davis Comprehension	(Carver, 1990a)	(.87)	.44	.85*
19. Washington Comprehension	(Carver, 1990a)	(.84)	.36	.79*
20. Davis Reading Test-Speed	(Carver & Darby, 1972)	.69	.32	(.89*)

Note: The factor loading that was predicted to be the highest of the three loadings for each test has an asterisk beside it. The factor loading which was actually the highest of the three loadings for each test is in parentheses. Therefore, when an asterisk is inside parentheses, (*), the prediction was confirmed.

Notice in Table 9-1 that the first 2 of the 7 accuracy measures (Numbers 1 and 2) loaded highest on the accuracy factory in accordance with what was predicted from the measure involved. Notice that the next five measures (Numbers 3 to 7) were reading vocabulary measures, and each one of them loaded highest on the accuracy factor in accordance with the theory presented in Chapter 4.

Also notice that all seven of the predictions associated with these accuracy measures were confirmed.

In Table 9-1, there were five rate measures (Numbers 8 to 12), and four of them loaded highest on the rate factor, as predicted. The Tinker Speed of Reading Test (Number 9) loaded higher on efficiency (.79) than it did on rate (.61). Four of these five predictions for the rate measures were confirmed.

In Table 9-1, there were eight traditional reading comprehension measures (Numbers 13 to 20), which were predicted to be efficiency measures. Four out of these eight measures involved the Nelson-Denny Reading Test (NDRT), Comprehension (Numbers 13, 14, 16, & 17), and each one of these four loaded highest on the efficiency factor, as predicted. The Iowa Test of Basic Skills (ITBS), Comprehension (Number 15) also loaded highest on efficiency as predicted. The Davis Reading Test, Speed (Number 20) loaded highest on the efficiency factor, as predicted. However, the other two comprehension tests that were predicted to be efficiency measures—Davis and Washington—loaded highest on the accuracy factor, and this was not predicted. However, the Davis Reading Test, Comprehension (Number 18) was a modified version of the Davis Reading Test; Palmer, MacLeod, Hunt, and Davidson (1985) modified this test for their research, and those data were reanalyzed by Carver (1990a). Therefore, this measure was not the same test as Davis Level (Number 1) or Davis Speed (Number 20). It seems likely that Palmer et al. extended the time limit so that it was measuring accuracy much more than rate (.87 vs. .44), thus making it load higher on accuracy than efficiency (.87 vs. .85). Also, the Washington Comprehension test had an extra long time limit so it seems likely that it was measuring accuracy much more than rate (.84 vs. .36), thus making the test measure accuracy more than efficiency (.84 vs. .79). Notice that six of the eight predictions involving the efficiency measures were confirmed.

In general, these factor analytic results obtained from the 1-2-3 approach provide strong correlational support for the theory that efficiency level, E_L, is composed of accuracy level, A_L, and rate level, R_L. Out of 20 predictions about the highest of the three factor loadings for each test, 17 of the 20 were confirmed. Furthermore, the three errant predictions were based upon descriptions of these tests, and it seems more reasonable to fault the descriptions instead of the theory. That is, any reading test can accent accuracy more than rate by raising the time limits, and this appears to explain why two of the reading comprehension tests that were predicted to be measures of efficiency were actually slightly better measures of accuracy. Also, the Tinker Speed of Reading test was predicted to be a measure of rate but it turned out to be a somewhat better measure of efficiency than rate. Because 85% of the predictions were definitely confirmed, and because the other 15% could reasonably be interpreted as also being supportive, it appears that the correlational evidence from the factor analytic studies strongly supports the part of the causal model which contends that A_L and R_L are the two proximal causes of reading achievement, or E_L.

Relations Among A_L, R_L, and E_L. For all of the evidence given in the preceding subsection involving factor analyses, the value of E_L', derived from A_L and R_L, involved the arithmetic average from Equation 9-2. That evidence suggested that the arithmetic average of A_L and R_L is highly valid as an indicant of E_L. Next, evidence will be presented directly relevant to the validity of Equation 9-1, using the geometric mean to average A_L and R_L for a measure of E_L.

Carver (1997) reported results from 97 students in grades 3 through 12 who had been given measures of A_L, R_L, and E_L, obtained from the ALT (see Chapter 4), the RLT (see Chapter 5), and the RELT (see Chapter 3), respectively. A_L and R_L correlated highly with E_L, .74 and .77, respectively. However, E_L' determined from substituting A_L and R_L into Equation 9-1 correlated even higher with E_L, that is, .83. These data provide strong correlational support for A_L (measured by a vocabulary test) and R_L (measured by a rate test) being the two proximal causes of E_L, as prescribed in Equation 9-1.

Additional evidence relevant to the validity of E_L' derived from Equation 9-1 comes from similar partial correlations involving 56 students who took the three measures noted above (ALT, RLT, & RELT) plus the ITBS-Comprehension test, which is purportedly another indicant of E_L (see Number 16 in Table 9-1). Using the ITBS-Comprehension test as the criterion, the E_L' measure correlated higher with it ($r = .85$) than did the RELT ($r = .67$) which was designed to be direct measure of E_L. So, a derived estimate of a construct, E_L', seems to be more valid than a direct measure of E_L. As explained earlier in Chapter 3, this unusual finding is probably partly due to the reliability of the RELT being lower than E_L' derived from the ALT and the RLT. The RELT required sustained concentration while reading passages that increased in difficulty, and there were only five two-choice questions on each passage, so it is likely that it was not highly reliable.

Given the theory that E_L is caused by A_L and R_L, or that general reading ability is caused by levels of comprehension (accuracy) and levels of speed (rate), it should follow that (a) reliable indicants of A_L should correlate highly (about .50 to .70) with reliable indicants of E_L, and (b) reliable indicants of R_L should correlate highly (about .50 to .70) with reliable indicants of E_L. Empirical support for the high relationship between A_L and E_L, and the high relationship between R_L and E_L, comes from the measures involved in the research reported earlier in connection with Table 9-1. As examples of the high correlations between indicants of A_L and E_L consider the following: (a) the correlation between the accuracy score on the Davis Reading Test, A_L, and the NDRT-Comprehension score, E_L, was .73 (Carver & Darby, 1972); (b) the correlation between NDRT-Vocabulary, A_L, and NDRT-Comprehension, E_L, was .65 (A. E. Cunningham, Stanovich, & Wilson, 1990); and (c) the correlation between the Washington Pre-College reading vocabulary measure, A_L, and the NDRT-Comprehension, E_L, was .67 (Palmer, et al., 1985). As examples of the high correlations between indicants of R_L and E_L consider the following: (a) the correlation between the rate of reading difficult words, R_L, and NDRT-Comprehension, E_L, was .59 (Cunningham, Stanovich, & Wilson, 1990), and (b) the correlation between an experimental measure of reading speed, R_L, and the NDRT-Comprehension, E_L, was .60 (Palmer, et al., 1985).

The relationship between R_L and E_L can also be studied by using the speed of naming isolated raudamatized words as an indicant of R_L, as was pointed out in Chapter 5. Research that involves this measure should find that it is substantially related to an indicant of E_L. Indeed, Mason (1978) found that "reading ability in mature readers is related to speed of word recognition" (p. 568), and then concluded that "reading comprehension cannot be divorced from rapid and accurate word recognition" (p. 579). Also, Chabot, Zehr, Prinzo, and Petros (1984) concluded from their research that "the development of rapid word recognition skills is the primary factor which distinguishes skilled from less skilled reading performance" (p. 160).

There are also data which on the surface seem to provide evidence counter to the purported causal relationship between R_L and E_L. According to Anderson and Freebody (1981), Thorndike (1973) found "in his study of reading comprehension in 15 countries, only modest correlations between performance on reading speed and comprehension tests" (p. 83), and they go on to say that "the median corrected correlations were .42 for 10-year-olds and .47 for 14-year-olds" (p. 83). However, the comprehension tests used by R. L. Thorndike (1973) seemed to provide more than ample time limits so they were more likely to be indicants of A_L, not E_L. Therefore, the above correlations of .42 and .47 are more likely relevant to the relationship between A_L and R_L, and are less likely to be relevant to the purported high relationship between R_L and E_L.

Additional data relevant to the hypothesis that A_L and R_L at Echelon 2 are the primary causes of E_L at Echelon 1, have been provided by M. D. Jackson and McClelland (1979). In their study of what they called the processing determinants of reading speed, they collected correlational data from 52 college students. Relevant to A_L, they measured the percentage of questions answered correctly after reading one long passage (4,286 words) and 10 short passages (about 317 words per passage); there were 10 short-answer questions on the long passage, and there were 3 short-answer questions on each of the 10 short passages, for a total of 30 questions on the short passages. So, there were two indicants of A_L, which will be called LongA_L (about 4,000 words, 10 items) and ShortA_L (about 3,000 words, 30 items). Relevant to R_L, they measured the rate of reading these passages in words per minute. So, there were two corresponding indicants of R_L, which will be called LongR_L and ShortR_L. Finally, they derived an "effective reading speed" by multiplying the comprehension score (percentage correct) by the speed score (wpm), and this would be an indicant of E_L. So, there were two corresponding indicants of E_L, called LongE_L and ShortE_L. From the correlations they reported, it was possible to compute the multiple correlation with LongE_L as the criterion and ShortA_L and ShortR_L as the predictors; the result was $R = .79$, which was as high as the reliability of the criterion as estimated from the correlation between LongE_L and ShortE_L, $r = .79$. The multiple R was even higher for LongA_L and LongR_L predicting ShortE_L; i.e., $R = .84$. These data suggest that all of the reliable variance in their measures of E_L' could be accounted for by their measures of A_L and R_L, which is highly consistent with A_L and R_L being the two causes of E_L.

Summary of Theory

The theory is that the two proximal causes of efficiency level, E_L, are accuracy level, A_L, and rate level, R_L, in accordance with the equation which holds that E_L is the average of the product of A_L and R_L, using the geometric mean as the method of averaging. It is being theorized, for example, that if a student is measured at $A_L = 8$, $R_L = 2$, and $E_L = 4$, at the beginning of the school year, and this student gains 1.0 GEs in A_L and 2.0 GEs in R_L during the year, then E_L will increase to 6.0 at the end of the school year (see Equation 9-1). So, it is being theorized that (a) there can be no increase in reading achievement, or E_L, without there being an increase in A_L or R_L, and (b) increases in A_L or R_L will automatically result in increases in reading achievement, or E_L, according to Equation 9-1.

Reading achievement is most often measured using a test that requires individuals to read increasingly difficult text both accurately and quickly, e.g., the Iowa Test of Basic Skills-Comprehension and the Nelson-Denny Reading Test-Comprehension. Therefore, a score on a reading achievement test is a measure of the accuracy of text comprehension, A, and it was shown in Chapter 3 that A is determined by A_L and R_L on standardized reading comprehension tests. Therefore, scores on these reading tests and rauding efficiency level are both reflecting the same ability because A and E_L are caused by the same two factors, namely, A_L and R_L. This idea that individual differences in reading achievement, reading comprehension, or general reading ability, are caused by the accuracy and rate of reading text can be traced as far back as Gates (1921), through Holmes (1954), M. D. Jackson and McClelland (1979), Perfetti (1985), and Mills and Jackson (1990).

Summary of Evidence

The empirical evidence supporting the existence of an accuracy level factor, a rate level factor, and an efficiency level factor in measures of reading ability is overwhelmingly positive. The evidence from factor analytic studies indicates that purported measures of accuracy level, such as unspeeded measures of reading comprehension (e.g., Davis-Level or DRP) and reading vocabulary measures (e.g., NDRT or ITBS), have consistently been found to load highest on an accuracy level factor (Carver, 1990a, 1992a, 1992b; Carver & Darby, 1972). Also, measures of rate level in these factor analytic studies (e.g., NDRT-Rate) have generally loaded highest on a rate level factor (Carver, 1972, 1990a, 1992a). Furthermore, most timed reading comprehension tests (e.g., NDRT-Comprehension, ITBS-Comprehension) load highest on an efficiency level factor (Carver, 1990a, 1992a, 1992b; Carver & Darby, 1972); however, some timed reading comprehension tests have more than ample time limits so they load highest on an accuracy level factor (see Table 9-1). Correlational evidence collected in a more experimental type of study—conducted by M. D. Jackson and McClelland (1979)—also indicates that all of the reliable variance in experimental measures of efficiency level, E_L, can be predicted from just two sources, a measure of accuracy level, A_L, and a measure of rate level, R_L.

Implications

There seems to be no theoretical or empirical reason to doubt that individual differences in reading achievement, or E_L, are composed of two subfactors. One subfactor is accuracy level, A_L, which can be measured by unspeeded tests of reading comprehension or measures of reading vocabulary. The other subfactor is rate level, R_L, which can be measured by tests of the rate of comprehension. These two subfactors—A_L and R_L—explain all, or almost all, of the variance in E_L, probably because A_L and R_L are the two proximal causes of E_L.

When reading achievement is to be measured, this construct should be described before the research is designed, so that the aspect of reading that the researcher wants to accent can be properly measured. If a test is selected that would seem to be an indicant of E_L, then it should be acknowledged that both A_L and R_L will be involved. It would be desirable for the researcher to have some empirical estimate of whether any particular test selected for use in a study reflected E_L more than A_L or R_L. From the standpoint of rauding theory and the causal model, it would often seem best to have an empirical measure of A_L and an empirical measure of R_L.

There seems to be no good reason for educators to ignore the likely influence of rate level upon reading achievement, or E_L. Low reading achievement for many students is likely to be due to low rate level, not low accuracy level, and all efforts to ignore low rate level as a probable major cause of low reading achievement should be resisted. If reading rate level is ignored as a factor affecting reading achievement, or E_L, then it is likely that there will be a failure to discriminate between reading measures that reflect accuracy level and reading measures that reflect efficiency level. Given what we know about reading achievement and how it has been measured, there is really no good excuse for reading educators to claim that they want to increase reading achievement but then make no distinctions among A_L, R_L, and E_L, especially because it is highly likely that A_L and R_L are the two primary causes of E_L.

Forget Me Nots

The two proximal causes of efficiency level, E_L, are accuracy level, A_L, and rate level, R_L. E_L is the average of A_L and R_L. For example, if a student is reading at the sixth-grade level ($A_L = 6$) and has a typical reading rate at the fourth-grade level ($R_L = 4$), then this student is likely to have a level of reading achievement at about the fifth-grade level ($E_L = 5$), because 5 is the average of 4 and 6.

CHAPTER

10

TWO CAUSES OF ACCURACY LEVEL

There are two proximal causes of accuracy level, A_L, and they are verbal level, V_L, and pronunciation level, P_L. This causal connection has been referred to earlier as the simple view of reading (see Gough & Tunmer, 1986). The simple view is that improving the reading ability of younger students is relatively simple. All you have to do is (a) improve their ability to comprehend spoken language, and (b) improve their ability to transform printed words into spoken language.

The simple view idea summarizes what educators can do to cause improvement in accuracy level, via teaching and learning. Educators have less control over the other parts of the causal model. The other parts are influenced by cognitive speed level, and there is no known way for educators to help individuals increase their cognitive speed. So, if we want to improve reading achievement, or E_L, then we need to focus upon the two factors that can be improved by teaching and learning, which are (a) the students ability to comprehend spoken language, V_L, and (b) the students ability to transform printed words into spoken language, P_L. However, V_L and P_L are not independently potent for increasing A_L for all readers, as will be described in much more detail in the following section. Then, these theoretical relationships will be compared to related ideas in the research literature. A subsequent section will present a summary of the empirical evidence relevant to the theory that V_L and P_L are two proximal causes of A_L.

Theoretical Relationships

Remember that A_L is (a) the level of text difficulty in GE units at which the thoughts can be accurately comprehended at the individual's rauding rate, R_r, and (b) an indicant of A_L is the population of words whose meaning is known out of context. Also, remember that V_L is (a) the level of verbal knowledge in GE units, and (b) an indicant of V_L is an estimate of the population of words whose meaning is known when they are spoken out of context. Finally, remember that P_L is (a) the size of the population of words that can be accurately pronounced when they are presented out of context, in GE units, and (b) an indicant of P_L would be a sampling of increasingly difficult words (lower frequency of usage).

As noted earlier, the simple view of reading is that listening ability and decoding ability determine reading ability. In the causal model, this translates into V_L and P_L being the causes of A_L, according to Equation 1-2 presented in Chapter 1. In order to investigate this causal hypothesis, it is necessary to discriminate between (a) an indirect measure of A_L, such as provided by the Accuracy Level Test (see Chapter 4), and (b) A_L predicted from measures of V_L and P_L. So, the A_L that is predicted will be symbolized with an attached prime (A_L'), so that

$$A_L' = \sqrt{V_L P_L} \qquad (10\text{-}1)$$

Theoretically, an indirect measure of A_L, such as the GE score on the ALT described earlier, should provide the same result as A_L derived from Equation 10-1 using a measure of listening level, or V_L, and a measure of decoding level, or P_L, that is, we should find that $A_L' = A_L$.

Increasing V_L will cause an increase in A_L because increasing the level of verbal knowledge or increasing the population of words known auditorily, audamatized words, will make this information comprehensible when these same words can be recognized in print. Increasing P_L will cause an increase in A_L, because increasing the number of words that can be accurately pronounced, will make more difficult text comprehensible in printed form, as long as these words can be understood when spoken. This means that A_L will be increased whenever the meaning of printed words in more difficult text are readily recognized, that is, when the words in more difficult text are raudamatized.

The relationships among V_L, P_L, and A_L can be explained at a deeper theoretical level using the following concepts: (a) the lexicon of audamatized words, or V_LWords, (b) the lexicon of pronounceamatized words, or P_LWords, and (c) the lexicon of the raudamatized words, or A_LWords (see Chapters 4, 6, and 7). Remember that the size of the lexicon of audamatized words, V_LWords, is purportedly an indicant of V_L when expressed in GE units, and remember that the Auding Accuracy Level Test, AALT, provides an estimate of the number of V_LWords and an estimate of V_L (see Chapter 6). Also, remember that the size of the lexicon of pronounceamatized words, P_LWords, is actually P_L when expressed in GE units, and remember that the Pronunciation Level Test, PLT, provides an estimate of the number of P_LWords and an estimate of P_L (see Chapter 7). Finally, remember that the size of the lexicon of raudamatized words, A_LWords, is purportedly an indicant of A_L when expressed in GE units, and remember that the Accuracy Level Test, ALT, provides an estimate of the number of A_LWords and an estimate of A_L (see Chapter 4).

When individuals have raudamatized all of their audamatized words, then these individuals will be described as having reached raudamaticity. This means that individuals who have less raudamatized words than audamatized words (A_LWords < V_LWords) are below raudamaticity, and individuals who have raudamatized all of their audamatized words (A_LWords = V_LWords) are at raudamaticity.

For most beginning readers, the size of the audamatized lexicon is very large relative to the size of the pronounceamatized lexicon because these students can understand hundreds of words when spoken but can pronounce very few printed words when presented out of context in a list. This relationship is depicted in Figure 10-1. Notice that V_LWords > P_LWords, as indicated by the size of their respective circles. Furthermore, most of the words that beginning readers have learned to pronounce are words that they know when spoken; most of their pronounceamatized words are also audamatized, and this is depicted in Figure 10-1 by showing that almost all of the P_LWords are also V_LWords. That is, beginning readers ordinarily do not know how to pronounce very many words that they do not know when spoken. The few P_LWords that are not A_L-Words are the words that can be correctly pronounced using pure cipher knowledge, that is, c_kWords as depicted in Figure 10-1. The overlap between the V_LWords and the P_LWords is likely to be the A_LWords, that is, it is likely that the words that are known when listening and can also be pronounced, are the words that can be rauded, or are raudamatized words. Notice in Figure 10-1 that there is an almost perfect correspondence between the A_LWords and the P_LWords, and this close correspondence should result in a very high correlation between indicants of P_L and indicants of A_L. Also notice that there is not a high correspondence between the V_LWords and the A_LWords and this low correspondence should result in a lower correlation between V_L and A_L for beginning readers. Furthermore, beginning readers are ordinarily below raudamaticity because their number of A_LWords do not approach their number of V_LWords.

For many intermediate readers, the size of the pronounceamatized lexicon has increased in size relative to the audamatized lexicon so that both lexicons are approximately the same size. Because almost all of the audamatized words are also raudamatized words, many of these individuals are at raudamaticity or are approaching raudamaticity. These relationships are depicted in Figure 10-2. Notice that the overlap of the V_LWords and the P_LWords again represents the A_LWords, which is almost the same size as the other two lexicons. This should result in a high correlation between V_L and A_L, and a high correlation between P_L and A_L. Again, notice that the relative size of the ciphermatized lexicon, or c_kWords, has also grown in size.

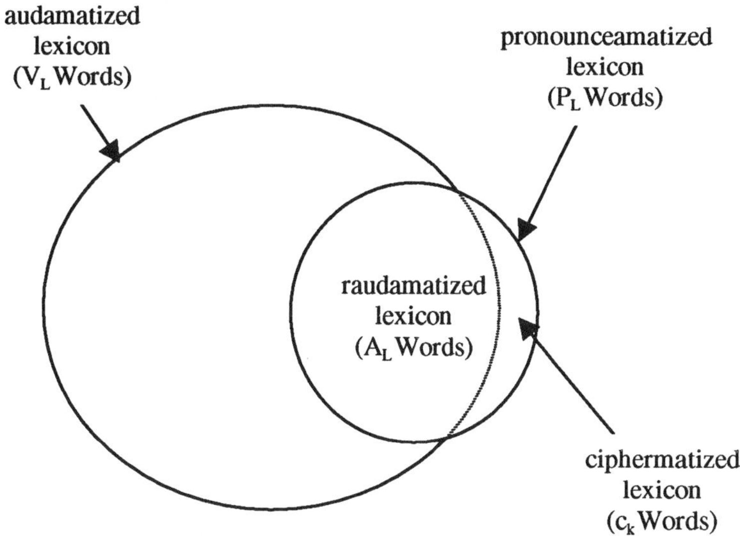

Figure 10-1. A graphic depiction of the relatively large audamatized lexicon, V_LWords, and the relatively small pronounceamatized lexicon, P_LWords, with the overlap representing an estimate of the relative size of the population of raudamatized words, A_LWords, for almost all beginning readers. Also, the P_LWords that are not A_LWords, are ciphermatized words, or c_kWords (see Equation 7-1 in Chapter 7).

For all advanced readers, the size of the pronounceamatized lexicon has increased even further relative to the growth in the audamatized lexicon so that all of the words in the audamatized lexicon are also included in the pronounceamatized lexicon. This relationship is depicted in Figure 10-3. Advanced readers have raudamatized all of their audamatized words so that the A_LWords and the V_LWords are the same words represented by the same circle in Figure 10-3. For all advanced readers, increases in the pronounceamatized lexicon will not increase the number of raudamatized words. This is because there is no chance that the correct pronunciation of a new word will be one that is already audamatized and can therefore be raudamatized with practice, because all of the audamatized words are already raudamatized. For all advanced readers, the correlation between V_L and A_L will be perfect because the V_LWords and the A_LWords are the same words. There will still be a high correlation between P_L and A_L, even though P_L is no longer a proximal cause of A_L because P_L has A_L as a component; P_LWords are still composed of A_LWords and c_kWords and P_L may still be the average of A_L and c_k for most of these readers (see Chapter 7). Therefore, P_L and A_L should still correlate substantially.

Again, all advanced readers have reached raudamaticity because they have raudamatized all of their audamatized words, A_LWords = V_LWords.

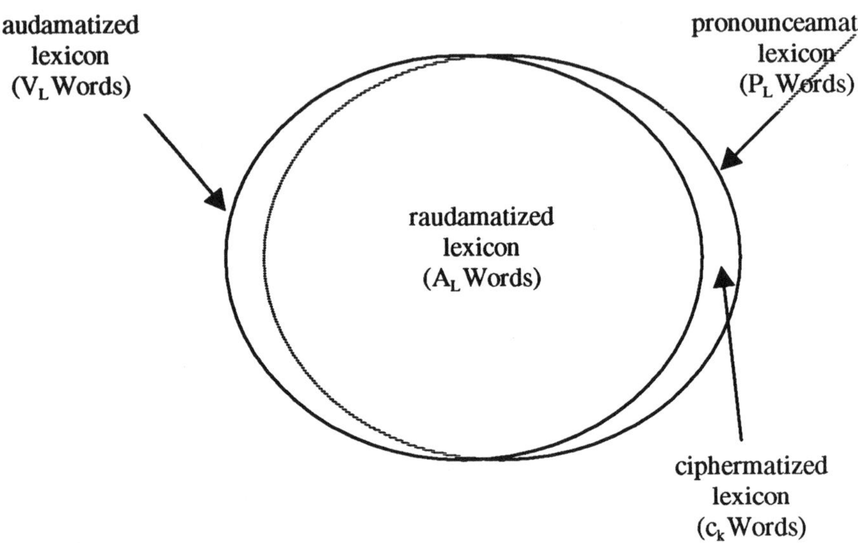

Figure 10-2. A graphic depiction of the large audamatized lexicon, V_LWords, and the large pronounceamatized lexicon, P_LWords, with the overlap representing an estimate of the relative size of the population of raudamatized words, A_LWords, for many intermediate readers. This figure portrays a situation where an individual is close to raudamaticity, that is, almost all audamatized words have been raudamatized. Again, the P_LWords that are not A_LWords are the c_kWords, which are the unknown words that can be pronounced using pure cipher knowledge (see Equation 7-1 in Chapter 7).

Once the point is reached where all of the A_LWords are V_LWords, then raudamaticity has been reached and increases in P_LWords will no longer have the same impact upon A_LWords. At this point, the size of the audamatized lexicon and the size of the raudamatized lexicon become equal, V_LWords = A_LWords, so V_L will correlate perfectly with A_L. This raudamaticity concept is very important because learning to pronounce more words is likely to increase A_L before an individual reaches raudamaticity, but instruction designed to help students learn to pronounce more words is not likely to increase A_L after the individual reaches raudamaticity, unless this instruction is also designed to increase V_L. This means that increasing P_L has a major causal effect upon A_L for individuals who are below raudamaticity, but increasing P_L will not increase A_L for individuals who are at raudamaticity.

All Advanced Readers

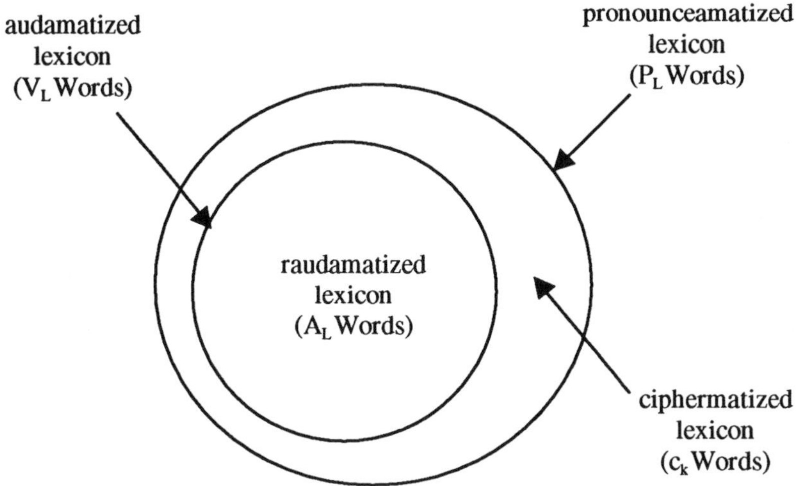

Figure 10-3. A graphic depiction of the large audamatized lexicon, V_LWords, and the larger pronounceamatized lexicon, P_LWords, with the overlap representing the size of the population of raudamatized words, A_LWords, for all advanced readers. That is, the V_LWords and the A_LWords are the same words. Again, the P_LWords that are not A_LWords are ciphermatized words, or c_kWords (see Equation 7-1 in Chapter 7).

For all those readers who are at raudamaticity, every new word should become audamatized, pronounceamatized, and raudamatized almost simultaneously, so that V_L, P_L, and A_L all increase at the same time. For example, consider a typical college student who encounters a new word such as "homoscedasticity." If the meaning of this word is not known, it does not matter much whether this individual can accurately pronounce this word on a list. What is important is that the meaning of the word be learned so that it can be comprehended in context, whether spoken or written; the word needs to be raudamatized so it can be rauded whenever it is encountered in context. Students who are at raudamaticity no longer have a pool of words that are known auditorily but not known visually, so that learning to pronounce "homoscedasticity" accurately (increase P_L) no longer increases the chances that the word can be understood in context. For individuals at raudamaticity, there are no words or concepts left in the audamatized lexicon that cannot be recognized in print, so all new words need to become audamatized, pronounceamatized, and raudamatized at approximately the same time.

Related Ideas

Introduction. As noted earlier, the causal model incorporates the simple view of reading so this connection with the simple view will be explained in more detail in this section, later. Also, previous theory relevant to the discrepancy between the ability to listen and comprehend and the ability to read and comprehend, is relevant to the causes of A_L. So, the connection between the listening-reading discrepancy and the proximal causes of A_L will be explained later in this section.

Simple View of Reading. The general idea that verbal level and pronunciation level determine accuracy level according to Equation 1-2 evolved from the simple view of reading (Gough & Tunmer, 1986), as noted in earlier chapters. According to Hoover and Gough (1990), the simple view is that "reading consists of only two parts, decoding and linguistic comprehension, both necessary for reading success, neither sufficient by itself" (p. 132). Juel, Griffith, and Gough (1986) have graphically depicted the simple view as word recognition and listening comprehension being the causes of reading comprehension.

There is already a great deal of data supporting the simple view (e.g., Chen & Vellutino, 1997; Dreyer & Katz, 1992; Juel, 1988). Furthermore, the idea has received support from various sources even when "simple view" is not mentioned. For example, Sticht, Beck, Hauke, Kleiman, & James (1974) presented a developmental model of auding and reading which was based upon the idea that skilled reading depends upon decoding well and listening well. Also, Carlisle (1983) stated that "reading comprehension cannot take place without these essential components—word recognition and language comprehension" (p. 188) and that "it is reasonable to consider decoding and language necessary if not entirely sufficient requirements for successful reading comprehension" (p. 188). Similarly, Daneman (1991) stated that "almost all reading problems are due to recognizing words and comprehending language" (p. 518). More recently, Vellutino, Scanlon, and Tanzman (1994) stated that their data "... provide strong documentation that adequate facility in word recognition is a prerequisite to adequate facility in reading comprehension and that, given the former, one's ability to read is dependent on adequate language comprehension" (p. 323).

In 1993a, the simple view of reading was merged with rauding theory by Carver; the simple view was modified slightly and was called Simple View II. Whereas the original simple view was presented in a form that was relevant to a reading process that occurs during 1 second of reading, Simple View II did not purport to be directly relevant to 1 second of reading. Instead, Simple View II focused on the gains that occur during 1 year of reading, measured in GE units. Empirical support was found for Simple View II (Carver, 1993a) in the form of reading ability (indicated by A_L) being the arithmetic mean of decoding ability (indicated by P_L) and listening ability (indicated by V_L).

It should be pointed out that Hoover and Gough (1990) hypothesized that reading was the *product* of linguistic comprehension and decoding, not the arithmetic average as used in Simple View II, above. In this regard, Carver (1993a) acknowledged the theoretical advantage of a "product" relationship but lamented that there was no apparent solution to the units of measurement problem; that is, in Simple View II if decoding level in GE units was multiplied by listening level in GE units, then reading level would be in GE units squared. Belatedly, Carver (1997) noticed that there was a solution to this problem, namely, take the square root of the product—which is the geometric mean of V_L and P_L. So, the simple view of reading as theoretically defined by Equation 1-2, does incorporate the product aspect of the original simple view. This product relationship is more satisfying from a theoretical standpoint because A_L will be zero whenever V_L or P_L equals zero. That is, if an individual has $P_L = 0$, then A_L must be zero no matter how high V_L is. However, it should be pointed out again that the difference between A_L' values calculated from the product equation (Equation 10-1), or from the equation using the arithmetic average of V_L and A_L, is more superficial than real in most situations because the correlation between the scores resulting from the two equations has been shown to be .99 (Carver, 1998c). Therefore, in many situations arithmetic averages may be as valid or more valid than the geometric averages presented in Chapter 1. That is,

$$E_L = (A_L + R_L)/2, \quad (10\text{-}2)$$
$$A_L = (V_L + P_L)/2, \quad (10\text{-}3)$$
and
$$R_L = (P_L + C_s)/2. \quad (10\text{-}4)$$

This arithmetic averaging in Equations 10-2, 10-3, and 10-4 produces almost exactly the same result as the geometric averaging involved in Equations 1-1, 1-2, and 1-3. Furthermore, it is much easier to measure variables on an interval scale as is required for Equations 10-2, 10-3, and 10-4, as compared to the ratio scale that is theoretically required for using the geometric means involved in Equations 1-1, 1-2, and 1-3.

The original simple view has been merged with rauding theory and upgraded twice (Carver, 1993a, 1997). It now needs to be upgraded again so that it is compatible with the concept of raudamaticity. The causal relationships between V_L and A_L and between P_L and A_L depend upon whether individuals are below or at raudamaticity. This upgraded version of the simple view still allows for V_L and P_L to be important determiners of A_L for beginning and intermediate readers who have not reached raudamaticity but when raudamaticity has been reached for any reader, then P_L drops out as a proximal cause of A_L. For beginning readers and intermediate readers who are below raudamaticity, then A_L does depend upon V_L and P_L. For all advanced readers, it is assumed they are at raudamaticity (the number of A_LWords equals the number of

V_LWords), so V_L and A_L are synergistic, and P_L is not a proximal cause of A_L (see Chapter 17).

In summary, the simple view of reading is no longer as simple as it was, but the upgrades seem to offer a closer connection to the realities involved.

Listening-Reading Discrepancy. Stanovich (1991) has discussed the idea of a discrepancy between listening and reading that is relevant to the equations that have been presented (see also Stanovich, 1988a). He says that if listening ability is high compared to reading ability, then decoding ability must be low, that is, "in subjects who show a large reading discrepancy from listening comprehension we have probably isolated—as closely as we ever will—a modular decoding problem" (p. 20). For example, suppose there is a student who is reading at the fourth-grade level, $A_L = 4$, and has a listening level at grade 6, $V_L = 6$. Because this student is reading at a level considerably below his/her listening level (4 vs. 6), then the decoding level of this student must be relatively low; according to Equation 10-3, this student would be at the second grade level in decoding, $P_L = 2$, because $4 = (6 + 2)/2$. The essence of the listening-reading discrepancy idea is mathematically summarized by Equation 10-3, that is, decoding must be lower than reading when listening is higher than reading because reading, or A_L, is the average of listening, or V_L, and decoding, or P_L. To the extent that evidence exists for the simple view of reading and this listening-reading discrepancy idea advanced by Stanovich, then evidence also exists for Equation 10-3.

The listening-reading discrepancy idea, discussed above, also has an unstated complement. It is as follows: those readers who show a large reading to decoding discrepancy, that is, high decoding ability relative to reading ability, will have a listening ability that is relatively low. Again, this relationship is a mathematical certainty as long as Equation 10-3 is valid. Those individuals with a decoding-reading discrepancy are often referred to as hyperlexics. They would be good candidates for being "word callers" (Dymock, 1993) because they could pronounce the words in many texts without having the verbal knowledge, or listening knowledge, necessary to understand the text. For example, if decoding is high relative to reading, such as $P_L = 8$ and $A_L = 5$, then listening must be low, such as $V_L = 2$, according to Equation 10-3. Hyperlexics are also likely to be individuals who are at raudamaticity (A_LWords = V_LWords); their lexicon of pronounceamatized words is likely to be much larger (maybe 2 or three times as large) as their lexicon of audamatized words (P_LWords much greater than V_LWords). Therefore these individuals need help with increasing the size of their audamatized lexicon, or V_LWords.

Summary of Theory

According to the causal model, the two proximal causes of accuracy level, A_L, are verbal level, V_L, and pronunciation level, P_L. This means that a low level of verbal knowledge (or a low level of listening comprehension) is likely to cause a low accuracy level for reading, which in turn, is likely to cause a low level of reading achievement. This also means that a low level of pronunciation knowledge (or low decoding skill) is likely to cause a low accuracy level for reading, which in turn is likely to cause a low level of reading achievement, or low E_L.

The mechanisms that explain the above relationships involve the lexicon of audamatized words, V_LWords, the lexicon of pronounceamatized words, P_LWords, and the lexicon of raudamatized words, A_LWords. It is theorized that the lexicon of raudamatized words is likely to be represented by the overlap between V_LWords and the P_LWords, that is, the audamatized words that can also be accurately pronounced out of context are likely to become raudamatized words with practice.

Beginning readers have a relatively large lexicon of audamatized words and a relatively small lexicon of pronounceamatized words, with almost all P_LWords being V_LWords. This means that beginning readers are seldom able to pronounce words that they cannot understand when listening. Thus, the number of P_LWords almost completely determines the number of A_LWords, or raudamatized words. Therefore, P_L is much more of a proximal cause of A_L than V_L for almost all beginning readers. Furthermore, there should be a very high correlation between P_L and A_L for beginning readers because the lexicon of P_LWords and the lexicon of A_LWords are almost identical, but the correlation between V_L and A_L should be much lower because the lexicon of V_LWords is much larger than the lexicon of A_LWords.

For many intermediate readers, the lexicon of P_LWords has grown so that it approximates the size of the lexicon of V_LWords, and these two lexicons highly overlap. The overlap between these two lexicons—V_L and P_L—again contains the lexicon of A_LWords, or the raudamatized words. These relationships among lexicons for intermediate readers suggest that (a) there should be a high correlation between V_L and A_L because almost all of the V_LWords are also A_LWords, and (b) there should be a high correlation between P_L and A_L because most of the P_LWords are also A_LWords.

For advanced readers, the lexicon of P_LWords has grown even further so that it completely overlaps the lexicon of V_LWords, that is, advanced readers can accurately pronounce all of the words in their lexicon of audamatized words. Therefore, for advanced readers there should be a perfect relationship between V_L and A_L because all of the audamatized words are also raudamatized words. When individuals have reached the point in their learning where all of their audamatized words have become raudamatized, it is said that they have reached raudamaticity. Advanced readers have achieved raudamaticity because all of their V_LWords are also A_LWords. Given this 100% overlap between V_LWords and A_LWords, it follows that perfectly reliable indicants of V_L and A_L should correlate perfectly for advanced readers.

This theory involving lexicons of words and their overlaps, requires that the causal model presented in Chapter 1 be qualified, because P_L is not an equally potent proximal cause of A_L for all readers. The potency of P_L as a proximal cause of A_L depends upon whether individuals are below or at raudamaticity. Almost all beginning readers are below raudamaticity, so P_L is much more dominant as a proximal cause of P_L than is V_L for these students. Some intermediate readers will be below raudamaticity and some will be at raudamaticity, so V_L and P_L are more equally potent as proximal causes of A_L for these readers. All advanced readers will be above raudamaticity, so P_L is not a proximal cause of A_L for them. This diminishing of causal potency for P_L, as P_L increases, can be predicted from the relationship between A_LWords and V_LWords, that is, individuals with A_LWords < V_LWords are below raudamaticity and individuals with A_LWords = V_LWords are at raudamaticity.

Equations 10-2, 10-3, and 10-4 presented in this chapter, are simpler versions of 1-1, 1-2, and 1-3 presented in Chapter 1, because arithmetic averages are simpler than geometric averages and give almost exactly the same results.

Summary of Evidence

Based upon the quality and quantity of supporting data that will be reviewed later, it appears reasonable to conclude that almost all of the reliable variance in measures of A_L can be accounted for by reliable measures of V_L and reliable measures of P_L, for lower graders, middle graders, and adults.

For lower graders, who are likely to consist of almost all beginning readers, it appears that almost all of the reliable variance in A_L can be explained by P_L. The correlations between measures of P_L and A_L generally are reported to be around .75 to .85 (Barr & Dreeban, 1983, r = .76, .70; Calfee & Piontkowski, 1981, r = 86; Chen & Vellutino, 1997, r = .86; Sears & Keogh, 1993, r = .85; Woodcock, 1973, r = .85, .86). The correlations between measures of V_L and A_L are much lower, generally averaging around .20 to .40 (Sticht & James, 1984, average of correlations for grade 1 was .35 and average for grade 2 was .40). With respect to most lower graders, it seems that almost all P_LWords are also A_LWords, and that is why the correlations between indicants of P_L and A_L in the lower grades are very high, around .80 to .90. On the other hand, only a relatively few of the V_LWords are A_LWords (see Figure 10-1), and that is why the correlations between indicants of V_L and A_L are relatively low, around .20 to .30.

For middle graders, including many students who are below raudamaticity and many students who are at raudamaticity, it appears that V_L and P_L contribute about equally to the variance of A_L. The correlations between measures of V_L and measures of A_L generally are around .70, varying from around .50 to .90 (Aaron, 1991, r = .62 to .74; Carver, 1998c, r = .72 to .87; Chen & Vellutino, 1997, r = .68, .81, .74; Curtis, 1980, r = .66, .74; Fletcher et al., 1994, r = .68; Hoover & Gough, 1990, r = .80, .87; Shany & Biemiller, 1995, r = .66; Sticht & James, 1984, r averages between .48 and .62). Furthermore, the correlations between measures of P_L and A_L are also generally around .70 (Fletcher et al., 1994, r = .72; Hammill & McNutt, 1980, r averaged .68; Shankweiler & Liberman, 1972, r = .72, .72, .77, .53; Shany & Biemiller, 1995, r = .62). The multiple correlations involving measures of V_L and P_L as predictors with measures of A_L as the criterion generally are around .80 to .90 (Chen & Vellutino, 1997, R = .82, .81, .75; Fletcher et al., 1994, R = .81; Shany & Biemiller, 1995, R = .91). It should also be remembered that all of the above correlations would have been even higher (probably around 1.00) if they had been corrected for the unreliability of the measures involved.

For adults, it appears that all, or almost all, of the variance in A_L can be explained by V_L (or vice-versa). When the correlations are corrected for attenuation they are at least .80 (Anderson & Fairbanks, 1937, corrected r = .87; Gernsbacher, Varner, & Faust, 1990, uncorrected r = .92; Larsen & Feder, 1940, corrected r = .80). Also, with respect to adults who are mostly advanced readers, such as college students, it seems that all V_LWords are also A_LWords (see Figure 10-3), and that is why the correlations between indicants of V_L and A_L are usually very high, around .80 to .90. Whenever the correlations between V_L and A_L have been lower than .80 to .90, there has been evidence from reliability estimates derived from correlating similarly measured variables, that V_L and A_L have been correlated as high as the reliabilities involved would allow (M. D. Jackson, & McClelland, 1979). Furthermore, whenever the mean scores for equivalent measures of V_L and A_L have been compared, these means have been approximately equal (Carver, 1973a, 1982; Hausfeld, 1981); these data further support the equivalency of V_L and A_L for most adults.

The theorized relationships among V_L, P_L, and A_L for beginning, intermediate, and advanced readers are almost perfectly consistent with the correlations that researchers have reported involving indicants of these constructs, for lower graders, middle graders, and adults.

Implications

Educators need to plan instruction in the lower grades to maximize the yearly gain in P_L for typical students. These students generally are below raudamaticity and can comprehend easy textual materials when they are read to them but they cannot comprehend these same materials in printed form, simply because they do not know how to pronounce the printed words.

In the middle grades, instruction should be designed to maximize the amount of gain in both verbal knowledge level and pronunciation knowledge level. The verbal knowledge gained by children in the middle grades, when listening, has a major impact upon their reading achievement. The gain in pronunciation knowledge by many children in the lower grades is also a potent cause of gain in reading achievement. However, when children reach raudamaticity, an increase in P_L is no longer a proximal cause of A_L or a potent cause of reading achievement. Therefore, educators need to estimate when raudamaticity has been reached for each individual so that instruction that is designed to cause growth in P_L can be discontinued and instruction designed to increase both V_L and P_L can begin.

For adults who are at raudamaticity, which includes most students in grade 8 and higher, it is verbal knowledge which needs extra attention from educators because these students have reached raudamaticity; for those students, gain in V_L is synonymous with gain in A_L, whereas gain in P_L does not cause gain in A_L unless it is accompanied by gain in V_L.

Forget Me Nots

The two proximal causes of accuracy level, A_L, are verbal level, V_L, and pronunciation level, P_L. A_L is the average of V_L and P_L. For example, if a student has a listening vocabulary at the sixth-grade level ($V_L = 6$) and can identify words at the fourth-grade level ($P_L = 4$), then this student is likely to have a fifth-grade reading level ($A_L = 5$), because 5 is the average of 6 and 4.

CHAPTER

11

TWO CAUSES OF RATE LEVEL

Because the rate level of an individual is purported to be a very important cause of high and low reading achievement, it is important to determine what can be done to improve R_L. In the causal model, it is theorized that the two proximal causes of improvement in rate level are pronunciation level and cognitive speed level. This means that the two factors that influence gain in R_L during a school year are the gain in P_L and the gain in C_s.

It is a relatively new idea that the rate at which individuals can accurately comprehend while reading can be improved by increasing their P_L or their C_s. In 1990a, Carver reviewed 100 years of research on reading rate and he theorized that there was only one primary factor influencing rate level, R_L, namely C_s. That is, Carver (1990a) never even considered that P_L might be a proximal cause of improvement in R_L, along with C_s.

In this chapter, the theoretical relationships among rate level, pronunciation level, and cognitive speed level will be examined in detail. Empirical evidence that is relevant to the relationships among these theoretical constructs will also be summarized.

Theoretical Relationships

Introduction. In the causal model, pronunciation level and cognitive speed level are the two proximal causes of R_L. Rate level has been hypothesized to be the average of pronunciation level and cognitive speed level, according to Equation 1-3 presented earlier in Chapter 1, or Equation 10-4 presented earlier in Chapter 10.

In order to investigate the above hypothesis, it is necessary to discriminate between an indirect measure of R_L, such as the Rate Level Test, RLT, provides (see Chapter 5), and R_L derived from P_L and C_s. So, R_L derived from measures of P_L and C_s will be symbolized with an attached prime ($R_L{'}$), that is,

$$R_L{'} = \sqrt{P_L C_s}\text{, or} \qquad (11\text{-}1)$$

$$R_L{'} = (P_L + C_s)/2 \qquad (11\text{-}2)$$

Theoretically, an indirect measure of R_L, such as the RLT described earlier, should provide the same result as R_L', derived from either Equation 11-1 or Equation 11-2; that is, we should find that $R_L' = R_L$.

Underlying the functional relationship expressed in the above equations is a more complex theoretical explanation involving raudamatized words. Remember that R_L is rauding rate, R_r, in GE units. Remember also that R_r is the rate at which individuals operate their rauding process, and that individuals normally operate their rauding process on relatively easy material. Relatively easy material contains words that have been raudamatized, that is, words that can be processed at the rauding rate, R_r. In order for individuals to increase their rauding rate, or the rate at which raudamatized words are processed during the execution of the rauding process, they must (a) increase their cognitive speed, which is their fastest speed of naming, or (b) increase their speed of recognizing letter patterns within words, even easy words that have already been overlearned. Their speed of recognizing letter patterns within pseudowords is called "pure decoding speed;" it will be symbolized as d_s when measured in GE units. Pure decoding speed, d_s, could also be considered as a measure of pure cipher speed because tasks involving pseudowords also involve pure cipher knowledge. The R_L construct will be hypothesized as being the average of d_s and C_s, that is,

$$R_L = (d_s + C_s)/2 \qquad (11\text{-}3)$$

If Equation 11-3 is valid, and Equation 10-4 is valid, then it follows that

$$d_s = P_L \qquad (11\text{-}4)$$

The next subsection will expand upon the theory that C_s is a proximal cause of R_L. Then, a subsection will be devoted more explicitly to the theory that P_L is a cause of R_L. Then, there will be a subsection which explains in more detail how d_s is related to P_L and R_L. Because spelling level, S_L, is a major indicant of P_L, a subsection will also be devoted toward the causal connection between S_L and R_L.

Theory about C_s and R_L. The idea that cognitive speed, or some similar thinking speed factor is likely to limit or influence reading rate is not new. As noted earlier in Chapter 8, the idea that some form of thinking rate limits reading rate goes back at least as far as Traxler (1934) who investigated the "speed of association of ideas" as a factor limiting reading rate. That early research relevant to cognitive speed and reading rate, has been described in considerable detail by Carver (1990a). One of the noteworthy studies reviewed by Carver was conducted by Buswell (1951); he hypothesized that "rate of silent reading varies directly with rate of thinking" (p. 339). Buswell also suggested that "the school should accept as satisfactory a slow rate of reading provided it is commensurate with the students' rate of thinking" (p. 339). Much later, Carver (1977) picked up on this same idea of Buswell's when he advanced Hypothesis 4 in his initial presentation of rauding theory; it was that "rauding rate (R_r) is limited by an individual's basic thinking rate" (p. 20). Also in 1977, Biemiller concluded from his research involving maximum oral reading rate for letters and words that "the abilities to quickly identify print and printed words appear to set a limit on how fast a child can read" (p. 245). Later, Ehri and Wilce (1983) considered digit naming speed as a baseline measure of how fast a child could recognize words; thus, Ehri and Wilce seem to be suggesting that an index of C_s be considered as an index of the limit of R_L.

The influence of C_s upon R_L is causal in the sense that the ability to name overlearned letters rapidly represents a basic ability to process language rapidly. Cognitive speed influences the rate at which individuals process words into the thoughts represented by sentences during the rauding process. Or, the fastest speed at which an individual can name randomized lists of letters should be one of the primary factors affecting how fast words can be lexically accessed, semantically encoded, and then integrated into the thoughts of sentences.

Naming words while reading silently (called silent speech or subvocalization) has long been considered an important aspect of the rauding process (see Carver, 1990a). The speed at which this naming can be done with words in sentences that are relatively easy for the individual, $A_L > D_L$, should be influenced by the basic speed at which individuals can transform stimuli into language or words. That is, how fast individuals can think about the names associated with colors or individual letters of the alphabet should have a major impact upon reading rate which involves how fast individuals can think about the names associated with strings of letters. In this regard, Rozin and Gleitman (1977) stated that "... thought is akin to sequential language, so that the speed of thinking is a major determiner of the speed of reading" (p. 65).

C_s is not being theorized as causal for R_L in the sense that Wolf (1991) meant when she noted that slower word recognition processes "... would indirectly impede more sophisticated, higher level processes such as reading comprehension by demanding more time" (p. 134). As has been mentioned before, when the rauding process is operating on relatively easy material, then all the words involved have been overlearned so that the type of causal mechanism hypothesized by Wolf should not be valid. Therefore, C_s is not being advanced as a causal factor in the sense that a slower operating cognitive speed distracts from the accurate comprehension of sentences during the rauding process. Instead, C_s is a proximal cause of R_L only in the sense that the ability to cycle fast through the processes associated with naming overlearned letters influences how fast an individual can cycle through similar processes associated with naming and comprehending overlearned words during the rauding process. C_s influences the rate at which a raudamatized word can be processed during reading. Similarly, pronouncing a word rapidly in a list of raudamatized words, is likely to reach an asymptotic rate after several practice trials or experiences, and this asymptotic rate for a particular individual is purported to be influenced by the individual's cognitive speed level, C_s.

It has been suggested by some researchers that naming speed is causal for verbal ability, that is, C_s is causal for V_L or A_L, but Sternberg and Powell (1983) contended that this was a matter of "dispute." The causal model presented in Chapter 1 does not allow for this type of relationship. Sternberg and Powell go on to say that "it seems likely to us that speed of lexical access plays some role in verbal comprehension, and what remains to be clarified is just what that role is" (p. 879). The causal model has advanced a clarifying answer to the mystery articulated by Sternberg and Powell. Namely, C_s is directly causal for R_L and indirectly causal for E_L. Because E_L is often used as a measure of verbal comprehension, this means that C_s is distally connected to E_L via the causal chain of $C_s \rightarrow R_L \rightarrow E_L$. However, if rate is not substantially involved in verbal comprehension, such as defined by the V_L construct, then there is little or no connection, that is, C_s and V_L are neither proximally nor distally connected in a casual chain. Evidence relative to the low relationship between C_s and V_L comes from partial correlations (controlling for age) between V_L and C_s for the data reviewed by Carver (1997); these correlations were as follows: (a) $r = .24$ for the 52 students in grades 3 through 5 (Study I), and (b) $r = .26$ for the 64 university students (Study III).

Theory about P_L and R_L. The influence of pronunciation level upon rate level is not obvious because P_L is an accuracy construct and R_L is a rate construct. However, the idea that individuals who have learned to make more connections between letter patterns and their corresponding sounds are also able to read faster does seem plausible. In this regard, Manis (1985) stated that "weak knowledge of letter-sound relations hampers progress toward rapid and automatic decoding among severely disabled readers (Ehri, 1980; Ehri & Wilce, 1983; Morrison & Manis, 1982)" (p. 88). Also, Aaron (1991) states that "poorly developed decoding skill, therefore, can impede the reading process by acting as a rate-limiting factor of reading comprehension at all age levels" (p. 179). These interpretations of Aaron (1991) and Manis (1985) are in accordance with the theorized causal influence of P_L upon R_L.

Theory about d_s, P_L, and R_L. This subsection will be devoted to a lengthy theoretical explanation of how P_L affects R_L via P_L affecting pure decoding speed, d_s, a construct introduced earlier. As noted earlier, pure decoding speed, d_s, is the speed at which individuals can recognize the most likely connections between letter patterns within printed pseudowords and their corresponding sounds, for example, the speed at which the letter pattern of "tion" is recognized and associated with the spoken sound of /shun/. Measures of d_s will be described next, and then its connections to previous theory and research in reading will be discussed.

The best indicants of pure decoding speed, d_s, are pseudoword tests that require individuals to pronounce lists of nonwords as fast as possible. Pronounceable nonwords, or pseudowords, that have never been seen before contain various letter combinations that appear in real words, such as bince, kure, and jast. The faster that individuals can accurately pronounce these pseudowords, the faster is their d_s. The faster they can recognize the sounds that are most likely to be associated with the pattern of letters within words, the higher will be their pure decoding speed.

A person who can correctly and quickly pronounce a pseudoword such as "trink" has an ability to rapidly associate a pattern of letters never seen before with a pattern of phonemes. In this regard, Perfetti, Finger, and Hogaboam (1978) have contended that "the persistent differences between skilled and less skilled readers in reaction times to words and pseudowords seem to be due to processes of verbal coding, including processes operating on subword units" (p. 739). Because subword units are what are involved in the construction of pseudowords, d_s is a construct that Perfetti, Finger, and Hogaboam regarded as important about 20 years ago. The speed of recognizing pseudowords was also recognized as important by Stanovich in 1980, as the following lengthy quote attests:

> The ability to rapidly recode print items into a phonological form also appears to be related to reading ..., even among relatively fluent adult readers .... Perhaps it is this relationship that accounts for finding that, for adults as well as children, the speed of naming pronounceable nonwords is one of the tasks that most clearly differentiates good from poor readers .... (p. 62)

The d_s construct seems to be a formal recognition of the above concept that Stanovich described about 20 years ago.

Data providing more direct support for the existence of d_s comes from Carver (1991). Children in grades 2 to 10 were tested using measures of C_s, R_L, and d_s; two factors were found—a cognitive speed factor and a rate level factor—and the C_s factor correlated .37 with the R_L factor. The measure of d_s, called Decoding Rate, loaded near zero on the cognitive speed factor, .06, and it loaded .77 on the rate level factor. This means that d_s is likely to be almost entirely learned or is educatable because it loaded highly on the R_L factor (.77 loading) but lowly on the cognitive speed factor (.06 loading). This result for d_s may be contrasted to the result for measures of R_L, such as (a) the Rate Level Test, RLT, which loaded .85 on the R_L factor and .61 on the C_s factor, (b) Maximum Oral Rate, which loaded .89 on the R_L factor and .43 on the C_s factor, and (c) the rate of naming a randomized list of words (Recognition Rate) which loaded .85 on the R_L factor and .61 on the C_s factor. Notice that all three of the latter indicants of R_L loaded highly on the R_L factor (.84 to .89), as would be expected, and all three also loaded substantially on the C_s factor (.41 to .61), as would also be expected since C_s is a proximal cause of R_L. In the context of these results, it seems to be very revealing that the measure of d_s loaded substantially on the R_L factor, .77, but loaded trivially on the C_s factor, .06. These results suggest that R_L is composed of two parts, one part is lowly related to cognitive speed (namely d_s) and the other part is cognitive speed (namely C_s), as was theorized earlier in the form of Equation 11-3.

The above hypothesized connection between P_L and d_s also seems to be supported by the contentions of Ehri (1994). She noted that "findings also support the idea that readers derive their knowledge of orthographic regularity from their knowledge of different words—perhaps those stored in lexical memory—rather than from exposure rate to words" (p. 342). This statement of Ehri's may be interpreted as indicating support for P_L being an indirect measure of knowledge about orthographic regularity, that is, Ehri seems to be contending that the more words an individual knows how to pronounce, higher P_L, the more orthographic knowledge they have. Increasing P_L should increase knowledge about orthographic regularity, and at the same time increase pure decoding speed. When d_s is increased, then all words can be read faster, even the very easy words that are found on indirect measures of R_L.

The construct of pure decoding speed can also be supported by reference to the theoretical ideas of Seidenberg and McClelland (1989). They contend that when words are read, they are recognized from subword units, or what they call "orthographic triplets" of neighboring letters. That is, each set of neighboring three letters in a word activates similar pronunciations. For example, *beak* activates *bean, bear, leak,* and *steak.* A neighborhood of letters is more readily recognized when the orthographic neighborhood is more activated. That is, they contend that words are recognized quicker and nonwords are pronounced faster when they contain subword units that have been recognized in many different words, many times.

The positive influence of word practice upon speed of word recognition would also be predicted from verbal efficiency theory (Perfetti, 1985). That is, a word that is practiced more will be recognized faster. Yet, if practice on words was the most important factor influencing speed of word recognition, then readers should get faster and faster as they get older from age 6 to age 90 because they will be practicing the same words over and over. Practice has to have a limit or an asymptote. Also, if the practice effect was extremely important as an individual difference factor affecting R_L, then it is not likely that the speed of reading pseudowords, d_s, would be highly related to R_L because each pseudoword is a letter string that has never been seen before, let alone practiced to asymptote. Yet, the rate at which these pseudowords can be read aloud correlates highly with indicants of R_L (r = .81 when corrected for attenuation, Carver, 1991). This fact suggests that it is probably the ability to quickly pronounce triplets of letters embedded in letter-strings that is important, whether the letter-strings form words that have been seen many times before or letter-strings that have never been seen before.

In summary, the theory is that increasing the number of words that can be accurately pronounced (increase P_L), will at the same time provide the individual with many new and different subword letter patterns associated with their corresponding subword sounds. These experiences will in turn increase pure decoding speed, d_s, because the more associations between letter patterns and their corresponding sounds, the faster an individual will be able to correctly pronounce a pseudoword which contains familiar letter patterns—even though the entire letter string has never been seen before. By increasing d_s, an individual will automatically increase rate level, because R_L is composed of d_s and C_s. An increase in implicit subword knowledge connecting letter patterns and sounds will also help to recognize all known real words faster, even relatively easy words that were overlearned years earlier. So, the reason that an accuracy construct such as P_L can have a major causal impact upon a rate construct such as R_L, is because increases in the number of words that can be accurately pronounced also results in an increase in implicit learning about spelling-sound correspondences at the subword level. This increase in d_s automatically causes an increase in rate level because R_L is the average of d_s and C_s (Equation 11-3).

Theory About S_L and R_L. Earlier in Chapter 7, a case was made for pronunciation knowledge level, P_L, and spelling knowledge level, S_L being equal. The ability to spell words correctly and the ability to recognize correct spellings quickly is also crucial for a fast rauding rate level, R_L.

This theoretical connection between orthographic knowledge and speed of word recognition has long been recognized by researchers. For example, Ehri (1980, 1985, 1987, 1991), and Reitsma (1989) have contended that quick recognition of a known word comes from accurate orthographic representation of the word in memory, that is, a knowledge of how the word is spelled. Recently, Share and Stanovich (1995) have articulated this theory as follows:

> ... accurate decoding leads to the complete phonological representation of a word becoming associated with its visual form. Such positive learning trials lead to the amalgamation of orthographic and phonological representations in memory ..., and the amalgamated orthographic representation is what eventually enables rapid and efficient processes of direct access to the lexicon. (p. 12)

Because P_L is highly associated with spelling knowledge, $P_L = S_L$ (see Chapter 7), this association helps to account for why the data support P_L being a causal factor for rauding rate level, R_L. Those individuals who can spell a larger population of words have at the same time learned to pronounce correctly a larger population of words, many of which are unknown in meaning, c_kWords. And, it is probably not possible to learn to pronounce a larger population of words without at the same time learning to spell a large population correctly, so that $S_L = P_L$.

It seems reasonable to hypothesize that there is a limit or asymptote for S_L or P_L affecting rauding rate, or R_L, and this limit occurs whenever individuals reach $S_L = 8$ or $P_L = 8$. (Note: According to Carver, 1997, this relationship was only expected to hold, up until P_L reached about grade level seven.) In the causal model presented in Chapter 1, P_L is hypothesized as a proximal cause of R_L up until $P_L = 8.0$, which is the P_L criterion for an advanced reader.

In summary, increasing S_L simultaneously increases P_L. This increase in the knowledge of letter patterns within words and their corresponding sounds when pronounced, causes an increase in d_s, which is the speed at which letter patterns can be quickly pronounced in pseudowords as well as all raudamatized words. This increase in d_s, due to an increase in spelling and pronunciation knowledge, in turn causes an increase in rauding rate level, because one component part of R_L is d_s.

Summary of Theory

From the causal model, it is being theorized that pronunciation level and cognitive speed level are the two proximal causes of rate level, according to Equation 1-3, or Equation 10-4. However, this relatively simple causal connection is complicated in several ways. First, spelling level, S_L, is an indirect measure of P_L, and is also a proximal cause of R_L. Second, there is assumed to be a causal relationship between P_L and pure decoding speed, d_s, such that $P_L = d_s$. Pure decoding speed, d_s, can be directly measured by how fast pseudowords can be pronounced; it seems to be influenced by how many intraword spelling patterns have been associated with sounds, such as the connections formed between sounds and triplets of letters as theorized by Seidenberg and McClelland (1989). Learning to spell and pronounce more words accurately out of context (an increase in S_L or P_L), will automatically mean more cipher knowledge such that pseudowords are pronounced more quickly (an increase in d_s). An increase in P_L will likely result in pseudowords being pronounced faster because an increase in P_L automatically means that more connections have been learned between patterns of letters within words; this increase in cipher knowledge automatically means that the sounds that go with these patterns will be recognized more quickly even when they are embedded within pseudowords. When d_s is increased, there will be an automatic increase in R_L because d_s is one of the component parts of R_L. Therefore, when it is theorized that P_L is a proximal cause of R_L, it should be recognized that this is somewhat of an oversimplification because it is hypothesized that an increase in P_L causes an increase in d_s

($P_L = d_s$), which automatically causes an increase in R_L because d_s is one part of R_L, according to Equation 11-3.

Summary of Evidence

In grade 2, indicants of P_L and C_s can predict indicants of R_L with a multiple *R* of .64 (from Bowers & Swanson, 1991) and a multiple *R* of .85 (from Bowers, 1993). These values of multiple R would undoubtedly increase considerably if they were corrected for the unreliability of the measures involved.

In the middle grades, it is known that (a) measures of P_L correlate substantially with measures of R_L (Barker, Torgesen & Wagner, 1992, $r = .67$; Biemiller, 1977, *r*'s from .55 to .92; Carver, 1997, $r = .58$; Shany & Biemiller, 1995, $r = .57$), (b) indicants of C_s correlate substantially with measures of R_L (Carver, 1997, $r = .60$; Shany & Biemiller, 1995, $r = .42$) and (c) indicants of P_L and C_s in combination are highly predictive of measures of R_L (Carver, 1997, $R = .66$; Shany & Biemiller, 1995, $R = .62$). These multiple *Rs* predicting R_L from P_L and C_s are probably about as high as the reliability of the measures involved would allow.

Also in the middle grades, indicants of pure decoding speed, d_s, have been found to correlate highly with indicants of R_L (Stanovich, Cunningham, & Feeman, 1984; $r = .70$ for grade 3 and $r = .85$ for grade 5). Furthermore, Carver (1991) administered measures of d_s, C_s, and R_L, and when all of the variables are corrected for attenuation, then d_s and C_s predict R_L with a multiple *R* of .97. These data from middle graders are highly consistent with Equation 11-3 which holds that R_L is the average of d_s and C_s.

A search of the relevant literature has resulted in the finding that measures of P_L and C_s each generally correlate higher with a measure of R_L than they correlate with each other (from Bowers, 1993; Bowers & Swanson, 1991; Carver, 1997; Shany & Biemiller, 1995). This pattern of correlations mitigates against C_s being causal for P_L or for P_L being causal for C_s.

For adults, it has been found that (a) spelling measures of P_L correlate substantially with measures of R_L (Holmes, 1954, $r = .47$ & $r = .50$), (b) measures of C_s correlate substantially with measures of R_L (Carver, 1997, $r = .67$), and (c) a C_s factor correlates substantially with an R_L factor (Carver, 1991, $r = .44$). Again, these correlations supporting P_L and C_s being causal for R_L would likely be much higher if corrected for the unreliability of the measures involved.

In summary, it appears likely that almost all of the reliable variance in how fast individuals can read relatively easy text, or how fast they can raud, R_L, can be explained or predicted, by (a) P_L and C_s in combination, (b) S_L and C_s in combination, or (c) d_s and C_s in combination. These data are consistent with the theory that (a) $S_L = P_L$, (b) $d_s = P_L$, and (c) P_L and C_s are the two proximal causes of R_L, according to the causal model.

Implications

Educators need to stop regarding spelling improvement primarily as a means to better writing, and start regarding spelling improvement as primarily a means to faster reading of known words. The accurate spelling of known words, and the rapid recognition of the correct spellings of these words, are ways to increase pronunciation knowledge, pure decoding speed, and rate level.

For beginning readers, invented spelling should be regarded as a good way for children to begin to associate letters with sounds. However, being able to spell words *correctly* will increase P_L, which is a proximal cause of R_L. Stated differently, inaccurate spelling of known words is likely to be a cause of low reading rate for many lower and middle graders.

Forget Me Nots

The two proximal causes of rate level, R_L, are pronunciation level, P_L, and cognitive speed level, C_s. R_L is the average of P_L and C_s. For example, if a student can identify words at the sixth-grade level ($P_L = 6$) and can rapidly name randomized letters at the fourth-grade level ($C_s = 4$), then this student is likely to have a normal reading rate around the fifth-grade level ($R_L = 5$), because 5 is the average of 6 and 4.

CHAPTER

12

TWO CAUSES OF VERBAL LEVEL

From the standpoint of education, this chapter and the one that follows are the two most important chapters in this book. These two chapters contain the theory relevant to the things that educators can do to improve instruction and learning, that is, teaching/learning relevant to verbal level is one root cause of high and low reading achievement. More specifically, this particular chapter will present the case that one of the main ways that educators can improve reading achievement is to increase the verbal knowledge of students.

It should come as no surprise that when educators are able to get students to listen to them as they tell them the things that they want them to know, they are having a major impact upon reading achievement. However, this increase in verbal knowledge due to teaching is also influenced by the aptitude of the students for learning and remembering what they have been told or taught.

In the causal model, the two factors at Echelon 4 that are purported to be causal with respect to verbal level are teaching/learning, T/L, and verbal knowledge aptitude, g_v; these two factors will be discussed in turn, and a short summary of evidence will also be presented.

Teaching/Learning

Introduction. In 1968, Carroll contended that most of education involves "learning from being told," either orally or in print. Similarly, the teaching/learning factor in the causal model primarily involves telling students the things that we want them to know. This telling involves language, ordinarily in the form of sentences. Carroll concluded that "What happens when a mature language user comprehends a single sentence, or fails to comprehend it, is the central problem in the analysis of learning from being told..." (p. 6). The following lengthy quotation from Carroll (1968) captures the conceptual nature of the teaching/learning factor as a major cause of improvement in verbal knowledge level, V_L:

> Traditional instruction characteristically uses the lecture method, along with plentiful reading assignments. Even in more 'progressive' educational settings which avoid the lectuıe method, much of the teacher's activity consists of asking questions and importing information verbally. To be sure, verbal instruction is often accompanied

> with supplemental aids—diagrams on the blackboard, charts, pictures, film strips, motion pictures, demonstration field trips, and the like. But language still functions in many of these. A picture without a caption is usually meaningless, and most educational films would be unintelligible without sound track or titles. It seems obvious that meaningful verbal discourse is the primary tool of teaching. We expect our students to learn most things by being told about them. (p. 1)

So, if we want the verbal level of students to improve at least one GE during a year of school, we had better tell them the things that are appropriate for them to know during the year, in a manner that they are likely to learn and also remember at the end of the year.

A review of techniques relevant to teaching and learning appropriate for increasing verbal knowledge is beyond the scope of this book. However, in Chapters 22 and 23 of this book, two approaches to reading instruction are reviewed in some detail, and their impact upon V_L is delineated. In the next subsection, the effect of teaching and learning vocabulary words will be addressed, because a primary indicant of V_L is a listening vocabulary test. Then, a brief subsection will be devoted to the measurement of the T/L factor.

Teaching Vocabulary. The decision about whether or not vocabulary words should be taught is inextricably tied to the complex relationship between vocabulary knowledge and reading comprehension (Nagy, 1988; Stahl, 1991; Stahl & Fairbanks, 1986). These complexities were tackled admirably by Anderson and Freebody in 1981; their ideas will be reviewed next and examined for relevance to the causal model. Then, some supplemental ideas advanced by Mezynski (1983) will be examined. Toward the end of this section, the general notion of vocabulary instruction will be discussed.

Anderson and Freebody (1981) said that the number of word meanings a reader knows "... enables a remarkably accurate prediction of this individual's ability to comprehend discourse" (p. 77). They asked *why* this was true, and then they reviewed three explanations—the instrumentalist hypothesis, the verbal aptitude hypothesis, and the knowledge hypothesis. Each of these hypotheses will be explained in more detail, and then evaluated in terms of the role of vocabulary knowledge in the causal model.

The instrumentalist hypothesis of Anderson and Freebody is that "individuals who score high on a vocabulary test are likely to know more of the words in most texts they encounter than low scoring individuals" (p. 80). Advocates of this hypothesis supposedly do not care much about "where vocabulary knowledge comes from but only that, once possessed, it helps the reader understand text" (p. 81). That is, knowing more words enables more text to be comprehended. It is obvious that this instrumentalist hypothesis is highly compatible with the causal model because A_L is directly influenced by V_L via the average of V_L and P_L (see Chapter 10). The equation for determining accuracy level, A_L, from V_L and P_L is instrumentalist in that the level of listening vocabulary, or verbal knowledge, V_L, has a mathematically precise effect upon A_L. The instrumentalist hypothesis can be translated into the causal model via the following causal connections: $\rightarrow V_L \rightarrow A_L \rightarrow A_r$. Increasing the number of words known when listening (higher V_L) has a causal impact upon rauding accuracy level (higher A_L) via Equation 1-2, or Equation 10-3, and an increase in A_L will result in higher accuracy of sentence comprehension when reading text once (higher A_r) via Equation 2-2. For those students at raudamaticity, including advanced readers, V_L and A_L become synonymous, so knowing more words (higher V_L and higher A_L) will result in higher accuracy of text comprehension during reading (higher A_r). Therefore, the causal model is highly compatible with their instrumentalist hypothesis.

The second hypothesis advanced by Anderson and Freebody was the verbal aptitude hypothesis, that is, "a person who scores high on such a test has a quick mind" (p. 81), and "with the same amount of exposure to the culture, this individual (with a quick mind) has learned more word meanings" (p. 81). Anderson and Freebody go on to claim that "... persons with large vocabularies are better at discourse comprehension because they possess superior mental agility" (p. 81). Part of this verbal aptitude hypothesis is compatible with the causal model and part is not. The part of the aptitude hypothesis which suggests a close connection between verbal aptitude and words known, is highly compatible with the causal connection between g_v and V_L in the causal model. That is, high g_v means high verbal knowledge aptitude in the form of the ability to learn verbal information, which is somewhat similar to the "quick mind" idea of Anderson and Freebody. However, the part of this aptitude hypothesis which suggests that higher verbal aptitude (higher g_v) causes higher text comprehension during a reading process (higher A_r) is not compatible with the causal model. A higher g_v is not a proximal cause of a superior processing ability. High g_v is a distal cause of rauding accuracy, A_r; high A_r can also be caused by high T/L at Echelon 4, high P_L at Echelon 3, and low D_L (see Equation 2-2).

The superior processing aspect of their verbal aptitude hypothesis is completely incompatible with rauding theory and the causal model. The rauding process is constant and equivalent across individuals in that all individuals are able to operate successfully the components of the rauding process—lexicon access, semantically encode, and sententially integrate—when the text is relatively easy for them, $A_L > D_L$. The operation of the rauding process is not directly affected by higher or lower g_v because low g_v individuals can operate their rauding process just as successfully as high g_v individuals. It is true that verbal knowledge aptitude, g_v, is a proximal cause of V_L, but it is not a proximal cause of A_L or A_r, as has been suggested by their verbal aptitude hypothesis.

The knowledge hypothesis advanced by Anderson and Freebody is that the person who knows more word meanings "has deeper and broader knowledge of the culture" (p. 81) and "it is this knowledge that is crucial for text understanding" (p. 81). This knowledge hypothesis translates very well into the causal model, as long as a slight twist is applied that acknowledges a distinction between listening vocabulary and reading vocabulary. It is listening vocabulary, V_L, that reflects the knowledge of the culture and its effect upon reading via accuracy level, A_L, is tempered by pronunciation level, P_L, for most lower graders and most middle graders via Equation 1-2, or Equation 10-3. Higher V_L reflects higher knowledge, that is, greater general knowledge or greater knowledge of the culture, and it is the amount of this knowledge which is usable in printed form, via A_L, that eventually impacts accuracy of text comprehension during reading, A_r. So, teaching students the meaning of new words has no long-term effect unless these words are more fully integrated into what a person knows generally, and then this learning will have a diluted impact upon A_L because P_L is another factor which influences A_L.

The above three hypotheses advanced by Anderson and Freebody (1981) have been elaborated upon and extended by Mezynski (1983). She added a fourth hypothesis, called the access hypothesis, which includes the "... skills involved in accessing word meanings and in using these meanings efficiently in text processing" (p. 254). She goes on to say that "the instructional implication of this perspective is that the amount of practice is a crucial variable in word acquisitions; instructed words must become part of the students repertoire to be useful in reading" (p. 254). She says that proponents of the access hypothesis regard the "automaticity" of word knowledge to be highly important. This hypothesis seems to imply that learning the meaning of words does not necessarily have a major impact upon comprehension, unless the words can be quickly accessed without diverting much attention to the words. So, the access hypothesis seems to embrace the general idea advanced by LaBerge and Samuels (1974), reviewed first in Chapter 4, that words must be automatized, otherwise the accuracy of comprehension will be lower due to the siphoning off of attention to word recognition when it is needed for comprehension. Still, the main intent of Mezynski seems to be a concern for the speed at which words can be processed.

This access hypothesis has an indirect connection to the causal model. In rauding theory, when a typical student in grade 5, for example, is given a relatively easy passage to read, e.g., $A_L = 5$ and $D_L = 3$, then it is assumed that *all* the words are raudamatized, that is, the passage can be read with high accuracy at the individual's rauding rate, R_r, so that diverted attention cannot be a factor affecting comprehension. When the same individual is given a relatively hard passage to read, e.g., $D_L = 7$, then the major factor limiting the accuracy of comprehension is not lack of attention, per se, but lack of relevant background knowledge and unknown vocabulary. In this regard, the research of Fleisher, Jenkins, and Pany (1979) demonstrated that automaticity of recognizing words in a passage is not a major factor limiting comprehension when the difficulty level of the passage is higher than the ability level of the individual, $D_L > A_L$.

After introducing this access hypothesis, along with the three advanced by Anderson and Freebody (1981), Mezynski (1983) goes on to give the implication of each hypothesis for teaching vocabulary. She says that "the instrumentalist hypothesis suggests that what is important is the number of words taught, the access hypothesis stresses practice as the crucial factor, and the knowledge hypothesis focuses on teaching words that are semantically related" (p. 255). With respect to the verbal aptitude hypothesis, she claims that it "contributes little from an instructional viewpoint" (p. 255).

The above assertions by Mezynski, about the teaching of vocabulary will be critiqued from the standpoint of the causal model and rauding theory. With respect to the instrumentalist hypothesis, it does seem important that many words be taught because learning more new words when listening increases V_L which will have a causal impact upon A_L and reading achievement, or E_L. With respect to the access hypothesis, it does seem important to practice pronounceamatized words that are audamatized words until they are quickly recognized, because this is what it takes to produce raudamatized words; more raudamatized words means an increase in A_L, as well as R_L and E_L. With respect to the knowledge hypothesis, it seems likely that teaching the meaning of new words in the context of new knowledge would increase V_L; however, it seems reasonable to question whether such a strategy is the most efficient one because teaching the meaning of many words by giving their definitions and an example of usage in a sentence may be sufficient to stimulate the integration of new words into knowledge (see Chapter 23). With respect to the verbal aptitude hypothesis, it has already been noted that it is most relevant to g_v, which helps or hinders teaching and learning designed to improve V_L.

After Mezynski reviewed the above four hypotheses and evaluated eight studies which investigated the effects of vocabulary training on reading comprehension, she then concluded that "students can often improve their performance on vocabulary tests, yet fail to improve on comprehension tests" (p. 275, 176). It will be helpful now to determine whether the above conclusion drawn by Mezynski is correct, that is, listening vocabulary, V_L, can be increased without rauding accuracy, A_r, increasing. Let us consider a hypothetical example given in terms of the causal model and rauding theory. Suppose we have two students at the beginning of grade 5 who are equal with respect to their scores on all the variables in the causal model. Both Student A and Student B have $V_L = 5.0$, $P_L = 3.0$, and $A_L = 3.9$. Both students are given the same fifth-grade level passage to read ($D_L = 5.0$). From Equation 2-2, we find that the accuracy of comprehension of this passage would be 60% for both students when it is read once at their rauding rate ($A_r = .60$). Suppose that during the fifth-grade year of school we give extensive oral vocabulary training to Student A, but Student B is given no special treatment. Let us assume that this oral vocabulary training is extremely effective so that by the beginning of grade 6, Student A has gained 3.0 GE units in verbal knowledge level ($V_L = 8.0$), whereas Student

B has gained 1.0 GE without any special instruction ($V_L = 6.0$). Let us also assume that both gained 1.0 GE in P_L so that $P_L = 4.0$ for both students at the beginning of sixth grade.

In the above example, it is possible to determine the accuracy level of each student at the beginning of grade 6 using Equation 1-2; Student A has $A_L = 5.7$, and Student B has $A_L = 4.9$. Now, the accuracy of text comprehension can be calculated for these two students when they read another passage at $D_L = 5$, as was done earlier at the beginning of grade 5. From Equation 2-2, Student A has 67% comprehension and Student B has 64% comprehension. Notice that Student A gained 3.0 GE units in vocabulary (from $V_L = 5.0$ to $V_L = 8.0$) whereas Student B gained only 1.0 GE (from $V_L = 5.0$ to $V_L = 6.0$), yet this big difference in their gain in V_L (3.0 vs. 1.0) only resulted in a 3% advantage in comprehension for Student A compared to Student B (67% vs. 64%). This hypothetical example illustrates why it makes sense for Mezynski to conclude from previously collected empirical data that increasing vocabulary level, V_L, has little or no effect upon reading comprehension. Even a large 2.0 GE advantage in V_L (6.0 vs. 4.0) only led to a 3% advantage in accuracy of text comprehension. Yet, it would be a mistake to conclude that the large 3.0 gain in V_L for Student A was a waste of time. This advantage of 3% means that Student A will almost always be comprehending slightly more than Student B. Furthermore, for students above the eighth grade level, most new knowledge will be obtained via reading so the advantage of Student A over Student B will be compounded over many, many hours of reading over years of time.

The above example also illustrates that gain in vocabulary, or V_L, is only part of the story when it comes to gain in accuracy level, A_L. In the example above, both students were equivalent in P_L and this drastically diluted the large gain in V_L for Student A. Even though Student A gained 3.0 in GE units in V_L and Student B only gained 1.0 GE units, Student A only enjoyed a 0.8 GE advantage in accuracy level by the start of sixth grade (5.7 vs. 4.9). This means that major improvements in V_L, or vocabulary knowledge, will be diluted by normal improvements in P_L when the final reading level is reached. Then, the small difference in percentage of comprehension when reading a passage (such as 67% vs. 64%) will be hard for an experimental study to discern without a very large sample size that makes the standard error of the means extremely small.

Measurement. At present there are no recommended techniques for measuring the teaching/learning factor, which is causal for V_L. Such a scale could be developed. At the top of the scale would be students who have attended schools where the best-known teaching and learning is taking place, and at the bottom would be students who have attended schools where the worst-known teaching and learning is taking place.

Although no standardized measure of T/L (for V_L) exists at present, it does seem reasonable to make inferences and assumptions about the quality and quantity of T/L from V_L and g_v. For example, students who have a very low V_L for their age but have a high g_v probably have had poor teaching and learning experiences.

Verbal Knowledge Aptitude

Introduction. In this section, the construct of verbal knowledge aptitude will be described in more detail. Then, measures of the construct will be considered, from a theoretical standpoint. Finally, empirical indicants of g_v will be described.

The Construct. There are large individual differences in what students can learn from what they are told. This aptitude for being able to learn verbal knowledge is called verbal knowledge aptitude, g_v, the other factor in Echelon 4 that is causal with respect to V_L. The g_v construct has been advanced to explain individual differences in gain in V_L for individuals at the same age when instruction designed to increase V_L is equal in quality and quantity.

Those individuals who are able to read several paragraphs and then repeat them almost verbatim probably have exceptionally high g_v, and may be labeled by others as having a photographic memory. Stated differently, using more common parlance, the low g_v individuals at a particular age are the ones you have to tell five times before you can be sure they have learned it well enough to remember it later, whereas the high g_v people are the ones you only have to tell once because they are able to learn verbal knowledge relatively quickly and remember it later.

The formal distinction between verbal knowledge level, V_L, and verbal knowledge aptitude, g_v, is a very important one. Students at the same age with low and high g_v still can achieve equally in V_L when the low-aptitude student receives extremely good instruction and the high-aptitude student receives extremely poor instruction. For example, it seems quite possible for a low g_v student in grade 4 to have $V_L = 4$ and a high g_v student in grade 4 also to have $V_L = 4$. This situation is likely to occur when the low g_v student has attended an excellent school system and comes from a family that encourages learning at home whereas the high g_v student has attended a school system that was chaotic and ineffective and comes from a family that did not encourage learning at home.

Measurement Theory. The theory underlying the measurement of verbal knowledge aptitude, g_v, will be divided into direct measures, indicants, and indirect measures.

Direct measures of g_v would involve tasks which discriminate among individuals with respect to their ability to learn and remember verbal knowledge in the form of words that have been presented auditorily more than a few seconds earlier. For example, one direct measure of g_v could require that individuals learn paired associations between (a) visual stimuli, such as objects or symbols, and (b) spoken responses, such as words. The words should be presented more than a few seconds earlier so that g_v is less dependent on short-term memory and more dependent on working memory capacity. The words should be relatively easy so as to provide a measure that is not readily amenable to improvement, or gain, due to educational intervention or instruction. A direct measure would also be in the form of stanines, or standard scores, that are based on age norms. At present, there are no standardized tests available that have been designed to provide a direct measure of g_v.

Indicants of g_v would include all tests measuring individual differences in learning and remembering words in auditorily presented material, as long as the measure is not likely to be amenable to gain due to instruction, or educational treatment. Indicants of g_v would include verbal aptitude tests, such as listening vocabulary tests that are designed to discriminate among individuals. For example, standardized listening vocabulary tests that are designed to measure intelligence are likely to be indicants of g_v, such as the vocabulary section of the Stanford-Binet, the vocabulary section of the Wechsler Intelligence Test for Children, and the Peabody Picture Vocabulary Test. These listening tests of verbal ability are likely to correlate highly with direct measures of g_v; these vocabulary intelligence tests are likely to correlate higher with g_v than V_L because of their focus upon maximizing individual differences and minimizing the effects of environment or education.

Indirect measures of g_v would be indicants that were scaled into stanines, or standard scores, based on age norms.

The distinction between aptitude measures, such as g_v, and achievement measures, such as V_L, is often difficult to make in practice. The main difference involves the purpose of the measure and how that purpose affects test construction. Indicants of verbal knowledge level, V_L, should have been designed to reflect varying amounts of achievement due to instruction or learning without trying to maximize the degree to which individuals differ from each other, as was the design for the Auding Accuracy Level Test, AALT, described in Chapter 6. Stated differently, a measure of V_L should be developed edumetrically (Carver, 1974), so that items are not thrown out during test development just because they did not discriminate highly between individuals. In contrast, indicants of g_v should be developed psychometrically so they discriminate highly between individuals at a particular age. Carver (1974) has given examples of how item selection techniques can tip the measure more toward achievement (edumetric) or aptitude (psychometric).

Using the above distinctions, standardized vocabulary tests that are designed to measure intelligence may be reasonably assumed to be indicants of g_v, whereas standardized vocabulary tests that are designed to measure achievement may be reasonably assumed to be good indicants of V_L. Again, empirical evidence would always be required when trying to adjudicate whether one of these hybrid measures was a better measure of g_v or V_L.

Relevant Tests. A good measure of g_v for beginning and intermediate readers would likely come from scores on the Visual-Auditory Learning subtest of the Woodcock Reading Mastery Test-Revised; it involves visual-verbal paired-associate learning of the names of ideographs.

A similar example of an indicant of g_v would come from the Memory for Names test which is part of the Woodcock-Johnson Psycho-Educational Battery-Revised (WJ-R). This test (Woodcock & Johnson, 1989) is described as measuring long-term retrieval. It requires individuals to learn and remember the names of previously introduced space creatures. Because this test requires that individuals remember the paired associations between symbols and their names, it should be an indicant of g_v.

A good test for measuring g_v in advanced readers is likely to be the reading-span test developed by Daneman and Carpenter (1980); they claim that their test measures working memory capacity. In advanced readers, remember that $V_L = A_L$ (see also Chapter 17), so reading measures and auding measures should give equal results. They had students read aloud a series of unrelated sentences and then they asked them to recall the last word in each sentence. From their instructions and descriptions, it can be surmised that their college students were being asked to learn and remember words that they read over 25 seconds earlier, which is a far longer length of time than most short-term memory research, either primary memory (inactive) or working memory (active)—as discussed more fully later in Chapter 20. Thus, their reading-span task seems to be measuring how well individuals can learn and remember words read earlier. It seems reasonable that the reading-span task they used would provide a measure of g_v for college students, because there should be little or no difference between measuring g_v with a reading task versus an auding task, as long as the sentences were relatively easy for the advanced readers. So, when Just and Carpenter (1992) comment that "the ability to answer a factual question about a passage correlates between .7 and .9 with reading span in various studies" (p. 123), this remark could be alternately interpreted as follows: an indicant of g_v correlated .7 to .9 with an indicant of A_L. With college students who have equivalent levels of reading and auding ($A_L = V_L$), this reading-span task would be considered an indicant of verbal knowledge aptitude, g_v, and the measure of reading they used would be considered an indicant of A_L, or V_L for advanced readers. Therefore, it seems likely that the reason they found such a high correlation was because g_v is a proximal cause of A_L in advanced readers.

Summary of Theory

The two purported causes of high and low verbal knowledge, V_L, are (a) teaching and learning experiences, T/L, and (b) verbal knowledge aptitude, g_v. Better teaching and learning experiences with respect to increasing verbal knowledge, will cause higher V_L. Furthermore, a higher aptitude for learning what was taught—higher g_v—will also cause higher V_L.

Verbal knowledge level, V_L, is also inextricably tied to the number of words known auditorily, V_LWords. Increasing the number of words known when listening will automatically increase V_L, and increasing V_L will automatically be associated with knowing more words when listening. Better teaching and learning with respect to verbal knowledge, or listening vocabulary, will increase V_L more, and therefore increase A_L more, and therefore increase reading achievement, or E_L. Stated differently, a root cause of low reading achievement, or low E_L, is poor teaching and learning experiences with respect to increasing verbal knowledge, or increasing listening vocabulary, via the causal chain of low V_L causes low A_L (see Chapter 10), and low A_L causes low E_L (see Chapter 9).

Verbal knowledge level, V_L, is also importantly affected by verbal knowledge aptitude, g_v, which is the aptitude for learning verbal information. This means that another root cause of low reading achievement, or low E_L, is a low verbal knowledge aptitude, or low g_v, via the causal chain of low g_v causes low V_L, low V_L causes low A_L, and low A_L causes low E_L.

Teaching students the meaning of more words auditorily, will also increase the accuracy of reading comprehension via the causal chain of T/L $\rightarrow V_L \rightarrow A_L \rightarrow A_r$. This theory is compatible with the three hypotheses of Anderson and Freebody (1981)—the instrumentalist hypothesis, the verbal aptitude hypothesis, and the knowledge hypothesis.

Summary of Evidence

Traditional verbal aptitude tests or traditional verbal intelligence tests (indicants of g_v) correlate highly with indicants of V_L (A. E. Cunningham & Stanovich, 1991, $r = .66$; Stancvich, Cunningham, & Feeman, 1984, $r = .65$). A reading-span test is purported to be a measure of g_v for advanced readers, and it has been found to correlate highly (.70 to .90) with an indicant of V_L, or A_L (Just & Carpenter, 1992).

In 1986, Stahl and Fairbanks conducted a meta-analysis of the effects of vocabulary instruction. They found that "vocabulary instruction does appear to have a significant effect on the comprehension of passages containing taught words" (p. 100), with a large effect size (ES = .97), on the average. Earlier it was noted in an example, that a larger increase in vocabulary (2 GE units) would only result in a 3% increase accuracy of comprehension, but this would be (a) for texts at a particular grade level, not texts that had the taught vocabulary in them, and (b) for listening vocabulary not reading vocabulary. With respect to the effect of vocabulary instruction on a standardized measure of vocabulary, Stahl and Fairbanks reported an ES value of .30, which is medium in size. Notice that this result could be interpreted as the effect of T/L at Echelon 4 upon A_L at Echelon 2, so it is not surprising that this distal effect was medium in size. With respect to the effect of giving definitions, emphasizing context, or a mixture of these two emphases, they found that "the methods that did appear to produce the highest effects on comprehension and vocabulary measures were methods that included both definitional and contextual information about each to-be-learned word (or 'mixed' methods)" (p. 101). These researchers concluded from this analysis of over 200 effect size measures that "the effects of vocabulary instruction are subtle and complex, but, given their potential effects on comprehension, they are worthy of further investigation" (p. 104). Translated into the constructs of the causal model, these findings of Stahl and Fairbanks seem to provide support for vocabulary instruction being effective as a T/L factor which increases V_L, A_L, and E_L.

Implications

Helping students learn the meaning of new words when listening is an excellent way to improve V_L. However, listening vocabulary instruction should not start until a student has reached raudamaticity—all audamatized words have been raudamatized. After students have learned to recognize in print all the words they know auditorily, then V_L, P_L, and A_L should be increased simultaneously by (a) learning the meaning of new words, (b) learning to spell these new words accurately, and (c) learning to recognize their correct spellings quickly. This strategy should be most effective in increasing A_L and R_L, and therefore should increase both A_r and E_L the most during a fixed length of instructional time. This strategy does not increase verbal aptitude, or g_v, and it does not cause an improvement in how the rauding process operates, but it does recognize that individual differences in g_v do influence how much is learned by teaching that is directed toward improving V_L. This strategy also recognizes that accessing the meaning of words quickly is an important aspect of the rauding process.

Forget Me Nots

The two proximal causes of verbal level, V_L, are teaching and learning, T/L, and verbal knowledge aptitude, g_v. That is, the amount of verbal knowledge individuals have depends upon (a) the quality and quantity of instruction directed toward their increasing verbal knowledge, and (b) their aptitude or ability to learn and remember verbal information.

CHAPTER

13

TWO CAUSES OF PRONUNCIATION LEVEL

This is the most important chapter in the entire book from the standpoint of reading educators. This chapter describes the two proximal causes of the part of reading achievement that is unique to reading, namely, pronunciation knowledge level, P_L. The preceding chapter was very important to educators in general because it dealt with improving verbal knowledge. But, the core of reading achievement for most beginning readers and many intermediate readers is their ability to transform printed language symbols into their spoken counterparts so that they can comprehend printed words as effectively as they can comprehend spoken words. Increasing P_L is the most effective way to increase reading achievement in those students who are below raudamaticity; a low P_L causes low reading achievement in two ways—via low A_L and via low R_L.

In the causal model, the two factors at Echelon 4 which are purported to be proximal causes of pronunciation level, P_L, are teaching/learning, T/L, and pronunciation aptitude, g_p. These two primary causal factors are sometimes discussed under other labels. For example, Vellutino (1979) has talked about an "experiential" factor (teaching/learning) and a "constitutional" factor (pronunciation aptitude). Similarly, Berninger and Abbott (1994) discussed a "treatment" factor (teaching/learning) and a "genetic" factor (pronunciation aptitude). The causality of both the teaching/learning factor and pronunciation aptitude factor on pronunciation level, P_L, was summarized by Neisser (1983) when he said the following:

> Some people need more teaching than others do. Even with a lot of teaching they may not reach the same level. (p. 62)

This chapter is mainly consistent with conventional wisdom about how to improve the ability of students to correctly identify words. However, it contains some unexpected interpretations. For example, in the causal model presented in Chapter 1, T/L and g_p are the two proximal causes of P_L and there are no distal causes presented, yet, a case will be made for P_L also having a distal cause. Another example of an unexpected interpretation involves phonological awareness (PA), that is, PA is interpreted as being of relatively minor importance with respect to causing high and low reading achievement.

The remainder of this chapter will expand upon the theory advanced in Chapter 1 and present data relevant to the two proximal causes of P_L that are located in Echelon 4—the teaching and learning factor, and pronunciation aptitude, g_p. Then, a special section will be devoted to the distal cause of P_L, noted above. Relevant empirical evidence will also be summarized.

Teaching/Learning

Introduction. The subsection which follows expands upon the teaching and learning relevant to increasing pronunciation knowledge level, P_L. Following that, there will be a subsection on the teaching of spelling. Finally, a lengthy subsection will be devoted to the influence of phonological awareness on P_L.

Teaching Pronunciation. The greatest gain each school year in pronunciation level is likely to come from teaching and learning which takes into account whether a student is below raudamaticity (A_LWords < V_LWords), or at raudamaticity (A_LWords = V_LWords). Remember that (a) P_L is P_LWords expressed in GE units, and (b) P_LWords are equal to A_LWords plus c_kWords (see Chapter 7). Those students who are below raudamaticity should receive reading instruction that focuses mainly upon increasing P_L during the school year, i.e., code-emphasis instruction that helps students increase (a) their pure lexical knowledge, A_LWords, and (b) their pure cipher knowledge, c_kWords. Those students who are at raudamaticity should receive instruction designed to increase V_L, P_L, and A_L, simultaneously (meaning-emphasis along with code-emphasis instruction, and an emphasis on raudamatizing words).

Almost all beginning readers will be below raudamaticity, and they will need to learn about phonemes in spoken words very early (Juel, Griffith, & Gough, 1986). They will also need to learn the names of the letters of the alphabet very early (Adams, 1990; Venezky, 1975). The teaching of reading should begin with helping students learn that there are correspondences between the letters in printed words and the sounds in spoken words; this is called the alphabetic principle (Rozin & Gleitman, 1977).

Beginning readers are likely to gain the most in P_L during a year of schooling if instruction is directed toward (a) increasing cipher knowledge, and (b) learning to pronounce and spell high-frequency words (Foorman, Francis, Novy, & Liberman 1991). Those students who do not know that spoken words have parts or phonemes that are represented by the letters of printed words, need to be taught this alphabetic principle (see Adams, 1990), and children who are at-risk especially need this help (Perfetti, Georgi, & Beck, 1993). However, there is no consensus with respect to the details of how best to help children in first grade learn this principle, although some of the details have been made explicit (Kameenui, 1996).

Learning the alphabetic principle simply means to learn that there are connections between the order of letters in words and the order of sounds in words, even though these connections or associations will not be perfectly consistent. This means that the concept of the alphabetic principle is almost an insight, or an Ah-Ha experience. In contrast, learning the cipher means learning the hundreds of specific connections between letter patterns within words and their corresponding sounds. Gough and Hillinger (1980) have noted that learning the cipher requires (a) the awareness of phonemes in spoken words, (b) the recognition of letters in printed words, and (c) learning the associations between letters and sounds. Learning the cipher refers to the activities that increase cipher knowledge, which automatically causes an increase in P_L via (a) an increase in pure lexical knowledge, or A_LWords, (b) an increase in pure cipher knowledge, or c_kWords, and (c) an increase in pure decoding knowledge, or d_kWords (see Chapter 7).

The learning described above can be accomplished via many different teaching activities, all of which build associations between printed words and their spoken counterparts via learning letter-to-sound correspondences or graphophonemic connections (Ehri, 1998). For example, having children write about their experiences will force them to spell words and make connections between letters and sounds. Teaching children, for example, that *put*, *pat*, and *pan* all have the same beginning sound whereas *pat*, *cat*, and *rat*, all have the same ending sounds will help them learn that the sounds within spoken words and the letters within printed words have correspondences that can be broken up and put together into other words. Most teaching activities that get students to learn to pronounce and spell more and more words accurately and quickly, should be highly effective in increasing P_L (e.g., see P. M. Cunningham, 1995).

By the time a student has progressed to $V_L = 3$ and $P_L = 3$, and therefore has become an intermediate reader, there should be no need for further emphasis on phoneme-grapheme correspondences or instruction in pure cipher knowledge. Instead, the greatest gains in P_L for those students below raudamaticity should be accomplished by activities which help each student learn to spell accurately and recognize quickly more of the words the student already knows auditorily. That is, P_L should increase the most for those students during a year of schooling when instruction is concentrated upon increasing the number of pronounceamatized words that are already audamatized so that those words can be raudamatized with practice. The more audamatized words that a student learns to pronounce, higher P_L, and subsequently raudamatizes, the higher A_L will be at the end of the year. Therefore, for students below raudamaticity in grades 3 to 7, there should be instructional activities which promote the accurate pronunciation of printed words whose meaning is known when they are spoken. Learning to quickly discern the correct spellings of these words in isolation is likely to represent an overlearning that will guarantee that these words can be accurately recognized out of context later, that is, P_L should show a high gain.

Once these intermediate students have learned how to quickly recognize in print all of the spoken words they know, they have reached raudamaticity and their instruction should change. Those students who are at raudamaticity need to increase their verbal knowledge and their pronunciation knowledge simultaneously. That is, these students need to (a) learn the meaning of new words and concepts, (b) learn to recognize these new words in print, and (c) practice these new words so their correct spellings can be recognized quickly. Their instruction should focus upon increasing V_L, P_L, and A_L at the same time, that is, a new word should be audamatized, pronounceamatized, and raudamatized almost simultaneously.

Students who have advanced to $V_L = 8$ and $P_L = 8$, have become advanced readers. All advanced readers are assumed to be at raudamaticity. Therefore, instruction designed to increase P_L purportedly will no longer have an effect upon accuracy level, A_L. These advanced readers can only profit from instruction designed to increase V_L, P_L, and A_L, simultaneously.

The point at which mastery of pronunciation occurs has not been agreed upon. Many researchers seem to argue that mastery has occurred when the alphabetic principle has been learned, or when the basics of phonological recoding have been learned so that the individual is in the orthographic phase of word learning. Typically, this would occur around the end of first grade, or for almost all children by the end of second grade (not for the disabled). Thus, mastery of pronunciation knowledge seemingly translates into the achievement which graduates a student from the category of alphabetic reader to orthographic reader. However, Carver (1998c) has presented data which he interpreted as challenging this idea because he found correlational evidence which suggested that pronunciation knowledge is still very important all the way up to $P_L = 8.0$. The correlation between pronunciation level, P_L, and accuracy level, A_L, was very high in grades 4, 5, and 6, that is, .77, .78, and .82, respectively. In this regard, Venezky (1976) has asserted that "the ability to apply letter-sound generalizations continues to develop at least through grade 8" (p. 22). Yet, the close connections between P_L and A_L in many middle graders is likely to be due to P_L being composed of A_L and c_k (see Equation 7-2), even though P_L is no longer causal for A_L after raudamaticity has been reached for many of the students in grades 4, 5, 6, and 7.

Teaching Spelling. One very important way to learn how to pronounce more words accurately is sometimes overlooked, that is, learning to spell more words accurately (Ehri, 1989a). Spelling is often considered to be a very important part of writing, but secondary to reading. In this regard, Gill (1992) noted that spelling was used to teach reading for almost 200 years, but "by the beginning of the 20th century, the tide has so turned that learning to spell was largely seen as incidental to learning to read" (p. 80). However, Shanahan (1984) studied reading and spelling in second-graders and fifth-graders, and then hypothesized that "... spelling instruction would have the greatest impact on reading instruction" (p. 475).

Evidence now exists which suggests that spelling words accurately is one of the most important parts of learning to decode words, for beginning readers (Ehri & Wilce, 1987b). In this regard, Perfetti (1991a) contends that "... the spelling of a given word by a child is the quality of its representation in terms of precision" (p. 38), and that "... spelling facility is the measure of quality" (p. 37). Finally, Henderson (1992) has contended that "... spelling, the alphabetic principle, and the orthographic features by pattern and meaning that flow from it, are the central core of literacy," and that "reading nourishes this gradually elaborating construct; writing automatizes it" (p. 23).

As noted in Chapter 7, the correlation between spelling knowledge and pronunciation knowledge is extremely high in grades 1 though 12 (Calfee, Lindamood, & Lindamood, 1973); measures of spelling knowledge level, S_L, were also considered to be excellent indirect measures of P_L, such that $S_L = P_L$. This means that as the spelling level of an individual increases then that person's pronunciation level will increase an equal amount in GE units, and if an individual's pronunciation level increases then that person's spelling level will also increase an equal amount in GE units, because reading words and spelling words rely on the same lexical representation (Perfetti, 1997). It is possible for good readers to be poor spellers in the sense that an individual could be above grade level in A_L (due to a very high V_L) but below grade level in S_L; but, it is theoretically impossible for a person to be below grade level in P_L but above grade level in S_L because $P_L = S_L$. In short, teaching individuals who are below raudamaticity to spell more of the words they know auditorily—audamatized words—should result in increases in P_L, A_L, R_L, and E_L. In this regard, Perfetti, (1997) has contended that "practice at spelling should help reading more than practice of reading helps spelling" (p. 31).

Gill (1992) has contended that "separate instruction for spelling and word recognition may well be redundant" and that "a true gain in sophistication of word knowledge, one that remains over time, yields gains in spelling and word recognition" (p. 102). These contentions of Gill support the idea that spelling level, S_L, is an indirect measure of P_L, and that instruction in how to spell more words is likely to increase P_L.

In summary, teaching spelling and learning to spell words correctly is a very important way to increase pronunciation level for students below raudamaticity. For students at raudamaticity, teaching spelling and learning to spell new words is only helpful if it coincides with learning the meaning of the new word.

Teaching Phonological Awareness. Teaching and learning, T/L, with respect to phonological awareness, PA, can improve PA but can this kind of T/L improve P_L? That is, PA can be improved through education or training by focusing upon discriminating the phonemes in spoken words (Foster et al., 1994). However, it is not clear that teaching children to break up spoken words into phonemes without also learning to associate letters with phonemes will substantially improve word recognition, or increase P_L. For example, Bradley and Bryant (1983) found that 5- and 6-year-olds who had scored low in PA a year earlier made a much higher gain in an indicant of P_L (spelling test) when they were given PA training that included letters, as compared to PA training without letters. It would be better to refer to PA training that includes letters, as alphabetic principle training or cipher training; Ehri (1998) might call this graphophonemic training. Using different terminology, the research of Bradley and Bryant can be summarized as follows: Cipher training dramatically improved P_L but PA training improved P_L a very small amount, if at all.

The reasons for the above results obtained by Bradley and Bryant (1983) can be explained by theory relating the following: cipher training, pure cipher training, PA, pure cipher knowledge, c_k, pure decoding knowledge, d_k, and pronunciation level, P_L. Cipher training would focus upon learning to pronounce and spell real words by learning correspondences between the letters within the words and the sounds within the words; cipher training is likely to have a large impact upon P_LWords—as was found by Bradley and Bryant—because it increases both A_LWords and c_kWords. Pure cipher training would focus upon learning correspondences between letters and sounds without much regard for how real words are pronounced, and this kind of training is likely to have a large impact upon c_kWords and d_kWords but a small impact upon A_L-Words. Similarly, PA training is likely to have its biggest impact upon c_kWords and d_kWords, and much less of an impact upon A_LWords, thereby having only a small or moderate effect upon P_L, as was found by Bradley and Bryant. There is likely to be a close connection between PA and c_k (and d_k) such that (a) increasing PA will increase c_k and d_k, (b) increasing c_k or d_k via pure cipher training will automatically increase PA, and (c) increasing P_L is likely to mean an increase in both A_LWords and c_kWords, which in turn is likely to result in an increase in PA.

Evidence relevant to the moderate effect that PA training has upon P_L comes from Lundberg, Frost, and Petersen (1988). They studied the effect of PA instruction given to around 200 preschoolers—15 to 20 minutes a day for a school year—with no involvement of letters or reading. There were around 150 comparable children in the control group. At the end of this year of instruction, they found a very large effect on a 53-item, phonological measure; they did not calculate any effect size measures but from the statistics they reported, Cohen's *d* was calculated to be large at 1.00 (.20, small; .50, medium; .80, large). This means that PA training had a large effect upon PA. With respect to P_L (as measured by a spelling test) at the end of first grade, there was a medium sized effect (d = .59) and this medium sized effect was also evident at the end of second grade (d = .46). These results suggest that a very lengthy PA treatment (over 35 hours) with preschoolers has a medium sized effect upon P_L. But, this result begs the question as to whether the effect upon P_L would have been very large if this 35 hours of instruction had included letters so that it was cipher training; a large effect for cipher training upon P_L would be predicted from the Bradley and Bryant (1983) results noted here.

In recent years, a great deal of success has been claimed for teaching PA. For example, Fielding-Barnsley (1997) contends that "the role of phonemic awareness in reading acquisition is well documented, as evidenced by successful intervention programs that have phonemic awareness as a control component (e.g., Ball & Blachman, 1991; Blachman, Ball, Black, & Tangel, 1994; Bradley & Bryant, 1983; Byrne & Fielding-Barnsley, 1991, 1993, 1995; A. E. Cunningham, 1990; Lundberg, Frost, & Petersen, 1988)" (p. 85). However, when the references cited above by Fielding-Barnsley were examined, it was found that almost all of the successful PA training cited actually taught PA along with letters. That is, it would be more appropriate to say that the above research showed the cipher training was effective in increasing P_L. In this regard, Christensen (1997) concluded from her research "that not only do phonological awareness and letter knowledge have independent positive relations with learning to read but they have an even greater impact on reading when they coincide" (p. 356).

Indeed, there seems to be no doubt that cipher training is effective in increasing P_L (Ehri, 1989a, 1992; Hatcher, Hulme & Ellis, 1994). Furthermore, evidence exists for the theory that PA instruction would be more effective in increasing pure cipher knowledge, or c_k, and less effective for increasing lexical knowledge, or A_L. In a 1997 study by Olson, Wise, Ring, and Johnson involving poor reading elementary students, they gave one group a great deal of instruction in PA and a control group received an equivalent amount of instruction that focused on increasing A_L. The results showed a big advantage for the PA group on a word attack measure (indicant of d_k and c_k) as would be predicted from the theory given above that asserted a reciprocally causal connection between PA and c_k. With respect to their indicant of P_L, the PA training showed a very small advantage. However, the group that received no PA training—but did receive a comparable amount of time engaged in training designed to increase A_LWords—gained much more on an indicant of A_L (a time-limited word identification test; see Chapter 4). (Note: These results are described in much more detail in Chapter 16.)

As soon as students have learned the alphabetic principle, and have learned to read more than a few words, it seems likely that PA becomes inextricably tied to their cipher knowledge in a reciprocally causal way. That is, the number of associations students have learned between letters within printed words and sounds within spoken words almost completely determines their knowledge of breaking up spoken words into sounds, which is called PA. Therefore, increasing PA will have to be associated with an increase in pure cipher knowledge, and increasing c_k will have to be associated with an increase in PA. If PA is highly related to c_k, then it must be equally related to pure decoding knowledge, d_k, because $c_k = d_k$; therefore, PA must also be highly related to P_L because d_k is part of P_L via Equation 7-4. Furthermore, PA must also be highly related to A_L and R_L because P_L is a proximal cause of both A_L and R_L. Thus, as children learn to read more and more words, they will automatically become more phonologically aware, that is, they will be able to take the first sound off of /hat/ and tell you that the word /at/ remains. They will be able to do this without any direct instruction in PA, that is, this awareness will be a byproduct of learning to pronounce more words that they know. Again, it is being contended that PA and c_k have a reciprocally causal relationship, and that relationship can explain why PA is so closely related to indicants of d_k, P_L, and A_L in grades 2 and higher.

Theory and evidence that PA and reading ability (d_k, P_L, A_L, and E_L) have a reciprocally causal relationship comes from several sources (Ehri, 1989b, 1998; McGuinness, McGuinness, & Donohue, 1995; Perfetti, 1991a; Perfetti, Beck, Bell, & Hughes, 1987; Perfetti, Georgi, & Beck, 1993; Vandervelden & Siegel, 1995). Evidence that a measure of PA and an indicant of P_L are highly related comes from Calfee, Lindamood, and Lindamood (1973) who found correlations in kindergarten through grade 12 which ranged from a low of .62 in grade 12 to a high of .77 in grade 5. If Calfee et al. had included a measure of pseudoword pronunciation, such as the Word Attack test in the Woodcock Reading Mastery Tests, then it is likely that the correlations with PA would have been even higher because this Word Attack test would have provided an indicant of cipher knowledge, or c_k. In this regard, Barker, Torgesen, and Wagner (1992) found that a phoneme deletion measure of PA correlated .70 with a measure of word attack (indicant of d_k) and PA correlated .61 with a measure of word identification (indicant of P_L)—for 87 third graders when the correlations were corrected for attenuation. For these data, notice that PA correlated slightly higher with d_k than it did with P_L (.70 vs. .61), and this is consistent with the theory that PA and c_k, or d_k, are related in a reciprocally causal way.

In 1997, Torgesen, Wagner, Rashotte, Burgess, and Hecht presented data relevant to the theory that once children have learned to pronounce more than a few words, then PA is an indicant of c_k. From this theory it would be predicted that from grade 2 or 3 on, if P_L is removed (or controlled for) when predicting A_L, R_L, or E_L, then there will be little variance left for PA to predict, or account for; because c_k is a part of P_L and PA is so closely associated with c_k, then PA should offer little or no uniqueness to the prediction of A_L, R_L, or E_L. In contrast, Torgesen et al. interpreted their data as indicating that PA "... did uniquely explain growth in a variety of reading skills ..." (p. 161). Their data involved 215 students tested in grades 2 and 4, plus 201 students tested in grades 3 and 5. These researchers, however, did not look at how much PA in grade 2 uniquely contributed to the prediction of A_L in grade 4, after the variance in P_L at grade 2 had been removed. These calculations were made and the answer is 2%, that is, PA in grade 2 only added 2% to the predictable variance in reading comprehension (or A_L) in grade 4, after the P_L variance in grade 2 had been removed. The corresponding contribution of PA in grade 3 to predicting A_L in grade 5 after removing P_L in grade 3, was also 2%. It can be seen that the unique contribution of PA to predicting A_L is quite small when P_L is controlled, only 2%. It appears that PA probably was not an important causal factor with respect to P_L in this Torgesen et al. research.

Also, in 1997, Torgesen, Wagner, and Rashotte studied the effectiveness of highly explicit instruction in phoneme awareness and phonological awareness; this PA instruction was "based almost exclusively on the *Auditory Discrimination in Depth* method developed by Patricia and Charles Lindamood (1984)" (p. 225). This was a 2-1/2 year prevention project involving 138 children who received instruction by 3 different methods. They reported that this intensive and explicit instruction in PA did not show "advantages in word-reading vocabulary or reading comprehension" (p. 217). Therefore, it seems reasonable to disregard PA as an important factor in the causal model, except it is likely to be a good indicant of g_p in kindergarten and early first grade, as will be explained later.

Pronunciation Aptitude

Introduction. This section describes and explains the theoretical construct called pronunciation aptitude, symbolized as g_p. Then, the theory associated with measuring pronunciation aptitude will be presented.

The Construct. The other factor at Echelon 4 that is causal with respect to pronunciation level is g_p. It is being theorized that individuals vary in their aptitude for being able to learn sound-symbol correspondences. The essence of g_p is in the ability to learn the sounds that often are associated with letters, syllables, and other spelling patterns. High g_p means that there is a higher gain in P_L with equal educational experiences or instruction—equal T/L. That is, the g_p construct is being advanced to explain individual differences in gains in P_L when equally motivated students experience the same quality and quantity of instruction.

The theory is that g_p is directly associated with the ability to learn the connections between letters within printed words and their corresponding sounds within spoken words. Manis et al. (1987) has shown that learning rules connecting visual symbols with spoken words is especially difficult for low P_L individuals (disabled) when the rules are inconsistent, or probabilistic. Individuals will learn these associations at different rates, that is, low g_p individuals will take more learning trials or experiences with these associations to learn them as compared to high g_p individuals. This g_p aptitude is distinct from the ability to learn to associate pairs of stimuli involving an auditory response and a visual stimulus (Vellutino, Steger, & Pruzek, 1973). Pronunciation aptitude is also slightly different from the ability to learn to associate a visual response with a visual stimulus (Vellutino, Harding, Phillips, & Steger, 1975). The g_p construct is also distinct from the ability to learn to associate a verbal response (e.g., /hegpid/) with nonsense letters (novel graphic symbols), which Vellutino, Harding, Phillips, and Steger (1975) found to discriminate between good and poor readers. The g_p construct is purported to be different from the ability to learn to associate a verbal response (spoken words or pseudowords) with a visual stimulus of any kind (meaningful objects or nonsense letters)—an aptitude which is likely to be more associated with verbal aptitude, g_v.

In kindergarten, the g_p construct is likely to be composed of two composite parts, an ability to recognize the fundamental sounds in spoken words (phoneme knowledge), and an ability to recognize letters in written words (letter knowledge). If a student cannot recognize the separate sounds within spoken words and cannot recognize the separate letters within written words, then the student will not be able to learn to associate the letters within words with their corresponding sounds, which is the essence of g_p. Learning the names of letters assures that the letters within words can be correctly perceived and discriminated from one another. This knowledge can be used to help students learn to associate letters in written words with phonemes within spoken words.

Once the student catches on to the alphabetic principle (that the order of letters within written words usually corresponds to the order of phonemes within spoken words), then the student has overcome a major hurdle down the long road of learning to pronounce many words. In this regard, Tunmer, Herriman, and Nesdale (1988) found that the product of phonological awareness and letter-name knowledge accounted for more variance in pseudoword knowledge, d_k, than the linear combination of the two variables alone. This means that either zero letter-name knowledge or zero phonological awareness would result in zero g_p, even if there was a great deal of the other.

Evidence that pre-reading PA correlates highly with P_L in later grades comes from Stuart and Masterson (1992) who found that the PA scores of 4-year old preschoolers correlated .68 and .75 with word reading and spelling (indicants of P_L) when they became 10-year olds. Also, Yopp (1995) found that PA in kindergarten correlated .78 with a reading vocabulary test (indicant of A_L) in sixth grade. It is being contended that this potency of PA in preschool and kindergarten for predicting later success in reading (higher P_L or A_L) comes from (a) PA being an indicant of g_p during this pre-reading period ($g_p \rightarrow P_L \rightarrow A_L$), and (b) PA being so closely related to pure cipher knowledge in the middle grades.

Measurement Theory. An ideal direct measure of pronunciation aptitude is likely to be one which measures the ability to learn and remember sounds that have been associated with pronounceable strings of letters. Such a measure would be scaled into stanines, or some other standard score that controlled for age. This ideal measure would be appropriate for students who have learned the alphabetic principle, that is, such a measure would not be appropriate for almost all students in kindergarten and many students in first grade.

As explained earlier, one indicant of g_p in kindergarten would be a measure of phonological awareness, PA, which is the ability to break up words into sounds. PA is a part of g_p, and is likely to be highly correlated with any direct measure of g_p. The high correlation often found between PA in kindergarten and later measures of reading ability (e.g., Yopp, 1995) is being theorized as partly due to PA being a part of g_p. Of course, if some kindergartners in a group are taught PA and others in the same group are not taught PA, so instruction is not constant or not approximately equal for everyone in the group, then PA would no longer be an indicant of g_p in this group, and would not correlate highly with later measures of reading ability. This means that tests that measure phonological awareness in kindergarten, for example, the Yopp-Singer Test of Phoneme Segmentation (Yopp, 1995), would provide indicants of g_p, for students who had not been taught PA.

In kindergarten, another indicant of g_p would be a measure of letter-naming knowledge. Those students who have learned more letters names are likely to have more g_p because learning to associate letters (having shapes that vary from one type of print to another) with their names (having sounds that vary from one person speaking them to another) is similar to what is involved in the g_p construct. For example, a capital "B" does not look like a lower case "b," and almost every printed form of these letters varies from one typeface to another, as well as background, color, size, etc. Furthermore, the correct response (oral pronunciation) to a printed letter "B" also varies considerably—one person may say /be/ so quickly it can hardly be discerned from /de/ and another person may say /beee/ so slowly, softly, and prolonged, that it may seem to have little in common with /be/.

Given that letter-name knowledge is an indicant of g_p for beginning readers, it is not surprising that it is highly predictive of later measures of reading ability (Bond & Dykstra, 1967; Chall, 1967). Stanovich (1986) has noted that "it has long been known that letter knowledge prior to entering school is a better predictor of initial reading acquisition than IQ: Chall, 1967; Richek, 1977; Stevenson et al., 1976" (p. 392). Again, one main reason why letter-naming accuracy in kindergarten correlates so highly with measures of reading ability is probably because this measure is an indicant of g_p, and is therefore an indicator of a very important factor which is directly causal for P_L. On the other hand, if the kindergartners with low g_p in a group are given a great deal of instruction in learning the letter names, whereas the kindergartners with high g_p in the group are given no instruction, then letter-naming accuracy would not be a good indicant of g_p in this group. However, in most kindergartens the amount of instruction in learning the letter names is relatively constant, or approximately equal across students. Therefore, a letter-name test, such as the Letter Identification Test from the Woodcock Reading Mastery Tests, would be an indicant of g_p, especially in groups where this knowledge varied considerably and members of the group did not vary drastically in the amount of instruction in letter-name knowledge.

A Distal Cause of P_L

Besides g_p and T/L being two proximal causes of P_L (at Echelon 4), there is another factor which exerts a distal causal effect upon P_L; it is V_L. This complication will be examined first for students below raudamaticity, and then it will be examined again for students who have reached raudamaticity.

For students who have not reached raudamaticity (A_LWords < V_LWords), the most gain in A_L due to a constant amount of instruction will come from instruction devoted entirely to P_L, i.e., lexical instruction and cipher instruction, without regard for instruction in the meaning of words, or instruction designed to increase V_L. However, this does not mean that V_L has no effect upon A_L for students below raudamaticity. In fact, students with higher V_L will have a larger lexicon of V_LWords which increases the probability that pure cipher learning will result in one of those words becoming pronounceamatized without any lexical instruction. That is, a word may be pronounced correctly in a list upon its first encounter due to cipher learning and if this same word is already in the audamatized lexicon, V_LWords, then it can become raudamatized with practice. On the other hand, this same word cannot become raudamatized if it is not already in the audamatized lexicon. Therefore, having a larger audamatized lexicon—more V_LWords—makes P_L instruction have a somewhat bigger effect upon A_L.

Increasing the number of pronounceamatized words automatically is associated with an increase in cipher knowledge, and this means that a side effect is an increase in ciphermatized words. These ciphermatized words will become raudamatized words if they are already audamatized and are subsequently practiced. Therefore, having a larger lexicon of audamatized words—more V_LWords—means a higher V_L which affects A_L via Equation 1-2 (A_L is the average of V_L and P_L). V_L is a proximal cause of A_L and a distal cause of P_L because A_L is also a proximal cause of P_L. Notice that this also means that A_L and P_L are reciprocally causal. Furthermore, an even more distal cause of a low P_L could be a low verbal aptitude, low g_v, or poor teaching and learning with respect to increasing verbal knowledge.

This distal effect of V_L on P_L can also be explained using mathematical relationships, given earlier, that is,

$$P_L = (A_L + d_k)/2, \text{ and} \qquad \text{(from 7-4)}$$
$$A_L = (V_L + P_L)/2 \qquad \text{(from 10-3)}$$

Notice that P_L depends on A_L from Equation 7-4, A_L and depends on V_L from Equation 10-5, so P_L depends on V_L. The two above equations can be solved for P_L as a function of V_L, with the result being

$$P_L = (V_L + 2d_k)/3 \qquad (13\text{-}1)$$

Notice P_L depends on 1/3 V_L and 2/3 d_k, according to this equation. This equation supplements the theory given earlier which explained how a low level of verbal knowledge, low V_L, could distally affect level of pronunciation knowledge, P_L, in a negative manner.

It should also be pointed out that there are four unknowns in Equations 7-4 and 10-3. Therefore, if values are known for two of these four variables, then the other two can be mathematically determined. For example, suppose a student scores at the second-grade level on a word attack test ($d_k = 2$) and at the fourth-grade level on a word identification test ($P_L = 4$). By substituting these values into Equation 7-4, it can be determined that this student is reading at the sixth-grade level ($A_L = 6$). Then, by substituting $A_L = 6$ and $P_L = 4$ into Equation 10-3, it can be determined that this student has an eighth-grade listening level ($V_L = 8$). Notice that once it is estimated how many words a student can identify, $P_L = 4$, and how many of these words were identified by pure cipher knowledge, $c_k = d_k = 2$, then that determines the reading level of the student, $A_L = 6$, as well as the listening level of the student, $V_L = 8$.

For students who have reached raudamaticity (A_LWords = V_LWords), instruction designed to increase P_L no longer has an independent causal effect upon A_L. This means that the distal effect that V_L has upon P_L is no longer important. It also means that A_L and P_L are no longer reciprocally causal; A_L is still causal for P_L but P_L is no longer causal for A_L.

Summary of Theory

The two proximal causes of pronunciation level, P_L, are (a) teaching and learning experiences, T/L, relevant to increasing pronunciation knowledge, and (b) pronunciation aptitude, g_p. It seems likely that poor teaching and learning experiences with respect to pronunciation knowledge can be overcome by a high aptitude for pronunciation, g_p. It also seems likely that a low pronunciation aptitude, low g_p, can be overcome by good teaching and learning experiences. However, those unfortunate individuals who have low pronunciation aptitude and also have poor teaching and learning experiences are highly likely to have low P_L, low A_L, low R_L, and low reading achievement, or low E_L.

For individuals who are below raudamaticity, reading instruction should focus upon increasing P_L, that is, should be code-emphasis instruction. These individuals need to learn to raudamatize their audamatized words by increasing their lexicon of pronounceamatized words. One way for these students to raudamatize words is to learn to spell audamatized words (pronounceamatize them) and then practice reading those words until they are overlearned.

Beginning readers must learn to discriminate among the letters within words and the sounds within words, and then learn the alphabetic principle which involves associations between the letters and sounds in words. The best teaching for almost all beginning readers would involve cipher training—helping students learn to pronounce words by helping them learn to associate letters in printed words with their corresponding sounds in spoken words. Beginning readers and intermediate readers who are below raudamaticity and are being taught by traditional approaches are usually asked to do a great deal of reading in materials that are at their level of ability, $D_L = A_L$. This is called matched rauding, and it is likely to contain audamatized words that will become pronounceamatized, and then raudamatized with practice.

Readers who have reached raudamaticity (such as many ESL students, many intermediate readers, and all advanced readers) cannot improve their reading achievement by learning to pronounce more isolated words. Instead, these students need to learn the meaning of new words and concepts, and then they need to learn to spell these words so they can be eventually raudamatized with practice, that is, they need to increase V_L, P_L, and A_L, almost simultaneously.

Learning how to pronounce new words is greatly influenced by g_p, which is the aptitude for learning the correspondences between letters and sounds in words. The best measures of pronunciation aptitude, g_p, would be those that (a) determine how well individuals can learn the connections between the letters within printed words and the sounds within spoken words, and (b) are not substantially influenced by teaching or learning experiences. In kindergarten, a test of phonological awareness, PA, would provide an indicant of g_p because pronunciation aptitude must be very low when there is little awareness of the separate sounds within words. A test of letter names would also provide an indicant of g_p in kindergarten because pronunciation aptitude must be low (a) when there is little awareness of the separate letters within a word, and (b) when a student is slow to learn the imperfect associations between the spoken sounds associated with letters.

After students have learned the alphabetic principle, then teaching PA to beginning readers, or pre-readers, without using letters and printed words produces little or no gain in P_L, and teaching PA with letters and words is more appropriately called cipher training. When individuals have learned the alphabetic principle and have learned to pronounce more than a few words, then PA is related to cipher knowledge in a reciprocally causal way. An increase in PA will automatically result in an increase in c_k; an increase in c_k will automatically result in an increase in PA. Because c_k is equal to pure decoding knowledge, d_k, and is also a component part of P_L, this means that PA is also connected to d_k and P_L—as well as measures of A_L, R_L, and E_L. For most students who have learned the alphabetic principle, PA is no longer an important concept with respect to the causal model because it is inextricably tied to cipher knowledge via c_k, d_k, and P_L.

Summary of Evidence

The best correlational evidence supporting T/L and g_p as the two proximal causes of P_L, comes from a study of first graders conducted by Barr and Dreeban (1983). Their indicant of T/L was a measure of the amount of instruction in phonics, called Phonics Coverage. Their indicant of g_p was called Aptitude, which measured how many phonics words and sight words were learned and remembered after a constant amount of instruction for all students. Their measure of P_L was called Phonics Learning, and it involved the correct pronunciation of two-, three-, and four-letter syllables. The correlational data they reported indicated that (a) T/L correlated .62 with P_L, and (b) g_p correlated .69 with P_L. Furthermore, T/L and g_p predict P_L with a multiple R of .79, thereby suggesting that almost all of the reliable variance in P_L probably would be explained by T/L and g_p if all the variables had been perfectly reliable.

The best evidence supporting g_p being a proximal cause of P_L comes from an experiment conducted by Ehri and Wilce (1979a). They taught first- and second-graders to learn oral responses to various stimuli. Their indicant of g_p (individual differences in the ability to learn to use correct spellings to remember sounds) correlated .75 with their indicant of P_L (a measure of word recognition), whereas other measures that were not indicants of g_p correlated much lower with P_L (.43, .36, and .41). Furthermore, their data supported the teaching of spelling to increase P_L because these beginning readers learned the paired associations between letters and sounds better when they were given the correct spellings of the sounds they were supposed to learn. That is, even beginning readers profit from the correct spellings of words as they learn how to pronounce them.

There is also considerable evidence that teaching poor readers to pronounce isolated words increases P_L (Williams, 1980), and teaching beginning readers to spell words increases P_L (Foorman et al., 1991). More evidence that teaching and learning directed toward P_L will increase P_L comes from Roth and Beck (1987). They used computers to help fourth-grade students who were low in reading achievement and low in socio-economic status become more proficient in decoding. For example, under time-dependent conditions, students selected a word ending from *ime*, *in*, and *ake* to go with *st* as a word beginning. The training involved 20-24 hours over a school year (8 months). Compared to controls, the poorer readers benefited from this training on measures of word attack skills (d_kWords) and reading vocabulary (A_LWords). But, there was no similar improvement on the reading achievement test (probably an indicant of E_L). Because E_L is also dependent on cognitive speed level, C_s, and verbal knowledge level, V_L, which were not part of the training, it is understandable that E_L would not show the same gain. The gain that they found in their measures which were indicants of d_k and A_L, can be taken as evidence that teaching and learning directed toward P_L will result in a gain in P_L—because d_k and A_L are the two components of P_L (see Chapter 7).

Phonological awareness, PA, has close connections to T/L and g_p at Echelon 4 in the causal model, plus P_L at Echelon 3. Teaching and learning, T/L, involving PA along with printed letters is very effective in increasing P_L but pure PA training (no printed letters) is not highly effective in increasing P_L (Bradley & Bryant, 1983; Lundberg, Frost, & Petersen, 1988). Instruction or training which increases P_L (without any direct instruction in PA), will produce increases in PA (Perfetti, Beck, Bell, & Hughes, 1987; Perfetti, 1991a). Individual differences in PA are highly related to P_L in kindergarten through grade 12 (Calfee, Lindamood, & Lindamood, 1973), probably because PA and c_k are related in a reciprocally causal manner, and c_k is a part of P_L (see Chapter 7).

PA instruction for poor readers in elementary school, as compared to instruction designed to increase V_L, P_L, and A_L, results in an advantage for pure decoding knowledge, d_k, but a disadvantage for A_L (Olson, Wise, Ring, & Johnson, 1997); this result provides evidence that an increase in PA results in an increase in cipher knowledge, but this increase in c_k is not as effective in increasing A_L as instruction in lexical knowledge, even though both types of instruction result in approximately equal gain in P_L.

PA in grade 2 adds only 2% to the prediction of A_L in grade 4, after P_L in grade 2 has been controlled, and PA in grade 3 adds only 2% to the prediction of A_L in grade 5 after P_L in grade 3 has been controlled (Torgesen, Wagner, Rashotte, Burgess & Hecht, 1997); this result suggests that PA does not add much to the prediction of P_L, because PA is incorporated into P_L via its reciprocal relationship with pure cipher knowledge, c_k.

Implications

Dependent variables in research that are only distally affected by our independent variables should be avoided. For example, Bradley and Bryant (1983) found a much bigger gain in spelling (or P_L) for their cipher training than they did for their reading ability measure (or A_L). According to the causal model, cipher training is a part of the T/L factor at Echelon 4 that is a proximal cause of P_L at Echelon 3, but cipher training is only a distal cause of A_L at Echelon 3. If Bradley and Bryant had only used an indicant of A_L, then the effect of their cipher training may have been disregarded.

Students with low pronunciation aptitude need to be given extra help with the teaching and learning experiences outlined above because it will take them much longer to learn the letter-sound correspondences within words; they will take much more practice to gain 1.0 GE units in P_L. Because this learning will be hard work for these low g_p individuals, it is more likely that they will try to avoid reading-related activities—such as reading, spelling, and writing—even though these activities are likely to help them gain more in P_L. Therefore, all T/L should be designed to overcome these major problems, using all kinds of encouragement for engaging in these kinds of activities which are necessary for improving P_L.

Forget Me Nots

The two proximal causes of pronunciation level, P_L, are teaching and learning, T/L, and pronunciation aptitude, g_p. That is, the amount of pronunciation knowledge that individuals have depends upon (a) the quality and quantity of teaching and learning directed towards increasing their pronunciation knowledge, and (b) their aptitude or ability to learn and remember how printed words are correctly pronounced.

CHAPTER

14

TWO CAUSES OF COGNITIVE SPEED LEVEL

Reading achievement is influenced by an individual's cognitive speed level, C_s, a construct that was described in Chapter 8. Now, the two factors at Echelon 4 which affect C_s, namely, age and cognitive speed aptitude, g_s, will be described in more detail.

Maturation, or age, affects cognitive speed level; educators have no control over this factor. Educators also have no control over the other factor at Echelon 4 which affects cognitive speed level, that is, cognitive speed aptitude, g_s. It is unfortunate that there is no known teaching/learning factor that influences C_s. No matter how good the quality or quantity of teaching and learning, reading achievement will always be limited by this factor that is relatively immune to improvement due to teaching and learning experiences.

As noted earlier in Chapter 8, C_s is cognitive speed expressed in GE units, whereas g_s is cognitive speed relative to age—expressed in stanines, or a standard score of some kind. In one sense, C_s and g_s are not separate factors because they correlate perfectly at a particular age. However, the failure to separate g_s from C_s, conceptually and empirically, has mislead several researchers; they have concluded erroneously, that naming speed, or cognitive speed, is not an important factor in reading—as will be explained in more detail later in this chapter.

These two factors at Echelon 4, age and g_s, which are the proximal causes of C_s, will be discussed in turn. Relevant empirical evidence will also be reviewed.

Age

It is being theorized that over the course of a year, typical students will gain one GE unit in C_s due to maturation, at least between the ages of 6 to 13 years, and possibly between the ages of 6 to 18 years. It is also being theorized that education or experience has a minimal or zero effect upon the amount of this yearly gain. How fast individuals can successfully transform overlearned stimuli into their names is not influenced by teaching or learning. So, the theory is that C_s increases a constant amount each year between age 6 and age 13, or between grade 1 and grade 8.

Data directly relevant to the effect of age upon C_s comes from the grade-by-grade data collected by Doehring (1976), and reanalyzed by Carver (1990a); the rate of letter naming increased a constant amount each year from grade 2 to grade 10. So, there is good evidence for the theory that C_s increases a constant amount each year between the ages of 6 and 13, or between grade 1 and grade 8.

Other evidence relevant to this theoretical claim comes from the administration of the Speed of Thinking Test, STT (see Chapter 8) to students in grades 2 through 8 of a private parochial school. The sample size, mean and SD for each grade level are presented in Table 14-1. Notice that the SDs were approximately equal at each grade, ranging from a low of 11.8 in grade 3 to a high of 17.4 in grade 5. Also, the correlation between grade (as Variable X) and STT raw score means (as Variable Y) in Table 14-1 was .99, indicating an almost perfect linear increase in STT from grade to grade. So, there is evidence that a test which purports to provide an indirect measure of C_s does increase a relatively constant amount between the grade 2 and grade 8. Not only does the arithmetic mean increase about the same amount each year of age, but the SD stays relatively constant.

Table 14-1
Means and Standard Deviations of the Speed of Thinking Test for Students in Grades 2 Through 8

Grade	*N*	*Mean*	*SD*
2	53	64.0	12.8
3	40	65.8	11.8
4	38	78.4	13.6
5	47	86.7	17.4
6	44	92.6	15.0
7	44	98.5	16.6
8	47	105.8	16.0

What is not clear from these data involving letter naming (Carver, 1990a) and the STT (Table 14-1) is whether this constant rate of increase, purportedly due to maturation, is the same for individuals above and below the mean. It is possible that the rate of increase for those above the mean is higher than the rate of increase (slope) for those below the mean. However, if this latter situation holds, then the variability within a grade should increase as the grade increases. Evidence relevant to whether variability increases as grade in school increases comes from the STT data presented earlier in Table 14-1; the SDs only increased from about 12 or 13 in grades 1, 2, and 3, to about 15 or 16 in grades 6, 7, and 8.

Other strong evidence linking C_s to age comes from Stanovich, Nathan, and Zolman (1988). They studied students in grades 3, 5, and 7 who had the same mean on the Reading Survey Test from the Metropolitan Achievement

Tests. They found that when they compared these students in grades 3, 5, and 7 on 26 variables, the biggest differences among the means was on the letter-naming variable. Letter naming was a latency variable which would be an indicant of C_s, as discussed in Chapter 8. Therefore, when an indicant of reading ability was held constant for students at 3 different ages, then they still differed considerably on a variable that is theoretically supposed to be importantly affected by age. Thus, these data support the theory that C_s increases a substantial amount yearly, due to maturation.

The consistency of gains in C_s within individuals from year to year is also shown by the data collected by Bowers (1993). She reported extremely high year-to-year correlations for digit naming speeds of 37 students. The R.A.N. digits measure (see Chapter 8) was administered to the students in her research in the fall of grade 3 and the fall of grade 4; the correlation between those two measures was .91. From the spring of grade 3 to the spring of grade 4, the corresponding correlation was .92. Lastly, but most impressively, the correlation was .91 between those two measures from the fall of grade 2 to the spring of grade 4. Notice that over a span of about $2^1/_2$ years, these two measures correlated .91; these two variables would correlate even closer to 1.00 if they were adjusted for their unreliability.

If the mean scores increase a constant amount each year, if the correlations between year-to-year scores is near perfect, and if the variability remains approximately the same each year, then the individuals have to gain a constant amount each year. There seems to be little doubt but that the means increase a constant amount each year considering the linear increase reported by Carver, (1990a) for the Doehring (1976) data. There seems to be little doubt but that the correlations between year-to-year scores are near perfect given the data of Bowers (1993), just noted. There seems to be little doubt but that the variability in the scores from year-to-year is relatively constant given the data presented earlier in Table 14-1. These results support the theory that education or learning has little effect upon C_s.

In summary, considering the evidence available at this time it appears that C_s is strongly affected by age, or maturation, at least from grades 2 through 8, and possibly from grades 1 through 12, or ages 6 to 18.

Cognitive Speed Aptitude

Individual differences in cognitive speed at a certain age have been defined as cognitive speed aptitude, g_s. Theoretically, these individual differences at each of ages 6 through 13 will correlate perfectly from year to year because the gain each year is constant between 6 and 13; the data collected by Bowers (1993), just reviewed, provided evidence for this theory. This means that if g_s is measured in standard score units, such as stanines, then the stanine that an individual has at age 7 (or grade 2), will be the same or approximately the same at age 13 (or grade 8).

The remainder of this section will be devoted to earlier theory and data relevant to g_s, presented in chronological order.

In 1971, R. B. Cattell named one of the factors he isolated, "cognitive speed," and he symbolized it as "g_s," as noted earlier in Chapter 8. The highest loadings on his g_s factor were from Writing Speed (.63), Backward Writing (.48), and Cancellation Speed (.46). Notice that none of these three variables involved measures of naming speed, which is the essence of C_s. He interpreted his findings as follows: "If intelligence is considered speed at all it is speed in more complex performances than those that are typically strongly loaded by g_s" (p. 108). This cognitive speed factor isolated by Cattell is not the same as the cognitive speed factor in the causal model, even though they have exactly the same name and identifying symbol. In the causal model, g_s is a measure of how quickly a series of overlearned objects or symbols can be named, not writing speed, backward writing speed, or cancellation speed.

In 1980, M. D. Jackson presented data relevant to the theory presented earlier that g_s, as measured by letter-naming speed, reflects a more general ability called cognitive speed. He studied skilled and less-skilled college readers as they performed on a latency version of the Posner task (e.g., aA have the same name and Ba have different names, as in the STT mentioned earlier). He also gave these college readers other speeded tasks that were similar, except they involved placing objects into categories and learning the nonsense syllable names of novel drawings. He interpreted his results as suggesting that (a) "better readers have faster access to memory representations for any meaningful visual pattern, and this advantage is not the result of more practice or experience with the particular items tested" (p. 683), and (b) "better readers are faster at accessing the names of characters, once the name is stored in memory and associated with the appropriate representation of the visual character" (p. 692). Notice that Jackson is saying that there is a general ability to access the names of symbols—not just letters or language symbols—because he used other speeded tasks that did not involve letter or digit naming. He also noted that the individual differences involved could not be explained by practice or experience. Thus, these interpretations of Jackson seem to support the case for g_s being more general so it is appropriate to call it cognitive speed. Finally, Jackson ended his research report dealing with the connection between naming speed and reading ability by suggesting that " ... no amount of practice may compensate the less-skilled reader" (p. 693). Translated, Jackson seems to be agreeing that cognitive speed is primarily an attribute of the individual that is not amenable to improvement via instruction or learning, which in turn supports the case for g_s being an aptitude which is education proof.

In 1988a, Stanovich reported upon a study that involved students in grades 3, 5, and 7 who were matched on reading ability using the GE scores on a reading test from the Metropolitan Achievement Tests. The third graders scored above grade level (GE = 4.35) while the seventh graders scored well below grade level (GE = 4.32). He referred to these three groups as CL matched because they were matched on comprehension level. Stanovich presented data which compared the three groups on 26 reading related measures. Most of the measures showed little discrimination among the three groups; the two highest discriminators were letter-naming time and articulation time. Stanovich summarized his results as follows:

> Table 6 indicates that only two of the variables differed significantly across the three CL-matched groups. Letter naming was significantly faster for older children. This variable was unrelated to reading ability (see Table 3). Thus, this study replicated the finding in our previous study and in the work of other investigators (e.g., N. E. Jackson & Biemiller, 1985) that letter-naming speed tracks chronological age more strongly than reading ability. The other variable to show a significant difference—articulation time—displayed a pattern similar to letter-naming time, although in even stronger form. As is clear from Tables 3 through 5, articulation time appears to be completely unrelated to reading ability. However, it is strongly related to chronological age. (p. 597)

Translated, Stanovich seems to be claming that his data show that C_s is not an important variable and does not belong in the causal model. However, these results from Stanovich actually support the causal model, when analyzed more closely. First, consider the reading measure; it is in a battery (Metropolitan) which claims that the time limits provided are generous so that the students will have time to attempt all of the items they are likely to answer correctly within the test's time limit. This means that this test is more likely to be a good indicant of accuracy level, or A_L. Therefore, it is not surprising that an indicant of C_s (letter-naming latency) does not correlate highly with an indicant of A_L (level of comprehension) from the Metropolitan because C_s is neither a proximal cause of A_L nor a distal cause of A_L. Indeed, this finding of a lack of a relationship between C_s and A_L provides support for the causal model. Furthermore, when Stanovich found that letter-naming speed (indicant of C_s) was highly related to age, this result provided support for age at Echelon 4 being a proximal cause of C_s.

Stanovich also noted that articulation speed was not related to reading ability but was highly related to age. Articulation speed is involved in measures of C_s that involve the speed of reading randomized letters of the alphabet, and it is also involved in the measure of R_L that involves reading an easy passage aloud as fast as possible. The measure of articulation speed that he used involved repeating a pair of words over and over, as fast as possible. It seems likely that any measure involving articulation speed will have a component that is specific to the task itself which may or may not be an inherit part of the construct being measured. That is, when C_s is measured by the Alphabet Rate

Test, ART (see Chapter 8), then there is likely to be a large articulation component that may or may not be part of C_s.

In 1997, Carver collected data that has been reanalyzed to find out how g_s relates to other variables. For 126 students in grades 3 to 7 (actually $2.9 < AgeGE < 8.0$), C_s was correlated with the other variables in Echelons 1, 2, and 3. However, these correlations were controlled for AgeGE, so the C_s variable is actually g_s, because C_s controlled for age is g_s. Cognitive speed aptitude, g_s, correlated highest with R_L ($r = .66$). This result is required by the causal model, and this result supports the causal model. Cognitive speed aptitude correlated second highest with E_L, efficiency level, and this would be expected because E_L is at the end of the causal chain of C_s R_L E_L; however, for these data, E_L was derived from measures of A_L and R_L using Equation 1-1, so this correlation of .58 is not independent of the .66 correlation with R_L. The other correlations with V_L, P_L, and A_L were much lower, ranging from .18 to .33, as would be expected because these variables are not in the same causal chain as g_s or C_s. That is, neither g_s nor C_s are proximal nor distal causes of V_L, P_L, and A_L so g_s would not be expected to be correlated substantially with these variables. These correlations are readily interpreted as providing support for the causal model, and they are comparable to similar data collected by other researchers, as will be discussed next.

Remember from Chapter 8 that the Posner task was presented as an indicant of C_s, that is, the Speed of Thinking Test, STT, involves the Posner task and it provides an indirect measure of C_s when scaled into GE units. Also, remember that the Posner task was used by E. Hunt (1978) to investigate verbal ability, or verbal speed. Research on this task was summarized by Anderson and Freebody (1981) as follows: "Hunt and his collaborators have found that this measure correlates .30 with standardized tests of verbal ability" (p. 82). For the data presented in the preceding paragraph, g_s correlated .18 with V_L, which is verbal knowledge level. Thus, it appears that g_s does not have a large relationship with verbal knowledge, or verbal ability ($r = .18$ and $r = .30$), when the latter concept is measured in a way that accents accuracy much more than speed. Also remember from Chapter 11 that many other researchers have found correlations around .30 to .40 between indicants of C_s and P_L, and these data replicate the .33 correlation between C_s and P_L for the data presented in the preceding paragraph.

Whenever an indicant of C_s has been related to a measure of IQ, the correlations are ordinarily small. Bowers, Steffy, and Tate (1988) found a correlation of .24 between digit naming speed and the average of five subtests on the WISC-R which load highest on *g*. Spring and Davis (1988) found a correlation of .20 between digit naming speed and WISC-Verbal IQ; for WISC-R performance IQ, the corresponding correlation was .04 .

Whenever g_s has been related to the Raven Progressive Matrices test, which is purportedly the best single measure of *g* (Jensen, 1982), the correlation has not been large—usually fluctuating around zero. Carver (1991) reported a negative partial correlation of -.26 between g_s (C_s controlled for school grade) and the Raven test for 41 students in grades 2 to 10. For the data reported earlier in this chapter for the 126 students in grades 3 to 7, the partial *r* between C_s and the Raven, controlling for age, was only .12.

In summary, the above data may be interpreted as indicating that g_s is a factor which together with age, determines cognitive speed level, C_s. This g_s factor is not substantially related to traditional indicators of intelligence, such as IQ tests that measure verbal ability or performance ability; this g_s factor is also not importantly related to the Raven test which measures *g*, or fluid intelligence, Gf.

Summary of Theory

The two proximal causes of cognitive speed level, C_s, are age and cognitive speed aptitude, g_s. Age, or maturation, affects C_s in that cognitive speed increases a constant amount each year of school, from about age 6 to maturity which is probably somewhere around age 13. Cognitive speed aptitude, g_s, is simply individual differences in C_s at each of the above ages, so g_s and C_s are not qualitatively different. C_s is cognitive speed scaled into GE units; g_s is cognitive speed scaled into standard scores, such as stanines, based upon the mean and SD at a particular age.

The best measure of g_s for most lower graders, middle graders, and adults is probably the rate of naming the letters of the alphabet, or digits, in random order. An indicant of g_s is the Posner task which requires individuals to quickly determine whether two letters have the same name when one is upper case and the other is lower case. Individuals improve each year in their cognitive speed, at least from around age 6 to age 13. So, the cognitive speed level, C_s, of individuals is completely determined from their age and their cognitive speed aptitude, g_s. This means that (a) if we know age and C_s, then we know g_s, and (b) if we know g_s and age, then we know C_s.

Summary of Evidence

With respect to age and C_s, it is known that (a) rate of letter naming increased a constant amount from grade 2 to grade 10 (see Carver, 1990a), (b) an indicant of C_s increased a constant amount each year in school from grade 2 to grade 8 (see Table 14-1), (c) within individual gain in digit-naming speed is probably relatively constant each year, because year-to-year longitudinal correlations have been found to be around .90 (Bowers, 1993), and (d) when students at different ages were matched on an indicant of A_L, then letter-naming speed (measure of C_s) was the best discriminator among 26 variables (Stanovich, 1988a; Stanovich, Nathan, & Zolman, 1988). Therefore, there is strong evidence that age, or maturation, causes a constant increase in C_s each year for each individual in school, at least between age 7 and age 13.

With respect to g_s, the earlier cognitive speed construct advanced by R. B. Cattell (1971) is more of a processing speed variable that is not the same as g_s in the causal model. The newer g_s construct represents the speed of naming a series of overlearned objects or symbols, not necessarily language symbols (M. D. Jackson, 1980). Earlier research on letter-naming speed has been interpreted as rendering g_s unimportant in reading research because it was lowly related to a standardized reading comprehension test (Stanovich, 1988a); however, these same data may be alternately interpreted as supporting cognitive speed aptitude because g_s should not be highly related to an indicant of reading level, or A_L, because g_s is neither a proximal or distal cause of A_L in the causal model. Finally, indicants of g_s (a) correlate lowly with indicants of V_L (E. Hunt, 1978), (b) correlate lowly with IQ (Bowers, Steffy & Tate, 1988; Spring & Davis, 1988), and (c) correlate lowly with the Raven Progressive Matrices Test (Carver, 1991).

Implications

It is very important that researchers keep the constructs of g_s and C_s separate when conducting research. For example, suppose Student A is a less-skilled reader in grade 6 with $C_s = 4$; therefore Student A has a low g_s. Suppose Student B is a skilled reader in grade 2 with $C_s = 3$; therefore Student B has a high g_s. Notice that the less-skilled reader (Student A) has a higher cognitive speed than the skilled reader (Student B), 4 vs. 3, yet, the less-skilled reader would not have a higher cognitive speed aptitude because g_s is measured in relationship to age. This kind of anomaly is easily sorted out and recognized if the concept of g_s is separated from the concept of C_s. However, without these two concepts, plus the recognition that C_s is not causal for A_L, it is easy to see how researchers such as Perfetti et al. (1978) and Stanovich (1981) could find no differences between skilled and less-skilled readers in digit naming speed. If the two groups—skilled and less-skilled—were selected by the researchers on a reading ability criterion that did not load on speed, such as A_L, then there is no reason to expect a difference in g_s, or in C_s, if both groups were the same age.

Forget Me Nots

The two proximal causes of cognitive speed level, C_s, are age and cognitive speed aptitude, g_s. That is, the cognitive speed level of a student depends upon the age of the student and the cognitive speed aptitude of the student.

PART IV

GENERAL RESEARCH EVIDENCE

This part of the book contains a review of theory and research relevant to the causal model involving lower-grade readers (Chapter 15), middle-grade readers (Chapter 16), and adults, or upper-grade readers (Chapter 17).

Earlier, in Part II (Chapters 3 to 8), each of the six constructs in Echelons 1 to 3 were described in detail, along with a summary of relevant research evidence. Then, in Part III (Chapters 9 to 14), two primary causes for a particular construct were discussed in each of the six chapters, along with a summary of relevant data. Now, in Part IV (Chapters 15 to 17), theory and data will be presented that is relevant to more than the individual pieces dealt with in earlier chapters. Part IV will contain research that is relevant to disparate parts of the causal model—such as distal causes and noncausal relationships. Also, research was summarized in Parts II and III that was directly related to the constructs and their proximal causes, whereas Part IV will include more detailed descriptions of research which will help to make the explanatory and predictive power of the causal model more easily understood. Finally, conclusions and implications will be drawn that are more specific to each of the three age categories of readers—lower graders, middle graders, and adults.

CHAPTER

15

LOWER-GRADE READERS

In this chapter, theory and research will be presented that is directly relevant to various constructs in the causal model when lower graders are involved. The research evidence presented in this chapter was not presented in earlier chapters for two reasons: (a) the data involved distal causes instead of proximal causes in the causal model, or (b) the data involved constructs that were neither distally nor proximally related in the causal chain.

Whereas the data presented in the earlier chapters were very supportive of the causal model, it was all correlational in nature. A unique feature of this chapter is that it also contains experimental data, or treatment research, which more directly supports the causal claims made in the model—as will be explained in detail later.

A lengthy section containing theory and research will be presented first, and a short section on implications will be presented.

Theory and Research

The theory and evidence relevant to lower graders and the causal model will be reviewed in chronological order.

In 1986, Juel, Griffith and Gough outlined a model of literacy acquisition which is mostly consistent with V_L, P_L, and A_L in the causal model, as well as c_k and d_k. This model included writing as well as reading, as end products. However, because the causal model presented in Chapter 1 focuses only upon reading achievement as an end product, the writing aspects of the Juel, Griffith, and Gough model will be disregarded. The bottom line of their model is directed toward reading comprehension, or A_L, which is purportedly determined by word recognition, or P_L, and listening comprehension, or V_L; this is the simple view of reading outlined in Chapter 10. They show no causal factors for listening comprehension, or V_L. However, they do show two factors as causal for word recognition, or P_L, namely, cipher knowledge and lexical knowledge. An indicant of cipher knowledge for them would be accuracy of pseudoword naming, and this is also consistent with pure decoding knowledge, d_k, being an indicant of c_k, or pure cipher knowledge, as explained earlier in Chapter 7. Lexical knowledge for them is the knowledge of how to pronounce words that violate the systematic relationships involved in the cipher. That is, lexical knowledge involves the ability to correctly pronounce irregular words, such as "laugh." Notice that in their model they are breaking P_L down into two parts, a general knowledge of letter-sound correspondences and a specific knowledge of how particular words are pronounced that do not follow the general knowledge. This theory is somewhat consistent with the theory presented earlier in Chapter 7 that P_L is composed of A_L and d_k, or lexical knowledge and cipher knowledge. However, the causal model holds that the proximal causes of P_L (as composed of d_k and A_L) are teaching/learning and pronunciation aptitude, g_p.

In 1985, N. E. Jackson and Biemiller reported results that are highly consistent with the following constructs in the causal model C_s, A_L, and R_L. They measured letter-naming time and scrambled-word reading time for 66 second graders. They also studied 97 kindergarten-age precocious readers. They summarized their results as follows:

> Within each group, letter naming and scrambled word reading times were correlated with text reading times. However, none of the reading time measures was strongly associated with precocious readers scores on a multiple-choice test of sentence reading comprehension. The precocious group named letters less rapidly than second graders did, but read words at the same speed as second graders and text faster (p. 196).

These lower-grade readers, just described, were given tests which were indicants of three constructs in the causal model. The reading times for letters is an indicant of C_s (see Chapter 8). The scrambled word and text reading time data were collected under maximum oral reading rate (MORR) conditions and are therefore indicants of R_L (see Chapter 5). The multiple-choice test of sentence reading comprehension was not timed and is therefore an indicant of A_L (see Chapter 4). Notice that Jackson and Biemiller have included measures of both of the constructs in Echelon 2, A_L and R_L, and one of the three constructs at Echelon 3, C_s.

With respect to their results for the second graders, their indicant of C_s correlated .67 with their indicant of R_L. This indicant of R_L came from their Test 1, which was very easy and did not involve words that the second graders did not know, a prerequisite for a good indicant of R_L involving only raudamatized words. So, these researchers found a correlation between C_s and R_L for second graders ($r = .67$) which is comparable to those reported earlier in Chapter 11 for students in grades 3 up to college students. Jackson and Biemiller also found that their precocious group (kindergartners) named letters less rapidly than the second graders, and this is also in accordance with the causal model. Remember that C_s is purported to vary directly with age (see Chapter 14), so that it is reasonable even for precocious kindergartners to have a lower C_s than second graders who are 2 years older. There is no reason to expect these kindergartners to be equal to the second graders on C_s because the procedure for selecting the precocious readers involved asking kindergarten teachers to identify students in their classes who were reading at or above the third grade level, i.e., $A_L = 3$ or higher. With this selection criterion, which also involved giving teachers a third-grade text to use in screening potential nominees, it is easy to see from the causal model that rate, in the form of E_L, R_L, or C_s, was not a selection factor. Therefore, it would be expected that these kindergartners, high in reading level or not, would not be as high in cognitive speed level, C_s, as second graders, and this finding is consistent with the causal model (see Chapter 14).

The finding by Jackson and Biemiller that the precocious kindergartners read text faster than second graders is also easily explainable in terms of the causal model. Reading text faster means higher R_L, or rate level. Because R_L is determined by both P_L and C_s, it is highly likely that the faster reading of text by the kindergartners was due to their having a much higher P_L than the second graders. Probably, they could not have gotten to the third grade level of A_L at such a young age without having a high pronunciation aptitude, g_p, which helped to cause a high P_L. Because they were reading at $A_L = 3$ or higher, it seems likely that many of them had $V_L = 4$ and $P_L = 4$ giving them $A_L = 4$. Notice that when $P_L = 4.0$ is combined with $C_s = 1.9$ the result is $R_L = 3.0$ (from Equation 10-3) which could easily make them higher than a typical second-grade class at $R_L = 2.5$. These data collected by Jackson and Biemiller (1985) are readily explained by references to the theorized relationships among g_p, C_s, P_L, A_L, and R_L in the causal model.

In 1988, Lundberg, Frost, and Petersen conducted an experimental treatment study that is relevant to T/L at Echelon 4, V_L and P_L at Echelon 3, and A_L at Echelon 2. This study was also described earlier in Chapter 13. These researchers gave instruction in phonological awareness to around 200 preschoolers for 15 - 20 minutes a day for the entire school year, and compared the results to a comparable control group. At the end of first grade and at the end of second grade, it was possible to calculate Cohen's *d* on an indicant of P_L (a spelling test); the values were 0.59 and 0.46 respectively. It seems likely that the two groups were comparable on V_L because at the end of the year of PA instruction, a test was given that measured language comprehension, and Cohen's *d* was .08. Given that the mean *d* for P_L was .52 (medium ES), and the *d* for V_L was .08, it follows that *d* for A_L should be around .30 (the average of .52 and .08). They did measure reading vocabulary in first and second grade, and the *d* values for this indicant of A_L were .19 and .28, for an average of .24. The average value of d from V_L and P_L was very close to the actual value of *d* (.30 vs. .24). Therefore, these data provide experimental evidence for V_L and P_L being the two proximal causes of A_L.

In 1991, Naslund and Schneider presented data from 92 German children who were given several tests in kindergarten and in grade 2, some of which seem to provide indicants of g_v, g_p, A_L and R_L. In kindergarten, they administered a measure of general verbal ability taken from a standardized intelligence test. This measure, which they called Verbal Ability, is likely to provide an indicant of verbal knowledge aptitude, g_v (see Chapter 12). Also in kindergarten, they administered several phonological awareness tests, which they combined into one phonological awareness measure. This measure is likely to provide an indicant of pronunciation aptitude, g_p, as explained earlier in Chapter 13. In second grade, they administered an untimed reading comprehension test which involved reading five short stories and answering 30 multiple-choice questions. This test would provide an indicant of accuracy level, A_L (see Chapter 4). Also in second grade, they asked students to read 30 four-letter words and 30 four-letter pseudowords as fast as they could, which should provide an indicant of rate level, R_L (see Chapter 5 and Chapter 11).

The relevant results are presented in Figure 15-1, using an outline of the causal model from Figure 1-5 in Chapter 1. Notice that almost all of the constructs in the causal model are represented in this figure, except a construct that was not measured in this research was not enclosed in a circle. P_L was omitted from the figure because it was not measured and it would have cluttered the figure. Notice in the figure that g_v correlated .35 with A_L; this moderate relationship is reasonable because g_v is a distal cause of A_L in the causal chain of $g_v \rightarrow V_L \rightarrow A_L$. The g_v variable only correlated .13 with R_L, and this low relationship is as expected since there is no causal chain between g_v and R_L. As for the g_p variable, it is a distal cause of A_L via the causal chain of $g_p \rightarrow P_L \rightarrow A_L$, and it is a distal cause of R_L via the causal chain of $g_p \rightarrow P_L \rightarrow R_L$. Thus, it is a reasonable finding for g_p to correlate .50 with A_L and .49 with R_L. The high correlation between A_L and R_L of .63 is reasonable given that P_L is a proximal cause of both A_L and R_L.

One reason for reviewing these data from Naslund and Schneider (1991) is to show how using the causal model puts their results into a very different perspective. With the advantage of hindsight and the causal model, it can be seen that it is likely that a much higher impact of g_v in kindergarten would have been evident if an indicant of V_L had been administered in grade 2. That is, the correlation between g_v and V_L is likely to have been .50 or higher. Furthermore, a much higher impact of g_p in kindergarten is likely to have been evident if an indicant of P_L had been administered in grade 2; the correlation between g_p and P_L is likely to have been much higher than .50. Nevertheless, these data collected by Naslund and Schneider (1991) may be interpreted as being in accordance with the causal model, even though the causal relationships investigated were distal, not proximal; their relationships skipped Echelon 3 and stretched from Echelon 2 to Echelon 4.

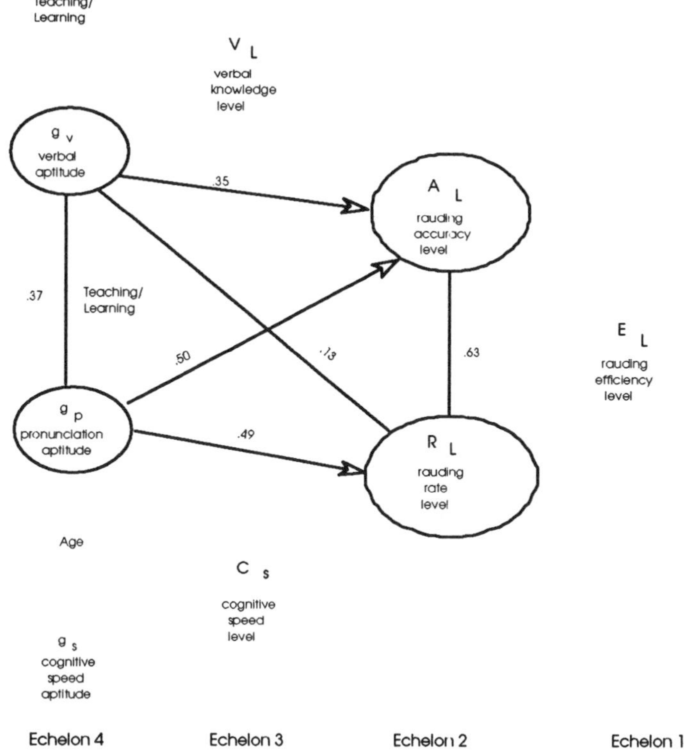

Figure 15 - 1. A graphic depiction of the correlational results reported by Naslund and Schneider (1991) in terms of the relevant constructs in the causal model.

In 1993, Uhry and Shepherd investigated the effect of teaching first graders to segment and spell words—in two 20-minute periods each week for 6½ months. This was an experimental treatment study, that is, not a descriptive study involving only correlations. They were investigating the effect of a particular teaching technique upon the pronunciation of words, or decoding. Translated into the context of the causal model, they were manipulating T/L at Echelon 4 to determine its effect. Thus, the effectiveness of this treatment should be most evident on pronunciation level. Indeed, an indicant of P_L—Woodcock Reading Mastery Tests-Word Identification—showed a very large effect size (ES) at the end of the school year. The experimental and control groups can be compared using Cohen's d; it was calculated to be 1.2. Because Cohen (1977) considers a *d* of .8 to be large, this was a very large effect of the teaching/learning factor at Echelon 4 upon P_L at Echelon 3.

Uhry and Shepherd also compared their experimental and control groups on the Listening Comprehension subtest of the Stanford Achievement Test, and found a small difference in favor of the control group instead of the experimental group (d = -0.2; small ES). Indeed, a zero (or near zero) ES would be expected because their decoding treatment is associated with a T/L factor for P_L in the causal model; therefore, their treatment would not be a proximal or distal cause of verbal level, V_L. They also compared their experimental and control groups on the Gates-MacGinitie Reading Test, which is likely to be an indicant of A_L in first grade because speeded reading achievement tests are rare or nonexistent in first grade. For this measure of A_L, Cohen's d was calculated for the means that were adjusted for pretest differences and it was .49; because d = .50 is a medium ES according to Cohen, this .49 value is a medium ES. So, T/L directed toward P_L resulted in a very large effect size for P_L, a small or negative effect size for V_L, and a medium effect size for A_L.

Figure 15-2 contains a graphic summary of Uhry and Shepherd's results, as translated into the causal model. Notice that their treatment is depicted by the arrow pointing to the teaching/learning circle and the arrow from that circle to the P_L circle. The effect size, ES, of this treatment upon P_L was found to be large, as noted above the P_L circle. However, the resulting effect upon A_L was medium in effect size because there was a small or negative effect upon V_L. The "ES = small" for V_L and the "ES = large" for P_L combined to produce an "ES = medium" for A_L.

These results would have been predicted from the causal model. If a treatment has a large effect upon P_L (d = 1.2) but no positive effect upon V_L (d = -0.2), then the net effect upon A_L would likely be medium in size (d = .49) because increases in A_L are due to an average of the gains in V_L and P_L. A large effect of a treatment upon P_L would not translate into a large effect upon A_L unless its other proximal cause, V_L, also increased more than a small amount. In this research, the average of the d values for P_L and V_L (1.2 and -0.2) was .50 which is almost exactly the d value for A_L (.49), as would be expected from the causal model. As noted earlier, these data provide *experimental results* which support the causal model, whereas most of the other data supporting the causal model has been correlational. This means that these data allow strong inferences to be made about V_L and P_L being the two proximal causes of A_L, because the effect of T/L upon P_L (d = 1.2) combined with the effect of this treatment upon V_L (d = -0.2) produced almost exactly the expected net effect upon A_L (d = .49).

In 1995, Stone and Brady conducted a study that seems to have involved five constructs from the causal model (g_v, g_p, P_L, C_s, & A_L), as depicted in Figure 15-3. They administered eight phonological processing tests, plus other tests, to 266 students in grades 2 and 3; these students as a group were at the boundary between lower graders and middle graders. The research employed a common design strategy whereby less-skilled readers were compared to one group matched on age and another group matched on "reading level." Group A was supposed to be the less-skilled reader group with Group B matched on age but reading better, and Group C matched on "reading level" but younger. The ages of the three groups, in grade equivalent units (AgeGE = Age - 5.4), were 3.4, 3.3, and 2.4, respectively. Notice that Groups A and B were almost exactly the same age whereas Group C was about 1 year younger.

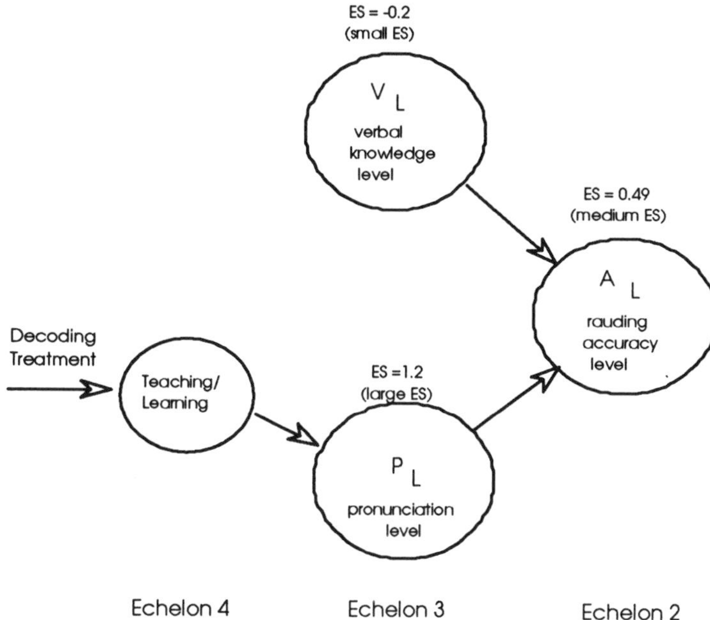

Figure 15-2. A graphic depiction of the effects associated with a decoding treatment administered by Uhry and Shepherd (1993) in terms of the relevant constructs in the causal model.

With respect to the results of the Stone and Brady research, the mean GE scores on the Word Identification test, from the Woodcock Reading Mastery Tests, Revised (WRMT-R), were 3.0, 5.0, and 2.8, respectively. Notice that Groups A and C were almost equal on this indicant of P_L, whereas Group B was about 2 GEs higher. This means that (a) Group A was LowP_L, that is, a little below average in P_L for their age (3.0 - 3.4 = -0.4), (b) Group B was considerably above average in P_L for their age, that is, HighP_L (5.0 - 3.3 = +1.7), and (c) Group C was a little above average for their age, that is, HighP_L (2.8 - 2.4 = +0.4). Group B had the highest ability-age difference (+1.7), Group C had the second highest ability-age difference (+0.4), and Group A had the lowest ability-age difference (-0.4)—in rank order from Group B to Group C to Group A. The above results for P_L compare favorably with the results for the three groups on a test which seems to be an indicant of pronunciation aptitude, g_p. This test was called the pseudoword imitation test, and it involved listening to tape-recorded pseudowords and then repeating them. This test involves the ability to learn and remember sounds in words and this ability represents part of the ability which defines pronunciation aptitude, g_p (see Chapter 13). On this later test, Group B scored the highest, 23.3, Group C second highest, 21.9, and Group A the lowest, 17.5—in rank order from B to C to A exactly like the P_L - AgeGE values noted above. These data are consistent with the causal connection between g_p and P_L in the causal model.

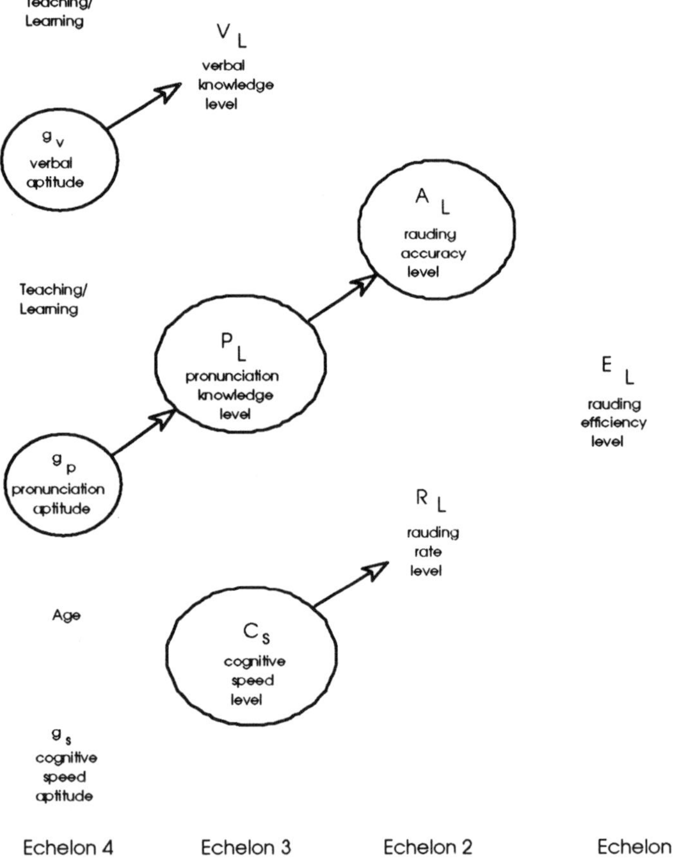

Figure 15-3. A graphic depiction of the measures administered by Stone and Brady (1995); the circled constructs in the causal model are the ones that were measured by Stone and Brady.

One of the tests administered by Stone and Brady (1995) was called Concurrent Processing, and it appears to be a good indicant of verbal aptitude, g_v. This test was an adaptation of the Daneman and Carpenter (1980) Reading Span test (see Chapter 12), except it did not involve reading, only listening to sets of tape-recorded sentences. Students listened to a series of sentences, and responded true or false after each. Then, students were supposed to remember the last word in each sentence. As explained in Chapter 12, this test should provide an indicant of g_v. The scores on this indicant of g_v for Groups A, B, and C were 18.2, 21.9 and 17.5, respectively. Unfortunately, there was no test administered which provided an indicant of verbal level, V_L, for comparison. However, g_v and g_p should be potent determiners of accuracy level, A_L, so it would be predicted that because Group A was the lowest on both g_v and g_p and Group B was the highest on g_v and g_p, then an indicant of A_L should be the highest for Group A and the lowest for Group B when A_L is compared to age. Indeed, this result was as expected, as indicated by the scores on the Passage Comprehension subtest from the WRMT-R—an indicant of A_L (see Chapter 4). Group B scored 4.5 which was the highest score compared to AgeGE (4.5 - 3.3 = +1.2), Group C scored 3.0 which was the second highest score compared to AgeGE (3.0 - 2.4 = +0.6), and Group A scored 3.3 which was the lowest score compared to AgeGE (3.3 - 3.4 = -0.1). These data also are consistent with the theorized causal connections involving g_v, g_p, and A_L.

Finally, it should be pointed out that Stone and Brady (1995) administered a rapid naming test, which involved the time (not rate) required to rapidly name pictured objects. This measure should provide an indicant of cognitive speed level, C_s (see Chapter 8). The time scores for Groups A, B, and C were 53.9, 48.1, and 58.4, respectively. Notice that Group C took the longest time to name, and this would be reasonable because (a) the groups were not selected on any variable which involved rate, such as C_s, R_L, or E_L, and (b) Group C was the youngest group (AgeGE = 2.4) . The lowest naming time was for Group B, which suggests that this better reading group probably had a higher cognitive speed level, C_s, than Group A which was the same age but was less skilled.

Given the clarity afforded from the vantage point of hindsight, it is obvious that if g_v was represented in this research, then some measure of V_L should have been administered to made the connection with A_L. It is also obvious that if C_s was measured then some measure of R_L or E_L should have been included because C_s is neither a proximal nor distal cause of any of the other measures administered in this research.

In 1998, Rupley, Willson, and Nichols purportedly tested rauding theory using structural equation modeling. They found fit indices above .95 for grades 1 and 2 (above .95 for grades 3 & 4, and above .90 for grades 5 & 6), which they interpreted as supporting rauding theory. However, they did not test the causal model of reading achievement as described in Carver (1997), which is almost exactly the same model as presented in Chapter 1. They included a measure of cognitive power (C_p) which was in an earlier model (Carver, 1990a), but has been dropped because of a lack of supporting evidence (see Chapter 20). Also, their measure of C_p was the Peabody Picture Vocabulary Test-Revised (PPVT-R), which was described in Chapter 12 as an indicant of g_v. In short, these data are only superficially relevant to the causal model of reading achievement, as described by Carver (1997) or as described in Chapter 1.

In 1999, Shankweiler et al. reported intercorrelations among indicants of V_L, P_L, A_L, and d_k, involving 361 children with reading problems whose ages were comparable to second and third graders. The correlations they reported involved reading variables that were composites. The reading comprehension variable, A_L, was the average score on 3 tests. The word reading variable, P_L, was the average score on 3 tests. The listening comprehension variable, V_L, involved only one test which probably was not highly reliable. Nevertheless, these indicants of V_L and P_L predicted A_L with a multiple R of .91, thus providing indirect support for Equation 10-3. Furthermore, these indicants of A_L and d_k predicted P_L with a multiple R of .96, thus providing indirect support for Equation 7-4. These data provide considerable support for the theory advanced in Chapter 13 that V_L, P_L, A_L, and d_k are so closely interconnected via Equations 7-4 and 10-3 that when values for two of these constructs are known, then the values of the other two can be determined mathematically.

Implications

In kindergarten, the best measures of the constructs in the causal model are probably quite different, as compared to middle graders and adults. A good indicant of g_v is likely to be an oral vocabulary test that was designed to maximize individual differences, such as the PPVT-R—as used by Dickinson and Smith (1994). A good indicant of g_p in kindergarten is probably a phonological awareness test, such as the Yopp-Singer test discussed earlier in Chapter 13 (Yopp, 1995). However another good indicant of g_p in kindergarten is probably letter-name knowledge—as used by Sears and Keogh (1993). A good correlate of g_s would be color naming (Denckla & Rudel, 1974) when the colors were overlearned and the rate of naming normed for age.

For kindergartners, V_L is probably best measured by an orally administered vocabulary test that is designed to measure achievement rather than individual differences. A good indicant of P_L would be a word-identification test that starts with very easy words, not letters; using letters on a word-identification test for kindergartners makes the test an indicant of g_p for the lower scoring students and an indicant of P_L for the higher scoring students.

The best indicant of C_s is probably a color-naming test, as was also suggested for g_s, above, except GE units should be used. A good indicant of A_L is probably a reading vocabulary test that starts with very easy words (very high frequency), or a sentence completion type of test such as the Passage Comprehension test from the Woodcock Reading Mastery Tests (see Chapter 4). A good indicant of R_L is probably a maximum oral reading rate measure (see Chapter 5) that involves very easy words in very easy sentences.

In kindergarten, a good indicant of E_L would be a silent reading comprehension test involving easy words and easy sentences that combined accuracy and rate; it is likely that a good indicant of E_L is almost impossible in kindergarten so that the best indicant of E_L would be derived from A_L and R_L via Equation 9-1 or Equation 9-2. The RELT (see Chapter 3) is not likely to provide a good indicant of E_L in kindergarten because almost all of the students will score 0, that is, they will not pass the test on the first-grade level passage so there will be no individual differences in E_L.

If the causal model is indeed valid, then it is not always necessary to include indicants of V_L or A_L when investigating hypotheses about the effect of a treatment designed to improve pronunciation level, P_L. If the treatment is highly effective, then it will be less effective in improving A_L because the large effect upon P_L is approximately cut in half in its effect on A_L—because V_L is not changed. It also seems likely that effective educational treatments in the past may have appeared to be ineffective because an indicant of E_L was used to assess effectiveness, thereby substantially diluting a large positive effect upon P_L, V_L, or both. Furthermore, this type of research may not have been published because it found no statistically significant difference between the experimental and control groups on a measure of E_L. Once again, it should be recognized that whenever V_L, P_L, or C_s are changed, the effects upon A_L, R_L, and E_L are likely to be mathematically determined by Equations 1-1, 1-2, and 1-3 (or Equations 10-2; 10-3, & 10-4), and these effects are likely to be diluted for the reasons just outlined. Therefore, unless there is some special extenuating circumstance, there may be no need to measure A_L, R_L, or E_L, because they are dependent upon V_L, P_L, and C_s.

If the causal model is valid, then it is questionable to measure how an indicant of g_v relates to A_L without also measuring V_L, and it is also questionable to measure how an indicant of g_p relates to A_L and R_L without also measuring P_L (e.g., see Naslund & Schneider, 1991). Furthermore, it is also questionable (a) to include measures of g_v from Echelon 4 but not measure V_L from Echelon 3, and (b) to include a measure of C_s from Echelon 3 but not include a measure of R_L at Echelon 2 or E_L at Echelon 1 (e.g., see Stone & Brady, 1995).

Forget Me Nots

There is a great deal of empirical data collected from lower-grade readers which supports the causal model.

CHAPTER

16

MIDDLE-GRADE READERS

The causal model depicted graphically in Chapter 1 is purported to be valid for many middle-grade readers, that is, those students who are between ages 8.4 and 13.3 years. When these ages are converted into GE units, then middle-grade readers are in grades 3 through 7, that is, 3.0 to 7.9. Almost all of the students in the middle grades (a) have learned the alphabetic principle, (b) have learned a great deal of cipher knowledge and know how to use phonological decoding skills, and (c) have a great deal of lexical knowledge. Most of these readers are intermediate readers. That is, they have verbal knowledge and pronunciation knowledge at the third-grade level or higher ($V_L \geq 3.0$ & $P_L \geq 3.0$). However, to be an intermediate reader, students cannot read so well that they have become an advanced reader, with $V_L \geq 8.0$ and $P_L \geq 8.0$.

In Chapter 10, it was theorized that both V_L and P_L were likely to be causal for A_L for those students who had not yet reached raudamaticity. However, for students who were at raudamaticity, P_L was not an independent factor that causally affected A_L. This means that classrooms of students in grades 3 to 7 probably have varying percentages of students that are below and at raudamaticity, with the percentage that is at raudamaticity increasing as the grade level becomes higher. When the causal model is applied to classrooms in these grades, then P_L probably is an independent causal factor for most students in grade 3 but it probably is not an independent causal factor for most students in grade 7. Nevertheless, when the causal model is applied to a sampling of students in grades 3 to 7, it is likely that it will provide a good fit to the data because relatively few students will be at raudamaticity.

Existing data will be presented from several research studies in the lengthy section which follows. These data were collected from middle-grade readers, and they involved proximal causes along with distal causes and noncausal relationships. The relevant evidence will be presented in chronological order.

Existing Data

In 1974, Schmidt and Crano reported correlations involving 3,944 middle-SES students in grades 4 and 6, who took the Iowa Test of Basic Skills, ITBS, and had (a) reading comprehension scores (indicants of E_L), (b) reading vocabulary scores (indicants of A_L), and (c) spelling scores (indicants of P_L). Notice that they had one measure at Echelon 3, P_L, one at Echelon 2, A_L, and the one at Echelon 1, E_L. When these students were in the fourth grade, A_L correlated .73 with E_L; when they were in the sixth grade the corresponding correlation was .81. With respect to the correlation between P_L and A_L, it was .58 in fourth grade and it was also .58 in sixth grade. The above correlations probably would have been higher if they had not excluded 1,501 lower-SES students; these lower-SES students were likely to have scored lower so their exclusion (a) restricts the range and lowers the correlations, and (b) excludes many students who were below raudamaticity and were likely to have had a closer relationship between P_L and A_L. Nevertheless, these data provide correlational evidence for a high relationship between A_L and E_L which supports the theory that A_L is a proximal cause of E_L. These correlational data also provide evidence for a substantial relationship between P_L and A_L which supports the theory that P_L and A_L are reciprocally causal (see Chapter 13) for many middle graders.

In 1979, Fleisher, Jenkins, and Pany conducted a study which involved several parts related to the causal model; these data have also been cited from a different perspective in earlier chapters. These researchers investigated whether poor readers would comprehend text better if they were trained to decode the words in the text more rapidly. They conceived their research as investigating the "strong form of the bottleneck hypothesis," which was that "... fast decoding is a sufficient condition for high comprehension" (p. 33). Their subjects were students in the fourth and fifth grades who were good and poor readers. The good readers scored at the seventh-grade level on the Metropolitan Achievement Tests (MAT); probably this translates into high E_L and/or high A_L. The poor readers scored at the second-grade level on the MAT—probably low A_L and/or low E_L. Both groups were given two passages to read which were around 100 words in length, and were at the 7.1 and 6.3 grade level of difficulty according to a readability formula (D_L = 6, 7). The poor readers were given the words in the text of one of the two passages and trained to decode those isolated words until they could read them out of context accurately, and at a rate of 90 words per minute or more. Then, they were given both the passages to read for comprehension.

They found that the poor readers learned to read the words in isolation much faster, from 43 wpm prior to training to 93 wpm after training. Their rate of reading these isolated words after training was almost as fast as the good readers read them at 100 wpm. Notice that this means that these slow readers could be trained to respond quite rapidly to isolated words, almost as rapidly as these good readers—probably because these poor and good readers did not differ drastically on cognitive speed level, C_s, because they were approximately the same age. When the poor readers were asked to read aloud the particular passage that they had been trained to decode the isolated words rapidly, they did read it faster, much faster than the untrained passage, 91 vs. 61 wpm. However, there was no evidence from three different comprehension measures that they comprehended the passage that they read any more accurately when they read faster; there was no difference in comprehension between the trained passage and the untrained passage. Furthermore, the good readers read the untrained passage much faster than the poor readers read either the trained passage or the untrained passage (168 wpm vs. 91 and 61 wpm), and the good readers comprehended their untrained passage much better than the poor readers comprehended either the trained or untrained passage (large effect sizes).

The above research of Fleisher, Jenkins, and Pany will be analyzed next from the standpoint of the causal model and rauding theory. First, it is likely that the text being read was very difficult for the poor readers because it was around the sixth- and seventh-grade level of difficulty (D_L = 6, 7); these poor readers were likely to have an accuracy level well below that, probably around A_L = 2 or 3. Their accuracy of comprehension, A, of any text could be predicted from the equations given in Appendix C. That is, if their A_L and R_L had been measured, and the time they spent reading text of known length and difficulty level had been measured, then accuracy of text comprehension, A, could be predicted quite accurately. Furthermore, this accuracy, A, probably would not change by some brief training on how fast the words could be read in isolation. There is no provision for that kind of improvement in the formulas involved in rauding theory. Furthermore, it is reasonable to interpret these data collected by Fleisher, Jenkins, and Pany as supporting rauding theory and the causal model because rauding accuracy, A_r, did not increase with this training. Theoretically, the only way that rauding accuracy can be improved is by improving A_L (see Equation 2-2). Because substantial increases in A_L are likely to occur only with many hours of instruction and learning over a year of time, in accordance with the T/L factors at Echelon 4 in the causal model, it is very unlikely that brief training procedures geared toward helping poor readers decode 100 words faster would increase A_L substantially.

This research can also be analyzed more closely from the standpoint of rate level, R_L. The reading rates reported in this research were oral reading rates, not silent. However, the silent reading rates were likely to be close to the oral reading rates of the good readers because most of the good readers were probably operating their rauding process on material that probably was not hard for them. Their rate was 168 wpm and that is likely to be around the fifth- or sixth-grade level (R_L = 5 or 6). The rate level of the poor readers is likely to be much lower, around R_L = 2 or 3. From the standpoint of rauding theory and the causal model there is no way that this treatment—designed to increase the rate at which the words in a 100-word passage at the sixth-grade level of difficulty could be pronounced accurately—would increase R_L in any substantive or measurable way; R_L can only be increased substantially by increasing P_L or C_s

over a year of time, and their brief treatment would not likely increase either P_L or C_s.

In 1991, A. E. Cunningham and Stanovich presented data from 134 students in grades 4, 5, and 6 who had been given several reading related tests. Four of their measures seemed to provide indicants of constructs in the causal model located in Echelons 2, 3, and 4, namely g_v, V_L, P_L, and A_L. Their Word Checklist was a vocabulary measure which consisted of 27 words (e.g., coin, grooming, and secretary) and 13 nonwords (disler, plabage, and wiltial), so the checking of more actual words and less nonwords would likely constitute an indicant of A_L. Their General Information test was "a probe of general world knowledge" (p. 267) and it consisted of 18 questions asked orally which required written answers; this variable would likely provide an indicant of V_L (see Chapter 6). Their spelling measure consisted of 20 words administered auditorily (e.g., sugar, succeed, chocolate) with written answers required; this variable should provide an indicant of P_L (see Chapter 7). They administered the Peabody Picture Vocabulary Test, Revised (PPVT-R), and it should be an indicant of g_v (see Chapter 12).

Figure 16-1 contains the causal model with the four constructs studied by Cunningham and Stanovich surrounded by circles, and the correlations between the constructs noted on the connecting lines. Notice that the correlation between V_L and A_L ($r = .43$) was not as high as most of those reported in Chapter 10; however, the indicant of A_L was a checklist that only took 5 minutes to administer and probably was low in reliability—a reliability estimate was not reported for this indicant of A_L. The correlation between the indicants of P_L and A_L was .68, which is highly consistent with P_L being reciprocally related to A_L for many middle graders.

With respect to Echelon 4 in Figure 16-1, g_v correlated .66 with V_L, as would be consistent with the causal model. Just as importantly, g_v correlated lower with A_L at Echelon 2 (.32) than it did with V_L at Echelon 3 (.66), and this is consistent with g_v being a proximal cause of V_L but a distal cause of A_L. These data from A. E. Cunningham and Stanovich (1991) provide results which are consistent with the causal model, and thereby may be said to provide correlational support for the causal model.

In 1997, Carver, presented data from 156 students in grades 2 to 11 (Study I, 52 students in grades 3 to 5; Study II, 104 students in grades 2 to 11). This research has also been described in earlier chapters, but from a different perspective. These data have subsequently been analyzed in a manner that involves only the middle graders, that is, 135 of the 156 students who were between AgeGE = 3.0 and AgeGE = 7.9, with a mean of 5.2 and an SD of 1.2. For these students, the intercorrelations among the 6 variables at Echelons 1, 2, and 3 have been determined—controlled for age. That is, Table 16-1 contains the partial correlations among all the variables, plus their means and SDs. Notice in Table 16-1 that V_L correlated .77 with A_L, and P_L correlated almost as highly with A_L, .66. P_L also correlated highly with R_L, .55; almost as highly as C_s correlated with R_L, .67. Again, these correlational data are consistent with the causal model; the high correlation between P_L and A_L is also consistent with P_L and A_L being reciprocally causal.

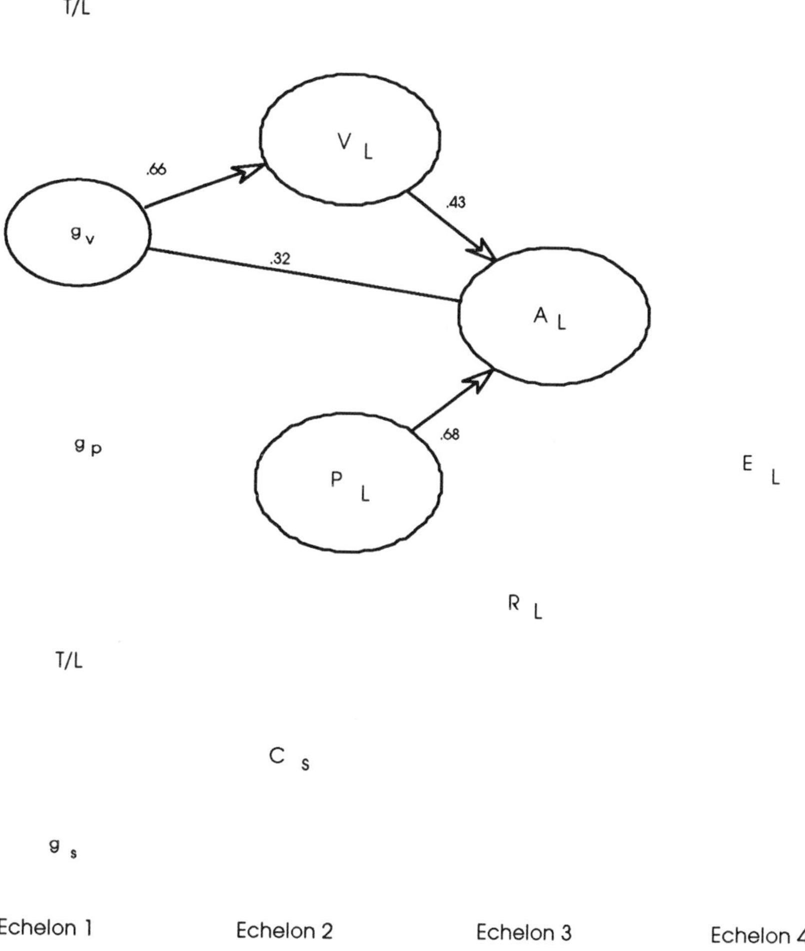

Figure 16-1. A graphic depiction of four constructs in the causal model that were measured by A. E. Cunningham and Stanovich (1991), with the simple correlations between the four circled constructs given on the lines connecting the pairs of constructs.

Also in 1997, Olson, Wise, Ring, and Johnson reported upon the effects of phonological awareness training. Their research involved T/L for P_L at Echelon 4, P_L (and d_k) at Echelon 3, and A_L at Echelon 2, for students in grades 2 to

5. The experimental treatment group received explicit, analytic phonological training. They were given "... many of the training procedures of the Lindamood Auditory Discrimination in Depth (ADD) program ..." (p. 238). The control group received no PA training. Both groups received computer-based remediation training and individuals in both groups were below the local 10th percentile in word recognition. The control group ($N = 45$) was given 18 hours of computerized help on a program called ROSS, which was described as follows:

> The children in the ROSS program read interesting stories on the computer and were trained to target difficult words with a mouse for decoding assistance so they could correctly identify the words. The difficulty level of the stories was continually adjusted, so that children required assistance on 2% to 5% of the words.
> (p. 237)

Table 16-1
Partial Correlations Among the Six Variables of Echelons 1,2, and 3 in the Causal Model for Students in the Middle Grades ($N = 135$)

Variable	V_L	P_L	C_s	A_L	R_L	E_L	*Mean*	*SD*
V_L; Verbal Level	1.00	.49	.27	.77	.37	.61	5.4	2.6
P_L; Pronunciation Level		1.00	.40	.66	.55	.68	5.0	2.7
C_s; Cognitive Speed Level			1.00	.35	.67	.60	5.4	2.4
A_L; Accuracy Level				1.00	.54	.83	5.3	2.5
R_L; Rate Level					1.00	.91	5.1	2.7
E_L; Efficiency Level						1.00	5.0	2.4

When reading on ROSS, the children were "... encouraged to target any word they were unsure of and to use the colors to help them sound out the word before clicking the mouse again for computer pronunciation of the segments, and again for the whole-word pronunciation if needed" (p. 239). Both the experimental and control groups received 7 hours of small group instruction, and both groups read on ROSS. The major difference between the two groups was that the control group spent 18 hours reading on ROSS while the experimental group spent only 8 hours reading on ROSS and 10 hours in the training on phonological awareness. They summarized their experimental design as follows:

> The primary reason for including the [control] condition was to have a comparison group that spent most of its time reading stories with decoding assistance for unfamiliar words, but that included the same amount of time with interesting small-group activities. Both small group and individualized computer time was the same for the two groups. What was different, and what we wanted to compare, was the effects of time spent in explicit phonological instruction and

> practice versus spending that practice time in accurate phonologically supported story reading. (p. 239, 240)

With respect to the results of the above research, the experimental treatment was effective in that the effect sizes for two measures of phonological awareness were extremely large (1.00 for the Lindamood Auditory Conceptualization test, and .77 for a phoneme deletion test). So, there is little doubt but that the individuals in the experimental group were more aware of the phonemes in words, using auditory measures that involved no reading. These researchers also measured the percent correct on a nonword reading test, which constituted an indicant of pure decoding knowledge, d_k, and it also had a very large effect size, 1.29. Therefore the experimental group which received the 10 hours of phonological awareness training gained much more in pure decoding knowledge, d_k. This result is consistent with the theory presented earlier in Chapter 13 that PA and c_k, or d_k, would be reciprocally related for students who had learned to read more than a few words.

Another test these researchers administered was an experimentally developed measure of time-limited word recognition, which was a "... difficulty-ordered list of words presented individually for 2 sec on the computer screen" (p. 245). This would constitute an indicant of A_L (see Chapter 4). For this A_L measure, there was an effect size of -.51, which was medium in size and favored the control group *not* the experimental group. Notice that these results suggest that there was a tradeoff in terms of treatment effectiveness—the experimental group had a large advantage with respect to pure decoding knowledge, d_k, and the control group had a medium advantage with respect to reading level, or A_L. It appears that the extra 10 hours that the control group received in learning how to pronounce increasingly difficult words was more effective in increasing accuracy level, A_L, which is a proximal cause of reading achievement, or E_L; the experimental treatment had a large effect upon d_k but this advantage was negated by a loss, relatively, in A_L.

Remember that Olson et al. also measured P_L. Before the treatment, both groups were around $P_L = 2.5$. The experimental group gained about 0.7 in GE units and the control group gained about 1.0 in GE units. It should be remembered that P_L is composed of d_k and A_L (see Chapter 7), and that P_L is likely to involve (a) some words that are accurately pronounced from cipher knowledge alone (uniquely c_k), (b) some words that are accurately pronounced from lexical knowledge alone (uniquely A_L), and (c) many words are accurately pronounced from the combination of cipher and lexical knowledge (combination of d_k and A_L). Therefore, if the experimental group gained more in d_k (and c_k) and gained less in A_L, then it is not clear how to predict what the net effect on P_L would be. However, the net effect should be relatively small because the gain in d_k for the experimental group would be offset by the gain in A_L for the control group because P_L is composed of d_k and A_L. In fact, there were two indicants of P_L and both had small effect sizes (PIAT, +.27; WRAT-R, +.15).

These data can be reasonably interpreted as providing support for the causal model because they are consistent with what would be predicted. A treatment that devoted a great deal of time to phoneme awareness and letter-sound knowledge, compared to a treatment that devoted a comparable amount of time to increasing A_L, produced a relatively large gain in phoneme awareness, PA, a relatively large gain in pure decoding knowledge, d_k, a relatively small gain in P_L, and a relative loss in A_L. A treatment that devotes more time to reading words in context, and learning about their pronunciation and their meaning, increased A_L more—probably by increases in both V_L and P_L. The large gain in d_k which resulted from phonological awareness training did not produce a very large gain in P_L because P_L is composed of both d_k and A_L. A treatment that focuses too much on d_k at the expense of lexical knowledge, or A_L, is likely to be at a disadvantage because increasing d_k provides too much of an accent on increasing pure cipher knowledge without regard for increasing lexical knowledge.

Olson et al. were able to give delayed posttests to 27 experimentals and 20 controls, 1 year later. The effect size for d_k remained large, .93, the effect size for A_L dropped to near zero, .01, and the effect size for P_L remained near zero, .13. This means that there was no booster effect on P_L or A_L associated with the relatively large gain in phonological awareness, or d_k. Then, these researchers did a 2-year follow-up on 19 experimentals and 17 controls There was still a large advantage for the experimentals on d_k, but the effect of P_L was near zero (.25 for PIAT and .00 for WRAT-R) and the effect on A_L was small, .22. Olson et al. contended that their results were in keeping with other researchers (Brown & Felton, 1990; Foorman, Francis, Shaywitz, Shaywitz, & Fletcher 1997; Lovett et al., 1994; Torgesen, Wagner, & Rashotte, 1997) in that "the more explicit phonologically based programs produced better phonological decoding, but not significantly better word recognition in most measures at the end of training" (p. 249).

In 1997, Torgesen, Wagner, Rashotte, Burgess, and Hecht presented simple correlations involving several indicants of constructs in the causal model—P_L, A_L, R_L & E_L—for students in grades 2, 3, 4, and 5. They conducted a two-part longitudinal study involving 215 students whom they tested in both grade 2 and grade 4, plus 201 students whom they tested in both grade 3 and grade 5. They measured phonological awareness, PA, and rapid naming in grades 1, 2, and 3, but not grades 4 and 5.

Figure 16-2 contains the causal model constructs at Echelons 1, 2, and 3 that Torgesen et al. measured in grades 4 and 5 along with the correlations between the pairs of these constructs for grade 4 and also for grade 5. For example, in grade 4 the correlation between the indicants of A_L and E_L was .82; the corresponding correlation for grade 5 was .76. Their indicant of E_L was a measure they called Word-Reading Efficiency. It involved a list of 104 words on a page which increased in difficulty (from high frequency, such as *up* and *he*, to low frequency, such as *repayment* and *permutation*); the students were given 45 seconds to name as many of the words correctly as they could. Their indicant of A_L was the Passage Comprehension measure from the Woodcock Reading Mastery Tests. Their indicant of R_L was a computer-administered latency measure of the speed at which 20 short exception words (e.g., lose, deaf, anchor) could be pronounced; only words correctly pronounced were used to calculate the average speed over all the words. The indicant of P_L was the Word Identification test from the Woodcock. In Figure 16-2, notice that the simple correlations between constructs and their proximal causes were all relatively large, ranging from .58 to .85. These data provide additional correlational support for the causal connections between these parts of the causal model.

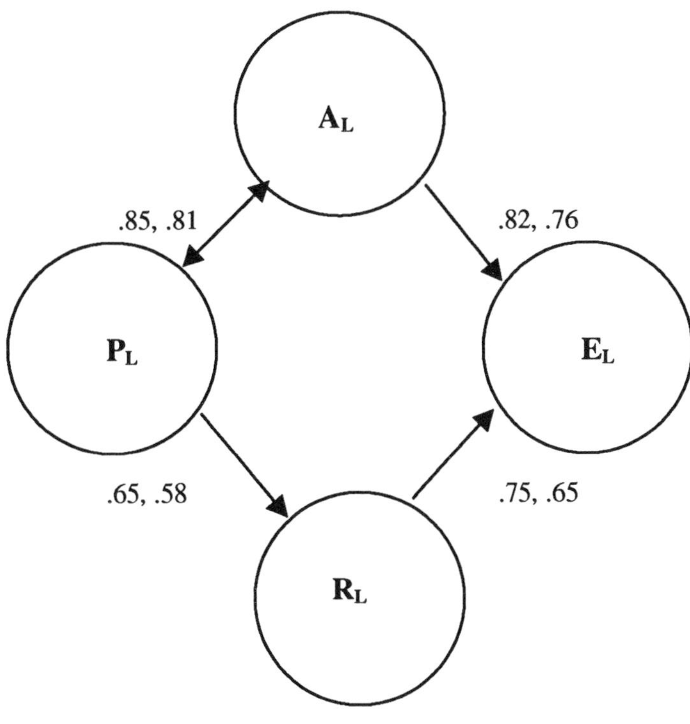

Figure 16-2. Simple correlations between indicants of constructs at Echelons 1, 2, and 3 for 215 students in grade 4 and 201 students in grade 5—taken from Torgesen, Wagner, Rashotte, Burgess, and Hecht (1997).

There are other results in this Torgesen et al. research which provide additional support for the causal model. When the multiple *R* was calculated for predicting E_L from A_L and R_L in grade 4, it was found to be .88; *R* increased to .93 when each simple correlation involved was corrected for attenuation prior to calculating multiple *R*. When the corresponding multiple *R* was calculated for grade 5, it was .80; it increased to .83 when corrected for attenuation. These data provide additional correlational support relevant to A_L and R_L being the proximal causes of E_L (see Chapter 9).

It should also be pointed out that one of the main conclusions drawn by Torgesen et al. (1997) was that rapid naming (an indicant of C_s) in grades 2 and 3 contributed little or nothing to the prediction of two-year growth in word identification, P_L, word attack, d_k, or reading comprehension, A_L. Those conclusions are perfectly in keeping with the causal model in that C_s is purported to be neither a proximal nor distal cause of P_L, d_k, or A_L. Therefore, these data may be interpreted as providing additional correlational support for this part of the causal model.

Furthermore, it should be noted that Torgesen et al. presented reading speed data (indicant of R_L) for students in grade 5, which on the surface, may seem to provide evidence against the causal model. They found that their indicant of C_s in grade 3 contributed only 1% unique variance to the prediction of their indicant of R_L in grade 5, after the variance accounted for by R_L in grade 3 had been removed. However, the gain in R_L due to a gain in C_s should be constant for each individual (see Chapter 11), that, is there should be no variation between individuals in their gains in C_s from year to year. Therefore, C_s should not contribute to the prediction of individual differences in gain because there are no individual differences in gain due to maturation. This means that these data are also consistent with the causal model and provide support for it.

Forget Me Nots

The data collected from middle graders are overwhelmingly consistent with the causal model.

CHAPTER

17

ADULT READERS

The causal model for most adult readers is not exactly the same as it was presented in Figure 1-5, Chapter 1. Adult readers were defined earlier as 8th graders and older, that is AgeGE $\geq$ 8.0 or age 13.4 and older; notice that this definition of an adult is at variance with a common requirement that individuals be age 16 and older. Most adults are at raudamaticity, and the causal model needs to be modified for all readers who are at raudamaticity. Furthermore, most adult readers have become advanced readers, that is, they have reached the eighth-grade level or higher on verbal level and pronunciation level ($V_L \geq$ 8.0, $P_L \geq$ 8.0), and all advanced readers are assumed to be at raudamaticity. Therefore, for most adults, the model needs to be modified because some of the constructs in the model no longer have the same proximal causes that they had for most lower-grade readers and most middle-grade readers.

In the next section, the new relationships between several of the constructs in the model will be delineated. Then, empirical data will be presented in the lengthy section that follows; these data will involve proximal, distal, and noncausal relationships that are relevant to the validity of the modified causal model.

Modified Causal Model

As was explained above, it has been theorized that all advanced readers are at raudamaticity, that is, they have raudamatized all of their audamatized words. Therefore, verbal level and accuracy level have become perfectly synergistic; an increase in one causes an increase in the other. This means that for individuals at this high level of cipher knowledge, $P_L \geq$ 8.0, it has been hypothesized that pronunciation level is no longer a proximal cause of accuracy level, A_L, and it is no longer a proximal cause of R_L, so P_L has been removed from the causal model along with its own proximal causes at Echelon 4. Furthermore, it has been hypothesized that these advanced readers have reached developmental maturity, so age is no longer a causal factor for C_s; therefore, g_s and C_s should correlate perfectly even when age varies among adults. These changes are depicted in Figure 17-1.

When $V_L \geq 8.0$ and $P_L \geq 8.0$, then $A_L = V_L$ and $R_L = C_s$.

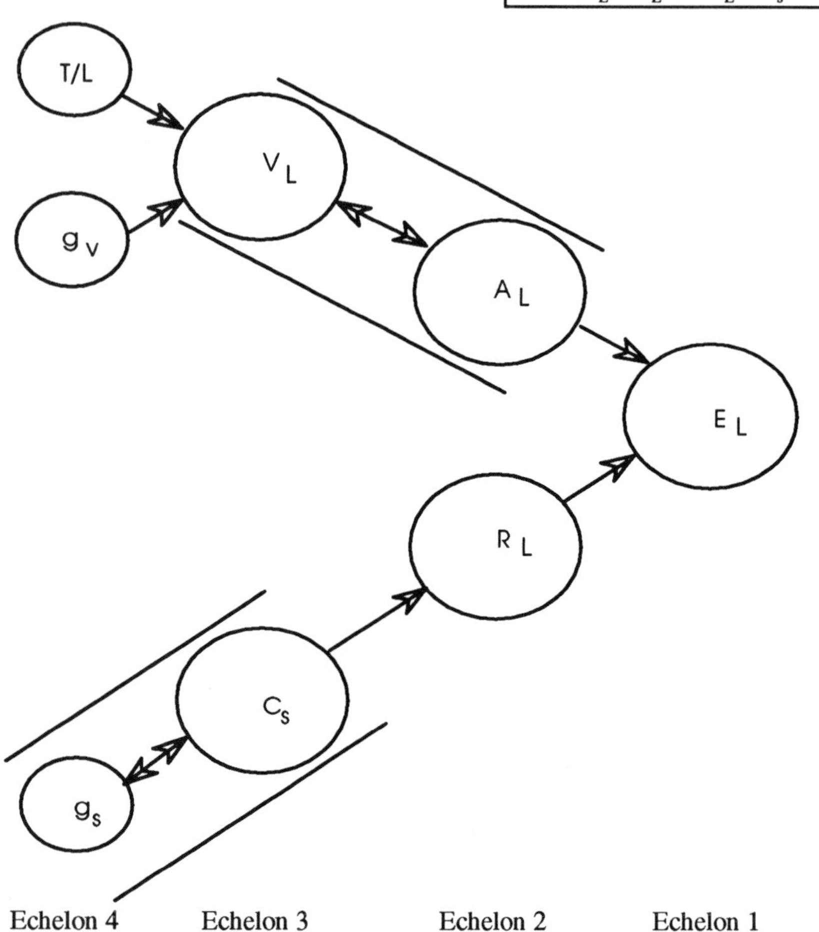

Figure 17-1. The modified causal model for many adult readers (Age $\geq$ 13.4) who are advanced readers ($V_L \geq 8.0$, $P_L \geq 8.0$). Note that (a) V_L and A_L have been joined by a line with double-headed arrows, and two enclosing lines, symbolizing the theory that V_L and A_L are synergistic and perfectly correlated, (b) P_L and its proximal causes at Echelon 4 are no longer in the model, and (c) g_s and C_s have also been joined by a line with double-headed arrows and two enclosing lines, symbolizing the theory that these two constructs are perfectly correlated because age is no longer a causal factor for C_s.

Notice also in Figure 17-1 that the line between V_L and A_L has an arrow on both ends signifying a synergistic relationship, or a reciprocally causal relationship. Learning new words and concepts when listening will ordinarily result in the same words and concepts being comprehended when they are read, and learning new words and concepts by reading will also ordinarily result in the same words and concepts being comprehended by listening. This means that when individuals learn to understand the meaning of a new word when listening (have audamatized the word), then that word will likely be recognized in print also, given the advanced reader's high level of pronunciation knowledge, or orthographic skill ($P_L \geq 8.0$). This also means that when an advanced reader learns the meaning (and pronunciation) of a new word in print, then that word will also be understood when listening because it is likely that the individual's high level of pronunciation knowledge will result in a pronunciation of the word that matches the way it is pronounced by others when it is spoken. This means that an increase in V_L will result in a corresponding increase in A_L and an increase in A_L will result in a corresponding increase in V_L. Notice that one long line has been drawn above V_L and A_L and another long line has been drawn below V_L and A_L to further signify the close connection between these two constructs for advanced readers.

Extensive data on the relationship between auding and reading has been reviewed by Sticht and James (1984), and these data support the equivalence of V_L and A_L at about the eighth-grade level. They concluded that (a) "up to the seventh grade, auding surpasses reading on the average, whereas at the seventh grade, one is equally likely to find auding surpasses reading and reading equal to or surpassing auding" (p. 305), and (b) "these data indicate that auding surpasses reading until a measured skill at the seventh-grade level is obtained; at that point, and beyond, there is equivalence in accuracy and efficiency of processing by ear and by eye" (p. 307). Support for this equivalence for advanced readers comes from Palmer et al. (1985), who noted that for college students "Reading speed is only moderately correlated with listening comprehension, but reading comprehension is indistinguishable from listening comprehension ability" (p. 59). Given the above theory and data, it appears reasonable to hypothesize that

$$\text{when } V_L \geq 8.0, \text{ and } P_L \geq 8.0, \text{ then } A_L = V_L \qquad (17\text{-}1)$$

This means that A_L is no longer the average of V_L and P_L for advanced readers; Equation 1-2 and Equation 10-3 no longer hold for advanced readers, because they have reached a point where they are able to comprehend everything in print that they can comprehend when spoken. For advanced readers, learning to pronounce more words cannot increase A_L because all of their audamatized words are already raudamatized.

It is also being hypothesized that when an individual reaches $P_L = 8.0$, then their cipher knowledge and lexical knowledge have reached a point where further increases cannot improve R_L. This means that there is a limit to the helpfulness of implicit learning of letter combinations and their associated sounds with respect to speed of word pronunciation. Learning how to pronounce and spell new words (increase P_L) will not increase how fast words are rauded (increase R_L) after P_L becomes equal to, or greater than 8.0. Therefore, when $P_L \geq 8.0$, then P_L drops out as a factor causing R_L, leaving only C_s as a causal factor, so that

$$\text{when } P_L \geq 8.0, \text{ then } R_L = C_s \qquad (17\text{-}2)$$

Equation 17-1 and 17-2 are presented as more refined hypotheses that are associated with the modified causal model presented in Figure 17-1; these two equations make explicit the theory that P_L is no longer causal for advanced readers who have $V_L \geq 8.0$ and $P_L \geq 8.0$. Equations 17-1 and 17-2 are also summarized in the statement enclosed in the box which is in the top right side of Figure 17-1.

Before reviewing relevant data, it should be noted that it has been estimated that about 55% of adults are advanced readers (see Chapter 18), and the modified causal model in Figure 17-1 is directly relevant to these adults. However, this modified model will not be relevant to the estimated 40% of adults who are intermediate readers, or the estimated 5% of adults who are beginning readers.

Empirical Data

Empirical evidence will be reviewed which is (a) directly relevant to adults and the casual connections in the modified causal model, and (b) relevant to non-adjacent and noncausal connections in the model. This evidence will be reviewed in chronological order.

In 1956, Webb and Wallon administered a reading test (indicant of A_L) and a listening test (indicant of V_L) to hundreds of men between the ages of 18 and 25 who had a minimum of 2 years of college, or equivalent, and had been accepted for naval flight training. It is likely that these adults with 2 years of college would be advanced readers, or they would not have done well enough on written tests to have been accepted for flight training. The textual materials involved were chosen to have low familiarity; they were taken from mythology. There were two forms of the test, each containing three stories (totaling 2,300 words) with 45 questions on Form I and 43 questions on Form II. The two relevant experimental conditions were (a) to listen to a tape recording of the stories, and (b) to read the story through once. For each of the two forms involving a total N of 536, the means were comparable under these two conditions. They concluded that "a single read-through of the material and hearing the material read once resulted in equally effective comprehension" (p. 239). These data support the comparability of V_L and A_L for advanced readers, and therefore support the comparability of V_L and A_L for most adults.

In 1979, M. D. Jackson and McClelland administered several measures to 52 freshmen and sophomores at a university; these data have been cited for other purposes in earlier chapters. They developed an indicant of efficiency level, E_L, on a long passage (4,286 words) by multiplying the speed that the passage was read (in words per minute) by the percentage correct on the corresponding 10 short-answer comprehension questions. They developed an indicant of accuracy level, A_L, from the answers to the 33 short questions on 11 paragraphs containing about 317 words each. They developed an indicant of rate level by measuring how fast these 11 paragraphs were read in words per minute. The indicant of A_L correlated .52 with the indicant of E_L, and the indicant of R_L correlated .72 with the indicant of E_L. Clearly, the product formula they used for creating E_L made it more highly related to R_L than A_L, probably because there was more variance in their rate measure. Nevertheless, these data may be considered as correlational support for A_L and R_L being proximal causes of E_L for advanced readers. They also developed a listening comprehension test (an indicant of V_L) on another set of 11 paragraphs designed to be equivalent to the ones just described as an indicant of A_L. They reported a correlation of .55 between this indicant of V_L and the indicant of A_L just described. This correlation of .55 is not as high as would have been expected from the modified causal model which holds that V_L and A_L are synonymous for adults. However, it was possible from their own data to estimate the reliability of the indicant of A_L for the short passages from its correlation with a similar indicant of A_L on the long passage; this reliability estimate was only .55. Therefore, V_L correlated as high with A_L as could be expected from the estimated reliability of A_L, and this may be interpreted as providing support for V_L and A_L being the same for adults.

In this research of Jackson and McClelland, they also measured letter-naming speed using latencies on a Posner type of task similar to the Speed of Thinking Test task described in Chapter 8; this variable provided an indicant of C_s. Unfortunately, Jackson and McClelland did not report the correlation between this indicant of C_s and an indicant of R_L. They did report the correlation between this indicant of C_s from Echelon 3 and the indicant of E_L from Echelon 1, just noted; this correlation between E_L and one of its distal causes was .45. The correlation between C_s and R_L likely would have been much higher because (a) C_s is a proximal cause of R_L and (b) E_L contains considerable variance due to A_L that is not causally affected by C_s.

In summary, these data collected by Jackson and McClelland provide correlational support for the part of the causal model for advanced readers which holds that V_L and A_L are synonymous. Their data also provide support for C_s being a distal cause of E_L.

In 1985, Palmer et al. reported a correlation between listening comprehension and reading comprehension of .82, for 91 sophomores and juniors in college who were likely to be advanced readers. They interpreted their results as follows: "Reading comprehension can be predicted almost perfectly by a listening measure" (p. 80). Therefore, these data provide support for $V_L = A_L$ in the modified causal model.

In 1990, A. E. Cunningham, Stanovich, and Wilson administered 22 reading-related measures to 76 introductory psychology students, and these measures included indicants of several constructs in the causal model. The Nelson-Denny Reading Test (NDRT) was administered, and the comprehension score (NDRT-Comp) on this test provided an indicant of E_L whereas the vocabulary score (NDRT-Vocab) provided an indicant of A_L. They also administered the NDRT as a listening test (ND-Listening), and this would be an indicant of V_L. Their best indicant of R_L came from a test they called the Easy Word RT; it measured latency of vocal reaction time (RT) for naming easy words after they appeared on a monitor. They measured latencies to naming 25 letters of the alphabet, and this would constitute an indicant of C_s. Because latency variables are time measures, instead of rate, correlations involving latencies will be reversed in sign, later, to facilitate communication.

Figure 17-2 contains the indicants of each construct, just mentioned, in the context of the modified causal model. To the right of the circle containing each theoretical construct is the name of the test used by these researchers, which is an indicant of the construct. Under each test name is an estimate of reliability. The split-half reliabilities reported by the researchers were used for V_L, A_L, and E_L. For C_s, the correlation between letter naming and number naming was used as the reliability estimate; this was lower than the split-half value reported (.78 vs. .93). For R_L, the correlation between Easy Word RT and Hard Word RT was used as the reliability estimate because the researchers did not report a reliability coefficient. The correlation between each pair of variables hypothesized to be causally related is given in Figure 17-2; following each correlation is the corrected value in parentheses.

These data in Figure 17-2 provide correlational support for A_L and R_L being the proximal causes of E_L, because the two corrected correlations were .79 (between A_L and E_L) and .64 (between R_L and E_L). The corrected correlation between V_L and A_L is .73, and the corrected correlation between C_s and R_L was .70. These two correlations should be closer to 1.00 according to the causal model. However, it is likely that the split-half reliabilities involved were inflated estimates of reliability; remember that the split-half estimate for Letter Naming RT was .93 whereas this variable only correlated on .78 with another variable that should be measuring exactly the same construct. The uncorrected intercorrelations involving the five variables (N = 76) depicted in Figure 17-2 were subjected to structural equation modeling with the causal relationships hypothesized as the arrows indicate. The Bentler and Bonett Normed Fit Index was .92. This relatively large goodness of fit for the modified causal model provides correlational support for this model.

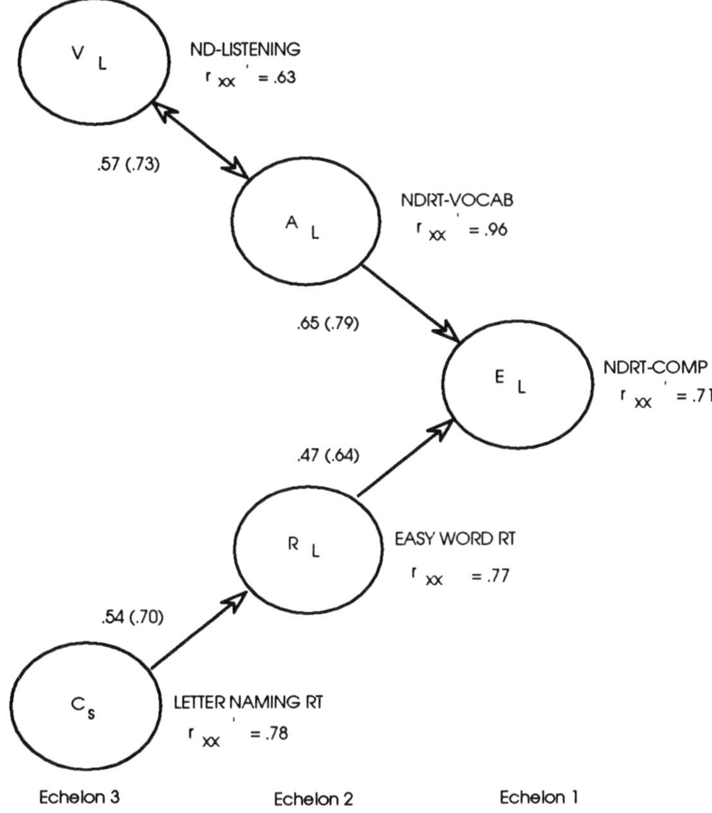

Figure 17-2. Correlations, reliabilities, and corrected correlations between indicants of constructs in the causal model, taken from test results reported by A. E. Cunningham, Stanovich, and Wilson (1990).

In 1994, Bell and Perfetti provided data relevant to most of the factors in the causal model, namely, E_L, A_L, R_L, V_L, P_L, C_s, and g_v. These researchers were interested in the components of reading, so they administered many different reading tasks. They reported means and standard deviations for three different groups on 46 variables. These data will be examined at length and in great detail because (a) they are extensive, and (b) they are directly relevant to almost all parts of the modified causal model.

The three comparison groups studied by Bell and Perfetti were selected using scores from the Scholastic Aptitude Test (SAT), which has a verbal score and a quantitative score. They had one high-skilled reading group that was high on SAT Verbal (M = 609) and high on SAT Quantitative (M = 593); this group will be labeled HiVerbalHiQuant. They had two low-skilled reading groups. One was low in SAT Verbal (M = 414) and low in SAT Quantitative

(M = 447); this group will be labeled LoVerbalLoQuant. The other low-skilled reading group was low on SAT Verbal (M = 419) and high on SAT Quantitative (M = 585); this group will be labeled LoVerbalHiQuant. On the Comprehension section of the Nelson-Denny Reading Test, NDRT, the mean percentile rank for the HiVerbalHiQuant group was very high at 86, whereas the mean percentile ranks for the other two groups were very low at 22 and 24, respectively. The groups were also formed to be approximately comparable on the Spatial Ability subtest of the Primary Mental Abilities Test. Bell and Perfetti contended that this made the three groups roughly comparable in performance IQ.

Before getting into the details of their results, three things should be pointed out. First, it was not clear how many students had to be tested in order to form these three groups with an N of 10, 9, and 10 respectively. Second, it was not exactly clear how they carried out this selection procedure involving four different criteria, simultaneously. Third, because scores on mathematics tests ought to correlate highly with fluid intelligence, Gf, and because performance IQ scores also should correlate highly with fluid intelligence, it is not clear what the end result is when these two indicants of Gf are forced to be uncorrelated by group selection. In spite of the problems just outlined, most of their results still fit the causal model, as will be explained later. One of the reasons why their data fit the causal model in spite of the strange selection procedures involving two indices of fluid intelligence is probably because Gf (whether measured by a mathematics test or performance IQ) is not a major factor according to the causal model (see Chapter 20).

By selecting the HiVerbalHiQuant group to be high on the Comprehension section of the Nelson-Denny, they were automatically high on efficiency level, E_L; so, this HiVerbalHiQuant group will also be referred to hereafter as the HiE_L group. By forcing the other two groups to be low on this same measure, they were automatically low on efficiency level, E_L. So, the LoVerbalLoQuant group will hereafter be labeled as the LoE_L1 group, and the LoVerbalHiQuant group will hereafter be labeled as the LoE_L2 group.

According to the causal model, if one group is higher than another on E_L, then the higher E_L group would also have to be higher on A_L and/or higher on R_L because A_L and R_L determine E_L. So, for the Bell and Perfetti data, the HiE_L group must also tend to be higher than the two low E_L groups on measures that would be indicants of A_L and/or R_L. Indeed, their data provided strong support for this theory. For example, on the Vocabulary section of the Nelson-Denny Reading Test, NDRT, which is an indicant of A_L, the mean of the HiE_L group was 89 and the means for the other two groups were 48 and 50, respectively. These differences in means can be compared much better using effect size, ES, measures, such as Cohen's *d*. This ES measure compares the differences between the means to standard deviations involved; for example, the difference between the means of the vocabulary scores for the HiE_L group and the LoE_L1 group (89 - 48 = 41) would be divided by an estimate of the population standard deviation derived from the SD of the HiE_L group (11.3) and the SD of the LoE_L1 group (22.3). In this situation, $d = 2.37$. This value of d can be judged as small, medium, or large using Cohen's (1977) criteria; that is, $d = .80$ is a large ES, .50 is medium, and .30 is small. Thus, we can see that $d = 2.37$ is an extremely large ES, suggesting that one major cause of the difference in E_L between the high and low E_L groups is an extra large difference in A_L. When the HiE_L group is compared to the other low group, LoE_L2, the d was almost exactly the same size, 2.25. And, when the two low E_L groups were compared to each other, then $d = .09$, indicating that they were comparable on A_L because ES was very small.

According to the causal model, if the two low E_L groups (LoE_L1 and LoE_L2) are approximately equal on E_L and A_L, as the results reported above indicated, then these same two groups would also have to be approximately equal on an indicant of R_L. A comparison of R_L between these two groups can be made using the reading rate data they reported. They measured the rate at which these students read 10 paragraphs, in words per minute. When the two low groups were compared on R_L, d was .09, indicating that ES was small. So, these data were consistent with the results that would have been predicted *a priori* from the causal model, and thereby provide support for this part of the causal model.

It is possible for the differences between the HiE_L group and the two low E_L groups to be completely accounted for by large differences in A_L that were just reported. However, it is also possible that the large differences in E_L are also caused by large differences in R_L. These differences in R_L were again measured using d; it was 1.28 for HiE_L compared to LoE_L1, and it was 0.90 for HiE_L compared to LoE_L2. Again, these are extremely large ES differences using Cohen's criteria ($d = .80$ for large). So, for these data, the large differences between the HiE_L group and the two low E_L groups were likely caused by the HiE_L group being much higher on both of the primary causes of E_L, namely, A_L and R_L.

The large group differences found above for vocabulary as an indicant of A_L, were replicated for another indicant of A_L that they reported. After their students read each of the 10 passages noted above (where rate was measured in words per minute) they also administered short-answer comprehension questions. So, this comprehension variable would also be an indicant of A_L. When d was calculated comparing the HiE_L group to the two low E_L groups on this comprehension indicant of A_L, it was 2.00 and 2.04, respectively, and it was only .38 when the two low E_L groups were compared with each other. So, from the causal model, it would be predicted that the results for the vocabulary measure would be replicated by an unspeeded accuracy of comprehension measure, and they were.

Bell and Perfetti also measured rate and comprehension as their students read long passages on science, history, and fiction. They described the measure on each passage as "a 30-point multiple choice comprehension test" (p. 246). Again these data should replicate the results for A_L just reported, and they did. The mean of the three values of *d* for the comparison between HiE_L and LoE_L1 for the three passages (science, history, fiction) was 1.23—a very large ES for A_L, again. The corresponding *d* for the comparison between HiE_L and LoE_L2 was 1.20—another very large ES for A_L. The corresponding *d* for the differences between the two low E_L groups was .22—a small ES which also replicates the A_L data from the vocabulary measure and the 10 short passages reported earlier.

When the same kind of *d* calculation as just described was performed on the rates in words per minute for reading these long passages, the *d* for comparing HiE_L with LoE_L1 was 1.23—which replicates the large ES for the R_L data reported above. When the corresponding *d* was calculated for the comparison between the HiE_L group and the LoE_L2 group, it was .55—a medium ES. This latter *d* value does not replicate the large ES found earlier. Also, the *d* for comparing the two low E_L groups was .50 which was also medium in ES. So, for this indicant of R_L, the HiE_L and LoE_L1 groups provided replicative evidence, but the LoE_L2 group did not. It seems likely that many of these students shifted out of their rauding process and into a learning process for this silent reading, and that is why these rate data did not support theory regarding R_L.

Another indicant of R_L administered by Bell and Perfetti (1994) was vocalization latencies of high-frequency words, low-frequency words, and pseudowords. For the high-frequency words, the accuracies were almost perfect, with group means of 99.5% and 99.0%, respectively. Therefore, the latencies for pronouncing these words should be an indicant of R_L, with little or no variation due to possible accuracy trade offs; the *d* values for comparing the HiE_L group with each of the two low E_L groups were .96 and 1.22, respectively. These are very large ES values for this indicant of R_L. The corresponding *d* values for comparing the two low E_L groups with each other was only .15, a small ES as predicted. So, these objective data relevant to rauding rate suggest that the HiE_L group included faster readers (high R_L) and that was a major cause of the large differences in E_L between the HiE_L and the two low E_L groups.

To summarize up to this point, the Bell and Perfetti data involved one group of highly efficient readers and two groups of lowly efficient readers, and the mean differences among the groups provided support for the causal model. For three separate types of indicants of A_L (vocabulary, accuracy of comprehension of short passages, accuracy of comprehension of long passages), all suggested that one major cause of the differences in E_L was differences in A_L. Also, for three indicants of R_L (rate of reading short passages, rate of reading long passages, and latency of responding to high-frequency words), almost all suggested that another major cause of the group differences in E_L was due to major differences in R_L. There was one exception to the consistency just noted, and it was the data for the rate of reading the long passages for one of the two lowE_L groups.

Now that those data have been presented relevant to A_L and R_L at Echelon 2 being the two proximal causes of E_L at Echelon 1, it is appropriate to move on to Echelon 3. Bell and Perfetti also administered measures that were indicants of V_L, P_L, and C_s. One indicant of V_L was a listening comprehension measure that involved listening to 10 short passages and then giving short-answer questions. Because these college students should be advanced readers, V_L should provide results that are equivalent to the A_L results, and they do. For this indicant of V_L, *d* was calculated to be 1.23 for the comparison between the HiE_L group and the LoE_L1 group—a very large ES for this V_L correlate. The corresponding *d* for the comparison between the HiE_L group and the LoE_L2 group was 1.54—another very large ES. The corresponding *d* for the comparison between the two low E_L groups was .32, which is a small ES.

The above V_L results were also replicated by a listening comprehension test given on the long passages in science, history, and fiction. The mean *d* value for the three passages comparing HiE_L with LoE_L1 was 1.33—again a very large ES for V_L. When the two low E_L groups were compared to each other, the LoE_L1 group was higher than the LoE_L2 group on one passage but it was lower on the two others, giving a mean *d* of .06—small ES. So, these V_L results from the listening comprehension tests given on the long passages replicates the V_L results from the listening comprehension tests given on the short passages. These comparable scores for V_L and A_L are consistent with the modified causal model which holds that for advanced readers, A_L and V_L are measuring the same factor.

In the modified causal model for advanced readers, P_L is purportedly not causal for A_L or R_L. Bell and Perfetti also administered seven measures of spelling accuracy—four types of regularly spelled words (common, familiar, unfamiliar, and obscure) and three types of irregularly spelled words (common, familiar, and unfamiliar). For the common regular words, each of the three groups got 100% correct. The best indicants of P_L would be how these groups spelled familiar and unfamiliar words that are spelled both regularly and irregularly. When the HiE_L group was compared to the LoE_L1 group by calculating the mean for the above four measures, then *d* is very large at 1.42. When the corresponding *d* was calculated for comparing the HiE_L group with the LoE_L2 group, it was large at .88. The corresponding *d* for comparing the two low E_L groups was .70. So, these data are mixed with respect to support for the modified causal model. The HiE_L group had higher P_L than the two lowE_L groups, even though P_L was not supposed to be causal, yet there was a difference in P_L between the two lowE_L groups which is relevant to the causal model because P_L is no longer a distal cause of R_L. It should be remembered, however, that indicants of P_L can still be expected to be related to indicants of A_L even though P_L is not causal for A_L; they will be related because A_L and c_k are components of P_L (from Chapter 7).

Next, the other major factor that is redundant with R_L in the modified causal model will be examined, namely, cognitive speed level, C_s. The indicant of cognitive speed administered by Bell and Perfetti was a variant of the Posner task (see Chapter 8); it involved latencies for deciding whether a pair of letters have the same name or not. For this task, they reported the latencies for each of the three groups when the name was the same. The HiE_L group was compared to each of the other two low E_L groups, and *d* was .95 and .91, respectively--large ES values. When the two low E_L groups were compared to each other *d* was .05, a very small ES. So, we find that the results for C_s are equivalent to the results for R_L, as would be predicted from the modified causal model.

Finally, Bell and Perfetti administered one measure that was relevant to Echelon 4, namely, the reading-span task which should be an indicant of g_v for adults who can read as well as they can aud (see Chapter 12). Remember that g_v is one of two major factors causing V_L, and, it should be a factor that helps explain differences in V_L. If the HiE_L group has higher V_L scores than the other two groups, then one factor that ought to be a cause of this would be higher g_v for the HiE_L group. Therefore, the earlier reported differences in V_L should be accompanied by a similar pattern of differences in an indicant of g_v, such as the reading-span measure. These college students were asked to read aloud sets of three to seven sentences and then recall the last word in the set of unrelated sentences read immediately before. However, they were not very good at this particular version of the task because the means and SDs for the three groups were very low on this scale from 0 to 7, that is, 2.35(.69), 1.78(.26), and 2.05(1.21), respectively. It seems that the sentences used for this task were too long and complex to yield enough variability; one of their example sentences was "When at last the eyes opened, there was no gleam of triumph, no shade of anger." With such low mean scores and such low standard deviations, it would not be surprising if no differences were found, or there were inconsistencies. When the HiE_L group was compared to each of the two low E_L groups, *d* was 1.10 and .31, respectively, and *d* was -.30 when the two low E_L groups were compared to each other. This means that there was a large ES when the HiE_L group was compared to LoE_L1 but the ES was small when the HiE_L group was compared to LoE_L2. Therefore, it can be seen that those results are only partially in accordance with what would be predicted from the causal model.

Parenthetically, it should be noted that Bell and Perfetti did not calculate any of the effect size measures reported earlier. Instead, they made dichotomous decisions about whether the means of their three groups were different or not, by first testing for statistical significance among the three means, and then when statistical significance was found, conducting paired comparisons. This procedure has been called a corrupt form of the scientific method (Carver, 1978), and it has recently been shown to be detrimental to the cumulation of knowledge by Schmidt (1996). Using effect size measures instead of statistical significance (Carver, 1993b), the data collected by Bell and Perfetti were, in general, highly supportive of the causal model, with a few exceptional results that were not supportive.

In 1998, Carver and Clark published three studies, one of which involved 128 community college students who were enrolled in reading improvement classes. For these 128 students, it was possible to reanalyze their data by selecting only the advanced readers ($V_L \geq 8.0$ and $P_L \geq 8.0$). For the 51 students who met this criterion, the correlation between the indicant of V_L and the indicant of A_L was .91, the mean of V_L was 12.3 (SD = 1.5) and the mean of A_L was 12.9 (SD = 1.7). This high correlation of .91 and the comparability of the means (12.3 vs. 12.9) is highly consistent with the theory that V_L and A_L are synergistic and comparable for advanced readers. For these adults who are advanced readers, the correlation between the indicant of C_s and the indicant of R_L was .81; the mean of C_s was 10.6 (SD = 3.0) and the mean of R_L was 9.5 (SD = 2.3). This high correlation of .81 between C_s and R_L is probably about as high as the reliabilities of both measures would permit. Furthermore, the means of these two variables, C_s and R_L, were roughly comparable (10.6 vs. 9.5). So, these data may also be interpreted as providing evidence for C_s being the only cause of R_L for advanced readers. P_L correlated only .21 with A_L, and only .29 with R_L, but this is misleading because almost all of these 43 advanced readers were at the top on this word-identification test (M = 8.6; SD = 0.83). In summary, these reanalyzed data from Carver and Clark (1998) provide support for the theory that $A_L = V_L$ and $R_L = C_s$ for adults who are advanced readers.

Out of the 128 adults involved in the Carver and Clark (1998) study just described, there were 77 who were not advanced readers. Their results should provide evidence relative to the validity of the causal model described in Chapter 1. For those 77 college students who were not advanced readers, V_L correlated .75 with A_L, and P_L correlated .60 with A_L; V_L and P_L predicted A_L with R = .86. Notice that V_L and P_L probably account for all of the reliable variance in A_L. For this group, P_L correlated .47 with R_L and C_s correlated .62 with R_L; P_L and C_s predicted R_L with R = .71. Notice that P_L and C_s probably account for almost all of the reliable variance in R_L. When the intercorrelations among V_L, P_L, and C_s, and A_L, R_L, and E_L were subjected to structural equation modeling, the Bentler and Bonett (1980) normed-fit-index was .97. However, this index would be inflated somewhat due to E_L being estimated from the geometric mean of A_L and R_L (using Equation 9-1). Nonetheless, these data collected from adults who were not advanced readers provided correlational support for the causal model presented in Chapter 1. Therefore, it appears that the causal model fits data collected from adults who are not advanced readers (N = 77), and the modified causal model also fits data collected from adults who are advanced readers (N = 51).

Implications

The reading achievement of adults who are advanced readers probably can only be increased by increasing verbal knowledge level; increasing their P_L is not likely to increase E_L via A_L or R_L, and R_L is likely to be completely determined by C_s which is not amenable to improvement via education or learning. However, many adults are not advanced readers, and read relatively poorly. Educators and researchers should recognize that for many of these poor-reading adults, their reading achievement, or E_L, probably can be improved via instruction and learning activities designed to increase P_L; these poor-reading adults are likely to be below the 8th grade level in P_L so that A_L and/or R_L probably can be improved by helping them learn to spell more of the words they know when listening so these words can become raudamatized with practice. Many poor-reading adults, however, are likely to be low in verbal knowledge, and verbal aptitude, so instruction designed to increase P_L would not be very effective unless it also was designed to increase verbal knowledge, V_L.

Forget Me Nots

The data collected from adults seem to fit the modified causal model of reading achievement very well, as long as the adults are likely to be advanced readers. That is, advanced readers have (a) equivalent reading and listening levels, $A_L = V_L$, and (b) have equivalent rate levels and cognitive speed levels, $R_L = C_s$. The reading achievement of advanced readers cannot be increased by instruction which focuses upon the pronunciation and spelling of more words.

PART V

DISABLED READERS

This part of the book contains two chapters relevant to disabled readers. Chapter 18 explains the rauding diagnostic system (RDS), which is based upon the causal model. In this system, three primary disabilities, two secondary disabilities, and three handicaps are diagnosed. These eight specific deficits can be determined from tests developed to measure constructs in the causal model. Empirical data will also be presented that is directly relevant to the validity of this system.

The rauding diagnostic system, RDS, has been developed in a manner that is consistent with the admonitions of Stanovich and Siegel (1994). They pointed out that it would be logical to determine if individuals were reading poorly using a psychometrically sound measure, and then determine if these poor readers differ with respect to other cognitive abilities. They also noted that this approach, although logically sound, had not yet been applied in the reading disability field. Again, this has been the logic underlying the development of the rauding diagnostic system since its beginnings (Carver, 1991).

After the details of the RDS have been described in Chapter 18, Chapter 19 compares this system to previous theory and research in the areas of dyslexia and reading disabilities.

CHAPTER

18

THE RAUDING DIAGNOSTIC SYSTEM

The causal model can be used to diagnose reading disabilities, and this is important from a practical standpoint. If we can improve upon our diagnosing of reading problems, then we should be able to solve more of those problems.

In this chapter, a diagnostic system will be described which uses efficiency level, E_L, to determine if an individual is a poor reader, that is, a reader who is so low in reading achievement that it is reasonable to conclude that this individual has a reading problem. If an individual does have a reading problem (low E_L for age), then the proximal causes of this problem are first determined. For those individuals who are very low in E_L at Echelon 1, then the cause of their problem is likely to be that they are low in A_L or low in R_L at Echelon 2. Those individuals who are low in A_L and/or low in R_L at Echelon 2 are likely to have these problems because they are low in V_L, P_L, and/or C_s at Echelon 3. An individual who is low in V_L is likely to have had poor teaching/learning experiences and/or be low in verbal aptitude, g_v. An individual who is low in P_L is likely to have had poor teaching/learning experiences and/or be low in pronunciation aptitude, g_p. An individual who is low in C_s is likely to have low g_s or be low in age.

Individuals who have low A_L or low R_L for their age will be defined as having a secondary disability in reading. Individuals who have low V_L, low P_L, or low C_s for their age will be defined as having a primary disability in reading. It may be possible to remediate the primary disabilities in V_L and P_L because they involve factors which are directly or indirectly influenced by teaching and learning experiences; the remediation of primary disabilities at Echelon 3 should automatically remediate the secondary disabilities at Echelon 2, and thereby increase reading achievement.

Individuals who have low g_v, low g_p, or low g_s will be defined as handicapped in reading. It is not likely that a g_v handicap, a g_p handicap, or a g_s handicap can be remediated because these conditions are likely to be associated with inherited brain structures. It should be remembered that a low aptitude—low g_v, g_p, or g_s—means that the individual is being compared to an average person of the same age, that is, low aptitude means low compared to other individuals at the same age.

In most cases, the diagnosed handicaps will probably best explain why a person has a reading problem. However, in some cases a person may have no handicaps, only poor teaching and learning experiences. In any event, the diagnosis should help to determine if low achievement in reading can be remediated, how to best remediate it, and how long it will take to remediate it. This system of diagnosing reading problems will be called the rauding diagnostic system, RDS.

Before presenting more of the details involved in the RDS, it will be helpful to review the age and ability categories used earlier in this book because the rauding diagnostic system is only appropriate in certain of these categories. Then, the RDS will be described in detail, and its relationship to diagnoses of dyslexia will be described. A section has also been devoted to remedial treatments recommended for each of the primary disabilities. Finally, empirical evidence relevant to the system will be presented.

Age, Skill, and Achievement

This section contains a review of the categorizations used with respect to age and rauding skill, as presented in Chapter 2, and how they relate to the rauding diagnostic system, RDS.

Figure 18-1 contains the operational definitions of the three age or grade categories (lower grade, middle grade, and adult) and the three rauding skill categories (beginning, intermediate, and advanced). For example, notice that (a) lower graders are below the third-grade level in AgeGE units, and (b) beginning readers are below the third-grade level, in V_L or P_L. Also notice that "No Diagnosis" has been placed in each of the three boxes representing lower graders. The RDS is not appropriate for lower graders (grade 2 and below; age less than 8.4 years), because the system requires an individual to be considerably lower than what would be expected for their age in order to have a disability. For example, it would be impossible for a first grader to be two GEs lower than expected because none of the tests provide scores lower than zero in GE units, so the RDS is not appropriate for them.

Also in Figure 18-1 are the same rough estimates given in Chapter 2 of the percentage of individuals in each age (or grade) category who are beginning, intermediate, and advanced readers. These frequency estimates have no direct ties to empirical data, and are given only to help clarify the relationship between the three age or grade categories and the three rauding skill categories.

Not mentioned in Figure 18-1 are the five categories of rauding achievement—Very Poor Readers, Poor Readers, Average Readers, Good Readers and Very Good Readers. These five categories of rauding achievement are defined with respect to the difference between E_L and age in GE units—called AgeGE. Individuals who have an E_L that is more than 2.0 GEs below their AgeGE are Very Poor Readers. Individuals who have an E_L that is 1.0 to 2.0 GEs below their AgeGE are Poor Readers. Individuals who have an E_L that is between 1.0 below and 1.0 above their AgeGE are Average Readers. Individuals who have an E_L that is 1.0 to 2.0 GEs above their AgeGE are Good Readers. Individuals who have an E_L that is more than 2.0 GEs above their AgeGE are Very Good Readers. For adults (AgeGE $\geq$ 8.0), their AgeGE is set at 8.0 so that their categories of rauding achievement are always in relationship to the eighth-grade level; for example, a Very Poor adult reader would have a E_L that is below 6.0. This means that most college students would be categorized as Very Good Readers because most would have an E_L that was at the tenth-grade level or higher (E_L = 10.1 or higher).

Age Categories	Rauding Skill Categories: BEGINNING Verbal level is less than 3.0 or pronunciation level is less than 3.0. ($V_L < 3.0$ or $P_L < 3.0$)	INTERMEDIATE Has progressed beyond being a beginning reader but has not yet become an advanced reader. ($V_L \geq 3.0$ & $P_L \geq 3.0$; $V_L < 8.0$ or $P_L < 8.0$)	ADVANCED Verbal level and pronunciation level must both be 8.0 or higher. ($V_L \geq 8.0$ & $P_L \geq 8.0$)
LOWER GRADERS (Below AgeGE 3.0) (Age < 8.4 years) (100%)	No Diagnosis (80%)	No Diagnosis (20%)	No Diagnosis (0%)
MIDDLE GRADERS (AgeGE 3.0 to 7.9) (8.4 yrs. < Age < 13.4 yrs.) (100%)	Use Rauding Diagnostic System (10%)	Use Rauding Diagnostic System (70%)	Use Rauding Diagnostic System (20%)
ADULTS (AgeGE 8.0 and above) (Age $\geq$ 13.4 yrs.) (100%)	Use Rauding Diagnostic System (5%)	Use Rauding Diagnostic System (40%)	Use Rauding Diagnostic System (55%)

Figure 18-1. Appropriateness of the reading diagnostic system for three age (or grade) categories and three rauding skill categories, with estimates of the percentages in each rauding skill category for each age category.

Categorizing individuals as Very Poor Readers when they are 2.0 GEs below age in GE units is a somewhat conventional practice. For example, in the *Encyclopedia of Human Intelligence*, Perfetti (1994) has given the following operational definition of dyslexia: "children are considered dyslexic if their reading achievement is sufficiently low relative to some standard (usually two grades below their grade level), and if the deficit cannot be accounted for by low IQ or a lack of opportunity to learn" (p. 924). Requiring individuals to be 2.0 GEs below grade level in reading achievement is comparable to requiring individuals to have an E_L score that is 2.0 GEs below AgeGE in order to be classified as a Very Poor Readers. The RDS is mostly appropriate for Poor and Very Poor Readers.

In summary, there are three age categories (lower graders, middle graders, & adults), three rauding skill categories (beginning, intermediate, & advanced), and five categories of rauding achievement (Very Poor, Poor, Average, Good, & Very Good). The RDS diagnoses reading disabilities for Poor and Very Poor Readers who are middle graders and adults.

Causal Model and the Diagnostic System

Introduction. The causal model, summarized in Chapter 1, contains the factors that purportedly cause high and low reading achievement, and these causal factors form the basis for the rauding diagnostic system. This system follows the logical strategy articulated by Stanovich and Siegel (1994)—noted earlier in the introduction to Part V. They state that: "One might have thought that researchers would have begun with the broadest and most theoretically neutral definition of reading disability—reading performance below some well-known and psychometrically sound test—and then proceeded to investigate whether there were poor readers with differing cognitive profiles within this broad group" (p. 25). Indeed, this is the strategy of the rauding diagnostic system. First, it is determined if individuals read poorly, that is, whether they are low in efficiency level, E_L, which also means low in reading achievement or general reading ability. As noted earlier, individuals with low E_L scores are categorized as Poor Readers (between 1 and 2 GEs below that expected for their age) or Very Poor Readers (2 GEs or more below that expected for their age).

The determination of rauding achievement is based on E_L, which is in Echelon 1 of the causal model (see Chapter 1). The description of the RDS, which follows, will be organized by reference to Echelons 1, 2, 3, and 4.

Echelon 1. Children who have E_L scores (in GE units) that are approximately equal to what would be expected from their age, or higher, are not considered as having a reading problem. That is, if their rauding achievement is Average, Good, or Very Good, then they are not considered as having a reading problem. It is possible that these students who read well, relative to their age, have scores that are low in other areas. They might be diagnosed as having a disability but this is not serious for them, and it should happen rarely; when it does happen it is likely to be due to unreliable scores. Furthermore, treatment would be questionable in these situations where a disability is diagnosed but the individual does not read poorly.

The diagnostic system is most appropriate for Very Poor Readers—those students with an E_L that is at least 2 GEs below that expected for their age

(AgeGE). AgeGE is their age in years minus 5.4; for example, a student in grade 5 who is 11.6 years old would have an AgeGE of 6.2 (11.6 - 5.4 = 6.2), which is sixth grade in GE units. Students with an E_L that is between 1 and 2 GEs below AgeGE are called Poor Readers, as noted earlier, and the RDS is also appropriate for these students. This means that the RDS is appropriate for individuals in grades 3 or higher with reading problems, that is, children who are poor readers because they are in the rauding achievement category of Poor Reader or Very Poor Reader. Again, it is a common practice to select a sample of reading-disabled children using the criterion of one or two grade levels below that expected from a child's age (e.g., see Bowers, Steffy, & Tate, 1988).

Echelon 2. The proximal causes of the reading problems of Poor Readers and Very Poor Readers, as determined from their low E_L score for their age, are theorized to be due to either a very low rauding accuracy level, A_L, or a very low rauding rate level, R_L—called secondary disabilities. Individuals are diagnosed as being disabled in rauding accuracy level when A_L is 2 or more GE units below their AgeGE; they are diagnosed as being disabled in rauding rate level when R_L is 2 more GE units below their AgeGE. Poor Readers and Very Poor Readers are highly likely to be accuracy disabled (DisabledA_L), rate disabled (DisabledR_L), or both (DisabledA_LR_L). The proximal causes of reading poorly (low E_L for age) are purported to be DisabledA_L, DisabledR_L, or DisabledA_LR_L.

Lovett (1984) seems to have been the first to advocate diagnosing readers as accuracy disabled and/or rate disabled, although her criteria for these disabilities were different from the criteria just described for the RDS.

Echelon 3. Next to be discussed are the factors in Echelon 3—V_L, P_L, C_s—which are purported to be the proximal causes of DisabledA_L, DisabledR_L, or DisabledA_LR_L.

Given that V_L and P_L are the two proximal causes of high and low A_L, in the causal model, it follows that individuals who are accuracy disabled, DisabledA_L, are highly likely to be disabled in verbal knowledge level (DisabledV_L), disabled in pronunciation level (DisabledP_L), or disabled in both (DisabledV_LP_L). In this diagnostic system, individuals with V_L at least 2 GE units below their AgeGE are DisabledV_L, and individuals with P_L at least 2 GE units below their AgeGE are DisabledP_L.

Given that P_L and C_s are the two proximal causes of R_L in the causal model, it follows that individuals who are rate disabled, DisabledR_L, are very likely to be disabled in pronunciation level, DisabledP_L, disabled in cognitive speed level (DisabledC_s), or disabled in both (DisabledP_LC_s). The operational definition of DisabledP_L was given earlier. The operational definition of DisabledC_s is as follows: C_s must be at least 2 GE units below AgeGE.

The three disabilities at Echelon 3—verbal, pronunciation, and cognitive speed—will be called primary disabilities because they are the proximal causes of the two secondary disabilities at Echelon 2. The two disabilities at Echelon 2—accuracy and rate—have been called secondary disabilities because they are secondary in importance to the three primary disabilities; they are secondary with respect to the diagnoses which are used to determine the treatments most likely to remediate the reading problems, or to increase reading achievement, E_L.

For some students, their reading comprehension difficulties are mainly due to general language comprehension difficulties (DisabledV_L). These students are also likely to be low in accuracy level, A_L. For other students who read poorly; it is their decoding and spelling that is poor (DisabledP_L). These students are also likely to be low in accuracy level, A_L, and rate level, R_L. Then, there are some students who have a problem with their speed of thinking, or cognitive speed (DisabledC_s). These students are also likely to be low in rate level, R_L.

Next, the proximal causes of the primary disabilities at Echelon 3 will be described; those causal factors will be derived from the root causes of reading achievement, at Echelon 4 in the causal model.

Echelon 4. As described in earlier chapters, there are three fundamental aptitudes at Echelon 4 that influence reading achievement, namely verbal knowledge aptitude, g_v, pronunciation aptitude, g_p, and cognitive speed aptitude, g_s. These three aptitudes influence how much individuals are able to profit from teaching and learning experiences with respect to improvement in reading achievement. These aptitudes will be measured using standard scores, or stanine units; stanines range from 1 to 9 with a mean of 5 and an SD of 2. Individuals with stanines 1 and 2 will be labeled as handicapped. For example, an individual with a stanine of 2 for g_v will be labeled as handicapped in verbal knowledge aptitude, or g_v handicapped. The three handicaps will be abbreviated as Handicapped/g_v, Handicapped/g_p, and Handicapped/g_s.

If stanine scores are rounded off to the nearest whole number, as they normally are, then a stanine of 2 would represent 1.5 SDs below the mean. This criterion of 1.5 SDs below the mean has been used elsewhere as a cutoff criterion for reading disability or dyslexia (e.g., see Shaywitz et al., 1992). So, stanine scores of 1 (2 SDs below the mean) and 2 (1.5 SDs below the mean) will be used as the criteria for being handicapped at Echelon 4. Because a stanine of 2.49 would round off to 2, and because this stanine of 2.49 represents 1.25 SDs below the mean, it follows that about 10% of a normally distributed aptitude would be classified as handicapped (actually 11%). Those individuals who had stanines of 3 could be considered as borderline handicapped and another approximately 10% would therefore be expected in this category (actually 12%). Those who had a stanine of 1 could be considered as severely handicapped and approximately 5% would be expected in this category (actually 4%).

When an individual is DisabledV_L, then the cause of this disability is likely to be Handicapped/g_v. However, it is possible that the individual is average or above in g_v but has had poor teaching and learning experiences.

When an individual is disabled DisabledP_L, then the cause of the disability is likely to be due to Handicapped/g_p. However, it is possible that a DisabledP_L individual is average or above in g_p but has been exposed to poor teaching and learning experiences. Also, it is possible that a DisabledP_L individual has low V_L (caused by low g_v and/or poor T/L for V_L) and this is the main cause of DisabledP_L (see Chapter 13).

An individual who is DisabledC_s is also likely to be Handicapped/g_s. This is likely because DisabledC_s means low in C_s compared to age and Handicapped/g_s also means low in C_s compared to age, that is, the only difference between DisabledC_s and Handicapped/g_s, is slightly different cut-off criteria.

In this diagnostic system, the most fruitful places to look for potential seems to be g_v, g_p, and g_s. Those individuals who are not handicapped in g_v, g_p, or g_s, are likely to have considerable potential with respect to reading achievement.

Adults. The adult criteria for rauding achievement categories were explained earlier as follows: Very Poor Reader (E_L at 5.9 and lower), Poor Reader (E_L from 6.0 to 7.0), Average Reader (E_L from 7.1 to 8.9), Good Reader (E_L from 9.0 to 10.0), and Very Good Reader (E_L 10.1 and higher).

The adult criterion for a disability in accuracy level is A_L = 5.9 and lower, and the corresponding criterion for rate level is R_L = 5.9 and lower.

The adult criteria for the primary disabilities are as follows: (a) disabled in verbal knowledge is V_L = 5.9 and lower, (b) disabled in pronunciation knowledge is P_L = 5.9 and lower, and (c) disabled in cognitive speed is C_s = 5.9 and lower. Because advanced readers must have $V_L \geq 8.0$ and $P_L \geq 8.0$, this means that advanced readers can only be disabled in C_s at Echelon 3. However, advanced readers could also be disabled in R_L at Echelon 2, due to a low C_s.

The system for diagnosing handicaps for adults is not different from the way they are diagnosed for middle graders. That is, standard scores or stanines for adults would be based upon adult norms so that a stanine of 1 or 2 would still define a handicap in g_v, g_p, or g_s.

Concluding Comments. The rauding diagnostic system may appear to be complex. However, it is being based only upon the connections among 12 circles in the causal model. The RDS is relatively simple compared to the reading diagnostic system advanced by Kibby (1995). He has presented a "diagnostic decision-making model" which involved 37 interconnected circles and boxes. In Kibby's system, the decisions are subjective, that is, two diagnosticians may follow the same model and still make quite different decisions. That system may be contrasted to the RDS which is designed to be as objective as possible, so that a computer can be programmed to make the decision about very poor reading, as well as specific disabilities and handicaps. An advantage of the RDS from a scientific standpoint is its falsifiability. That is, it would be relatively difficult to falsify the diagnostic system outlined by Kibby, but it will be relatively easy to find evidence against the RDS because it contains much less subjectivity.

The RDS and Dyslexia

Introduction. The rauding diagnostic system will be related to dyslexia in this section. In the RDS, the possible combinations involving handicaps involve what is often called dyslexia. In the remainder of this section, the RDS definition of dyslexia will be given, and then this definition will be related to other definitions of dyslexia.

RDS Definitions. Individuals who have trouble learning the sound-symbol correspondences involved in reading printed words but have no trouble acquiring verbal knowledge auditorily are often labeled as having dyslexia. Therefore, individuals who are Handicapped/g_p, but not Handicapped/g_v, will be defined as having dyslexia. Many of the individuals who have been studied in the past with severe dyslexia are also likely to have been Handicapped/g_s. Therefore, individuals who are handicapped in both pronunciation aptitude and cognitive speed aptitude but not handicapped in verbal aptitude (Handicapped/g_pg_s, Not-Handicapped/g_v), will also be defined as having dyslexia and will be referred to as "severe dyslexics." Those dyslexics who are not handicapped in cognitive speed will be referred to as a "mild dyslexics." So, in the RDS, dyslexia includes two subcategories—mild dyslexia and severe dyslexia.

Low pronunciation aptitude, low g_p, is the core of dyslexia under the RDS definition. Dyslexics will learn to pronounce words slower than normals (Not-Handicapped/g_p). This definition of dyslexia is consistent with Vellutino (1979) who considers the dyslexic's problem of confusing b and d (or *was* and *saw*) as being due to the fact that they do not always remember "which verbal label is associated with which printed symbol" (p. 124). Notice that this deficiency is consistent with the concept of a low pronunciation aptitude, g_p. The research of Snowling, Goulandris, and Defty (1996) also supports this definition of dyslexia in that they found that a group of dyslexic children (lowP_L, averageIQ) made less gain in reading pseudowords (less gain in d_k) over a 2- year period, as compared to a group of younger students who were likely to have been average with respect to g_p.

If there is no information about an individual that is directly relevant to g_v, g_p, and g_s, from Echelon 4 in the causal model, then probable dyslexia can be determined from Echelon 3 information. That is, individuals who are DisabledP_L are likely to be Handicapped/g_p, individuals who are not DisabledV_L are not likely to be Handicapped/g_v, and individuals who are DisabledC_s are likely to be Handicapped/g_s. Therefore, an individual who is DisabledP_L but not DisabledV_L will be diagnosed as a "probable mild dyslexic," and an individual who is DisabledP_LC_s but not DisabledV_L will be diagnosed as a "probable severe dyslexic." It should be acknowledged that the concept of a "probable dyslexic" was advanced by Vellutino (1987), but his definition of a probable dyslexic was different from the one used here in the RDS.

In the RDS, a hyperlexic is defined as an individual with low g_v but not low g_p (Handicapped/g_v, Not-Handicapped/g_p). These individuals are likely to be able to pronounce many words very well even though they do not know what the words mean when they hear them spoken. In this regard, Ellis (1985) has said that hyperlexia "... occurs in individuals who are generally retarded but who show a surprising competence in reading aloud" (p. 184). The definition of hyperlexia in the RDS is also in keeping with the following one given by Leong (1993), after reviewing the work of several researchers:

> The consensus finding of these authors is that hyperlexia is not so much a syndrome-specific phenomenon resulting from pathological impairment. Rather, hyperlexia should be defined as a pervasive developmental reading/language disorder characterized by intense and precocious interest in oral reading together with a significant deficit in language comprehension and development .... (p. 92)

Notice that the above RDS definition of hyperlexia as handicapped in verbal aptitude is commensurate with the above "significant deficit in language comprehension and development," and the lack of a deficit in pronunciation aptitude is likely to be associated with an early interest in oral reading.

Other Definitions. In this subsection, the above RDS definitions of dyslexia will be compared to earlier formal definitions of dyslexia.

In the *Encyclopedia of Human Intelligence*, Leckliter (1994) has reviewed several explicitly stated definitions of dyslexia. He began by saying that "dyslexia is a language disorder characterized by difficulty in decoding the written word into its spoken form" (p. 376). This encyclopedia definition given by Leckliter is somewhat consistent with mild dyslexia, that is, Handicapped/g_p, Not-Handicapped/g_v. However, this definition would also be consistent with a definition which required a handicap in g_p, but was silent on whether any other handicaps were involved. Furthermore, this definition would also be compatible with an individual who was DisabledP_L. So, this definition of dyslexia by

Leckliter suffers from ambiguity when translated into the specifics of rauding diagnostic system.

Leckliter goes on to say that some specialists operationally define dyslexia as requiring that an individual score 2 or more years behind their grade placement on standardized reading tests. Notice that this second definition presented by Leckliter would be somewhat comparable to a Very Poor Reader (low E_L for age) in the RDS. Leckliter also says that "currently most educational and psychological practices prefer classifications based on 15- or 16-point differences between ability and achievement test score" (p. 379). Notice that this third definition of Leckliter's is the most common one because it tends to require a normal or above IQ score and a very low score in reading achievement; this is the definition that Siegel (1988) and Stanovich (1991) have argued so strongly against (see Chapter 19).

Leckliter gives a fourth definition of dyslexia: "by definition, people with dyslexia are of at least average intelligence but read at a level below that expected for their ability" (p. 381). This fourth definition is the classic conceptual definition, and it is also the one operationalized the most in research (e.g., Shaywitz et al., 1992). Individuals diagnosed as dyslexic under this fourth definition are likely to be the same individuals diagnosed in the RDS as having mild dyslexia, *if* the measure of intellectual ability, or IQ is highly loaded on verbal knowledge or verbal aptitude, and *if* the measure of reading is highly loaded on pronunciation or spelling. In fact, it would be difficult to score high on an intelligence test and be low on verbal knowledge aptitude, g_v, or low on listening level, V_L, because intelligence tests administered individually (not group tests) ordinarily involve no reading of words, only oral communication.

Next, let us consider the recent working definition of dyslexia provided by a 1994 Orton Dyslexic Society Research Committee (Lyon, 1995):

> Dyslexia is one of several distinct learning disabilities. It is a specific language-based disorder of constitutional origin characterized by difficulties in single word decoding, usually reflecting insufficient phonological processing. These difficulties in single word decoding are often unexpected in relation to age and other cognitive and academic abilities; they are not the result of generalized developmental disability or sensory impairment. Dyslexia is manifest by variable difficulty with different forms of language, often including, in addition to problems with reading, a conspicuous problem with acquiring proficiency in writing and spelling. (p. 9)

The above definition of dyslexia by the Orton Society will henceforth be labeled Dyslexia1994. The RDS definition of dyslexia is very close to that of Dyslexia1994. Notice that Dyslexia1994 is a disorder of constitutional origin, and that idea fits closely with mild dyslexics being handicapped in pronunciation aptitude and severe dyslexics also being handicapped in cognitive speed aptitude. Furthermore, Dyslexia1994 says that the disorder is characterized by difficulties in single word decoding, which is a natural result of Handicapped/g_p causing DisabledP_L. Dyslexia1994 asserts that these word decoding problems "... are often unexpected in relation to age and other cognitive and academic abilities," and this fits nicely with mild dyslexics having no handicap in verbal knowledge aptitude; if individuals are not handicapped in g_v, they are likely to be normal or above in verbal level, called an "academic ability" in the definition above. Finally, Dyslexia1994 says that these characteristics of dyslexia are likely to result in poor reading, writing, and spelling, and this fits nicely with the idea that mild dyslexia will likely cause DisabledP_L, and severe dyslexia will cause DisabledP_LC_s, which in turn will cause poor general reading ability or low E_L for age. Also, poor "single word decoding" automatically means poor spelling (word encoding), because S_L equals P_L (Equation 7-5). Poor spelling would likely cause problems in writing because it would be very difficult to write well when one has to expend great attention and mental energy on how each word should be spelled.

In summary, the above definition of dyslexia given by the Orton Society, Dyslexia1994, is highly compatible with the RDS definitions of mild and severe dyslexia derived from the causal model. However, the one aspect about Dyslexia1994 that is conspicuously missing is any mention of a rate problem. Rate level, R_L, is likely to be low due to the characteristics of mild dyslexia (low $g_p \rightarrow$ low $P_L \rightarrow$ low R_L), and rate is likely to be severely retarded by the double deficit characteristics of severe dyslexia (low $g_p \rightarrow$ low $P_L \rightarrow$ low R_L, plus low $g_s \rightarrow$ low $C_s \rightarrow$ low R_L).

It should be noted that under the RDS definition of dyslexia, several types of individuals can be diagnosed as dyslexic who have been excluded in the past, namely, IQ under 90, socioeconomically disadvantaged, inadequate opportunity to learn to read, and severe neurological or physical disability. The only traditionally excluded group that would still be excluded under the RDS definition are those individuals with sight and hearing problems (poor vision despite corrective lenses and poor hearing despite hearing aid).

With respect to excluding certain kinds of individuals from having dyslexia, Ellis (1985) has contended that "if we are to use the term 'dyslexia,' then *anyone* with unexpected reading problems must be eligible" (p. 172). The RDS does allow more individuals to be categorized as dyslexic than the Dyslexia1994 definition, and this is in keeping with the above admonition by Ellis.

Remedial Treatment

Introduction. In the RDS, the type of treatment recommended depends upon the primary disability. It is recommended that individuals who are DisabledV_L be given a V_L remedial treatment which focuses upon increasing verbal knowledge, vocabulary knowledge, and/or knowledge of the English language. It is recommended that individuals who are DisabledP_L be given a P_L remedial treatment which focuses upon helping the individual learn how to pronounce more known words correctly and learning correspondences between letters and sounds, or graphemes and phonemes; this instruction could take the form of learning word attack skills, learning to spell known words accurately, and learning to recognize correct spellings quickly. It is recommended that individuals who are DisabledC_s be given plenty of time to read and listen during instruction because they are likely to be slower than most children.

In the RDS, the time required for remediation of a disability in V_L will be slower for individuals who are Handicapped/g_v. Furthermore, the remediation time for those individuals diagnosed as having a disability in P_L will be slower for individuals who are Handicapped/g_p and even slower for individuals who are Handicapped/$g_v g_p$. Finally, the remediation time for those individuals diagnosed as having a disability in C_s, or Handicapped/g_s, will be slow, and it will be extremely slow for individuals who are Handicapped/$g_v g_p g_s$.

In the remainder of this section, the above RDS treatment recommendations will be compared to recommendations about treatment given in the research literature.

Visual Problems. In the past, dyslexia has often been considered to be a visual perception problem, such as reversing b and d or pronouncing "dog" as /god/. The relevant research in this area of visual perception was reviewed in 1987 by Vellutino. He recounted that in 1925, Orton suggested that the cause of dyslexia was a deficiency in the visual systems but that research conducted since then has indicated that dyslexia is a subtle language deficiency, e.g., problems with breaking words into their component sounds. Vellutino admirably reviewed the research on the hypothesized visual causes of poor reading, and then concluded that they have no support. Also with regard to visual problems, Rayner (1983) studied eye movements and dyslexia, and he concluded that "my observations of a number of dyslexics (including those whose eye movements we have recorded) and the general literature on eye movements and dyslexia lead me to believe that eye movements are not the cause of dyslexia" (p. 169).

Remember that the rauding diagnostic system does not include any measures of visual problems, that is, it assumes poor eyesight has been corrected by glasses so that visual perception is not an important variable. Therefore, visual perception problems including eye movements are not part of the RDS, and are not recommended for treatment.

Spelling Treatment. Juel (1983) has shown that learning versatile letter combinations, such as the "ea" in "pear" and "bear" speeds up the identification of words above and beyond their ease of decodability. It seems likely that most students will gradually learn these orthographic redundancies via spelling but that the Handicapped/g_p students do not learn them as well or as fast. Therefore, dyslexic students are likely to learn these kinds of orthographic redundancies at a much slower rate. However, it seems likely that learning to spell most of the words they know when listening would help these individuals increase their P_L, which in turn would improve A_L, R_L, and E_L. So, spelling is a recommended treatment for those individuals who are diagnosed as DisabledP_L in the RDS.

Trait Trainability. The three aptitudes at Echelon 4—g_v, g_p, and g_s—are assumed to be education proof. That is, it is assumed that educational training or instruction would not be able to improve an individual's score on measures of these aptitudes. They are psychological traits which differ between individuals at the same age, similar to height as a physical trait.

Research studies which tried to improve psychological abilities in students who had deficits were reviewed in 1979 by Arter and Jenkins. They summarized their conclusions as follows: "After reviewing over 100 separate studies covering a wide range of auditory, visual, and psycholinguistic training programs, one finds little evidence to support the trainability of underlying psychological abilities" (p. 540). Therefore, the assumption that g_v, g_p, and g_s cannot be improved by instruction, or educational treatments, seems to have some empirical support.

None of the disabilities diagnosed in the RDS are likely to be remediated by treatments focused on traits.

Aptitude-Treatment Interaction. In 1977, Cronbach and Snow advanced the idea of an aptitude-treatment interaction, which is directly relevant to whether instruction should focus on strengths or weaknesses. These researchers were interested in whether the best type of instruction, or treatment, depended upon the aptitude of the individual. This idea is relevant to instruction based upon the RDS. Remember, a person who is low in verbal aptitude, low g_v, is likely to be low in verbal knowledge level, and that those who are low in V_L are supposed to be given a type of instruction designed to increase verbal knowledge. Remember also that a person who is low in pronunciation aptitude, low g_p, is likely to be low in pronunciation knowledge level, and those who are low in P_L are supposed to be given a type of instruction designed to increase pronunciation knowledge. So, the instructional strategy based upon the RDS could be called a disability-treatment interaction in that the best treatment depends upon the type of disability; however, because the disabilities are likely to be due to specific low aptitudes, then there is likely to be an indirect connection with an aptitude-treatment interaction.

At present, there is no research evidence to support an aptitude-treatment interaction (ATI) in the area of reading; for example, Speece (1993) noted the "disappointing fate" of ATI research. This problem has been addressed by Stanovich (1993b) who noted that "... outside the pioneering work of Lyon

(1985), there are very few data on differential response to treatment" (p. 285). Stanovich goes on to say that "this is not a trivial gap in our knowledge," and "differential treatment effects are, in large part, the raison d'être of special education" (p. 286). This means that there are no sound empirical data showing that individuals who are diagnosed as having one type of reading problem improve more or less from a specific type of treatment; stated differently, there is little or no evidence that one type of treatment (such as decoding instruction) improves decoding any more than another type of treatment that does not involve decoding. By analogy, we have no evidence that radiation therapy eliminates cancer more effectively than does vitamin therapy. At the present time, such a degree of ignorance would not be tolerated in medical science; it should not be tolerated in the scientific study of reading where the human development of children is the victim of this ignorance.

Empirical Evidence

The empirical evidence directly relevant to the RDS will be presented in chronological order.

In 1997, Carver presented data that were collected using Version 2.0 of the Computer Assisted Reading Diagnosis (CARD); these data have been reviewed several times earlier from a different perspective. The test battery involved in the data collection included many tests from which indicants of E_L, A_L, R_L, V_L, P_L, and C_s can be derived. Those data collected in the research described in 1997 have been reanalyzed using the RDS, as described earlier in this chapter.

In Study I, CARD data were collected from 52 students in grades 3 to 5, and in Study II, CARD data were collected from 104 students in grades 2 to 11. Table 18-1 contains the results of a reanalysis of those data collected from students in grades 2 to 11. These 156 students have been categorized into three categories of rauding achievement based upon the five rauding achievement categories: poor readers (including Poor and Very Poor) average readers (Average), and good readers (including Good and Very Good); these categories were based upon an indirect measure of E_L derived from measures of A_L and R_L using Equation 9-1. These students have also been categorized with respect to whether they have 0, 1, 2, or 3 of the possible primary disabilities, that is, a verbal disability, a pronunciation disability, or a cognitive speed disability. For example, notice that (a) there were 5 students who had all 3 primary disabilities, and they were all poor readers, and (b) there were 84 students with no primary disabilities and only 4 of them were poor readers.

The data in Table 18-1 can be aggregated in a manner that summarizes the results in a more revealing manner. If a student has no disabilities at Echelon 3 (no primary disabilities), then the student has a 95% probability of being an average or good reader. If the student has just one disability at

Echelon 3, then the student only has a 51% chance of being an average or good reader, a precipitous drop. If a student has 2 disabilities at Echelon 3, then the student has only a 25% chance of being an average or good reader. Finally, if a student has 3 disabilities at Echelon 3, then the student has no chance (0%) of being an average or good reader. These data make the case rather dramatically for disabilities in V_L, P_L, and C_s being the three primary causes of poor reading ability, or poor reading achievement. That is, students who are not disabled in verbal knowledge level, pronunciation level, or cognitive speed level are not at risk for being a poor or very poor reader (.05 probability), whereas students who have just one of these disabilities are at risk (.49 probability). Furthermore, students who have two of these disabilities are highly likely to be a poor or very poor reader (.75 probability), whereas students who have all three of these disabilities seem certain to be a poor or very poor reader (1.00 probability).

Table 18-1
A Contingency Table Relating Three Levels of Rauding Achievement to the Number of Primary Disabilities Existing in 156 Students in Grades 2 to 11 ($N = 156$).

Number of Primary Disabilities	*Rauding Achievement* Poor	Average	Good	*Total*
0	4	58	22	84
1	19	19	1	39
2	21	7	0	28
3	5	0	0	5
Total	49	84	23	156

In 1998, Carver and Clark reported upon the administration of the CARD to 128 community college students who were attending reading improvement classes at a community college; these data were reviewed in earlier chapters from different perspectives. These students were asked to attend these classes if they did not receive relatively high scores on a standardized reading achievement test. These adult data collected by Carver and Clark (1998) have been reanalyzed using the criteria presented earlier for age categories, rauding skill categories, rauding achievement categories, and rauding disability. In this group of 128 students enrolled in reading improvement classes at a community college, all were categorized as adults. With respect to rauding skill categories, 5% were beginning readers, 55% were intermediate readers, and 40% were advanced readers. With respect to the rauding achievement categories, 12% were Very Poor Readers, 5% were Poor Readers, 23% were Average Readers, 16% were Good Readers, and 43% were Very Good Readers. With respect to the secondary disabilities, 2% were DisabledA_L, 20% were DisabledR_L, 2% were DisabledA_LR_L, and 75% had no secondary disabilities. Notice that 22% of this group of 128 were disabled in R_L but only 4% were disabled in A_L; it appears that a relatively slow rauding rate is the main cause for their relatively low scores on a reading achievement test.

For these 128 individuals, the probability (*p*) of being a poor reader (Poor or Very Poor) can be calculated under the following conditions: (a) if there were no primary disabilities, *p* was .04 (4/91), (b) if there was one primary disability, *p* was .39 (12/31), and (c) if there were either two or three primary disabilities, *p* was 1.00 (6/6). Notice that as the number of primary disabilities increase, then the probability of being a Poor Reader or a Very Poor Reader increases dramatically from .04 for no primary disabilities to 1.00 for two or three disabilities. These data may be interpreted as providing support for the theory underlying the RDS which holds that the primary disabilities are primarily responsible for high and low reading achievement.

Summary of Theory

The causal model of reading achievement has implications for the diagnosis and remediation of reading problems, and the improvement of efficiency level, E_L, in poor readers. The rauding diagnostic system, RDS, is based upon the causal model. Poor readers are defined as those individuals who have low E_L for their age. The causes of low E_L are accuracy and rate disabilities at Echelon 2 in the causal model. The causes of the accuracy and rate disabilities—called secondary disabilities—are three primary disabilities at Echelon 3—verbal, pronunciation, and cognitive speed. The root causes of these three primary disabilities are likely to be three corresponding handicaps in Echelon 4, that is, a handicap in verbal aptitude, a handicap in pronunciation aptitude, and a handicap in cognitive speed aptitude.

An individual who has a handicap in pronunciation aptitude but does not have a handicap in verbal aptitude is called a mild dyslexic. An individual who has handicaps in both pronunciation aptitude and cognitive speed aptitude but does not have a handicap in verbal aptitude is called a severe dyslexic.

The best way to remediate a verbal disability, or increase V_L, is to help those students learn more words and concepts. The best way to remediate a pronunciation disability, or increase P_L, is to help those students overlearn the spellings of all the words they know when listening, that is, learn to accurately and rapidly recognize the correct spellings of all the words they know when auding.

Summary of Evidence

The definitions of mild and severe dyslexia in the RDS are compatible with encyclopedia definitions of dyslexia (Leckliter, 1994), and are compatible with the recent Orton Society definition of dyslexia (Lyon, 1995). However, the

RDS definition of dyslexia is focused upon aptitudes, not achievements. Furthermore, the RDS definition of severe dyslexia requires a handicap in cognitive speed aptitude, whereas speed or rate has not been explicitly mentioned previously in formal definitions of dyslexia.

From the research of Carver (1997) and Carver and Clark (1998), it appears that the probability of being a poor reader is very small if the individual does not have a primary disability (about .05), much larger if the individual has one primary disability (about .50), higher if the individual has two primary disabilities (about .75), and a virtual certainty if the individual has three primary disabilities (about 1.00).

Implications

The diagnosis of dyslexia and other reading disabilities by using IQ-discrepancy formulas needs to be discontinued because it appears to be theoretically unjustified and because there is no sound evidence that this system of diagnosis leads to higher reading achievement. The RDS system should be tried because it is more logical from a theoretical standpoint and because it seems likely to produce higher gains in reading achievement when it is combined with the recommended differential treatments.

Forget Me Nots

The rauding diagnostic system, RDS, uses the causal model to diagnose specific disabilities and handicaps in poor readers. The RDS also diagnoses mild and severe dyslexia in a more systematic manner.

CHAPTER

19

RESEARCH ON DYSLEXIA AND DISABILITIES

This chapter examines more closely how the rauding diagnostic system, RDS, is related to the traditional concepts of dyslexia, disabilities, and diagnoses used by researchers. There is a plethora of research definitions of dyslexia and reading disabilities, each including different types of individuals. When these concepts that are used in traditional research are compared to the constructs used in the RDS, it seems that the RDS could be considered a major upgrade. The RDS clarifies existing concepts and incorporates them into a systematic and organized framework. It seems more likely that we can conduct research that will help individuals overcome their severe reading problems, if we take advantage of the organizing clarity offered by the RDS.

In the following section, several of the concepts of dyslexia that have been used by researchers will be compared to dyslexia as defined within the RDS (see Chapter 18). Then, several of the concepts of disabled readers that have been used by researchers will be critiqued from the standpoint of the RDS.

Dyslexia

Introduction. Many of the different conceptions of dyslexia held by researchers, will be examined by reference to specific constructs in the causal model. For example, the first traditional research concept to be discussed is one that also defines mild dyslexia in the RDS, namely, low g_P but not low g_V (see Chapter 18). This definition will provide the context for comparisons with the other research conceptions of dyslexia that follow.

Low g_P But Not Low g_V. The conception of dyslexia in the RDS as low g_P but not low g_V seems to be consistent with the essence of the phonological-core variable-difference model of Stanovich (1988a). In this model, Stanovich explains that both the garden-variety poor reader and the dyslexic share a phonological deficit, which is the core of both their reading problems, but that the dyslexic does not share with the garden-variety reader any other reading-related deficit—such as low g_V.

The definition of dyslexia in the RDS as primarily a deficit in pronunciation aptitude (low g_P), is also very much in keeping with Rosenberger (1992) who has contended that "dyslexia is a specific aptitude deficit, leading to underachievement in reading by children of otherwise normal intelligence" (p. 193). Rosenberger goes on to say that "dyslexic children who receive proper tutorial support acquire essential literacy skills despite a shortage of the aptitude that makes learning to read easier for their normal classmates" (p. 193). These latter ideas of Rosenberger are consistent with the part of Echelon 4 which holds that low pronunciation aptitude can be ameliorated by teaching and learning so that P_L might be normal, or average. Excellent teaching and sustained learning can often offset the specific aptitude deficit that makes it more difficult to achieve normally in reading. Stated differently, a dyslexic has a very low pronunciation aptitude (Handicapped/g_P), but this does not guarantee that this individual will (a) have a pronunciation level disability, DisabledP_L, (b) have an accuracy level disability, DisabledA_L, (c) have a rate level disability, DisabledR_L, or (d) be a very poor reader—low E_L for age.

In summary, the RDS definition of mild dyslexia seems to be consistent with traditional research conceptions of dyslexia, except that the RDS definition is much more precise, that is, Handicapped/g_P but Not-Handicapped/g_V.

Low P_L But Not Low V_L. An individual who is low in P_L but not low in V_L (DisabledP_L, Not-DisabledV_L) has been defined as a probable dyslexic in the RDS. In this regard, Bowers, Steffy, and Tate (1988) state that "the prototypical dyslexic is a child whose oral language ability is well developed, but whose reading of written language is unexpectedly poor; if oral and written language abilities are commensurate, then there can be no unexpected reading failure" (p. 307). Translated into the causal model, the above statements seem to mean that typical dyslexics are individuals with high V_L for their age but low P_L for their age, and that there can be no unexpected reading failure for individuals who have V_L and P_L equal to that expected for their age. In short, this research definition of a prototypical dyslexic seems to be very similar to a probable mild dyslexic in the RDS.

Low d_k. Pure decoding knowledge, d_k, or pseudoword reading accuracy, is considered by many to be a potent variable in diagnosing dyslexics (e.g., Leong, 1993). Yet, it is not directly involved in the RDS because d_k is considered to be a component of P_L (see Chapter 13)—a component which is amenable to improvement via teaching and learning. Accuracy scores on a pseudoword reading test are not education proof; scores on such a test should show important gains due to instruction in decoding, spelling, and word attack. Therefore, d_k is considered to be influenced by g_P and T/L at Echelon 4 because d_k is a component of P_L at Echelon 3. The potency of d_k for diagnosing dyslexia in the RDS lies in (a) its close relationship to g_P and (b) d_k is a component of P_L.

Rack, Snowling, and Olson (1992) reviewed studies relevant to low d_k being the critical component of dyslexia. Their hypothesis was "that dyslexic children have a specific deficit in phonological reading processes" (p. 28). More specifically, they reviewed research relevant to their "phonological deficit hypothesis" where poor readers were matched with younger readers on a word recognition measure (an indicant of P_L), and then compared on their accuracy of pronunciation of novel words and pronounceable nonwords (pseudowords); they said that they used "nonword reading as our index of phonological reading skill" (p. 32). So, their measurement of phonological reading skill seems to be highly similar to what is measured by pure decoding knowledge, d_k, as defined in Chapter 13. In the view of Rack, Snowling, and Olson, "the development of word recognition is constrained by poor phonological decoding, although dyslexics may ultimately acquire word-specific knowledge despite their poor phonological skills" (p. 29).

These research data which Rack et al. have contended "provide extremely strong evidence for the phonological deficit hypothesis" may be alternatively interpreted as providing indirect support for defining a dyslexic as a person who is low in pronunciation aptitude, low g_P.

Low P_L. Some researchers have defined dyslexics by their low scores on word-identification tests, that is, low on an indicant of P_L. An example of this practice comes from the research of Siegel, Share, and Geva (1995). They operationally defined dyslexics in their research as having IQ scores higher than 80 but scores below the 25th percentile on a word identification test, the Wide Range Achievement Test (WRAT). Because high IQ scores are likely to mean high g_V and V_L, and because their word-identification test is an indirect measure of P_L, their definition of dyslexia might be regarded as similar to one discussed earlier as low P_L but not low V_L. However, because students with IQs below 70 usually are not in regular classrooms in school, their definition of dyslexia would amount to being low in P_L. Furthermore, because their definition of a poor reader mainly involved an indicant of P_L, it seems likely that this research on dyslexics actually was more likely to involve individuals who were DisabledP_L with little regard for g_V or V_L. Therefore, this research by Siegel, Share, and Geva illustrates how low P_L, or DisabledP_L, has been used to define dyslexia. On the surface, their definition of dyslexia appears to be similar to probable mild dyslexia in the RDS, but their definition is relatively weak with respect to being sure that their dyslexics were not also DisabledV_L. In the RDS, there must be some direct evidence that individuals are not DisabledV_L before they are diagnosed as "probable mild dyslexic."

It should also be pointed out that low P_L has also been used to define an individual as reading disabled (e.g., Metsala, 1997), whereas low P_L individuals are defined as pronunciation disabled in the RDS.

Low g_s. Low cognitive speed aptitude (low g_s) has been identified as an important factor in defining dyslexia. Wimmer (1993) says that "a finding of importance for the theoretical characterization of speed dyslexia is the low association between numeral-naming speed and performance on the phonemic segmentation task (pseudoword spelling, vowel substitution)" (p. 28), and "it appears questionable to subsume naming speed impairments (in particular, naming speed for overlearned alphanumeric symbols) under phonological impairments" (p. 28). Notice Wimmer is arguing for a special kind of dyslexia, which he calls speed dyslexia (or Handicapped/g_s), and he is arguing that this kind of dyslexia should not be considered a phonological problem, or a pronunciation problem (or a part of Handicapped/g_P). Evidence that traditionally diagnosed dyslexics are often Handicapped/g_s, comes from Elbro (1991) who reported that "... the dyslexic subjects in the present study were slower at the automatized naming test when compared to normal readers at the same age" (p. 238).

In summary, low g_s individuals seem to have been referred to in the research literature as speed dyslexics. In the RDS, this concept of speed dyslexic has been integrated into the diagnosis of a severe dyslexic. However, a so-called speed dyslexic might also be Handicapped/g_V, but in the RDS a severe dyslexic cannot be Handicapped/g_V.

Low A_L or E_L. One way to operationally define dyslexia is to require a low score on a reading measure. For example, consider the research of Shaywitz et al. (1992). They concluded from their study of 414 children that "... no distinct cutoff point exists to distinguish children with dyslexia clearly from children with normal reading ability; rather the dyslexic children simply represent the lower portion of a continuum of reading capabilities" (p. 148). Notice that their criterion for dyslexia seems to be somewhat similar to being a Poor Reader or a Very Poor Reader (Low E_L for age), or being DisabledA_L in the RDS. Rather than make dyslexia synonymous with a low score on a reading measure (low A_L or E_L for age), the RDS requires that the dyslexic be at the lower portion of the continuum for pronunciation aptitude, g_P, but not in the lower portion of the continuum for verbal aptitude, g_V.

Subtypes of Dyslexia. The concepts of phonological dyslexics and surface dyslexics as subtypes (see Castles & Colthart, 1993) were recently endorsed by Stanovich, Siegel, and Gottardo (1997). These two subtypes of dyslexia will be critically examined using the RDS.

Stanovich et al. interpreted their data involving reading disabled (RD) children and reading-level (RL) controls as providing support for the subtype of a phonological dyslexic who has deficits in pseudoword naming, phonological sensitivity, working memory, and syntactic processing. They also stated that "the surface dyslexics, in contrast, displayed a cognitive profile remarkably similar to that of the RL controls" (p. 114). In their research, both the phonological dyslexics and the surface dyslexics scored equally low on a word-identification test, or equally low in pronunciation knowledge (equally low

P_LWords). However, the phonological dyslexics scored high on exception words, that is, they knew how to correctly pronounce more real words than pseudowords (high A_LWords but low d_kWords), whereas the surface dyslexics scored high on pseudowords relative to exception words (low A_LWords but high d_kWords). Remember that P_LWords equal A_LWords plus c_kWords (Equation 7-1, and that c_k equals d_k (Equation 7-3).

In order to analyze further these two dyslexic subtypes, fictitious data have been created for a phonological dyslexic (Student A) and a surface dyslexic (Student B); these fictitious data are presented in Table 19-1. Both students are at the end of grade 5 in school (GE = 5.9), and score equally low on a word-identification test (P_L = 3.0), that is, both are disabled in pronunciation knowledge, DisabledP_L. Notice that the phonological dyslexic, Student A, scored lower on a word attack test (d_k = 2.0), whereas the surface dyslexic, Student B, scored considerably higher on the word attack test (d_k = 4.0). The other scores in Table 19-1 for A_L and V_L are consistent with theoretical relationships noted in earlier chapters, that is, the A_L score was derived using Equation 7-4 (P_L is the arithmetic mean of d_k and A_L), and V_L was derived using Equation 10-3 (V_L is the arithmetic mean of V_L and P_L).

Table 19-1
A Phonological Dyslexic and a Surface Dyslexic Who are Both in Grade 5 (GE = 5.9) With Identically Low Pronunciation Level But Differing in d_K, A_L, and V_L

Student	*Subtype*	d_k	P_L	A_L	V_L
A	phonological dyslexic	2.0	3.0	4.0	5.0
B	surface dyslexic	4.0	3.0	2.0	1.0

d_K = pure decoding knowledge, or the grade equivalent (GE) score on the Word Attack test from the Woodcock Reading Mastery Test (WRMT).
P_L = pronunciation knowledge level, or the GE score on the Word Identification test from the WRMT.
A_L = rauding accuracy level, or the GE score on the Passage Comprehension test from the WRMT.
V_L = verbal knowledge level, or the GE score on the General Information subtest from the Peabody Individual Achievement Test.
P_L = $(A_L + d_K)/2$ (Equation 7-4).
A_L = $(V_L + P_L)/2$ (Equation 10-3)

If both the phonological dyslexic and the surface dyslexic have equally low values for P_L, whereas the phonological dyslexic is lower in d_k and the surface dyslexic is higher in d_k, then it automatically follows that the phonological dyslexic must be higher in A_L and the surface dyslexic must be lower in A_L. Translated into the values given in Table 19-1, the phonological dyslexic has d_k (pseudoword accuracy) lower than pronunciation knowledge level ($2.0 < 3.0$), therefore, rauding accuracy level must be higher than P_L ($4.0 > 3.0$). Conversely, the surface dyslexic has d_k higher than P_L ($4.0 > 3.0$), therefore, rauding accuracy level must be lower than P_L ($2.0 < 3.0$). Again, these relationships among P_L, A_L, and d_k depicted in Table 19-1 must follow given that P_L is the average of d_k and A_L, according to Equation 7-4 in Chapter 7.

Stated differently, the distinguishing characteristic of phonological dyslexics is their low pseudoword knowledge compared to their knowledge of how to correctly pronounce real words ($d_k < P_L$); this automatically means that their word knowledge must be higher than their pronunciation knowledge ($P_L < A_L$), according to Equation 7-4. Similarly, the distinguishing characteristic of surface dyslexics is their high pseudoword knowledge compared to their knowledge of how to correctly pronounce real words ($d_k > P_L$); this automatically means that their pronunciation knowledge must be higher than their knowledge of the meaning of printed words ($P_L > A_L$). So, the phonological dyslexic has very low d_k, low P_L, and higher A_L ($d_k < P_L < A_L$), and the surface dyslexic has high d_k, low P_L, and very low A_L ($d_k > P_L > A_L$). This pattern should hold according to (a) the descriptions of the phonological dyslexic and the surface dyslexic given by Stanovich et al. (1997), and (b) the theoretical relationships among P_L, d_k, and A_L given in Chapter 7.

Given these characteristics of phonological dyslexics ($d_k < P_L < A_L$) and surface dyslexics ($d_k > P_L > A_L$), then it necessarily follows from Equation 10-3 that phonological dyslexics will have a level of verbal knowledge that is higher than their knowledge of the meaning of words ($V_L > A_L$), and surface dyslexics will have a level of verbal knowledge that is much lower than their knowledge of the meaning of words ($V_L < A_L$). Even though phonological dyslexics are very low in word-identification knowledge, DisabledP_L, they are even lower in pseudoword knowledge, $d_k < P_L$, and have the pattern of $d_k < P_L < A_L < V_L$; Student A fits this pattern with $d_k = 2.0$, $P_L = 3.0$, $A_L = 4.0$, and $V_L = 5.0$. Surface dyslexics are also very low in word-identification knowledge, DisabledP_L, but they are higher in pseudoword knowledge, $d_k > P_L$, and have a pattern of $d_k > P_L > A_L > V_L$; Student B fits this pattern with $d_k = 4.0$, $P_L = 3.0$, $A_L = 2.0$, and $V_L = 1.0$.

Given that a phonological dyslexic is DisabledP_L with $d_k < P_L < A_L < V_L$, it follows that a phonological dyslexic is likely to be Handicapped/g_p (because d_k is very low) and Not-Handicapped/g_V (because V_L is relatively high). Therefore, the phonological dyslexic is also likely to be diagnosed as a dyslexic in the RDS. However, a phonological dyslexic could be further diagnosed into two subtypes using the RDS—a mild dyslexic or a severe dyslexic.

Given that a surface dyslexic is DisabledP_L with $d_k > P_L > A_L > V_L$, it follows that a surface dyslexic is likely to be Not-Handicapped/g_P (because d_k is not low) and is likely to be Handicapped/g_V (because V_L is very low). Therefore, the traditionally diagnosed surface dyslexic is not likely to be diagnosed as a dyslexic at all in the RDS, either mild or severe, because a dyslexic in the RDS system (a) must be Handicapped/g_P, and (b) must not be Handicapped/g_V.

Notice that the phonological dyslexic (Handicapped/g_P) and the surface dyslexic (Handicapped/g_V) are likely to represent only two of six subtypes that are possible at Echelon 4 of the causal model. There would be four other possible subtypes, namely, Handicapped/g_s, Handicapped/$g_V g_P$, Handicapped/$g_V g_s$, Handicapped/$g_P g_s$, and Handicapped/$g_V g_P g_s$.

In the RDS, the traditional subtypes of a phonological dyslexic and surface dyslexic can be explained in terms of root causes at Echelon 4 in the causal model. The phonological dyslexic is likely to have inherited low pronunciation aptitude and that is the main cause of being DisabledP_L, whereas the surface dyslexic is likely to have inherited low verbal aptitude, and that is the main cause of being DisabledP_L. However, Stanovich et al. have contended that "surface dyslexia may arise from ... exceptionally inadequate reading experience" (p. 123), that "such children lack word-specific knowledge that is normally acquired by reading" (p. 123), and that "phonological dyslexia will be more refractory to treatment than surface dyslexia" (p. 124). It should not go unnoticed that these conclusions drawn by Stanovich et al. are not consistent with the preceding theoretical analysis of phonological and surface dyslexics using the RDS. Instead of predicting that a surface dyslexic can be remediated more easily or more quickly than a phonological dyslexic, the RDS would require a knowledge of V_L, P_L, and C_s at Echelon 3 and a knowledge of g_V, g_P, and g_s at Echelon 4. In the RDS, there is no *a priori* reason to predict that students who are Handicapped/g_P (phonological dyslexics) have less potential for remediation than students who are Handicapped/g_V (surface dyslexics). Furthermore, in the RDS there would be four more subtypes of handicap combinations at Echelon 4, that are similar to the phonological dyslexic and the surface dyslexic, and these possible combinations of handicaps would be much more critical with respect to remediation potential.

Finally, it should be noted that the phonological dyslexic is also likely to have a listening-reading discrepancy, which Stanovich (1991) contended was an alternative way to measure potential instead of an IQ-reading discrepancy. In Table 19-1, the phonological dyslexic had a listening-reading discrepancy ($V_L = 5.0$; $A_L = 4.0$), and therefore should have high potential. On the other hand, the surface dyslexic did not have a listening-reading discrepancy ($V_L = 1.0$; $A_L = 2.0$), and therefore should not have high potential. Notice that Stanovich et al. (1997) seem to be suggesting that the phonological dyslexics have less potential even though these individuals are likely to have a listening-reading discrepancy, which according to Stanovich (1991) means more potential. Also, notice that the surface dyslexics purportedly have more potential even though they are not likely to have a listening-reading discrepancy, which Stanovich (1991) has suggested would make them have less potential. The possibility of these kinds of internal inconsistencies would seem to be minimized using the RDS.

Concluding Comments. It is clear that most of the constructs in the causal model have been used previously by researchers to define dyslexia—g_v, g_P, g_s, V_L, P_L, A_L, and E_L. It seems likely that much more progress will be made in understanding dyslexia and helping dyslexics read better if most researchers will operationally define dyslexia in a manner which assures that the same phenomenon is being studied. Under the RDS, it is possible to study probable mild dyslexics (DisabledP_L, Not-DisabledV_L) and probable severe dyslexics (DisabledP_LC_s, Not-DisabledV_L) and be relatively sure we are studying two specific forms of dyslexia. However, until there are reliable and valid measures of all three aptitudes—g_V, g_P, and g_s—there will be no way to conduct research on dyslexics as defined in the RDS and as defined by most researchers.

Disabilities

Introduction. Reading disabilities are a subset of a more general area called learning disabilities. It has been noted by Lyon (1993) that the development of a valid system for diagnosing learning disabilities is the most important problem facing scientists in that area, and that "... the field must undertake a systematic effort to establish a precise definition for the disorder and a theoretically based classification system that is open to empirical scrutiny" (p. xvii). So, diagnosing learning disabilities, such as reading disabilities, appears to be recognized as an area that needs improvement in order to make progress with respect to the treatment of these disorders.

In the field of reading, it is important to understand better how to remediate reading disabilities because it has been estimated from the National Adult Literacy Survey that about 90 million adults in the United States have serious reading problems (Kirsch, Jungeblut, Jenkins, & Kolstad, 1993). These literacy data were summarized in TIME magazine (1993) as follows: "roughly 90 million Americans over age 16—almost half that category's total population are, as far as most workplaces are concerned, basically unfit for employment" (p. 75). If almost all reading problems are caused by a general cognitive deficit, such as Handicapped/$g_Vg_Pg_s$, which makes remediation extremely difficult and costly, then it may not be practical to put time and resources into any treatments designed to remediate reading disabilities. On the other hand, if most reading problems are due to specific deficits which are amenable to specific remedial treatments, and the rate of improvement is predictable from specific aptitudes, then the costs of remediation can be estimated and subsequently funded if deemed to be a priority.

Poor readers are said to be disabled in the RDS if they have deficits at Echelons 2 and 3 in the causal model. This means that poor readers are defined as having low general reading ability for their age, but that a disabled reader has a more specific disability in an area that is assumed to be a secondary cause of E_L at Echelon 2 or a primary cause of E_L at Echelon 3. At Echelon 2, an individual may be disabled in A_L, and/or disabled in R_L—the two secondary disabilities. At Echelon 3, an individual may be disabled in V_L, disabled in P_L, or disabled in C_s—the three primary disabilities. In the RDS, an individual can have a disability in A_L, R_L, V_L, P_L, C_s or any combination of these five constructs at Echelons 2 and 3.

This RDS system of diagnosing several disabilities is somewhat compatible with Vellutino, Scanlon and Tanzman (1994) who have contended that not all reading disabilities are alike. They have presented the case that other factors such as orthographic skill, speed of reading, and vocabulary may be components of reading. Notice that (a) orthographic skill probably is highly related to DisabledP_L, (b) speed of reading probably is highly related to DisabledR_L, and (c) vocabulary probably is highly related to DisabledV_L.

In the RDS, disabilities can be remediated by teaching and learning, and this conception of disabilities is compatible with the findings of Williams (1980). She found that learning-disabled children (who were given explicit training in phoneme analysis and phoneme blending, letter-sound correspondences, and decoding), learned general decoding strategies and were able to decode a novel combination of letters not presented in the training. Because most of these children were likely to have been Handicapped/g_P and DisabledP_L, these data suggest that this type of handicap or disability does not mean that these individuals cannot improve in decoding, or P_L, with instruction.

In the remainder of this section, the RDS will be compared to several other methods that researchers have used to define disabilities.

Age-Achievement Discrepancy. It is a common practice for researchers to select reading-disabled subjects using a cutoff of one or two grade levels below expected grade level for the child's age (e.g., Bowers, Steffy, & Tate, 1988), as was mentioned in Chapter 18. The system of diagnosing disabilities in the RDS has used age-achievement discrepancies; individuals must be 2 GEs below average for their age to be considered as disabled in A_L, R_L, V_L, P_L, and C_s. The decision to define disabilities in the RDS as two grade equivalents below that expected from age in GE units is in keeping with the contention by Ellis (1985) that reading-related deficits are more like obesity than measles. That is, disabilities do not involve a discrete entity like the measles but do involve a graded continuum like weight in pounds (also see Stanovich, 1988b). It must never be forgotten that any attempt to study the frequency of occurrence of disabilities depends directly on these cutoff criteria. Furthermore, it is possible that a cutoff criterion of 1.5, or 1.0, would work better than 2.0 GEs.

Disabled Readers. The RDS is generally compatible with earlier conceptions of reading disabilities except that the RDS is more specific, as just noted. Disabled readers in the RDS can have quite different configurations of specific disabilities at Echelons 2 and 3. Thus, the RDS may be regarded as an upgrade of more conventional ideas about reading disabilities.

The above-mentioned RDS upgrade is quite different from the approach taken by Lipson and Wixson (1986). They took issue with much of the earlier research on reading disabilities; they said that this research "must move away from the search for causative factors within the reader and toward the specification of the conditions under which different readers can and will learn" (p. 129). Notice that the causal model and the rauding diagnostic system would not have been developed had this advice been heeded. The causal model represents the end result of a search for factors within the reader which cause high and low reading achievement, namely, g_V, g_P, and g_s, as well as a recognition that there are also environmental conditions (teaching and learning) which also drastically affect what readers can and will learn. This same general idea was recently articulated by Spear-Swerling and Sternberg (1996) who contended that a reading disability "arises from the interaction between environmental factors and the child's intrinsic characteristics" (p. 311).

The approach of Lipson and Wixson seems to assure that education and psychology are opposing and mutually exclusive approaches—that if researchers properly focus upon instruction then they should disregard or denigrate individual differences in aptitudes. Or, if one dares to focus upon individual differences in aptitudes (psychology) then one would be disregarding or denigrating instructional effects (education). Indeed, this dichotomy between education and psychology is the same pitfall that Cronbach (1957) was warning about in his treatise about the dichotomy between experimental and correlational psychology that was mentioned at the outset of this book. Instead, it seems likely that there will be more growth in reading achievement when those in charge of instruction understand how factors inside the child (g_v, g_P, & g_s) and factors outside the child (teaching and learning) combine to produce growth.

It should be pointed out again that the RDS system of diagnosing reading disabilities almost completely disregards the traditional "unexpected" ideas inherent in a traditional concept of reading-disabled children. That is, traditionally a child is only labeled disabled if reading achievement is unexpectedly low based upon IQ or listening. For example, Stanovich (1991) explains that children who do not comprehend spoken language well would not be expected to read well, so "such children are not reading disabled" (p. 21). This means that it is common to use the term "disabled" for unexpectedly low reading achievement, yet a "disability" in the rauding diagnostic system has nothing to do with expectancy, except for expectancy based on age.

Garden-Variety Poor Readers. The concept of a "garden-variety poor reader" was introduced by Gough and Tunmer (1986) to isolate the type of poor reader who was low in listening, language, or verbal knowledge, and also low in decoding or pronunciation knowledge. In their system of categorization, or diagnosis, the garden-variety poor readers (Disabled$V_L P_L$) (a) were kept separate from the poor readers who were called "dyslexic" because dyslexics were low in decoding knowledge but not low in listening knowledge (DisabledP_L, Not-DisabledV_L), and (b) were kept separate from the poor readers who were called "hyperlexic" because hyperlexics were low in listening knowledge but not low in decoding knowledge (DisabledV_L, Not-DisabledP_L). Notice that a dyslexic in their system of diagnosis would be considered a probable mild dyslexic in the RDS, and their hyperlexic would be considered a probable hyperlexic in the RDS.

The RDS may be regarded as an upgrade of the system of diagnosing dyslexics, hyperlexics, and garden-variety poor readers because it includes C_s at Echelon 3, and therefore allows probable mild dyslexics to be differentiated from probable severe dyslexics who are also DisabledC_s.

IQ-Achievement Discrepancy. Disabilities in reading have often been diagnosed as a large discrepancy between reading ability, or reading achievement, and IQ. That is, if a person had a relatively high IQ and a relatively low achievement in reading, then this person is likely to be diagnosed as having a reading disability. Translated into the RDS, individuals would have a disability if they were not low in IQ but they were DisabledP_L, or DisabledA_L, or were a Very Poor Reader. This subsection will contain a review of some of the research literature relevant to the IQ-Achievement discrepancy and how it relates to the RDS, in chronological order.

In 1989, Siegel contended that "IQ is irrelevant to the definition of learning disabilities." In this article, she attacked the theoretical relevance of IQ to defining a reading disability, and she presented empirical data showing that disabled readers and nondisabled readers were drastically different at each IQ level on word identification or decoding. That is, there was a big difference between these two groups at each of the low, medium, and high IQ levels, and there was little or no relationship between decoding ability and IQ within either group. Again, she concluded that "on logical grounds, IQ test scores are not necessary for the definition of learning disabilities" (p. 469), mainly because "there are no differences among children of different IQ levels in basic cognitive processes" (p. 478). Translated into the terminology of the rauding diagnostic system, Siegel found that the differences between low P_L individuals and high P_L individuals was the same at each level of IQ. This means that IQ is not importantly related to one of the primary causes of high and low reading achievement.

Also in 1989, Stanovich had a theoretical article published entitled "Has the learning disabilities field lost its intelligence?" He asserted that "Siegel's data are not airtight, nor are they completely unambiguous in their interpretation" (p. 488), but her arguments are "in the tradition of recent empirical work that has highlighted the challenges facing advocates of the LD concept: Produce the data that indicate different cognitive processing in dyslexic and garden-variety poor readers reading at the same level, the data indicating that these two groups of poor readers have a differential educational prognosis, and the data indicating that they respond differently to certain educational treatments" (p. 488). This statement can be translated several ways. First, Stanovich seems to contend that researchers should be required to show that probable dyslexics (DisabledP_L, Not-DisabledV_L) and garden-variety poor readers (DisabledV_LP_L) have different cognitive processing, or operate their rauding process in a different manner. Notice that this is counter to rauding theory, including the causal model and the RDS, because both probable dyslexics (DisabledP_L, Not-DisabledV_L) and garden-variety poor readers (DisabledV_LP_L) purportedly operate their rauding process similarly as long as the text being read is relatively easy, $A_L > D_L$. Second, Stanovich is contending that researchers need to be able to show that probable mild dyslexics and garden-variety poor readers have a different educational prognosis. In the RDS, this differential prognosis would be that the probable mild dyslexics would likely be able to gain more than garden-variety poor readers in a fixed amount of time from remedial treatment because the probable mild dyslexics are likely to be handicapped in only one area (Handicapped/g_P) rather than two areas for the garden-variety poor readers (Handicapped/g_Vg_P).

In 1994, Fletcher et al. continued the investigation of the validity of the IQ-achievement discrepancy as a means of determining reading disability. They studied 199 children aged 7.5 to 9.5 who were categorized using two different IQ-achievement formulas into five groups: standard score discrepancy only, regression discrepancy only, both standard score and regression discrepancy, low achievement, and not reading impaired. They compared these five groups on 9 cognitive variables related to reading proficiency. They concluded the following:

> Results did not support the validity of discrepancy versus low achievement definitions. Although differences between children with impaired reading and children without impaired reading were large, differences between those children with impaired reading who met IQ-based discrepancy definitions and those who met low reading achievement definitions were small or not significant. (p. 6)

These results and conclusions again are compatible with the rauding diagnostic system because these results suggest that it is not important to use an IQ-achievement discrepancy to diagnose a reading disability because those identified as reading disabled will differ little in relevant cognitive skills from those identified from their low achievement.

In summary, the RDS system of diagnosing disabilities is not compatible with diagnosing disabilities from IQ-achievement discrepancies, and this is consistent with a considerable amount of evidence that IQ is not helpful in diagnosing reading disabilities. It appears that the IQ-achievement method of diagnosing reading disabilities has no empirical support. Therefore, the RDS seems to be consistent with the most recent theory and data which holds that IQ scores are not useful for diagnosing disabilities in reading.

Listening-Reading Discrepancy. Listening level, or verbal level, can be used to estimate what Stanovich (1991) called "unlocked potential," that is, the amount of growth in accuracy level, A_L, that could be expected "... if the decoding deficit that was the proximal cause of the disability were to be totally remediated" (p. 22). If teaching and learning were successfully focused on remediating the disability in pronunciation level, DisabledP_L, then it is reasonable to expect that the accuracy level, A_L, of students to approach or equal their verbal level, V_L. So, in this sense, listening level can be thought of as representing unlocked potential. However, the traditional concept of potential seems to fit more closely with high or low aptitudes at Echelon 4; the potential for successful remediation of low reading achievement cannot be high if any of these three aptitudes is low, especially g_P, which is the most likely cause of being DisabledP_L (Carver & Clark, 1998). Therefore, we have the semantic problem of saying that the severe dyslexics (Handicapped/g_Pg_s, Not-Handicapped/g_V) have high potential for reading well, because V_L is higher than P_L, when in fact, severe dyslexics are likely to require many hours of teaching and learning in order to show much growth in E_L.

A diagnostic procedure based upon the discrepancy between listening comprehension scores, or V_L, and reading comprehension scores, or A_L, was implemented by Aaron (1991). He concluded that "the results suggest that this diagnostic procedure has potential utility" (p. 178). In the RDS, these individuals with higher listening-reading discrepancies (higher V_L - A_L) are very likely to be DisabledP_L but Not-DisabledV_L (from Equation 10-3), and are therefore likely to be classified as probable mild dyslexics or probable severe dyslexics.

In summary, when researchers diagnose individuals as having a disability because they have a large listening-reading discrepancy, then it is very likely that these individuals would be diagnosed as probable mild dyslexics or probable severe dyslexics in the RDS. Therefore, using listening-reading discrepancies to diagnose disabilities has been directly incorporated into the RDS.

Spelling Disability. The close connection between spelling and reading, or between spelling knowledge and pronunciation knowledge (Equation 7-5), is sometimes challenged by those who advocate the existence of a specific spelling disability or deficit (Frith, 1984; Jorm, 1983; Nelson & Warrington, 1974; Newman, Fields, & Wright, 1993). For example, Frith (1980) has contended that there are "poor spellers who are good readers" (p. 514). In this regard, Joshi and Aaron (1990) studied college students who appeared to be poor spellers but good readers. They found these college students to be "... inefficient readers who committed numerous errors in reading function words, low frequency and unfamiliar words, and pronounceable nonwords" (p. 107). They went on to summarize their results and conclusions as follows: "There appears to be a trade off between speed and comprehension in reading and by slowing down considerably, the 'poor spellers but good readers' attain an acceptable level of comprehension" (p. 107). These results are consistent with the theory that (a) spelling knowledge is an indicant of P_L, (b) a spelling disability is not a separate disability from DisabledP_L, and (c) low spelling knowledge, or DisabledP_L, is a cause of slow reading, or DisabledR_L.

In the RDS, individuals who are disabled in pronunciation level, are purported to be equally disabled in spelling level. That is, individuals who are low in pronunciation knowledge for their age are purported to be equally low in spelling knowledge for their age, that is $P_L = S_L$ (see Chapter 7). There are no individuals who are relatively low in the number of words they can accurately pronounce for their age but are not relatively low in the number of words they can accurately spell for their age, even though almost all individuals can accurately pronounce more words than they can accurately spell. On the other hand, it is quite possible for some individuals to know how to spell a relatively low number of words for their age (low S_L and equally low P_L) but be able to read considerably better; this is because reading level, or A_L, is caused by both V_L and P_L. For example, when $V_L = 6$ and $P_L = 2$, then $A_L = 4$ (see Equation 10-3). Therefore, individuals with these scores in grade 3 may be regarded as good readers ($A_L = 4$ is above grade level) but poor spellers ($P_L = 2$ is below grade level). However, individuals with the scores in this example are more likely to be in a higher grade, such as grade 6 so that they are below grade level in reading because $A_L = 4$ and $P_L = 2$. Therefore, they are more likely to be diagnosed as probable mild dyslexic (DisabledP_L, Not-DisabledV_L). This means that individuals who are very poor spellers for their age are likely to be diagnosed in the RDS as probable mild dyslexics, or as probable severe dyslexics, even though some of these very poor spellers could be average or above in reading level. Therefore, the traditional concept of a spelling disability has been incorporated into the RDS, except it is defined more precisely as being disabled in P_L.

Slow Readers. Compton and Carlisle (1994) say that there are "... compelling arguments for considering speed as a central factor in the identification of reading disabilities" (p. 117). They reviewed a number of research studies and concluded that (a) "the single most important finding of this review is that a comparatively slow rate of word reading is characteristic of RD students" (p. 133), and (b) "the results of our literature review suggest that it is time for clinicians/practitioners to begin to consider word reading speed as an important factor associated with the diagnosis of reading disabilities" (p. 134). These ideas about using slow rates of reading words to diagnose reading disabilities are highly compatible with a rate disability in the RDS, that is, DisabledR_L. The remainder of this subsection will contain the views of other researchers which support the diagnosis of a rate disability, in chronological order.

In 1983, Juel stated that "there is much evidence indicating that mastery of rapid context-free word identification is one of the major factors that separates good from poor readers (Biemiller, 1977; Lesgold & Perfetti, 1978; Liberman & Shankweiler, 1979; Pace & Golinkoff, 1976; Perfetti, 1977; Perfetti & Hogaboam, 1975; Perfetti & Lesgold, 1977; Shankweiler & Liberman, 1972)" (p. 307). Because the speed of identifying context-free words is an indicant of R_L (see Chapter 5), it follows that Juel's remarks are highly compatible with an R_L disability in the RDS.

In 1984, Lovett seems to be the first to explicitly talk about a rate disability, as was noted earlier. She considered accuracy and rate disabilities to be subtypes of dyslexic children. Her research included two groups, both of which came from a population of poor readers referred to a special treatment program at a children's hospital. The group she called Accuracy Disabled was selected because they scored low on word recognition tests, that is, low P_L; so, in the RDS, her Accuracy Disabled group would be called pronunciation disabled at Echelon 3, or DisabledP_L. Her Rate Disabled group was selected because they scored low on reading speed measures but were about average or above on the word recognition tests; so, her Rate Disabled group would be DisabledR_L but not DisabledP_L, and this would make them likely to be DisabledC_s at Echelon 3. Notice that her two groups were not selected in a parallel fashion because her Accuracy Disabled group did not have to be average or above on the reading speed measures. Indeed, from the data presented by Lovett, it is clear that her Accuracy Disabled group contained slower readers than the Rate Disabled group; the mean reading rate on the Gilmore Oral Reading Test was 85 wpm for the Accuracy Disabled and 92 wpm for the Rate Disabled.

It can be surmised from this discussion that even though Lovett used the terms "accuracy disabled" and "rate disabled," they were not similar in concept to the corresponding terms used in the rauding diagnostic system. Her Accuracy Disabled group was closer to being pronunciation disabled, DisabledP_L, and her Rate Disabled group was probably closer to being DisabledC_s. So, it appears that the concepts of DisabledA_L and DisabledR_L are new even if the terms "accuracy disabled" and "rate disabled" are not. Still, Lovett was the first to point out that accuracy and rate were important dimensions to separate when dealing with dyslexia, and this is in keeping with DisabledA_L and DisabledR_L being secondary disabilities in the RDS.

In 1995, Share and Stanovich stated that "we know unequivocally that less-skilled readers have difficulty turning spellings into sounds" (p. 7), and that "this processing deficit is revealed by the most reliable indicator of reading disability: difficulty in rapidly and accurately reading pseudowords ..." (p. 7). Measures of the speed of accurately pronouncing pseudowords was defined as pure decoding speed, d_s, which is a component of R_L (see Chapter 11). Therefore, these comments by Share and Stanovich can be translated into an argument for diagnosing DisabledR_L because d_s is a major component of R_L, and they contend that low d_s is an indicator of a reading disability.

In summary, diagnosing rate disabilities in the RDS is quite compatible with the findings of other researchers who have contended that being a slow reader is an important indicator of reading disability. Therefore, the prior concept of a rate disability has been incorporated into the RDS via DisabledR_L.

Double-Deficit. Low decoding ability and low naming speed ability comprise what Wolf and Bowers have called the double-deficit hypothesis (Bowers, Sunseth, & Golden, 1999; Wolf, 1997). This hypothesis is that the most severe reading disabilities are due to deficits in both decoding and naming speed, and that deficits in one but not both areas result in a less severe reading problem. This double-deficit hypothesis almost perfectly coincides with the RDS definition of probable severe dyslexia—DisabledP_LC_s, Not-DisabledV_L. Therefore, earlier research supporting the double-deficit hypothesis may also be interpreted as supporting the causal model relevant to dyslexia.

In summary, this double-deficit hypothesis has been incorporated into the RDS via a probable severe dyslexic, or DisabledP_LC_s but Not-DisabledV_L.

Summary

In the preceding two sections of this chapter, the handicaps and disabilities of the RDS have been compared to the definitions of dyslexia and disability used by researchers. A summary of those comparisons will be presented in this section, in an attempt to better organize and better summarize the similarities and differences that exist between the RDS and previous diagnostic procedures.

When all of the previous diagnoses studied by researchers are considered, it becomes obvious that almost all of the constructs in the causal model have been used. Measures of reading achievement in the IQ-Achievement Discrepancy type of diagnosis have involved E_L, yet the RDS does not involve IQ measures. The listening-reading discrepancy is not directly involved in the RDS, but it is indirectly involved when diagnosing disabilities in V_L, P_L, and A_L. The concept of a rate disability advanced by Lovett (1984) is included in the RDS, even though the criteria used for DisabledR_L are quite different from the criteria used by Lovett. Many researchers have used low scores on word recognition tests, or spelling tests, to diagnose reading disabilities, and this practice is incorporated into the RDS via being disabled in P_L. The double-deficit diagnosis advanced by Wolf (1997) is incorporated into the RDS via a disability in both P_L and C_s. The diagnosis of dyslexia has also been studied using concepts and measures that implicate P_L, g_P, g_V, and g_s. As noted earlier, the RDS involves most of the previous concepts and measures used in the diagnosis of reading problems.

Table 19-2 contains a list of traditional diagnoses, that is, earlier concepts investigated in the research literature, and their translated counterparts in the RDS. For example, an individual diagnosed as having a reading disability using traditional concepts, could be a Very Poor Reader, DisabledA_L, or DisabledP_L. This table summarizes most of the two previous sections on dyslexia and disabilities.

Table 19-2
Traditional Diagnoses and Their RDS Counterparts

Traditional Diagnoses	*RDS Counterparts*
Reading disability	Very Poor Reader, or DisabledA_L, or DisabledP_L.
IQ-Achievement discrepancy	IQ vs. E_L, or IQ vs. A_L.
Rate disability	DisabledR_L, or low d_K.
Listening-reading discrepancy	V_L vs. A_L, or DisabledP_L but Not-DisabledV_L.
Double-deficit	DisabledP_LC_s.
Dyslexic	DisabledP_L, or Handicapped/g_P, or DisabledP_L but Not-DisabledV_L, or Handicapped/g_P but Not-Handicapped/g_V, or DisabledP_LC_s, or DisabledP_LC_s but Not-DisabledV_L.
Phonological dyslexic	Handicapped/g_P
Surface dyslexic	Handicapped/g_V
Garden-variety poor reader	DisabledV_LP_L.
Hyperlexic	DisabledV_L but Not-DisabledP_L.

Table 19-3 contains a similar summary except it is organized in the reverse, that is, for each RDS diagnosis, there are traditional names, labels, and concepts that may be used to describe individuals with this diagnosis. For example, for individuals diagnosed as DisabledP_L in the RDS, they might be described as dyslexic or as having a deficit in word recognition, or spelling.

Table 19-3
Traditional Names, Labels, or Concepts Likely to be Used to Describe Each RDS Diagnosis

RDS Diagnosis	*Traditional Names, Labels, or Concepts*
DisabledA_L	poor reader
DisabledR_L	slow reader
DisabledA_LR_L	very poor reader
DisabledV_L	low verbal ability, poor vocabulary, or hyperlexic
DisabledP_L	word identification deficit, spelling deficit
DisabledC_s	naming speed deficit, or speed dyslexic
DisabledV_LP_L	garden-variety poor reader
DisabledV_LC_s	(none)
DisabledP_LC_s	dyslexic, or a double-deficit
Disabled$V_LP_LC_s$	garden-variety poor reader
Handicapped/g_v	Surface dyslexic, low verbal aptitude, or low verbal IQ
Handicapped/g_P	phonological dyslexic, low phonological skills, low phonological awareness
Handicapped/g_s	slow thinker
Handicapped/g_vg_P	low aptitude for reading
Handicapped/g_vg_s	(none)
Handicapped/g_Pg_s	severe dyslexic
Handicapped/$g_vg_Pg_s$	low mental ability

The information in Tables 19-2 and 19-3 summarizes how the RDS incorporates almost all of the earlier conceptions of dyslexia and reading disabilities, but upgrades these conceptions in ways that are clearer, more refined, and more organized.

Forget Me Nots

Previous ideas about reading disability and dyslexia held by researchers have involved all of the theoretical constructs in the causal model; the rauding diagnostic system has upgraded and organized the best of these ideas.

PART VI

THREE NON-CAUSAL FACTORS

This part of the book describes and evaluates three factors that have been considered to be important in the past for causing high reading achievement, namely, intelligence (Chapter 20), volume of reading (Chapter 21), and the whole-language approach to reading instruction (Chapter 22). These three factors have been designated as non-causal because a case will be made that each is not an important cause of high reading achievement.

CHAPTER

20

INTELLIGENCE AND READING

What is the relationship between intelligence and reading? The answer to this question is of great theoretical importance because many people in education consider intelligence to be an indication of whether the student is reading up to potential or not. The answer is also of great practical importance because the decision as to whether a student receives special services in a school district often depends upon the discrepancy between a score on an IQ test and a score on a reading achievement test. Furthermore, it has been contended by some reading researchers (e.g., Lohnes & Gray, 1972) that "reading experts must understand intelligence to understand reading" (p. 475). In short, intelligence is often considered to be a major factor causing high and low reading achievement.

Whether or not intelligence causes high and low reading achievement depends upon what is meant by intelligence and what is meant by reading achievement. For example, one of the most popular conceptions of intelligence seems to have little to do with rauding efficiency level, E_L, but this popular concept of intelligence does have an important relationship to traditional standardized tests of reading comprehension.

In this chapter, the various meanings of intelligence will be considered first. Then, the complex relationship between intelligence and reading achievement will be explained. There will also be a section on traditional reading comprehension tests. Later, other topics that are related to intelligence and the causal model will be examined, i.e., IQ-achievement discrepancy and the relationship between memory and reading.

What is Intelligence?

Theorists have given many explanations about the nature of intelligence, and what is known and unknown about it (e.g., see Neisser et al., 1996). Rather than reviewing the historical record, which may be found elsewhere (Sternberg, 1994), only those concepts of intelligence will be considered which (a) are measurable in a reliable manner, (b) have current research support, and (c) are relevant to the causal model.

The most recent and most exhaustive empirical study of intelligence was a meta-analysis conducted by Carroll (1993) who factor analyzed data from more than 460 different data sets. He summarized this massive data analysis effort by presenting what he called a structure of cognitive abilities, with three stratums. Stratum III was the highest level and it included only one factor, called general intelligence. At Stratum II were eight subfactors, called fluid intelligence, crystallized intelligence, general memory and learning, broad visual perception, broad auditory perception, broad retrieval ability, broad cognitive speediness, and processing speed. Carroll noted that the order of importance of these eight subfactors is given by the order they occupy in the list given above, that is, fluid intelligence contributes the most to general intelligence and processing speed the least in terms of the "strength of domination." Underneath each of the eight subfactors of general intelligence at Stratum II were many sub-subfactors, located in Stratum I. For example, under the subfactor called fluid intelligence at Stratum II were such sub-subfactors as general sequential reasoning, induction, and quantitative reasoning at Stratum I.

When Carroll listed fluid intelligence and crystallized intelligence as the most important subfactors of general intelligence in his structure of cognitive abilities, he was in accordance with recent Gf - Gc theory (Woodcock, 1994). Gf is often the symbol used for the concept of fluid intelligence and Gc is often the symbol used for crystallized intelligence, as these concepts were advanced by Cattell (1963). Gf, or fluid intelligence, is an abstract reasoning kind of factor that involves drawing inferences with respect to novel tasks. Gc, or crystallized intelligence, is a knowledge type of factor that reflects education and experience. This Gf-Gc theory was extended by Horn and Cattell (1966). In 1994, Horn succinctly presented the latest version of this theory; it has been expanded to include 10 interacting but somewhat separate factors, the most important of which are Gf, fluid eduction, and Gc, acculturated knowledge--also known as fluid and crystallized intelligence, respectively, as noted earlier. The other eight factors in this theory of several intelligences (instead of one general intelligence) are visual processing, auditory processing, processing speed, correct decision speed, short-term memory, long-term memory, visual sensory detection, and auditory sensory detection. These 10 intelligences of Gf - Gc theory roughly correspond to the 8 Stratum II subfactors of Carroll (1993), noted earlier. Both of these theoretical models presented by Carroll and Cattell-Horn include Gf and Gc as the most important factors. However, Gf-Gc theory deprecates the usefulness of general intelligence as a single scientific concept--termed *g* by Spearman (1904)--which is at Stratum III in Carroll's (1993) model.

To summarize, up to this point, intelligence may be viewed as being comprised of many sub-subfactors by reference to Carroll's Stratum I. Or, intelligence may be viewed as being organized into several intelligences by reference to Carroll's Stratum II which contains 8 factors or Horn's 10 factors (see Gustafsson, 1994), keeping in mind that fluid and crystallized intelligence, Gf and Gc, are considered to be more important. Finally, 8 - 10 intelligences can also be organized into one general factor according to Carroll, called *g*, or general intelligence. Next, the concept of intelligence will be analyzed further by examining how it is measured.

The concept of *g*, general intelligence, cannot be measured directly in theory; *g* must be the first general factor derived from a factor analysis of general cognitive ability tests. However, the Raven Progressive Matrices (RPM) test is widely considered to be the purest and best single indicant of *g* (Court, 1994; Gustafsson, 1994; Jensen, 1982). The RPM was developed by Raven who was a student of Spearman. It contains complex patterns in the form of matrices with one piece missing from the matrix; there are multiple choices for which piece best completes the matrix or pattern. This test has consistently been shown to load highly on the *g* factor, typically better than .80 (Court, 1994). On the other hand, the RPM is also considered to be a measure of Gf, or fluid intelligence (Court, 1994). Notice that the RPM can be alternately thought of as (a) the best indicant of *g*, and (b) the best indicant of Gf which is the primary subfactor of *g*, and a measure of one of the two most important factors in the Gf-Gc model. With respect to crystallized intelligence, Gc, one of the best measures is generally considered to be a vocabulary test, such as the Mill Hill Vocabulary Test or the Peabody Picture Vocabulary Test (PPVT).

Of course, intelligence can also be measured by IQ tests, such as the Wechsler Intelligence Scale for Children (WISC), the Stanford-Binet Intelligence Scale, and the Wechsler Adult Intelligence Scale (WAIS). Each of these measurement scales contain a battery of tests that can be interpreted as providing indicants of various Stratum II subfactors in the Carroll model or many of the 10 factors in the Gf-Gc model. The Stanford-Binet averages the scores over all the tests in the battery (or factors), and gives a single IQ score—which therefore provides a measure similar in concept to general intelligence, *g*. On the other hand, both of the Wechsler measurement scales divide their test batteries into two sections, performance and verbal, which correspond roughly to fluid and crystallized intelligence; they give an IQ score for each of these two factors that correspond roughly to Gf and Gc, and then they give an overall IQ that is the average of these two factors. So, for the two Wechsler tests a number of tests are administered which are somewhat similar to Carroll's 8 Stratum II factors and Horn's 10 factors, then the scores on these tests are averaged in two areas, representing the two most important factors (fluid and crystallized), and then these two are averaged again into something similar to the single Stratum III factor, that is, Spearman's *g*.

Intelligence and Reading Achievement

Introduction. In this section, reading achievement will be related to general intelligence, fluid intelligence, and crystallized intelligence, after each of these intelligences have been described in much more detail.

General Intelligence. Empirical data relevant to *g* and the causal model have been collected which directly support the decision to exclude general intelligence from the model. Carver (1998c) has administered the RPM along with other tests which measure many of the constructs in the causal model. These data indicate that the RPM does not add to the prediction of E_L once that V_L, P_L, and C_s have been entered as predictors. Furthermore, almost all of the reliable variance in E_L could be accounted for by these three factors—V_L, P_L, and C_s—at Echelon 3; therefore, there does not seem to be any need or any room for *g* to be included in Echelon 3 of the causal model. Also, for middle graders, college readers, and poor reading community college students, the RPM correlated around .30 or lower with V_L, P_L, and C_s, so it appears that *g* is not a likely candidate for being an important causal factor at Echelon 4.

These data suggest that there are no compelling theoretical or empirical reasons to include *g* as an important factor causing high or low reading achievement when reading achievement is taken to mean rauding efficiency level, E_L. Stated differently, if you have two students in grade 2, one of whom obtains an average score on the Raven test and the other obtains a high score on this test, there is no compelling evidence that we should predict that in Grade 6, for example, the high Raven student will have a higher efficiency level score, E_L. The theory underlying the causal model is that E_L in grade 6 will be greatly affected by the three aptitudes of the students in grade 2—g_v, g_p, and g_s—as well as their teaching and learning experiences in grades 3 to 6. But, their scores on the RPM, as an indicator of *g* or general intelligence, will be of little consequence for growth in E_L.

General intelligence does not have to be measured by the Raven test, however. The operational definition of *g* requires several tests for its derivation (Detterman, 1982), and an IQ score is a number which is an average of the scores from several different tests that sample several intelligences (Lezak, 1988). Also, as noted earlier, the most popular IQ tests, such as the Stanford-Binet, WISC, and WAIS, all sample cognitive abilities or several intelligences that are similar to the 8 Stratum II factors of Carroll or the 10 factors in the Gf-Gc theoretical model.

The empirical relationship between IQ scores and reading ability has been studied by Hammill and McNutt (1981). From their meta-analysis of 34 studies, involving the WISC Full Scale IQ and reading ability, they found a median correlation of .44. From their meta-analysis of 33 studies involving the IQ score on the Stanford-Binet and reading ability, they found a median correlation of .46.

If these IQ tests had sampled cognitive abilities, or several intelligences, in a way that included verbal aptitude, g_v, pronunciation aptitude, g_p, and cognitive speed aptitude, g_s, then we might expect the relationship between single IQ scores and E_L to be high. In fact, however, most IQ tests sample a variety of cognitive abilities or several intelligences which include (a) some that are likely to be closely related to g_v, (b) none that are likely to be related to g_p, (c) some that may be related to g_s, and (d) many others that are not closely related to any of the factors in the causal model. Therefore, from this task analysis of IQ tests, it could be predicted that an IQ score would not be highly related to measures of reading ability because these scores contain too many subfactors, or too many intelligences not closely related to reading ability. It could also be predicted that IQ scores would not be unrelated to reading ability because IQ scores do contain subfactors that are closely related to g_v, or verbal aptitude. Therefore, the .44 and .46 average correlations found in research by Hammill and McNutt (1981), seem to be consistent with this theoretical analysis of IQ tests and reading achievement.

In summary, from a theoretical standpoint there is no reason to expect *g*, or a single IQ score from a battery of IQ tests, to be more important than g_v, g_p, or g_s in the causal model. The IQ score is usually an average of several intelligences, few of which are directly causal with respect to reading achievement. A battery of individual intelligence tests ordinarily do not involve reading in an important way, that is, individuals are not required to read lists of words, sentences, or paragraphs. Therefore, the only reason such measures could be expected to be related to reading achievement, or E_L, would be because some of the intelligences being measured require an auditory knowledge of words and language (g_v or V_L) and some of the tests involve speed which could be indirectly or lowly related to cognitive speed aptitude, g_s. If intelligence means general intelligence, and if reading achievement means efficiency level in the causal model, then intelligence does not seem to be an important factor causing high and low reading achievement. General intelligence is not an important cause of E_L, at least as long as (a) *g* is measured by the single best measure available, the RPM, or (b) *g* is measured by an IQ score derived from a battery of tests, such as the Stanford-Binet, the WISC, or the WAIS.

Fluid Intelligence. The essence of fluid intelligence, called Gf in the Cattell-Horn model, is the ability to solve novel and complex problems, or the ability to reason abstractly, or the ability to draw inferences. Remember that Gf is the primary subfactor of *g* according to Carroll (1993). The Raven Progressive Matrices test, RPM, and the Block Design subtest of the WISC-R test are often considered to be the two most direct measures of Gf (Snow & Yalow, 1982). E. Hunt (1978) has articulated the essence of Gf abilities as being demonstrated by tasks that require "the ability to make inferences, draw relations, and develop hypotheses, but that do not appear to be determined by cultural factors" (p. 125), and he says that "verbal intelligence tests typically have fairly low loadings on the Gf factor" (p. 125). In this regard, Sternberg (1986) contends that "we need to separate out the processes of reasoning from the processes of perception, on the one hand, and the influence of knowledge, on the other, if we wish to obtain a relatively pure measure of reasoning ability" (p. 20).

Reasoning ability is the single concept that seems to capture the essence of fluid intelligence. If reading is actually reasoning, as E. L. Thorndike

(1917) and R. L. Thorndike (1974) have argued, then Gf ought to predict reading ability quite well. R. L. Thorndike (1974) concluded that it was primarily meager reasoning ability, or meager intellectual skills, that limited reading comprehension, not deficiencies in more specific and readily teachable skills. However, this argument for Gf being a potent cause of reading achievement was severely criticized by Carver (1973b) because the empirical findings involved reading tests that were actually reasoning tests, as will be explained in more detail later in this chapter. More recent criticism of the idea that reading is reasoning comes from Stanovich (1992), who contended that efficient word recognition, or lexical access, is central to the complex act of reading, and that "... lexical access in fluent readers is not at all like reasoning or problem solving" (p. 3).

The concept of Gf has also been studied under the rubric of "cognitive power," that is, fluid intelligence also represents cognitive power. The general idea of cognitive power seems to have been first advanced by R. B. Cattell (1971) under the rubric of "power intelligence" (p. 108). Later, Carver (1990a) theorized that cognitive power (C_p), as measured by the RPM, was a major factor at Echelon 3 in the causal model, a proximal cause of A_L and R_L. However, Carver (1997) dropped C_p from the causal model after a research study was conducted in 1993 (that was published later, 1998c); these latter data were reviewed in the preceding subsection on general intelligence. They will be reviewed again, in more detail.

Three studies relevant to Gf (or C_p) and reading were reported (Carver, 1998c); all of these studies involved the RPM and indicants of E_L, or reading achievement. In Study I, 62 college students were given the RPM and the CARD, which provided indicants of E_L, A_L, R_L, V_L, P_L, and C_s. In Study II, the same tests were given to 36 students in grades 3 to 10. In Study III, the same tests were given to 49 students in grades 3 to 11. In Studies II and III, the correlations involved were all controlled for grade in school using partial correlations. The RPM correlated with E_L at .41, .41, and .26, respectively, in the three studies. In all three studies the RPM did not add to the prediction of E_L after V_L, P_L, and C_s had been entered into a hierarchical regression analysis. It was concluded that the RPM, or Gf, did not belong at Echelon 2 or Echelon 3 of the causal model. With respect to Echelon 4, the correlations between the RPM and measures of V_L, P_L, and C_s were (a) .23, .16, and .23, respectively, in Study I, (b) .43, .42, and .03, respectively, in Study II, and (c) .39, .02, and .07, respectively, in Study III. Notice that the RPM correlated .23 to .43 with V_L, .02 to .42 with P_L, and .03 to .23 with C_s. These correlations seem to be too low to consider the RPM (or Gf) as being an important causal factor at Echelon 4. That is, it is assumed that a good measure of g_v will correlate higher with V_L, and a good measure of g_p will correlate higher with P_L.

These low correlations between the RPM and C_s, or g_s, suggest that Gf and g_s are almost completely independent intelligences. Indeed, in another research study, Carver (1991) found that C_s (or g_s) correlated lowly with the RPM. Therefore, those data suggest that g_s and Gf are relatively independent aptitudes or intelligences. In this regard, Spring and Davis (1988) found that a measure of naming speed, which was an indicant of g_s, correlated .04 with a measure of fluid intelligence, Gf; this is more evidence that these two aptitudes are actually separate intelligences, one of which (g_s) affects E_L indirectly via rate level, R_L, and the other (Gf) does not directly affect E_L.

In summary, fluid intelligence, Gf, has not been shown to correlate highly with measures of E_L, A_L, R_L, V_L, P_L, or C_s (Carver, 1998c). Furthermore, there are no compelling theoretical reasons to expect fluid intelligence to be highly related to rauding efficiency level, E_L, because reasoning ability does not seem to be a potent factor involved in rauding, or E_L.

Crystallized Intelligence. As noted earlier, one of the best measures of a person's learned knowledge, or crystallized intelligence, Gc, is a vocabulary test. Therefore, it follows that vocabulary tests are likely be highly related to general intelligence, because vocabulary tests measure Gc, and Gc is a major part of *g*, general intelligence. The high relationship between vocabulary, Gc, and general intelligence, *g*, has been articulated by Anderson and Freebody (1981), as follows:

> The strong relationship between vocabulary and general intelligence is one of the most robust findings in the history of intelligence testing. Terman (1918), for instance, reported a correlation of .91 between mental age (as assessed by the Stanford Revision of the Binet-Simon Scale) and the vocabulary subscale. On this basis he suggested that the vocabulary measure alone constitutes a good estimate of performance on the entire scale and thus could be used as a short measure. (p. 77)

Anderson and Freebody found that in 18 studies the "... correlations between vocabulary subtest scores and total test scores on a number of different IQ and achievement tests have ranged from .71 to .98" (p. 78), with a median of .83.

At first glance, it might seem that crystallized intelligence, Gc, and verbal knowledge level, V_L, in the causal model might be the same thing because both involve tests of listening vocabulary. So, verbal level, V_L, may be alternately considered to be an indicant of crystallized intelligence, Gc. In this regard, Carroll (1993) lists Listening Ability as an underlying factor for crystallized intelligence, so listening level and Gc seem to be almost the same theoretical concept. Therefore, in the sense that Gc is listening ability, then Gc is a distal cause of efficiency level, E_L, according to the causal model. Yet, V_L is measured in a manner that separates achievement from aptitude so it is misleading to consider Gc as synonymous with V_L as a causal factor for E_L. It would be more in keeping with the concept of Gc to associate it with verbal aptitude, g_v, as an individual difference factor, or a trait, as was noted earlier in Chapter 12.

Crystallized intelligence also has a great deal in common with A_L, or accuracy level. A_L is a measure of the level of comprehension accuracy and therefore it has a great deal in common with one of the Gc subfactors listed by Carroll (1993), namely, Reading Comprehension. Furthermore, crystallized intelligence, Gc, has another Carroll sub-subfactor called Reading Decoding which is likely to be highly related to g_p and/or P_L. Finally, Gc has a sub-subfactor called Reading Speed which makes it overlap with rate level, R_L.

Notice that crystallized intelligence, Gc, is broad enough to overlap with all the components at Echelon 2—A_L and R_L—as well as two of the three components at Echelon 3—V_L and P_L—plus two of the three aptitude factors at Echelon 4—g_v and g_p. Not included in Gc is cognitive speed level, C_s, or cognitive speed aptitude, g_s. This latter factor in the causal model has no direct counterpart in Carroll's model, although it could be a sub-subfactor of Broad Cognitive Speediness or Processing Speed, the 7th and 8th factors in Stratum II.

Earlier it was concluded that general intelligence, *g*, and its primary component, fluid intelligence, Gf, were not importantly related to reading achievement as reflected by efficiency level, E_L. Now, we can conclude that crystallized intelligence, Gc, is defined so broadly that it includes reading achievement. That is, it seems to be impossible to separate reading achievement, or E_L, from crystallized intelligence, Gc. This is due to the fact that (a) reading level, A_L, and rate level, R_L, completely determine efficiency level, E_L, or reading achievement, and (b) A_L and R_L are subfactors of Gc because they measure the ability to comprehend when reading (Reading Comprehension) and the ability to read fast and comprehend (Reading Speed).

Concluding Comments. General intelligence, *g*, does not have a large or important causal connection to efficiency level, E_L. Furthermore, the most important component of general intelligence, called fluid intelligence, Gf, also does not have a large or important causal connection to E_L. That is, neither *g* nor Gf have an important causal impact upon efficiency level, E_L. Furthermore, there is no empirical evidence that *g* is closely related to reading achievement, when IQ scores are used as an indicant of *g*. Also, there is no empirical evidence that Gf is an important cause of E_L when the RPM is used as an indicator of Gf. However, the second most important component of *g*, is crystallized intelligence, and it pervades the causal model because A_L, R_L, V_L, P_L, g_v, and g_p seem to be constructs that would be subsumed under the Gc factor at Stratum II of Carroll's model. It should be noted that measures of A_L, R_L, V_L, P_L, g_v, and g_p would all involve words, or language, and this is the primary reason that they all would be subsumed under crystallized intelligence.

Traditional Reading Comprehension Tests

Now that the relationship between intelligence (*g*, Gf, and Gc) and E_L has been described, it is important to see how that relationship changes when a traditional reading comprehension test is used as an indicant of E_L. The relationship becomes even more complicated.

Whenever reading achievement was mentioned earlier in this chapter, it was usually qualified by connecting it to efficiency level. As E_L has been defined, it can be measured in a manner that involves little or no abstract reasoning, novel problem solving, or drawing inferences, which are the main ingredients of fluid intelligence, Gf. However, it has also been noted earlier that standardized reading achievement tests, or standardized reading comprehension tests, provide indicants of E_L. Therefore, the relationship between intelligence and reading achievement becomes more complicated because typical standardized reading comprehension tests often involve inferential questions—which measure Gf—and literal questions—which do not measure Gf.

Literal questions are those which can ordinarily be answered correctly by those individuals who have read and understood the thoughts in the sentences of the text. That is, literal questions are likely to be appropriate for measuring whether rauding has occurred. However, individuals who raud the text still might not be able to answer the inferential questions because these questions are likely to require varying degrees of fluid intelligence, Gf. Indeed, the description of Gf given by Horn (1994) is as follows: "... measured in tasks requiring inductive, deductive, conjunctive, and disjunctive reasoning to arrive at understanding of relations among stimuli, to comprehend implications, and to draw inferences" (p. 443). Notice that asking inferential questions on a standardized test of reading comprehension would be one excellent way to measure Gf. Therefore, the more inferential questions there are on a standardized reading comprehension test, the more likely (a) the test is measuring Gf, and (b) the test will correlate highly with measures of Gf, such as the Raven test described earlier.

Besides the use of inferential questions on traditional reading tests, another complicating factor involves situations where the text to be read is relatively difficult for the reader, $D_L > A_L$. In these situations, which are prevalent, the text cannot be rauded so the reader will have to shift into a learning process. This means that even the literal questions are likely to involve problem solving and abstract reasoning when the text is relatively hard for the reader. Because most reading achievement tests involve texts that are relatively difficult for many of the examinees and because many of the test questions are of the inferential type, this means that scores on these traditional reading achievement tests often are likely to be substantially related to fluid intelligence.

It has been known for many years that traditional reading comprehension tests are notorious for measuring reasoning ability. This connection between traditional reading comprehension tests and reasoning ability is why R. L. Thorndike (1974) found evidence to support E. L. Thorndike's (1917) claim that reading was basically a reasoning process. It was noted earlier that Carver (1973b) studied this connection. He concluded the following:

> It is not surprising that if reading is measured by passages and questions that obviously require reasoning, then reading is bound to appear to be reasoning. (p. 50)
> For example, most of the correlations between the STEP Reading Test and the SCAT Test (an intelligence test) are reported to be above .80, according to the manual for the test. (p. 51)
> Consider ... the following categories of items given in the manual for the STEP Reading Test: reproduce ideas, translate ideas and make inferences, analyze motivation, analyze presentation and criticize. (p. 52)
> Hopefully, the next fifty years will not find reading researchers in the same embarrassing situation of concluding from reading test data that the ability to answer reasoning-type questions on paragraphs mainly involves the ability to reason. (p. 55)

Whereas traditional reading comprehension tests are likely to require a great deal of reasoning or inferencing, the rauding process is a basic reading process that involves minimal inferencing on-line, that is, during the process. The rauding process is generally operated on relatively easy text. If the text being read is relatively difficult, $D_L > A_L$, then the readers are likely to shift to a learning process, as noted earlier. In this type of learning situation there is likely to be off-line processing devoted to inferences designed to solve the problem of what certain words mean and what each sentence means. This view of the various processes involved in reading is highly compatible with the theorizing of Perfetti (1993) who contends that during ordinary reading, inferencing on-line is minimal. He states that ordinary reading involves "... making sure that all pronouns are immediately attached to antecedents and making sure that each sentence can connect to some preceding sentence stored in memory," and that "everything else is postponed until later, examined off-line as the reader prepares to paraphrase, summarize, or answer some question about what was read" (p. 183).

Notice that an attempt is being made to clarify the relationship between intelligence and reading achievement by making a distinction between E_L and traditional reading comprehension tests that involve a great many inferences. This relationship can get even more complicated when it is remembered that traditional standardized reading comprehension tests are ordinarily timed tests, so they also involve rate level, R_L. Therefore, even if the reading achievement test involved all inferential questions, it still may not correlate extremely highly with a measure of Gf because the Gf measure would not correlate highly with the R_L part of E_L. Therefore, any conclusions about the connection between intelligence and reading achievement needs to be very specific about how reading achievement is measured.

Now that the relationships among *g*, Gf, and traditional standardized reading comprehension tests have been explained, Gc will be considered. It is the second most important subfactor of general intelligence, and it is empirically determined from the same factors that are causal for reading achievement, namely, accuracy level, A_L, rate level, R_L, verbal level, V_L, pronunciation level, P_L, verbal aptitude, g_v, and pronunciation aptitude, g_p. Therefore, many measures of *g*, such as IQ tests, will have a moderate relationship with measures of reading achievement because crystallized intelligence, Gc, is involved in both IQ and the measure of reading achievement. It seems likely that if the IQ scores involve several tests involving language, Gc, then there will be at least a moderate relationship with traditional standardized reading comprehension tests.

It can be seen from this discussion that the relationship between intelligence and reading achievement depends upon the particular measure of intelligence (*g*, Gf, Gc, or other of the several intelligences) and the particular measure of reading achievement (a direct measure of E_L, or a traditional standardized test of reading comprehension). Table 20-1 summarizes the expected range of relationships. For example, the highest relationship expected between intelligence and reading achievement (correlations around .80 to .90) would be between (a) an untimed printed group IQ test that involved mainly Gf and Gc, and (b) an untimed reading comprehension test that involved only inferential questions. In Table 20-1, the lowest expected relationship between intelligence and reading achievement (correlations around .20 to .40) would involve an untimed test of fluid intelligence, such as the RPM, and a timed, or speeded, reading achievement test that contains only literal questions.

Data indirectly relevant to the predictions made in Table 20-1, come from Stanovich, Cunningham, and Feeman (1984). They reported the correlational results of "a wide (but certainly not exhaustive) sampling of relatively recent studies" which "employed a variety of IQ tests, reading achievement tests, age levels, and subject populations" (p. 279). The median correlation for various grade categories were as follows: grade 1, $r = .46$ ($N = 29$ studies); grade 2, $r = .46$ ($N = 18$ studies); grade 3, $r = .46$ ($N = 13$ studies); grades 4 - 8, $r = .61$ ($N = 29$ studies); grade 9 and above $r = .66$ ($N = 6$ studies). They summarized these data as follows: "It would appear that a typical value in the early grades would fall into the .3 - .5 range (figures consistent with Chall's 1967 review of earlier literature) and in the .45 - .65 range for middle grades" and "most are within the range of .3 - .7" (p. 279). The lower correlations found in the lower grades (.3 - .5) are likely to be due to individual IQ tests that involve no reading and unspeeded reading achievement tests that have few inferential questions on them. The higher correlations in the middle and upper grades are likely to be due to (a) more group-administered IQ tests that require reading, and (b) the use of reading achievement tests that have more inferential questions on them.

Table 20-1
Summary of the Expected Correlations Between Various Types of Intelligence Measures and Various Types of Reading Achievement Measures

If the measure of intelligence	*and the reading achievement measure*	*then the correlation is likely to be*
is an untimed printed group IQ test, which measures mostly fluid intelligence, Gf, and crystallized intelligence, Gc,	is untimed with all inferential questions.	extremely high (around .80 to .90).
is an individual IQ test that samples mostly language tasks and measures Gc,	is untimed with many inferential questions.	very high (around .70 to .80).
is an individual IQ test that samples across several intelligences besides Gf and Gc but has many language subtests, such as the WAIS,	is a timed test with an even mixture of inferential and literal questions, such as many standardized reading comprehension tests for adults,	moderate to high (around .60 to .70).
is an individual IQ test that samples several intelligences but measures Gf quite well, such as the Stanford-Binet and the WISC,	is a timed test that has more literal questions than inferential,	moderate (around .40 to .50).
is an untimed test of fluid intelligence, such as the RPM,	is a timed test that has all literal questions,	low to moderate (around .20 to .40).

Data relevant to the predicted high relationship between intelligence and reading achievement comes from R. L. Thorndike in 1973 (reviewed earlier in Chapter 4). The intelligence measure was a reading vocabulary test that would load highly on Gc and the reading achievement test involved ample time limits with both literal and inferential questions. The correlations he reported have been corrected for attenuation due to unreliability, and are as follows: $r = .91$ for 10-year olds; $r = .88$ for 14-year olds; $r = .91$ for 17 - 18-year olds. Notice that these correlations are extremely high between an indicant of Gc and an unspeeded measure of reading achievement.

Table 20-1 helps explain how it is possible to find very high correlations between intelligence and reading achievement along side of very low correlations in the research literature. For example, Torgesen (1985) has stated that "we do know that tests of general intelligence predict reading achievement very well" (p. 352). Contrast this statement with Stanovich (1984) who said that "intelligence tests like the Raven, which do not directly tap a recognized subskill of reading, but are instead measures of the abstract reasoning ability or 'mental energy' that supposedly is the quintessence of *g* ... are generally poor predictors of reading ability" (p. 298). Torgesen can be correct about a high relationship if the measures of general intelligence load highly on both Gf and Gc and the measures of reading achievement are untimed group tests that include many inferential questions, or include literal questions on relatively hard texts. Stanovich can also be correct about a low relationship when the measure of intelligence is the Raven—which is the best single indicant of general intelligence—and the reading achievement tests are timed and/or involve mainly literal questions on texts that are not highly difficult.

In summary, it is being hypothesized that all of the reliable variance in the size of the correlations between intelligence test scores and reading achievement test scores can be accounted for by considering several factors known to influence the relationship. With respect to the intelligence tests, the correlation with reading achievement, or E_L, becomes higher when the intelligence test (a) loads highly on Gc, (b) loads lowly on Gf, and (c) involves reading (such as group tests instead of individual tests). With respect to reading achievement tests, the correlation with intelligence becomes higher (a) when the reading achievement test is more of a power test than a speeded test, (b) when the passages for the readers being tested become more difficult, and (c) when more inferential questions are involved. The correlation between measures of intelligence and reading achievement will be low (around .20 to .40), when (a) the intelligence test is individually administered and loads lowly on Gc and highly on Gf, and (b) the reading achievement test is a speeded test with literal questions on relatively easy passages. The correlation between measures of intelligence and reading achievement will be very high (around .80 to .90), when (a) the IQ test loads highly on Gc and also loads highly on Gf, and (b) the reading achievement test is a power test with inferential questions on relatively difficult passages.

IQ-Achievement Discrepancy

One topic that is highly relevant to intelligence and reading achievement is the use of a discrepancy between an IQ score and a reading achievement score to determine a reading disability, as was discussed earlier in Chapter 19. In this section, the IQ-Achievement discrepancy will be examined again, now that the multiple meanings of intelligence and reading achievement are clearer.

A reading disability has often been determined by the degree of discrepancy between an IQ score and a reading achievement score, or reading expectancy has been predicted from intelligence measures using formulas (Hoffman, 1980). For example, one way to do this is to require a 20 point discrepancy when both measures have the same standard score scale with a mean of 100 and a standard deviation of 15. If one student had an IQ of 95 and a reading achievement score of 80, this 15 point discrepancy would not be enough to qualify for a reading disability. The theory underlying this procedure is that the

IQ score represents potential so that those students who read far below their potential (more than 20 points, for example) are said to have a disability. This procedure of identifying potential from an aptitude-achievement discrepancy has been attacked by several researchers (e.g., Fletcher et al., 1994; Francis et al., 1996; Shaywitz, 1996; Shaywitz et al., 1992; Siegel, 1988, 1989; Spear-Swerling & Sternberg, 1996; Stanovich, 1989, 1991), as was mentioned earlier in Chapter 19.

It was noted earlier that the score on individually administered IQ tests, such as the Stanford-Binet, WISC, and WAIS is an average over several intelligences, and many of these intelligences are not importantly causal for reading achievement. For example, fluid intelligence and spatial intelligence are not highly important individual difference factors that cause high or low reading achievement, yet they are important parts of most IQ tests. Therefore, students with extremely high spatial intelligence (IQ = 150) are likely to have a total IQ score that is much higher than their reading achievement, yet in no way does that mean that these students are not reading up to their potential. Students who score high on an IQ test mainly because they have high spatial ability are not likely to gain in E_L quickly with remedial instruction because their high spatial ability is not very helpful to them when they read. Yet, a student who reads poorly and has high scores on g_v, g_p, and g_s probably has had poor teaching/learning experiences and therefore would likely gain in E_L quickly with the appropriate remedial instruction. So, the theoretical rationale underlying the use of an IQ score as an indicator of reading potential or expected reading achievement is not sound. There are no sound reasons for averaging over several intelligences and using the results as an indicator of potential. Too often this spurious indicator of potential is likely to suggest high potential when in fact low potential exists.

With respect to IQ measuring potential, Berninger & Abbott (1994) state that "it is often assumed that IQ is a good predictor of rate of future learning, but this assumption must be tested empirically to determine if IQ predicts which children respond to a particular treatment or how fast a child moves through a treatment protocol" (p. 174). There are no known existing data which supports the theory that IQ predicts rate of growth in reading due to treatment. In fact, the data collected by Vellutino et al. (1996) indicates that IQ does not predict growth in reading ability due to treatment.

Memory Capacity and Reading Achievement

Memory capacity has generally been considered a basic part of intelligence. For example, short-term memory is measured by the Memory for Digits subtest on the Stanford-Binet, and the Digit Span subtest on the Wechsler tests. In recent years, a great deal of research has been done on working memory and its relationship to reading (e.g., see Gathercole & Baddeley, 1993; Hulme & Mackinzie, 1992). For some researchers, working memory is almost synonymous with short-term memory (STM) as measured by a digit span test. For others researchers, STM can be divided into a passive part, which can be measured by a test of digit span, and an active part, which cannot be measured by digit span but can be measured by backward digit span. The active part of working memory refers to the ability to hold some items in mind while working on them. So, backward digit span involves a task that measures active working memory because when the digits 7, 3, 1, and 9 are said aloud to individuals, for example, and then they are asked to repeat them backwards, they must be able to hold 7, 3, 1, and 9 in memory while saying 9, 1, 3, and 7. The longer the string that can successfully be repeated, the larger the working memory capacity (WMC).

Empirical evidence has been presented for the theory that the higher the ability to reason, the higher the WMC (Kyllenon & Crystal, 1990). Furthermore, the Raven Progressive Matrices, RPM, test which was cited earlier as the single best measure of general intelligence, *g*, and one of the best measures of fluid intelligence, Gf, involves a great deal of WMC (Just & Carpenter, 1992).

Evidence has also been collected which is directly relevant to WMC and the causal model. Carver (1998c) related WMC to reading by developing a measure of WMC that was based on one of the tasks used in the research of Kyllenon and Crystal (1990). This test was given to 62 college students, and this measure of WMC correlated highest with a passive STM measure, .66, and second highest with the RPM, .49. It correlated .41 with an indicant of efficiency level, E_L, but when it was entered into a hierarchical regression analysis (H.R.A.) after V_L, P_L, and C_s, it contributed 0% to the prediction of E_L. This measure of WMC correlated .34 with V_L, .25 with P_L, and .32 with C_s. For these advanced readers, it appeared that WMC did not belong at Echelons 2 or 3, and its correlations with V_L, P_L, and C_s at Echelon 3 were only moderate (around .30) so it was not considered to be a major causal factor at Echelon 4.

In this research by Carver, data was also reported from a group of 36 students in grades 3 to 10, who were given the same tests as described above. When grade in school was controlled in all the correlations, WMC correlated only .21 with the RPM for these younger students, but it correlated .50 with E_L. However, in another H.R.A., after entering grade in school, V_L, P_L, and C_s, the measure of WMC contributed 0% variance to the prediction of E_L. It was concluded that WMC did not belong in Echelons 2 and 3 of the causal model. However, WMC did correlate .42 with V_L, .50 with P_L, and .33 with C_s. Therefore, WMC seemed to provide a candidate for inclusion at Echelon 4 for these students in grades 3 to 10.

In another study in this same research reported by Carver, 49 students in grades 3 to 11 were given the same battery of tests except the test of WMC was modified so that the letters and numbers remained on the screen for 3 seconds instead of 1 second. This time the measure of WMC correlated .33 with the

RPM, which is still relatively low for two tests which purportedly measure the same thing. The measure of WMC correlated .47 with E_L, and this replicated fairly closely Studies I and II at .41 and .50. For the third time, an H.R.A. was conducted, and WMC contributed 0% variance to the prediction of E_L after entering grade in school, V_L, P_L, and C_s. So, it did not appear that WMC should be included in Echelons 2 and 3. This time, the correlations for students in grades 3 to 11 with V_L, P_L, and C_s were lower at .21, .36 and .21, respectively. So, the importance of WMC as an important causal factor at Echelon 4 could not be replicated.

These data suggest that WMC is not an important enough factor to be included in the causal model because it did not compete successfully with V_L, P_L, and C_s at Echelon 3, and it did not consistently correlate high enough with V_L, P_L, and C_s to be included at Echelon 4.

It should also be noted that in the three studies examined above, two measures of passive STM were also included. One involved a measure of letter span administered by a computer involving keyboard responses, and the other involved a parallel version of the same letter span test administered orally with oral responses. In all three studies, neither measure of STM contributed more than 1% variance to the prediction of E_L after entering V_L, P_L, and C_s, so it was concluded that neither belonged at Echelons 2 and 3 for either the college students or the younger readers. For all three studies, the median of the 18 correlations involving V_L, P_L, C_s and these two STM measures was .30; this was considered to be too low to consider passive STM as an important causal factor at Echelon 4. This decision to omit STM from the causal model would seem to be supported by Turner and Engle (1989) who state that:

> The digit span has been assumed to reflect output from short-term memory and is a ubiquitous component of intelligence tests (Wechsler, 1944). However, it does not correlate well with performance on such higher level tasks as reading comprehension (Perfetti & Lesgold, 1977) or even the amount of information estimated to be represented in primary or secondary memory (Martin, 1978). (p. 127)

In summary, short-term memory and working memory capacity have been related to all the factors in the causal model in Echelons 1, 2, and 3, for middle graders, upper graders, and college students. Neither STM nor WMC added a substantial amount of unique variance to the prediction of reading achievement, E_L, over and above V_L, P_L, and C_s. Furthermore, neither STM nor WMC consistently correlated high enough with V_L, P_L, and C_s to be seriously considered as root causes of reading achievement at Echelon 4. Therefore, memory capacity, STM & WMC, does not seem to be important enough to be included in the model as a separate causal factor.

Summary of Theory

There are three aptitudes, or intelligences, that strongly influence reading achievement, or E_L; they are verbal knowledge aptitude, g_v, pronunciation knowledge aptitude, g_p, and cognitive speed aptitude, g_s. Notice that these three aptitudes may also be considered as three of many intelligences, or three of many cognitive abilities. Verbal aptitude, g_v, is usually represented in an intelligence test battery by verbal measures such as vocabulary tests that do not require reading. Pronunciation aptitude, g_p, usually is not represented in intelligence test batteries. Cognitive speed aptitude, g_s, is also not represented in intelligence test batteries because a direct measure of g_s requires the speed of naming a series of overlearned stimuli; the speeded tests in an IQ battery usually involve tasks that involve abilities less directly related to reading, such as perceptual speed.

Because an IQ score is generally derived from many different intelligence tests, each measuring a different cognitive ability, this single IQ score represents an average of 6 to 10 different intelligences, or cognitive abilities. Therefore, the IQ score is an overall score, or average score, that is a measure of general intelligence, *g*. An IQ score, or *g*, is not highly related to reading achievement, or E_L, because it contains many intelligences, or subfactors, that are not related to E_L, such as spatial intelligence.

The two main cognitive abilities that comprise IQ, or *g*, are fluid intelligence, Gf, and crystallized intelligence, Gc. Gf is not an important factor causing high and low reading achievement, or E_L, because high levels of abstract reasoning are not required for a high rauding efficiency level. Gc, or crystallized intelligence, represents what has been learned, and it is indistinguishable from E_L, that is, E_L is part of Gc. Therefore, it would be confusing to theorize that Gc is causal for E_L because E_L is part of Gc. This means that general intelligence (*g* or IQ) is composed primarily of two factors, one of which is not causal for high reading achievement, or E_L, and the other is almost indistinguishable from E_L. Stated differently, E_L is not importantly affected by Gf whereas E_L is part of Gc.

An untimed standardized reading comprehension test which contains passages that are difficult to understand and questions that require a great deal of abstract reasoning to answer correctly, is not a good measure of reading achievement, or E_L. These kinds of reading achievement tests are actually general intelligence tests in disguise, or IQ tests, because they are measuring the two primary ingredients of *g*, namely, fluid intelligence and crystallized intelligence. If a time limit is placed on this kind of a reading achievement test, so that it becomes speeded, then it will be more related to cognitive speed aptitude, g_s, and therefore less related to measures of Gf and Gc.

The size of the relationship between intelligence tests and reading achievement tests depends upon (a) the extent to which the measure of intelligence involves Gf, Gc, g_v, g_p, and g_s, and (b) the extent to which the measure of reading achievement involves inferential questions, difficult to comprehend passages, and a time limit that makes the test speeded. More specifically, E_L is not importantly related to Gf, the main component of general intelligence and a primary part of most IQ tests. Out of all existing kinds of intelligence, or cognitive abilities, there are only three that are important root causes of high and low E_L; they are g_v, g_p, and g_s.

Summary of Evidence

Correlations between measures of intelligence and measures of reading achievement are (a) very low when the measure of intelligence is an indicant of Gf, such as the Raven test, and the measure of reading achievement is a good indicant of E_L (Carver, 1998c), and (b) very high when the measure of intelligence is a reading vocabulary test, Gc, and the measure of reading achievement is an unspeeded standardized reading comprehension test (R. L. Thorndike, 1973). IQ measures usually include tests that measure Gf and Gc, and these measures correlate moderately with traditional reading comprehension tests (Hammill & McNutt, 1981).

Gf, as indicated by the RPM, does not contribute importantly to the variance in E_L after the variance predictable from V_L, P_L, and C_s (at Echelon 3) have been accounted for (Carver, 1998c). Furthermore, the RPM does not correlate highly with V_L, P_L, or C_s (Carver, 1998c).

Implications

Researchers who study the relationship between intelligence and reading achievement need to be cognizant of what type or types of intelligence are being measured (such as Gf, Gc, g_v, g_p, or g_s) and what aspect of reading achievement is being measured (such as a unspeeded test involving inferential questions on difficult passages, or a speeded test that measures efficiency level, E_L). Most importantly, researchers need to be cognizant of whether the measure of reading achievement is a good indicant of efficiency level, or not.

IQ tests should not be used to measure potential in reading, and should not be used to determine who gets special help in reading. IQ tests should not be used in this manner because there is no research evidence which supports this type of usage, and there is a great deal of research evidence which indicates that IQ tests are invalid when used in this manner.

Forget Me Nots

The relationship between intelligence and reading achievement (a) is very high when measures of fluid intelligence and crystallized intelligence are involved and the measure of reading achievement is unspeeded with inferential questions, and (b) is very low when measures of IQ, or fluid intelligence, are involved and the measure of reading achievement involves rauding efficiency level, E_L. Reading achievement seems to be a measure of crystallized intelligence. Intelligence is best considered as having a non-causal connection with reading achievement, or E_L, whether general intelligence, fluid intelligence, or IQ.

CHAPTER

21

VOLUME OF READING

If we can get students to read more (higher volume) during a school year, will that cause an increase their reading achievement? Most teachers and many researchers will answer "yes" to this question. However, the evidence is mixed. Under certain limited conditions a higher volume of reading is likely to cause an increase reading achievement, or E_L, but in typical reading situations a higher volume of reading is not likely to cause an increase in reading achievement.

Later in this chapter, theory and research relevant to volume of reading will be presented. Then, the classroom practice of sustained silent reading (SSR) will be described, and relevant research will be reviewed. Finally, the concept of "print exposure" will be described, and relevant research will be reviewed.

Theory

In 1990a, Carver presented a causal model which had thoughts rauded (T_r) as a proximal cause of both reading level, A_L, and rate level, R_L. Thoughts rauded, T_r, was a concept indistinguishable from volume of reading. This means that volume of reading occupied the central position in the causal model of reading achievement—the position that P_L now occupies (see Figure 1-5 from Chapter 1). Subsequent research and theory development forced volume of reading out of the causal model, and forced P_L into its prominent place.

The effect of a high volume of reading will be analyzed taking several theoretical factors into account. Most importantly, the effect depends upon whether the reading involves (a) material that is relatively easy, $A_L > D_L$ (called easy rauding), (b) material that is at the individual's level of ability, $A_L = D_L$ (called matched rauding), or (c) material that is relatively hard, $D_L > A_L$ (called hard reading). The effect of a high volume of reading also depends somewhat upon whether the individual is a beginning, intermediate, or advanced reader. These complicating factors need to be elaborated.

The main problem with increasing the volume of reading is that most students will increase their amount of reading in relatively easy materials, $A_L > D_L$, called "easy rauding." High volumes of easy rauding are not likely to increase substantially either V_L, P_L, or A_L. Verbal knowledge level, V_L, cannot be increased by easy rauding, because students will not encounter any words they do not already know auditorily, that is, they cannot increase their V_LWords because they will not encounter any words that are not already audamatized when they read relatively easy material (see Carver, 1994b). Pronunciation knowledge, P_L, cannot be increased by easy rauding because students will not encounter any words that they do not already know how to pronounce, that is, they cannot increase their P_LWords because they will not encounter any new words in relatively easy material that are not already pronounceamatized. Finally, all words in relatively easy materials are already raudamatized words, therefore A_L cannot increase during easy rauding. This means that students who spend a great deal of time reading relatively easy novels—called recreational reading—will not gain more in V_L, P_L, or A_L, than students who spend an equal amount of time watching television or playing basketball.

It is difficult to understand how reading old known words could increase the number of new unknown words that can be accurately and quickly recognized. Or, stated differently, there is no obvious mechanism whereby the repeated reading of old raudamatized words will somehow result in the raudamatization of new words without ever encountering these new words in print. Thus, a high volume of reading relatively easy material during a school year is not likely to result in an increase in verbal level, V_L, or pronunciation level, P_L, or accuracy level, A_L. This means that a high volume of recreational reading involving fictional books is not likely to increase A_L or R_L. Therefore, it is not likely that reading achievement, or E_L, will be increased by a high volume of easy rauding.

It does seem likely that a low volume of easy rauding will keep fine tuned (practiced to asymptote) the ability to recognize overlearned words rapidly, for any reader. Individuals need to engage in a low volume of easy rauding in order to *maintain* all of their raudamatized words at their rauding rate, that is, maintain P_L and A_L at their achieved levels without losses occurring due to a lack of practice.

Whereas a high volume of easy rauding is not likely to improve reading achievement, a high volume of matched rauding is likely to improve reading achievement, or E_L. If students can be induced to read texts that are at their level of ability, $D_L = A_L$, then they are more likely to increase their pronunciation knowledge and their accuracy level. For students below raudamaticity, a high volume of matched rauding is likely to increase P_L and A_L, because these students will encounter audamatized words that they can learn to pronounce (increase P_LWords) and eventually raudamatize with practice (increase A_L. Words). That is, students who are below raudamaticity can benefit from high volumes of matched rauding because a few new words will be encountered—about 1 new word every 100 words of text when $A_L = D_L$ (Carver, 1994b).

For students who are at raudamaticity, a high volume of matched rauding is also likely to increase reading achievement, or E_L. The new words that these students encounter will not be known auditorily, but they will often be able to infer their meanings from context. If these students engage in a high volume of matched rauding, they are likely to increase V_L, P_L, and A_L (a) by learning the meaning of a new word from context, (b) by figuring out how to pronounce this word, and (c) by practicing the words via several encounters until it reaches raudamaticity. If V_L and P_L are increased, then A_L and R_L must be increased; therefore, E_L must also be increased, according to the causal model. This means that a high volume of matched rauding should increase reading achievement, or E_L, for all students, whether they are below or at raudamaticity. However, it is not easy, from a teaching standpoint, to get students to read texts that are at matched difficulty. It is much easier to get students to engage in large volumes of recreational reading because they ordinarily will choose books to read that involve easy rauding.

Hard reading involves texts that have high difficulty levels relative to the ability of the reader, $D_L > A_L$. Getting students to tackle relatively hard material and stick with it without becoming frustrated and giving up, is not an easy challenge to meet. In this regard, Jorgeson (1977) found correlations of .23 and .25 between the relative difficulty of the material that students were asked to read and the number of behavior problems in the classroom. These correlations are not large but when all of the factors which cause misbehavior are considered, this seems to be one of the contributing factors. That is, when students are asked to read relatively hard texts (materials that are at their frustration level), it should not be surprising that aggressive behaviors arise in some of the students.

Beginning readers and intermediate readers should not be asked to engage in hard reading because this will be too frustrating for them. When these students try to read relatively hard material they are likely to encounter many unknown words, that is, audamatized words that have not been pronounceamatized, plus words that have not yet been audamatized. This kind of reading may be so frustratingly difficult that an aversion to reading is learned. These readers should not be given relatively hard texts to read because they are likely to learn to avoid reading under these conditions.

With respect to advanced readers, they are all purported to be at raudamaticity. The main way for these readers to increase their reading achievement, or E_L, is probably by engaging in a high volume of hard reading. That is, by studying relatively hard materials, they are likely to increase V_L and A_L, which in turn will increase E_L.

Table 21-1 summarizes the recommendations regarding volume of reading at various levels of relative difficulty of text for beginning, intermediate, and advanced readers. Notice that a low volume of easy rauding is recommended for beginning, intermediate, and advanced readers, in order to maintain all of their raudamatized words at asymptote. Also notice that high volumes of matched rauding is recommended for beginning, intermediate, and advanced readers, in order to help increase the number of raudamatized words, and thereby increase reading achievement, or E_L. Finally, notice that hard reading is not recommended for beginning and intermediate readers, but it is recommended for advanced readers. Hard reading is likely to be very frustrating for beginning and intermediate readers, and not an effective way to increase reading achievement, or E_L. On the other hand, hard reading is likely to be the main way that advanced readers can increase their reading achievement, via increasing V_L and A_L simultaneously, by learning new words and concepts that can eventually become raudamatized with practice.

Table 21-1
Recommended Volume of Reading at Varying Levels of Relative Difficulty for Beginning, Intermediate, and Advanced Readers

Relative Difficulty of Text Being Read	*Beginning Readers (Below Raudamaticity)*	*Intermediate Readers (Below & At Raudamaticity)*	*Advanced Readers (At Raudamaticity)*
Relatively Easy, $D_L < A_L$, called "easy rauding"	Low Volume	Low Volume	Low Volume
Matched Difficulty, $D_L = A_L$, called "matched rauding"	High Volume	High Volume	High Volume
Relatively Hard, $D_L > A_L$, called "hard reading"	(Zero Volume)	(Zero Volume)	High Volume

Research

Most of the research relevant to volume of reading and reading achievement prior to 1992 has been reviewed by Carver and Leibert (1995). They noted that Ingham (1981) "flooded" two schools with books and found that the test scores for these students were negligibly different from the students in two control schools. They also critiqued a study by Taylor, Frye, and Maruyama (1990) involving fifth and sixth graders keeping daily logs and concluded that "those data provide little or no encouragement for theory and practice that advocates more silent reading to increase growth in reading ability because only 2-3% of the variance was associated with home and school reading, and even this evidence remains correlational" (p. 30). Carver and Leibert also noted that Elley (1991) provided evidence that reading library books helps second-language learners become better readers, but those data may not generalize to first-language users because these students were likely to be engaged in matched rauding, not easy rauding. None of the studies reviewed by Carver and Leibert provided evidence that a high volume of easy rauding causes an increase in reading achievement.

Carver and Leibert (1995) also reported upon the results of a research study that they conducted. They studied the gain in reading achievement, E_L, for a group of 43 students in grades 3, 4, and 5 who read relatively easy fiction during 6 weeks of summer school, 2 hours a day. This 60 hours of nominal reading time did not result in their having higher reading achievement as measured by a test designed to indicate efficiency level, E_L. The control group was 107 students in the same school who did not participate in the high volume of supervised summer reading. Carver and Leibert summarized the findings of all of their research as follows: "Considering all the data collected, we found no solid or consistent evidence that students in a summer reading program who engaged in reading relatively easy library books for 6 weeks gained in their reading level, vocabulary, rate, or efficiency" (p. 46). They go on to evaluate the relevant theory and practice as follows:

> This idea of learning to read better by reading has some of the same qualities as lifting oneself up by one's bootstraps, a paradox that has been called the reading bootstrap. The reading bootstrap effect seems to be impossible for students engaged in easy rauding. (p. 46)
>
> Given the above results and interpretations, the instructional practice of allocating 2-3 hours of class time each week to free reading seems to be questionable. If most of this time could be made less free by inducing students to read books that are measured to be at or above the reading level of the student, then *maybe* this practice would result in gain in general reading ability. (p. 46)
>
> As long as we hear the truism that the best way to learn to read is to read, and as long as substantial amounts of classroom time are devoted to the free reading of library books, we should continue to be embarrassed that we have no solid experimental data supporting the reading bootstrap or the instructional practices based upon it. (p. 46)

The above research by Carver and Leibert (1995) is relevant to the contention of Smith (1992) who stated that: "if children are reading with interest and without difficulty, they are learning to read (and learning other useful things as well)" (p. 440). Indeed, this is what Carver and Leibert (1995) thought they would find when they designed this research where students read books of their choice each day in the summer reading program; Carver (1990a) even advanced the construct of volume of reading as a core causal factor, as was noted earlier. However, there was no evidence that the level of reading achievement of these students increased due to this book reading that involved students spending more hours reading "with interest and without difficulty." Instead, the correlation that Carver and Leibert reported between reading volume and reading achievement ($r = .42$) is more likely to be causal in the other direction. It seems much more likely that the students who came into the summer reading program at higher levels of reading achievement choose to read more during the time set aside for reading.

The above .42 correlation that Carver and Leibert reported between reading volume and reading achievement, or E_L, was found under structured conditions where everyone was encouraged and constrained to be engaged in recreational book reading, and alternative behaviors were discouraged. Surely, this correlation would increase under more normal situations where children could choose to read a book, watch TV, play a game, talk on the phone, etc., after school and on weekends. That is, it seems even more likely that students with higher reading achievement, higher E_L, would choose to spend more time at school and more time at home engaged in reading popular books than students with lower reading achievement because this activity is easier and therefore more fun for them. Again, it seems much more likely that higher reading achievement is a cause of higher volumes of reading than higher volumes of reading is a cause of higher reading achievement.

Sustained Silent Reading

The classroom practice of having students involved in uninterrupted sustained silent reading was suggested by L. C. Hunt (1967), and then later, McCracken (1971) referred to this practice as Sustained Silent Reading (SSR). For SSR, a teacher usually sets aside a certain period of class time, such as 20 to 30 minutes, for all students to read a book of their own choosing and read it silently for enjoyment and reading practice.

In 1980, Sadoski reviewed the history and rationale underlying sustained silent reading. He summarized the rationale as follows: "... students who read tend to become better readers, and the best way to develop reading ability is not through assessment or isolated skills drill, but by reading" (p. 154). However, he did note that "none of the theorists or researchers have suggested replacing reading instruction with Sustained Silent Reading" (p. 155).

According to the theory presented earlier, SSR would have minimal effects upon reading achievement, or E_L, unless there was some assurance that the students were selecting books to read that were at their own level of reading ability, i.e., matched difficulty or $D_L = A_L$. Because most students would probably choose a relatively easy novel to read for recreation during this period, it is not likely that SSR would improve E_L over a control group that worked on math problems, for example. Furthermore, if the class had no systematic spelling instruction, then it is likely that E_L would be increased much more by a control group that was encouraged to work on learning to spell more of the their audamatized words.

The research studies on SSR reviewed by Sadoski were pre-experimental; they were not designed with good control groups covering a long treatment (e.g., Farrell, 1982). Unfortunately, a good research study of the effect of SSR upon reading achievement has not been found.

Print Exposure

In research on the volume of reading by Stanovich and colleagues, the term "print exposure" has replaced the term "volume of reading" (e.g., Stanovich & Cunningham, 1993). Stanovich (1986) has drawn attention to print exposure as a major factor which purportedly causes improvement in reading achievement. He contends that "many things that facilitate further growth in reading comprehension ability—general knowledge, vocabulary, syntactic knowledge—are developed by reading itself" (p. 364). He went on to suggest that volume of reading had a bootstrapping effect: "The effect of reading volume on vocabulary growth, combined with the large skill differences in reading volume, could mean that a 'rich-get-richer' or cumulative advantage phenomenon is almost inextricably embedded within the developmental course of reading progress" (p. 381). So, the concept of print exposure and its possible effects, must be closely examined to see if it confirms or denies the theory presented earlier about reading volume.

In 1989, Stanovich and West theorized further about print exposure. They contended that the primary effect of more print exposure is upon orthographic knowledge, that is, knowledge of how words are spelled. Notice that an increase in this kind of knowledge should result in an increase in P_L, or an increase in the number of words that can be recognized or pronounced correctly. Thus, their theory about print exposure can be summarized as follows: students who read more books during the school year will gain more in P_L. Notice that this theory about print exposure is not restrictive with respect to what difficulty level of material is being read. Yet, the relative difficulty of material, D_L - A_L, would seem to be a crucial factor interacting with print exposure, as contended at the outset of this chapter. If individuals read relatively easy books, that is, easy rauding or recreational reading, then it is difficult to see how they could increase P_L when all of the words they encounter are already raudamatized words. Because students are not likely to encounter any new words when they read high volumes of relatively easy recreational books, it is difficult to understand how P_L could increase.

Stanovich and West also developed a measuring instrument which was designed to measure "print exposure," and thereby allow them to investigate their theoretical ideas about higher print exposure causing higher gain in P_L. This instrument was called the Author Recognition Test (ART). It required examinees to check "yes" or "no" beside 100 names indicating whether or not the person was a popular writer or author. Out of the 100 names, 50 were popular authors who purportedly would be known by most individuals who read a great deal because these 50 individuals are best-selling authors who have sold hundreds of thousands of books, e.g., Steven King, Judith Krantz, and Isaac Assimov. An attempt was made to avoid authors who are regularly studied in the school curriculum. Also on the list of 100 names were 50 names of people who are not popular authors but instead were authors of published research in reading.

An instrument similar to the ART, described above, was also developed for children, by A. E. Cunningham and Stanovich (1990). It was called the Title Recognition Test (TRT). The TRT contains a list of 39 items, 25 of which are the actual titles of children's books, and 14 are foils, or pseudo titles. These lists of book titles contain such books as *Make Way for Ducklings* for first graders and *The Lion, The Witch, and The Wardrobe* for middle graders; some of the book titles are nonexistent foils so the test can be objectively scored, and a correction for guessing applied. The rationale is that individuals who score higher on this test have a higher volume of reading, or a higher degree of print exposure, because they would have had to have read more of these books in order to correctly identify more of them on the test. And, the more books they have read (higher volume of reading), the higher the number of book titles they can recognize. Translated, this theory seems to suggest that print exposure is a proximal cause of P_L, and therefore should occupy a circle in the causal model at Echelon 4 with an arrow directed toward P_L.

It does not seem possible for a person to spend 100 hours or 1000 hours, for example, reading popular fiction from many different authors, and experience a substantial gain in P_L, or A_L, or E_L. These gains would seem to be very unlikely because this type of reading involves relatively easy material and would contain few new spelling patterns. So, from the standpoint of rauding theory, it does not seem likely that this kind of increased print exposure—reading more light fiction—would increase P_L, or A_L, or R_L, or E_L.

The ART and the TRT, just described, have been used to conduct a great deal of research on print exposure during recent years. Therefore, it seemed important to critically examine the validity of these instruments.

The ART and the TRT are checklist tests which require individuals to remember the names of book authors and the titles of books. Higher scores on these tests no doubt will indicate higher print exposure but higher scores are also likely to reflect a higher verbal knowledge level—higher V_L—and higher verbal knowledge aptitude—higher g_v. That is, individuals who can correctly check more authors and titles are also likely to have more knowledge about books and authors, higher V_L, and be able to learn this verbal knowledge better—have higher g_v. Individuals with higher V_L are likely to correctly check more of the authors and titles whether or not they have read the correctly checked book; they are more likely to learn and remember authors and titles from conversations with people who have read the books, from seeing the book on a library shelf, and from seeing publicity about authors and books, whether or not the books have been read. Thus, the ART and the TRT measures are likely to be indicants of g_v and V_L as much as indicants of the number of popular books read. The more that these instruments measure g_v and V_L (not involving reading), the less valid they are for being an indicant of print exposure, or an indicant of the amount of recreational reading done by an individual. This means that print exposure is confounded with g_v and V_L, so further investigation and confirmation would be needed to determine whether a high-scoring individual had high print exposure.

The validity of these instruments can be evaluated by their correlations with other more direct measures of recreational reading, and by their correlations with nonprint measures such as indicants of g_v and V_L. With respect to more direct measures of recreational reading or print exposure, Allen, Cipielewski, & Stanovich (1992) found that the ART correlated .52 with the amount of time engaged in book reading as indicated by daily diary records, for 63 fifth grade students. This correlation of .52 is a respectable validity coefficient, but it is not a high validity coefficient. With respect to nonprint measures, Allen, Cipielewski, & Stanovich found that the ART correlated .47 with an indicant of V_L (a nonreading, composite measure of general knowledge) for the same 63 fifth graders noted above. This correlation of the ART with a nonprint measure was almost as high as it correlated with a standardized reading comprehension test (.47 vs. .52), thus suggesting that the ART is measuring nonprint verbal knowledge as much as it is measuring print exposure.

In general, the validity of the ART and the TRT as measures of print exposure are suspect because they have not been found to correlate highly with direct measures of the volume of print exposure, and they have been found to correlate with nonprint measures of verbal knowledge about as high as they have correlated with direct measures of print exposure.

The most important way to evaluate the ART and TRT as indicants of print exposure is to examine the evidence relevant to whether print exposure as measured by these tests should be at Echelon 2, Echelon 3, or Echelon 4 in the causal model. This evidence will be examined next.

With respect to Echelon 2, is there evidence that the ART or the TRT can add to the prediction of indicants of E_L, after the variance in A_L and R_L has been accounted for? If these data exist, then it would constitute evidence that the ART and the TRT were measuring a construct that belonged at Echelon 2 in the causal model. Stanovich and Cunningham (1993) have collected relevant data. They administered the ART plus a similar Magazine Recognition Test (MRT) and a similar Newspaper Recognition Test (NRT) to 268 college students, along with an indicant of A_L (general knowledge) and an indicant of E_L (Nelson-Denny Reading Test-Comprehension). The ART combined with the two other measures of print exposure did not add to the prediction of the indicant of E_L after the indicant of A_L had been entered in a hierarchical regression analysis (added 0% to the predictable variance). Therefore, these data do not support the ART as a causal factor at Echelon 2.

With respect to Echelon 3, is there evidence that the ART and TRT are highly related to A_L, and can add to the prediction of A_L after the variance in V_L and P_L have been accounted for? In 1989, Stanovich and West found that an indicant of A_L (measure of passage comprehension) correlated .36 with the ART, for 180 undergraduates. This is not a large correlation. Furthermore, the ART did not add substantially to the prediction of A_L after indicants of P_L (word identification and spelling) were entered in a hierarchical regression analysis (added 1%).

Later in 1991, A. E. Cunningham and Stanovich administered measures that provided indicants of V_L, P_L, and A_L. A reanalysis of their data revealed that the TRT did add 6% to the predictable variance in A_L after entering age plus V_L and P_L in a hierarchical regression analysis. However, the indicant of A_L was a vocabulary measure that involved the same response technique as the TRT—the real words were supposed to be checked in a list containing both real words and nonwords. This measure of A_L is of questionable validity as an indicant of A_L. It is also possible that the reason that 6% was added to the prediction was because the TRT was contributing variance unique to the response technique, that is, a checklist measure.

In 1993, Stanovich and Cunningham found that the ART plus two other print exposure measures in a composite correlated .85 with an indicant of A_L—which was also a composite of four checklist measures of general knowledge. On the surface, this result would seem to suggest that print exposure should be in Echelon 3 in the causal model because it correlated so highly with an indicant of A_L at Echelon 2. However, these data deserve closer scrutiny. These college students were likely to be advanced readers, given their description as coming from two large state universities—one of which was described as "one of the most selective public institutions in North America" (p. 212). Therefore, A_L and V_L are likely to be equal (see Chapter 17), so that the indicant of A_L in this research is also an indicant of V_L. Remember that the ART is also likely to be an indicant of V_L, as contended earlier. It seems likely that these purported measures of print exposure are measuring verbal knowledge as much as they are measuring print exposure, and that is why they correlated so highly with an indicant of A_L.

In 1996, Hall, Chiarello, and Edmondson administered a measure of print exposure (a combination of the ART, MRT, and NRT), an indicant of A_L (115 item multiple-choice test on cultural literacy), an indicant of g_v (SAT-Verbal), and an indicant of V_L (TV-exposure composite). In their results, it was found that the print exposure composite did not add a substantial amount of variance to the prediction of the indicant of A_L, after the indicants of g_v and V_L had been entered—only 2% added. This small amount of variance added to the prediction of A_L, after the variance attributable to g_v and a nonprint variable (TV-exposure composite) has been accounted for, does not support the case for this measure of print exposure belonging at Echelon 3.

Also with respect to Echelon 3, it is important to ask if the ART or the TRT adds to the prediction of R_L after the variance in P_L and C_s have been accounted for? In the 1989 study of Stanovich and West, noted earlier, the ART did not add substantially to the prediction of R_L (reaction times to regular words) after the indicants of P_L had been entered into a hierarchical regression analysis (added 1%). These data do not support the addition of print exposure to Echelon 3 as a proximal cause of rate level at Echelon 2.

With respect to Echelon 4, it is important to ask if there evidence that the ART and the TRT are highly related to P_L? In 1989, Stanovich and West found that an indicant of P_L (a measure of word identification) correlated .50 with the ART (N = 180 undergraduate students). This correlation represents a large effect size and thereby supports print exposure as a proximal cause of P_L for college students; however, this is a moot point because P_L is purportedly no longer a causal factor affecting reading achievement for those students who are likely to have reached raudamaticity. Remember that P_L is a part of A_L according to Equations 7-2 and 7-4, so P_L and A_L should correlate highly for advanced readers, even though P_L is not a cause of A_L.

In 1990, A. E. Cunningham and Stanovich found that an indicant of P_L (word identification) correlated .37 with the TRT, for third and fourth graders. This correlation represents a moderate effect size and thereby provides some support for print exposure being a teaching/learning factor that affects P_L.

In 1993, A. E. Cunningham and Stanovich found that an indicant of P_L (word identification) correlated .64 with the TRT for a group of 26 first graders; this is a high correlation which seems to support volume of reading as a cause of P_L for beginning readers. However, it is quite possible that the TRT for first graders is more of a reading test, or a measure of A_L. That is, those students who can pronounce the words and recognize their meaning in the titles on the test were more likely to underline the actual titles of books, thus making the TRT an indicant of A_L.

These data relevant to the effects of print exposure upon P_L, A_L, R_L, and E_L are not conclusive. It seems to be at least equally plausible that higher P_L, A_L, R_L, and E_L are causing students to read more, or engage in more print exposure.

Summary of Theory

A high volume of reading is likely to result in higher reading achievement under some conditions. Whether or not a high volume of reading increases reading achievement, or E_L, depends primarily upon the relative difficulty of the material being read. If the material is relatively easy, $D_L < A_L$, then a high volume of reading will not increase reading achievement, because no new words will be encountered. If the material is at matched difficulty, $D_L = A_L$, then a high volume of reading will increase reading achievement because it is likely that a few new words will be encountered and eventually raudamatized.

If the material is relatively hard, then a high volume of reading cannot be recommended for beginning readers or intermediate readers because it will be slow and frustratingly difficult. However, this kind of hard reading is probably the main way that advanced readers can increase their reading achievement, or E_L.

Easy rauding, or time spent engaged in reading novels and other light fiction, should be considered as recreational reading, because a high volume of this kind of reading will not increase reading achievement, or E_L.

Summary of Evidence

Typical students in grades 3, 4, and 5 who spend 20 to 30 hours reading relatively easy books do not gain in reading achievement, or E_L (Carver & Leibert, 1995). There is no good evidence that sustained silent reading, SSR, in elementary school classrooms increases reading achievement, or E_L.

The recent evidence involving print exposure measured by author recognition checklists and title recognition checklists (e.g., Stanovich & Cunningham, 1993) has not been definitive with respect to whether higher scores represent a cause of higher reading achievement or whether higher reading achievement represents a cause of higher scores on these checklists.

Scores on an Author Recognition Test, ART, and a Title Recognition Test, TRT, (a) have not been shown to be highly related to time engaged in book reading (Allen, Cipielewski, & Stanovich, 1992), (b) have been shown to be substantially related to nonprint measures (Allen, Cipielewski, & Stanovich, 1992), (c) have been shown to add little or no variance to the prediction of E_L after entering indicants of A_L and R_L (Hall, Chiarello, & Edmondson, 1996, Stanovich & Cunningham, 1993), (d) have usually been shown to add little or nothing to the prediction of A_L and R_L, after measures of V_L, P_L, and C_s have been entered into the prediction (Hall, Chiarello, & Edmondson, 1996; Stanovich & West, 1989)—but there have been exceptions (A. E. Cunningham & Stanovich, 1991), and (e) have been found to correlate from around .35 to .65 with indicants of P_L (A. E. Cunningham & Stanovich, 1990, 1993; Stanovich & West, 1989).

In general, existing data do not support theory which holds that sustained silent reading, or a high volume of print exposure, increases reading achievement, or E_L. These data also do not support theory which holds that encouraging students to engage in high volumes of recreation reading will increase reading achievement, or E_L. Finally, these data are not definitive with respect to the conditions under which a high volume of reading will or will not increase reading achievement, because it is mostly correlational.

Implications

Experimental treatment studies need to be conducted (not correlational) which determine (a) whether higher amounts of recreational book reading causes higher P_L, higher A_L, and higher E_L, or (b) whether higher P_L, A_L, and E_L cause higher amounts of recreational book reading. We need to know if high achievers are more likely to find recreational book reading to be interesting and rewarding (easier, faster, and therefore more fun) so they engage in it more frequently, whereas low achievers in reading are more likely to find the reading of fiction to be boring and unrewarding (harder, slower, and more frustrating). We need to know if extra recreational book reading does in fact cause extra gain in reading achievement, because (a) the causal model holds that this kind of easy rauding will not increase reading achievement, or E_L, and (b) many teaching and learning activities are predicated on the assumption that this kind of easy rauding does increase reading achievement, or E_L.

Given the current status of theory and research, educators need to discontinue all sustained silent reading programs in middle grade classrooms until there is direct experimental evidence that SSR causes higher reading achievement; otherwise these programs should be regarded as recreational and the educational equivalent of recess for most students. High volumes of easy rauding should not be recommended for any student as a way to increase reading achievement.

Forget Me Nots

A high volume of reading relatively easy texts, such as reading light fiction for recreation, is not likely to increase reading achievement because no new words or concepts will be learned.

CHAPTER

22

WHOLE-LANGUAGE APPROACH

In recent years, the whole-language approach to reading instruction has been used by many teachers in the lower grades (kindergarten, first grade, and second grade). This approach will be described, and then it will be evaluated as a possible cause of high reading achievement, using the knowledge that has been acquired by scientists during the last 20 years. This approach to teaching beginning readers will also be evaluated by comparing it to the causal model; it is relevant to the two teaching and learning factors in Echelon 4 of the model as described in Chapter 1. Before continuing, it should be acknowledged that some advocates of whole language have referred to it as an approach (e.g., Weaver, 1988), but most have referred to these ideas and recommended activities as a philosophy, a theory, or a movement (Altwerger, Edelsky, & Flores, 1987; K. S. Goodman, 1986; Watson, 1989).

It is likely that the whole-language approach causes students to read slower (lower R_L). It is also likely that the whole-language approach is one of the causes of low reading achievement, or low E_L, for students with low pronunciation aptitude. The advantages and disadvantages of this approach, which has been popular in reading instruction, will be closely examined in this chapter.

Description

Introduction. In this section, the whole-language approach will be described by reviewing its theoretical background, and by reporting how it is purported to be implemented in the classroom.

Theoretical Background. The theory underlying the whole-language approach can be traced back to 1967, when K. S. Goodman argued that reading was a "psycholinguistic guessing game." He contended that "efficient reading does not result from precise perception and identification of all elements, but from skill in selecting the fewest, most productive cues necessary to produce guesses which are right the first time" (p. 260). This guessing hypothesis formed the core of whole-language theory.

More of the theoretical foundation underlying whole-language is provided by the top down reading model of Smith (1971). One of his ideas was that "the more difficulty a reader has with reading, the more he relies on the visual information; this statement applies to both the fluent reader and the beginner" (p. 221). Smith thought that good readers were able to correctly predict or guess words from a sampling of letters within words and a sampling of words within sentences, without having to look at all the letters or all the words. This process supposedly worked because of the semantic and syntactic redundancy of nonvisual information, and it supposedly worked quicker than looking at all the letters or looking at all the words.

Later, in 1979, K. S. Goodman and Y. M. Goodman added the following details to the guessing hypothesis:

> ... readers try to get meaning as efficiently as possible using minimal time and energy. That involves sampling from available cues, predicting syntactic structures and subsequent graphic cues, confirming or disconfirming predictions, correcting when necessary, and accommodating the developing sense as new information is decoded. (p. 149)

The whole-language approach is grounded in this guessing hypothesis which purports to describe the reading process used by a fluent reader. However, the whole-language approach involves much more than the guessing hypothesis. Bergeron (1990) reviewed the whole-language literature and summarized its core as follows: "Construction of meaning, wherein an emphasis is placed on comprehending what is read; functional language, or language that has purpose and relevance to the learner; the use of literature in a variety of forms; the writing process, through which learners write, revise, and edit their written works; learning experience, such as motivating enthusiasm, and interest" (p. 319).

It seems reasonable to summarize the theoretical basis of the whole-language approach in the following five tenets:

1. Learning to read is natural just like learning to talk is natural, that is, both are natural uses of language to communicate; children do not need to be taught to listen and they also do not need to be taught to read (K. S. Goodman & Y. M. Goodman, 1979).
2. Because reading is natural, it should be learned in natural settings that involve actual authentic language situations, for example, real books should be used not contrived books such as basal readers (K. S. Goodman, 1992; Smith, 1976).
3. Good readers guess the words they do not know using context, not sound-it-out or decoding strategies (Smith, 1979), and all readers should be taught to do this (K. S. Goodman, 1967; Smith, 1979).
4. Teaching children to decode isolated words by getting them to pay attention to the letters in the words is wrong because this is not natural, that is, we do not teach children to talk by teaching them syllables or phonemes (K. S. Goodman & Y. M. Goodman, 1979).

5. Writing is a natural way to communicate and helping children learn to write to communicate is an important aspect of learning to read (K. S. Goodman & Y. M. Goodman, 1979).

Before continuing, it should be pointed out that advocates of whole-language often contend that their approach includes many other important aspects or tenets, such as child-centered education and teacher empowerment, but these aspects are more relevant to instruction in general instead of reading instruction in particular (see Adams, 1991; K. S. Goodman, 1986; Stanovich, 1993a).

Implementation in Classrooms. The whole-language approach to the teaching of reading is primarily used in kindergarten and grade 1, but it also has many advocates in grade 2. That is, it is mostly relevant to beginning readers in the lower grades.

Harste and Burke (1977) seem to be the first to use the term "whole-language" to describe this approach as it is implemented in classrooms, but they credit the ideas of K. S. Goodman (1967) as foundational. They described whole language as "language based" wherein "good readers" are those who choose language-appropriate substitutions when encountering a word they do not know as they read text. For example, a child being taught by a teacher following the whole-language approach might substitute the spoken word /channel/ for the printed word "canal" in the following sentence: Men haul things up and down the canal in big boats. That is, a student who substituted /channel/ when reading this sentence aloud would be considered a good reader by a whole-language type of teacher because this word "sounds like language and retains the author's meaning" (p. 38). In this approach, reading means to construct meaning from language represented by graphic symbols (letters).

Harste and Burke contrast the whole-language approach just described with two other approaches, *decoding* and *skills.* In the decoding approach, they say that "reading is perceived as an offshoot of oral language, the chief accomplishment of which is dependent upon developing and manipulating relationships between the sounds of speech and their graphic symbols" (p. 35). They say that a good reader as perceived by a teacher following the decoding approach would be one who substituted the spoken word /cannel/ in the example sentence given above. That is, a decoding teacher would consider the substitution of /cannel/ as good because of the high grapheme-phoneme correspondence with "canal" even though "cannel" is not a word and does not make any sense in the context of the sentence. For teachers using the decoding approach, reading means the skill of turning the letters embedded in words into their corresponding sounds. It should be pointed out that "teaching phonics" would be considered a decoding approach by Harste and Burke. That is, phonics is a decoding approach to the teaching of reading; phonics also usually involves learning rules about sound-symbol correspondences.

In the *skills* approach to reading instruction, reading is described as one of four language arts—listening, speaking, reading, and writing—which are a collection of discrete skills. Children are expected to learn to pronounce printed words and then use them appropriately in text, by developing a basic sight vocabulary that involves learning word-recognition skills. Harste and Burke explain that a teacher using the skills approach would consider a student to be a good reader who substituted the spoken word /candle/ for "canal" in the example above. That is, a skills approach teacher would consider the substitution of /candle/ as good because "candle" was a word that probably was learned earlier by the student. This substituted word looks something like "canal," and it is not highly important that it does not preserve the meaning of the sentence. The skills approach is described as focusing upon grammar, comprehension, vocabulary, and word recognition.

Harste and Burke have explicated the whole-language approach by describing the kind of reading that a teacher tries to foster in the classroom. The things that whole-language teachers do in a classroom in order to get this kind of reading have been described in an International Reading Association publication entitled "Whole-language Across the Curriculum: Grades 1, 2, 3," edited by Raines (1995). She states that: "Teachers who have a whole-language perspective operate their classrooms with an abundance of children's literature, use a writing process approach, usually organize the curriculum in integrated, thematic units, teach strategies approaches to inquiry, and find authentic meaningful ways for children to communicate about their lives and what they are learning" (p. 2).

A typical day in a classroom taught by the whole-language approach has been described by Clarke (1987) as follows:

> ... work in personal journals, small group discussion of current events, "quiet time" for reading, "show-and-tell," conferences with the teacher or a parent volunteer on recently read or written books, a brief "lecture" by the teacher on "story leads" followed by individual work on short stories. (p. 386)

The whole-language approach stresses motivation to read, that is, making learning to read interesting, functional, and fun; this is done, for example, by having children write down rules for the care of class pets, by using message boards for notes from teachers to children, and by using games that involve reading (see K. S. Goodman & Y. M. Goodman, 1979).

The preceding description of the activities expected in whole-language classrooms has not mentioned the activities that generally do not occur. The following quotation from Ehri (1996) gives a more complete picture of the things that do and do not occur:

> Common practices of whole-language instruction are daily journal writing, with beginners encouraged to invent spellings of unfamiliar words, and lots of silent and oral reading of real literature. Whereas these practices are prescribed, others are prohibited: no work sheets, no phonics drills or memorization, no reading words

> on flash cards, no testing to see what students have learned about letters or sounds or words or reading. Beginners are expected to figure out how the letter-sound system works incidentally as they hear, read, and write meaningful text. (p. 196, 197)

Evaluation

Introduction. Now that the whole-language approach to the teaching of reading has been described, it will be evaluated from several standpoints. First, the guessing hypothesis will be scrutinized closely because it is the foundation of the theory underlying this approach. Second, the effect of avoiding any direct instruction regarding the alphabetic principle will be examined. Third, this approach will be evaluated by comparing it to the causal model described in Chapter 1. Fourth, the five tenets of this approach will be analyzed in terms of the research literature. Fifth, research evidence will be reviewed. Sixth, the connection between science and the whole-language approach will be closely examined.

Guessing Hypothesis. When the whole-language approach was described earlier, the guessing hypothesis was explained as follows: Good readers do not look at all the letters in each word and they do not look at all the words in each sentence, but instead, they guess at the meaning of words from the context using a sampling of letters and a sampling of words. Smith (1979) says that guessing from context is a "preferred strategy for beginners and fluent readers alike; it is the most efficient manner in which to read and learn to read" (p. 67). Both Goodman and Smith contend that when better readers guess at a word while reading orally, the word they come up with is usually one which preserves the meaning of the sentence. However, when poorer readers guess at unknown words they often do not make good use of the context to come up with a word that is meaningful in the sentence.

K. S. Goodman (1967) developed his guessing hypothesis from an earlier research study (K. S. Goodman, 1965) where he asked elementary students to read texts orally. He presented details of the errors (which he called "miscues") made by a child in grade four who was given the opening paragraphs from a story in a sixth-grade basal reader. The child guessed at unknown words and substituted words that preserved the meaning. In this research, it appears that Goodman used a passage that was just difficult enough for a "good" reader to make some reasonable guesses from context for some unknown words, but it was too difficult for a "poor" reader to come up with reasonable guesses from context. He reported that the students he studied made less errors when reading words in context, as compared to reading them out of context in an isolated list—60 to 80% less errors. In 1991, Nicholson replicated this research of K. S. Goodman's using more appropriate controls, and he concluded that "... the evidence now suggests that only poor and younger average readers clearly read better in context" (p. 449).

K. S. Goodman collected his data relevant to the guessing hypothesis in 1965, and there has been no evidence collected since then which supports the guessing hypothesis. But, there has been a great deal of evidence collected since then which has shown the guessing hypothesis to be false. From eye movement data, the evidence shows that skilled readers (advanced readers) who are given relatively easy texts to read, are paying attention to every letter in every word (see review by Carver, 1990a). Advanced readers look at (fixate upon) almost every word in the text and if one letter in each word they are looking at is omitted, then their rate drops dramatically; their rate is cut by about 50% (Rayner, Inhoff, Morrison, Slowiaczek & Bertera, 1981). There has been no evidence collected which confirms that advanced readers are sampling, predicting, or guessing what words will come next. Instead, there is evidence showing that when good readers are fixating upon one word and the next word in the periphery is changed in meaning, then these good readers are not likely to notice this difference (Rayner, 1975); they will not skip over the next word and guess at its meaning, but instead will fixate upon it so as to know for sure what the word is. Researchers have found that when good readers are fixating upon a word in a sentence and the text is removed, they will correctly guess the next word only 24 to 31% of the time (McConkie & Hogaboam, 1985). This low percentage of guessing correctly is exactly what would be expected from the redundancy of the language using the data reported by Carver (1976).

During typical reading, it is true that some short words may not be fixated upon, for example, short functional words such as *the, a, an*, or, *at*. However, this fact does not necessarily mean that the word is skipped by the reader. It is likely that these words are perceived in the periphery of a fixation and phonologically activated, that is, subvocalized. In this regard, Perfetti, Zhang, and Berent (1992) have presented theory and data supporting the principle that "... across writing systems, encounters with most printed words (exceptions restricted to a short list of sign-like words) automatically lead to phonological activation, beginning with phoneme constituents of the word and including the word's pronunciation" (p. 231). Another related principle of Perfetti, Zhang, and Berent is that "activated phonology serves memory and comprehension, with phonological rehearsal but not the activation itself under reader control" (p. 231). Some of the data they reported in support of these principles involved Chinese students reading text composed of Chinese characters. They found that Chinese text involving many tongue twisters was read 20% more slowly than control text, thereby indicating a phonological effect involving "phonological codes in working memory, the same as in English" (p. 239).

This research provides a strong case against the guessing hypothesis. The evidence indicates a rather automatic phonological activation of each perceived printed word, and the evidence indicates that skilled readers tend to fixate upon almost every word. Thus, there is good evidence that advanced readers are (a) paying attention to all the letters within words, (b) are not guessing at any of the words but instead are fixating upon almost every word, and (c) are pronouncing each word in the text, internally. Rayner & Pollatsek (1989) have noted that the earlier ideas about guessing using graphophonic, syntactic, and semantic cues have failed to recognize that graphophonic cueing "is more central or important to the process of learning to read than are the others" (p. 351).

A great deal of empirical data collected from good readers or skilled readers has not supported the sampling, predicting, and guessing ideas that K. S. Goodman and Smith advanced in the 1960s and 1970s. On the other hand, this more recent research does provide support for two of the original hypotheses underlying rauding theory (Carver, 1977), namely, that (a) "during rauding each successive word in a sentence is checked to determine whether a complete thought is being successfully formulated" (p. 14), and (b) "the internal articulation of each successive word in a sentence (internal speech) is an aid to comprehension during both reading and auding" (p. 16).

The efficiency of reading that K. S. Goodman and Y. M. Goodman (1979) talk about (quoted earlier) does not come from guessing, predicting, or sampling. Instead, the high efficiency comes from looking at each word and rapidly recognizing all the letters in each word. In order to become an advanced reader, children must eventually learn the correct spellings of words (Adams & Bruck, 1995). This ability of advanced readers to read fast (300 words per minute, 5 words per second) comes from overlearning the pronunciation that corresponds to the spelling of a word, that is, the raudamatizing of over 20,000 words.

Ironically, researchers have also found that it is the poorer readers who have to do more guessing and predicting, instead of the better readers (e.g., Stanovich, 1986). It is the poorer readers who are continually forced to read text that is relatively hard for them so they have to guess at many unknown words. The better readers are seldom forced to read hard text, so they guess less, predict less, and sample less. Stanovich (1986) reviewed the guessing hypothesis and the evidence relevant to good and poor readers. and he found evidence for his interactive-compensatory model. That is, he found that it is true that this kind of guessing from context can aid comprehension, but that poorer readers tend to use context as much or more than good readers as an aid to word recognition when relative difficulty is controlled. When the material being read was relatively hard, it would make sense that all readers (good and poor) would use context as an aid to word recognition and the comprehension of the thoughts in sentences.

In 1990, Liberman and Liberman critiqued the whole-language approach and a code-emphasis approach (which is a decoding approach), and they summarized the guessing model of K. S. Goodman's as follows:

> Put with admirable succinctness by Goodman himself, the Whole-language assumption is that reading is a "psycholinguistic guessing game" (Goodman, 1976). By this, Goodman means that (presumably skilled) readers merely sample the print; apprehending some

> words and skipping others. Then, using their normal and natural language processes, they guess at the message by taking advantage of context, their knowledge of the world, or indeed, anything else that will spare them the inconvenience of actually reading what the writer had, in fact, written. As we shall see later, this leads the Whole-language people to advocate actually *teaching* the child to guess. (p. 62)

With respect to teaching children to guess, Liberman and Liberman provide the following quote from the 1988 Spring issue of the Whole-language Teachers Newsletter:

> Foremost on the list of Don'ts are sound-it-out and look-for-familiar-word-parts-within-the-word because these activities divert the reader's attention from meaning .... Good Things to Do include skip it, use prior information ... read ahead, re-read, or put in another word that makes sense. (p. 69)

Notice that guessing from context is being elevated to a "must do" status; any attempt by the student to use cipher knowledge is being relegated to a "don't do" status.

Stanovich (1993a) reviewed the research evidence relevant to contextual guessing and early reading development, and then in 1995, Share and Stanovich conducted another review. Share and Stanovich concluded that (a) "it should be clear from the previous review that a foundational tenet of whole-language instruction in many incarnations — that guessing words based on the previous context of a passage is an efficacious way of reading and of learning to read — is markedly at variance with the empirical evidence" (p. 30), and (b) ".. the empirical evidence has falsified the basic prediction that skilled readers rely more on context for word recognition than poor readers" (p. 30). Share and Stanovich go on to say that "it seems inconceivable that we will continue wasting energy on the 'reading wars' simply because we cannot get both sides to say, simultaneously, 'some teachers overdo phonics' and 'some children need explicit instruction in alphabetic coding" (p. 34). Translated, these contentions of Share and Stanovich mean that the ability to predict or correctly guess upcoming words is *not* a factor that belongs in the causal model; the ability to predict or guess words does not belong at Echelons 1, 2, 3, or 4 because there is absolutely no evidence that contextual guessing is an important cause of high reading achievement.

In summary, the contextual guessing hypothesis that was first broached in 1967 has not been supported by research conducted in the subsequent years. On the contrary, there is a considerable body of research data which indicates that this hypothesis is not valid, and should be rejected. Good readers use their knowledge of letter-sound correspondences when they encounter a word, and poor readers use contextual guessing more than good readers. Furthermore, there is no evidence that the teaching of contextual guessing leads to higher reading achievement.

Alphabetic Principle. In general, the whole-language approach undervalues the importance of helping beginning readers learn the alphabetic principle, which is learning the somewhat systematic connections between the letters in words and the sounds they represent. Learning the alphabetic principle was regarded as very important over 30 years ago by Fries (1963). He contended that "... modern English spelling is not hopelessly chaotic" (p. 169). He explained the implications of the alphabetic principle as follows:

> Most ... spelling is patterned. It is basically phonemic in its representation with *patterns of letters*, rather than single *letters*, as the *functioning units* of the representation. (p. 169)

Later, in 1990, Liberman and Liberman made it clear that teachers need to teach the alphabetic principle. They contended that one big reason, among many, for not understanding text is its difficulty, and that teaching children to regard individual words as not very important to know so they can be skipped or guessed is a poor remedy for lack of comprehension. They concluded their critique of the whole-language and code-emphasis approaches as follows:

> Given the nature of language, it is simply inconceivable that texts can be understood except by taking account of the words they comprise. Teaching the children what they need to know in order to read these words fluently must be the primary aim of reading instruction. What they need to know, and what their experience with language has not taught them, is no more and no less than the alphabetic principle. (p. 72)

Liberman and Liberman have made it clear that whole-language teachers who refuse to teach children about letter-sound correspondences are likely to be a major cause of low reading achievement in many beginning readers. This surmissal was recently reinforced by Scanlon and Vellutino (1997) who studied the cognitive abilities of 151 kindergartners, their reading instruction in grade 1, and their word recognition and word attack skills at the end of grade 1. They concluded that kindergarten teachers should help children learn the alphabetic principle to increase the probability of success for beginning readers.

Most students in whole-language classrooms will learn the alphabetic principle even if it is not directly taught because these students spend a great deal of time writing words. Learning to write words requires that the words be spelled, and spelling words in a readable way is not likely to occur without learning some letter-sound correspondences. However, all students are not likely to learn this principle quickly, especially those with low pronunciation aptitude, g_P. Therefore, it seems likely that low g_P students will gain less in P_L

(and A_L, R_L, and E_L) during a school year under the whole-language approach. Therefore, it seems reasonable to hypothesize that the whole-language approach is itself a cause of low reading achievement for many students.

Causal Model. The whole-language approach will be evaluated next by examining how it relates to the causal model.

In Echelon 4 of the causal model, there are two teaching/learning factors; the first one is directly associated with verbal knowledge level, V_L, and the second one is directly associated with pronunciation knowledge level, P_L. The whole-language approach is meaning-emphasis oriented, and very closely connected to the teaching/learning factor that is a proximal cause of V_L. A decoding approach is a code-emphasis oriented, and is very closely associated with the teaching/learning factor that is a proximal cause of P_L.

The whole-language approach focuses upon helping students improve their verbal knowledge by reading, just like they improve their verbal knowledge by listening. For example, Raines (1995) states that "whole-language programs use children's own language, employ activities and materials that are meaningful to the children, and give them opportunities to develop, refine, further develop, and further refine their language, respecting them as constructors of concepts" (p. 7). Therefore, the whole-language approach to reading instruction is likely to increase the listening level, or V_L, of a classroom of typical students more than a decoding approach. Because whole-language is directed toward language improvement or verbal knowledge, and because V_L is an indicator of verbal knowledge level, it follows that classrooms taught by the whole-language approach are likely to gain more in V_L during a school year, as long as the classrooms are equal with respect to g_v, g_p, and g_s.

A code-emphasis approach focuses upon teaching and learning experiences that are directly relevant to decoding, or identifying isolated words. Therefore, it seems likely that students taught with this type of focus will gain more in pronunciation level, P_L, during a year, compared to students taught by the whole-language approach. This means that code-emphasis classrooms should have lower V_L but higher P_L, whereas whole-language classrooms should have higher V_L but lower P_L.

One theoretical prediction that can be made from the causal model, as it applies to the whole-language approach, is that students taught under this approach should read slower than students taught under a code-emphasis approach. That is, students taught under the whole-language approach should read slower than a comparison group which received instruction designed to help children pronounce isolated words. The reason that students taught by the whole-language approach should read slower is because their lower P_L automatically means a lower R_L in the causal model. This likely disadvantage has not been seriously considered by educators or researchers. In the past, the reading rate of students has not been considered to be very important by most reading educators, or even most reading researchers. For example, there have been two Handbooks of Reading Research published in the last 15 years (Barr, Kamil, Mosenthal, & Pearson, 1991; Pearson, 1984) and neither book has had a chapter on reading rate and neither has reviewed research on reading rate. If rate level, R_L, is not considered important by the researchers most closely connected with reading instruction, then it is easy to see how this negative side effect of whole-language instruction could be overlooked. The likely detrimental effect that the whole-language approach has upon rate level, R_L, should be seriously considered by researchers and teachers.

Tenets. In this section, the whole-language approach will be evaluated by citing research literature relevant to the five numbered tenets that were presented earlier.

Tenet No. 1 was that learning to read is natural, just like learning to talk, and that in every culture almost all children learn the language of the culture without any formal instruction (K. S. Goodman & Y. M. Goodman, 1979). In opposition to this tenet, it has been noted that all cultures have spoken language, but many cultures have no written language, and that the cultures having written languages also have many students who can talk but do not learn to read even with formal instruction; reading and writing seem to be unnatural acts that are desirable and have to be taught formally (see Gough & Hillinger, 1980; Liberman & Liberman, 1990).

Tenet No. 2 was that reading should be learned using real books and authentic communication tasks. This tenet seems to have no sound evidence to support it. That is, there is no sound evidence that reading achievement is higher if students are taught this way, as compared to a phonics approach (see Perfetti, 1991b), for example, or as compared to a basal approach (Stahl & Miller, 1989; Stahl, McKenna, & Pagnucco, 1994). Furthermore, McKenna, Stratton, Grindler, and Jenkins (1995) found that there was no evidence that the whole-language approach improved the attitude of students toward reading.

Tenet No. 3 was that good readers guess at unknown words in text using context so this means that beginning readers should be taught to guess at unknown words using context. As was documented earlier, this guessing hypothesis has not had any research support since it was advanced in 1967 by K. S. Goodman (Stanovich, West, & Feeman, 1981; West & Stanovich, 1978). In this regard, Henderson (1992) contended that "... reading is a psycholinguistic knowledge game and not a guessing game at all" (p.3).

Tenet No. 4 is that teaching children to decode using isolated words is detrimental to learning to read (K. S. Goodman & Y. M. Goodman, 1979). This tenet is mostly inconsistent with teaching children the alphabetic principle and represents a crucial difference between the whole-language approach and code-emphasis approaches. McKenna, Robinson, and Miller (1990) articulated these differences as follows: "the key distinction separating whole-language theorists from their counterparts is the position that explicit, skill-by-skill decoding instruction should have no role in the teaching of reading" (p. 4). All the evidence that has been accumulated indicates that this tenet is wrong (e.g., Evans & Carr, 1985). Teaching children the alphabetic principle along with cipher knowledge has been shown to be very helpful—as a way of increasing pronunciation and spelling knowledge (Bradley & Bryant, 1983; Williams, 1980), as a successful addition to Reading Recovery instruction (Iversen & Tunmer, 1993), and as an addition to whole-language instruction (Castel, Riach, & Nicholson, 1994). It should be acknowledged that K. S. Goodman (1986) has contended that the whole-language approach does not ignore phonics and that students should be taught phonics generalizations in context. However, it is not clear how this can be done effectively without presenting words out of context to be sure that students are learning to pronounce words using letter-sound correspondences instead of context cues.

Tenet No. 5 is that having beginning readers write to communicate is helpful to them learning to read (K. S. Goodman & Y. M. Goodman, 1979). The effect of writing upon reading is complex (Shanahan & Lomax, 1988), but there is as yet no scientific evidence that having children write many sentences improves their reading achievement more than some control condition that does not involve this kind of writing. However, because writing involves spelling, and spelling helps children learn to decode, or learn the cipher, it is likely that a certain unknown amount of sentence writing is helpful.

In summary, these five tenets of the whole-language approach have little or no empirical support whereas there is a great deal of research evidence that is counter to Tenet No. 3 and Tenet No. 4. The scientific evidence indicates that teaching children about letter-sound correspondences helps them read better, and that reading is not a psycholinguistic guessing game for good readers.

Research Evidence. General research evidence will be reviewed next, relevant to the whole-language approach.

In 1989, Stahl and Miller conducted a meta-analysis of 117 research studies in kindergarten and first grade where whole-language and language experience approaches were compared to basal-based instruction. They found that these two approaches were "approximately equal in their efforts" (p. 27).

In 1991, Vellutino reviewed research "bearing on the theoretical foundations of code-oriented versus whole-language approaches to reading instruction..." (p. 437), and drew the following conclusions:

> Research findings, on balance, tend to favor the major theoretical premises on which code-emphasis approaches to reading instruction are based and are at variance with the major theoretical premises on which whole-language approaches are based. However, the findings do not preclude the compatibility of certain features of both approaches. (p. 437)
>
> The implications of the research for teaching children to read should be apparent. The most basic dictate seems to be that instruction that

> promotes facility in word identification is vitally important to success in reading. Accordingly, instruction that facilitates phoneme awareness and alphabetic coding is vitally important to success in reading. However, there is nothing in the research that precludes the use of whole-language-type activities in teaching reading, such as the use of context for monitoring and predictive purposes, vocabulary enrichment to imbue printed words with meaning, discussion that would encourage reading for comprehension, integration of reading, writing, and spelling to concretize the relationships between and among these representational systems, and so forth. Conversely, the research runs counter to exclusive versions of either whole-language or code-oriented approaches to reading instruction. In other words, the research supports a balanced approach. (p. 442)

In 1994, Stahl, McKenna, and Pagnucco reviewed the literature relevant to the effects of whole-language instruction, and they concluded that "... whole-language approaches are not a magic bullet: Teachers will not automatically become more effective merely by adopting a particular philosophy toward instruction" (p. 181).

With respect to existing evidence, it seems clear that there is no basis for considering whole-language to be the best approach for increasing reading achievement (Biemiller, 1994; Pressley, 1994; Stahl, McKenna, & Pagnucco, 1994). The best approach would have to teach the alphabetic principle in kindergarten or first grade. The best approach would not require beginning readers to read words that they do not know by guessing a word that fits the context.

Science. The whole-language approach to reading instruction seems to be implemented by many teachers, (a) in spite of research results which indicate that the theory underlying this approach to be fundamentally wrong, and (b) in spite of research which indicates that teaching the alphabetic principle will produce better readers. This inconsistency suggests that political issues may play a bigger role in reading instruction than does science.

Adams (1991) has pointed out that the whole-language movement has involved the following important issues: "... (1) teacher empowerment; (2) child-centered instruction; (3) integration of reading and writing; (4) disavowal of the value of teaching or learning phonics; and (5) subscription to the view that children are naturally predisposed toward written language acquisition" (p. 41). Later, Adams and Bruck (1995) advocated that the issues associated with the political empowerment of teachers must be disentangled from the issues associated with the best ways to teach reading. They contend that:

> ... this disentangling cannot take place so long as there exists an anti-research spirit within the whole-language movement. Many of the leaders of this movement actively discredit traditional scientific research approaches to the study of reading development and more specifically to the evaluation of their programs. The movement's

> anti-scientific attitude forces research findings into the backroom, making them socially and thereby, intellectually unavailable to many educators who are involved in whole-language programs. (p. 18)

A big disadvantage of mixing politics and science in reading instruction is that decisions about the best way to improve reading achievement, or E_L, may be made on the basis of vested interests instead theory and supporting evidence, In this regard, McKenna, Stahl, and Reinking (1994) have observed the following:

> ... whole-language proponents tend to see research as essentially political and to believe that unfavorable findings require a political not necessarily a research response (Shannon, 1994). Political responses include attacks on the motives of the researchers, ignoring unfavorable research, and deligitimatizing researchers. The results of these strategies may be to draw the whole-language community closer together, but they also tend to alienate those not in the community. (p. 219)

The tendency of many whole-language advocates to disregard the basic tenets of science has also been noted by other researchers (Pressley & Rankin, 1994).

On the other hand, K. S. Goodman (1989) has contended that "the practice of whole-language is solidly rooted in scientific research and theory" (p. 207). Yet, he cited no experimental studies showing (a) that the whole-language approach works better, (b) that children taught under this approach have higher reading achievement, or (c) that the guessing hypothesis is valid. He goes on to say that when whole-language teachers are asked about proof that what they are doing works, they "... have a right to answer that the proof is in their classrooms and their pupils" (p. 213). Ordinarily a scientific approach to evidence in education requires more than the opinion of anyone, even a teacher. Ordinarily, the best scientific evidence in education does not come from the anecdotal reports of teachers who participate in a particular whole-language classroom, but comes from studies with control groups—so we are not fooled or biased by our own theories, hypotheses, or vested interests. This is the main contribution that science makes.

For K. S. Goodman (1989), science seems to be equated with theory because all of the examples he gave about science involved theoretical ideas, and none involved research studies designed to determine if the whole-language approach produces better readers than another approach. Neither K. S. Goodman nor Smith, nor any of the more vocal advocates of the whole-language approach (e.g., Edelsky, 1990), have conducted any scientifically sound research to determine if children do learn to read better if (a) they always are given natural texts to read in school, (b) they are taught to guess at words they do not know from context, and (c) they are not directly taught about the alphabetic principle using words in isolation. These are fundamental hypotheses associated with the whole-language approach but most of its leaders seem to show disdain for collecting evidence using the best methods of science (e.g., experimental and control groups) to find out if these ideas and practices are valid.

Scientists should be applauded for setting forth theory and hypotheses that seem to make sense but are eventually shown to be mostly wrong, because that is one major way that scientific progress is made. However it is not acceptable in science, to disregard evidence against theory or hypotheses, no matter whether the disregard is due to ignorance or arrogance. Those who disregard conflicting evidence are behaving more like politicians or religionists instead of scientists. For example, none of the evidence cited earlier which shows that the contextual guessing hypothesis is wrong, was ever acknowledged in the later writings by Goodman (1992), Smith (1992), or Harste (1989), who have been leaders in the whole-language movement.

Scientists do not believe what they want to believe, no matter how enticing the theory; they believe what they have to believe based upon the best data that have been collected using the best known methodological controls so they will not be fooled by their wants, desires, or needs. That is, when the data or evidence do not fit the theory, then the theory must be changed, modified, or discarded. Almost all scientists who have studied whole-language theory and the scientifically collected evidence that is relevant to it, seem to agree that whole-language theory must be modified. For example, Pressley and Rankin (1994) argue that "... whole-language is a dated philosophy not well supported by scientific analyses of reading and reading instruction" (p. 157). There is no scientific evidence to support the theory that learning to read and write is as natural as learning to talk and listen. There is no evidence that teaching students about letter-sound correspondences in isolated words is harmful to learning to read better. The scientific evidence that has been collected does not support the guessing hypothesis as it applies to good and poor readers.

What is noteworthy, and somewhat astounding, is that the main proponents of whole-language theory have not considered any of the negative evidence that might be helpful in modifying their theoretical ideas. Yet, it would seem reasonable to modify whole-language theory in the following important way: Respect for language and respect for learners shown by reading real books does not preclude the use of instruction time to teach letter-sound correspondences in isolated words because this modification yields better readers (see Spiegel, 1992). The evidence certainly supports this type of balanced approach to reading instruction, yet this evidence seems to have been disregarded or dismissed as not relevant by many whole-language advocates—this is unacceptable behavior from the standpoint of scientists.

Whole-language theory has all the earmarks of religious dogma that is immune from being modified by evidence. In fact, an article by Smith (1992) suggests that scientifically collected evidence is not even to be considered, as the following excerpt attests:

> The great debate may never end. But perhaps it never should. The most productive way to deal with fundamental educational controversies might be to take them into every school and every community where they can be dissected, discussed, and honestly argued. The endless debate over teaching reading could serve to keep teachers—and the public at large—conscious of the profound importance and delicacy of the noble art of teaching. (p. 441)

Notice that in the quote above—which was the concluding paragraph in the article—Smith never mentioned using evidence collected by scientists as a way to inform debates or to find out the best ways to teach children to read. This is a basic shortcoming associated with many advocates of the whole-language approach. Whenever the leaders of any ideological movement discourage definitive research, then it is likely that the movement is fueled by ignorance, or it has political or religious goals that are threatened by the more dispassionate goals of science, which are to find out if there is sound evidence to support the ideas.

Summary of Whole-Language Theory and Practice

The theoretical ideas underlying the whole-language approach have been articulated by K. S. Goodman (1967) and Smith (1971), and then elaborated upon in later writings (e.g., K. S. Goodman & Y. M. Goodman, 1979; Smith, 1979). This theory is that learning to read is natural, just like learning to talk; children learn to talk by being immersed in oral language and are not instructed in the nuances of phonemes and syllables, so children will similarly learn to read if they are immersed in written language (books) and are not instructed in the nuances of grapheme to phoneme correspondences using isolated words. Furthermore, this theory is that good readers are able to sample letters and words from context and correctly guess at unknown words so poor readers can learn to become good readers by guessing at the meaning of unknown words.

The whole-language approach to reading instruction is often used in the lower grades—kindergarten, first grade, and second grade. The leaders and strongest advocates of this approach urge teachers to avoid any instruction that involves learning to pronounce isolated words by learning letter-sound correspondences because this is not whole-language, which involves comprehending the meaning associated with whole words and whole sentences. Instead, teachers are urged to make all reading instruction more meaningful (a) by having children read real books, not basal readers, and (b) by having them guess at all the unknown words they encounter by inserting a word that makes sense in the context of the sentence or text. They also encourage children to write down messages, stories, or experiences that are meaningful to them, without putting a great deal of emphasis on the correct spelling of these words.

Summary of Relevant Causal Model Theory

The largest gains in reading achievement during a year come from teaching and learning experiences that improve V_L and P_L the most. In the early grades, the greatest gains in A_L, R_L, and E_L are likely to come from instruction that focuses upon increasing P_L because learning to pronounce printed words that are known auditorily will increase A_L the most. The whole-language approach is used most often in the early grade classrooms, and it is primarily devoted to increasing V_L via instruction that emphasizes meaning and language improvement. This approach to instruction is not likely to produce the greatest gains in reading achievement because it deprecates direct instruction on isolated words or letter-sound correspondences that is likely to produce large gains in P_L.

Code-emphasis instruction designed to increase P_L is likely to produce a double-dividend in most beginning readers and many intermediate readers because an increase in P_L produces an increase in both A_L and R_L, which are the two factors which cause increases in reading achievement, or E_L. Because the whole-language approach tends to deprecate activities designed to increase the pronunciation of isolated words (increase P_L), this means that this approach is likely to produce lower than optimal gains in reading achievement. Most importantly, the lack of attention to decoding, or to the correct pronunciation and correct spelling of isolated words, is likely to produce lower gains in P_L. In turn, lower P_L causes a lower reading level and a slower reader—lower A_L and lower R_L—which in turn causes lower reading achievement, or E_L.

Good readers (high E_L for age) and poor readers (low E_L for age) operate the same rauding process when they read relatively easy material, $A_L > D_L$, and neither good readers nor poor readers engage in contextual guessing during rauding because all of the words they encounter have been raudamatized. When students in a particular grade in school are given texts to read at a level of difficulty that is approximately equal to the grade they are in (e.g., fourth graders given fourth-grade level material), then the good readers in that grade are likely to be able to raud the text without engaging in contextual guessing because the text is relatively easy for them, $A_L > D_L$. However, the poor readers in that grade are likely to engage in contextual guessing because the material is relatively hard for them, $D_L > A_L$; the text is likely to contain several unknown words and that poor readers try to figure out from context. Similarly, even the good readers in a particular grade will also use contextual guessing for unknown words when they are given relatively hard material, $D_L > A_L$.

Teaching students to guess at unknown words from context without using pronunciation knowledge, or cipher knowledge, is likely to be a root cause of low reading achievement, that is, poor teaching and learning with respect to P_L.

Summary of Evidence

The theory that good readers use context more than poor readers has been shown to be invalid in several research studies (Stanovich, West, & Feeman, 1981; West & Stanovich, 1978). Contextual guessing is used more by poor readers than it is by good readers, because good readers can accurately and rapidly recognize most of the words they encounter from their spellings without guessing at them from context (Stanovich, 1986; 1993a). Teaching children to decode using isolated words is helpful to reading achievement (Calfee & Piontkowski, 1981; Evans & Carr, 1985; Williams, 1980). This means that there is evidence that instruction which helps children learn the alphabetic principle improves reading achievement. Stated differently, teaching children to be aware of the somewhat systematic correspondences between the letters within words and the sounds within words is helpful to learning to read (Bradley & Bryant, 1983; Castel, Riach, & Nicholson, 1994; Iversen & Tunmer, 1993). There is no evidence that learning to read is a natural process that can be learned by most students the same way they learn to talk (Gough & Hillinger, 1980; Liberman & Liberman, 1990). There is no consistently sound evidence that reading achievement will be higher if students are taught by a whole-language approach (Stahl, McKenna, & Pagnucco, 1994; Stahl & Miller, 1989). The theory underlying the whole-language approach is considered to be a disproven theory by scientists who make decisions based upon research evidence in reading (Stanovich, 1993a).

Implications

Educators need to make sure that beginning readers are (a) given direct instruction in learning the alphabetic principle, (b) are taught many of the consistencies between letters and sounds, especially for consonants, and (c) are encouraged to learn to spell words correctly even though invented spellings may be helpful in kindergarten and first grade. The whole-language approach must be modified by incorporating what has been learned by researchers using the best known methods of science, otherwise it will continue to include activities that are likely to cause lower reading achievement.

Forget Me Nots

The whole-language approach to reading instruction is not a root cause of high reading achievement mainly because it places too much emphasis on contextual guessing at the expense of teaching the alphabetic principle using isolated words.

PART VII

THE LAST PART

This last part contains two chapters. Chapter 23 advances a new approach to reading instruction, called the rauding approach, and it is based on the content of all the preceding chapters; the rauding approach seems to have great potential as a root cause of high reading achievement. Chapter 24 contains a summary of all of the theory and research presented in this book, along with the conclusions that have been drawn.

CHAPTER

23

THE RAUDING APPROACH

The causal model of high and low reading achievement has stimulated a new approach to reading instruction; it is called the rauding approach. This approach is quite conventional in the sense that it encourages children to learn to spell all the words they know, and it encourages book reading. However, the rauding approach is also a radical one in the sense that (a) it does not encourage students to guess at the pronunciation of words, either from context or from phonics rules, and (b) it depends upon a computer for practical implementation. It should be pointed out that the computer has been used to teach skills related for reading for over 25 years (e.g., see Atkinson, 1974), so the rauding approach may also be considered as conventional from this standpoint.

It seems likely that the implementation of the rauding approach in the early and middle grades will produce the most gain in reading achievement, or E_L, during a school year. Therefore, it would seem to deserve close scrutiny.

In this chapter, the rauding approach will be described, and then it will be evaluated by comparing it to other approaches—whole-language, phonics, skills, decoding, and balanced—which purport to cause high reading achievement.

Description

Introduction. The rauding approach has been designed so that it supplements most of the instructional practices currently used by the best teachers in kindergarten, grade 1, and grade 2 (Pressley, Rankin, & Yokoi, 1995), such as (a) learning the alphabetic song and learning letter names in kindergarten, (b) reading big books in kindergarten and first grade, and (c) teaching story writing and morphemes-structural analysis for decoding in grades 1 and 2.

One of the facets of the rauding approach that makes it drastically different is its recommendations about guessing unknown words in text. Therefore, this topic will be discussed at length, later in this section. The rauding approach is also somewhat unique in its focus upon learning to spell words correctly, not for the purpose of writing better but for the purpose of reading better. Another facet of the rauding approach which is unique when compared to most traditional approaches to reading instruction is its emphasis on learning to recognize the correct spellings of words rapidly. Helping students learn to spell all of their audamatized words and helping them learn to recognize correct spellings rapidly, is called raudamaticity training; this training will be explained in detail later in this section.

One aspect of the rauding approach that is not unique is vocabulary training, that is, helping students learn the meaning of new words. However, in this approach as soon as the meaning of a new word is learned, the student is given raudamaticity training until the new word can be recognized quickly. This new approach to vocabulary instruction is also described in more detail, later.

Finally, the goals of the rauding approach will be described. It is necessary to describe the goals, so that various approaches can be compared with respect to determining which one is best.

Guessing Unknown Words. Most approaches to the teaching of reading encourage children to guess at the pronunciation of unknown words, but this is not done in the rauding approach. Instead, children should be told how to pronounce new words before they have to read them by themselves. This means that in the rauding approach, a student would not be asked to read a particular story until the student has been told how to pronounce all the words in the story. Whenever possible and practical, students should not have to guess at words they are asked to read. This does not mean that students should be punished or chided when they do guess at unknown words. Instead, it means that in the rauding approach, instruction is planned so that students are rarely asked to read words that they have not already been taught how to pronounce. Furthermore, when a student does encounter an unknown word during instruction, a teacher using this approach would tell the student how to pronounce this word without requiring that the student guess from context or guess by trying to sound it out. For example, before a beginning reader is asked to read aloud a children's trade book or a story in a basal reader, the student should be told how to pronounce every word in this book; ideally, the child would have been given practice in pronouncing all of the words in isolation first.

Because the instructional strategy just outlined is so drastically counter to almost all current reading instruction, and likely to be highly controversial, a great deal more explanation, justification, and discussion will be provided in the following paragraphs.

There is a big disadvantage associated with guessing the wrong pronunciation of words, as the following quotations from Olson, Wise, Ring, and Johnson (1997) attest:

> Children with poor phoneme awareness and phonological decoding skills are likely to make many errors when attempting to decode new words on their own. If those errors are not corrected, they result in negative learning trials that constrain the development of a sight vocabulary for those words. (p. 236, 237)

> In addition to problems created by those negative learning trials, the children's obvious frustration in reading probably led to much less reading practice as compared to normal readers. (p.237)

So the biggest disadvantage of teaching children to guess—either from context or from letter-sound correspondences—is that these guesses are likely to be wrong most of the time for most readers (> 50%), and they are likely to be wrong almost all the time (> 90%) for the poorer readers. Context is a very poor determiner of a word; even college students get only around 30% correct guesses at successive words in the sentences of eighth-grade level material (Carver, 1976). Letter-sound correspondences are also very poor determiners of how a word is pronounced, especially for beginning readers who will encounter many sight words that are irregular in their letter-sound correspondences, such as "laugh." Therefore, children are being set up for failure when we ask them to guess at words they do not know how to pronounce in print. We are making the learning task unnecessarily difficult, and we are making it a highly frustrating experience for those children with low aptitudes for learning to read (low g_v, low g_p, and low g_s).

A student does not have to be frustrated by trying to sound out a word, in order to learn letter-sound correspondences. On the other hand, learning the letter-sound correspondences does help students learn how to pronounce a new word in a few trials, and then this pronunciation knowledge helps them remember it later (Ehri & Wilce, 1979a). Learning to spell words correctly also helps students learn letter-sound correspondences, and practicing the correct pronunciation of words after they have been told how to pronounce them helps them learn letter-sound correspondences.

It should be pointed out that poor readers do not guess because it is their nature or habit to guess; poor readers guess because they are usually given texts to read that are relatively hard for them. On the other hand, the good readers do not guess because they are usually given texts to read that are relatively easy, thereby containing no unknown words. If poor readers are given relatively easy texts to read, they will not guess, and if good readers are given relatively hard texts to read, they will guess.

Furthermore, there seems to be no evidence that forcing children to guess at the pronunciation of words is a necessary or optimal aspect of reading instruction. As educators, we should try to make reading as easy, as fast, and as much fun as possible. The forced guessing associated with the whole-language approach and the phonics approach is likely to make reading hard, slow, and frustrating for many students. This guessing is also likely to be less effective from a learning standpoint, compared to simply telling the student how to pronounce a word.

As an instructional practice, teaching children to guess at unknown words would be modified drastically in the rauding approach. Students should be taught to guess only as a last resort, only when they cannot find out what the word is by any other means. That is, determining the correct pronunciation and meaning of unknown words is so important under the rauding approach that guessing is not encouraged due to its high probability of being incorrect. An attempt would be made to tell students how to pronounce a word before they are asked to read it. However, under the practical constraints of a classroom, it is not always possible to find out from the teacher or someone else how to pronounce a word upon demand; in those situations, which should be rare by design, the student would be encouraged to guess at an unknown word using context and letter-sound correspondences.

In summary, neither good readers nor poor readers are asked to guess at the pronunciation of words in the rauding approach. Both good and poor readers should be given texts that contain audamatized words whose pronunciation has been practiced so that these words can become raudamatized with further practice. All words in these texts will be known so none need to be guessed. Relatively hard texts should not be given to either good or poor readers to read during reading instruction, so neither the good nor the poor readers will be forced to guess at the pronunciation of unknown words.

Raudamaticity Training. Helping students learn to quickly recognize in print all of the words they know when they hear them spoken, is called raudamaticity training. The words that require raudamaticity training are those audamatized words that have not yet been raudamatized. First, the audamatized words of a particular student need to be identified. Second, this student must learn to spell each of these audamatized words accurately. Third, this student must learn to recognize rapidly the correct spelling of each audamatized word. Notice that raudamaticity training does not try to increase V_L (listening vocabulary), but it does try to increase P_L (word identification) and A_L (reading vocabulary), simultaneously.

The identification of the lexicon of audamatized words that require raudamaticity training can be estimated in two steps. First, the raw score on the Auding Accuracy Level Test (see Chapter 6) can be used to estimate the number of words on the Carroll, Davies, and Richman (1971) ranked list that have been audamatized; this would be an estimate of the number of V_LWords. Second, the raw score on the Accuracy Level Test (see Chapter 4) can be used to estimate the number of words on the Carroll et al. ranked list that have been raudamatized; this would be an estimate of the number of A_LWords. The words on the Carroll et al. ranked list that are V_LWords but are not A_LWords would be the words that require raudamaticity training. For example, suppose the raw score on the AALT indicated that an individual would know the meaning of almost all the words on the Carroll et al. ranked list from 1 to 8,100. Suppose the ALT indicated that this individual had learned the meaning of all printed words between ranks 1 and 5,700. In this example, the words between ranks 5,700 and 8,100 would be in the lexicon of words that require raudamaticity training, that is, the 2,400 words would be the ones that need to be raudamatized.

Once the words have been identified which require raudamaticity training, then the students can begin learning to spell each of these words. The first hurdle for a student is learning to spell an audamatized word accurately. If an audamatized word cannot be spelled accurately, or at least close to 100% accuracy, then it is unlikely it will ever become raudamatized. This accent upon spelling accuracy in raudamaticity training is consistent with the theoretical ideas of Ehri and Wilce (1987a) who have contended that word recognition and spelling rely on similar sources of knowledge.

Notice that the rauding approach elevates the importance of knowledge about the letters in a word. Knowing how to spell a word relatively accurately is extremely important with respect to being able to recognize it rapidly, at the rauding rate of the individual. Words whose spellings are not known will probably be identified using context and/or using letter-sound cues, and this process is likely to take extra time or the word will be recognized incorrectly.

The debilitating effect of not knowing just one letter of a word was dramatically portrayed in the research of Rayner et al. (1981), and referenced earlier in Chapter 22. Using computerized eye movement technology, these researchers programmed the words presented on the screen so that one letter in each word would be left blank—the letter that was fixated upon. They found that when college students read this text that contained one blank letter in each word, then the rate of reading dropped approximately 50%. This experimentally induced spelling problem for skilled readers induced a slowness of reading rate that is similar to that of dyslexics. It is highly likely that much of the slow reading of dyslexics is due to their not being able to spell many of the words in the text they are reading. They are likely to be engaging in a psycholinguistic guessing game which is excruciatingly slow.

The spelling part of raudamaticity training could be accomplished in a traditional manner by assigning spelling words on Monday that must be spelled correctly on Friday's test. However, this type of group instruction cannot be directed toward the V_LWords that are not A_LWords because it would be too labor intensive for a teacher to try administer individual spelling instruction and individual spelling tests. The only way that raudamaticity training can be made practical is by use of a computer. The computer can be programmed to administer only those audamatized words that were not raudamatized for a particular student, and the computer could also help the student learn to spell each word—an untiring tutor.

As explained above, the first hurdle of raudamaticity training for a student is learning to spell an audamatized word correctly. After that hurdle has been overcome for a short list of words, then the student needs to learn to recognize these words rapidly—the second hurdle. Again, a computer would be most effective for helping students learn to recognize correct spellings rapidly. For example, a list of words could be presented one at a time to a student with one-half of the words spelled correctly and the other half spelled incorrectly. The student would be required to press one key to indicate a correct spelling and another key to indicate an incorrect spelling. The student would be required to keep working on a list of words until an appropriate criterion of raudamaticity for the student had been reached. For example, Ehri and Wilce (1983) present data to show that "digit-naming speed is the appropriate baseline for assessing unitized levels of responding to words" (p. 9). In this regard, Manis (1985) was able to get fifth and sixth graders to learn to recognize new words as fast as highly familiar words in only three practice sessions.

Raudamaticity training should continue until all of the V_LWords had been raudamatized, at which point it is said that raudamaticity has been reached for that individual. When raudamaticity is reached, then raudamaticity training for that individual has been completed so it should be stopped.

Raudamaticity training produces raudamatized words, and the importance of raudamatized words has long been recognized. As early as 1978, Hogaboam and Perfetti found that practice on pseudowords improved decoding speed equally for good and poor readers. This can be interpreted as support for the ability of poor readers to learn to pronounce words quickly via practice. Furthermore, in Perfetti's 1985 book on verbal efficiency theory, he contended that efficient text comprehension is dependent on rapid and accurate word recognition, which is consistent with helping students convert audamatized words into raudamatized words. The following ideas of Perfetti (1988) also seem to be consistent with raudamaticity training:

> As for the amount-of-practice component, it should come as no surprise that an hour or two of training is simply not enough. The fluency of a skilled reader has been achieved over hundreds of encounters with specific letter patterns. There are not likely to be dramatic gains from quick "training experiments" but there may be gains from useful instructional events extended over much longer periods. (p. 179)
>
> I suggest that what is learned is not fast responding to words nor even attention-free responding to words. What is learned is thousands of specific word forms (the lexicon) and thousands of orthographic patterns that support access to the lexicon. Speed of processing and low-attention processing are by-products of this overlearning. (p. 139)

This verbal efficiency theory of Perfetti's suggests that instruction and learning which increases the number of words in the raudamatized lexicon may take hundreds of hours. This kind of mastery of hundreds or thousands of printed words not only means that these specific words will be raudamatized, but "thousands of orthographic patterns" will be learned. Thus, raudamaticity training not only increases A_LWords, it also increases (a) pure cipher knowledge, c_k, and (b) pure decoding knowledge, d_k. Perfetti also would seem to agree that this learning process is likely to increase rate level, R_L, because all known words will be recognized faster due to this practice on orthographic patterns. That is, an increase in P_L is likely to cause an increase in d_s, or pure decoding speed, which is a component part of R_L. Again, these ideas of Perfetti's seem to provide theoretical support for raudamaticity training.

It is assumed that giving students practice in recognizing isolated words as fast as possible will eventually result in these words being read faster in context. Evidence to support this hypothesis comes from the research of Fleisher, Jenkins, and Pany (1979); this research has been reviewed in earlier chapters from different perspectives. These researchers had poor readers in grades 4 and 5 practice saying an isolated list of words taken from a paragraph. This practice resulted in a big increase in the rate at which these words could be read in random order, from 43 wpm (SD = 15) for the control group to 93 wpm (SD = 10) for the trained group. Notice that the effect size for this improvement is extremely large, over 3 SDs. The most important result, however, was the effect of this training program upon the rate at which the words could be read in context. The improvement was again a very large effect size—over 1 SD—from 61 wpm (SD = 22) for the control group, compared to 91 wpm (SD = 26) for the trained group. In summary, these data support the theory that training students to accurately and quickly recognize words in isolation will transfer to faster reading rates when the words are read in context.

Raudamaticity training is likely to involve a great deal of "skill and drill" which is the antithesis of recommended instruction by many reading educators (e.g., Spiegel, 1992). However, the importance of this type of practice in reading beyond accuracy was emphasized almost 100 years ago by Huey (1908/1968) when he stated that "repetition progressively frees the mind from attention to details, makes facile the total act, shortens the time, and reduces the extent to which consciousness must concern itself with the process" (p. 104). Also, Newell and Rosenbloom (1981) have pointed out that "almost always, practice brings improvement, and more practice brings more improvement", (p. 1). For a few students, this may be a bitter pill to swallow but it also helps them recover the quickest from their ailment, which is a large gap between listening and reading (between V_LWords and A_LWords), or a large gap between P_L and C_s, which causes a needlessly low rate level, R_L. It might take 50 to 100 hours of raudamaticity training for a dyslexic to gain one GE in P_L, A_L, or R_L. This estimate is consistent with the following statement by Mikulecky (1990): "Award winning adult literacy programs report that it takes 50 to 100 hours for an adult to move from the 9-year-old level to the 10-year-old level" (p. 306). For most students, however, raudamaticity training is likely to be relatively fun because the computer will be a tutor which helps them to learn in small steps, and they are likely to be successful in their learning most of the time, thereby increasing motivation.

While engaged in raudamaticity training, students should be encouraged to engage in about 15 minutes of easy rauding each day (low volume; see Chapter 21), so they can maintain all of their raudamatized words at their rauding rate. It should be pointed out that in most traditional approaches to reading instruction, students who have not reached raudamaticity often have to engage in frustratingly hard reading so they encounter words in their functional lexicon that can be practiced until they reach raudamaticity.

Finally, raudamaticity training is likely to be needed by most individuals who have been diagnosed as pronunciation disabled, DisabledP_L, in the rauding diagnostic system (see Chapter 18). This training should accomplish what Adams (1990) considered to be most important for being a "fluent" reader; she said that the "most critical factor in fluent reading is the ability to recognize letters, spelling patterns, and whole words effortlessly, automatically, and visually" (p.54).

Vocabulary Training. When beginning readers and intermediate readers have reached raudamaticity, then they are ready for vocabulary training. More new words need to be added to the lexicon of words whose meaning is known. So, learning new vocabulary words becomes top priority in the rauding approach once a student has reached raudamaticity (all of their audamatized words have become raudamatized). Vocabulary training strives to increase V_L (listening vocabulary), P_L (word identification), and A_L (reading vocabulary), simultaneously.

The most practical way to conduct vocabulary training would be to use the computer to introduce new words (see Leong, 1993), by giving a definition and by using the word in a sentence. Whenever the student has learned the meaning of a short list of new words, then this list would undergo raudamaticity training, as described earlier.

The vocabulary instruction advocated in the rauding approach is one that gives a definition of the word along with the word being used in a sentence, or a few sentences. This instruction would start with the words on the Carroll et al. list (described earlier), that are ranked lower than the point at which raudamaticity was reached. Then, it would continue with lower ranked words. After a short list of these words had passed a criterion for mastery, such as 90%, then these newly learned words would undergo raudamaticity training until they were all raudamatized. It is this raudamaticity training on vocabulary words that makes vocabulary training in the rauding approach unique. After these new vocabulary words are raudamatized, it would be expected that the student would engage in a high volume of matched rauding (see Chapter 21), so these newly learned words would be encountered in text, and a breadth of meanings would be learned.

An overview of the role of instruction in fostering vocabulary development has been given by Graves (1987). He noted that vocabulary instruction was frequently a very small part of most elementary reading programs. He contended that more instruction was needed even if it was relatively brief for each new word being taught. He said "the value of brief instruction is suggested if one considers brief instruction to be the initial encounter in the series of encounters that are necessary to fully learn the word" (p. 169). The brief instruction for each word in the rauding approach is supplemented by students being engaged in matched rauding in their school work, so that the newly learned words can be encountered in many contexts and learned in depth.

In 1992, Graves updated his ideas about what the elementary vocabulary curriculum should be. Most of his ideas are compatible with vocabulary training in the rauding approach. One of his ideas is not compatible. He stated that "students learn something like 3,000 to 4,000 words each year, many more words than can be taught directly" (p. 115). This idea deserves close scrutiny because the rauding approach purports to be able to teach students how to read all the words they need to be able to read, in order to become an advanced reader. A case will be made in the following paragraphs that it is possible to directly teach all the words that are needed to gain about 3,000 words each year.

From the Accuracy Level Test, ALT, described in Chapter 4, it can be learned from the test manual that a raw score of 50 produces a GE score of 7.9 and an estimated reading vocabulary of 20,000 words. Notice that this estimate of 20,000 words learned in seven years (grades 1-7) is about 3,000 words per year, and this is highly compatible with the estimate used by Graves of 3,000 to 4,000 words per year. This 20,000 word estimate from the ALT comes from the Carroll et al. (1971) rankings, and includes many words besides basic words, such as *walk, walks, walked*, and *walking*. When the words that are not basic words are eliminated from this 20,000, then there are only about 6,200 basic words left. So, there are only around 6,200 basic words that need to be learned during the first 7 years of school; this is 886 words per year, or about 30 words per week during 30 weeks of school. This means that only 6 basic words need to be learned each day of school. Therefore, it is not unreasonable in the rauding approach to set as a goal, the raudamatization of 6 basic words each day of school for a typical student in grades 1-7.

If this goal is accomplished, than a student at the end of grade 7 will likely have learned to read 20,000 words, and thus score as high as $A_L = 7.9$ at the end of grade 7. Furthermore, the reaching of this goal via raudamaticity training and vocabulary training is also likely to mean that $V_L > 8.0$ and $P_L > 8.0$, so that these students will have become advanced readers at the end of grade 7. Therefore, it is likely to be somewhat misleading for Graves to state that 3,000 words per year are more than can be directly taught because most of these words can be derived from only 6 basic words directly taught each day in school via raudamaticity training and vocabulary training under the rauding approach.

With respect to the goal of improving P_L and A_L simultaneously during vocabulary training, Perfetti (1983) has presented theory which may be interpreted as strongly supportive. He has contended that computer-based instruction can be used to improve the breath of vocabulary, that is, knowledge about more words rather than an in-depth knowledge of fewer words—breadth over depth. Perfetti concluded his commentary dealing with computer-based reading instruction as follows:

> My view of the evidence suggests that lower-level skills of decoding and word knowledge are critical in verbal functioning. They are also teachable. Both accuracy and speed of processing can be taken as instructional objectives. Though there are many ways to teach *word knowledge*, there is evidence that even loosely organized semantic content can be learned to a highly generalized degree, affecting comprehension, for example. There is enough evidence to guide computer instruction. (p. 161)

Experimental evidence supporting this type of vocabulary training comes from Tan and Nicholson (1997). They selected 42 below-average readers between the ages of 7 and 10 years. They gave an experimental group about 2 hours of instruction that involved learning the meaning of words (such as "lemonade") and also learning to recognize these words within 1 second using flashcards. This instruction improved the rate and accuracy with which they read passages that contained the trained words, as compared to the control group.

In most traditional approaches to reading instruction, students have to read relatively hard texts so they can encounter new words and try to figure out their meanings from (a) context, (b) a dictionary, or (c) by being told orally. In the rauding approach, students are encouraged to engage in matched rauding, $D_L = A_L$, so that a newly learned word from vocabulary training is encountered in a variety of contexts and eventually raudamatized in almost all contexts. Many students are likely to forget the meaning of these newly learned vocabulary words if they do not encounter them again quite soon in their school books or their auditory experiences; each subsequent encounter with one of these words is assumed to reinforce the depth of its meaning so that V_L, P_L, A_L, R_L, and E_L, will in fact increase quite substantially over a year of this vocabulary training.

In summary, in the rauding approach those students who have reached raudamaticity are given vocabulary training using a computer (which includes raudamaticity training). For those students this kind of training is likely to produce the highest gains in reading achievement, via increases in V_L, P_L, A_L, R_L, and E_L.

Goals. The first goal of the rauding approach is to increase the number of raudamatized words for individuals each day. For example, on the average, early graders and middle graders should increase their raudamatized words by about 6 each day. After raudamaticity has been reached, then vocabulary training would continue to be used to increase the number of raudamatized words by 6 each day of school.

It should be noticed that achieving raudamaticity is a goal similar to helping students learn to read as well as they can listen, a goal often advocated by researchers (Gleitman & Rozin, 1977; Stanovich 1991, 1993b; Sticht, 1972). However, this goal should be considered as secondary in the rauding approach. The accomplishment of this goal might be monumental for dyslexics but it would be fruitless for many ESL students, as well as all those students who are disabled in verbal knowledge, including hyperlexics. These latter students are likely to reach raudamaticity rather quickly, but still be poor readers (low E_L for age). Thus, reaching raudamaticity is not a primary goal for many students who have low verbal knowledge for their age.

The second goal of the rauding approach is to help students in the early grades become intermediate readers ($V_L \geq 3.0$ and $P_L \geq 3.0$) as soon as possible, but at least by the beginning of grade 3. Intermediate readers have learned all the fundamentals of reading. They have passed a milestone with respect to learning to read, so they can also begin reading to learn. They should be able to begin to increase their verbal knowledge level, V_L, by reading (as well as by listening).

The third goal of the rauding approach—the main goal—is to help individuals become advanced readers as soon as possible, at least by the eighth grade. This means that the main goal of the rauding approach is to help students reach $V_L = 8$ and $P_L = 8$ as soon as possible in the middle grades, but at least by grade 8. From kindergarten on, the main goal is to help as many children as possible become advanced readers as soon as possible. Students who become advanced readers are likely to be able to comprehend most of the thoughts (64% or more) in material written at the eighth-grade level of difficulty ($D_L = 8$) when the material is read at their own rauding rate. That is, advanced readers should be able to lexically access, semantically encode, and sententially integrate each word in eighth-grade level text, $D_L = 8$, at their own rauding rate.

When this main goal of reading instruction has been achieved, a student can fully participate as a citizen by being able to read and comprehend almost all newspaper articles and news magazine articles (Carver, 1975). Advanced readers should be able to inform themselves on any issue relevant to being a good citizen. They should be able to read well enough to enjoy almost all the great literature as well as popular fiction. These advanced readers should be able to educate themselves by checking out books from the library upon almost any topic. Finally, they should be able to become even better readers by continuing their education. Advanced readers have reached a standard of excellence in reading that makes it no longer appropriate for them to receive instruction directly relevant to rauding.

Concluding Comments. The historical roots of the rauding approach can be traced as far back as Fries (1963). He called his method of teaching reading, a "spelling pattern" approach; because it developed "the connections between alphabetic signs of reading and the sound patterns of talk" (p. 201). He goes on to say that his approach "... centers upon developing the habits of high speed recognition responses to English spelling patterns, that constitute the process of reading" (p. 189). To achieve those high-speed recognition responses, he contended that "all the experience lying back of the conclusions presented in this book seems to justify the assertion that only a tremendous amount of practice on reading materials that have been adequately programmed and streamlined to lead the developing reader by small steps through all the important sets of spelling-patterns will lead to the high-speed recognition responses of efficient reading" (p. 205, 206). Fries also says that in learning to read, individuals must develop "... habits of high-speed recognition response to the identification features of the spelling-patterns that represent the word patterns ..." (p. 170). It is obvious that these ideas of Fries are highly consistent with the rauding approach which features raudamaticity training, and vocabulary training which includes raudamaticity training.

The roots of the rauding approach are also firmly located in verbal efficiency theory, as developed by Perfetti (1985), in that the rauding approach embraces verbal efficiency. The rauding approach is also consistent with the findings and interpretations of Vellutino, Scanlon, and Spearing (1995) who studied oral vocabulary, accuracy of decoding, and rapid naming in second graders and fifth graders, and concluded that "while the present findings suggest that limitations in vocabulary development may not often be the primary source of reading difficulty in beginning readers, it is quite likely a source of such difficulties in other children" (p. 89).

The rauding approach is also consistent with what has traditionally been regarded as good instruction. McCormick (1994) has summarized various components of good instruction as follows:

> It previously has been hypothesized that certain instructional frameworks will promote literacy among reading disabled students—for example, employing a one-to-one mode of instruction (Bloom, 1984), using materials with levels of difficulty appropriate to the student (Jorgeson, 1977), providing increased opportunity for reading responses (Allington & Johnston, 1989), and designing programs to promote generalization of instruction (Johnston & Allington, 1991). Indeed, research has confirmed many of these variables as causal to success with students whose reading difficulties are mild or moderate (e.g., Pinnell, 1989). (p. 158)

In accordance with these components of good instruction, the rauding approach does employ one-to-one instruction or tutorial learning via the computer as a tutor. It also determines the instructional level of the student and uses instructional materials at that level of difficulty. Furthermore, the rauding approach provides for student responses in that the student is likely to be responding many times per minute, and receiving immediate feedback regarding the correctness of these responses. However, the rauding approach has not been designed to promote generalization of instruction in the same sense as intended in the quotation by McCormick. But, it has been designed to work with words that students are likely to encounter quite often in their curriculum materials, so in this sense there should be a great deal of generality of instruction. Therefore, it appears that the rauding approach to reading instruction is based upon sound instructional principles for promoting literacy among students in general, as well as reading disabled students.

Evaluation

Introduction. In this section, the rauding approach will be evaluated quite extensively by comparing it to several approaches to reading instruction, namely, whole-language, phonics, decoding, skills, and balanced; these other approaches will be evaluated as well.

Whole-Language. In the last chapter, the whole-language approach was described and evaluated in considerable detail. In this subsection, both the rauding approach and the whole-language approach will be evaluated via direct comparisons.

As noted in the last chapter, guessing at the pronunciation of unknown words is a fundamental part of the whole-language approach, and this guessing is considered to be optimal when it is done from context by guessing a word that preserves the meaning of the sentence; also, students are not encouraged to make guesses based upon letter-sound correspondences. In contrast, the rauding approach tries to teach students how to pronounce all the words they will encounter in texts, before they are given the texts to read; guessing is not an issue, either from context or from letter-sound correspondences, because students are given training in how to pronounce words before they are asked to read them in context.

The whole-language approach focuses upon the teacher making learning to read and write as meaningful and natural as possible. In contrast, the rauding approach focuses upon computerized reading instruction designed to increase pronunciation knowledge in most beginning readers, and designed to increase both verbal knowledge and pronunciation knowledge in students who have reached raudamaticity.

The whole-language approach avoids teaching children how to pronounce or spell words in lists—out of the context of sentences—because this is not naturally occurring language; also, this approach considers any instruction which is directed toward increasing pronunciation knowledge out of the context of naturally occurring language or sentences, to be counter to good reading instruction. In contrast, the rauding approach is directed toward increasing P_L in readers who have not reached raudamaticity by helping them learn to pronounce and spell lists of words they already know when listening.

In the whole-language approach, teachers expect children to learn new vocabulary words from context, that is, from reading relatively hard text—called hard reading. In contrast, the rauding approach advocates the direct teaching of word definitions to those students who have reached raudamaticity.

In the whole-language approach, students are usually given real books to read—not basal readers designed for instruction. These books, mostly fictional stories in trade books, usually contain many words that beginning readers do not know how to pronounce. Therefore, these books may be relatively hard to read. In contrast, the rauding approach involves matched rauding (see Chapter 21).

In the whole-language approach, no attention is paid to the speed at which words are recognized or text is read. It is understandable that speed of word recognition, or rate level, is ignored because students are doomed to read very slowly when they are given relatively hard texts to read; they must try to figure out how to pronounce words from context. It is also understandable that rate of reading is ignored when the entire focus is upon comprehending the text; the stress in the whole-language approach is upon high accuracy of text comprehension (high A), even when the student is given relatively hard text. In contrast, the rauding approach is primarily concerned with increasing the number of words in a student's lexicon of raudamatized words, each day of school.

In the whole-language approach, a fundamental goal is to make reading interesting and enjoyable by having lower graders read children's books—real books—written by the best authors; making reading meaningful and enjoyable is so important under the whole-language approach that gain in reading achievement is often a secondary goal, or not a goal at all. In contrast, the rauding approach has gain in reading achievement as its primary goal, with enjoyment being a secondary goal. Students are never given texts to read that are relatively hard for them. Instead, they are given raudamaticity training which is designed to be administered in small steps so that students are successful most of the time. Under the rauding approach, students are never frustrated by being asked to take part in activities wherein they are unsuccessful, or wrong, most of the time. This design for success in the rauding approach should result in risk-taking, task persistence, and other encouraging behaviors related to achievement in reading. On the other hand, students who are low in pronunciation aptitude or low in verbal knowledge aptitude are likely to be frustrated by the whole-language approach because they are continually asked to pronounce words that they cannot figure out from context. It seems likely that most beginning readers will find reading to be more enjoyable in the rauding approach, because they will read faster, they will find reading to be easier, and they will have more successes than failures.

The main reason that the whole-language approach is effective in increasing reading achievement in some students is probably because it requires that writing be taught along with reading. Writing messages and stories requires students to spell words, and it is this spelling which helps many students learn the alphabetic principle, and increase their cipher knowledge, without being explicitly taught. This spelling required in writing is very helpful for increasing P_L in students who are at least average in pronunciation aptitude; for low pronunciation aptitude students this spelling that is required in writing sentences is likely to be very frustrating and not an effective way to increase P_L. Learning to spell words accurately and recognize correct spellings rapidly is a fundamental part of the rauding approach.

Phonics Approach. The phonics approach to reading instruction will be described first, and then it will be compared to the rauding approach, later.

The phonics approach is used mainly in the early grades. It stresses the learning of grapheme-phoneme correspondences, usually including the learning of rules about these correspondences. For example, students might be taught the rule that silent *e* at the end of a word makes the main vowel say its name (e.g., wide). Another example of a phonics rule is that when two vowels go walking, the first one does the talking; however, this rule only works in about one fourth of the words containing two consecutive vowels.

According to Stahl, Duffy-Hester, and Stahl (1998) "good phonics instruction should not teach rules" (p. 341). Furthermore, the rules that are explicitly taught in a typical phonics approach are not exactly what students need to learn, according to Gough, Juel, and Griffith (1992). These latter researchers contend that all students need to learn the systematic connections between letters and sounds, no matter what approach has been used in their instruction (phonics, whole-language, etc.). In their terminology, students must learn the "orthographic cipher of English." Students must "master the system by which printed words are mapped onto spoken words" (p. 39), and they call this "learning the cipher." They go on to say that "... the rules of phonics are explicit, few in number, and slow" (p. 39), whereas "the rules of the cipher are implicit, very numerous, and fast" (p. 39). For example, when individuals learn the cipher instead of phonics rules, they learn that the first four letters in "chord" and "chore" are pronounced differently, depending upon the fifth letter; they learn that the pronunciation of phonemes depends upon not only on a letter but also the neighborhood of letters. Although typical phonics instruction has the advantage of forcing children to attend to the letters of words and the sounds they represent, this approach is not an efficient way to learn to read; too much time is spent learning rules that can only be applied rarely with success, and then too slowly. Instead of learning rules under the phonics approach, the child should learn letter-sound associations that usually work. That is, bag is composed of three sounds, one for each letter. However, it is not /buh/ /a/ /guh/, as might be taught in a phonics lesson. Instead, it is /ba/ and /ag/ put together.

Whereas students are taught rules about letters in words and their corresponding sounds in the phonics approach, the rauding approach includes no learning of phonics rules. In the phonics approach, beginning readers spend a great deal of time learning how to pronounce isolated words, but there is ordinarily no stress on learning how to spell words. In contrast, all students who have not reached raudamaticity (including almost all beginning readers), spend a great deal of time learning to pronounce and spell isolated words in the rauding approach.

In the phonics approach, there is no time devoted to learning the meaning of new words, that is, vocabulary development is not part of the phonics approach. In contrast, the rauding approach stresses vocabulary training for those students who have reached raudamaticity.

In the phonics approach, there is a need to get students to read text that is relatively hard for them so they can practice on trying to pronounce new words. In contrast, beginning readers in the rauding approach are not asked to do hard reading; they are always given texts which contain words that they have already practiced pronouncing, most of which have been learned during raudamaticity training.

In the phonics approach, there is no attention paid to the speed of word recognition, or the rate of reading. This is understandable, because this approach ordinarily involves students being asked to read relatively difficult text that requires them to frequently stop and try to figure out how to pronounce a new word. Rate is not an important factor. Learning to correctly pronounce new words by applying rules that have been learned is very important in the phonics approach—no matter how slowly this is accomplished. In contrast, students who are taught under the rauding approach learn to pronounce the spoken words they know very quickly—during raudamaticity training.

In the phonics approach, there is no stress on making reading enjoyable. The phonics approach can only be applied by asking students to solve difficult puzzles, that is, asking them to try to figure out how to pronounce words they have never seen before; this is a difficult and frustrating task even for adults who are advanced readers. In contrast, students would never be asked to read relatively hard text under the rauding approach so they should always find reading to be easier, faster, and more enjoyable. Furthermore, raudamaticity training and vocabulary training are designed so that students will be successful in their learning most of the time. It seems likely that the students with high pronunciation aptitude will be successful most of the time under the phonics approach, and therefore they may find it to be as enjoyable as the rauding approach. However, for all readers besides those with high g_p, it is likely that they will find the rauding approach to be more enjoyable because they will be more successful and less frustrated.

Decoding Approach. Some may want to equate the decoding approach to phonics instruction. Both involve learning spelling to sound correspondences (that often are regular). The decoding approach (or the alphabetic coding approach) also involves learning sound-symbol correspondences and the alphabetic principle, but it does not involve the explicit learning of rules. Furthermore, the decoding approach avoids teaching students, erroneously, that there is a one-to-one correspondence between letters and sounds.

The decoding approach incorporates that part of phonics which does not involve the learning of abstract rules, but it also puts more of a focus upon learning to spell words so they can be more accurately recognized. Again, spelling knowledge helps individuals learn how to pronounce a word, and thereby retrieve its previously stored meaning (Ehri & Wilce, 1979a). Therefore, the decoding approach is somewhat similar to the rauding approach with respect to spelling instruction. However, the rauding approach has upgraded the decoding approach by using a computer to implement the spelling instruction.

The decoding approach includes instruction devoted to isolated words and the guessing of unknown words; it also requires that students be given relatively hard texts to read. In contrast, students taught under the rauding approach are not encouraged to guess at unknown words, whether isolated or in context, and are not given texts to read that are relatively hard, as explained several times earlier.

In the decoding approach, there is no attention paid to words that are not known when listening, that is, no attention is paid to vocabulary development or increasing V_L. This means that the decoding approach is only appropriate for students who have not reached raudamaticity. It also means that this approach is mostly relevant to beginning readers who are not ESL students and are not disabled with respect to verbal knowledge level. In contrast, the rauding approach is relevant to all beginning readers and all intermediate readers because it focuses upon increasing P_L and A_L for those who have not reached raudamaticity and it focuses upon increasing V_L, P_L, and A_L for those who have reached raudamaticity.

The decoding approach includes a concern for recognizing words rapidly, or overlearning them via spelling and practice. In this regard, the decoding approach is similar to the rauding approach. The only difference is that the rauding approach incorporates the use of a computer for individualized instruction, so as to increase the recognition speed more systematically and more effectively via raudamaticity training.

In the decoding approach, there is no inherent concern for making reading more enjoyable. Remember that the decoding approach still requires that students try to guess at new words using their decoding knowledge. Therefore, the decoding approach depends upon students being given relatively hard materials so that they can learn to pronounce most new words without help, by sounding them out. This approach is likely to be difficult, slow, and frustrating for most readers, especially those with low pronunciation aptitude. In contrast, the rauding approach strives to make reading relatively easy, relatively fast, and relatively fun by never asking students to read relatively hard material, and by making sure students are mostly successful during raudamaticity training and vocabulary training.

Skills Approach. As noted earlier in Chapter 22, the skills approach focuses upon teaching decoding, vocabulary, spelling, grammar, and comprehension as discrete skills. Students are given lessons in decoding and grammar; they are also given lessons in how to comprehend text. Those lessons are often delivered to students via workbooks or worksheets which require written responses from students.

The decoding lessons in the skills approach are likely to incorporate many of the same word attack strategies as was described earlier in the phonics approach or decoding approach. The vocabulary lessons are likely to include definitions of words and then these same words used in sentences, much like the rauding approach. The spelling lessons are likely to involve lists of words whose spelling must be studied and tested periodically, somewhat similar to the rauding approach. The grammar lessons are likely to involve learning about sentence construction and the parts of speech, which is not included in the rauding approach because grammar instruction is more directly relevant to writing than to reading. The comprehension lessons are likely to include activities that involve direct instruction in how to comprehend text better, which is completely counter to the rauding approach.

MacGinitie (1991) has provided the following critique of the traditional skills approach to reading instruction:

> ... consider the fad of breaking down reading into objectives and skills. It was perfectly reasonable and, indeed, salutary to think about exactly what we were trying to accomplish. It was perfectly reasonable and, indeed, salutary to think about what children needed to be able to do before asking them to do something more advanced. But it was *not* reasonable to ignore goals that could not be stated in objective terms, to impose a fancied sequence where a real one could not be found, to break down tasks into skills so numerous that neither the student nor the teacher could see the ultimate objective, to require students to practice component skills that were difficult only because they had been deprived of their natural context. (p. 57)

The skills approach, with its devotion to a scope and sequence chart, is very different from the rauding approach.

In the skills approach, decoding, spelling, and vocabulary are taught directly, and this is somewhat similar to the raudamaticity training and vocabulary training that comprise the rauding approach. However, the skills approach also strives to teach study skills that purportedly increase reading comprehension when studying relatively hard text, via prediction activities, metacognitive activities, and main idea activities; these skills and activities are not part of the rauding approach and are counter to it. It is likely that students taught under the rauding approach will gain more in reading achievement because they will not be wasting time engaged in comprehension activities—prediction, question generation, and main idea—that are highly questionable with respect to causing gains in reading achievement, or E_L (see Carver, 1992c). Again, the teaching of these study strategies is more relevant to the learning and memorizing gears (see Chapter 2).

As an example of direct instruction in comprehension, consider the research by Palinczar and Brown (1984). They presented the results of a study on what they called reciprocal teaching (RT). This comprehension-fostering strategy was modeled for students so they would learn to employ the practices of question generation, summarization, prediction, and clarification when they read. They reported large gains for the group that received RT, as compared to three control groups. However, Carver, (1987a) pointed out that the larger gain for the RT group could have been due to these students learning study habits that stimulated them to spend more time reading and studying the test passages. That is, because no time limits were mentioned, it seems likely that the RT group simply learned to study harder thereby increasing their accuracy of text comprehension, A, by increasing the time they spent on the text (see Appendix C). If so, there would be little or no advantage for the RT group on a standardized reading comprehension test that had a time limit where many students would not have time to finish the test.

A meta-analysis of reciprocal teaching, RT, was conducted by Rosenshine and Meister (1994). They reviewed 16 studies that compared reciprocal teaching, RT, to a control group. Out of the 16 studies, there were 9 that compared RT to a control group using a standardized test; for those data they reported a median effect size of .32. They did not report whether they used the same measure as Glass (1976), or whether they used Cohen's *d* (Cohen, 1977). However, both measures are likely to produce similar results so that Cohen's criteria can be used to interpret whether the ES was small (.20), medium (.50), or large (.80). Notice that this .32 effect size is very close to what Cohen would interpret as small. These researchers also reported the median ES for 10 of the 16 studies that used a reading comprehension test developed by the experimenter; it was .88, which can be interpreted as large using Cohen's criteria. Rosenshine and Meister considered several reasons for why the standardized test resulted in a small ES (.32), and the experimenter test resulted in the much larger ES (.88). However, they never considered the most obvious reason given earlier by Carver (1987a). That is, the experimenter tests were not timed whereas the standardized tests were timed. This means that the standardized tests were likely to be an indicant of reading achievement, or E_L, and there was a very small effect of reciprocal teaching upon reading achievement, or E_L. Therefore, there was probably no substantial increase in general reading ability that resulted from RT. Instead, the RT treatment probably induced these students to increase the amount of time they spent reading the passages on the test, which would increase the accuracy of text comprehension, A, on the experimenter tests (see Appendix C). This meta-analysis of RT by Rosenshine and Meister may be reasonably interpreted as providing evidence that direct instruction by teachers in question generation, summarization, prediction and clarification does *not* result in substantial increases in reading achievement. The part of the skills approach which emphasizes direct instruction in reading comprehension, seems to suffer from a lack of sound supporting evidence.

It should be noted that Dole, Duffy, Roehler, and Pearson (1991) have recommended that students be taught five comprehension strategies. They are: (a) determining importance, (b) summarizing information, (c) drawing inferences, (d) generating questions, and (e) monitoring comprehension. These strategies are relevant to studying relatively hard texts, $D_L > A_L$, and are therefore relevant to a learning process (Gear 2) and a memorizing process (Gear 1). However, these comprehension strategies are not relevant when individuals read normally, that is, operate their rauding process on relatively easy texts, $A_L > D_L$, and should not be taught in the lower or middle grades to beginning and intermediate readers. In this regard, it is notable that Pressley, Wharton-McDonald, Mistretta-Hampton, and Echevarria (1998) found that seven "competent" and three "really exceptional" teachers in grades 4 and 5 did not include substantive amounts of comprehension-strategy instruction in their language arts instruction, as observed over a 6-month period. These comprehension strategies are only appropriate for advanced readers who increase their reading achievement primarily by reading relatively hard texts (see Chapter 21). Therefore, the rauding approach should be used until individuals have become advanced readers, and then these comprehension strategies should be taught as part of a study skills curriculum.

It should not go unnoticed that direct instruction in comprehension for beginning and intermediate readers is completely counter to rauding theory, which emphasizes the common comprehension process used in reading and auding. It is not necessary to teach children how to comprehend texts that are read aloud to them when all of the words are audamatized words. Likewise, it is not necessary to teach children how to comprehend texts that they read themselves when all of the words are raudamatized words.

In summary, the rauding approach is compatible with some parts of the skills approach but incompatible with other parts. The rauding approach agrees with skills instruction that focuses upon the teaching of vocabulary, but the teaching of vocabulary in the rauding approach is likely to be more effective because (a) it can be individualized using a computer, and (b) it includes the raudamatization of the newly learned words. The rauding approach is incompatible with direct instruction in comprehension skills because it is highly questionable whether this instruction time is useful in increasing V_L, P_L, A_L, R_L, or E_L in beginning and intermediate readers.

Balanced Approach. There are no data currently available that unequivocally indicates that one approach to reading instruction is best. Stahl (1997) has reviewed various approaches to the teaching of reading and he concluded that "it should be obvious by now that none of these approaches is 'best' ..." (p. 25). However, all the data indicate that an approach which includes an emphasis on learning alphabetic coding, or cipher training, is probably best for beginning readers (e.g., Foorman, Francis, Novy, & Liberman, 1991). Many researchers are calling for a balanced approach, that is, a balance between meaning emphasis in the whole-language approach and code emphasis in the phonic approach (e.g., Biemiller, 1994; Vellutino, 1991), and this balanced approach does have some empirical support (Calfee & Piontkowski, 1981; Evans & Carr, 1985).

An approach that qualifies as a balanced approach is the one advocated by P. M. Cunningham (1995). She says that what she advocates is quite different from the "old phonics" because "it is not rules, jargon, and worksheets" (p. 192). Her balanced approach is highly compatible with the rauding approach so it will be described in some detail.

In the first and second grades, Cunningham recommended that 120 minutes a day be devoted to four blocks of instruction, 30 minutes each. She described three of the blocks as follows:

> Basal Block—which involves teacher-guided reading and discussion of selections from basal readers and trade books; Writing Block—which follows a writing process format; Self-Selected Block—in which children choose what they want to read from a wide range of books and other reading materials.
> (p. 192)

Elsewhere P. M. Cunningham (1992) described the fourth Block as follows: "The Working With Words Block includes a daily word wall chanting/writing activity designed to help children develop automatic reading and spelling of the highest frequency words and a daily Making Words activity designed to help them learn that words are made up of letters which form predictable spelling patterns ..." (p. 29).

It should be noted that the computerized implementation of the rauding approach could be substituted for this Working With Words Block, thereby integrating the rauding approach with this balanced approach of Cunningham's. This Working With Words block involves learning to read and spell words automatically, and this is a goal of raudamaticity training in the rauding approach. It seems likely that the computerization of this 30 minutes would make this instruction more effecting in increasing P_L, because it would be individualized instead of a group activity, thereby matching instruction to the level of the student.

This approach of Cunningham's is balanced in the sense that it incorporates the reading of literature and language training, inherent in the whole-language approach (meaning emphasis), along with the teaching of decoding or letter-sound correspondences (code emphasis). She has contended that we must "... promote balanced literacy instruction" (p. 192).

Cunningham developed her balanced approach so that it is compatible with "what we know about how good readers read words" (p. 184). She summarized that research knowledge as follows:

> Readers look at virtually all of the words and almost all of the letters (Rayner & Pollatsek, 1989; McConkie, Kerr, Reddix, & Zola, 1987). (p. 23)
> Readers usually recode printed words into sound (P. M. Cunningham & Cunningham, 1978; Tannenhaus, Flanigan & Seidenberg, 1980; McCutchen, Bell, France & Perfetti, 1991). (p. 23)
> Readers recognize most words immediately and automatically without using context (LaBerge & Samuels, 1974; Perfetti, 1985; Stanovich, 1980, 1986, 1991; Samuels, 1988; Nicholson, 1991). (p. 23)
> Readers accurately and quickly pronounce infrequent, phonetically regular words (Perfetti & Hogaboam, 1975; Hogaboam & Perfetti, 1978; Daneman, 1991). (p. 23)
> Readers use spelling patterns and analogy to decode words (Adams, 1990; Goswami & Bryant, 1990). (p. 24)
> Readers divide big words as they see them based on interletter frequencies (Mewhort & Campbell, 1981; Seidenberg, 1987). (p.24).

These principles are quite consistent with the rauding approach, especially the emphasis on the reading of all the words on a page, the use of the spelling of a word (all the letters) to recognize it, the saying of the words to oneself when reading, and the rapid recognition of words without relying on context.

As an advocate of the balanced approach, Cunningham has also recommended that before children come to school (a) they should be read to, and (b) they should learn the names of many of the letters. With this pre-school help, these students have less to learn when they reach school. Cunningham also notes that "phonemic awareness is critical to success in beginning reading (Bryant, Bradley, MacClean, & Crossland, 1989; Perfetti, 1991a)" (p. 25), and she recommends "... lots of exposure to nursery rhymes and books which make words sound fun" (p. 26), and "... sound manipulation games which help children figure out the critical relationship between words and phonemes" (p. 26). P. M. Cunningham (1992) points out that "children who can decode well will learn sight words better (Ehri, 1991; Jorm & Share, 1983; Stanovich & West, 1989)" (p. 26), which further justifies the teaching of the alphabetic principle, plus spelling. She goes on to contend that "lots of successful reading is essential for readers to develop automaticity and rapid decoding (Samuels, 1988; Stanovich & West, 1989; Juel, 1990; Clay, 1991)" (p. 26).

If the balanced approach recommended by Cunningham is supplemented 30 minutes each day by the rauding approach administered by a computer during her Working With Words Block, then children ought to be learning to read in a very effective and efficient manner in the early grades. During this 30 minutes of raudamaticity instruction, students will be learning to quickly recognize new printed words each day. These words are likely to be used in the Writing Block, and thereby their spellings will be reinforced. Students are also likely to choose books to read for themselves in the Self-Selected Block which contain the words they have learned to spell and recognize quickly. This reading will maintain and reinforce their accurate and rapid recognition. During the teacher-guided reading block, students should also be learning about how words are pronounced, that is, they should be getting direct instruction in the cipher. In shared reading with predictable big books, they should be learning sounds that usually go with letters and how to blend sounds (fat, rat, cat & pan, ran, man), and they should be learning about prefixes and suffixes, as Cunningham (1995) has admirably described in great detail.

In summary, the balanced approach primarily consists of a merger between the decoding approach (code-emphasis) and the whole-language approach (meaning-emphasis). In the code-emphasis part, phonics rules are not included but there is an emphasis on the accurate and rapid recognition of isolated words—which is contrary to the whole-language approach. Also, there are no workbooks or worksheets, which is part of the skills approach. The balanced approach to the teaching of reading outlined by P. M. Cunningham (1995) can be easily merged with the rauding approach so that her 30 minutes a day devoted to Working With Words consists of raudamaticity training for most beginning readers. This means that students in the early grades should gain the most in P_L, A_L, R_L, and E_L if they are given instruction following the balanced approach outlined by Cunningham supplemented by the rauding approach administered by a computer for 30 minutes a day.

One big advantage to supplementing this balanced approach with the rauding approach (balanced-rauding approach) is that reading instruction is much more individualized for beginning readers; students are given raudamaticity training at their own instructional level, and then when they reach raudamaticity they are given vocabulary training at their own instructional level. Another big advantage of using the balanced-rauding approach in the early grades is that students are less likely to be asked to read relatively hard texts, and are more likely to find reading to be easy, fast, and fun, even if they have a low pronunciation aptitude or a low verbal aptitude.

Whereas the balanced-rauding approach is most appropriate in the lower grades for beginning readers, the rauding approach is much more appropriate on its own in the middle grades where some students need raudamaticity training and some students need vocabulary training. In the middle grades, the rauding approach can be used for 30 minutes a day as an upgrade of the skills approach. Then, for another hour each day students can work on language arts activities such as learning grammar and writing letters and stories. The big advantage of the rauding approach is that it is (a) useful as a supplement to the balanced approach in the lower grades, and (b) useful as the main way to teach reading in the middle grades.

Implications

Any approach to the teaching of reading should (a) include instruction designed to help children learn the alphabetic principle, (b) include instruction that helps children learn how to pronounce isolated words correctly, but does not depend upon phonics rules, (c) include instruction in spelling words correctly, (d) include learning activities that help students recognize correct spellings rapidly, and (e) include activities that help children learn the meaning of new words, after they have learned to recognize in print all of the words they know when they hear them spoken.

Forget Me Nots

The rauding approach is purportedly a root cause of high reading achievement. It uses raudamaticity training and vocabulary training to help beginning and intermediate readers learn to raudamatize at least 6 new words each day of school. When this approach is combined with the balanced approach in the lower grades, there should be higher gains in reading achievement each year, as compared to other approaches, such as whole-language, phonics, decoding, and skills. In the middle grades, the rauding approach should produce higher reading achievement than any other approach.

CHAPTER

24

SUMMARY AND CONCLUSIONS

The causes of high and low reading achievement have been explained in previous chapters using the causal model outlined in Chapter 1. This final chapter will summarize (a) the causal model, (b) the *modified* causal model as it applies to advanced readers, (c) the rauding system for diagnosing disabilities and handicaps, (d) the less important factors that are not in the causal model, (e) the rauding approach to reading instruction and how it compares to other approaches, and (f) the interconnections among the theoretical constructs in rauding theory. Conclusions will also be drawn based upon the theory and research evidence given in earlier chapters.

Causal Model

Introduction. The causal model was described in the earlier chapters by first focusing upon reading achievement, or E_L at Echelon 1, and then describing (a) the secondary causes of E_L at Echelon 2, (b) the primary causes of E_L at Echelon 3, and (c) the root causes of E_L at Echelon 4. This section will summarize the causal model in reverse order; Echelons 1 and 2 will be summarized last, and Echelons 3 and 4 will be summarized first.

Verbal Knowledge. In the causal model, a very important root cause of high and low reading achievement is teaching and learning directed toward increasing verbal knowledge. Educators can have a major impact upon the reading achievement of students via this teaching/learning construct in the causal model. Students cannot achieve highly in reading without having high levels of verbal knowledge. When verbal knowledge level is measured in GE units, it is symbolized as V_L and referred to as "verbal level."

Verbal level, V_L, can be measured by a test designed to sample all the knowledge individuals have in the form of words, in GE units. An indicant of V_L would be a test of general knowledge, administered auditorily. Another indicant of V_L would be a listening comprehension test. A third indicant would be a vocabulary test administered auditorily so that pronunciation knowledge would not be required. The V_L construct has been measured in previous research by the Auding Accuracy Level Test, AALT, which is a vocabulary test administered auditorily. This test measures how many words an individual knows when the words are spoken, or heard. Words that an individual knows auditorily are called audamatized words, or V_LWords, and the number of V_LWords scaled into GE units provides a measure of V_L.

Reading instruction in school can have a major impact upon V_L, but a great deal of verbal knowledge should be learned before schooling starts, and a great deal of verbal knowledge should be acquired outside of reading instruction in school. Learning the meaning of spoken words and gaining the knowledge associated with spoken words is one of the main activities involved in education. Therefore, the effectiveness of education can be measured by the gain in V_L each year. However, not all students are equal with respect to their ability to gain verbal knowledge. Individuals vary considerably in how quickly they can learn verbally, and this aptitude is called verbal knowledge aptitude; it is symbolized as g_v and referred to as "verbal aptitude."

It is being theorized that V_L depends upon two proximal causes—teaching /learning activities and verbal aptitude, g_v. Those students with high g_v and good teaching/learning have a good chance of achieving high in reading, whereas those students with low g_v and poor teaching/learning are more likely to be low in reading achievement.

At present there is no available standardized test designed to measure g_v in the causal model. Such a measure would involve learning verbal information. For adults who can learn from printed words as easily as they can learn from spoken words, the reading-span test would seem to provide an indicant of g_v. On this test, a student is asked to read sentences and then remember the last word in each sentence. A listening version of this test should provide an indicant of g_v for students in the early and middle grades.

Pronunciation Knowledge. The most important root cause in the causal model is the teaching and learning that is directed toward increasing pronunciation knowledge, P_L. The number of printed words that can be pronounced correctly in a list of unrelated words is pronunciation knowledge, and when this knowledge is measured in grade equivalent units it is called pronunciation knowledge level, P_L. A word that can be pronounced correctly by a particular individual when it is encountered in an unrelated list of words is said to be a pronounceamatized word. The lexicon of pronounceamatized words is called P_LWords, and the number of P_LWords expressed in GE units is pronunciation knowledge level, P_L; it is usually referred to as "pronunciation level." P_L can be measured directly by sampling the population of printed words and then finding out how many of these words an individual can pronounce.

There are several measures that provide indicants of P_L. Word identification tests, which measure the accuracy of pronouncing increasingly difficult words, provide indicants of P_L—such as the Word Identification test in the Woodcock Reading Mastery Tests. Spelling tests also provide indicants of P_L, that is, spelling tests provide scores that correlate highly with the number of printed words that an individual can correctly spell—such as the Wide Range Achievement Test-Spelling. The best measure of P_L, at present, is probably the Pronunciation Level Test, PLT, because it systematically samples words from the population of printed words. The PLT is a standardized test that has been designed to measure the P_L construct in the causal model. However, it should also be pointed out that the number of words that an individual can spell in GE units, S_L, is also a good measure of P_L, that is, $S_L = P_L$.

P_L is an extremely important construct in the causal model. Reading instruction is a teaching/learning factor that has a major impact upon gain in reading achievement via increases in P_L. For example, one of the biggest problems with the whole-language approach to reading instruction is that it avoids teaching activities designed to have a direct impact upon gain in P_L. One of the main ways to compare different approaches to reading instruction is by the amount of gain in P_L during a school year. However, the quality and quantity of reading instruction is not the only factor which influences gain in P_L during a year. The pronunciation aptitude, g_p, of the student also has a major influence upon gain in P_L. Individuals vary considerably in how quickly they can learn the somewhat consistent connections between letters in words and sounds in words, and this aptitude for learning the probabilistic sound-symbol relationships in words is called g_p.

Notice that P_L has two proximal causes—teaching/learning activities and pronunciation aptitude, g_p. Those students with high g_p and good teaching/learning are very likely to be high achievers in reading, whereas students with low g_p and poor teaching and learning activities are very likely to be low achievers in reading.

At present, there is no available standardized test designed to measure g_p in the causal model. Such a measure would involve learning to associate sounds with symbols. For students in the early grades who have not yet learned all the names of the letters of the alphabet, letter-naming accuracy would likely provide an indicant of g_p. Letter-naming accuracy is necessary for being able to learn correspondences between the letters and sounds in words—the essence of g_p. For a group of students who have received similar teaching and learning activities relevant to learning the names of the letters of the alphabet, variation in their accuracy of naming letters should be due mainly to g_p. That is, learning the less than perfect connections between the graphic symbols representing letters (such as B and b) and the sounds used to name these letters (such as /bee/ and /beeee/) is a task that is similar to the one described earlier for measuring g_p.

Another indicant of g_p in the early grades would be a measure of phonological awareness, or PA. One measure of PA involves asking an individual what word remains after removing the first sound from another word, for example, /at/ is the word that remains when the first sound is removed from /cat/. PA would provide an indicant of g_p in the early grades because PA is necessary for g_p; it is impossible for an individual to have an aptitude for learning the inconsistent connections between the sounds within spoken words and the letters within printed words if the individual is not aware of the sounds within spoken words.

So, a measure of letter-naming accuracy and a measure of phonological awareness are likely to provide good indicants of g_p in the early grades. However, these measures would not provide a direct measure of g_p because they are highly influenced by teaching and learning activities; a direct measure of g_p would not be substantially influenced by teaching and learning. That is, a good measure of g_p would be education proof, but letter-naming accuracy is not education proof and measures of PA are not education proof.

Giving children help in learning the names of the letters of the alphabet is one of the first steps in learning to read, and those students who score high on a letter-name test in kindergarten are usually the same students who score high on P_L in grade 2. However, it is a mistake to (a) give a letter-naming test in kindergarten, (b) find out who scored low, (c) give the low scorers extra help so they score high on the test when it is given a second time, and (d) then predict that these original low scorers will score high on P_L at the end of second grade. Letter-naming accuracy in kindergarten correlates highly with P_L in first and second grade because it is usually a good indicant of g_p, and g_p is a proximal cause of gain in P_L. Most researchers now recognize that teaching letter-naming accuracy does not automatically make a student have a high aptitude for learning to read.

A situation seemingly similar to letter-naming has arisen with phonological awareness. Because PA in kindergarten correlates so highly with P_L in grade 2, it is being hypothesized that teaching PA to students in kindergarten and grade 1 will make them score high on P_L in grade 2. It seems more likely that PA is an indicant of g_p in the early grades and that is why it correlates highly with P_L. Although some knowledge of PA is necessary for g_p, and PA is necessary for making large gains in P_L, the kind of teaching that is likely to be the most effective for increasing P_L is PA teaching that also involves letters and words. The most effective way to increase PA and P_L is to teach the alphabetic principle, or to administer cipher training. Individuals need to learn the connections between letter patterns and sounds in words, or between graphemes and phonemes in words, and this is called cipher learning. Beginning readers need to learn the alphabetic principle and they need to learn cipher knowledge, and this is done most effectively when both letters and sounds are involved, not just the sounds in PA instruction.

Typical beginning readers know the meaning of many words when listening but they know how to pronounce very few printed words; the size of their lexicon of audamatized words is much larger than the size of their lexicon of pronounceamatized words. Therefore, instruction for beginning readers needs to be focused upon increasing the number of pronounceamatized words, or increasing P_LWords and P_L, as noted earlier. In this regard, it should also be pointed out that the whole-language approach to reading instruction emphasizes meaning, and therefore focuses more upon V_L, whereas the phonics approach to reading instruction emphasizes the code, and therefore focuses more upon P_L. The best reading instruction probably emphasizes (a) learning the cipher for those students who have more audamatized words than pronounceamatized words, and (b) learning the meaning of words for those students who have learned to pronounce all of their audamatized words.

Cognitive Speed. Another root cause of high and low reading achievement is cognitive speed, which is the fastest rate at which an individual can name a series of overlearned objects or symbols, in items per minute. Cognitive speed aptitude, g_s, is cognitive speed compared to same-age peers. That is, the g_s construct is measured by the fastest speed at which an individual can name a series of overlearned objects or symbols, such as colors, digits, or letters, when compared to other individuals at the same age. For beginning readers who have not yet learned to name digits or letters accurately, the best measure of g_s would probably be a color-naming test. For most individuals in grade 2 or higher, the best measure of g_s would be digit naming speed or letter naming speed. This g_s construct has been measured in previous research on the causal model by the Alphabet Rate Test, ART.

Cognitive speed aptitude and the individual's age, are the two proximal causes of cognitive speed level, symbolized as C_s. Cognitive speed aptitude, g_s, is measured in standard score units, whereas cognitive speed level, C_s, is the same ability measured in grade equivalent, GE, units.

Primary and Root Causes. Cognitive speed level, along with verbal level and pronunciation level, discussed earlier, are the three primary causes of high and low reading achievement. Individuals who have high V_L, P_L, and C_s for their age have a very high probability of being high achievers in reading, whereas individuals who have low V_L, P_L, and C_s for their age have a very high probability of being low achievers in reading.

Whereas V_L, P_L, and C_s are the three primary causes of high and low reading achievement, the root causes are the proximal causes of V_L, P_L, and C_s. That is, the six root causes of reading achievement are as follows: (a) teaching and learning designed to increase verbal knowledge, (b) verbal knowledge aptitude, g_v, (c) teaching and learning designed to increase pronunciation knowledge, (d) pronunciation aptitude, g_p, (e) cognitive speed aptitude, g_s, and (f) age. Educators cannot change four of these six root causes, namely g_v, g_p, g_s, and age. Educators can cause changes in two of these six root causes, namely, teaching and learning designed to increase verbal knowledge, and teaching and learning designed to increase pronunciation knowledge.

Reading educators have their biggest impact on typical students via teaching and learning designed to increase pronunciation knowledge, P_L. Educators in the lower and middle grades need to recognize that reading achievement for most students is determined primarily by V_L, P_L, and C_s. The two main avenues that educators have for influencing reading achievement is by teaching and learning activities that cause gain in V_L and P_L. Yet, everyone must recognize that reading achievement is also influenced heavily by four factors that educators cannot influence—verbal aptitude, pronunciation aptitude, cognitive speed aptitude, and age. It should also be pointed out that even though two proximal causes of P_L are pronunciation aptitude, g_p, and teaching and learning designed to increase P_L, it turns out that V_L is a distal cause of P_L. That is, low P_L can also be indirectly caused by low V_L.

Secondary Causes. The deterministic influence that V_L, P_L, and C_s have upon reading achievement, or E_L, involves two very important intervening constructs, namely, rauding accuracy level and rauding rate level. Rauding accuracy level is symbolized as A_L and is usually referred to as "accuracy level." It is the highest level of text difficulty, D_L, that an individual can accurately read when the text is read at the individual's rauding rate, R_r. An individual's rauding rate is the rate at which the rauding process is operated. When an individual's rauding rate is expressed in GE units it is called "rauding rate level," which is symbolized as R_L and usually referred to as "rate level."

A_L, or accuracy level, is similar to the traditional concepts of reading level or instructional level. An unspeeded reading comprehension test, such as the Passage Comprehension test from the Woodcock Reading Mastery Tests, would provide a measure of A_L. Also, the untimed Degrees of Reading Power test would provide an indicant of A_L because it involves reading increasingly difficult passages that must be accurately comprehended. A reading vocabulary test would also provide an indicant of A_L. Another indicant of A_L would be the number of raudamatized words, or A_LWords, scaled into GE units; raudamatized words are words that individuals know in print and can recognize at their normal reading rate. Previous research on the causal model has used the Accuracy Level Test, ALT, to measure A_L; it is a reading vocabulary test with scores scaled into GE units.

A_L has two proximal causes and they are V_L and P_L. This means that verbal level and pronunciation level determine accuracy level, and this is similar to the simple view of reading which holds that listening and decoding determine reading. The theory that V_L and P_L determine A_L can be summarized and expressed precisely as follows: A_L is the average of V_L and P_L. For example, suppose (a) it is determined from the Auding Accuracy Level Test, AALT, that an individual is at the tenth-grade level in verbal knowledge, $V_L = 10$, and (b) it is determined from the Pronunciation Level Test, PLT, that this individual is at the fourth-grade level in pronunciation knowledge, $P_L = 4$; then, this individual would be at the seventh-grade level in rauding accuracy, $A_L = 7$, because 10 plus 4 divided by 2 is 7. Notice that educators have little or no control over the accuracy level of students, except by their influence upon their verbal level and their pronunciation level, because V_L and P_L determine A_L.

It should be noted that A_L is another proximal cause of P_L, that is, A_L and P_L have a reciprocally causal relationship not depicted in Figure 1-5 given in Chapter 1. It turns out that P_LWords equal A_LWords plus c_kWords; A_LWords are those P_LWords that can be pronounced because they are raudamatized words and c_kWords are those P_LWords that are not raudamatized but can be pronounced from pure cipher knowledge. When c_kWords are scaled into GE units, this construct is called pure cipher knowledge and is symbolized as c_k; P_L is also equal to the average of A_L and c_k. Therefore, P_L is influenced by A_L which in turn is influenced by V_L; as noted earlier, this makes V_L a distal cause of P_L via the causal influence V_L has upon A_L.

R_L, or rate level, is similar to the traditional concept of the normal reading rate of an individual expressed in GE units. R_L can be measured by the relatively constant rate at which individuals read texts that are relatively easy for them, $A_L > D_L$. There is a great deal of research data supporting the constancy of reading rate, or R_L, when (a) individuals are asked to read normally, (b) the text is relatively easy, (c) rate is measured in standard words per minute, Wpm, and (d) the individuals know that there will be no tests given on what was read. There are also research data involving text processing which show that individuals do vary their reading rate, but this research has involved learning processes and memorizing processes, not typical reading or the rauding process. Furthermore, earlier research data involving latency of isolated word recognition has suggested that individuals recognize words faster when they are given with more context. However, under typical reading situations involving relatively easy text, individuals reach a limit with respect to how fast they can accurately comprehend so that variations in text difficulty, redundancy, or word frequency have little or no effect on typical reading rate.

One of the reasons that reading rate is constant for individuals during typical reading is probably because their eye movements have become habituated at the rauding rate. These rhythmic eye movements are called apping; they involve a fixation upon almost every word during the rauding process, which allows every word to be perceived, lexically accessed, semantically encoded, and sententially integrated; apping allows printed words in sentences to be comprehended just as fast as when they are auded, or just as fast as when each word is presented in the center of a computer screen for a length of time equal to the individual's rauding rate. Another reason why individuals tend to read relatively easy text at a constant rate is because all of these words have been raudamatized by the individual. That is, each of these words has been overlearned to asymptote, so the word can be processed no faster without losing accuracy of comprehension. Even poor readers can successfully operate their rauding process on relatively easy text at their rauding rate because all of the words in this text have been raudamatized—overlearned due to numerous practice trials. Raudamatized words are audamatized words that have been practiced in print well beyond the point where they can be recognized without much attention, that is, well beyond automaticity.

An indicant of R_L would be the speed at which a list of raudamatized words can be read; traditional measures of decoding speed would likely provide a good indicant of R_L because those measures usually involve the speed at which a list of known words can be read. Previous research on the causal model has used the Rate Level Test, RLT, as a measure of R_L; it measures how fast the words that belong in easy sentences can be chosen—scaled into GE units. Another good objective measure of R_L is the fastest rate at which relatively easy text can be read aloud, scaled into GE units.

R_L also has two proximal causes and they are pronunciation level and cognitive speed level. The theory that P_L and C_s determine R_L can be summarized and expressed precisely as follows: R_L is the average of P_L and C_s. For example, suppose (a) it is determined from the Pronunciation Level Test, PLT, that an individual is at the fourth grade level in pronunciation knowledge, P_L = 4, and (b) it is determined from the Alphabet Rate Test, ART, that this individual is at the second-grade level in cognitive speed, $C_s = 2$, then, this individual would be at the third grade level in rauding rate, $R_L = 3$, because 4 plus 2 divided by 2 is 3. Notice that educators have little or no control over the rate level of a student, except by their influence upon their pronunciation level; because P_L and C_s determine R_L, and C_s cannot be influenced by educators, this means that educators have to increase P_L if they want to increase rate level, R_L.

Reading Achievement. The two constructs just described, accuracy level and rate level, determine the reading achievement of a student. The traditional concept of reading achievement has been refined, upgraded, and replaced in the causal model by rauding efficiency level, which is symbolized by E_L and referred to as "efficiency level." E_L is the highest level of text difficulty, D_L, that can be accurately comprehended when the text is presented at a rate that is equal to the difficulty level, that is, $R_L = D_L$. For example, individuals with $E_L = 9$ can accurately comprehend text at the ninth-grade level of difficulty, $D_L = 9$, when it is presented for a length of time that is equal to a ninth-grade reading rate, $R_L = 9$. Indicants of E_L can be obtained from traditional standardized tests of reading comprehension such as the Comprehension section of the Nelson-Denny Reading Test or the Comprehension section of the Iowa Test of Basic Skills. Previous research on the causal model has used the Rauding Efficiency Level Test, RELT, as a direct measure of E_L; it involves answering comprehension questions after reading passages at varying levels of difficulty at varying rates such that $R_L = D_L$.

The direct causal impact that accuracy level and rate level have upon efficiency level can be summarized and expressed precisely as follows: E_L is the average of A_L and R_L. For example, using the values from the two previous examples, $A_L = 7$ and $R_L = 3$, then $E_L = 5$ because 7 plus 3 divided by 2 is 5. Notice that the rauding accuracy level of an individual, $A_L = 7$, and the rauding rate level of the individual, $R_L = 3$, completely determine the reading achievement of the individual, or $E_L = 5$; A_L and R_L are called secondary causes of E_L.

It should not go unnoticed that V_L, P_L, and C_s also completely determine E_L. In the previous example, $V_L = 10$, $P_L = 4$, and $C_s = 2$ completely determined reading achievement, or $E_L = 5$; V_L, P_L, and C_s are called primary causes of E_L. Remember also that the proximal causes of V_L, P_L, and C_s are called the six root causes of reading achievement; they are as follows: (a) teaching/learning, T/L, directed toward V_L, (b) verbal aptitude, g_v, (c) teaching/learning, T/L, directed toward P_L, (d) pronunciation aptitude, g_p, (e) age, and (f) cognitive speed aptitude, g_s.

Modified Causal Model

The causal model of reading achievement needs to be modified when individuals have become advanced readers. This means that the causal model does not work exactly as it was described earlier for individuals who have reached the eight grade level for verbal knowledge and pronunciation knowledge ($V_L \geq 8.0$ and $P_L \geq 8.0$). It is hypothesized that all advanced readers ($V_L \geq 8.0$ and $P_L \geq 8.0$) are above raudamaticity so P_L is not a causal factor for them, and $A_L = V_L$. Because P_L is no longer a proximal cause of A_L, then V_L becomes the only proximal cause of A_L, so that $A_L = V_L$. This means that there is a reciprocally causal relationship between V_L and A_L for advanced readers.

P_L also drops out as a proximal cause of R_L for advanced readers; individuals keep learning new words as college students but they are not likely to keep increasing their rauding rate. There is a theoretical limit at which learning new sounds that are associated with new letter patterns increases the raudamatized asymptote for all words. Stated differently, increases in P_L no longer results in increases in pure decoding speed, d_s, after the eighth grade level is reached. This means that P_L is no longer a proximal cause of either A_L or R_L for advanced readers.

When students become developmentally mature, or adults, then age is no longer is a proximal cause of C_s. Therefore, for advanced readers who are adults, g_s and C_s become synonymous, and C_s is the only proximal cause of R_L, such as $R_L = C_s$.

This means that for adults who are advanced readers, P_L is no longer a primary cause of reading achievement, leaving only V_L and C_s as primary causes. Increasing verbal knowledge automatically increases rauding accuracy level because $A_L = V_L$. R_L cannot be increased because it is determined solely by C_s, and C_s has reached its developmental limit. For advanced readers, the only way that educators can improve their reading achievement, or E_L, is by increasing their verbal knowledge, V_L.

Diagnosis

The causal model is also helpful for diagnosing reading problems, or determining the causes of low reading achievement. Those individuals who have low reading achievement for their age are called poor readers; the causal model can be used to diagnose the disabilities of poor readers. Individuals with disabilities were described as those who are 2 GEs or more below their grade level in A_L, R_L, V_L, P_L, or C_s.

Poor readers (low E_L for age) are likely to be disabled in rauding accuracy level, rauding rate level, or both A_L and R_L. Because V_L and P_L are causal for A_L, this means that those individuals who are DisabledA_L are likely to be DisabledV_L, DisabledP_L, or DisabledV_LP_L. Because P_L and C_s are causal for R_L, this means that those individuals who are DisabledR_L are likely to be DisabledP_L, DisabledC_s, or DisabledP_LC_s. Because V_L, P_L, and C_s are causal for A_L and R_L, this also means that those individuals who are DisabledA_LR_L are likely to be DisabledV_LP_L, DisabledP_LC_s, DisabledV_LC_s, or Disabled$V_LP_LC_s$. Notice that there are several kinds of disabilities and many possible combinations of disabilities. However, if an individual is disabled in V_L, then special teaching and learning activities designed to increase verbal knowledge can be administered to remediate this particular disability. If the individual is disabled in P_L, then special teaching and learning activities designed to increase pronunciation knowledge can be administered to remediate this particular disability. If the individual is disabled in C_s, then there is no educational intervention that can be administered to remediate this particular disability.

Individuals who are disabled in V_L are not likely to make quick gains in V_L due to remedial treatment if they have a low verbal aptitude, low g_v. An individual with a low verbal aptitude can be described as being handicapped, that is, Handicapped/g_v. Similarly, individuals who are disabled in P_L are not likely to make quick gains in P_L due to a remedial treatment if they have a low pronunciation aptitude, low g_p. An individual with a low pronunciation aptitude can also be described as being handicapped, that is, Handicapped/g_p. Those individuals who are disabled in C_s are automatically handicapped in cognitive speed, Handicapped/g_s, and are not likely to make quick gains due to any remedial treatment.

Mild dyslexics are defined as individuals who are Handicapped/g_p but are not Handicapped/g_v. Notice that mild dyslexics are not verbally handicapped but they are pronunciation handicapped. This means that they are likely to learn verbal knowledge quite normally (make normal yearly gains in V_L) but they are likely to learn pronunciation knowledge slowly (make below normal gains in P_L).

Severe dyslexics are defined as individuals who are Handicapped/g_pg_s but are not Handicapped/g_v. Notice that severe dyslexics are not verbally handicapped but they are handicapped in both pronunciation and cognitive speed. This means that they might learn verbal knowledge normally (make normal yearly gains in V_L), but they are likely to learn pronunciation knowledge extremely slowly because they are handicapped in both pronunciation and cognitive speed.

It is theoretically possible to remediate both mild dyslexics and severe dyslexics by helping them to reach a level of reading achievement that is not below average for their age. By diagnosing the specific disabilities and specific handicaps of poor readers, using the causal model, it seems to be more likely that an effective remedial treatment can be prescribed, and a more realistic estimate of time required for remediation can be given.

Less Important Factors

Introduction. There are a number of traditional factors, concepts, and measures that have not been included as causal constructs in the causal model, such as intelligence, volume of reading, pseudoword knowledge, reading comprehension, the reading process, fluency, and automaticity. Each of these less important factors will be discussed in turn.

Intelligence. Not included in this causal model is any factor directly related to what is typically measured by intelligence tests. IQ scores determined from intelligence tests represent an average score over a battery of cognitive ability factors. This battery often includes an indicant of verbal aptitude, or g_v, but this battery usually does not include an indicant of pronunciation aptitude, g_p, or an indicant of cognitive speed aptitude, g_s. An IQ score is ordinarily an average of aptitudes and achievements that is not highly related to any of the three specific aptitudes that cause high and low reading achievement, namely, g_v, g_p, and g_s. This means that intelligence, as it is typically measured, does not belong in the causal model because it is a global factor that does not have a substantial effect upon high and low reading achievement.

Many tests of intelligence, or cognitive abilities, include measures of fluid intelligence, Gf, and crystallized intelligence, Gc. Gf is not an important factor causing high and low reading achievement, whereas Gc is indescriminable from reading achievement, or E_L.

Volume of Reading. A second factor that is not directly represented in the causal model is volume of reading, or print exposure. This factor was included in an earlier version of the causal model, but it has been omitted in this latest version because the evidence obtained from research was not supportive. It seems more likely that reading achievement causes a higher volume of reading, rather than a higher volume of reading being a cause of higher reading achievement. When students are encouraged to read more library books, during periods of uninterrupted sustained silent reading, for example, it is likely that they will choose to read relatively easy books. Because these books are not likely to include any unknown words, neither V_L nor P_L can be increased.

Pseudowords. A third factor not directly represented in the causal model is the ability to pronounce pseudowords. However, the pronunciation of these kinds of words has not been completely ignored in the model. The accuracy of pronunciation of increasingly difficult pseudowords is a measure of pure decoding knowledge, and has been symbolized as d_k. When d_k is expressed in GE units, as is often the case for standardized word attack tests, it has been hypothesized that pronunciation level, P_L, is equal to the average of d_k and A_L. So, the number of pronounceamatized words is the average of raudamatized words and pseudomatized words when all three are expressed in GE units, that is, P_L, A_L, and d_k.

Pseudoword pronunciation accuracy, d_k, has not been included as one of the main factors affecting high and low reading achievement, or E_L, because d_k is a component part of P_L which *is* one of the main factors affecting reading achievement, or E_L. Yet, one of the most important contributions of this causal model is the hypothesized connections between the accuracy of pronouncing pseudowords, d_k, and the other three variables that are directly represented in the causal model—V_L, P_L, and A_L. That is, there are mathematically lawful relationships among the following:

(a) level of general knowledge, or verbal level, V_L,
(b) reading level, level of reading comprehension, reading vocabulary level, or accuracy level, A_L,
(c) level of word identification, level of spelling knowledge, or pronunciation level, P_L, and
(d) level of word attack, level of pseudoword decoding, or pure decoding knowledge, d_k.

These lawful relationships were expressed earlier as follows:

$$P_L = (A_L + d_k)/2, \text{ and} \qquad \text{(from Equation 7-4)}$$
$$A_L = (V_L + P_L)/2 \qquad \text{(from Equation 10-3)}$$

For example, the above values of V_L, A_L, P_L, and d_k can be estimated from the following measures:

(a) GE score on the General Information test from the Peabody Individual Achievement Test as an indirect measure of V_L,
(b) GE score on Passage Comprehension test from the Woodcock Reading Mastery Tests as an indirect measure of A_L,
(c) GE score on the Word Identification test from the Woodcock Reading Mastery Tests as an indirect measure of P_L, and
(d) GE score on the Word Attack test from the Woodcock Reading Mastery Tests as an indirect measure of d_k.

If two of the values of V_L, A_L, P_L, and d_k are known, then the other two can be mathematically determined from Equations 7-4 and 10-3. For example, suppose it can be determined that a fifth grader is at the third-grade level for word identification ($P_L = 3$) and at the second-grade level for word attack ($d_k = 2$). It can be determined from Equation 7-4 that this student is likely to be at the fourth-grade level for reading level ($A_L = 4$). Then, it can be determined from Equation 10-3 that this student is at the fifth-grade level for listening comprehension ($V_L = 5$). Therefore, pronouncing pseudowords accurately has a mathematically precise relationship to reading level, or A_L, but d_k is best considered as not being a proximal cause of A_L.

These relationships involved the accuracy of pronouncing a list of difficulty-ordered pseudowords. The speed at which pseudowords can be pronounced has been called pure decoding speed, and symbolized as d_s. This factor has been incorporated into the causal model as one of the components of rauding rate level. That is, R_L is theorized to be composed of two parts, d_s and C_s. This means that the rate at which individuals can operate their rauding process is determined by one factor that is highly influenced by learning, d_s, and another factor that is independent of learning, C_s. Furthermore, it has been hypothesized that $d_s = P_L$, in GE units, so that increasing the number of words that can be identified causes an equivalent increase in pure decoding speed.

Notice that pronouncing pseudowords has indirect connections to the causal model (a) via accuracy of pseudoword pronunciation, d_k, being a component of P_L, and (b) via speed of pseudoword pronunciation, d_s, being a component of R_L.

Reading Comprehension. It should not go unnoticed that the causal model focuses directly upon improving reading achievement, or E_L, and does not focus directly upon improving reading comprehension. The concept of reading comprehension is usually somewhat vague but it often means the accuracy of comprehension, A, that is associated with reading text for a minute, or longer. There are several factors that influence the accuracy of comprehension, A, in those situations: (a) the accuracy level of the individual, A_L, (b) the rate level of the individual, R_L, (c) the difficulty level of the text, D_L, (d) the length of the text being read, T_p, and (e) the time allowed for reading the text, t. Once the text is selected and the time limit allowed for reading is fixed, then the accuracy of text comprehension, A, depends solely upon the rauding accuracy level and rauding rate level of the individual, A_L and R_L. So, the two factors that educators can have some effect upon in this situation are A_L and R_L. Therefore, A_L and R_L directly determine accuracy of text comprehension, A, and A_L and R_L also directly determine reading achievement, or E_L, in the causal model

When A_L and R_L are known, then (a) reading achievement is determined according to a mathematical average (either Equation 1-1 or Equation 10-2), and (b) the accuracy of comprehension of a piece of text, A, can also be determined by a mathematical formula (see Appendix C). This means that the two proximal causes of reading achievement, or E_L, are also the same two proximal causes of the accuracy of comprehension of text, A. Therefore, when educators are doing their best to improve reading achievement during a year of schooling, they are also doing their best to improve the accuracy of comprehension during a minute or more of text reading. A_L and R_L are two constructs which explain growth in reading achievement during a year of reading or schooling, and these same two constructs also explain accuracy of reading comprehension during 1 minute of reading text; A_L and R_L determine E_L, and A_L and R_L also determine A. Therefore, reading comprehension has been incorporated into the causal model indirectly via A_L and R_L being the two proximal causes of accuracy of text comprehension, A.

The Reading Process. Earlier research in reading has often focused upon "the" reading process, as if there was only one reading process. The causal model is based upon the theory that there are many reading processes that could be involved when individuals are reading texts. However, there are five basic reading processes, called scanning, skimming, rauding, learning, and memorizing. The one process that is typically or normally used by individuals is the rauding process; it involves the three components for processing each word in text—lexical access, semantic encoding, and sentential integrating. Notice that the rauding process involves understanding the complete thoughts in the sentences of text by processing each word through the same three components which culminate with sentential integration, or sentence comprehension. Everyone uses these same three components when the rauding process is operating. Furthermore, when individuals are given relatively easy text to read, then they are likely to operate their rauding process (see Appendix B). The words in relatively easy text should be raudamatized words, that is, words that have been overlearned to an asymptote, which is the individual's rauding rate. This means that all individuals are likely to use the same rauding process when they are asked to read relatively easy text because all of these words have been raudamatized and can be accurately comprehended at the rauding rate.

Given this view of the rauding process, it follows that both good and poor readers successfully operate their rauding process on relatively easy material. This means that it would be fruitless to look for a broken or malfunctioning reading process to explain why some readers are good (high E_L for age) and some readers are poor (low E_L for age). The reason there are poor readers does not have anything to do with a malfunctioning reading process. Indeed, poor readers are likely to comprehend text quite well (a) when the text they read is relatively easy, $A_L > D_L$, and (b) when relatively easy text is read aloud to them. The reason why there are poor readers (low E_L for age) is because they have had poor teaching and learning experiences with respect to verbal knowledge or pronunciation knowledge, or they have low g_v, g_p, or g_s. Stated differently, poor readers have low E_L because (a) they have a low verbal knowledge level, (b) they have a low pronunciation level, or (c) they have a low cognitive speed level. Finally, it can also be said that poor readers have a low E_L because they have a low rauding accuracy level or a low rauding rate level.

The way to help poor readers become better readers is to (a) help them increase their verbal knowledge level and their pronunciation knowledge level so they can accurately read text at a higher difficulty level (increase A_L), or (b) help them increase their pronunciation level so they can increase their rauding rate (increase R_L). If we are successful in helping poor readers become good readers (increased E_L), then they will still be operating the same rauding process the same way they did when they were poor readers. The difference will be that they will be operating it faster than they were before and they will be operating it more accurately on texts at higher levels of difficulty.

The A_L and R_L constructs in the causal model also help explain and predict what happens during 1 second of reading, or what happens during the fraction of a second that an individual looks at a word during a reading process. If reading involves text that is relatively hard, $D_L > A_L$, then normal or typical reading is not likely to be involved. So, the A_L of the individual can be compared to the D_L of the text to determine whether typical reading is likely to be involved during 1 second of reading; this typical reading involves the rauding process. If a word is not presented long enough for the individual to lexically access it, semantically encode it, and sententially integrate it, then the rauding process cannot be involved. The amount of time needed in milliseconds to operate the rauding process on a standard length word can be determined by dividing rauding rate, in Words per minute units, into 60,000. For example, if an individual has a rauding rate level of 16, that is, $R_L = 16$, then this can be converted into a rauding rate of 267 Wpm (see Appendix D). Then, 60,000 is divided by 267 to give 225; this individual would need 225 milliseconds to raud this standard length word. If less than 225 milliseconds were allowed, this individual would not be able to operate his/her rauding process. Notice that information derived from A_L and R_L can be used to determine whether the rauding process is possible during research involving 1 second or less of reading. The A_L and R_L constructs are therefore relevant to the most important reading process, called the rauding process, which involves 1 second of reading, 1 minute of reading, and 1 year of reading.

Fluency. The traditional concept of fluency has not been included in the causal model. The concept of a fluent reader has been upgraded and replaced by the concept of rauding. When individuals are engaged in the rauding process during silent reading they are ordinarily understanding the thoughts in sentences as they read the words at their rauding rate, so they may be said to be reading fluently, or rauding. However, fluency is usually associated with accurate oral pronunciation at a reasonable rate, along with proper expression, so that a listener could easily comprehend also. A high quality of oral rendition is not directly relevant to the causal model, so the concept of fluent reading, has been replaced by the concept of rauding, which is the rauding process being accurately executed at the rauding rate when reading silently.

The concept of fluency has also been replaced by Maximum Oral Reading Rate as a measure of rauding rate level, R_L. That is, individuals who can read relatively easy text aloud very quickly, for their age, are also likely to be considered as fluent readers.

Automaticity. The concept of automaticity has been replaced in the causal model. The original automaticity idea referred to the ability of an individual to read text fluently without extra attention being directed toward word recognition. The overload on attention supposedly distracted individuals from comprehension. This original concept of automaticity was supposedly an attribute of individuals, that is, some individuals had more automaticity than others or some individuals could learn to process text with a minimum of attention paid to the letters and words.

Several researchers have upgraded the automaticity concept in recent years by pointing out that it is the words that are automatized, not the individuals. An automatized word is one that can be recognized without excessive attention demands. That is, each individual has some words that are automatized and some that are not automatized. Furthermore, several researchers have pointed out that an automatized word still can be recognized at a faster rate if it is practiced beyond being the point where it is recognized with little attention.

These concepts of automaticity and automatized words have been replaced by the concept of raudamatized words. Raudamatized words are those words that have been practiced and overlearned to an asymptote, which is the rauding rate of the individual. Further practice on these raudamatized words will not result in their being recognized any faster during the rauding process. Raudamatized words are therefore automatized words that have been practiced to a higher rate. This means that raudamatized words have nothing directly to do with attention demands because they have been practiced to a much higher rate of recognition than is required for being regarded as being automatized. Furthermore, raudamatized words do not represent an attribute of the individual, but represent a property of a particular word for a particular individual.

Another theoretical construct in the causal model that has connections to automaticity is cognitive speed level. As noted earlier, C_s is measured by the fastest naming speed for a series of overlearned stimuli, such as colors, objects, letters, and digits; researchers using these measures have often contended that they have been investigating automaticity. C_s is an attribute of the individual, and therefore could be regarded as a measure of automaticity as it was originally conceived.

It can be seen that automatized words and automaticity have been replaced in the causal model by raudamatized words and cognitive speed.

Reading Instruction

Introduction. The causal model of reading achievement has stimulated a new approach to the teaching of reading, or reading instruction; it is called the rauding approach and it will be summarized next. Then, this new approach will be compared to other approaches, namely, whole-language, phonics, decoding, skills, and balanced.

Rauding Approach. The rauding approach has been developed to produce the highest gains in reading achievement each year in school during the early and middle grades. The type of instruction given to an individual under this approach depends upon whether the individual is below or at raudamaticity. Those individuals who are below raudamaticity, should be given raudamaticity training. Those individuals who have reached raudamaticity, or are said to be at raudamaticity, are given vocabulary training. Therefore, the rauding approach to reading instruction consists of raudamaticity training and vocabulary training.

Raudamaticity training involves the raudamatization of audamatized words. This means that words whose meanings are known when listening are practiced until they can be recognized quickly in print. This practice is done in two steps. Step 1 involves learning to spell the audamatized word. Step 2 involves learning to recognize the correct spelling rapidly. For these individuals who are below raudamaticity, raudamaticity training has no effect on V_L because all the words involved in the training are already audamatized words. However, each word that is raudamatized during raudamaticity training will result in a small increment in P_L and A_L, which in turn will result in an increment in reading achievement, or E_L. The only practical way to administer this training efficiently, is by using a computer.

As soon as individuals have raudamatized all of their audamatized words, raudamaticity training is stopped and vocabulary training is started. Vocabulary training in the rauding approach involves learning the meaning of new words plus raudamaticity training. During this training, a new word is defined and used in the context of a sentence. At the same time that the meaning of the word is learned, the spelling of the word is learned and it is also learned to be recognized quickly. The only practical way to administer vocabulary training efficiently, is also by using a computer.

For those individuals at raudamaticity, the vocabulary training just described will increase verbal knowledge, pronunciation knowledge, and accuracy level. When the meaning of a new word is learned, V_L increases, and when this word is raudamatized, P_L and A_L increases. Therefore, vocabulary training should result in simultaneous increases in V_L, P_L, and A_L. However, vocabulary training needs to be supplemented with large volumes of matched rauding (reading involving $D_L = A_L$), so that these newly learned words are likely to be encountered in texts. Experiencing these newly learned words in texts should (a) provide practice that mitigates against forgetting, and (b) provide breadth for the meaning of the word so it can be rauded in many different contexts.

The rauding approach is recommended for 30 minutes a day starting in first grade, or as soon as students have learned the alphabetic principle. The first goal of this approach is to raudamatize 6 new words each day of school. The second goal is to help a student become an intermediate reader by the end of grade 2 or the beginning of grade 3, that is, achieve $V_L = 3.0$ and $P_L = 3.0$. The third and most important goal, is to help a student become an advanced reader as soon as possible, at least by the end of grade 7 or the beginning of grade 8, that is, achieve $V_L = 8.0$ and $P_L = 8.0$. As soon as a student has become an advanced reader, the individual no longer needs special help with reading achievement; at this point, the rauding approach has achieved its goal and the 30 minutes a day of instruction should be stopped. Notice that the rauding approach has been designed to be appropriate for all beginning and intermediate readers, but it is not appropriate for advanced readers.

Another important feature of the rauding approach is that is does not encourage students to guess at the pronunciation of a word, either from context or from cipher knowledge. These guesses are likely to be wrong, and this requires relearning. More importantly, asking students to read materials that contain unknown words makes reading frustratingly difficult. Instead, students taught under the rauding approach are ordinarily asked to read texts which contain words which have undergone raudamaticity training, and need to be practiced in context. If a student happens to encounter an unknown word, then the student should be told how to pronounce it. The rauding approach has been designed to make reading easy, fast, and fun, not hard, slow, and frustrating.

Next, the rauding approach will be compared to several other more traditional approaches to the teaching of reading—whole-language, phonics, decoding, skills, and balanced.

Whole-Language Approach. In the whole-language (WL) approach, students are given very little instruction relevant to learning the alphabetic principle, a prerequisite for the rauding approach. Students in typical WL classrooms are never asked to learn about words in isolation, as is done in the rauding approach. A fundamental part of the WL approach is giving students texts to read which include unknown words, and then teaching them to guess at the meaning of those words from context; this kind of instruction is to be completely avoided, if possible, under the rauding approach so that reading is made easy, fast, and fun. The WL approach is especially appropriate for the early grades, whereas the rauding approach is especially appropriate for students in both the early grades and the middle grades. The WL approach puts an emphasis on the meaning of words, and de-emphasizes any instruction which focuses upon the correct pronunciation of words in isolation; WL is a meaning-emphasis approach, not a code-emphasis approach. In comparison, the rauding approach is a code-emphasis approach for those students below raudamaticity (increase P_L), and it is a meaning-emphasis approach for those students above raudamaticity (increase V_L). The WL approach encourages writing but does not emphasize the correct spelling of words, whereas the rauding approach emphasizes the correct spelling of words and also emphasizes the rapid recognition of the correct spellings of words.

Phonics Approach. The phonics approach is a code-emphasis approach that typically involves learning abstract rules about the spelling of words and their pronunciation. The phonics approach tries to teach students how to pronounce unknown words by helping them try to figure out how they should be pronounced from their spellings. In contrast, the rauding approach does not ask students to pronounce unknown words; instead, students are told how to pronounce each new word, and they learn to recognize the word from practice or experience with its own particular spelling. In the rauding approach, students implicitly learn cipher knowledge from learning to spell more and more words, and they are not asked to learn abstract rules about spellings-to-sound correspondences. The phonics approach makes reading slow and frustratingly difficult for most students, whereas the rauding approach should make the reading of text easy, fast, and fun because the words being read have already undergone raudamaticity training. The phonics approach is directed toward increasing P_L for all students, whereas the rauding approach is directed toward increasing P_L for students below raudamaticity and increasing V_L and P_L for students at raudamaticity. The phonics approach does not put an emphasis on the correct spelling of words nor the rapid recognition of correct spellings, whereas correct spellings and rapid recognition is fundamental in the rauding approach. The phonics approach is only appropriate in the lower grades whereas the rauding approach is appropriate in both the lower and middle grades for most students.

The Decoding Approach. The decoding approach is similar to the phonics approach in that both are code-emphasis, but the decoding approach focuses upon learning cipher knowledge implicitly, rather than by explicitly taught rules. Both the decoding approach and the rauding approach emphasize learning the correct spelling of words. The decoding approach, however, emphasizes the guessing of unknown words as a strategy for learning the cipher, whereas the rauding approach strives to eliminate this kind of guessing. The decoding approach has as its main goal, an increase in P_L for all readers, whereas the rauding approach only has this goal for students below raudamaticity. The decoding approach disregards learning the meaning of new words, which is the emphasis of the rauding approach for those students above raudamaticity (increase V_L and P_L). The decoding approach is only appropriate in the early grades for students who are trying to become intermediate readers, whereas the rauding approach is also appropriate for students in the middle grades who are trying to become advanced readers.

Skills Approach. The skills approach attempts to teach decoding, spelling, and vocabulary, and is thereby similar to the rauding approach. However, the skills approach ordinarily involves worksheets, whereas the rauding approach uses computers. Also, the rauding approach is very systematic in the sense that help with decoding, spelling, and vocabulary is individually administered so that decoding and spelling help is given for audamatized words, and vocabulary help is given for words that are not audamatized. The skills approach also emphasizes teaching comprehension skills, such as prediction activities, metacognitive activities, and main idea activities; this is not done in the rauding approach because these activities are not likely to increase V_L, P_L, A_L, R_L, or E_L for beginning or intermediate readers.

Balanced Approach. The balanced approach has much in common with the rauding approach in that it attempts to be both meaning-emphasis and code-emphasis—trying to include the best from the whole-language approach and the phonics approach. The balanced approach eliminates teaching children to guess at words only from context. It also eliminates the learning of explicit phonics rules. However, the balanced approach retains the guessing of words using decoding knowledge, so it is quite different from the rauding approach in this respect. The balanced approach does emphasize the correct spelling of words, and learning to recognize words rapidly, but it does not advocate doing this individually with the systematic efficiency afforded by a computer. The balanced approach is limited to the early grades, and it makes no systematic instructional decisions based upon whether or not a student has reached raudamaticity.

The balanced approach is most effective in kindergarten and first grade for those students who are learning the rudiments of the cipher, that is, learning to be aware of letters, learning to be aware of phonemes, and learning the correspondences between letters and sounds in words. Once students have learned the alphabetic principle, then the rauding approach can be used 30 minutes a day to supplement the balanced approach. Once students have reached raudamaticity, then the balanced approach is no longer appropriate. So, in the early grades the best approach seems to be a balanced/rauding approach until raudamaticity is reached. For all students who are above raudamaticity, the balanced approach is not appropriate whereas the rauding approach continues to be appropriate until a student becomes an advanced reader.

Rauding Theory Constructs

The development of the causal model of reading achievement has involved the creation of new rauding theory constructs and symbols, such as d_k and d_s. Given below is a list of 16 theoretical constructs and their symbols, along with corresponding traditional concepts and measured variables.

(a) E_L, rauding efficiency level,
reading achievement,
general reading ability,
(b) A_L, rauding accuracy level,
reading level,
reading vocabulary,
score on an individualized passage comprehension test,
score on a time-limited word identification test,
(c) R_L, rauding rate level,
score on a reading rate test,
decoding speed for a list of easy words,
fastest rate of reading relatively easy text aloud,
(d) V_L, verbal knowledge level,
level of listening comprehension,
listening vocabulary,
score on a general knowledge test given auditorily,
(e) P_L, pronunciation knowledge level,
score on a word identification test,
level of spelling knowledge,
orthographic knowledge,
(f) C_s, cognitive speed level,
naming speed,
thinking speed,
verbal speed,

(g) c_k, pure cipher knowledge,
accuracy of correctly pronouncing unknown real words,
(h) d_k, pure decoding knowledge,
accuracy of pronouncing pseudowords,
score on an untimed word attack test,
(i) d_s, pure decoding speed,
rate of pronouncing pseudowords,
(j) D_L, difficulty level of text,
score from using a readability formula on text,
(k) A, accuracy of text comprehension,
(l) R, rate of text comprehension,
time allowed to read text,
average rate of reading text of known length,
(m) E, efficiency of text comprehension,
(n) A_r, rauding accuracy,
percentage comprehension when reading text once,
(o) R_r, rauding rate,
typical silent rate of reading text once,
(p) E_r, rauding efficiency, and
efficiency when reading text once.

This list of 44 concepts, measured variables, and constructs are lawfully related; they have been organized and interrelated via mathematical formulas involving the 16 symbols for the theoretical constructs. The specific mathematical formulas involved are as follows: (a) Equations 10-2, 10-3, and 10-4 which interrelate E_L, A_L, R_L, V_L, P_L, and C_s, (b) Equations 7-2, 7-3, and 7-4 which interrelate P_L, A_L, c_k, and d_k, (c) Equation 11-3 which interrelates R_L, d_s, and C_s, (d) Equation 2-2 which interrelates A_r, A_L, and D_L, (e) Equation B-1 (from Appendix B) which interrelates E, A, and R, and (f) Equations C-1, C-3, and C-4 (from Appendix C) which interrelate A, A_r, R_r, and R.

Again, it appears that most of the important constructs and variables involved in reading are lawfully connected via mathematical formulas; this allows rauding theory to be more readily falsified when it is not valid. For example, by solving equations algebraically, it can be determined that the reading level of students in GE units, A_L, is equal to 0.67 times their listening vocabulary in GE units, V_L, plus 0.33 times their accuracy of pronouncing a difficulty-ordered list of pseudowords in GE units, d_k. Another example would be a student at the ninth-grade level of listening and the seventh-grade level of word identification who is given 8.1 minutes to read a fifth-grade level passage containing 1,667 standard words; this student will comprehend 56% of the sentences in this passage—provided that this student has a rate of pronouncing pseudowords at the second-grade level and a rate of naming randomized letters of the alphabet at the sixth-grade level (see Table C-3 in Appendix C, Equation 10-3, and Equation 11-2).

Conclusions

This causal model, which describes the factors which cause high and low reading achievement, represents a challenge to many traditional ideas in reading. Those challenges are summarized in the list of conclusions which follow:

(a) there is nothing wrong with the typical reading process of poor readers because they use the same sentence comprehension process as good readers,
(b) beginning readers should not be asked to guess at the pronunciation of unknown words, whether from context or from phonics rules, because this guessing is likely to be wrong too often,
(c) beginning and intermediate readers should not be taught comprehension-strategy skills, or study skills, because these students should not be asked to read texts that are hard for them to comprehend,
(d) IQ should not be used to diagnose reading disabilities or dyslexia because it is not an important factor affecting reading achievement,
(e) a high volume of silent reading is a very poor way to increase the reading achievement of most students because too much time will be spent reading books that contain no new words,
(f) fluency should not be a goal of reading teachers because reading aloud with expression should be a goal of speech teachers,
(g) automaticity should be discontinued as an important concept in reading because (a) students cannot learn to be more automatic when reading, and (b) lack of attention capacity is not a cause of low reading achievement,
(h) traditional approaches to the teaching of reading, such as whole-language, phonics, skills, and balanced, will always be a cause of low reading achievement in certain students because these approaches fail to discriminate between those who need to learn how to pronounce more words and those who need to learn the meaning of more words, and
(i) students should be taught the correct spellings of the words they know when listening because this will help them to learn to read these words faster.

Forget Me Nots

Reading achievement has been upgraded by a theoretical construct which is called rauding efficiency level—symbolized as E_L. Efficiency level, E_L, also represents general reading ability and is similar to what is being measured by most standardized tests of reading comprehension.

A model has been developed to help explain the causes of high and low reading achievement, or E_L. According to this causal model, two secondary causes of high and low E_L are rauding accuracy level, A_L, and rauding rate level, R_L. The three primary causes of high and low E_L are verbal level, V_L, pronunciation level, P_L, and cognitive speed level, C_s. The six root causes of high and low E_L are (a) teaching and learning relevant to increasing verbal level, (b) verbal aptitude, (c) teaching and learning relevant to pronunciation level, (d) pronunciation aptitude, (f) age, and (g) cognitive speed aptitude. Individuals who are low in verbal aptitude, pronunciation aptitude, and cognitive speed aptitude have handicaps that are likely to cause reading disabilities that prevent high achievement in reading.

The rauding approach to reading instruction was stimulated by the causal model. This approach has been developed to improve two of the root causes in this model, namely, teaching and learning relevant to increasing verbal level plus teaching and learning relevant to increasing pronunciation level. If the rauding approach is used in grades 1 through 7, it is likely that more students will achieve at high levels, or become advanced readers, by the time they reach the eighth-grade. This approach uses a computer to help students learn to spell, pronounce, and quickly recognize all the words they know when listening; then, students are helped (a) to learn the meaning of new words, (b) learn how to pronounce and spell these new words, and (c) learn how to recognize quickly those new words when they are read.

The causal model just outlined, along with the rauding approach to reading instruction, are part of rauding theory. This theory strives to describe, explain, predict, and control the typical reading of individuals by interrelating the most important concepts, measured variables, and constructs using mathematical formulas. This theory of rauding is a theory of normal reading that can be used by researchers, teachers, and others to increase the number of advanced readers, that is, to lessen the number of low achievers in reading.

APPENDIX A

THE EARLIER CONSTRUCTS OF RAUDING THEORY

Table A-1 contains the most important theoretical constructs in rauding theory that existed prior to the development of the causal model presented in Chapter 1. Notice that efficiency level, E_L, which is the focus of the causal model, is listed in Table A-1 as an earlier research concept, along with accuracy level, A_L, and rate level, R_L.

Table A-1
Constructs from Earlier Rauding Theory Research with Symbols and Related Traditional Concepts

Symbol	*Construct*	*Related traditional concept*
D_L	Difficulty level	Readability of text
A	Accuracy of text comprehension	Percent comprehension of text
R	Rate of text comprehension	Average rate, or time allowed to read text
E	Efficiency of text comprehension	Text reading efficiency
A_r	Rauding accuracy	Individual's accuracy of comprehension (during time spent reading text once)
R_r	Rauding rate	Individual's typical rate of reading (during time spent reading text once)
E_r	Rauding efficiency	Individual's efficiency of reading (during time spent reading text once)
A_L	Rauding accuracy level	Individual's reading level in GE units (can be measured by standardized vocabulary tests)
R_L	Rauding rate level	Individual's typical reading rate in GE units (can be measured by standardized rate tests)
E_L	Rauding efficiency level	Individual's reading achievement, or general reading ability, in GE units (can be measured by standardized reading comprehension tests)
D_L-A_L	Relative difficulty	Difficulty of the text for the individual

The first construct in Table A-1, called difficulty level, D_L, is simply the readability of a piece of text, or a passage, in grade equivalent (GE) units. The last construct in the table is relative difficulty, D_L - A_L, and it is a measure of how difficult the material is for the particular individual reading it. If the relative difficulty, D_L - A_L, is positive (greater than 0), then the textual material is relatively hard ($D_L > A_L$), and if the relative difficulty is negative (less than 0) then the textual material is relatively easy ($D_L < A_L$). It should be noted that the relative easiness of textual material is the reverse, A_L - D_L, with positive values indicating relatively easy text, that is, text is relatively easy if $A_L > D_L$.

The relative difficulty of text (or relative easiness) is very important in rauding theory because individuals are not expected to be able to operate their rauding process successfully on relatively hard material, $D_L > A_L$. Individuals should not be given relatively hard material if the purpose of the research is to study the rauding process. Individuals can successfully operate their rauding process on relatively easy material because all of the words should be raudamatized words, that is, words that can be rauded at the rauding rate.

In prior research on rauding theory, individuals have been asked to read text and their accuracy of comprehension of that text has been measured; the percentage (or proportion) of sentences in the text that has been comprehended is called the accuracy of text comprehension, and this construct is symbolized as A. In this reading situation, rate of text comprehension (amount of text divided by the time to read the text) is symbolized as R, and the corresponding efficiency of text comprehension is symbolized as E. Sometimes, researchers have fixed time limits that do not allow individuals enough time to finish reading a piece of text, or they give them extra time so they can go back and reread some or all of the text. In these reading situations involving fixed time limits, it is helpful to have more precise constructs that refer to the comprehension that occurs during the first reading of text. For example, if an individual is only given enough time to finish half (50%) of the sentences in a piece of text—the accuracy of comprehension of the part of text that was read once may be 80% but the accuracy of comprehension of the entire piece of text may only be 40% (A = .40). So, a theoretical construct is needed that refers to the accuracy of comprehension that accompanies the rauding process; it is called rauding accuracy, and it is symbolized as A_r. In the example given above, $A_r = .80$. In these situations, the rate that the rauding process was executed is called the rauding rate, and it is symbolized as R_r; the efficiency that accompanied the rauding process is called rauding efficiency, and it is symbolized as E_r.

Notice in Table A-1 that when E, A, and R are accompanied by a subscript "r", then the construct refers to what happened during the time the rauding process was executed on the text that was covered. When E, A, and R are accompanied by a subscript "L" then the construct refers to a rather stable attribute of the reader that does not vary with the particular text being read, and is subject to substantial change or improvement only after months or a year of teaching or learning. When E, A, and R are not accompanied by a subscript, then the construct refers to a particular piece of text during the time allowed for reading, without regard for whether the rauding process was used to read the text once, and without regard for whether enough time was allowed to finish reading the piece of text.

When these theoretical constructs are used, then the relationships among them are lawful (see Appendix B) and mathematical equations can be used to predict the accuracy of comprehension (see Appendix C).

APPENDIX B

THE THREE LAWS OF RAUDING THEORY

There are three laws underlying rauding theory (Carver, 1981) and they will be reviewed in turn.

Law I is that *individuals attempt to comprehend thoughts in passages at a constant rate, called the rauding rate, unless they are influenced by situation-specific factors to change that rate.* Using symbols to represent constructs, this means that ordinarily $R = R_r$, or that the rate of comprehending a passage, R, is ordinarily the individual's rauding rate, R_r. When individuals are reading normally, their rate of comprehension of a passage, R, is typically the same rate as they operate their rauding process, R_r. On some occasions, individuals may shift gears (Carver, 1990a) to another reading process so that R is no longer equal to R_r, such as when (a) the instructions induce scanning, skimming, learning, or memorizing processes, (b) the objective consequences involve verbatim recall or a search for a targeted word rather than simply comprehending the complete thoughts in the sentences, or (c) the material is relatively hard, $D_L > A_L$. Also, the rate of comprehending, R, is not likely to equal the rauding rate, R_r, in research situations where individuals are not given enough time to finish reading the text, or they are given an unlimited amount of time so they can study the text, or read it more than once.

Law II is that *the efficiency of passage comprehension depends upon the accuracy of passage comprehension and the rate of passage comprehension.* Using symbols to represent constructs, Law II is:

$$E = AR \qquad \text{(B-1)}$$

The efficiency of comprehension, E, is the product of the accuracy of comprehension, A, and the rate of comprehension, R. For example, if an individual reads the sentences in a text at the rate of 20 standard sentences per minute (R = 20 Spm), and comprehends 80 out of 100 standard length sentences (A = .80), then this individual's efficiency of comprehension would be 16 standard sentences per minute (E = AR = .80 x 20 = 16).

Law III is that *the most efficient rate of comprehending thoughts in a passage is the rauding rate.* Using symbols to represent constructs, this means that when $R = R_r$, then $E_{max} = E_r$. When $R = R_r$, the rauding process is operating on the text at the rauding rate, and the efficiency which accompanies this rate, E_r, is the maximum possible efficiency, E_{max}. If the text is read by the individual at any other rate besides R_r, so that R is not equal to R_r, then the resulting efficiency of comprehension, E, will be less than E_r, or $E < E_r$. In other words, the rauding rate, R_r, is the optimal rate because the efficiency of comprehension, E, at all other rates besides R_r is lower.

A great deal of empirical evidence supports the above three laws (e.g., Carver, 1982, 1983, 1984, 1985a, 1985b), and most of this supporting research has been reviewed and summarized in later publications (Carver, 1990a, 1997).

APPENDIX C

THE EQUATIONS OF RAUDING THEORY

The equations of rauding theory (Carver, 1981) have been empirically validated (see Carver, 1990a, 1997), and they will be reviewed and updated in this appendix. These equations allow the accuracy of text comprehension, A, to be determined, or predicted.

The accuracy of text comprehension, A, is determined by rate, in the form of R and R_r, along with rauding accuracy, A_r. The equations for determining A will be presented under two time conditions, which are called "restricted" and "ample."

Under the restricted time condition, the individual does not have time to finish reading the text, that is, the average rate the text is presented for reading, R, is faster than the rauding rate of the reader, $R > R_r$. The equation for determining the accuracy of text comprehension under this restricted time condition is as follows:

$$A = A_r R_r (1/R) \qquad \text{(C-1)}$$

This equation may also be said to be appropriate when the time allowed to read the text (t) is less than the time needed to raud the text (t_r) at the individuals rauding rate, R_r. So, Equation C-1 is valid when $t < t_r$. The value of t_r is determined by obtaining the length of the text being read, that is, the number of thoughts in the passage (T_p), and then dividing by the rauding rate, R_r, of the individual; this means that $t_r = T_p/R_r$. The value of T_p is measured in standard length sentences and the value of R_r is measured in standard length sentences per minute so that rauding time, t_r, is in minutes. R is the average rate the text was presented for reading, or $R = T_p/t$.

A hypothetical example will now be given for using Equation C-1 under the restricted time condition. Suppose an individual is given a passage to read that contains 20 standard length sentences ($T_p = 20$). One standard length sentence is 16.67 standard words in length and a standard word is 6 character spaces in length, so this example passage is 333 standard words in length. Suppose the individual has a rauding rate of 14 Sentences per minute ($R_r = 14$ Spm). In this example, the amount of time the individual would need to read the passage once at his/her rauding rate would be determined as follows: $t_r = T_p/R_r = 20/14 = 1.42$ minutes. Also, suppose the individual is given 1.25 minutes to read the passage ($t = 1.25$). Because R is the length of the text divided by the time allowed to read the text (T_p/t), then in this example, R =

20/1.25 = 16, or 16 standard sentences per minute. This is an example of a restricted time condition ($t < t_r$), because the individual would need 1.42 minutes to finish reading the passage once, but would have to stop reading after 1.25 minutes, because t = 1.25. Restricted time conditions are also those where $R > R_r$, and R would be greater than R_r in this example, because R = 16 Spm and R_r = 14 Spm. In this example, let us also assume that the rauding accuracy of the individual is 80% for this particular piece of text (A_r = .80). Therefore, when A_r = .80, R_r = 14, and R = 16, then Equation C-1 becomes

$$A = (.80)(14)(1/16) = .70 \tag{C-2}$$

So, the accuracy of comprehension of these 20 sentences (or 333 Words) under this restricted time condition, would be 70%. Table C-1 contains a summary of this example explaining how the accuracy of text comprehension, A, can be determined under these restricted time conditions.

Under the ample time condition for reading text, the individual has more than enough time to finish reading the text, that is, $R < R_r$, or $t > t_r$. This means that the time allowed for reading, t, is greater than the time needed to finish the passage once at the individual's rauding rate, t_r, so the average rate of presenting the text is less than the rauding rate, $R < R_r$. Under all ample time conditions, wherein $R < R_r$ or $t > t_r$, the equation for determining the accuracy of text comprehension is:

$$A = (1/R)/[(1/R) + i], \tag{C-3}$$

where

$$i = (1/R_r)[(1/A_r) - 1] \tag{C-4}$$

The "i" in Equations C-3 and C-4 represents the inefficiency constant; it is the constant amount of inefficiency associated with having more than enough time to read a passage once at the rauding rate (Carver, 1977). The inefficiency constant is first calculated in Equation C-4, and then used in Equation C-3, along with R, to determine accuracy of text comprehension, A.

A hypothetical example will be given next for the ample time condition. Suppose the time allowed for reading in the example given earlier is increased to 1.67 minutes (t = 1.67), so $R = T_p/t$ = 20/1.67 = 12. From Equation C-4, the value of i can be calculated as follows:

$$i = (1/14)[(1/.80) - 1] = .0179 \tag{C-5}$$

By substituting i = .0179 into Equation C-3, it can be determined that

$$A = (1/12)/[(1/12) + .0179] = .82 \tag{C-6}$$

Table C-1
An Example of How the Accuracy of Text Comprehension Can be Determined Under Restricted Time Conditions

---

Given:

$T_p = 20$. This means that the number of standard length sentences in a piece of text is 20, or that the number of standard length words is 333, or that the number of character spaces in the text is 2,000.

$t = 1.25$. This means that the individual is given 1.25 minutes, or 1 minute and 15 seconds to read the 333 Words in the text.

$R = T_p/t = 20/1.25 = 16$. This means that the average rate at which the text is presented for reading is 16 Sentences per minute (or 267 Words per minute).

$R_r = 14$. This means that the individual doing the reading in this example has a rauding rate of 14 Sentences per minute (or 233 Words per minute).

$t_r = T_p/R_r = 20/14 = 1.42$. This means that this individual would need 1.42 minutes to finish reading the 20 Sentences (or 333 Words) at his/her rauding rate.

$R > R_r$. This means that because $R = 16$ and $R_r = 14$, then this is a restricted time condition; therefore, Equation C-1 should be used to determine the accuracy of text comprehension, A.

$t < t_r$. This means that because $t = 1.25$ and $t_r = 1.42$, then not enough time has been allowed to finish reading the text using the rauding process; therefore, this is another way to determine that this is a restricted time condition that requires Equation C-1.

$A_r = .80$. This means that this individual has an accuracy level, A_L, that allows this difficulty level of text, D_L, to be read with 80% comprehension, when the individual is allowed to finish reading the text once at his/her own rauding rate.

Calculations:

$$A = A_r R_r (1/R) \qquad \text{(C-1)}$$

$$A = (.80)(14)(1/16) = .70 \qquad \text{(C-2)}$$

This means that it can be predicted that this individual would comprehend 70% of the thoughts, or sentences, in this piece of text that is 333 Words in length when only 1.25 minutes are allowed to read this text.

So, the accuracy of comprehension of these 20 sentences under this ample time condition, would be 82%. Table C-2 contains a summary of this example explaining how the accuracy of text comprehension can be determined under ample time conditions.

There is a great deal of empirical support for the theoretical relationships used to determine the accuracy of text comprehension, A, as expressed in Equations C-1, C-3, and C-4 (Carver, 1977, 1984, 1985a, 1985b). In these equations, $1/R$, R_r, and A_r completely determine the accuracy that a passage will be comprehended, A. Next, $1/R$, R_r, and A_r will be described in more detail.

Table C-2
An Example of How the Accuracy of Text Comprehension Can be Determined Under Ample Time Conditions

Given:

$T_p = 20$. (This is a given value; see Table C-1.)

$t = 1.67$. This means that 1.67 minutes is allowed to read the text, *not* 1.25 minutes as was the case for the example in Table C-1.

$R = T_p/t = 20/1.67 = 12.0$. This means that the average rate at which the text is presented for reading is 12 Sentences per minute.

$R_r = 14$. (This is a given value; see Table C-1.)

$t_r = 1.42$. (This value is calculated from T_p and R_r; see Table C-1.)

$R < R_r$. This means that because $R = 12.0$ and $R_r = 14$, then this is an ample time condition; therefore, Equations C-3 and C-4 should be used to determine the accuracy of text comprehension, A.

$t > t_r$. This means that because $t = 1.67$ and $t_r = 1.42$, then more than enough time has been allowed to finish reading the text using the rauding process; therefore, this is another way to determine that this is an ample time condition that requires Equations C-3 and C-4.

$A_r = .80$. (This is a given value; see Table C-1.)

Calculations:

$i = (1/R_r)[(1/A_r) - 1]$ (C-4)

$i = (1/14)[(1/.80) - 1] = .0179$ (C-5)

$A = (1/R)/[(1/R) + i]$ (C-3)

$A = (1/12)/[(1/12) + .0179] = .82$ (C-6)

This means that it can be predicted that this individual would comprehend 82% of the thoughts, or sentences, in this piece of text that is 333 Words in length when 1.67 minutes are allowed for reading this text.

The value of 1/R is the average time allowed for reading each standard length sentence in the text, in minutes per Sentence. In the restricted time example given earlier, R = 16 Spm. Therefore, 1/R = .0625 minutes per Sentence (or 3.75 seconds per Sentence, or 225 milliseconds per standard word, or 267 standard words per minute, or 267 Wpm).

The value of R_r for an individual can be estimated from the Rate Level Test, as described in Chapter 5; when R_r is expressed in grade equivalent, GE, units, then it is rate level, R_L (see Appendix D).

The value of A_r (which is rauding accuracy and should not be confused with rauding accuracy level, A_L) depends upon the relative difficulty of the material, $A_L - D_L$. The value of D_L (in GE units) for a particular text can be determined from a measure of difficulty, or readability (Carver, 1975, 1994b; Carver & Leibert, 1995; Klare, 1963). The relationship between rauding accuracy, A_r and the relative easiness of the text, A_L - D_L, was empirically determined by Carver (1990b) to be as follows:

$$A_r = 0.04\,(A_L - D_L) + 0.64 \qquad \text{(C-7)}$$

Notice that the accuracy of comprehension of a piece of text is A_r when the text is read once at the individual's rauding rate, and it depends upon the relative easiness of the text, A_L - D_L; the value of A_r depends upon A_L and D_L. The value of A_r can be used to determine the accuracy of text comprehension, A, when an individual is given a fixed amount of time to read a piece of text, using Equations C-1, C-3, and C-4 described earlier. So, A depends on A_r, and A_r depends upon A_L and D_L. Therefore, A depends upon (a) the rauding accuracy level of the individual, A_L, (b) the rauding difficulty level of the text, D_L, (c) the rauding rate level of the individual (R_L or R_r), and (d) the average rate, R, at which the passage is presented for reading (sentences in text divided by the time allowed for reading in minutes).

In summary, when A_L and D_L are known, then A_r can be determined from Equation C-7. When R_L is known, R_r can be determined in Sentences per minute from Appendix D. When the length of the passage in standard sentences is known, T_p, and the time allowed for reading is known, t, then R can be determined from T_p/t. Given A_r (from Equation C-7), given R_r (from Appendix D), and given R (from the length of the passage, T_p, and the time allowed to read, t), then Equations C-1, C-3, and C-4 can be used to determine the accuracy of comprehension of the passage, A.

The predictive power of the relationships expressed in these equations can be illustrated using another example. Suppose the length of the text in thoughts, T_p, is 100 standard sentences (1,667 standard words) and the text is at the fifth-grade level of difficulty, or $D_L = 5.5$. Suppose the individual has (a) an eighth-grade accuracy level, or $A_L = 8.5$, and (b) a fourth-grade rate level, $R_L = 4.5$. Suppose the time, t, that this individual was allowed to read the text was 8.1 minutes. In order to predict the accuracy of comprehension, A, we first need to know whether the time condition is restricted ($R > R_r$) or ample ($R < R_r$). R would be T_p/t, or 100/8.1 = 12.3 Spm, and R_r would be determined from $R_L = 4.5$ to be 150 Wpm or $R_r = 9.0$ Spm (see Appendix D). Because R = 12.3 Spm is greater than $R_r = 9.0$ Spm, this means that we need to use Equation C-1 for this restricted time condition.

The values needed for Equation C-1 are A_r, R_r, and R. A_r can be determined from Equation C-7 to be as follows:

$$A_r = .04\,(8.5 - 5.5) + .64 = .76 \qquad \text{(C-8)}$$

R_r was determined earlier to be 9.0. R was determined earlier to be 12.3. So, A can be determined by substituting these values into Equation C-1, as follows:

$$A = (.76)\,(9.0)\,(1/12.3) = .56 \qquad \text{(C-9)}$$

This means that this individual who has an eighth-grade reading level and a fourth-grade normal reading rate (A_L = 8.5; R_L = 4.5) would be expected to comprehend 56% of the Sentences (A = .56) in this 1,667 word passage (T_p = 100) written at the fifth grade level of difficulty (D_L = 5.5), when reading it normally for 8.1 minutes, or when operating his/her rauding process on this piece of text for 8.1 minutes. Table C-3 contains a summary of this example explaining how the accuracy of text comprehension can be determined under restricted time conditions when the accuracy level of the individual and the difficulty level of the text is known.

Given that A_r can be predicted from A_L and D_L, using Equation C-7, it is possible to substitute the value of A_r determined from Equation C-7 into Equation C-1 so that A is a function of A_L and D_L. Also, the R term in Equation C-1 can be replaced by the length of the passage, T_p, divided by the time allowed to read the passage, t. With these substitutions, Equation C-1 becomes

$$A = [.04(A_L - D_L) + .64]\, R_r \frac{t}{T_p} \qquad \text{(C-10)}$$

From this equation, it can be seen that when individuals are given a fixed amount of time to read a passage that is not enough time to finish reading it, then the accuracy of text comprehension, A, will increase as (a) A_L increases, (b) D_L decreases, (c) R_r increases, (d) t increases, and (e) T_p decreases. This means that individuals will comprehend more of a certain text under a fixed time limit when their reading level is higher, the difficulty level of the text is lower, their normal reading rate is higher, the fixed amount of time allowed to read is higher, and the length of the text is shorter.

The predictive power of the equations given earlier will be illustrated again, using a hypothetical class of seventh-graders. Suppose a new history textbook is being considered—its difficulty level has been estimated to be at the seventh-grade level (D_L = 7.5), and its length has been estimated to be 3750 Sentences. Suppose the class has been administered the Accuracy Level Test (see Chapter 4) and the Rate Level Test (see Chapter 5), and the resulting averages for the class were A_L = 7.9, R_L = 7.2 (so R_r = 11.1 as interpolated from Appendix D). From the length of the text (3,750 Sentences) and R_r (11.1 Sentences per minute), it can be estimated that it would take these students as a group an average of 338 minutes (3750/11.1 = 338), or 5.6 hours, to finish reading the book once at their normal rate. The relative easiness of this text,

$A_L - D_L$, would be 7.9 - 7.5 = + 0.4. From this 0.4 value, rauding accuracy can be estimated from Equation C-7 to be 0.66; $A_r = .66$. That is,

$$A_r = .04\ (7.7 - 7.5) + .64 = .66 \qquad \text{(C-11)}$$

Table C-3
An Example of How the Accuracy of Text Comprehension Can be Determined Under Restricted Time Conditions When the Accuracy Level of the Individual and the Difficulty Level of the Text is Known

---

Given:

$T_p = 100$. This means that the length of the text is 100 standard sentences, or 1,667 standard words.

$t = 8.1$. This means that the individual is given 8.1 minutes, or 8 minutes and 6 seconds, to read these 1,667 Words in the text.

$R = 100/8.1 = 12.3$. This means that the average rate at which the text is presented for reading is 12.3 Sentences per minute (or 206 Words per minute).

$R_L = 4.5$; $R_r = 9.0$. This means that the individual's rauding rate is 150 Wpm, or $R_r = 9.0$ Sentences per minute (see Appendix D).

$t_r = T_p/R_r = 100/9.0 = 11.1$. This means that 11.1 minutes would be required for this individual to read these 1,667 Words when using his/her rauding process.

$R > R_r$. This means that because $R = 12.3$ and $R_r = 9.0$, then this is a restricted time condition; therefore, Equation C-1 should be used to determine the accuracy of text comprehension, A.

$t < t_r$. This means that because $t = 8.1$ and $t_r = 11.1$, then not enough time has been allowed to finish reading the text using the rauding process; therefore, this is another way to determine that this is a restricted time condition that requires Equation C-1.

$A_L = 8.5$. This means that is has been determined that this individual can accurately comprehend text at the eighth grade level.

$D_L = 5.5$. This means that the text being read by the individual is at the fifth-grade level of difficulty.

Calculations:

$A_r = .04\ (A_L - D_L) + .64$ (C-7) $A_r = .04\ (8.5 - 5.5) + .64 = .76$ (C-8)

$A = A_rR_r(1/R)$ (C-1) $A = (.76)(9.0)(1/12.3) = .56$ (C-9)

This means that this individual who is at the eighth-grade level of accuracy (A_L = 8.5) can comprehend 76% of this text ($A_r = .76$) at the fifth-grade level of difficulty ($D_L = 5.5$) when the individual is allowed to finish reading the text once at his/her rauding rate ($t_r = 11.2$). But, when only 8.1 minutes are allowed to read these 1,667 Words of text, then only 56% of the thoughts, or sentences, in this text will be comprehended.

So, it can be estimated that typical students in this class would take about 5 ½ hours to read this history book once, and as a group they would comprehend 66% of it, on the average, because $A_r = .66$ from Equation C-11.

In this example, the accuracy of text comprehension can also be estimated for this group when they are encouraged to read the book twice, thus taking 676 minutes instead of 338 minutes (R = 3750/676 = 5.55). Then, from Equation C-4,

$$i = (1/11.1)\,[(1/0.66) - 1] = .0464 \qquad \text{(C-12)}$$

and from Equation C-3,

$$A = \frac{1/5.55}{(1/5.55)+.0464} = .80 \qquad \text{(C-13)}$$

So, it would be predicted that, on the average, this class would comprehend 80% of this textbook if each person read it twice, taking an average of about 11 hours. Table C-4 contains a summary of this example explaining how the accuracy of text comprehension can be determined under ample time conditions when the accuracy level of the individual and the difficulty level of the text is known.

From the constructs and equations of rauding theory plus the empirical techniques for measuring these constructs, the accuracy of text comprehension, A, can be predicted quite precisely. Rate, as indicated by R and R_r, are very important determinants of the accuracy of text comprehension, A, along with the relative easiness of the text (A_L - D_L). As the time allowed for reading the text increases (t increases, or 1/R increases), then the accuracy of comprehension of an individual increases for a particular text. When everyone is given the same amount of time to read the text and everyone has the same rate level, R_L, then individuals who have higher accuracy levels, A_L, will have higher accuracy of text comprehension. When everyone is given the same amount of time to read the text and when everyone has the same accuracy level, A_L, then individuals who have higher rauding rates, R_r, will also have higher accuracy of text comprehension. When everyone has the same accuracy level, everyone has the same rate level, and everyone is given the same amount of time to read the text, then textbooks that are at lower levels of difficulty, D_L, will be read with higher accuracy of comprehension, A.

In summary, the equations of rauding theory can be used to predict the accuracy of text comprehension, A, as long as there are valid estimates of the following: (a) the length of the text in standard length sentences, T_p, (b) the difficulty level of the text, D_L, in GE units, (c) the rauding accuracy level of the individual, A_L, in GE units, (d) the rauding rate of the individual, R_r, in standard length sentences per minute, and (e) the time allowed to read the text, t, in minutes.

Table C-4
An Example of How the Accuracy of Text Comprehension Can be Determined Under Ample Time Conditions When the Accuracy Level of the Individual and the Difficulty Level of the Text is Known

---

Given:

$T_p = 3{,}750$. This means that the length of the text is 3,750 standard sentences, or 62,512 Words.

$t = 676$. This means that the group is given 676 minutes, or 11.3 hours, to read the 62,512 Words in the text.

$R = 3{,}750/676 = 5.55$. This means that the average rate at which the text is presented for reading is 5.55 Sentences per minute (or 92 Wpm).

$R_L = 7.2$; $R_r = 11.1$. This means that the mean rauding rate for the group is 184 Wpm, or 11.1 Sentences per minute, or is at the seventh-grade level in GE units.

$t_r = T_p/R_r = 3{,}750/11.1 = 338$. This means that 338 minutes would be required for the average individual in this group to read these 62,512 Words when the rauding process was used.

$R < R_r$. This means that when $R = 5.55$ and $R_r = 11.1$, then this is an ample time condition; therefore, C-2 and C-3 should be used to determine the accuracy of text comprehension, A.

$t > t_r$. This means that because $t = 676$ and $t_r = 338$, then more than enough time has been allowed to finish reading the text once at the rauding rate; therefore, this is another way to determine that it is an ample time condition allowing Equation C-3 and C-4 to be used.

$A_L = 7.9$. This means that the average accuracy level for this group was 7.9, or the seventh-grade level.

$D_L = 7.5$. This means that the text being read by this group was at the seventh-grade level of difficulty.

Calculations:

$A_r = .04\,(A_L - D_L) + .64$	(C-7)	$A_r = .04(7.9 - 7.5) + .64 = .66$	(C-11)
$i = (1/R_r)[(1/A_r) - 1]$	(C-3)	$i = (1/11.1)[(1/.66) - 1] = .0464$	(C-12)
$A = (1/R)/[(1/R) + i]$	(C-2)	$A = (1/5.55)/[(1/5.55) + .0464] = .80$	(C-13)

This means that the average individual in this group, who is at the seventh-grade level of accuracy, $A_L = 7.9$, can comprehend 64% of this text at the seventh-grade level of difficulty, $D_L = 7.5$, when this average individual is allowed to finish reading the text once at his/her rauding rate, $t_r = 338$. But, when 676 minutes are allowed to read these 62,512 Words of text, then 80% of the thoughts, or sentences, in this text will be comprehended.

APPENDIX D

CONVERSIONS AMONG UNITS OF RAUDING RATE

Rauding rate level, R_L, which is in GE units, can be converted into rauding rate, R_r, which is in standard words per minute, Wpm, or standard sentences per minute, Spm. Table D-1 contains the conversions among units of rauding rate, that is, among GE units, Wpm units, and Spm units. For example, it can be determined from Table D-1 that an individual who is rauding at the fourth-grade level ($R_L = 4.5$), has a rauding rate of 150 Wpm, or 9.0 Spm.

These values in Table D-1 have been derived from Appendix A of Carver (1994c), which is an upgrade of a similar conversion table given in Appendix B of Carver (1990a).

Table D-1
Converting Rate Level, R_L (Grade Equivalent Units), Into Rauding Rate in Wpm (Standard Words Per Minute) and Spm (Standard Sentences Per Minute)

R_L (GE units)	R_r (Wpm units)	R_r (Spm units)
1.5	112	6.7
2.5	125	7.5
3.5	137	8.2
4.5	150	9.0
5.5	162	9.7
6.5	175	10.5
7.5	188	11.3
8.5	201	12.1
9.5	213	12.8
10.5	227	13.6
11.5	238	14.3
12.5	251	15.1
13.5	263	15.8
14.5	277	16.6
15.5	289	17.3
16.5	302	18.1
17.5	315	18.9
18.5	326	19.6

APPENDIX E

LIST OF NUMBERED EQUATIONS

$$E_L = \sqrt{A_L R_L} \tag{1-1}$$

$$A_L = \sqrt{V_L P_L} \tag{1-2}$$

$$R_L = \sqrt{P_L C_s} \tag{1-3}$$

$$t_r = \frac{60{,}000}{R_r} \tag{2-1}$$

$$A_r = .04\,(A_L - D_L) + .64 \tag{2-2}$$

$$A = [.04(A_L - D_L) + .64]\, R_r\, (t/T_p) \tag{3-1}$$

$$P_L \text{Words} = A_L \text{Words} + c_k \text{Words} \tag{7-1}$$

$$P_L = (A_L + c_k)/2 \tag{7-2}$$

$$d_k = c_k \tag{7-3}$$

$$P_L = (A_L + d_k)/2 \tag{7-4}$$

$$S_L = P_L \tag{7-5}$$

$$E_L' = \sqrt{A_L R_L} \tag{9-1}$$

$$E_L' = (A_L + R_L)/2 \tag{9-2}$$

$$A_L' = \sqrt{V_L P_L} \tag{10-1}$$

$$E_L = (A_L + R_L)/2 \tag{10-2}$$

$$A_L = (V_L + P_L)/2 \tag{10-3}$$

$$R_L = (P_L + C_s)/2 \tag{10-4}$$

$$R_L' = \sqrt{P_L C_s} \quad (11\text{-}1)$$

$$R_L' = (P_L + C_s)/2 \quad (11\text{-}2)$$

$$R_L = (d_s + C_s)/2 \quad (11\text{-}3)$$

$$d_s = P_L \quad (11\text{-}4)$$

$$P_L = (V_L + 2d_k)/3 \quad (13\text{-}1)$$

When $V_L \geq 8.0$ and $P_L \geq 8.0$, then $A_L = V_L$ (17-1)

When $P_L \geq 8.0$, then $R_L = C_s$ (17-2)

$$E = AR \quad (B\text{-}1)$$

$$A = A_r R_r\,(1/R) \quad (C\text{-}1)$$

$$A = (.80)(14)(1/16) = .70 \quad (C\text{-}2)$$

$$A = (1/R)/[(1/R) + i] \quad (C\text{-}3)$$

$$i = (1/R_r)[(1/A_r) - 1] \quad (C\text{-}4)$$

$$i = (1/14)[(1/.80) - 1] = .0179 \quad (C\text{-}5)$$

$$A = (1/12)/[(1/12) + .0179] = .82 \quad (C\text{-}6)$$

$$A_r = 0.04\,(A_L - D_L) + 0.64 \quad (C\text{-}7)$$

$$A_r = .04\,(8.5 - 5.5) + .64 = .76 \quad (C\text{-}8)$$

$$A = (.76)\,(9.0)\,(1/12.3) = .56 \quad (C\text{-}9)$$

$$A = [.04(A_L - D_L) + .64]\,R_r \frac{t}{T_p} \quad (C\text{-}10)$$

$$A_r = .04\,(7.7 - 7.5) + .64 = .66 \quad (C\text{-}11)$$

$$i = (1/11.1)\,[(1/0.66) - 1] = .0464 \quad (C\text{-}12)$$

$$A = \frac{1/5.55}{(1/5.55)+.0464} = .80 \quad (C\text{-}13)$$

GLOSSARY

accuracy level: (see rauding accuracy level.)

accuracy of comprehension: proportion of thoughts in text, or a passage, that were comprehended; symbolized as A; number of thoughts, or sentences, in a passage that were comprehended during reading or auding per the total number of thoughts, or sentences, in the passage.

actual rate: rate of comprehension, R, when the rate at which the words are presented is directly manipulated, e.g., by use of motion picture film or time-compressed speech; the rate that accompanies a manipulated rate.

actual words: a count of the number of words in a passage when a word is defined as the letter string between two blank spaces except that two words separated by a hyphen is counted as two words; contrast with standard word.

adult: grade 8 and above, or age 13.4 years and older.

advanced reader: verbal level and pronunciation level of grade 8 and higher ($V_L \geq 8.0$ and $P_L \geq 8.0$).

alphabet: written shapes (letters) which comprise printed words and often represent the separate vowel and consonant phonemes of a language; the English alphabet contains 26 letters.

alphabetic principle: sequences of letters in a printed word (graphemes) usually correspond to sequences of sounds (phonemes) in the word when it is spoken; learning the alphabetic principle means to comprehend the connection between letters and phonemes, that is, that each letter in a word usually has something to do with a unit of sound (called a phoneme); note that the successive letters in words are not associated perfectly with the successive units of sounds (phonemes) in words because there is not a one-on-one correspondence between letters and phonemes—there are 26 letters and around 40 phonemes—and because some words are irregular words or sight words that do not have regular grapheme-phoneme correspondences.

A_L Words: known printed words; printed words whose meaning is known; an estimate of the size of the lexicon of raudamatized words.

apping: automatic pilot for prose; eye movements during normal reading that have become habitual and rhythmic and therefore require little or no attention; habitual eye movements during the execution of the rauding process which assures that almost every word will be fixated upon and that each word will be perceived and processed through the three components of lexical access, semantic encoding, and sentential integration.

audamatized words: words that an individual can readily comprehend when they are spoken, or presented auditorily.

auding: listening to orally presented words, letters, or other language symbols in order to comprehend, or gain information or knowledge.

automatized words: words that can be recognized in print with very little memory capacity devoted to attention.

average rate: rate of comprehension, R, when presentation time is directly manipulated instead of rate, e.g., by allowing an individual to read a passage for a fixed amount of time; the passage presentation rate that accompanies an attempt to allow the rauding process to proceed at the rauding rate; contrast with actual rate.

basic reading processes: the five basic reading processes in rauding theory are scanning, skimming, rauding, learning, and memorizing; the reading processes most often used on text, or passages.

beginning reader: verbal level or pronunciation level below grade 3 ($V_L < 3$ or $P_L < 3$).

cipher: the somewhat consistent connections between the letters within printed words and their corresponding sounds within spoken words.

cipher knowledge: knowledge of the imperfect regularities between the letters within printed words and their corresponding sounds within spoken words; compare to lexical knowledge which is a knowledge of the meaning of real words, usually printed words; for some, phonics knowledge.

ciphermatized words: unknown real words that can be correctly pronounced in isolation using cipher knowledge; also symbolized as c_kWords.

c_kWords: words whose meaning is not known when listening but can be correctly pronounced in isolation using cipher knowledge; c_kWords = P_LWords - A_LWords.

cognitive power: basic ability to solve intellectual problems; symbolized as C_p; similar to fluid intelligence.

cognitive speed: fastest speed that a series of simple overlearned stimuli can be named, in items per minute.

cognitive speed aptitude: a trait or inherited ability to quickly manipulate or process verbal information; symbolized as g_s; ability to name a series of overlearned stimuli rapidly, when compared to individuals who are the same age.

cognitive speed level: fastest speed of naming a series of simple stimuli which have been overlearned, in grade equivalent units; symbolized as C_s; basic rate of thinking about verbal material; similar to verbal speed, naming speed, or speed of thinking.

complete thought: the meaning contained in a sentence or independent clause.

comprehending: understanding or grasping the meaning.

context: words that appear in meaningful sentences or paragraphs, as opposed to words that appear in lists where there are no clues that help determine the meaning of a word or help determine how the word is pronounced.

correlate: a variable that is substantially related to another variable.

crystallized intelligence: cultural knowledge, or breadth and depth of previously learned information; symbolized as Gc.

decoding: using letter-sound correspondences to pronounce a printed word or a pseudoword; phonological recoding; grapheme-phoneme conversion; for some, decoding is not occurring unless the meaning of a correctly pronounced word is known; for some, decoding can occur while reading silently; for some, decoding only occurs for regular words, such as "stop"; for some, decoding also occurs for irregular words such as "show"; for some, decoding means the same as word recognition or word identification; see pure decoding knowledge, or d_k.

difficulty flexibility: the purported ability of an individual to decrease or increase reading rate as the difficulty of the material increases or decreases.

difficulty level: rauding difficulty level of the passage in grade equivalent units; symbolized as D_L; a measurement of text readability; rauding difficulty of text as indicated by the Rauding Scale of Prose difficulty, or some other readability technique such as the Dale-Chall formula or the Fry readability graph.

direct measure: a measure designed from a definition of a theoretical construct, so it is measured in the units of the construct; contrast with an indicant or an indirect measure.

DisabledV_L: those students who have a verbal knowledge level, V_L, that is below their age in GE units; those reading disabled students who are exceptionally low for their age in their ability to comprehend when listening.

d_k: pure decoding knowledge; knowledge of how to pronounce increasingly difficult printed pseudowords when scaled into GE units.

d_kWords: printed pseudowords that can be accurately pronounced; individual differences in d_kWords should be highly related to individual differences in c_kWords, so that d_k is equal to c_k in GE units.

easy rauding: operating the rauding process on relatively easy material, $A_L > D_L$.

efficiency level: (see rauding efficiency level)

efficiency of comprehension: number of thoughts comprehended in a passage per the amount of time allowed for reading or auding; symbolized as E; product of accuracy of comprehension, A, and rate of comprehension, R.

ESL students: English as a Second Language students who have learned a language other than English first, and are now trying to learn English as a second language.

fact recalling: finding a word in memory, recognizing its meaning within the sentence, integrating the word into the complete thought of the sentence, storing the thoughts well enough that they can be recognized later, and rehearsing the thoughts or facts sufficiently that they can be freely recalled later.

fluid intelligence: ability to reason, think abstractly, and solve novel problems; symbolized as Gf.

functional lexicon: words which can be correctly pronounced in context but cannot be correctly pronounced in a list of unrelated words.

gear shifting: changing from one of the five basic reading processes to another; changing from one basic reading process to another.

GE: grade equivalent, that is, scores transformed so they represent a level equivalent to a certain grade in school.

general intelligence, *g*: composite or average of several separate intelligences, or cognitive abilities; the single factor that results from a factor analysis of several cognitive abilities; best represented empirically as the single IQ score on an IQ test which contains several subtests.

hard reading: attempting to read and comprehend text that is relatively hard, $D_L > A_L$.

idea remembering: finding a word in memory, recognizing its meaning within the sentence, integrating the word into the complete thought of the sentence, and storing the thought well enough that there is a good probability that it can be remembered later.

indicant: a correlate of a direct measure of a theoretical construct that does not have the same units of measurement as the theoretical construct; an indicator, an index, or a marker of a construct or concept, but not a direct measure.

indirect measure: an indicant that has been scaled into the same units as the theoretical construct that it purports to measure; contrast with a direct measure.

inefficiency constant: index of the amount of inefficiency associated with having more than enough time to execute the rauding process once on a passage; symbolized by *i*; depends upon rauding rate and rauding accuracy.

intermediate reader: verbal level and pronunciation level above grade 2 but below grade 8 ($V_L \geq 3.0$ and $P_L \geq 3.0$; $V_L < 8.0$ or $P_L < 8.0$).

learning process: one of the five basic reading processes; to read text so that its meaning will be remembered at a later time, possibly on a multiple-choice test; involves the reading of sentences in passages that are relatively difficult in order to comprehend them; a model learning process can be described as involving lexical access, semantic encoding, sentential integration, and idea remembering, which operates at a rate around 200 Wpm for college students.

lexical access: finding a word in memory; word identification; to recognize a known word, except "word recognition" often means to pronounce a word correctly whether it has been previously stored in memory or not; a pseudoword that has never been seen before cannot be lexically accessed.

lexical knowledge: knowledge of printed real words; the lexicon of printed words that are known and can be recognized in isolation; the lexicon of raudamatized words, or A_L Words; compare to cipher knowledge which is the knowledge of the correspondences between letters and sounds in words.

lower grader: below grade 3, or below age 8.4 years.

matched rauding: attempting to operate the rauding process on textual material that is equal in difficulty level to accuracy level, that is, $D_L = A_L$.

memorizing process: one of the five basic reading processes; a series of steps carried out on the words of a passage so as to increase the probability that the words, facts, ideas, or thoughts can be freely recalled on a subsequent occasion; implementation of those activities which are most likely to result in the recall of information; often involves the word-for-word recall of a passage either in written or oral form; a model memorizing process has been described as involving the components of lexical access, semantic encoding, sentential integration, idea remembering, and fact recalling, which operates at about 138 Wpm for college students.

middle grader: student in grades 3 to 7, or between age 8.4 and age 13.4 years.

operating: carrying out the components or steps of a process.

optimal rate: the rate of comprehension, R, associated with the maximum efficiency of comprehension, E; the optimal rate of comprehension for most individuals is theorized to be their rauding rate, R_r; college students tend to average around 300 Wpm for their rauding rate, R_r, and their optimal rate tends to be this same rate.

orthographic knowledge: knowing the correct spelling of words; explicitly or implicitly knowing about the rules for how letters can be ordered within words, e.g. in English, q is almost always followed by *u* and *ch* frequently occurs but *hc* almost never occurs.

passage: a set of connected thoughts usually in the form of related sentences and sometimes organized in paragraphs; a body of prose material or text, either in spoken or written form.

phonemes: smallest unit of sound in spoken words.

phonetics: a system by which each separate unit of sound (phoneme) that occurs in a language is identified; for example, a phonetic system in English would need around 40 different symbols to represent each different sound in words; phonetics is not concerned with how words are spelled in printed form.

phonics: a study of the relationship between the units of sound in spoken words (phonemes) and their corresponding letters in printed words (graphemes).

phonics approach: a method of teaching reading which focuses upon learning how to pronounce words correctly, usually by learning rules that connect letters to sound; synthetic phonics programs, for example, focus upon blending /puh/, /ah/, and /tuh/ into the spoken word /pat/; analytic phonics programs, for example, focus on presenting a written word, such as "pat," and having the student say /puh/, /ah/, /tuh/.

phonological recoding: correctly pronouncing unknown printed words and pseudowords by using letter-sound correspondences; for some, means the same as "decoding"; phonological recoding cannot occur while reading silently; the purest measure of phonological recoding is generally considered to be an accuracy measure of the ability to pronounce pseudowords.

P_L Words: printed words that can be correctly pronounced by an individual; the lexicon of pronounceamatized words for an individual.

presentation time: amount of reading time for a passage, either as allowed or spent depending upon whether time is fixed or free to vary; symbolized as t; usually measured in minutes.

process: a series of progressive and independent steps or components designed to accomplish a goal; a phenomenon that continuously changes with time, usually cyclic or algorithmic in nature.

process flexibility: the sifting of gears from one reading process to another in order to accomplish a goal that is best accomplished by the components of a certain reading process.

pronounceamatized words: those words which can be accurately pronounced by an individual; the lexicon of real words that can be correctly pronounced, without regard for whether the meaning of the word is known; P_L Words.

pronunciation knowledge aptitude: the ability of an individual to learn the less than perfect connections between the letters within printed words and the sounds within spoken words when compared to other individuals at the same age; symbolized as g_p.

pronunciation knowledge level: pronunciation level; the number of words an individual can correctly pronounce, measured in GE units; symbolized as P_L; the lexicon of words that can be accurately pronounced in GE units; determined by cipher knowledge and lexical knowledge; similar to what is measured by word-identification tests or word-recognition tests; the number of pronounceamatized words, or P_L Words, measured in GE units.

pseudoword: a string of letters put together in a manner that is pronounceable but has no meaning; a pronounceable nonword, such as "velf" or "contorpously."

pure cipher knowledge: the number of printed words that are unknown when listening that can be accurately pronounced; called c_kWords; symbolized as c_k when measured in grade equivalent (GE) units; highly related to pure decoding knowledge, d_k, which is the accuracy of pronouncing pseudowords that increase in difficulty; c_k and d_k are hypothesized as being equal (in GE units).

pure decoding knowledge: ability to pronounce accurately, increasingly difficult pseudowords; symbolized as d_k when expressed in GE units; reflects the number of pseudowords that can be accurately pronounced, called d_kWords.

pure decoding speed: ability to pronounce pseudowords accurately and rapidly even though they have never been seen before; symbolized as d_s.

purpose flexibility: the purported ability to change reading rate as the purpose for reading changes so as to be better able to accomplish the purpose.

rate flexibility: the purported ability to change reading rate as difficulty and purpose change.

rate level: (see rauding rate level)

rate of comprehension: rate of passage presentation; symbolized as R; number of complete thoughts in a passage that are encountered or presented per the amount of time allowed for reading or auding; measured by standard length sentences per minute, that is, Sentences per minute (Spm); often reported as actual words per minute, wpm, or standard length words per minute, Wpm.

raud: comprehension of all or almost all of the consecutively encountered thoughts or sentences during reading or auding; comprehending about 64% or more of the complete thoughts encountered during the operation of the rauding process.

raudamaticity: the point at which an individual has learned to quickly recognize in print all of his/her audamatized words; all of the words in an individual's lexicon of audamatized words can be accurately comprehended in print at the individual's rauding rate; all audamatized words are also raudamatized words.

raudamaticity level: below raudamaticity means an individual has not reached raudamaticity, and at raudamaticity means that an individual has reached raudamaticity.

raudamatization: the speed of word recognition or word identification reached by an individual when (a) the word can be processed during rauding at the rauding rate, or (b) further experience or practice with a particular word does not result in a faster speed for that word.

raudamatized words: those printed words that can be recognized in print at the rauding rate of the individual; words that can be recognized in print very quickly because they have been overlearned via many practice trials or experiences.

rauder: one who rauds or attempts to raud; a person who is operating the rauding process.

rauding: refers to those frequently occurring language comprehension situations where most of the thoughts being presented in the form of sentences are being comprehended as they are encountered; reading with high comprehension; attending to each consecutive word in sentences and comprehending each consecutively encountered complete thought in a passage; operating the rauding process and comprehending about 64% or more of the thoughts in a passage; executing the rauding process on relatively easy material ($A_L > D_L$) at the rauding rate (R_r).

rauding accuracy: accuracy of comprehension when the rauding process is operated on a passage at the rauding rate; symbolized as A_r.

rauding accuracy level: the highest level of passage difficulty, D_L, at which individuals can comprehend at least 64% of the thoughts when operating their rauding process at their rauding rate, R_r; symbolized as A_L; indicated by a GE score on an unspeeded test, such as Woodcock Reading Mastery Tests-Passage Comprehension or the Accuracy Level Test (reading vocabulary tests are indicants of A_L).

rauding achievement category: Very Poor (E_L is more than 2 GEs below age), Poor (E_L is 1 to 2 GEs below age), Average (E_L is between 1 GE below and 1 GE above age), Good (E_L is 1 to 2 GEs above age), and Very Good (E_L is more than 2 GEs above age).

rauding efficiency: efficiency of comprehension when the rauding process is operated on a passage at the rauding rate, R_r; symbolized as E_r.

rauding efficiency level: the highest level of passage difficulty, D_L, at which individuals can accurately comprehend ($A > .64$) when the passage is presented at a rate commensurate with that difficulty level; symbolized as E_L; traditional standardized tests of reading comprehension are indicants of E_L; general reading ability, or reading achievement.

rauding process: the process used by an individual to comprehend each consecutively encountered complete thought in a passage; involves the components of lexical access, semantic encoding, and sentential integration; one of the five basic reading processes; for college students this process operates at a rate around 300 Wpm. (Note: According to rauding theory, when individuals operate their rauding process on a passage, it involves perceiving and internally articulating each consecutive word in a passage in an attempt to comprehend each consecutive sentence and thereby understand the thoughts in the passage that the author intended to communicate; during reading the rauding process also includes a fixation centered on almost every word in a passage.)

rauding rate: the relatively constant rate at which individuals read when they are operating their rauding process; symbolized as R_r; the fastest rate at which an individual can accurately read ($A > .64$) relatively easy passages; fastest rate at which an individual can successfully operate the rauding process, $A > .64$, on relatively easy passages; highest rate at which all or almost all of the consecutively encountered sentences in passages can be comprehended. (Note: According to rauding theory, rauding rate is also an optimal rate, and the normal rate of reading relatively easy material.)

rauding rate level: the rauding rate, R_r, in grade equivalent units; symbolized as R_L; the average rauding rate of individuals at each rauding accuracy level, A_L; can be measured by the Rate Level Test.

rauding skill category: beginning ($V_L < 3.0$ or $P_L < 3.0$), intermediate ($V_L \geq 3.0$ and $P_L \geq 3.0$; $V_L < 8.0$ or $P_L < 8.0$), and advanced ($V_L \geq 8.0$ and $P_L \geq 8.0$).

reading: looking at visually presented words, letters, or other language symbols to gain information or knowledge.

reading achievement: the ability to accurately comprehend increasingly difficult material under speeded or timed conditions; general reading ability, or E_L; often measured by standardized tests of reading comprehension.

reading comprehension: the comprehension or understanding associated with reading; could refer to one, some, or all of the following: (a) rauding accuracy level, A_L, (b) rauding efficiency level, E_L, (c) rauding accuracy, A_r, (d) rauding efficiency E_r, (e) accuracy of comprehension, A, and (f) efficiency of comprehension, E.

reading disability: traditionally considered to be a deficit in reading achievement despite normal sensory abilities, educational opportunity, and intelligence; in rauding theory, a low GE relative to age in the following: accuracy level, A_L, rate level, R_L, verbal level, V_L, pronunciation level, P_L, or cognitive speed level, C_s.

reading process: any of a number of different processes used in reading to accomplish different goals.

reading rate: speed of reading under any reading process; could refer to rate of comprehension, R, or rauding rate, R_r.

relative difficulty: the rauding difficulty level of the text in relationship to the rauding accuracy level of the reader; symbolized as $D_L - A_L$.

relative easiness: the rauding accuracy of the reader in relationship to the rauding difficulty level of the text; symbolized as $A_L - D_L$.

relatively easy: text, or passages, at a difficulty level, D_L, which is below the accuracy level, A_L of the reader ($A_L > D_L$).

relatively hard: text, or passages, at a difficulty level, D_L, which is above the accuracy level, A_L, of the reader ($D_L > A_L$).

scanning process: one of the five basic reading processes; a reading process which involves looking at each individual word simply to recognize it; involves only lexical access; a model scanning process can be described as involving a search for a target word in a passage—for college students this process operates around 600 Wpm.

semantic encoding: finding a word in memory and also recognizing its meaning as it is used in the sentence; attaching a contextually relevant meaning to a word.

Sentences per minute (Spm): rate determined from a count of the number of standard sentences in a passage divided by presentation time in minutes.

sentential integrating: finding a word in memory, recognizing its meaning as it is used in the sentence, and integrating the word with the prior words to form the complete thought represented by the sentence in the context of a passage.

skimming process: one of the five basic reading processes; those reading processes which involve a sampling of the population of information to learn more about that body of information; involves skipping words when done in connection with passages; a series of steps carried out on the words in a passage so as to increase one's general knowledge about the information contained in the passage; involves sampling words or phrases and inferring about what was skipped; a model skimming process can be described as involving lexical access and semantic encoding in order to find two consecutive words in a passage whose order has been reversed—this process can be successfully operated by college students at around 450 Wpm.

spelling knowledge level: the number of words an individual can spell correctly scaled into GE units; symbolized as S_L.

standard sentence: 100 character spaces; symbolized as S; 16 2/3 standard length words; also signified by the capitalized word "Sentence."

standard word: six character spaces; symbolized as W; six consecutive characters including letters and punctuation marks with one blank space after each word and two blank spaces after each sentence also counted as characters; also signified by "Words"; sometimes defined as five letters.

studying: activities involving the basic reading processes, possibly supplemented by productive activities such as note taking, underlining, reciting, and outlining which are used as part of a strategy for increasing one's understanding or future recall of the information in a passage.

text: printed sentences, paragraphs, or passages that are coherent or meaningfully related to each other.

verbal knowledge aptitude: the ability to learn verbal information or gain verbal knowledge; symbolized as g_v.

verbal knowledge level: an individual's amount of verbal knowledge measured in GE units; symbolized as V_L; similar to level of listening comprehension; similar to the number of spoken words known by an individual; symbolized as $AudA_L$ in earlier versions of rauding theory; the number of V_L Words scaled into GE units.

V_L Words: known spoken words; words whose meaning is known when listening; the lexicon of audamatized words.

Word: a standard length word; a standard word; six characters spaces counting each letter, punctuation mark, one character space after each word, and two character spaces after each sentence.

word: any one of the thousands of entries in a dictionary; the letter strings between two blank spaces in a sentence (except for two words separated by a hyphen).

word-for-word reading: a reading process in which an attempt is made to lexically access, semantically encode, and sententially integrate every word in a passage; the rauding process is word-for-word reading and most learning processes and memorizing processes also involve word-for-word reading. (Note: This definition should not be confused with another usage that means a perfect oral rendition of a passage.)

Words per minute (Wpm): rate determined from a count of the standard words in a passage divided by the presentation time in minutes.

words per minute (wpm): reading rate determined from a count of the actual number of words in a passage divided by the presentation time in minutes.

REFERENCES

Aaron, P. G. (1991). Can reading disabilities be diagnosed without using intelligence tests? *Journal of Learning Disabilities, 24*(3), 178-186, 191.

Adams, M. J. (1990). *Beginning to read.* Cambridge, MA: MIT Press.

Adams, M. J. (1991). Why not phonics and whole language? In W. Ellis (Ed.), *All language and the creation of literacy* (pp. 40-53). Baltimore: Orton Dyslexia Society.

Adams, M. J., & Bruck, M. (1995). Resolving the "great debate." *American Educator,* Summer, 9-20.

Alexander, P. A., Schallert, D. L., & Hare, V. C. (1991). Coming to terms: How researchers in learning and literacy talk about knowledge. *Review of Educational Research, 61,* 315-343.

Allen, L., Cipielewski, J., & Stanovich, K. E. (1992). Multiple indicators of children's reading habits and attitudes: Construct validity and cognitive correlates. *Journal of Educational Psychology, 84*(4), 489-503.

Allington, R. L., & Johnston, P. H. (1989). Coordination, collaboration, and consistency: The redesign of compensatory and special education interventions. In R. Slavin, N. Madden, & N. Karweit (Eds.), *Preventing school failure: Effective programs for students at risk* (pp. 320-354). Boston: Allyn & Bacon.

Altwerger, B., Edelsky, C., & Flores, B. M. (1987, November). Whole Language: What's new? *The Reading Teacher,* 144-154.

Anderson, J. H., & Fairbanks, G. (1937). Common and differential factors in reading vocabulary and learning vocabulary. *Journal of Educational Research, 30,* 317-324.

Anderson, R. C. (1972). How to construct achievement tests to assess comprehension. *Review of Educational Research, 42,* 145-170.

Anderson, R. C., & Freebody, P. (1981). Vocabulary knowledge. In J. T. Guthrie (Ed.), *Comprehension and teaching: Research reviews* (pp. 77-117). Newark, DE: International Reading Association.

Anderson, R. C., & Pearson, P. D. (1984). A schema-theoretic view of basic processes in reading. In P. D. Pearson (Ed.), *Handbook of reading research* (pp. 255-292). New York: Longman.

Arter, J., & Jenkins, J. R. (1979). Differential diagnostic-prescriptive-teaching: A critical appraisal. *Review of Educational Research, 49,* 517-555.

Assink, E., & Kattenberg, G. (1993). Computerized assessment of verbal skill. *Journal of Psycholinguistic Research, 22,* 427-444.

Atkinson, R. C. (1974). Teaching children to read using a computer. *American Psychologist, 29*(3), 169-178.

Ball, E. W., & Blachman, B. A. (1991). Does phoneme awareness training in kindergarten make a difference in early word recognition and developmental spelling. *Reading Research Quarterly, 26*(1), 49-66.

Ballantine, F. A. (1951). Age changes in measures of eye-movements in silent reading. In *Studies in the psychology of reading* (University of Michigan Monographs in Education No. 4, pp. 67-114). Ann Arbor: University of Michigan Press.

Barker, T. A., Torgesen, J. K., & Wagner, R. K. (1992). The role of orthographic processing skills on five different reading tasks. *Reading Research Quarterly, 27,* 334-345.

Barr, R., & Dreeban, R. (1983). *How schools work.* Chicago: University of Chicago Press.

Barr, R., Kamil, M. L., Mosenthal, P. B., & Pearson, P. D. (Eds.). (1991). *Handbook of reading research.* New York: Longman.

Bear, R. M., & Odbert, H. S. (1940). Experimental studies of the relation between rate of reading and speed of association. *Journal of Psychology, 10,* 141-147.

Beck, I. L., & Carpenter, P. A. (1986). Cognitive approaches to understanding reading: Implications for instructional practice. *American Psychologist, 41,* 1098-1105.

Beck, I. L., McKeown, M. G., & Omanson, R. C. (1987). The effects and uses of diverse vocabulary instructional techniques. In M. G. McKeown & M. L. Curtis (Eds.), *The nature of vocabulary acquisition* (pp. 147-163). Hillsdale, NJ: Lawrence Erlbaum Associates Associates.

Bell, L. C., & Perfetti, C. A. (1994). Reading skill: Some adult comparisons. *Journal of Educational Psychology, 86,* 244-255.

Bentler, P. M., & Bonett, D. G. (1980). Significance tests and goodness-of-fit in the analysis of covariance structures. *Psychological Bulletin, 88,* 588-606.

Bergeron, B. S. (1990). What does the term whole language mean? Constructing a definition from the literature. *Journal of Reading Behavior, 22,* 301-329.

Berninger, V. W., & Abbott, R. D. (1994). Redefining learning disabilities: Moving beyond aptitude-achievement discrepancies to failure to respond to validated treatment protocols. In G. R. Lyon (Ed.), *Frames of reference for the assessment of learning disabilities* (pp. 163-184) Baltimore: Brookes.

Betts, E. A. (1946). *Foundations of reading instruction.* New York: American Book.

Biemiller, A. (1977). Relationships between oral reading rates for letters, words, and simple text in the development of reading achievement. *Reading Research Quarterly, 13,* 223-253.

Biemiller, A. (1994). Some observations on beginning reading instruction. *Educational Psychologist, 29,* 203-209.

Blachman, B. A., Ball, E., Black, S., & Tangle, D. (1994). Kindergarten teachers develop phoneme awareness in low-income inner-city classrooms: Does it make a difference? *Reading and Writing: An Interdisciplinary Journal, 6,* 1-17.

Bloom, B. (1984). The 2 sigma problem: The search for methods of group instruction as effective as one-to-one tutoring. *Educational Researcher, 13*(6), 4-17.

Bond, G. K., & Dykstra, R. (1967). The cooperative research program in first grade reading instruction. *Reading Research Quarterly, 2,* 5-142.

Bowers, P. G. (1993). Text reading and rereading: Determinants of fluency beyond word recognition. *Journal of Reading Behavior, 25*(2), 133-153.

Bowers, P. G. (1995). Tracing symbol naming speed's unique contributions to reading disabilities over time. *Reading and Writing: An Interdisciplinary Journal, 7,* 189-216.

Bowers, P. G., Steffy, R. A., & Swanson, L. B. (1986). Naming speed, memory, and visual processing in reading disability. *Canadian Journal of Behavioral Science, 18,* 209-223.

Bowers, P. G., Steffy, R., & Tate, E. (1988). Comparison of the effects of IQ control methods on memory and naming speed predictors of reading disability. *Reading Research Quarterly, 23,* 304-319.

Bowers, P. G., Sunseth, K., & Golden, J. (1999). The route between rapid naming and reading progress. *Scientific Studies of Reading, 3*(1), 31-53.

Bowers, P. G., & Swanson, L. B. (1991). Naming speed deficits in reading disability: Multiple measures of a singular process. *Journal of Experimental Child Psychology, 51,* 195-219.

Bradley, L., & Bryant, P. E. (1983). Categorizing sounds and learning to read: A causal connection. *Nature, 301,* 419-421.

Brown, J. S., & Felton, R. H. (1990). Effects of instruction on beginning reading skills in children at risk for reading disability. *Reading and Writing: An Interdisciplinary Journal, 2,* 223-241.

Bryant, P. E., Bradley, L., Maclean, M., & Crossland, I. (1989). Nursery rhymes, phonological skills and reading. *Journal of Child Language, 16,* 407-428.

Buswell, G. T. (1951). Relationship between rate of thinking and rate of reading. *School Review, 49,* 339-346.

Byrne, B., & Fielding-Barnsley, R. (1991). Evaluation of a program to teach phonemic awareness to young children. *Journal of Educational Psychology, 83,* 451-455.

Byrne, B., & Fielding-Barnsley, R. (1993). Evaluation of a program to teach phonemic awareness to young children: A 1-year follow-up. *Journal of Educational Psychology, 85* 104-111.

Byrne, B., & Fielding-Barnsley, R. (1995). Evaluation of a program to teach phonemic awareness to young children: A 2- and 3-year follow-up and a new preschool trial. *Journal of Educational Psychology, 87,* 488-503.

Cadenhead, K. (1987). Reading level: A metaphor that shapes practice. *Phi Delta Kappan, 68,* 436-441.

Calfee, R. C., Lindamood, P., & Lindamood, C. (1973). Acoustic-phonetic skills and reading—kindergarten through twelfth grade. *Journal of Educational Psychology, 64,* 293-298.

Calfee, R. C., & Piontkowski, D. C. (1981). The reading diary: Acquisition of decoding. *Reading Research Quarterly, 16*(3), 346-373.

Campito, J. S. (1994). Verbal ability. In R. J. Sternberg (Ed.), *Encyclopedia of human intelligence* (pp. 1106-1115). New York: Macmillan.

Carlisle, J. F. (1983). Components of training in reading comprehension for middle school students. *Annals of Dyslexia, 33,* 187-202.

Carroll, J. B. (1968). On learning from being told. *Educational Psychologist, 5*(2), 1, 5-10.

Carroll, J. B. (1993). *Human cognitive abilities: A survey of factor-analytic studies.* Cambridge: Cambridge University Press.

Carroll, J. B., Davies, P., & Richman, B. (1971). *Word frequency book.* New York: Houghton Mifflin.

Carver, R. P. (1970). Effect of "chunked" typography upon reading rate and comprehension. *Journal of Applied Psychology, 54,* 288-296.

Carver, R. P. (1971a). Pupil dilation and its relationship to information processing during reading and listening. *Journal of Applied Psychology, 55*(2), 126-134.

Carver, R. P. (1971b). Evidence for the invalidity of Miller-Coleman readability scale. *Journal of Reading Behavior, 4*(3), 42-47.

Carver, R. P. (1972, August). Speed readers don't read; they skim. *Psychology Today,* 22-30.

Carver, R. P. (1973a). Understanding, information processing, and learning from prose materials. *Journal of Educational Psychology, 64*(1), 76-84.

Carver, R. P. (1973b). Reading as reasoning: Implications for measurement. In W. H. MacGinitie (Ed.), *Assessment problems in reading* (pp. 44-56). Newark, DE: International Reading Association.

Carver, R. P. (1974). Two dimensions of tests: Psychometric and edumetric. *American Psychologist, 29,* 512-518.

Carver, R. P. (1975). Measuring prose difficulty using the Rauding Scale. *Reading Research Quarterly, 11,* 660-685.

Carver, R. P. (1976). Word length, prose difficulty, and reading rate. *Journal of Reading Behavior, 8,* 193-204.

Carver, R. P. (1977). Toward a theory of reading comprehension and rauding. *Reading Research Quarterly, 13,* 8-63.

Carver, R. P. (1978). The case against statistical significance testing. *Harvard Educational Review, 48,* 378-399.

Carver, R. P. (1981). *Reading comprehension and rauding theory.* Springfield, IL: Charles C. Thomas. (Reprint, 1987. Kansas City, MO: Revrac.)

Carver, R. P. (1982). Optimal rate of reading prose. *Reading Research Quarterly, 18,* 56-88.

Carver, R. P. (1983). Is reading rate constant or flexible? *Reading Research Quarterly, 18,* 190-215.

Carver, R. P. (1984). Rauding theory predictions of amount comprehended under different purposes and speed reading conditions. *Reading Research Quarterly, 19,* 205-218.

Carver, R. P. (1985a). How good are some of the world's best readers? *Reading Research Quarterly, 20,* 389-419.

Carver, R. P. (1985b). Measuring absolute amounts of reading comprehension using the rauding rescaling procedure. *Journal of Reading Behavior, 17*(1), 29-53.

Carver, R. P. (1987a). Should reading comprehension skills be taught? *Yearbook of the National Reading Conference, 36,* 115-126.

Carver, R. P. (1987b). *Manual for the Rauding Efficiency Level Test.* Kansas City, MO: Revrac.

Carver, R. P. (1989). Silent reading rates in grade equivalents. *Journal of Reading Behavior, 21*(2), 155-166.

Carver, R. P. (1990a). *Reading rate: A review of research and theory.* New York: Academic Press.

Carver, R. P. (1990b). Predicting accuracy of comprehension from the relative difficulty of material. *Learning and Individual Differences, 2,* 405-422.

Carver, R. P. (1990c). Rescaling the Degrees of Reading Power test to provide valid scores for selecting materials at the instructional level. *Journal of Reading Behavior, 22*(1), 1-18.

Carver, R. P. (1991). Using letter-naming speed to diagnose reading disability. *Remedial and Special Education, 12*(5), 33-43.

Carver, R. P. (1992a). What do reading standardized reading comprehension tests measure in terms of efficiency, accuracy, and rate. *Reading Research Quarterly, 27,* 346-359.

Carver, R. P. (1992b). The three factors in reading ability; Reanalysis of a study by Cunningham, Stanovich, and Wilson. *Journal of Reading Behavior, 24*(2), 173-190.

Carver, R. P. (1992c). The effect of prediction activities, prior knowledge, and text type upon the amount comprehended: Using rauding theory to critique schema theory. *Reading Research Quarterly, 27*(2), 165-174.

Carver, R. P. (1992d). Reliability and validity of the Speed of Thinking Test. *Educational and Psychological Measurement, 52,* 125-134.

Carver, R. P. (1992e). Reading rate: Theory, research, and practical implications. *Journal of Reading, 36*(2), 84-95.

Carver, R. P. (1993a). Merging the simple view of reading with rauding theory. *Journal of Reading Behavior, 25,* 439-455.

Carver, R. P. (1993b). The case against statistical significance testing, revisited. *Journal of Experimental Education, 61,* 287-292.

Carver, R. P. (1994a). *Technical manual for the Accuracy Level Test.* Kansas City, MO: Revrac.

Carver, R. P. (1994b). Percentage of unknown vocabulary words in text as a function of the relative difficulty of the text: Implications for instruction. *Journal of Reading Behavior, 26,* 413-437.

Carver, R. P. (1994c). *Technical manual for the Rate Level Test.* Kansas City, MO: Revrac.

Carver, R. P. (1996). *Technical manual for version 3.0 of the Computer Assisted Reading Diagnosis.* Kansas City, MO: Revrac.

Carver, R. P. (1997). Reading for one second, one minute, or one year from the perspective of rauding theory. *Scientific Studies of Reading, 1*(1), 3-43.

Carver, R. P. (1998a). *Manual for the Rauding Efficiency Level Test, Revised.* Kansas City, MO: Revrac.

Carver, R. P. (1998b). Relating reading achievement to intelligence and memory capacity. In W. Tomic & J. Kingma (Eds.) *Advances in cognition and educational practice* (Vol. 5, pp. 143-174). Greenwich, CT: JAI Press.

Carver, R. P. (1998c). Predicting reading level in grades 1 to 6 from listening level and decoding level: Testing theory relevant to the simple view of reading. *Reading and Writing: An Interdisciplinary Journal, 10,* 121-154.

Carver, R. P., & Clark, S. W. (1998). Investigating reading disabilities using the rauding diagnostic system. *Journal of Learning Disabilities, 31*(5), 143-174.

Carver, R. P., & Darby, C. A., Jr. (1971). Development and evaluation of a test of information storage during reading. *Journal of Educational Measurement, 8*(1), 33-44.

Carver, R. P., & Darby, C. A., Jr. (1972). Analysis of the chunked reading test and reading comprehension. *Journal of Reading Behavior, 5,* 282-296.

Carver, R. P., & Leibert, R. E. (1995). The effect of reading library books at different levels of difficulty upon gain in reading ability. *Reading Research Quarterly, 30*(1), 26-48.

Castel, J. M., Riach, J., & Nicholson, T. (1994). Getting off to a better start in reading and spelling: The effects of phonemic awareness instruction within a whole language program. *Journal of Educational Psychology, 86,* 350-357.

Castles, A., & Colthart, M. (1993). Varieties of developmental dyslexia. *Cognition, 47,* 149-180.

Cattell, J. M. (1886). The time it takes to see and name objects. *Mino, 11,* 63-65.

Cattell, R. B. (1963). Theory of fluid and crystallized intelligence: A critical experiment. *Journal of Educational Psychology, 54*(1), 1-22.

Cattell, R. B. (1971). *Abilities: Their structure, growth, and action.* Boston: Houghton Mifflin.

Cermak, L. S. (1983). Information processing deficits in children with learning disabilities. *Journal of Learning Disabilities, 16,* 599-605.

Chabot, R. J., Zehr, H. D., Prinzo, O. V., & Petros, T. V. (1984). The speed of word recognition subprocesses and reading achievement in college students. *Reading Research Quarterly, 19*(2), 147-161.

Chall, J. S. (1967). *Learning to read: The great debate.* New York: McGraw-Hill.

Chall, J. S. (1983). *Stages of reading development.* New York: McGraw-Hill.

Chen, R. S., & Vellutino, F. R. (1997). Prediction of reading ability: A cross validation study of the simple view of reading. *Journal of Literacy Research, 29*(1), 1-24.

Christensen, C. A. (1997). Onset, rhymes, and phonemes in learning to read. *Scientific Studies of Reading, 1*(4), 341-358.

Clarke, M. A. (1987). Don't blame the system: Constraints on "whole language" reform. *Language Arts, 64,* 384-396.

Clay, M. M. (1991). *Becoming literate: The construction of inner control.* Portsmouth, NH: Heinemann.

Cohen, J. (1977). *Statistical power analysis for the behavioral sciences.* New York: Academic Press.

Coke, E. U. (1974). The effects of readability on oral and silent reading rates. *Journal of Educational Psychology, 66,* 406-409.

Coleman, E. B. (1990). Just and Carpenter's theory of reading: Length and eye fixations. In R. P. Carver *Reading rate: A review of theory and research* (pp. 459-462). New York: Academic Press.

Compton, D. L., & Carlisle, J. F. (1994). Speed of word recognition as a distinguishing characteristic of reading disabilities. *Educational Psychology Review, 6*(2), 115-141.

Court, J. H. (1994). Raven Progressive Matrices. In R. J. Sternberg (Ed.) *Encyclopedia of human intelligence* (pp. 916-917). New York: Macmillan.

Cronbach, L. J. (1957). The two disciplines of scientific psychology. *American Psychologist, 12,* 671-684.

Cronbach, L. J. (1977). *Educational Psychology.* New York: Harcourt, Brace, Jovanovich.

Cronbach, L. J., & Snow, R. E. (1977). *Aptitudes and instructional methods: A handbook for research on interactions.* New York: Irvington.

Cunningham, A. E. (1990). Explicit versus implicit instruction in phonemic awareness. *Journal of Experimental Child Psychology, 50,* 424-444.

Cunningham, A. E., & Stanovich, K. (1990). Assessing print exposure and orthographic processing skill in children: A quick measure of reading experience. *Journal of Educational Psychology, 82,* 733-740.

Cunningham, A. E., & Stanovich, K. E. (1991). Tracking the unique effects of print exposure in children: Associations with vocabulary, general knowledge, and spelling. *Journal of Educational Psychology, 83,* 264-274.

Cunningham, A. E., & Stanovich, K. E. (1993). Children's literacy environments and early word recognition subskills. *Reading and Writing: An Interdisciplinary Journal, 5,* 193-204.

Cunningham, A. E., Stanovich, K. E., & Wilson, M. R. (1990). Cognitive variation in adult college students differing in reading ability. In T. H. Carr & B. A. Levy (Eds.), *Reading and its development: Component skills approaches* (pp. 129-159). New York: Academic Press.

Cunningham, P. M. (1992). What kind of phonics instruction will we have? *Yearbook of the National Reading Conference, 41,* 17-31.

Cunningham, P. M. (1995). *Phonics they use: Words for reading and writing* (2nd Ed.). New York: Harper Collins.

Cunningham, P. M., & Cunningham, J. W. (1978). Investigating the print to meaning hypothesis. *Yearbook of the National Reading Conference, 27,* 116-120.

Curtis, M. E. (1980). Development of components of reading skill. *Journal of Educational Psychology, 72,* 656-669.

Curtis, M. E. (1987). Vocabulary testing and vocabulary instruction. In M. G. McKeown & M. E. Curtis (Eds.), *Nature of vocabulary acquisition* (pp. 37-51). Hillsdale, NJ: Lawrence Erlbaum Associates.

Daneman, M. (1991). Individual differences in reading skills. In R. Barr, M. Kamil, P. Mosenthal, & P. D. Pearson (Eds.), *Handbook of reading research: Vol. II* (pp. 512-538). New York: Longman.

Daneman, M., & Carpenter, P. A. (1980). Individual differences in working memory and reading. *Journal of Verbal Learning and Verbal Behavior, 19,* 450-466.

Danks, J. (1980). Comprehension in listening and reading. In F. B. Murray (Ed.), *Reading and understanding* (pp. 1-39). Newark, DE: International Reading Association.

Davis, F. B. (1972). Psychometric research on comprehension in reading. *Reading Research Quarterly, 7,* 628-678.

Davis, J. M., & Spring, C. (1990). The digit naming speed test: Its power and incremental validity in identifying children with specific reading disabilities. *Psychology in the Schools, 27,* 15-22.

Denckla, M. B. (1972). Color-naming defects in dyslexic boys. *Cortex, 8,* 164-176.

Denckla, M. B., & Rudel, R. G. (1974). Rapid "automatized" naming of pictured objects, colors, letters, and numbers by normal children. *Cortex, 10,* 186-202.

Denckla, M. B., & Rudel, R. G. (1976). Rapid "automatized" naming (R.A.N.): Dyslexia differentiated from other learning disabilities. *Neuropsychologia, 14,* 471-479.

Detterman, D. K. (1982). Does "g" exist? *Intelligence, 6,* 99-108.

Dickinson, D. K., & Smith, M. W. (1994). Long-term effects of preschool teachers' book readings on low income children's vocabulary and story comprehension. *Reading Research Quarterly, 29*(2), 105-124.

Doehring, D. G. (1976). Acquisition of rapid reading responses. *Monographs of the Society for Research in Child Development, 41*(2), 1-54.

Dolch, E. M. (1948). *Problems in reading.* Champaign, IL: Gerard Press.

Dole, J. A., Duffy, G. G., Roehler, L. R., & Pearson, P. D. (1991). Moving from the old to the new: Research on reading comprehension and instruction. *Review of Educational Research, 61,* 239-264.

Dreyer, L. G., & Katz, L. (1992). An examination of "the simple view of reading." *Yearbook of the National Reading Conference, 41,* 169-176.

DuBois, P. H. (1932). A speed factor in mental tests. *Archives of Psychology, 141,* 5-38.

Dymock, S. (1993). Reading but not understanding. *Journal of Reading, 37*(2), 86-91.

Edelsky, C. (1990). Whose agenda is this anyway? A response to McKenna, Robinson, and Miller. *Educational Researcher, 19,* 7-11.

Ehri, L. C. (1980). The development of orthographic images. In U. Frith (Ed.), *Cognitive processes in spelling* (pp. 311-388). London: Academic.

Ehri, L. C. (1985). Effects of printed language acquisition on speech. In D. R. Olson, N. Torrance, & A. Hildyard (Eds.), *Literacy, language, and learning: The nature and consequences of reading and writing* (pp. 333-367). Cambridge, UK: Cambridge University Press.

Ehri, L. C. (1987). Learning to read and spell words. *Journal of Reading Behavior, 19,* 5-31.

Ehri, L. C. (1989a). Movement into word reading and spelling: How spelling contributes to reading. In J. Mason (Ed.), *Reading and writing connections* (pp. 65-81). Boston: Allyn & Bacon.

Ehri, L. C. (1989b). The development of spelling knowledge and its role in reading acquisition and reading disability. *Journal of Learning Disabilities, 22,* 356-365.

Ehri, L. C. (1991). Development of the ability to read words. In R. Barr, M. L. Kamil, P. B. Mosenthal, & P. D. Pearson (Eds.), *Handbook of reading research: Vol. 2* (pp. 512-538). White Plains, NY: Longman.

Ehri, L. C. (1992). Reconceptualizing the development of sight word reading and its relationship to recoding. In P. B. Gough, L. C. Ehri, & R. Treiman (Eds.), *Reading acquisition* (pp. 13-39). Hillsdale, NJ: Lawrence Erlbaum Associates.

Ehri, L. C. (1994). Development of the ability to read words: Update. In R. Ruddell, M. Ruddell, & H. Singer (Eds.), *Theoretical models and the processes of reading* (4th Edition, pp. 323-358). Newark, DE: International Reading Association.

Ehri, L. C. (1996). Researching how children learn to read: Controversies in science are not like controversies in practice. In G. C. Brannigan (Ed.), *The enlightened educator* (pp. 179-204). New York, NY: McGraw-Hill, Inc.

Ehri, L. C. (1997). Learning to read and learning to spell are one and the same, almost. In C. Perfetti, L. Rieben, & M. Fayel (Eds.), *Learning to spell: Research, theory and practice across languages* (pp. 237-270). Hillsdale, NJ: Lawrence Erlbaum Associates.

Ehri, L. C. (1998). Research on learning to read and spell: A personal-historical perspective. *Scientific Studies of Reading, 2*(2), 97-114.

Ehri, L. C., & Wilce, L. S. (1979a). The mnemonic value of orthography among beginning readers. *Journal of Educational Psychology, 71*(1), 26-40.

Ehri, L. C., & Wilce, L. S. (1979b). Does word training increase or decrease interference in a Stroop task? *Journal of Experimental Child Psychology, 27,* 352-364.

Ehri, L. C., & Wilce, L. S. (1983). Development of word identification speed in skilled and less skilled beginning readers. *Journal of Educational Psychology, 75*(1), 3-18.

Ehri, L. C., & Wilce, L. S. (1987a). Cipher versus cue reading: An experiment in decoding acquisition. *Journal of Educational Psychology, 79*(1), 3-13.

Ehri, L. C., & Wilce, L. S. (1987b). Does learning to spell help beginners learn to read words? *Reading Research Quarterly, 22,* 47-65.

Elbro, C. (1991). Differences in reading strategies reflect differences in linguistic abilities. *International Journal of Applied Linguistics, 1*(2), 228-244.

Elley, W. B. (1991). Acquiring language in a second language: The effect of book based programs. *Language Learning, 41,* 375-411.

Ellis, A. W. (1985). The cognitive neuropsychology of developmental (and acquired) dyslexia: A critical study. *Cognitive Neuropsychology, 2*(2), 169-205.

Ellis, N. C., & Miles, T. R. (1978). Visual information processing as a determinant of reading speed. *Journal of Research in Reading, 1*(2), 108-120.

Evans, M., & Carr, T. (1985). Cognitive abilities, conditions of learning, and the early development of reading skill. *Reading Research Quarterly, 20,* 327-350.

Farr, R. (1968). The convergent and discriminant validity of several upper level reading tests. *Yearbook of the National Reading Conference, 17,* 181-191.

Farrell, E. (1982). SSR as the core of a junior high program. *Journal of Reading, 26,* 48-51.

Fielding-Barnsley, R. (1997). Explicit instruction in decoding benefits children high in phonemic awareness and alphabet knowledge. *Scientific Studies of Reading, 1*(1), 85-98.

Fleisher, L. S., Jenkins, J. R., & Pany, D. (1979). Effects on poor readers comprehension of training in rapid decoding. *Reading Research Quarterly, 15*(1), 30-48.

Fletcher, J. M., Shaywitz, S. E., Shankweiler, D. P., Katz, L., Liberman, I. Y., Steubing, K. K., Francis, D. J., Fowler, A. E., & Shaywitz, B. A. (1994). Cognitive profiles of reading disability: Comparison of discrepancy and low achievement definitions. *Journal of Educational Psychology, 86*(1), 6-23.

Foorman, B. R., Francis, D. J., Novy, D. M., & Liberman, D. (1991). How letter-sound instruction mediates progress in first-grade reading and spelling. *Journal of Educational Psychology, 83,* 456-469.

Foorman, B. R., Francis, D. J., Shaywitz, S. E., Shaywitz, B. A., & Fletcher, J. M. (1997). The case for early reading interventions. In B. Blachman (Ed.), *Foundations of reading acquisition and dyslexia* (pp. 243-264). Mahwah, NJ: Lawrence Erlbaum Associates.

Forster, K. I. (1970). Visual perception of rapidly presented word sequences of varying complexity. *Perception and Psychophysics, 8,* 215-221.

Foster, K. D., Erickson, G. C., Foster, D. F., Brinkman, D., & Torgesen, J. K. (1994). Computer administered instruction in phonological awareness: Evaluation of the Daisy Quest program. *Journal of Research and Development in Education, 27,* 126-137.

Francis, D. J., Stuebing, K. K., Shaywitz, S. E., Shaywitz, B. A., & Fletcher, J. A. (1996). Developmental lag versus deficit models of reading disability: A longitudinal, individual growth curves analysis. *Journal of Educational Psychology, 88*(1), 3-17.

Frase, L. T. (1967). Learning from prose material: Length of passage, knowledge of results, and position of question. *Journal of Educational Psychology, 56,* 266-272.

Fries, C. C. (1963). *Linguistics and reading.* New York: Holt, Rinehart, & Winston.

Frith, U. (1980). Unexpected spelling problems. In U. Frith (Ed.), *Cognitive processes in spelling* (pp. 495-515). London: Academic.

Frith, U. (1984). Specific spelling problems. In R. N. Malatosha & H. A. Whitaker (Eds.), *Dyslexia: A global issue* (pp. 83-103). The Hague, Netherlands: Martinium Nijhoff.

Fuchs, L. S., Fuchs, D., & Deno, S. L. (1982). Reliability and validity of curriculum-based informal reading inventories. *Reading Research Quarterly, 18,* 6-26.

Gates, A. I. (1921). An experimental and statistical study of reading and reading tests. *Journal of Educational Psychology, 12,* 303-314.

Gathercole, S. E., & Baddeley, A. D. (1993). *Working memory and language.* Hillsdale, NJ: Lawrence Erlbaum Associates.

Gernsbacher, M. A., Varner, K. R., & Faust, M. E. (1990). Investigating differences in general comprehension skill. *Journal of Experimental Psychology: Learning, Memory, and Cognition, 16,* 430-445,

Gibson, E. L., & Levin, H. L. (1975). *The psychology of reading.* Cambridge, MA: MIT Press.

Gill, J. T. (1992). The relationship between word recognition and spelling. In S. Templeton & D. R. Bear (Eds.), *Development of orthographic knowledge and the foundations of literacy: A memorial festschrift for Edmund H. Henderson* (pp. 79-104). Hillsdale, NJ: Lawrence Erlbaum Associates.

Glass, G. V. (1976). Primary, secondary, and meta-analysis of research. *Educational Researcher, 5*(10), 3-8.

Gleitman, L. R., & Rozin, P. (1977). The structure and acquisition of reading I: Relations between orthographics and the structure of language. In A. S. Reber & D. L. Scarborough (Eds.), *Toward a psychology of reading* (pp. 1-53). Hillsdale, NJ: Lawrence Erlbaum Associates.

Goodman, K. S. (1965, October). A linguistic study of cues and miscues in reading. *Elementary English*, 639-643.

Goodman, K. S. (1967, May). Reading: A psycholinguistic guessing game. *Journal of Reading Specialists*, 259-271.

Goodman, K. S. (1976). Reading: A psycholinguistic guessing game. In H. Singer & R. Ruddell (Eds.), *Theoretical models and processes of reading* (pp. 497-508). Newark, DE: International Reading Association.

Goodman, K. S. (1986). *What's whole in whole language?* Portsmouth, NH: Heinemann.

Goodman, K. S. (1989). Whole-language research: Foundations and development. *Elementary School Journal, 90*(2), 207-221.

Goodman, K. S. (1992). I didn't found whole language. *The Reading Teacher, 46*(3), 188-199.

Goodman, K. S., & Goodman, Y. M. (1979). Learning to read is natural. In L. B. Resnick & P. A. Weaver (Eds.), *Theory and practice of early reading, Vol. I.* Hillsdale, NJ: Lawrence Erlbaum Associates.

Goswami, U., & Bryant, P. (1990). *Phonological skills and learning to read.* East Sussex, UK: Lawrence Erlbaum Associates.

Gough, P. B. (1972). One second of reading. In J. F. Kavanaugh & I. G. Mattingly (Eds.), *The relationships between speech and reading* (pp. 321-358). Cambridge, MA: MIT Press.

Gough, P. B. (1984). Word recognition. In P. D. Pearson (Ed.), *Handbook of reading research* (pp. 225-254). New York: Longman.

Gough, P. B., & Hillinger, M. L. (1980). Learning to read: An unnatural act. *Bulletin of the Orton Society, 30,* 179-196.

Gough, P. B., & Juel, C. (1991). The first stages of word recognition. In L. Rieben & C. A. Perfetti (Eds.), *Learning to read: Basic research and its implications* (pp. 47-56). Hillsdale, NJ: Lawrence Erlbaum Associates.

Gough, P. B., Juel, C., & Griffith, P. L. (1992). Reading, spelling, and the orthographic cipher. In P. B. Gough, L. C. Ehri, & R. Treiman (Eds.), *Reading acquisition* (pp. 35-48). Hillsdale, NJ: Lawrence Erlbaum Associates.

Gough, P. B., & Tunmer, W. (1986). Decoding, reading, and reading disability. *Remedial and Special Education, 1,* 6-11.

Graesser, A. C., Hoffman, N. L., & Clark, L. F. (1980). Structural components of reading time. *Journal of Verbal Learning and Verbal Behavior, 19,* 135-151.

Graves, M. F. (1987). The roles of instruction in fostering vocabulary development. In M. G. McKeown & M. E. Curtis (Eds.), *The nature of vocabulary acquisition* (pp. 165-184). Hillsdale, NJ: Lawrence Erlbaum Associates.

Graves, M. F. (1992). The elementary vocabulary curriculum: What should it be? In M. J. Dreher & W. H. Slater (Eds.), *Elementary school literacy: Critical issues* (pp. 101-131). Norwood, MA: Christopher-Gordon.

Gustafsson, J-E. (1994). *General intelligence.* In R. J. Sternberg (Ed.), *Encyclopedia of human intelligence.* New York: Macmillan.

Hall, V. C., Chiarello, K. S., & Edmondson, B. (1996). Deciding where knowledge comes from depends on where you look. *Journal of Educational Psychology, 88,* 305-315.

Hammill, D. D., & McNutt, G. (1980). Language abilities and reading: A review of the literature on their relationships. *Elementary School Journal, 80,* 269-277.

Hammill, D. D., & McNutt, G. (1981). *The correlates of reading: The consensus of thirty years of correlational research.* Austin, TX: Pro-Ed.

Harste, J. C. (1989). The future of whole language. *Elementary School Journal, 90,* 243-249.

Harste, J. C., & Burke, C. L. (1977). A new hypothesis for reading teacher research: Both teaching and learning of reading are theoretically based. *Yearbook of the National Reading Conference, 26,* 32-40.

Hatcher, P., Hulme, C., & Ellis, A. W. (1994). Ameliorating early reading failure by integrating the teaching of reading and phonological skills: The phonological linkage hypothesis. *Child Development, 65,* 41-57.

Hausfeld, S. (1981). Speeded reading and listening comprehension for easy and difficult materials. *Journal of Educational Psychology, 73,* 312-319.

Henderson, E. H. (1992). The interface of lexical competence and knowledge of written words. In S. Templeton and D. R. Bear (Eds.), *Development of orthographic knowledge and the foundations of literacy: A memorial festschrift for Edmund H. Henderson* (pp. 1-30). Hillsdale, NJ: Lawrence Erlbaum Associates.

Hill, W. R. (1964). Influence of direction upon the flexibility of advanced college readers. *Yearbook of the National Reading Conference, 13,* 119-125.

Hoffman, J. V. (1978). Relationship between rate and reading flexibility. *Reading World, 17,* 325-328.

Hoffman, J. V. (1980). The disabled reader: Forgive us our regressions and lead us not into expectations. *Journal of Learning Disabilities. 13,* 2-6.

Hogaboam, T. W., & Perfetti, C. A. (1978). Reading skills and the role of verbal experience in decoding. *Journal of Educational Psychology, 70,* 717-729.

Holmes, J. A. (1954). Factors underlying major reading disabilities at the college level. *Genetic Psychology Monographs, 49,* 3-95.

Hoover, W., & Gough, P. (1990). The simple view of reading. *Reading and Writing: An Interdisciplinary Journal, 2,* 127-160.

Horn, J. L. (1994). Theory of fluid and crystallized intelligence. In R. J. Sternberg (Ed.), *Encyclopedia of human intelligence* (pp. 443-451). New York: Macmillan.

Horn, J. L., & Cattell, R. B. (1966). Refinement and test of the theory of fluid and crystallized intelligence. *Journal of Educational Psychology, 57,* 253-270.

Huey, E. B. (1908). *The psychology and pedagogy of reading.* New York: Macmillan (Republished: Cambridge, MA: MIT Press, 1968).

Hulme, C., & Mackinzie, S. (1992). *Working memory and severe learning difficulties.* Hillsdale, NJ: Lawrence Erlbaum Associates.

Hunt, E. (1978). Mechanics of verbal ability. *Psychological Review, 85,* 109-130.

Hunt, E., Davidson, J., & Lansman, M. (1981). Individual differences in long-term memory access. *Memory and Cognition, 9,* 599-608.

Hunt, L. C., Jr. (1967). Evaluation through teacher-pupil conferences. In T. C. Barrett (Ed.), *Evaluation of children's reading achievement* (pp. 111-125). Newark, DE: International Reading Association.

Ingham, J. (1981). *The Bradford book flood experiment.* London: Heinemann.

Iversen, S., & Tunmer, W. E. (1993). Phonological processing skills and the Reading Recovery Program. *Journal of Educational Psychology, 85*(1), 112-126.

Jackson, M. D. (1980). Further evidence for a relationship between memory access and reading ability. *Journal of Verbal Learning and Verbal Behavior, 19,* 683-694.

Jackson, M. D., & McClelland, J. L. (1975). Sensory and cognitive determinants of reading speed. *Journal of Verbal Learning and Verbal Behavior, 14,* 575-589.

Jackson, M. D., & McClelland, J. L. (1979). Processing determinants of reading speed. *Journal of Experimental Psychology: General, 108*(2), 151-181.

Jackson, N. E., & Biemiller, A. J. (1985). Letter, word, and text reading times of precocious and average readers. *Child Development, 56*(1), 196-206.

Jensen, A. R. (1982). The chronometry of intelligence. In R. J. Sternberg (Ed.), *Advances in the psychology of human intelligence, Vol. 1* (pp. 255-310). Hillsdale, NJ: Lawrence Erlbaum Associates.

Johnston, P., & Allington, R. (1991). Remediation. In R. Barr, M. L. Kamil, P. Mosenthal, & P. D. Pearson (Eds.), *Handbook of reading research: Vol. 2* (pp. 984-1012). New York: Longman.

Jorgenson, G. W. (1977). Relationship of classroom behavior to the accuracy of the match between material difficulty and student ability. *Journal of Educational Psychology, 69,* 24-32.

Jorm, A. F. (1983). *The psychology of reading and spelling disabilities.* London: Routledge & Kegan Paul.

Jorm, A. F., & Share, D. L. (1983). Phonological recoding and reading acquisition. *Applied Psycholinguistics, 4,* 103-147.

Joshi, R. M., & Aaron, P. G. (1990). Specific spelling disability: Factual or artifactual? *Reading and Writing: An Interdisciplinary Journal, 2,* 107-125.

Juel, C. (1983). The development and use of mediated word identification. *Reading Research Quarterly, 18,* 306-327.

Juel, C. (1988). Learning to read and write: A longitudinal study of 54 children from first through fourth grades. *Journal of Educational Psychology, 80,* 437-447.

Juel, C. (1990). Effects of reading group assignment on reading development in first and second grade. *Journal of Reading Behavior, 22,* 233-254.

Juel, C., Griffith, P. L., & Gough, P. B. (1986). Acquisition of literacy: A longitudinal study of children in first and second grade. *Journal of Educational Research, 78,* 243-255.

Just, M. A., & Carpenter, P. A. (1980). A theory of reading: From eye fixations to comprehension. *Psychological Review, 87,* 329-354.

Just, M. A., & Carpenter, P. A. (1992). A capacity theory of comprehension: Individual differences in working memory. *Psychological Review, 99*(1), 122-129.

Kagan, J. (1982). Retrieval difficulty in reading disability. *Topics in Learning and Learning Disability, 3,* 75-83.

Kameenui, E. J. (1996). Shakespeare and beginning reading: The readiness is all. *Teaching Exceptional Children, 27*(2), 77-81.

Keenan, J. M., & Brown, P. (1984). Children's reading rate and instruction as a function of the number of propositions in a text. *Child Development, 55,* 1556-1569.

Kibby, M. W. (1995). *Practical steps for informing literacy instruction: A diagnostic decision making model.* Newark, DE: International Reading Association.

Kintsch, W. (1994). Text comprehension, memory, and learning. *American Psychologist, 49,* 294-303.

Kintsch, W., & Keenan, J. (1973). Reading rate and retention as a function of the number of propositions in the base structure of sentences. *Cognitive Psychology, 5,* 257-274.

Kirsch, I. S., Jungeblut, A., Jenkins, L., & Kolstad, A. (1993). Adult literacy in America. (U.S. Government Printing Office Stock Number GPO 065-000-00588-3) Washington, DC: National Center for Educational Statistics, U.S. Office of Education. Prepared by Educational Testing Services, Princeton, NJ.

Klare, G. R. (1963). *The measurement of readability.* Ames, IA: Iowa State University Press.

Kyllenon, P. C., & Crystal, R. B. (1990). Reasoning ability is (little more than) working-memory capacity?! *Intelligence, 14,* 389-433.

LaBerge, D., & Samuels, S. J. (1974). Toward a theory of automatic information processing in reading. *Cognitive Psychology, 6,* 293-323.

Larsen, R. P., & Feder, D. D. (1940). Common and differential factors in reading and learning comprehension. *Journal of Education, 31,* 241-252.

Leckliter, I. N. (1994). Dyslexia. In R. J. Sternberg (Ed.), *Encyclopedia of human intelligence* (pp. 376-386). New York: Macmillan.

Lehrl, S., & Fischer, B. (1990). A basic information psychological parameter (BIP) for the reconstruction of concepts of intelligence. *European Journal of Personality, 4,* 259-285.

Lennon, R. T. (1962). What can be measured? *The Reading Teacher, 15,* 326-337.

Leong, C. K. (1993). Towards developing a framework for diagnosing reading disorders. In R. M. Joshi & C. K. Leong (Eds.), *Reading disabilities: Diagnosis and component processes* (pp. 85-131). Boston: Kluwer.

Lesgold, A. M., & Perfetti, C. A. (1978). Interactive processes in reading comprehension. *Discourse Processes, 1,* 323-336.

Levin, H., & Kaplan, E. L. (1970). Grammatical structure and reading. In H. Levin & J. P. Williams (Eds.), *Basic studies on reading* (pp. 110-133). New York: Basic Books.

Levine, S. L., & Osbourne, S. (1989, April). Living and learning with dyslexia. *Phi Delta Kappan,* 594-598.

Lezak, M. D. (1988). IQ: R.I.P. *Journal of Clinical and Experimental Neuropsychology, 10,* 351-361.

Liberman, I. Y., & Liberman, A. M. (1990). Whole language vs. code emphasis: Underlying assumptions and their implications for reading instruction. *Annals of Dyslexia, 40,* 51-76.

Liberman, I. Y., & Shankweiler, D. (1979). Speech, the alphabet, and teaching to read. In L. B. Resnick & P. Weaver (Eds.), *Theory and practice of early reading* (Vol. 2, pp. 109-132). Hillsdale, NJ: Lawrence Erlbaum Associates.

Lindamood, C. H., & Lindamood, P. C. (1984). *Auditory discrimination in depth.* Austin, TX: PRO-ED.

Lipson, M. Y., & Wixson, K. K. (1986). Reading disability research: An interactionist perspective. *Review of Educational Research, 56*(1), 111-136.

Lloyd, J., & McKelvie, S. J. (1992). Effects of spatial disruptions on reading speed for fast and slow readers. *Journal of General Psychology, 119,* 229-235.

Lohnes, P. R., & Gray, M. M. (1972). Intelligence and the cooperative reading studies. *Reading Research Quarterly, 7,* 466-476.

Lorsbach, T. C., & Gray, J. W. (1986). Item Identification speed and memory span performance in learning-disabled children. *Contemporary Educational Psychology, 11,* 68-78.

Lovett, M. W. (1984). A developmental perspective on reading dysfunction: Accuracy and rate criteria in the subtyping of dyslexic children. *Brain and Language, 22,* 67-91.

Lovett, M. W., Borden, S. L., DeLuca, T., Lacerenza, L., Benson, N. J., & Brackstone, D. (1994). Treating the core deficits of developmental dyslexia: Evidence of transfer of learning after phonologically- and strategy-based training programs. *Developmental Psychology, 30*(6), 805-822.

Lundberg, I., Frost, J., & Petersen, P. P. (1988). Effects of an extensive program for stimulating phonological awareness in preschool children. *Reading Research Quarterly, 23,* 263-284.

Lyon, G. R. (1985). Educational validation studies of learning disability subtypes. In B. P. Rourke (Ed.), *Neuropsychology of learning disabilities* (pp. 228-250). New York: Guilford Press.

Lyon, G. R. (1993). Preface. In G. R. Lyon, D. B. Gray, J. F. Kavanaugh, & N. A. Krasnegor (Eds.), *Better understanding learning disabilities* (pp. xvii-xix). Baltimore: Brookes.

Lyon, G. R. (1995). Toward a definition of dyslexia. *Annals of Dyslexia, 45,* 3-27.

MacGinitie, W. H. (1991, March). Reading instruction: Plus ca change... . *Educational Leadership,* 55-58.

Mackworth, J. F. (1963). The duration of the visual image. *Canadian Journal of Psychology, 17*(1), 62-81.

Manis, F. R. (1985). Acquisition of word identification skills in normal and disabled readers. *Journal of Educational Psychology, 77,* 78-90.

Manis, F. R., Savage, P. L., Morrison, F. J., Horn, C. C., Howell, M. J., Szeszulski, P. A., & Holt, L. K. (1987). Paired associate learning in reading-disabled children: Evidence for a rule-learning deficiency. *Journal of Experimental Child Psychology, 43,* 25-43.

Martin, M. (1978). Memory span as a measure of individual differences in memory capacity. *Memory and Cognition, 6*(2), 194-198.

Mason, M. (1978). From print to sound in mature readers as a function of reader ability and two forms of orthographic regularity. *Memory and Cognition, 6,* 568-581.

Masson, M. E. J. (1986). Comprehension of rapidly presented sentences: The mind is quicker than the eye. *Journal of Memory and Language. 25,* 588-604.

McConkie, G. W., & Hogaboam, T. W. (1985). Eye position and word identification during reading. In R. Groner, G. W. McConkie, & C. Manz (Eds.), *Eye movements and information processing* (pp. 159-192). Amsterdam: Elsevier/North-Holland.

McConkie, G. W., Kerr, P. W., Reddix, M. D., & Zola, D. (1987). Eye movement control during reading: The location of initial eye fixations on words (Technical Report No. 406). Champaign, IL: Center for the Study of Reading, University of Illinois.

McConkie, G. W., & Zola, D. (1984). Eye movement control during reading: The effect of word units. In W. Prinz & A. F. Sanders (Eds.), *Cognition and motor processes* (pp. 63-74). Berlin, Germany: Springer-Verlag.

McCormick, S. (1994). A nonreader becomes a reader: A case study of literacy acquisition by a severely disabled reader. *Reading Research Quarterly, 29*(2), 157-176.

McCracken, R. A. (1971). Initiating sustained silent reading. *Journal of Reading, 14,* 521-524, 582-583.

McCutchen, D., Bell, L. C., France, I. M., & Perfetti, C. A. (1991). Phoneme-specific interference in reading: The tongue-twister effect revisited. *Reading Research Quarterly, 26,* 87-103.

McGuinness, D., McGuinness, C., & Donohue, J. (1995). Phonological training and the alphabet principle: Evidence for reciprocal causality. *Reading Research Quarterly, 30,* 830-852.

McKenna, M. C., Robinson, R. D., & Miller, J. W. (1990). Whole language: A research agenda for the nineties. *Educational Researcher, 19*(8), 3-6.

McKenna, M. C., Stahl, S. A., & Reinking, D. (1994). A critical commentary on research, politics, and whole language. *Journal of Reading Behavior, 26,* 211-233.

McKenna, M. C., Stratton, B. D., Grindler, M. C., & Jenkins, S. J. (1995). Differential effects of whole language and traditional instruction on reading attitudes. *Journal of Reading Behavior, 27*(1), 19-44.

Metsala, J. L. (1997). Spoken word recognition in reading disabled children. *Journal of Educational Psychology, 89,* 159-169.

Mewhort, D. J. K., & Campbell, A. J. (1981). Toward a model of skilled reading: An analysis of performance in tachistoscopic tasks. In G. E. MacKinnon & T. G. Waller (Eds.), *Reading research: Advances in theory and practice: Vol. 3* (pp. 39-118). New York: Academic Press.

Mezynski, K. (1983). Issues concerning the acquisition of knowledge: Effects of vocabulary training on reading comprehension. *Review of Educational Research, 53,* 253-279.

Mikulecky, L. (1990, December). National adult literacy and lifelong learning goals. *Phi Delta Kappan,* 304-309.

Miller, G. R., & Coleman, E. B. (1971). The measurement of reading speed and the obligation to generalize to a population of reading materials. *Journal of Reading Behavior, 4*(3), 48-56.

Miller, J. R., & Kintsch, W. (1980). Readability and recall of short prose passages: A theoretical analysis. *Journal of Experimental Psychology: Human Learning and Memory, 6,* 335-354.

Mills, J. R., & Jackson, N. E. (1990). Predictive significance of early giftedness: The case of precocious reading. *Journal of Educational Psychology, 82,* 410-419.

Mitchell, D. C., & Green, D. W. (1978). The effects of context and content on immediate processing in reading. *Quarterly Journal of Experimental Psychology, 30,* 609-636.

Morrison, F. J., & Manis, F. R. (1982). Cognitive processes and reading disability: A critique and proposal. In C. J. Brainerd & M. Pressley (Eds.), *Verbal processes in children: Progress in cognitive development* (pp. 59-83). New York: Springer-Verlag.

Morse, W. C. (1951). A comparison of the eye-movements of average fifth- and seventh-grade pupils reading materials of corresponding difficulty. In *Studies in the psychology of reading* (University of Michigan Monographs in Education No. 4, pp. 1-64). Ann Arbor: University of Michigan Press.

Nagy, W. E. (1988). *Teaching vocabulary to improve reading comprehension.* Newark, DE: International Reading Association.

Naslund, J. C., & Schneider. W. (1991). Longitudinal effects of verbal ability, memory capacity, and phonological awareness on reading performance. *European Journal of Psychology of Education, 6,* 375-392.

Neisser, U. (1983, May). A conversation with Ulric Neisser. *Psychology Today,* 54-62.

Neisser, U., Boodoo, G., Bouchard, T. L., Jr., Boykin, A. W., Brody, N., Ceci, S. J., Halpern, D. F., Loehlin, J. C., Perloff, R., Sternberg, R. J., & Urbina, S. (1996). Intelligence: Knowns and unknowns. *American Psychologist, 51*(2), 77-101.

Nelson, N. E., & Warrington, E. K. (1974). Developmental spelling retardation. *British Journal of Psychology, 65,* 265-274.

Newell, N., & Rosenbloom, P. S. (1981). Mechanisms of skill acquisition and the law of practice. In J. R. Anderson (Ed.), *Cognitive skills and their acquisition* (pp. 1-55). Hillsdale, NJ: Lawrence Erlbaum Associates.

Newman, S., Fields, H., & Wright, S. (1993). A developmental study of specific spelling disability. *British Journal of Educational Psychology, 63,* 287-296.

Nicholson, T. (1991). Do children read words better in context or in lists? A classic study revisited. *Journal of Educational Psychology, 83,* 444-450.

Olson, R. K., Datta, H., Gayan, J., & DeFries, J. C. (1999). A behavior-genetic analysis of reading disabilities and component processes. In R. Klein & P. McMullen (Eds.), Converging methods for understanding reading and dyslexia. Cambridge, MA: MIT Press.

Olson, R. K., Wise, B., Ring, J., & Johnson, M. (1997). Computer-based remedial training in phoneme awareness and phonological decoding: Effects on the posttraining development of word recognition. *Scientific Studies of Reading, 1*(3), 235-253.

Orton, S. T. (1925). "Word Blindness" in school children. *Archives of Neurology and Psychiatry, 14,* 581-615.

Pace, A. J., & Golinkoff, R. M. (1976). Relationship between word difficulty and access of single word meaning by skilled and less skilled readers. *Journal of Educational Psychology, 68,* 760-767.

Palinczar, A. S., & Brown, A. L. (1984). Reciprocal teaching of comprehension-fostering and comprehension-monitoring activities. *Cognition and Instruction, 1*, 117-175.

Palmer, J., MacLeod, C. M., Hunt, E., & Davidson, J. E. (1985). Information processing correlates of reading. *Journal of Memory and Language, 24*(1), 59-88.

Pearson, P. D. (1984). *Handbook of reading research.* New York: Longman.

Perfetti, C. A. (1977). Language comprehension and fast decoding: Some psycholinguistic prerequisites for skilled reading. In J. Guthrie (Ed.), *Cognition, curriculum, and comprehension* (pp. 20-41). Newark, DE: International Reading Association.

Perfetti, C. A. (1983). Reading, vocabulary, and writing: Implications for computer-based instruction. In A. C. Wilkinson (Ed.), *Classroom computers and cognitive science* (pp. 145-163). New York: Academic Press.

Perfetti, C. A. (1985). *Reading ability.* New York: Oxford University Press.

Perfetti, C. A. (1988). Verbal efficiency in reading ability. In M. Daneman, G. E. MacKinnon, & T. G. Waller (Eds.), *Reading research: Advances in theory and practice: Vol. 6* (pp. 109-143). New York: Academic.

Perfetti, C. A. (1989). There are generalized abilities and one of them is reading. In L. B. Resnick (Ed.), *Knowing, learning, and instruction: Essays in honor of Robert Glaser* (pp. 307-335). Hillsdale, NJ: Lawrence Erlbaum Associates.

Perfetti, C. A. (1991a). On the value of simple ideas in reading instruction. In S. Brady & D. Shankweiler (Eds.), *Phonological processes in literacy: A tribute to Isabelle Y. Liberman* (pp. 211-218). Hillsdale, NJ: Lawrence Erlbaum Associates.

Perfetti, C. A. (1991b). The psychology, pedagogy, and politics of reading. *Psychological Science, 2*(20), 70-76.

Perfetti, C. A. (1993). Why inferences might be restricted. *Discourse Processes, 16*, 181-192.

Perfetti, C. A. (1994). Reading. In R. J. Sternberg (Ed.), *Encyclopedia of human intelligence* (pp. 923-930). New York: Macmillan.

Perfetti, C. A. (1997). The psycholinguistics of spelling and reading. In C. A. Perfetti, L. Rieben, & M. Fayol (Eds.), *Learning to spell: Research, theory, and practice* (pp. 21-38). Mahwah, NJ: Lawrence Erlbaum Associates.

Perfetti, C. A., Beck, I. L., Bell, L. C., & Hughes, C. (1987). Phonemic knowledge and learning to read are reciprocal: A longitudinal study of first grade children. *Merrill-Palmer Quarterly, 33*, 283-319.

Perfetti, C. A., Finger, E., & Hogaboam, T. W. (1978). Sources of vocalization latency differences between skilled and less skilled young readers. *Journal of Educational Psychology, 70*, 730-739.

Perfetti, C. A., Georgi, M. C., & Beck, I. L. (1993). Implications of the Pittsburgh study for issues of risk. In H. Grimm & H. Skowronek (Eds.), *Language acquisition problems and reading disorders: Aspects of diagnosis and intervention* (pp. 193-209). Berlin: da Gruyter.

Perfetti, C. A., & Hogaboam, T. (1975). Relationship between single word decoding and reading comprehension skill. *Journal of Educational Psychology, 67*, 461-469.

Perfetti, C. A., & Lesgold, A. M. (1977). Discourse comprehension and sources of individual differences. In M. A. Just & P. A. Carpenter (Eds.), *Cognitive processes in comprehension* (pp. 141-183). New York: Wiley.

Perfetti, C. A., & Roth, S. F. (1981). Some of the interactive processes in reading and their role in reading skill. In A. M. Lesgold & C. A. Perfetti (Eds.), *Interactive processes in reading* (pp. 269-297). Hillsdale, NJ: Lawrence Erlbaum Associates.

Perfetti, C. A., Zhang, S., & Berent, E. (1992). Reading in English and Chinese: Evidence for a universal phonological principle. In R. Frost & L. Katz (Eds.), *Orthography, phonology, and meaning* (pp. 227-248). Amsterdam: Elsevier/North-Holland.

Pinnell, G. S. (1989). Success of at-risk children in a program that combines reading and writing. In J. Mason (Ed.), *Reading and writing connections* (pp. 237-259). Boston: Allyn & Bacon.

Posner, M. I., & Mitchell, R. F. (1967). Chronometric analysis of classification. *Psychological Review, 74*, 392-409.

Potter, M. C., Kroll, J. F., & Harris, C. (1980). Comprehension and memory in rapid sequential reading. In R. S. Nickerson (Ed.), *Attention and performance, VIII* (pp. 395-418). Hillsdale, NJ: Lawrence Erlbaum Associates.

Pressley, M. (1994). State-of-the-science primary-grades reading instruction or whole language? *Educational Psychologist, 29,* 211-216.

Pressley, M., & Rankin, J. (1994). More about whole language methods of reading instruction for students at risk for early reading failure. *Learning Disabilities Research and Practice, 9,* 157-168.

Pressley, M., Rankin, J., & Yokoi, L. (1995). A survey of instructional practices of primary teachers nominated as effective in promoting literacy (Report No. 41). University of Georgia and University of Maryland: National Reading Research Center.

Pressley, M., Wharton-McDonald, R., Mistretta-Hampston, J., & Echevarria, M. (1998). Literacy instruction in 10 fourth- and fifth-grade classrooms in upstate New York. *Scientific Studies of Reading, 2*(2), 159-194.

Rack, J., Snowling, M., & Olson, R. (1992). The nonword reading deficit in developmental dyslexia: A review. *Reading Research Quarterly, 27*(1), 29-53.

Raines, S. C. (1995). *Whole language across the curriculum.* Newark, DE: International Reading Association.

Rayner, K. (1975). The perceptual span and peripheral cues in reading. *Cognitive Psychology, 7,* 65-81.

Rayner, K. (1983). Eye movements, perceptual spans, and reading disability. *Annals of Dyslexia, 33,* 163-173.

Rayner, K. (1997). Understanding eye movements in reading. *Scientific Studies of Reading, 1*(4), 317-340.

Rayner, K., & Duffy, S. A. (1986). Lexical complexity and fixation times in reading: Effects of word frequency, verb complexity, and lexical ambiguity. *Memory and Cognition, 14*(3), 191-201.

Rayner, K., Inhoff, A. W., Morrison, R. E., Slowiaczek, M. L., & Bertera, J. H. (1981). Masking of foveal and parafoveal vision during eye fixations in reading. *Journal of Experimental Psychology: Human Perception and Performance, 7*(1), 167-179.

Rayner, K., & Pollatsek, A. (1989). *The psychology of reading.* Englewood Cliffs, NJ: Prentice Hall.

Rayner, K., Raney, G. E., & Pollatsek, A. (1995). Eye movements and discourse processing. In R. F. Lorch, Jr. & E. J. O'Brien (Eds.), *Sources of coherence in reading* (pp. 9-35). Hillsdale, NJ: Lawrence Erlbaum Associates.

Reitsma, P. (1983). Printed word learning in beginning readers. *Journal of Experimental Child Psychology, 36,* 321-339.

Reitsma, P. (1989). Orthographic memory and learning to read. In P. G. Aaron & R. M. Joshi (Eds.), *Reading and writing disorders in different orthographic systems* (pp. 51-73). The Netherlands: Kluwer.

Richek, M. (1977). Readiness skills that predict initial word learning using two different methods of instruction. *Reading Research Quarterly, 13,* 200-222.

Rosenberger, P. B. (1992). Dyslexia—is it a disease? *The New England Journal of Medicine, 326*(3), 192-193.

Rosenshine, B., & Meister, C. (1994). Reciprocal teaching: A review of the research. *Review of Educational Research, 64,* 479-530

Rost, D. H. (1989). Reading comprehension: Skill or skills. *Journal of Research in Reading, 12*(2), 85-113.

Roth, S. F., & Beck, I. L. (1987). Theoretical and instructional implications of the assessment of two microcomputer word recognition programs. *Reading Research Quarterly, 22*(2), 197-218.

Rothkopf, E. Z. (1966). Learning from written materials: An exploration of the control of inspection behavior by test-like events. *American Educational Research Journal, 3,* 241-249.

Rothkopf, E. Z., & Coatney, R. P. (1974). Effects of context passages on subsequent inspection rates. *Journal of Applied Psychology, 59,* 679-682.

Royer, J. M., Greene, B. A., & Sinatra, G. M. (1987, February). The sentence verification technique: A practical procedure for testing comprehension. *Journal of Reading,* 414-422.

Royer, J. M., Hastings, C. N., & Hook, C. (1979). A sentence verification technique for measuring reading comprehension. *Journal of Reading Behavior, 11,* 355-363.

Rozin, P., & Gleitman, L. (1977). The structure and acquisition of reading II: The reading process and the acquisition of the alphabetic principle. In A. S. Reber & D. L. Scarborough (Eds.), *Toward a psychology of reading* (pp. 55-141). Hillsdale, NJ: Lawrence Erlbaum Associates.

Rupley, W. H., Willson, V. L., & Nichols, W. D. (1998). Exploration of the developmental components contributing to elementary school children's reading comprehension. *Scientific Studies of Reading, 2*(2), 143-158.

Sadoski, M. (1980). Ten years of uninterrupted sustained silent reading. *Reading Improvement, 17,* 153-156.

Samuels, S. J. (1988). Decoding and automaticity: Helping poor readers become automatic at word recognition. *The Reading Teacher, 41,* 756-760.

Sassenrath, J. M. (1972). Alpha factor analyses of reading measures at the elementary, secondary, and college levels. *Journal of Reading Behavior, 5,* 304-316.

Scanlon, D. M., & Vellutino, F. R. (1997). A comparison of the instructional backgrounds and cognitive profiles of poor, average, and good readers who were initially identified as at risk for reading failure. *Scientific Studies of Reading, 1*(3), 191-215.

Schmidt, F. L. (1996). Statistical significance testing and cumulative knowledge in psychology: Implications for training of researchers. *Psychological Methods, 1,* 115-129.

Schmidt, F. L., & Crano, W. D. (1974). A test of the theory of fluid and crystallized intelligence in middle- and low-socioeconomic-status children. *Journal of Educational Psychology, 66,* 255-261.

Schustack, M. W., Ehrlich, S. F., & Rayner, K. (1987). Local and global sources of contextual facilitation in reading. *Journal of Memory and Language, 26,* 322-340.

Sears, S., & Keogh, B. (1993). Predicting reading performance using the Slingerland procedures. *Annals of Dyslexia, 43,* 78-89.

Seidenberg, M. S. (1987). Sublexical structures in visual word recognition: Access units or orthographic redundancy. In M. Coltheart (Ed.), *Attention and performance XII: The psychology of reading* (pp. 245-263). Hillsdale, NJ: Lawrence Erlbaum Associates.

Seidenberg, M. S., & McClelland, J. L. (1989). A distributed, developmental model of word recognition and naming. *Psychological Review, 96,* 522-568.

Shanahan, T. (1984). Nature of the reading-writing relation: An exploratory multi-variate analysis. *Journal of Educational Psychology, 76,* 466-477.

Shanahan, T., & Lomax, R. G. (1988). A developmental comparison of three theoretical models of reading-writing relationship. *Research in the Teaching of English, 22*(2), 196-212.

Shankweiler, D., & Liberman, I. Y. (1972). In J. F. Kavanagh & I. G. Mattingly (Eds.), *Language by eye and by ear* (pp. 293-318). Cambridge, MA: MIT Press.

Shankweiler, D., Lundquist, E., Katz, L., Stuebing, K. K., Fletcher, J. M., Brady, S., Fowler, A., Dreyer, L. G., Marchione, K. E., Shaywitz, S. E., & Shaywitz, B. A. (1999). Comprehension and decoding: Patterns of association in children with reading difficulties. *Scientific Studies of Reading, 3*(1), 69-94.

Shannon, P. (1994). People who live in glass houses. In C. B. Smith (Ed.), *Whole language: The debate* (pp. 97-120). Bloomington, IN: ERIC.

Shany, M. J., & Biemiller, A. (1995). Assisted reading practice. *Reading Research Quarterly, 30,* 382-395.

Share, D. L., & Stanovich, K. E. (1995). Cognitive processes in early reading development: Accommodating individual differences into a model of acquisition. *Issues in Education, 1,* 1-57.

Shaywitz, S. E. (1996, November). Dyslexia. *Scientific American,* 98-104.

Shaywitz, S. E., Escobar, M. D., Shaywitz, B. A., Fletcher, J. M., & Makuch, R. (1992). Evidence that dyslexia may represent the lower tail of a normal distribution of reading ability. *New England Journal of Medicine, 326*(3), 145-150.

Siegel, L. S. (1988). Evidence that IQ scores are irrelevant to the definition and analysis of reading disability. *Canadian Journal of Psychology, 42,* 201-215.

Siegel, L. S. (1989). IQ is irrelevant to the definition of learning disabilities. *Journal of Learning Disabilities, 22,* 468-478.

Siegel, L. S., Share, D. L., & Geva, E. (1995). Evidence for superior orthographic skills in dyslexics. *Psychological Science, 6,* 250-253.

Smith, F. (1971). *Understanding reading: A psycholinguistic analysis of reading and learning to read.* New York: Holt, Rinehart, and Winston.

Smith, F. (1976). Learning to read by reading. *Language Arts, 53,* 297-299, 322.

Smith, F. (1979). *Reading without response.* New York: Teachers College Press.

Smith, F. (1992, February). Learning to read: The never ending debate. *Phi Delta Kappan*, 432-411.

Smith, F., & Holmes, D. L. (1971). The independence of letter, word, and meaning identification in reading. *Reading Research Quarterly, 6,* 394-415.

Snow, R. E., & Yalow, E. (1982). Education and intelligence. In R. J. Sternberg (Ed.), *Handbook of human intelligence* (pp. 493-585). New York: Cambridge University Press.

Snowling, M. J., Goulandris, N., & Defty, N. (1996). A longitudinal study of reading development in dyslexic children. *Journal of Educational Psychology, 88,* 653-669.

Spear-Swerling, L., & Sternberg, R. J. (1996). *Offtrack: When poor readers become "learning disabled."* Boulder, CO: Westview Press.

Spearman, C. (1904). "General intelligence," objectively determined and measured. *American Journal of Psychology, 15,* 201-293.

Speece, D. L. (1993). Broadening the scope of classification research: Conceptual and ecological issues. In G. R. Lyon, D. G. Gray, J. F. Kavanagh, & N. A. Krasnegor (Eds.), *Better understanding learning disabilities* (pp. 57-72). Baltimore: Brookes.

Spiegel, D. L. (1992). Blending whole language and systematic direct instruction. *The Reading Teacher, 46*(1), 38-44.

Spring, C., & Capps, C. (1974). Encoding speed, rehearsal, and probed recall of dyslexic boys. *Journal of Educational Psychology, 66,* 780-786.

Spring, C., & Davis, J. M. (1988). Relations of digit naming speed with three components of reading. *Applied Psycholinguistics, 9,* 315-334.

Spring, C., & Farmer, R. (1975). Perceptual span of poor readers. *Journal of Reading Behavior, 7,* 297-305.

Spring, C., & Perry, L. (1983). Naming speed and serial recall in poor and adequate readers. *Contemporary Educational Psychology, 8,* 141-145.

Stahl, S. A. (1991). Beyond the instrumentalist hypothesis: Some relationships between word meanings and comprehension. In P. Schwanenfluegel (Ed.), *The psychology of word meanings* (pp. 157-178). Hillsdale, NJ: Lawrence Erlbaum Associates.

Stahl, S. A. (1997). Instructional models in reading: An introduction. In S. A. Stahl, & D. A. Hayes, *Instructional models in reading* (pp. 1-29). Mahwah, NJ: Lawrence Erlbaum Associates.

Stahl, S. A., Duffy-Hester, A. M., & Stahl, K. A. D. (1998). Theory and research into practice: Everything you wanted to know about phonics (but were afraid to ask). *Reading Research Quarterly, 33*(3), 338-355.

Stahl, S. A., & Fairbanks, M. (1986). The effects of vocabulary instruction: A model-based meta-analysis. *Review of Educational Research, 56,* 72-110.

Stahl, S. A., McKenna, M. C., & Pagnucco, J. R. (1994). The effects of whole-language instruction: An update and a reappraisal. *Educational Psychologist, 29*(4), 175-186.

Stahl, S. A., & Miller, P. D. (1989). Whole language and language experience approaches for beginning reading: A quantitative research synthesis. *Review of Educational Research, 59,* 87-116.

Stanovich, K. E. (1980). Toward an interactive-compensatory model of individual differences in the development of reading fluency. *Reading Research Quarterly, 16,* 32-71.

Stanovich, K. E. (1981). Relationships between word decoding speed, general name-retrieval ability, and reading progress in first-grade children. *Journal of Educational Psychology, 73,* 809-815.

Stanovich, K. E. (1984). The interactive-compensatory model of reading: A confluence of developmental, experimental, and educational psychology. *Remedial and Special Education, 5,* 11-19.

Stanovich, K. E. (1986). Matthew effects in reading: Some consequences of individual differences in the acquisition of literacy. *Reading Research Quarterly, 21*(4), 360-407.

Stanovich, K. E. (1988a). Exploring the differences between the dyslexic and the garden-variety poor reader: The phonological-core variable-difference model. *Journal of Learning Disabilities, 21,* 590-612.

Stanovich, K. E. (1988b). Science and learning disabilities. *Journal of Learning Disabilities, 21*(4), 210-214.

Stanovich, K. E. (1989). Has the LD field lost its intelligence? *Journal of Learning Disabilities, 22,* 487-492.

Stanovich, K. E. (1991). Discrepancy definitions of reading disability: Has intelligence led us astray? *Reading Research Quarterly, 26*(1), 7-29.

Stanovich, K. E. (1992). The psychology of reading: Evolutionary and revolutionary developments. *Annual Review of Applied Linguistics, 12,* 3-10.

Stanovich, K. E. (1993a). Romance and reality. *The Reading Teacher, 47,* 280-291.

Stanovich, K. E. (1993b). The construct validity of discrepancy definitions of reading disability. In G. R. Lyon, D. B. Gray, J. F. Kavanaugh, & N. A. Krasnegor (Eds.), *Better understanding of learning disabilities* (pp. 273-307). Baltimore: Brookes.

Stanovich, K. E., & Cunningham, A. E. (1993). Where does knowledge come from? Specific associations between print exposure and information acquisition. *Journal of Educational Psychology, 85,* 211-229.

Stanovich, K. E., Cunningham, A. E., & Feeman, D. J. (1984). Intelligence, cognitive skills, and early reading progress. *Reading Research Quarterly, 19,* 278-303.

Stanovich, K. E., Feeman, D. J., & Cunningham, A. E. (1983). The development of the relation between letter-naming speed and reading ability. *Bulletin of the Psychomic Society, 21,* 199-202.

Stanovich, K. E., Nathan, R. G., & Vala-Rossi, M. (1986). Developmental changes in the correlates of reading ability and the developmental lag hypothesis. *Reading Research Quarterly, 21,* 267-283.

Stanovich, K. E., Nathan, R. G., & Zolman, J. E. (1988). The developmental lag hypothesis in reading longitudinal and matched reading-level comparisons. *Child Development, 59,* 71-86.

Stanovich, K. E., & Siegel, L. S. (1994). Phenotypic performance profile of children with reading disabilities: A regression-based test of the phonological-core variable-difference model. *Journal of Educational Psychology, 86,* 24-53.

Stanovich, K. E., Siegel, L. S., & Gottardo, A. (1997). Converging evidence for phonological and surface subtypes of reading disability. *Journal of Educational Psychology, 89,* 114-127.

Stanovich, K. E., & West, R. F. (1979). The effect of orthographic structure on the word search performance of good and poor readers. *Journal of Experimental Child Psychology, 28,* 258-267.

Stanovich, K. E., & West, R. F. (1989). Exposure to print and orthographic processing. *Reading Research Quarterly, 34,* 402-433.

Stanovich, K. E., West, R. F., & Feeman, D. J. (1981). A longitudinal study of sentence context effects in second grade children: Test of an interactive compensatory model. *Journal of Experimental Child Psychology, 32,* 185-199.

Stauffer, R. C. (Ed.) (1967). *The first grade reading studies: Findings of individual investigations.* Newark, DE: International Reading Association.

Sternberg, R. J. (1986). The future of intelligence-testing. *Educational Measurement Issues and Practice, 5*(3), 19-22.

Sternberg, R. J. (1987). Most vocabulary is learned from context. In M. G. McKeown & M. E. Curtis (Eds.), *The nature of vocabulary acquisition* (pp. 89-105). Hillsdale, NJ: Lawrence Erlbaum Associates.

Sternberg, R. J. (1994). *Encyclopedia of human intelligence.* New York: Macmillan.

Sternberg, R. J., Conway, G. E., Ketron, J. I., & Berstein, M. (1981). People's conceptions of intelligence. *Journal of Personality and Social Psychology: Attitudes and Social Cognition, 41,* 37-55.

Sternberg, R. J., & Powell, J. S. (1983). Comprehending verbal comprehension. *American Psychologist, 38,* 878-893.

Stevenson, H., Parker, T., Wilkinson, A., Hegion, A., & Fisk, E. (1976). Longitudinal study of individual differences in cognitive development and scholastic achievement. *Journal of Educational Psychology, 68,* 377-400.

Sticht, T. G. (1972). Learning by listening. In R. O. Freedle & J. B. Carroll (Eds.), *Language comprehension and the acquisition of knowledge* (pp. 285-314). New York: Wiley.

Sticht, T. G., Beck, L. J., Hauke, R. N., Kleiman, G. M., & James, J. H. (1974). *Auding and reading: A developmental model.* Alexandria, VA: Human Resources Research Organization.

Sticht, T. G., Hooke, L. R., & Caylor, J. S. (1982). Literacy, oracy, and vocational aptitude as predictors of attrition and promotion in the armed services (Professional Paper 2-82). Alexandria, VA: Human Resources Research Organization.

Sticht, T. G., & James, J. H. (1984). Listening and reading. In P. D. Pearson (Ed.), *Handbook of reading research* (pp. 293-317). New York: Longman.

Stone, B., & Brady, S. (1995). Evidence for phonological processing deficits in less-skilled readers. *Annals of Dyslexia, 45,* 51-78.

Stroud, J. B. (1945). Rate of visual perception as a factor in rate of reading. *Journal of Educational Psychology, 36,* 487-498.

Stuart, M., & Masterson, J. (1992). Patterns of reading and spelling in 10-year-old children related to prereading phonological abilities. *Journal of Experimental Child Psychology, 54,* 168-187.

Tan, A., & Nicholson, T. (1997). Flashcards revisited: Training poor readers to read words faster improves their comprehension of text. *Journal of Educational Psychology, 89*(2), 276-288.

Tannenhaus, M. K., Flanigan, H., & Seidenberg, M. S. (1980). Orthographic and phonological code activation in auditory and visual word recognition. *Memory and Cognition, 8,* 513-520.

Taylor, B. M., Frye, B. J., & Maruyama, G. M. (1990). Time spent reading and reading growth. *American Educational Research Journal, 27,* 351-362.

Terman, L. M. (1918). Vocabulary test as a measure of intelligence. *Journal of Educational Psychology, 9,* 452-466.

Thorndike, E. L. (1917). Reading as reasoning: A study of mistakes in paragraph reading. *Journal of Educational Psychology, 8,* 323-332.

Thorndike, R. L. (1973). *Reading comprehension education in fifteen countries.* New York: Wiley.

Thorndike, R. L. (1974). Reading as reasoning. *Reading Research Quarterly, 9*(2), 135-147.

Thurstone, L. L. (1946). A note on a reanalysis of Davis' reading tests. *Psychometrika, 11,* 185-188.

TIME Magazine (1993, September 20). Adding up the under-skilled. Education section, p. 75.

Torgesen, J. K. (1985). Memory processes in reading disabled children. *Journal of Learning Disabilities, 18,* 350-357.

Torgesen, J. K., & Houck, D. (1980). Processing deficiencies of learning-disabled children who perform poorly on the digit span test. *Journal of Educational Psychology, 72,* 141-160.

Torgesen, J. K., Wagner, R. K., & Rashotte, C. A. (1997). Prevention and remediation of severe reading disabilities: Keeping the end in mind. *Scientific Studies of Reading, 1,* 217-234.

Torgesen, J. K., Wagner, R. K., Rashotte, C. A., Burgess, S., & Heckt, S. (1997). Contributions of phonological awareness and rapid automatic naming ability to the growth of word-reading skills in second- to fifth-grade children. *Scientific Studies of Reading, 1,* 161-185.

Traxler, A. E. (1934). The relationships between rate of reading and speed of association. *Journal of Educational Psychology, 25,* 357-365.

Tunmer, W. E., Herriman, M. L., & Nesdale, A. R. (1988). Metalinguistic abilities and beginning reading. *Reading Research Quarterly, 23,* 134-158.

Turner, M. L., & Engle, R. W. (1989). Is working memory capacity task dependent? *Journal of Memory and Language, 28,* 127-154.

Uhry, J. K., & Shepherd, M. J. (1993). Segmentational spelling instruction as part of a first-grade reading program: Effects on several measures of reading. *Reading Research Quarterly, 28,* 218-233.

Valencia, S. W., & Stallman, A. C. (1989). Multiple measures of prior knowledge: Comparative predictive validity. *Yearbook of the National Reading Conference, 38,* 427-436.

Vandervelden, M. C., & Siegel, L. S. (1995). Phonological recoding and phoneme awareness in early literacy: A developmental approach. *Reading Research Quarterly, 30,* 854-875.

Vellutino, F. R. (1979). *Dyslexia: Theory and research.* Cambridge, MA: MIT Press.

Vellutino, F. R. (1987). Dyslexia. *Scientific American, 256*(3), 34-41

Vellutino, F. R. (1991). Introduction to three studies on reading acquisition: Convergent findings on theoretical foundations on code-oriented versus whole-language approach to reading instruction. *Journal of Educational Psychology, 83,* 437-443.

Vellutino, F. R., Harding, C. J., Phillips, F., & Steger, J. A. (1975). Differential transfer in poor and normal readers. *The Journal of Genetic Psychology, 126,* 3-18.

Vellutino, F. R., Scanlon, D. M., Sipay, E. R., Small, S. G., Pratt, A., Chen, R., & Denckla, M. B. (1996). Cognitive profiles of difficult-to-remediate and readily remediated poor readers: Early intervention as a vehicle for distinguishing between cognitive and experiential deficits as basic causes of specific reading disability. *Journal of Educational Psychology, 88,* 601-638.

Vellutino, F. R., Scanlon, D. M., & Spearing, D. (1995). Semantic and phonological coding in poor and normal readers. *Journal of Experimental Child Psychology, 59,* 76-123.

Vellutino, F. R., Steger, J. A., & Pruzek, R. M. (1973). Inter- vs. intra-sensory deficit in paired associate learning in poor and normal readers. *Canadian Journal of Behavioral Science, 5*(2), 111-123.

Venezky, R. L. (1975). The curious role of letter names in reading instruction. *Visible Language, 9,* 7-23.

Venezky, R. L. (1976). *Theoretical and experimental base for teaching reading.* The Hague: Mouton.

Venezky, R. L. (1977). Research on reading processes: A historical perspective. *American Psychologist, 32,* 339-345.

Wagner, R. K., Torgesen, J. K., & Rashotte, C. A. (1994). Development of reading-related phonological processing abilities: New evidence of bi-directional causality from a latent variable longitudinal study. *Developmental Psychology, 30,* 73-87.

Walsh, D. J., Price, G. G., & Gillingham, M. G. (1988). The critical but transitory importance of letter naming. *Reading Research Quarterly, 23*(1), 108-122.

Watson, D. J. (1989). Describing and defining whole language. *Elementary School Journal, 90*(2), 129-141.

Weaver, C. (1988). *Reading process and practice: From socio-psycholinguistics to whole language.* Portsmouth, NH: Heinemann.

Webb, W. B., & Wallon, E. J. (1956). Comprehension by reading versus hearing. *Journal of Applied Psychology, 40,* 237-240.

Wechsler, D. (1944). *The measurement of adult intelligence.* Baltimore: Williams and Wilkins.

West, R. F., & Stanovich, K. E. (1978). Automatic contextual facilitation in readers of three ages. *Child Development, 49,* 717-727.

West, R. F., Stanovich, K. E., & Mitchell, H. R. (1993). Reading in the real word and its correlates. *Reading Research Quarterly, 28*(1), 35-50.

Williams, J. P. (1977). Building conceptual and cognitive strategies into a reading curriculum. In A. S. Reber & D. L. Scarborough (Eds.), *Toward a psychology of reading* (pp. 257-288). Hillsdale, NJ: Lawrence Erlbaum Associates.

Williams, J. P. (1980). Teaching decoding with an emphasis on phoneme analysis and phoneme blending. *Journal of Educational Psychology, 72*(1), 1-15.

Wimmer, H. (1993). Characteristics of developmental dyslexia in a regular writing system. *Applied Psycholinguistics, 14,* 1-33.

Wolf, M. (1991). Naming speed and reading: The contribution of the cognitive neurosciences. *Reading Research Quarterly, 26*(2), 123-141.

Wolf, M. (1997). A provisional, integrative account of phonological and naming speed deficits in dyslexia: Implications for diagnosis and intervention. In B. Blackhman (Ed.), *Foundations of reading acquisition and dyslexia* (pp. 49-66). Mahwah, NJ: Lawrence Erlbaum Associates.

Wolf, M., Bally, H., & Morris, R. (1986). Automaticity, retrieval processes, and reading: A longitudinal study in average and impaired readers. *Child Development, 57,* 988-1000.

Woodcock, R. W. (1973). *Manual for the Woodcock Reading Mastery Tests.* Circle Pines, MN: American Guidance Service.

Woodcock, R. W. (1990). Theoretical foundations of the WJ-R measures of cognitive ability. *Journal of Psychoeducational Assessment, 8,* 231-258.

Woodcock, R. W. (1994). Measures of fluid and crystallized theory of intelligence. In R. J. Sternberg (Ed.), *Encyclopedia of human intelligence* (pp. 452-456. New York: Macmillan.

Woodcock, R. W., & Johnson, M. B. (1989). *Tests of Cognitive Ability.* Allen, TX: DLM Teaching Resources.

Yopp, H. K. (1995). A test for assessing phonemic awareness in young children. *The Reading Teacher, 49*(1), 20-29.

Zuber, B. L., & Wetzel, P. A. (1981). Eye movement determinants of reading rate. In B. L. Zuber (Ed.), *Models of oculomotor behavior and control* (pp. 193-208). Boca Raton, FL: CRC Press.

Zwick, R. (1987). Assessing the dimensionality of NAEP reading data. *Journal of Educational Measurement, 24,* 293-308.

AUTHOR INDEX

A

Aaron, P. G. (1991), 151, 156, 270; Also 271
Abbott, R. D., 175, 292
Adams, M. J. (1990), 29, 176, 338, 352; (1991), 313, 323
Adams & Bruck (1995), 317, 323
Alexander, P. A., Schallert & Hare (1991), 91
Allen, L., Cipielewski & Stanovich (1992), 306, 309
Allington, R. L. & Johnston (1989), 342
Altwerger, B., Edelsky & Flores (1987), 311
Anderson, J. H. & Fairbanks (1937), 151
Anderson, R. C. (1972), 49, 50, 54
Anderson & Freebody (1981), 68, 72, 94, 136, 164, 166, 167, 172, 197, 285
Anderson & Pearson (1984), 39, 41
Arter, J. & Jenkins (1979), 253
Assink, E. & Kattenberg (1993), 106
Atkinson, R. C. (1974), 321

B

Baddeley, A. D., 293
Ball, E. W. & Blachman (1991), 181
Ballentine, F. A. (1951), 87
Bally, H., 124
Barker, T. A., Torgesen & Wagner (1992), 106, 161, 182
Barr, R. & Dreeban (1983), 150, 189
Barr, Kamil, Mosenthal & Pearson (1991), 321
Bear, R. M. & Odbert (1940), 115
Beck, I. L. & Carpenter (1986), 5, 26
Beck, McKeown & Omanson (1987), 72; Also 105, 176, 182, 189, 190
Beck, L. J., 146
Bell, L. C. & Perfetti (1994), 231, 234; Also 182, 189, 352
Benson, N. L., (Lovett, et al.), 222
Bentler, P. M. & Bonett (1980), 237
Berent, E., 316
Bergeron, B. S. (1990), 312
Berninger, V. W. & Abbott (1994), 175, 292
Berstein, M., 93
Bertera, J. H., 316, 335
Betts, E. A. (1946), 61, 62, 71
Biemiller, A. (1977), 85, 114, 155, 161, 272; (1994), 323. 351; Also 151, 161, 196, 204
Blachman, B. A., Ball, Black & Tangle (1994), 181
Black, S., 181
Bloom, B. (1984), 342
Bond, G. K. & Dykstra (1967), 185
Bonett, D. G., 237
Boodoo, G., (Neisser, et al.), 272
Borden, S. L., (Lovett, et al.), 222
Bouchard, T. L., (Neisser, et al.), 279
Bowers, P. G. (1993), 161, 194, 198; (1995), 124
Bowers, Steffy & Swanson (1986), 124
Bowers, Steffy & Tate (1988), 119, 124, 197, 199, 245, 259, 266
Bowers, Sunseth & Golden (1999), 273
Bowers & Swanson (1991), 124, 161
Boykin, A. W., (Neisser, et al.), 279
Brackstone, D., (Lovett, et al.), 222
Bradley, L. & Bryant (1983), 180, 181, 190, 322, 328; Also 352
Brady, S., (Shankweiler, et al.), 212
Brinkman, D., 179
Brody, N., (Neisser, et al.), 279
Brown, A. L., 349
Brown, J. S. & Felton (1990), 222
Brown, P., 87
Bruck, M., 317, 323
Bryant, P. E., Bradley, Maclean & Crossland (1989), 352; Also 180, 181, 190, 322, 328, 352
Burgess, S., 110, 182, 190, 222, 223, 224
Burke, C. L., 313
Buswell, G. T. (1951), 15, 115, 154
Byrne, B. & Fielding-Barnsley (1991), 181; (1993), 181; (1995), 181

C

Cadenhead, K. (1987), 63
Calfee, R. C., Lindamood & Lindamood (1973), 110, 179, 182, 190
Calfee & Piontkowski (1981), 150, 328, 351
Campbell, A. J., 352
Campito, J. S. (1994), 93
Capps, C., 113, 116, 123, 124
Carlisle, J. F. (1983), 146; Also 271
Carpenter, P. A., 5, 16, 26, 32, 171, 173, 211, 293
Carr, T., 322, 328, 351
Carroll, J. B. (1968), 163; (1993), 72, 75, 84, 88, 92, 110, 116, 279, 283, 285, 286
Carroll, Davies & Richman (1971), 68, 108, 334
Carver, R. P. (1970), 48; (1971a), 87; (1971b), 87; (1972), 25, 138; (1973a), 151; (1973b), 284, 288; (1974), 50, 97, 170; (1975), 341, 388; (1976), 66, 82, 87, 316, 333; (1977), 3, 5, 115, 155, 317, 386, 387; (1978), 237; (1981), 5,

33, 76, 87, 383, 385; (1982), 14, 77, 124, 151, 384; (1983), 78, 84, 87, 384; (1984), 384, 387; (1985a), 384, 387; (1985b), 384, 387; (1987a), 349; (1987b), 54, 55, 59, 68; (1989), 83; (1990a), 5, 14, 24, 26, 28, 29, 33, 63, 76, 78, 81, 82, 83, 84, 87, 115, 126, 133, 134, 138, 153, 154, 155, 193, 194, 198, 212, 284, 298, 302, 316, 383, 384, 385, 395; (1990b), 32, 34, 61, 69; (1990c), 67; (1991), 80, 81, 83, 84, 120, 121, 125, 157, 158, 161, 198, 199, 239, 285; (1992a), 13, 53, 59, 72, 85, 129, 133, 138; (1992b), 13, 133, 138; (1992c), 41; (1992d), 121; (1992e), 25, 78; (1993a), 101, 146, 147; (1993b), 237; (1994a), 19, 68; (1994b), 62, 79, 299, 388; (1994c), 76, 83, 395; (1996), 83, 84; (1997), 5, 11, 14, 15, 28, 33, 135, 147, 156, 160, 161, 197, 211, 212, 218, 254, 257, 284, 384, 385; (1998a), 54; (1998b); 124; (1998c), 96, 131, 147, 151, 178, 282, 284, 285, 293, 296
Carver & Clark (1998), 95, 108, 237, 255, 257, 270
Carver & Darby, Jr. (1971), 59; (1972), 59, 133, 135, 138
Carver & Leibert, (1995), 301, 302, 309, 388
Castel, J. M., Riach & Nicholson, (1994), 322, 328
Castles, A. & Colthart (1993), 261
Cattell, J. M. (1886), 113
Cattell, R. B. (1963), 280; (1971), 115, 195, 199, 284; Also 280
Caylor, J. S., 72, 98
Ceci, S. H., (Neisser, et al.), 279
Cermak, L. S. (1983), 125
Chabot, R. J., Zehr, Prinzo, & Petros, (1984), 136
Chall, J. S. (1967), 185, 289; (1983), 92
Chen, R. S. & Vellutino, (1997), 146, 150, 151; Also (Velluntino, et al.) 17, 292
Chiarello, K. S., 307, 309
Christensen, C. A. (1997), 181
Cipielewski, J., 306, 309
Clark, L. F., 33
Clark, S. W., 95, 108, 235, 255, 257, 270
Clarke, M. A. (1987), 57, 314
Clay, M. M. (1991), 352
Coatney, R. P., 87
Cohen, J. (1977), 207, 349
Coke, E. U. (1974), 87
Coleman, E. B. (1990), 32; Also 87
Colthart, M., 261
Compton, D. L. & Carlisle, (1994), 271
Conway, G. E., 93
Court, J. H. (1994), 281
Crano, W. D., 215
Cronbach, L. J. (1957), 18, 49, 91, 267; (1977), 130
Cronbach & Snow, (1977), 253
Crossland, I., 352
Crystal, R. B., 293
Cunningham, A. E. (1990), 181
Cunningham & Stanovich, (1990), 305, 308. 309; (1991), 172, 218, 219, 307, 309; (1993), 308, 309;
Cunningham, Stanovich & Wilson (1990), 135, 136, 230, 231
Also, 124, 161, 172, 289, 304, 306, 307, 309
Cunningham, J. W., 352
Cunningham, P. M. (1992), 351, 352; (1995), 177, 351, 353
Cunningham & Cunningham (1978), 352
Curtis, M. E. (1980), 124, 151; (1987), 71

D

Daneman, M. (1991), 146, 352
Daneman & Carpenter (1980), 16, 171, 211
Danks, J. (1980), 4
Darby, C. A., Jr., 59, 133, 135, 138
Datta, H., 17
Davidson, J., 114, 134, 136, 227, 229
Davies, P., 68, 108, 334
Davis, F. B. (1972), 53
Davis, J. M., & Spring (1990), 119, 124
Also 124, 197, 199, 285
DeFries, J. C., 17
Defty, N., 248
DeLuca, T., (Lovett, et al.), 222
Denckla, M. B. (1972), 116
Denckla & Rudel (1974), 113, 116, 120, 212; (1976), 123, 124
Also (Velluntino, et al.), 17, 292
Deno, S. L., 63

Detterman, D. K. (1982), 282
Dickinson, D. K. & Smith (1994), 212
Doehring, D. G. (1976), 85, 193, 194
Dolch, E. M. (1948), 48
Dole, J. A., Duffy, Roehler & Pearson (1991), 30, 350
Donohue, J., 182
Dreeban, R., 150, 189
Dreyer, L. G. & Katz (1992), 146
Also (Shankweiler, et al.), 212
DuBois, P. H. (1932), 115
Duffy, G. G., 30, 350
Duffy, S. A., 73
Duffy-Hester, A. M., 345
Dykstra, R., 185
Dymock, S. (1993), 148

E

Echevarria, M., 350
Edelsky, C. (1990), 324; Also 311

Edmonson, B., 307, 309
Ehri, L. C. (1980), 156, 159; (1985); 159; (1987), 159; (1989a), 178, 181; (1989b), 182; (1991), 159, 352; (1992), 181; (1994), 158; (1996), 314; (1997), 103; (1998), 177, 180 182
Ehri & Wilce (1979a), 189, 333, 347; (1979b), 66; (1983), 66, 67, 72, 114, 155, 156, 336; (1987a), 104, 335; (1987b), 179
Ehrlich, S. F., 32
Elbro, C. (1991), 261
Elley, W. B. (1991), 301
Ellis, A. W. (1985), 249, 251, 266; Also 181
Ellis, N. C., & Miles (1978), 124
Engle, R. W., 294
Erickson, G. C., 179
Escobar, M. D., 246, 250, 261, 292
Evans, M. & Carr (1985), 322, 328, 351

F

Fairbanks, G., 151
Fairbanks, M., 164, 173
Farmer, R., 123, 124
Farr, R. (1968), 53, 59
Farrell, E. (1982), 303
Faust, M. E., 151
Feder, D. D., 151
Feeman, D. J., 124, 161, 172, 289, 321, 328
Felton, R. H., 222
Fielding-Barnsley, R. (1997), 181
Fields, H., 271
Finger, E., 124, 157, 199
Fisher, B., 119
Fisk, E., 185
Flanigan, H., 352
Fleisher, L. S., Jenkins & Pany (1979), 31, 166, 216, 337
Fletcher, J. M., Shaywitz, Shankweiler, Katz, Liberman, Steubing, Francis, Fowler & Shaywitz (1994), 151, 269, 292
Also 212, 222, 246, 250, 261, 292
Flores, B. M., 311
Foorman, B. R., Francis, Novy, & Liberman (1991), 176, 189, 351
Foorman, B. R., Francis, Shaywitz, Shaywitz & Fletcher (1997), 222
Forster, K. I. (1970), 82
Foster, D. F., 179
Foster, K. D., Erickson, Foster, Brinkman & Torgesen (1994), 179
Fowler, A. E., (Fletcher, et al.), 151, 269, 292; (Shankweiler, et al.), 212
France, I. M., 352
Francis, D. J., Stuebing, Shaywitz, Shaywitz & Fletcher (1996), 292
Also 151, 176, 189, 222, 269, 292, 351
Frase, L. T. (1967), 33
Freebody, P., 68, 72, 94, 136, 164, 166, 167, 172, 197, 285
Fries, C. C. (1963), 65, 319, 341
Frith, U. (1980), 111, 271; (1984) 271
Frost, J., 180, 181, 190, 205
Frye, B. J., 301
Fuchs, D., 63
Fuchs, L. S., Fuchs & Deno (1982), 63

G

Gates, A. I. (1921), 131, 137
Gathercole, S. E. & Baddeley (1993), 293
Gayan, J., 17
Georgi, M. C., 176, 182
Gernsbacher, M. A., Varner & Faust (1990), 151
Geva, E., 260
Gibson, E. L. & Levin (1975), 25
Gill, J. T. (1992), 178, 179
Gillingham, M. G., 124
Glass, G. V. (1976), 349
Gleitman, L. R. & Rozin (1977), 341
Also 115, 155, 176
Golden, J., 273
Golinkoff, R. M., 272
Goodman, K. S. (1965), 315, 316; (1967), 87, 311, 312, 313, 315, 321, 326; (1976), 317; (1986), 311, 313, 322; (1989), 42, 324; (1992), 42, 57, 312, 325
Goodman & Goodman (1979), 25, 312, 313, 314, 317, 321, 322, 326
Goodman, Y. M., 25, 312, 313, 314, 317, 321, 322, 326
Goswami, U. & Bryant (1990), 352
Gottardo, A., 261, 263, 264
Gough, P. B. (1972), 29; (1984) 87
Gough & Hillinger (1980), 177, 321, 328
Gough & Juel (1991), 105
Gough, Juel & Griffith (1992), 102, 103, 345
Gough & Tunmer (1986), 15, 140, 146, 268
Also 15, 34, 103, 104, 146, 147, 151, 176, 203
Goulandris, N., 248
Graesser, A. C., Hoffman & Clark (1980), 33
Graves, M. F. (1987), 338; (1992), 339
Gray, J. W., 124
Gray, M. M., 279

Green, B. A., 49, 54
Green, D. W., 88
Griffith, P. L., 34, 102, 103, 104, 146, 176, 203, 345
Grindler, M. C., 321
Gustafsson, J-E. (1994), 280, 281

H

Hall, V. C., Chiarello & Edmondson (1996), 307, 309
Halpern, D. F., (Neisser, et al.), 279
Hammill, D. D. & McNutt (1980), 93, 151; (1981), 282, 283, 296
Hardy, C. J., 184
Hare, V. C., 91
Harris, C., 82
Harste, J. C. (1989), 325
Harste & Burke (1977), 313
Hastings, C. N., 49
Hatcher, P., Hulme & Ellis (1994), 181
Hauke, R. N., 146
Hausfeld, S. (1981), 151
Heckt, S., 110, 182, 190, 222, 223, 224
Hegion, A., 185
Henderson, E. H. (1992), 179, 321
Herriman, M. L., 184
Hill, W. R. (1964), 78, 87
Hillinger, M. L., 177, 321, 328
Hoffman, J. V. (1978), 75, 87; (1980), 291
Hoffman, N. L., 133
Hogaboam, T. W. & Perfetti (1978), 117, 336, 352; Also 124, 157, 199, 272, 316, 352
Holmes, D. L., 85
Holmes, J. A. (1954), 51, 59, 72, 76, 131, 137, 161
Holt, L. K., (Manis, et al.), 183
Hook, C., 49
Hook, L. R., 72, 98
Hoover, W. & Gough (1990), 15, 146, 147, 151
Horn, C. C. (Manis, et al.), 183
Horn, J. L. (1994), 280, 287
Horn & Cattell (1966), 280
Houck, D., 124
Howell, M. J., (Manis, et al.), 183
Huey, E. B. (1908), 48, 337
Hughes, C., 182, 190
Hulme, C. & Mackinzie (1992), 293
Also 181
Hunt, E. (1978), 94, 117, 118, 197, 199, 283
Hunt, Davidson & Lansman (1981), 114
Also, 134, 136, 207, 229
Hunt, L. C., Jr. (1967), 303

I

Ingham, J. (1981), 301
Inhoff, A. W., 316, 335
Iversen, S. & Tunmer (1993), 322, 328

J

Jackson, M. D. (1980), 195, 199
Jackson & McClelland (1975), 25; (1979), 124, 136, 137, 138, 151, 229
Jackson, N. E. & Biemiller (1985), 196, 204
Also 131, 137
James, J. H., 146, 150, 151, 227
Jenkins, L., 265
Jenkins, S. J., 321
Jensen, A. R. (1982), 197, 281
Johnson, M., 70, 72, 181, 190, 219, 332
Johnson, M. B., 171
Johnston, P. H. & Allington (1991), 342
Jorgenson, G. W. (1977), 300, 342
Jorm, A. F. (1983), 271
Jorm & Share (1983), 352
Joshi, R. M. & Aaron (1990), 271
Juel, C. (1983), 252, 272; (1988), 146; (1990), 352
Juel, Griffith & Gough (1986), 34, 103, 104, 146, 176, 203
Jungeblut, A., 265
Just, M. A. & Carpenter (1980), 32; (1992), 171, 173, 293
Also 102, 103, 105, 345

K

Kagan, J. (1982), 125
Kameenui, E. J. (1996), 176
Kamile, M. L., 321
Kaplan, E. L., 87
Kattenberg, G., 106
Katz, L., 146, 151, 212, 269, 292
Keenan, J. M. & Brown (1984), 87
Keogh, B., 150, 212
Kerr, P. W., 352
Ketron, J. I., 93
Kibby, M. W. (1995), 247
Kintsch, W. (1994), 26, 27
Kintsch & Keenan (1973), 87; Also 33
Kirsch, I. S., Jungeblut, Jenkins & Kolstad (1993), 265
Klare, G. R. (1963), 388
Kleiman, G. M., 146
Kolstad, A., 265
Kroll, J. F., 82
Kyllenon, P. C. & Crystal (1990), 293

L

LaBerge, D. & Samuels (1974), 31, 63, 72, 85, 107, 166, 352

Lacerenza, L., (Lovett, et al.), 222
Lansman, M., 114
Larsen, R. P. & Feder (1940), 151
Leckliter, I. N. (1994), 249, 256
Lehrl, S. & Fischer (1990), 119
Leibert, R. E., 301, 302, 309, 388
Lennon, R. T. (1962), 52
Leong, C. K. (1993), 249, 259, 338
Lesgold, A. M. & Perfetti (1978), 272
Also 272, 294
Levin, H. & Kaplan (1970), 87; Also 25
Levine, S. L. & Osbourne (1989), 90
Lezak, M. D. (1988), 282
Liberman, A. M., 317, 319, 321, 328
Liberman, D., 176, 189, 351
Liberman, I. Y. & Liberman (1990), 317, 319, 321, 328
Liberman & Shankweiler (1979), 272
Also 151, 172, 269, 292
Lindamood, C. H. & Lindamood (1984), 183
Lindamood, P. C., 110, 179, 182, 183, 190
Lipson, M. Y. & Wixson (1986), 267
Lloyd, J. & McKelvie (1992), 87
Loehlin, J. C., (Neisser, et al.), 279
Lohnes, P. R. & Gray (1972), 279
Lomax, R. G., 322
Lorsbach, T. C. & Gray (1986), 124
Lovett, M. W. (1984), 245, 272, 273
Lovett, Borden, DeLuca, Lacerenza, Benson & Brackstone (1994), 222
Lundberg, I., Frost & Petersen (1988), 180, 181, 190, 205
Lundquist, E., (Shankweiler, et al.), 212
Lyon, G. R. (1985), 253; (1993), 265; (1995), 250, 256

M

MacGinitie, W. H. (1991), 348
Mackinzie, S., 293
Mackworth, J. F. (1963), 116
Maclean, M., 352
MacLeod, C. M., 134, 136, 227, 229
Makuch, R., 246, 250, 261, 292
Manis, F. R. (1985), 156, 336
Manis, Savage, Morrison, Horn, Howell, Szeszulski, & Holt (1987), 183
Also 156
Marchione, K. E., (Shankweiler, et al.), 212
Martin, M. (1978), 294
Maruyama, G. M., 301
Mason, M. (1978), 136
Masson, M. E. J. (1986), 26, 82
Masterson, J., 184
McClelland, J. L., 25, 29, 124, 136, 137, 138, 151, 158, 160, 229
McConkie, G. W. & Hogaboam (1985), 316
McConkie, Kerr, Reddix & Zola (1987), 352
McConkie & Zola (1984), 82
McCormick, S. (1994), 342
McCracken, R. A. (1971), 303
McCutchen, D., Bell, France & Perfetti (1991), 352
McGuinness, C., 182
McGuinness, D., McGuinness & Donohue (1995), 182
McKelvie, S. J., 87
McKenna, M. C., Robinson & Miller (1990), 321
McKenna, Stahl & Reinking (1994), 324
McKenna, Stratton, Grindler & Jenkins (1995), 321
Also 321, 323, 328
McKeown, M. G., 72
McNutt, G., 93, 151, 282, 283, 296
Meister, C., 349
Metsala, J. L. (1997), 260
Mewhort, D. J. K. & Campbell (1981), 352
Mezynski, K. (1983), 164, 166, 167
Mikulecky, L. (1990), 337
Miles, T. R., 124
Miller, G. R. & Coleman (1971), 87
Miller, J. R. & Kintsch (1980), 33
Miller, J. W., 321
Miller, P. D., 321, 322, 328
Mills, J. R. & Jackson (1990), 131, 137
Mistretta-Hampton, J., 350
Mitchell, D. C. & Green (1978), 88
Mitchell, H. R., 98
Mitchell, R. F., 118, 120
Morris, R., 124
Morrison, F. J. & Manis (1982), 156; Also (Manis, et al.), 183
Morrison, R. E., 316, 335
Morse, W. C. (1951), 87
Mosenthal, P. B., 321

N

Nagy, W. E. (1988), 164
Naslund, J. C. & Schneider (1991), 206, 213
Nathan, R. G., 124, 193, 199
Neisser, U. (1983), 175
Neisser, Boodoo, Bouchard, Jr., Boykin, Brody, Ceci, Halpern, Loehlin, Perloff, Sternberg & Urbina (1996), 279
Nelson, N. E. & Warrington (1974), 271

Nesdale, A. R., 184
Newell, N. & Rosenbloom (1981), 337
Newman, S., Fields & Wright (1993), 271
Nichols, W. D., 211
Nicholson, T. (1991), 315, 352; Also 322, 328, 340
Novy, D. M., 176, 189, 351

O

Odbert, H. S., 115
Olson, R. K., Datta, Gayan & DeFries (1999), 17
Olson, Wise, Ring & Johnson (1997), 70, 72, 181, 190, 219, 332
Also 259, 260
Omanson, R. C., 72
Orton, S. T. (1925), 252
Osbourne, S., 90

P

Pace, A. J. & Golinkoff (1976), 272
Pagnucco, J. R., 321, 323, 328
Palinczar, A. S. & Brown (1984), 349
Palmer, J., MacLeod, Hunt & Davidson (1985), 134, 136, 227, 229
Pany, D., 31, 166, 216, 337
Parker, T., 185
Pearson, P. D. (1984), 321; Also 30, 39, 41, 321, 350
Perfetti, C. A. (1977), 272; (1983), 339; (1985), 13, 29, 37, 51, 59, 81, 85, 88, 131, 137, 158, 336, 342, 352; (1988), 37, 39, 40, 336; (1989), 52, 58; (1991a), 65, 66, 72, 101, 107, 179, 182, 190, 352; (1991b), 321; (1993), 288; (1994), 243; (1997), 179
Perfetti, Beck, Bell & Hughes (1987), 182, 190
Perfetti, Finger & Hogaboam (1978), 124, 157, 199
Perfetti, Georgi & Beck (1993), 176, 182
Perfetti & Hogaboam (1975), 272, 352
Perfetti & Lesgold (1977), 272, 294
Perfetti & Roth (1981), 28
Perfetti, Zhang & Berent (1992), 316
Also 117, 231, 234, 272, 336, 352
Perloff, R., (Neisser, et al.), 279
Perry, L., 124
Petersen, P. P., 180, 181, 190, 205
Petros, F., 184
Phillips, F., 184
Pinnell, G. S. (1989), 342
Piontkowski, D. D., 150, 328, 351
Pollatsek, A., 88, 317, 352
Posner, M. I. & Mitchell (1967), 118, 120
Potter, M. C., Kroll & Harris (1980), 82
Powell, J. S., 94, 95, 156
Pratt, A., (Velluntino, et al.), 17, 292
Pressley, M. (1994), 323
Pressley & Rankin (1994), 324, 325
Pressley, Rankin & Yokoi (1995), 331
Pressley, Wharton-McDonald, Mistretta-Hampston & Echevarria (1998), 350
Price, G. G., 124
Prinzo, O. V., 136
Pruzek, R. M., 184

R

Rack, J., Snowling & Olson (1992), 259, 260
Raines, S. C. (1995), 314, 320
Raney, G. E., 88
Rankin, J., 324, 325, 331
Rashotte, C. A., 110, 182, 183, 190, 222, 223, 224
Rayner, K. (1975), 316; (1983), 252; (1997), 82
Rayner & Duffy (1986), 73
Rayner, Inhoff, Morrison, Slowiaczek & Bertera (1981), 316, 335
Rayner & Pollatsek (1989), 317, 352
Rayner, Raney & Pollatsek (1995), 88
Also 32
Reddix, M. D., 352
Reinking, D., 324
Reitsma, P. (1983), 104; (1989), 159
Riach, J., 322, 328
Richek, M. (1977), 185
Ring, J., 70, 72, 181, 190, 219, 332
Robinson, R. D., 321
Roehler, L. R., 30, 350
Rosenberger, P. B. (1992), 258
Rosenbloom, P. S., 337
Rosenshine, B. & Meister (1994), 349
Rost, D. H. (1989), 53, 59
Roth, S. F. & Beck (1987), 105, 189
Also 28
Rothkopf, E. Z. (1966), 33
Rothkopf & Coatney (1974), 87
Royer, J. M.,Greene & Sinatra (1987), 49, 54
Royer, Hastings & Hook (1979), 49
Rozin, P. & Gleitman (1977), 115, 155, 176; Also 341
Rudel, R. G., 113, 116, 120, 124, 212
Rupley, W. H., Willson & Nichols (1998), 211

S

Sadoski, M. (1980), 303
Samuels, S. J. (1988), 352; Also 31, 63, 72, 85, 107, 166, 352
Sassenrath, J. M. (1972), 53
Savage, P. L., (Manis, et al.), 183
Scanlon, D. M. & Vellutino (1997), 319

Also, 17, 103, 107, 146, 266, 292, 342
Schallert, D. L., 91
Schmidt, F. L. (1996), 237
Schmidt & Crano (1974), 215
Schneider, W., 206, 213
Schustack, M. W., Ehrlich & Rayner (1987), 32
Sears, S. & Keogh (1993), 150, 212
Seidenberg, M. S. (1987), 352
Seidenberg & McClelland (1989), 29, 158, 160
Also 352
Shanahan, T. (1984), 178
Shanahan & Lomax (1988), 322
Shankweiler, D. & Liberman (1972), 151, 272
Shankweiler, Lundquist, Katz, Stuebing, Fletcher, Brady, Fowler, Dreyer, Marchione, Shaywitz & Shaywitz (1999), 212
Also 151, 269, 272, 292
Shannon, P. (1994), 324
Shany, M. J. & Biemiller (1995), 151, 161
Share, D. L. & Stanovich (1995), 31, 159, 273, 318; Also 260, 352
Shaywitz, B. A., 151, 212, 222, 246, 250, 261, 269, 292
Shaywitz, S. E. (1996), 292
Shaywitz, Escobar, Shaywitz, Fletcher & Makuch (1992), 246, 250, 261, 292
Also 151, 212, 222, 269, 292
Shepherd, M. J., 207, 209
Siegel, L. S. (1988), 250, 292; (1989), 268, 292
Siegel, Share & Geva (1995), 260
Also 182, 239, 244, 261, 263, 264
Sinatra, G. M., 49, 54
Sipay, E. R., (Velluntino, et al.), 17, 292
Slowiaczek, M. L., 316, 335
Small, S. G., (Velluntino, et al.), 17, 292
Smith, F. (1971), 85, 87, 311, 326; (1976), 312; (1979), 312, 315, 326; (1992), 302, 325
Smith & Holmes (1971), 85
Smith, M. W., 212
Snow, R. E. & Yalow (1982), 283; Also 253
Snowling, M. J., Goulandris & Defty (1996), 248
Also 259, 260
Spearing, D., 342
Spear-Swerling, L. & Sternberg (1996), 267, 292
Spearman, C. (1904), 280
Speece, D. L. (1993), 253
Spiegel, D. L. (1992), 325, 337
Spring, C. & Capps (1974), 113, 116, 123, 124
Spring & Davis (1988), 124, 197, 199, 285
Spring & Farmer (1975), 123, 124
Spring & Perry (1983), 124
Also 119, 124
Stahl, K. A. D., 345
Stahl, S. A. (1991), 164; (1997), 64, 350
Stahl, Duffy-Hester & Stahl (1998), 345
Stahl & Fairbanks (1986), 164, 173
Stahl, McKenna & Pagnucco (1994), 321, 323, 328
Stahl & Miller (1989), 321, 322, 328
Also 324
Stallman, A. C., 40, 41
Stanovich, K. E. (1980), 30, 65, 66, 85, 87, 88, 157, 352; (1981), 117, 124, 199; (1984), 290; (1986), 71, 185, 304, 317, 328, 352; (1988a), 148, 195, 199, 258; (1988b), 267; (1989), 269, 292; (1991), 148, 250, 264, 265, 267, 270, 292, 341, 352; (1992), 284; (1993a), 313, 318, 328; (1993b), 253, 341
Stanovich & Cunningham, (1993), 304, 306, 307, 309
Stanovich, Cunningham & Feeman (1984), 161, 172, 289
Stanovich, Feeman & Cunningham (1983), 124
Stanovich, Nathan & Vala-Rossi (1986), 124
Stanovich, Nathan & Zolman (1988), 193, 199
Stanovich & Siegel (1994), 239, 244
Stanovich, Siegel & Gottardo (1997), 261, 263, 264
Stanovich & West (1979), 80; (1989), 304, 306, 307, 308, 309, 352
Stanovich, West & Feeman (1981), 321, 328
Also 31, 98, 135, 136, 159, 172, 218, 219, 230, 231, 273, 305, 306, 307, 308, 309, 318, 321, 328
Stauffer, R. C. (1967), 35
Steffy, R. A., 119, 124, 197, 199, 245, 259, 266
Steger, J. A., 184
Sternberg, R. J. (1986), 283; (1987), 68; (1994), 279
Sternberg, Conway, Ketron & Berstein (1981), 93
Sternberg, R. J. & Powell (1983), 94, 95, 156
Also 267, 279, 292
Steubing, K. K., (Fletcher, et al.), 151, 269, 292; (Shankweiler, et al.), 212
Stevenson, H., Parker, Wilkinson, Hegion & Fisk (1976), 185
Sticht, T. G. (1972), 3, 341
Sticht, Beck, Hauke, Kleiman & James (1974), 146
Sticht, Hooke & Caylor (1982), 72, 98
Sticht & James (1984), 150, 151, 227

Stone & Brady (1995), 73, 208, 210, 211, 213
Stratton, B. D., 321
Stroud, J. B. (1945), 115
Stuart, M. & Masterson (1992), 184
Sunseth, K., 273
Swanson, L. B., 124, 161
Szeszulski, P. A., (Manis, et al.), 183

T

Tan, A. & Nicholson (1997), 340
Tangle, D., 181
Tannenhaus, M. K., Flanigan & Seidenberg (1980), 352
Tanzman, M. S., 103, 107, 146, 266
Tate, E., 119, 124, 197, 199, 245, 259, 266
Taylor, B. M., Frye & Maruyama (1990), 301
Terman, L. M. (1918), 285
Thorndike, E. L. (1917), 283, 288
Thorndike, R. L. (1973), 72, 136, 290, 296; (1974), 53, 59, 284, 288
Thurstone, L. L. (1946), 72
TIME Magazine (1993), 265
Torgesen, J. K. (1985), 123, 290
Torgesen & Houck (1980), 124
Torgesen, Wagner & Rashotte (1997), 183, 222
Torgesen, Wagner, Rashotte, Burgess & Heckt (1997), 110, 182, 190, 222, 223, 224; Also 106, 161, 179, 182
Traxler, A. E. (1934), 115, 154
Tunmer, W. E., Herriman & Nesdale (1988), 184 Also, 15, 140, 146, 268, 322, 328
Turner, M. L. & Engle (1989), 294

U

Uhry, J. K., & Shepherd (1993), 207, 209
Urbina, S., (Neisser, et al.), 279

V

Valencia, S. W., & Stallman (1989), 40, 41
Valla-Rossi, M., 124
Vandervelden, M. C. & Siegel (1995), 182
Varner, K. R., 151
Vellutino, F. R. (1979), 175, 248; (1987), 249, 252; (1991), 322, 351
Vellutino, Harding, Phillips & Steger (1975), 184
Vellutino, Scanlon, Sipay, Small, Pratt, Chen & Denckla (1996), 17, 292
Vellutino, Scanlon & Spearing (1995), 342
Vellutino, Scanlon & Tanzman (1994), 103, 107, 146, 266
Vellutino, Steger & Pruzek (1973), 184
Also 146, 150, 151, 319
Venezky, R. L. (1975), 176; (1976), 178; (1977), 28

W

Wagner, R. K., Torgesen & Rashotte (1994), 124; Also 106, 110, 161, 182, 183, 190, 222, 223, 224
Wallon, E. J. 228
Walsh, D. J., Price & Gillingham (1988), 124
Warrington, E. K., 271
Watson, D. J. (1989), 311
Weaver, C. (1988), 311
Webb, W. B. & Wallon (1956), 228
Wechsler, D. (1944), 294
West, R. F. & Stanovich (1978), 321, 328
West, Stanovich & Mitchell (1993), 98
Also 80, 304, 306, 307, 308, 309, 321, 328, 352
Wetzel, P. A., 87
Wharton-McDonald, R., 350
Wilce, L. S., 66, 67, 72, 104, 114, 155, 156, 179, 189, 333, 335, 336, 347
Wilkinson, A., 185
Williams, J. P. (1977), 88; (1980), 189, 266, 322, 328
Willson, V. L., 211
Wilson, M. R., 135, 136, 230, 231
Wimmer, H. (1993), 260
Wise, B., 70, 72, 181, 190, 219, 332
Wixson, K. K., 267
Wolf, M. (1991), 113, 116, 118, 155; (1997), 273, 274
Wolf, Bally & Morris (1986), 124
Woodcock, R. W. (1973), 110, 150; (1990) 115; (1994), 280
Woodcock & Johnson (1989), 171
Wright, S., 271

Y

Yalow., E., 283
Yokoi, L., 331
Yopp, H. K. (1995), 184, 185, 212

Z

Zehr, H. D., 136
Zhang, S., 316
Zola., D., 82, 352
Zolman, J. E., 193, 199
Zuber, B. L. & Wetzel (1981), 87
Zwick, R. (1987), 53, 59

SUBJECT INDEX

A

A (see accuracy of comprehension)
Accuracy level, A_L, 6-18, 129-139
see *Glossary*, 399
causes of, 140-152
construct, 61-62
implications, 73, 152
low, 261
related concepts, 62-67
related ideas, 146-148
tests, 67-71
theoretical relationships, 140-145
theory and evidence, 71-73
Accuracy of comprehension, A, 385-393
see *Glossary*, 399
Adults, 35-37
data, 228-238
implications, 238
modified causal model, 225-228
rauding achievement, 247
Advanced readers, 15, 35-37, 143-145
see *Glossary*, 399
modified causal model, 225-228
Age, 35-36, 242-244
cause of C_s, 192-194
Age-achievement discrepancy, 266-267
AgeGE, 245
A_L (see accuracy level)
Alphabetic principle, 319-320
A_LWords, 141-145
(also see raudamatized words)
Apping, 81-82
see *Glossary*, 399
Aptitude-treatment interaction, 253-254
A_r (see rauding accuracy)
Audamatized words, 92, 102
see *Glossary*, 399
lexicon, 141-145
Auding, 3, 4
see *Glossary*, 399
Automaticity, 63-65, 118-119, 370-371
Automatized words, 65-66
see *Glossary*, 400
Autonomous lexicon, 65-66, 107-108
Average rate, R, 379
see *Glossary*, 400

B

Balanced approach, 350-353, 374-375
Basic information processing (BIP), 119-120
Basic reading processes, 24-28
see *Glossary*, 400
Beginning readers, 35-37, 142-143
see *Glossary*, 400

C

Causal model
detail, 11-18
diagnostic system, 244-248
modified, 225-228, 363-364
primary, 359-360
overview, 6-11
root causes, 359-360
secondary, 360-362
summary, 355-363
whole-language approach, 320-321, 327
Causation, 127
Cipher, 102-103, 177
Cipher knowledge, 102-103
Ciphermatized words, 100-102
see *Glossary*, 400
lexicon, 141-145
c_k (see pure cipher knowledge)
c_kWords, 100, 102, 142-145
(also see ciphermatized words)
Cognitive performance speed, 115-116
Cognitive power, 284
see *Glossary*, 400
Cognitive speed, 113-359
see *Glossary*, 400
Cognitive speed aptitude, g_s, 12, 18, 194-198, 359
see *Glossary*, 400
definition, 194
implications, 199
low, 260-261
theory and evidence, 198-199
Cognitive speed level, C_s, 8-18, 153-159
see *Glossary*, 400
age, 192-194
causes of, 192-200
cognitive speed aptitude, 194-198
construct, 113-114
implications, 125-126
related concepts, 114-120
tests, 120-122
theory and evidence, 122-125, 198-199
Complete thought, 5
see *Glossary*, 400
Comprehension, 379-393
(see accuracy of comprehension, A; rate of comprehension, R; efficiency of

comprehension, E; rauding accuracy, A_r; rauding efficiency, E_r; accuracy level, A_L; efficiency level, E_L)
Conclusions, 377
Constant rate, 75-80
Constructs, 6-18, 375-376
earlier, 379-381
elaborated, 45-126
measures, 19-21
Crystallized intelligence, Gc, 280-281, 285-286
see *Glossary*, 400
and reading comprehension tests, 287-291
C_s (see cognitive speed level)

D

Decoding, 104-105
rapid single-word, 80-81
speed, 117-118
Decoding approach, 346-347, 374
instruction, 313
Difficulty level, 13-14, 179-180
see *Glossary*, 401
Direct measures, 18-21
see *Glossary*, 401
Disabled readers, 239-276
diagnosis, 364-365
disabilities, 265-275
double-deficit, 273
dyslexia, 258-264
RDS, 267-268
slow, 272
summary, 273-275
DisabledA_L, 245
DisabledC_s, 245-246
DisabledP_L, 245-246
DisabledR_L, 245
slow, 272
DisabledV_L, 245-246
d_k (see pure decoding knowledge)
d_k Words, 100-102
see *Glossary*, 401
D_L (see difficulty level)
Double-deficit, 273
d_s (see pure decoding speed)
Dyslexia
other definitions, 249-251
phonological, 261-265
RDS definitions, 248-249
research, 258-265
subtypes, 261-265
surface, 261-265
treatment, 251-254

E

E (see efficiency of comprehension)
Easy rauding, 298-301
see *Glossary*, 401
Echelons, 13-18, 244-247
Efficiency level, E_L, 6-18
see *Glossary*, 401
causes of, 129-139
construct, 47-49
factor analytic research, 132-135
implications, 138-139
low, 261
related concepts, 49-53
relation to A_L and R_L, 135-137
tests, 54-58
theory and evidence, 58-60, 137-138
Efficiency of comprehension, E, 379-380, 383
see *Glossary*, 401
E_L (see efficiency level)
Equations of rauding theory, 385-393
list of, 397-398
E_r (see rauding efficiency)
Eye movements, 81-82

F

Fact recalling,
see *Glossary*, 401
Fact-rehearsing, 24-28
Fluency, 5, 370
Fluid intelligence, Gf, 56, 280-281, 283-285
see *Glossary*, 401
and reading comprehension tests, 287-291
definition, 283
Functional lexicon, 107-108
see *Glossary*, 402

G

g (see general intelligence)
Gc (see crystallized intelligence)
Gears, 24-28
Gear shifting, 78
see *Glossary*, 402
General intelligence, *g*, 280-283
see *Glossary*, 402
reading comprehension tests, 287-291
General knowledge, 91
General reading ability, 6-18, 51-52
Gf (see fluid intelligence)
Goals, 340-341
Good readers, 242-244
g_p (see pronunciation knowledge aptitude)
g_s (see cognitive speed aptitude)

Guessing hypothesis, 312
evaluation, 315-319
rauding approach, 332-334
g_v (see verbal knowledge aptitude)

H

Hard reading, 298-301
see *Glossary*, 402
Handicapped, 246-247
Handicapped/g_p, 246-247
Handicapped/g_s, 246-247
Handicapped/g_v, 246-247

I

Idea-remembering, 24-28
see *Glossary*, 402
Indicant, 18-21
see *Glossary*, 402
Indirect measure, 18-21
Inefficiency constant, 386
see *Glossary*, 402
Intelligence, 365-366
and reading, 279-297
and reading comprehension tests, 287-291
implications, 296
theory and evidence, 295-296
Intermediate readers, 35-37, 142, 144
see *Glossary*, 402
IQ-achievement discrepancy, 268-270, 291-292

L

Laws
first, 383
second, 383
third, 77, 383
Learning process, 24-28
see *Glossary*, 402
Lexical access, 24-28
see *Glossary*, 402
Lexical knowledge, 103-104
see *Glossary*, 402
Listening (see auding)
Listening comprehension, 92-93
Listening knowledge, 91
Listening-reading discrepancy, 148, 264-265, 270
Listening vocabulary, 91
Lower-graders, 35-37
see *Glossary*, 403
implications, 212-213
theory and research, 203-212

M

Matched rauding, 298-301
see *Glossary*, 403
Maximum oral reading rate, 84
Memorizing process, 24-28
see *Glossary*, 403
Memory capacity
and reading achievement, 292-294
Middle-graders, 35-37
see *Glossary*, 403
data, 215-224
see *Glossary*, 402

N

Naming speed, 15, 116-118

O

One minute of reading, 33-34
One second of reading, 28-33
One year of reading, 34-35
Optimal rate, 384
see *Glossary*, 403
Orthographic knowledge, 105-107
see *Glossary*, 403

P

Phonics approach, 345-346, 373-374
see *Glossary*, 403
Phonological awareness, 184-185
teaching, 179-183
P_L (see pronunciation knowledge level)
P_LWords, 141-145
(also see pronounceamatized words)
Poor readers, 242-244
garden-variety, 268
Print exposure, 304-308
Pronounceamatized words, 99-102
see *Glossary*, 404
lexicon, 141-145
Pronunciation knowledge aptitude, g_p, 12, 16
see *Glossary*, 404
construct, 183-184
low, 258
measurement, 184-186
Pronunciation knowledge level, P_L, 8-18, 140-152, 153-159, 176, 356-359
see *Glossary*, 404
construct, 99-101
implications, 111-112
low, 259, 260
related concepts, 101-108
tests, 108-109
theory and evidence, 110-111
Pronunciation level (see pronunciation knowledge level)
Pseudowords, 366-367

(see also pure decoding knowledge and pure decoding speed)
Pure cipher knowledge, c_k, 100, 102
see *Glossary*, 404
Pure decoding knowledge, d_k
see *Glossary*, 404
low, 259
Pure decoding speed, d_s, 154, 156-159
see *Glossary*, 405

R

R (see rate of comprehension)
Rate level, R_L, 7-18, 129-139
see *Glossary*, 404
causes of, 153-162
construct, 76-77
conversions among units, 395
implications, 88-89, 162
related concepts, 78-82
tests, 82-86
theoretical relationships, 153-160
theory and evidence, 86-88, 160-162
Rate of comprehension, R, 383-393
see *Glossary*, 405
rate of text comprehension, 379-380, 383, 385-393
Raudamaticity, 299-301
see *Glossary*, 405
Raudamaticity training, 334-338
goals, 340-341
vocabulary training, 338-340
Raudamatized words, 62-67, 79-80, 102
see *Glossary*, 405
lexicon, 141-145
Rauding, 3-5
Rauding accuracy, A_r, 34, 388-389
see *Glossary*, 406
Rauding accuracy level (see accuracy level)
see *Glossary*, 406
Rauding achievement, 242-244
see *Glossary*, 406
Rauding approach, 371-373
description, 331-343
evaluation, 343-353
Rauding diagnostic system, 239, 241-257, 364-365
causal model and, 244-248
dyslexia, 248-251
evidence, 254-256
implications, 257
treatment, 251-254
theory and evidence, 256-257
Rauding efficiency, E_r, 379-380
see *Glossary*, 406
Rauding efficiency level, E_L (see efficiency level)
see *Glossary*, 406
Rauding process, 24-28
see *Glossary*, 406
inducing, 27-28
Rauding rate, R_r, 379-380, 383-384, 385-393
see *Glossary*, 406
conversions among units, 395
Rauding rate level, R_L, (see rate level)
see *Glossary*, 406
Rauding skill, 242-244
see *Glossary*, 407
Rauding theory, 3-5, 378
Readability (see difficulty level)
Reading, 3-5
and intelligence, 279-297
Reading ability
factors, 52-53
Reading achievement, 6-18, 362-363
see *Glossary*, 407
and memory capacity, 292-294
Reading comprehension, 367-368
Reading comprehension tests
standardized, 49-51
traditional, 287-291
Reading rates, 24-28
Reading disability (see disabled readers)
see *Glossary*, 407
Reading level, 62-63
Reading process, 31-33, 368-370
see *Glossary*, 407
Reading rate 78
see *Glossary*, 407
Reading vocabulary, 68, 71
Relative difficulty, 298-301, 380
see *Glossary*, 407
Relatively easy, 298-301
see *Glossary*, 407
Relatively hard, 298-301
see *Glossary*, 407
R_L (see rate level)
R_r (see rauding rate)

S

Scanning process, 24-28
see *Glossary*, 407
Schema theory, 39-42
Science
and whole-language approach, 323-326
Semantic encoding, 24-28
see *Glossary*, 407
Sentences per minute, 395

Sentence integrating, 25
see *Glossary*, 407
Silent rate
typical, 83
Simple view, 146-148
Skimming process, 24-28
see *Glossary*, 408
Skill, 35-36
rauding, 242-244
Skills approach, 348-350, 374
S_L (see spelling level)
Spelling
disability, 271
level, 103, 159-160
pattern, 341-342
teaching, 178
training, 334-338
treatment, 252-253
Spelling knowledge, 103
Spelling level, 103, 159-160
Standard sentences
see *Glossary*, 408
Standard word
see *Glossary*, 408
Standard words per minute, Wpm, 395
Studying, 39-41
see *Glossary*, 408
Sustained silent reading, SSR, 303-304

T

Thinking speed, 115
Teaching/learning
cause of P_L, 176-186
cause of V_L, 163-169
implications, 173, 190-191
measurement, 168, 184-186
phonological awareness, 179-184
pronunciation, 176-178
spelling, 178-179
theory and evidence, 172-173, 187-190
Thoughts rauded, T_p, 298

U

Unitized speed, 66
Unitized words, 66-67

V

Verbal ability, 93-94, 117-118
Verbal comprehension, 94
Verbal efficiency theory, 37-39
Verbal intelligence, 94
Verbal knowledge aptitude, g_v, 12, 16
see *Glossary*, 408
construct, 169
implications, 173
measurement, 170-171
not low, 258-259
tests, 171-172
theory and evidence, 172-173
Verbal knowledge level, V_L, 8-18, 140-152, 355-356
see *Glossary*, 408
causes of, 163-174
construct, 90-92
distal cause of P_L, 186-187
implications, 98
not low, 259
related concepts, 92-95
tests, 95-97
theory and evidence, 97-98
Verbal level (see verbal knowledge level)
Verbal speed, 117-118
V_L (see verbal knowledge level)
V_LWords, 141-145
(also see audamatized words)
Vocabulary
(see reading vocabulary and listening vocabulary)
teaching, 164-168
training, 338-340
Volume of reading, 366
print exposure, 304-308
research, 301-303
sustained silent reading, 303-309
theory, 298-301
theory and evidence, 308-309

W

Whole language, 42
approach, 373
causal model, 327
description, 311-315
evaluation, 315-326, 343-345
evidence summary, 328
summary, 326
tests, 57
Word identification, 101-102
Word recognition, 101-102
speed, 81
Words per minute (Wpm), 395
see *Glossary*, 409
words per minute (wpm)
see *Glossary*, 409
World knowledge, 91